10 Real SAT®s

10 Real SAT®s

College Entrance Examination Board, New York

Editor/Writer: Cathy Claman
Program Manager: Moira McArdle
Project/Production Manager: Jason Roth
Book Design: Alan Harmon Design
Additional Interior Revisions: Julia Selinger
Cover Design: Rich Koch
Special thanks: Alison Amdur, Lisa Andrews, Betty Keim, Parlan McGaw, Susan Merrill, and Virginia Perrin of the College Board, and Jim Baswell, Marilyn W. Bonner, Edward W. Curley, Rose Horch, Carol A. Jackson, Nontas Konstantakis, Melvin Y. Kubota, Gerry May, Ralph Pantozzi, Donald E. Powers, and Gloria E. Weiss of Educational Testing Service

The College Board is a national nonprofit membership association dedicated to preparing, inspiring, and connecting students to college and opportunity. Founded in 1900, the association is composed of more than 3,800 schools, colleges, universities, and other educational organizations. Each year, the College Board serves over three million students and their parents, 22,000 high schools, and 5,000 colleges, through major programs and services in college admission, guidance, assessment, financial aid, enrollment, and teaching and learning. Among its best-known programs are the SAT®, the PSAT/NMSQT™, the Advanced Placement Program® (AP®), and Pacesetter®. The College Board is committed to the principles of equity and excellence, and that commitment is embodied in all of its programs, services, activities, and concerns.

Copies of this book (item # 006542) are available from your bookseller or may be ordered from College Board Publications, Two College Way, P.O. Box 1100, Forrester Center, WV 25438-4100, (tel.: 800 323-7155). The price is $18.95 per copy. Purchase orders above $25 are accepted.

Editorial inquiries concerning this book should be addressed to the College Board, 45 Columbus Avenue, New York, NY 10023-6992.

International Standard Book Number: 0-87447-654-2

Library of Congress Card Catalog Number: 00-131952

9 8 7 6 5 4 3 2

Distributed by Henry Holt and Company, LLC.

Contents

Preface

Created by the experts who develop the SAT® I: Reasoning Test, this book is intended first and foremost to explain clearly what the SAT is and to give you an opportunity to become familiar with the different types of questions on the test. You'll discover a variety of strategies both for approaching the SAT as a whole and for tackling specific types of questions. Our goal is not to prescribe a hard-and-fast method for taking the test, but to give you the tools to approach the SAT with confidence and optimism. While every effort has been made to ensure that the contents of this book are as up-to-date as possible, we urge you to consult the free publication, *Taking the SAT I: Reasoning Test*, for the most current information on the test.

10 Real SATs is packed with the information, strategies, tips, and practice that the experts know will help you do your best on the SAT. The amount of material may seem overwhelming. We suggest that you break up your use of the book over several weeks, or study different chapters at your own pace.

How This Book Is Organized

Chapters 1, 2, and 3 offer a general introduction to the SAT I: Reasoning Test, as well as valuable test-taking strategies. You won't learn how to "psych out" the test, but you will develop sound techniques to do your best in what, for some, can be a stressful situation. These beginning chapters should also help you create realistic expectations for your performance on the SAT. We recommend trying out the different techniques using either the practice verbal and mathematics questions given in Chapters 4–15, or other SAT test-preparation materials.

Chapters 4–15 deal specifically with the verbal and mathematics sections of the SAT. They contain in-depth discussions for each type of question on the test with effective tips and strategies for answering them. You should become familiar with the questions, the test instructions, and the kind of answers required. Pay particular attention to the Student-Produced Response (Grid-in) questions in Chapter 14. The answers to these questions must be given in specific formats. You should also become familiar with the paired Reading Passage format in Chapter 7, which requires you to answer questions comparing and contrasting two related passages.

Sample questions with explanations are provided for each type of verbal and math question. Chapter 8 includes additional practice for each type of verbal question; Chapter 15 includes practice for each type of mathematics question.

Chapter 11, "Mathematics Review," describes the concepts and operations that will appear on the SAT. It is not intended to replace a solid high school mathematics program, but should help you identify your strengths and areas in which you need further review. Use the techniques you are most comfortable with to solve mathematics problems and don't be concerned if your methods are different from the ones given in this book. On the other hand, if you have difficulty with particular types of problems, studying the solutions to sample questions may help you develop the skills needed to solve similar problems in the future.

This book also includes Chapter 16, a special chapter devoted specifically to the PSAT/NMSQT™ (Preliminary SAT/National Merit Scholarship Qualifying Test). Chapter 16 presents a complete description of the PSAT/NMSQT, including sample questions and explanations for the writing skills section introduced in October 1997.

The last chapter, Chapter 17, contains 10 editions of the SAT. But, just because we include 10 full SATs doesn't mean you must practice on all of them. Consider taking the tests selectively. For example, if you feel your weakness is critical reading, focus your practice more on these questions than on the others. It is essential, however, that you take at least one full practice test under timed conditions to get an idea of the stamina and concentration required to complete the test successfully.

How This Book Can Help You

10 Real SATs provides you with ample opportunity for practicing with the different types of questions that appear on the SAT. While the best preparation for the test is still a solid course of study in high school, the practice questions should help you, your teachers, parents, and counselors identify your strengths and those areas in which you need to work. In this sense, it should help you with long-term preparation for the SAT. On the other hand, the tips, notes, and recaps let you find and review important information quickly before you take the test.

The staff of the College Board hopes that you find this book easy to use and helpful. If you have specific comments or questions, please write to us at: College Board SAT Program, P.O. Box 62000, Princeton, NJ 08541-6200, or e-mail us at: sat@info.collegeboard.org.

Chapter 1

Introducing the SAT

About the SAT

Every year, two million students who apply to college take the SAT. Colleges require the SAT because it measures skills that you need for academic and career success. When colleges consider your application, they take into account many factors:

- your academic record
- your participation in school activities and sports
- letters of recommendation
- your best personal qualities
- your SAT test scores

Specifically, the SAT is designed to help predict your freshman grades in college, so that admission officers can make appropriate decisions about your chances of succeeding academically at their colleges.

Who Develops the Test?

The SAT is a program of the College Board. Founded in 1900, the College Board is an association of schools and colleges whose aim is to help students make the transition to higher education. Educational Testing Service (ETS) develops and administers the SAT for the College Board.

An SAT Committee made up of College Board members is responsible for overseeing the development of the test. Committee members are typically high school and college educators. Test questions are written by outside experts and ETS staff and reviewed by the SAT Committee.

Why This Is the Only Book You'll Need

Other books may claim to have the inside story on the SAT, but only *10 Real SATs* includes actual test questions from cover to cover. Other books may contain some real questions and questions that look like the real thing, but other publishers must create many of the questions in their books. Every single question in this book was developed for the SAT or has appeared on an actual test. Other major test-preparation publishers recommend *10 Real SATs* as essential practice for the SAT.

In addition to real practice, this book includes invaluable test-taking strategies from the people who know the SAT better than anyone else — the people who develop the test.

What's in the SAT

The SAT includes both verbal and math sections, with a total of six types of questions.

Types of Questions

Verbal	No.	Math	No.
Sentence Completions	19	Five-Choice	35
Analogies	19	Quantitative Comparisons	15
Critical Reading	40	Grid-ins*	10
Total	78	Total	60

*(Student-Produced Responses)

Timing

The SAT is three hours long and consists of seven test sections:

3 Verbal Sections	3 Math Sections
30 minutes	30 minutes
30 minutes	30 minutes
15 minutes	15 minutes

1 More Verbal or Math
Equating Section**
30 minutes

**The equating section will not count toward your final score. It is used to try out new questions for future editions of the SAT and to help make sure that your test scores are comparable to scores on other editions of the SAT. You won't be able to tell which section this is.

Preparing for the Test

Test preparation can be divided into two broad categories: short-term and long-term.

- Short-term preparation gets the quickest results.
- Long-term preparation has the biggest potential payoff.

Short-Term Preparation

Short-term preparation focuses on the test itself. It includes specific test-taking tips and techniques, including:

- Knowing what to expect from the test: what types of questions, how many questions, in what order.
- Knowing the test directions.
- Learning how to pace yourself.
- Learning when and how to guess.
- Knowing how to identify the easiest questions.
- Learning specific approaches for each of the six types of test questions.

These are the types of tips and hints you'll find in Chapter 2.

Short-term preparation is designed to make sure that you correctly answer every question that you currently have the ability to answer.
Short-term preparation can gain you some points on the test. But alone it doesn't help you become a more able student.

Long-Term Preparation

Long-term preparation focuses on your overall academic performance. It's designed to improve your abilities — to help you gain the skills necessary to answer more difficult questions. Long-term preparation includes things you can and should be doing all year, such as:

- Reading effectively: gives you the ability to figure out what the author means as well as what the author says.
- Improving your vocabulary: gives you tools to figure out new words from the context in which they are used.

- Developing your problem-solving abilities: helps you figure out what to do and how to do it, and helps you get started on challenging problems when you seem to be stumped.

Remember, short-term preparation helps you correctly answer all the questions you already can. Long-term preparation, on the other hand, can actually help you improve your abilities so that you can answer even more questions correctly. Ultimately, long-term preparation can have the greatest effect both on your scores and on how well you'll do in college.

Prepare by Practicing on the PSAT/NMSQT

The PSAT/NMSQT includes the same types of verbal and math questions as the SAT I: Reasoning Test plus writing skills questions like those on the SAT II: Subject Test in Writing. But the PSAT/NMSQT is shorter than the SAT—2 hours and 10 minutes. And, because the PSAT/NMSQT includes math and verbal questions interchangeable with those found in the SAT, it provides one of the best opportunities for practice. In addition, by taking the PSAT/NMSQT you can qualify for scholarships sponsored by the National Merit Scholarship Corporation and other scholarship programs. For more information about the PSAT/NMSQT, see Chapter 16.

What To Take on the Day of the Test

On the day of the test, arrive at the test center between 8:00 and 8:15 a.m. Remember to take the following items:

- Admission ticket
- Photo ID
- #2 pencils and erasers
- Approved calculator
- Watch

Gaining Points

Based on statistical findings of Educational Testing Service (ETS) and the College Board, your SAT scores will probably go up a little if you take the test more than once. But a gain is not guaranteed. The higher your first test score, the less likely you are to improve and the smaller the improvement is likely to be. Also, taking the test more than a couple of times will probably not bring about continued score gains.

Improving your overall abilities through long-term preparation can result in higher scores.

Tips: Things You Should Do

1. Make sure you're familiar with the test.
2. Make sure you're familiar with the tips and techniques in this book.
3. Practice.
4. Limit your test-specific preparation to 12 to 20 hours, at most. This can be done reasonably close to the time you take the test—within a month or two.
5. Work on your long-term preparation. Use the strategies in this book throughout your high school career.
6. Continue to work hard in school.

Understanding Your Scores

This section is designed to clear up a lot of mysteries surrounding the SAT — how the test is scored, what the scores mean, and how the scores should be used.

The SAT Scoring System

SAT scores are calculated as follows:

1. A fraction of the multiple-choice questions answered wrong is subtracted from the total number of right answers.
2. No points are added or subtracted for unanswered questions.
3. Nothing is subtracted for wrong answers to grid-ins.
4. If the resulting score includes a fraction, the score is rounded to the nearest whole number.

Your score is then converted into a 200 (lowest) to 800 (highest) scaled score using a statistical process called *equating*. Scores are equated to adjust for minor differences between test editions. Equating assures you and colleges that a score of 450 on one edition of the test indicates the same ability level as 450 on another edition. The SAT is *not* marked on a curve.

Score Range

No test can ever measure your skills precisely, but it can provide good estimates. If you took many editions of the test within a short time, your scores would tend to vary, but not too far above or below your actual abilities. The score range is an estimate of how your scores might vary if you were tested many times. The SAT score range is usually about 32 points above and below your specific numerical score, and it indicates the range in which your true abilities probably fall.

Your Scores

Test Date: OCTOBER 20XX

R= Recentered score (test dates on or after April 1, 1995)
See reverse side for information.

SAT I: Reasoning Test	Score	Score Range	Percentiles College-bound Seniors	
			National	State
Verbal	R 550	520-580	64	68
Mathematical	R 540	510-570	60	67

Jane L Henderson
761 Valley Forge Avenue
Valley Forge PA 00032

Percentiles

In addition to the scaled SAT score, you'll also get a percentile score. This compares your scores to the scores of other students who took the test. The comparison is given as a number between 1 and 99 that tells what percentage of students earned a score lower than yours. For example, if your percentile is 53, it means that out of every 100 test takers in the comparison group, you performed better than 53 of them.

Your percentile changes depending on the group with which you are being compared. For the SAT, your national percentile (all recently graduated college-bound seniors from across the nation who took the test) is often higher than your state percentile (all recently graduated college-bound seniors from your state who took the test). That's mainly because the national group contains a larger, more diverse group of test takers.

Using Your Scores

Along with your score, score range, and percentile score, the SAT score report gives you the following information:

- Raw score information for different types of verbal and math questions — the number you got right, wrong, or omitted. Use this information to analyze your performance.
- Profiles of up to four colleges or universities to which you asked that your scores be sent. These profiles include institutional characteristics, what high school preparation is required, freshman admission policies, and cost/financial aid information. If you fill out the Student Descriptive Questionnaire, that information will also be included.

Guides such as *The College Handbook* often provide information about SAT scores of enrolled freshmen. (Your score report will also contain this information.) If your scores are in the range of the scores at a campus you are interested in, you will probably be able to handle the academic challenge there. If your scores fall far below, you may be in for a struggle. If your scores are much higher, you may not be academically challenged at that campus.

You should not, however, select a college simply because your scores match the profile of students already enrolled there. A particular college may offer a unique program or social environment that makes it right for you.

Student Services

You can order these services when you register for the SAT, or you can use the order form that is sent with your score report.

Question and Answer Service

For the disclosed administrations (specified in the *Registration Bulletin*), this service provides you with a computer-generated report that lists the question number, the correct answer, your answer, the type of question, and the difficulty level of that question. You will also receive the actual questions from the edition of the test you took, so you can review your performance on that test.

Student Answer Service

This service is available if the Question and Answer Service is not offered. The Student Answer Service provides your answer, the correct answer, the type of question, and the difficulty level of that question. This service does not provide the test questions but can help you identify types of questions on which you performed well or poorly.

Student Search Service®

The Student Search Service helps colleges find prospective students. When you take the PSAT/NMSQT, you can ask to be included in this free Search. Here's how it works:

When you indicate on the answer sheet that you want to be part of the Search, your name is put in a data base along with other information you provide: address, high school grade-point average, Social Security number, intended college major, and projected career.

Colleges and scholarship programs then use the Search to help them locate and recruit students with characteristics they are interested in.

Things to keep in mind about the Student Search Service:

- Your participation is voluntary. You may take the test without participating in the Search.
- Colleges participating in the Search do not receive your PSAT/NMSQT scores. They can ask for the names of students within certain score ranges, but your exact score is not reported.
- Being contacted by a college is not the same as being admitted. You can be admitted only after you apply. The Student Search Service is a means by which colleges reach prospective students, that's all.
- You may also participate in the Student Search Service when you take the SAT I, SAT II, or Advanced Placement (AP®) Examinations.

Chapter 2

Test-Taking Strategies

Test-Taking Rules

Follow these rules to gain all the points you possibly can.

Before the Test

- **Learn the directions for all six question types.** Take some time to read the directions for the different types of questions carefully. That way, you won't lose time reading the directions on the day you take the SAT. You'll feel more confident and be less likely to make careless errors because you will understand the instructions.

During the Test

- **Eliminate choices.** If you don't know the correct answer to a question, try eliminating wrong choices. It's sometimes easier to find the wrong answers than the correct one. On some questions, you can eliminate all the choices until you have only the one correct answer left. In other cases, eliminating choices can help you think your way through to the correct answer. If you can eliminate one choice as definitely wrong, guess an answer from among the remaining choices.
- **Guess when you can eliminate at least one choice.** If you can eliminate even one answer, you increase your chances of getting a question right. With each correct answer you gain one point; if you leave the answer blank you get no points; if your answer is wrong you only lose 1/4 of a point.
- **Don't spend too much time on any one question.** All questions are worth the same number of points. So if you can't answer a question without spending a long time figuring it out, go on to the next one. If you aren't sure about how to answer a question, or you don't know where to begin, stop working on that question. You may have time to come back to it later.
- **Don't lose points to carelessness.** No matter how frustrated you are, don't pass over questions without at least reading through them. And be sure to consider all the choices in each question. You could lose points on easy questions through careless errors. Take each question as it comes and avoid careless mistakes:

1. Answer the question asked. For example, if the question asks for the area of a shaded region, don't answer with the unshaded area.
2. Always read all the answers to a verbal question before choosing your answer.
3. For math questions, especially word problems, check that your answer makes sense. Is a discount higher than the original price? Is the average age of a high school student 56 years old?
4. Again for math, check your work from the beginning. If you can, use a *different* method than the one you used to get the answer. If you use the same method, you may make the same mistake twice.
5. Try to work at an even, steady pace. Keep moving, but not so quickly that you make careless mistakes.

- **Answer all the easy questions you can before moving on to the harder ones.** Once you know where the easy and hard questions are located (see "Pacing and Timing," page 15), be sure to answer the easy questions before tackling the more time-consuming questions. All questions are worth the same amount.
- **Use your test booklet as scratch paper.** While you have to keep your *answer sheet* neat and free of stray marks, you can mark up your test booklet. You can write whatever you want, wherever you want, in the section of the booklet you're working on. You will not receive credit for anything written in the booklet, however. How should you use your test booklet?
  - Mark each question that you don't answer so that you can easily go back to it later.
  - When working on a question, put a line through each choice as you eliminate it.
  - Mark sections, sentences, or words in reading passages.
  - In math, make drawings to help you figure out word problems. Mark key information on graphs. Add information to drawings and diagrams as you figure.

- **Check your answer sheet regularly to make sure you are in the right place.** Losing your place on the answer sheet can be a major problem that will affect your score. To prevent this, check the number of the question and the number on the answer sheet every few questions. Check them carefully every time you skip a question.

Recap: Test-Taking Rules

Before the Test

- Learn the directions for all six question types.

During the Test

- Eliminate choices.
- Guess when you can eliminate at least one choice.
- Don't spend too much time on any one question.
- Don't lose points to carelessness.
- Answer all the easy questions you can before moving on to the harder ones.
- Use your test booklet as scratch paper.
- Check your answer sheet regularly.

Pacing and Timing

Pacing is based on the idea that each question on the test takes a certain amount of time to read and answer. If you had unlimited time, or very few questions to answer, pacing would not be a problem.

Good test takers also develop a sense of timing to help them complete the test. The goal is to spend time on the questions that you are most likely to answer correctly and leave some time for review at the end of the testing period.

Strategies for Pacing

Following are some basic pacing strategies that will help ensure that you don't lose time on the SAT and that you'll have time to consider all the questions you have the ability to answer:

- **Keep moving.** Don't spend so much time puzzling out hard questions that you lose the time to find and answer the easier ones. Work on less time-consuming questions before moving on to more time-consuming ones. Remember to mark the questions as you work on them, especially the ones you want to go back to. Also, cross out choices you can eliminate as you move through the test. This will save time when you return to those questions later.
- **Questions arranged from easy to hard.** The questions on the SAT (and the PSAT/NMSQT) are organized from easy to hard (except for Critical Reading questions). This means that within a group of questions, for example Analogies, the easier ones come first and the questions get more difficult as you move along. If you find that the questions of one type are getting too difficult, quickly read through the rest of the questions in that group to see if there are others you can answer. Then go on to the next group of questions in that section. (Again, this does not apply to Critical Reading questions: a difficult Critical Reading question might be followed by an easier one — see Chapter 7.)
- **Spend time on the questions that you have the best chance of getting right.** Some question types take longer to answer than others. Most students find that they can answer Analogies in the least time, that Sentence Completions take longer, and that Critical Reading questions take the longest time to answer.

- **Keep track of time during the test.** The SAT includes seven sections requiring three hours. You should develop the habit of occasionally checking your progress through the test, so that you know when you are one-fourth of the way through the time allotted for a section, halfway through, and when you have five minutes left. If you finish a section before time is called, use the remaining time to check your answers and erase any stray marks on your answer sheet.
- **Know which questions are best for you.** After practicing the different types of questions on the tests in this book, you will probably know which type is your best. You might want to begin with that type of question rather than at the beginning of the section. If you do this, however, be sure to mark what was skipped and go back and do the questions you passed over.
- **Remember that all questions are worth the same.** The score value for a correct answer is the same regardless of the type of question or the difficulty of the question. So go through an entire section, answering questions that you know or can answer quickly and skipping questions for which you know you will need more time. Be careful to mark the skipped questions in your test booklet and leave the ovals on the answer sheet blank to avoid marking answers to the wrong questions.

A Recommended Approach to Pacing

Practice using the following pacing approach on the actual SATs included in this book:

1. Set up a schedule for progress through each test section. Know when you should be one-quarter of the way through and halfway through the section. Every now and then, check your progress against your schedule.

   [NOTE: Some questions take less time than others. So if you have 30 minutes to answer 30 questions, it does NOT necessarily work out to one minute per question. For example, if you take 10 minutes to answer 10 Analogies you are working too slowly. If, however, you take 10 minutes to read a passage and answer 10 questions on it, you are working at, or faster than, the speed you should be.]

2. Begin to work as soon as the testing time begins. Keep your attention focused on the test. Don't daydream.

3. Don't ponder over alternatives on the first pass through a section. Answer questions you are sure of first; mark those questions you are unsure of in the test booklet so you can easily locate them later. When you skip a question, make sure to mark your answers to later questions in the appropriate ovals on the answer sheet.
4. Go back and try the questions you skipped, using a guessing strategy if necessary.
5. In the last few minutes, check your answers to avoid careless mistakes.
6. Check your answer sheet to make sure that there are no stray marks and that all erasures are clean.

Pacing

- Keep moving.
- Questions are arranged from easy to hard.
- Spend time on the questions that you have the best chance of getting right.
- Keep track of time during the test.
- Know which questions are best for you.
- All questions are worth the same.

Guessing Strategies

Guessing on the SAT when you're not sure of an answer is a good idea if you have an effective strategy.

Understanding how the test is scored will help you develop an effective strategy for the multiple-choice questions and for the math questions that are not multiple choice and for which *you* supply an answer. Each correct answer on the SAT is worth one point.

Multiple-choice questions

When you are not sure of an answer to a multiple-choice question, eliminate all the answer choices that you know are wrong and guess from the remaining ones. The more choices you can eliminate, the better your chance of choosing the right answer and earning one point. To correct for random guessing, a fraction of a point is subtracted for each incorrect answer. Because of this, random guessing probably won't improve your score. In fact, it could lower your score. If you *can't* eliminate any choice, move on. You can return to the question later if there is time.

Student-produced-response math questions

For the math questions that are not multiple choice, fill in your best guess. You lose no points for incorrect answers to these problems. If you have no idea how to approach a problem, move on. You can return to it later if there is time.

Examples Using Real SAT Questions

The following SAT questions provide examples of how these guessing strategies work.

Verbal Guessing Example — Sentence Completion

He was ---- businessman, but in his personal life he was kind, thoughtful, and ---- .

(A) a competent . . self-centered

(B) an avaricious . . menacing

(C) a scrupulous . . tactful

(D) a ruthless . . magnanimous

(E) an amiable . . compassionate

Guessing explanation:

Start with the second blank in the sentence: He was ---- businessman, but in his personal life he was kind, thoughtful, and ---- . The word must be positive because it is in a series with the words *kind* and *thoughtful*. The second words in (A) and (B) — self-centered and menacing — are both negative, so you can

eliminate those two choices. That leaves (C), (D), or (E) as possible correct answers, giving you one chance in three of getting it right. Pick your guess.

Even though you may get this particular question wrong, it is to your advantage to guess if you can eliminate one or more of the answer choices as definitely wrong. The correct answer is (D).

Math Guessing Example — Multiple Choice

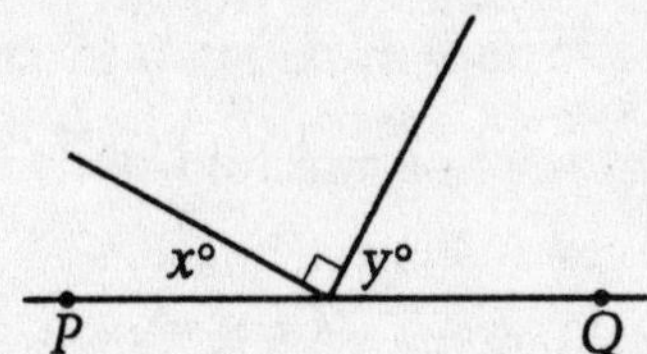

In the figure above, PQ is a straight line. Which of the following must be true about x and y?

(A) $x + y = 180$
(B) $90 + x = 180 - y$
(C) $90 + x = y$
(D) $2x = y$
(E) $2y = x$

Guessing explanation:

Which of the answer choices can you eliminate by estimation? Clearly, the answer cannot be choice A because both $x°$ and $y°$ are less than 90°. Cross off choice (A). Choice (B) looks possible, but what about (C)? It's pretty obvious that (C) is not the answer, because $90 + x$ is greater than y. Cross off choice (C). Choice (D) looks possible, so don't cross it off. But choice (E) is not possible, so cross it off. Now you're left with only two possible answers, (B) and (D). If you were simply guessing, you are now faced with only two choices and have a 50-50 chance of answering it correctly.

If you notice that $x° + y°$ must equal 90°, and examine choice (B), you will see that $90 + x = 180 - y$ simplifies to $x + y = 90$. Therefore, the correct answer is choice (B).

eliminate one more choice. That leaves (C), (D), or (E) as possible correct answers, giving you one chance in three of getting it right with your guess.

Even though you may get this particular question wrong, it is to your advantage to guess if you can eliminate one or more of the answer choices as definitely wrong. The correct answer is (D).

Math Reasoning Example — Multiple Choice

In the figure above, [illegible] are straight lines. Which of the following must be true?

[illegible]

Answer explanation

Which of the answer choices can you eliminate by estimation? [illegible] the answer cannot be [illegible] both [illegible] than 0, [illegible] choice (A). Choice (B) looks possible, but what about (C)? It's pretty obvious that (C) can't be the answer because [illegible] is greater than [illegible]. Choice (D) looks possible, so don't cross it off, but choice (E) is not possible, so cross it off. Now you're left with only two possible answers, (B) and (D). If you were simply guessing, you're now faced with only two choices and have a 50-50 chance of answering it correctly.

If you notice that [illegible] must equal [illegible] and examine choice (B), you will see that [illegible] simplifies to [illegible]. Therefore the correct answer is choice (B).

Chapter 3

Psyching Yourself Up

Your SAT results depend on how much you know and on how well you can put what you know to work. But your results can also reflect how you feel. Nerves, distractions, poor concentration, or a negative attitude can pull down your performance.

Relaxation Techniques

Being nervous is natural. Being nervous, by itself, isn't really a problem. A bit of a nervous edge can keep you sharp and focused. Too much nervousness, however, can keep you from concentrating and working effectively.

Here are some techniques you can use to keep your nerves in check.

Before the Test

You can start your psychological preparation the day before the test:

- Get a good night's sleep.
- Have everything that you need for the test ready the night before:
  - The appropriate ID, which must include your photo, or a brief description of you. The description must be on school stationery or a school ID form, and you must sign it in front of your principal or guidance counselor, who must also sign it.
  - Admission ticket
  - #2 pencils
  - Calculator with fresh batteries
- Make sure you know the way to the test center and any special instructions for finding the entrance on Saturday or Sunday.
- Leave yourself plenty of time for mishaps and emergencies.
- If you're not there when the test starts, you can't take the test.

Think Positively

Getting down on yourself during the test does more than make you feel bad. It can rob you of the confidence you need to solve problems. It can distract you. If you're thinking that you aren't doing well, you aren't thinking about the question in front of you. Think positive thoughts that will help you keep up your confidence and focus on each question.

Keep Yourself Focused

- Try not to think about anything except the question in front of you.
- If you catch yourself thinking about something else, bring your focus back to the test, but congratulate yourself. You have just demonstrated that you are in control.

Concentrate on Your Own Work

The first thing some students do when they get stuck on a question or find themselves running into a batch of tough questions is to look around to see how everyone else is doing. What they usually see is that others are filling in their answer sheets.

"Look at how well everyone else is doing . . . . What's wrong with me?" If you start thinking this way, try to remember:

- Everyone works at a different pace. Your neighbors may not be working on the exact question that has puzzled you.
- Thinking about what someone else is doing doesn't help you answer even a single question. In fact, it takes away time you should be using on the test.

Put the Test in Perspective

The SAT is important, but how you do on one test will not determine whether you get into college.

- The test is only one factor in the college admission decision.
- High school grades are considered more important than the SAT by most college admission officers.
- Nonacademic admission criteria are important, too. These include things like extracurricular activities and personal recommendations. College admission officers at individual colleges will usually be glad to discuss the admission policies at their institutions with you.
- If you don't do as well as you wanted to, you can take the test again.

Remember You're in Control

Developing a plan for taking the SAT will keep you in control during the test: practice each type of question, remember that the easier questions generally come first in each section, and learn how to pace yourself and guess wisely. If you're in control, you'll have the best chance of getting all the points you deserve.

Chapter 4

About Verbal Questions

The verbal sections of the SAT contain three types of questions:

- Sentence Completions
- Analogies
- Critical Reading

Sentence Completions are fill-in questions that test your vocabulary and your ability to understand fairly complex sentences. Analogies focus on the relationships between pairs of words; they measure your reasoning ability as well as the depth and breadth of your vocabulary. Critical Reading questions are based on passages 400 to 850 words long. The content of the passages is drawn from the humanities, the social sciences, and the natural sciences. Narrative passages (prose fiction or nonfiction) also are used in the test.

The three types of verbal questions are designed to test how well you understand the written word. Your ability to read carefully and to think about what you read is crucial to your success in college. In college, you will have to learn a great deal on your own from your assigned reading. And that's just as true in mathematics and science and technical courses as it is in "reading" courses like literature, philosophy, and history. Verbal skills are fundamental building blocks of academic success.

Strategies for Tackling the Questions

About half of the verbal questions are Sentence Completions and Analogies. Work on these first in any section that includes all three types of verbal questions. But don't spend half your time on them, because the Critical Reading passages take a lot more time. As you work on one of the 30-minute verbal sections, you may want to use the following strategy:

- Begin with the first set of Sentence Completions. Answer as many questions as you can. Mark the others with a question mark (?) or an X. A question mark means you have a good chance of answering the question with a little more time. An X means you don't think you'll have much chance of answering the question correctly.
- Move on next to the Analogy questions and work through them the same way you worked through the Sentence Completions.

- Go back and take a second, quick look at the questions you marked with a question mark. Answer the ones you can without spending lots of time.
- Then move on to the Critical Reading passages and questions.
- **Important:** One 15-minute verbal section includes *only* Critical Reading questions.

Even when questions of one type become difficult to answer, give the rest of them a quick read before you skip ahead to the next type. All Sentence Completion and Analogy questions are based in part on your knowledge of vocabulary, and you never can tell when you might hit on a word that you know. It doesn't take long to read these questions and you may pick up a correct answer or two.

If you have time to go back to some of the more difficult questions that you skipped, try eliminating choices. Sometimes you can get to the correct answer that way. If not, eliminating choices will at least allow you to make educated guesses.

Consider related words, familiar sayings and phrases, roots, prefixes, and suffixes. If you don't know what a word means right away, stop for a moment to think about whether you have heard or seen a word that might be related to it.

You might get help from common sayings and phrases. If you don't know a word but are familiar with a phrase that uses it, you might be able to figure the word out.

For instance, you might not immediately remember what the words *ovation* and *annul* mean. But you probably would recognize them in the phrases *a standing ovation* and *annul a marriage*. If you can recall a phrase or saying in which a word is used, you may be able to figure out what it means in another context.

Building Vocabulary Skills

Building vocabulary takes time, but it doesn't take magic. The single most effective thing you can do to build your vocabulary, over time, is to read a lot. Your teachers and librarians will be more than happy to recommend a variety of helpful and enjoyable reading materials for you.

In addition to reading, there are many other things you can do to improve your vocabulary. The suggestions offered here are presented in outline form, but vocabulary building is a long-term effort. If you succeed, the results will go a long way toward helping you reach your academic goals, including and beyond getting good SAT verbal scores.

- When you read to improve your vocabulary, have a dictionary and a pencil handy. Each time you encounter a word you don't know, stop. Try to figure out what it means from the context. If you can't figure the word out, look it up and make a note of it.
- When you look up a word in the dictionary, pay attention to the different definitions and the contexts in which each is appropriate.
- Practice your expanding vocabulary by using the new words you have learned in your reading with your friends and in your school writing assignments.
- Pay close attention to roots, prefixes, and suffixes.
- Check your school or local library and/or bookstore for vocabulary-building books. Almost all of them include lists of common roots, prefixes, and suffixes.
- Memorizing the meanings of roots, prefixes, and suffixes will be more helpful than memorizing individual words.
- Apply your knowledge of foreign languages, especially those related to Latin, such as Spanish, French, and Italian. English has many cognates, or words with similar meanings, from these languages.
- Work crossword puzzles.
- Play Scrabble or Boggle.
- Play word-find games.

Tip:

If you take the time to do vocabulary-building work every time you read, you may not get much reading done or enjoy your reading as fully as you should. So set aside a reasonable amount of time, perhaps half an hour, for vocabulary building two or three times a week. If you keep it up week-in and week-out, month after month, you'll be surprised at how much you will add to your vocabulary in a year's time.

Chapter 5

Sentence Completion Questions

Sentence Completion questions require a broad vocabulary plus the ability to understand the logic of sentences that are sometimes quite complex. There is no short, simple approach to Sentence Completions. But there are a number of strategies that will help you through even the toughest questions.

The box below gives an example of the kind of questions that will appear on the test, and the directions for Sentence Completions.

Each sentence below has one or two blanks, each blank indicating that something has been omitted. Beneath the sentence are five words or sets of words labeled A through E. Choose the word or set of words that, when inserted in the sentence, best fits the meaning of the sentence as a whole.

Example:

Medieval kingdoms did not become constitutional republics overnight; on the contrary, the change was ---- .

(A) unpopular
(B) unexpected
(C) advantageous
(D) sufficient
(E) gradual

The correct answer is (E).

Explanation:

The first part of the sentence says that the kingdoms did not change *overnight*. The second part begins with *on the contrary* and explains the change. So the correct answer will be a word that describes a change that is *contrary* to an *overnight* change. Gradual change is *contrary* to *overnight* change.

- Sentence Completion questions can have one or two blanks, but each sentence, as a whole, still counts as only **one** question.
- Some of the questions are straightforward vocabulary questions. Others require that you know more than just the meanings of the words involved. They also require that you understand the logic of fairly complicated sentences.
- Most Sentence Completions involve compound or complex sentences, that is, sentences made up of several clauses. In many cases, to answer the question correctly you have to figure out how the parts of the sentence—the different clauses—relate to each other.

Here are some examples of the different types of Sentence Completion questions you will see:

Example 1: A one-blank vocabulary-based question

This type of question depends more on your knowledge of vocabulary than on your ability to follow the logic of a complicated sentence. You still need to know how the words are used in the context of the sentence, but if you know the definitions of the words involved, you almost certainly will be able to select the correct answer.

These one-blank vocabulary-based questions tend to be relatively short, usually not more than 20 words.

Ravens appear to behave ---- , actively
helping one another to find food.

(A) mysteriously
(B) warily
(C) aggressively
(D) cooperatively
(E) defensively

The correct answer is (D).

Explanation:

This sentence asks you to look for a word that describes how the ravens behave. The information after the comma restates and defines the meaning of the missing word. You are told that the

ravens *actively help one another*. There is only one word among the choices that accurately describes this behavior — *cooperatively*.

Example 2: A two-blank vocabulary-based question

You will also find some two-blank sentences with rather straightforward logic but challenging vocabulary.

Both ---- and ---- , Wilson seldom spoke and never spent money.

(A) vociferous..generous
(B) garrulous..stingy
(C) effusive..frugal
(D) taciturn..miserly
(E) reticent..munificent

The correct answer is (D).

Explanation:

In this sentence, the logic is not difficult. You are looking for two words that describe Wilson. One of the words has to mean that he *seldom spoke* and the other that he *never spent money*. The correct answer is *taciturn..miserly*. Taciturn means "shy, unwilling to talk." Miserly means "like a miser, extremely stingy."

Example 3: A one-blank logic-based question

Success in answering these questions depends as much on your ability to reason out the logic of the sentence as it does on your knowledge of vocabulary.

After observing several vicious territorial fights, Jane Goodall had to revise her earlier opinion that these particular primates were always ---- animals.

(A) ignorant
(B) inquisitive
(C) responsive
(D) cruel
(E) peaceful

The correct answer is (E).

Explanation:

To answer this question, you have to follow the logical flow of the ideas in the sentence. A few key words reveal that logic:

- First, the introductory word **After** tells you that the information at the beginning of the sentence is going to affect what comes later. The word **After** also gives an order to the events in the sentence.
- Second, the word **revise** tells you that something is going to change. It is going to change **after** the events described at the beginning of the sentence. So the events at the beginning really cause the change.
- Finally, the end of the sentence — **her earlier opinion that these particular primates were always ---- animals** — tells you what is changing. The word filling the blank should convey a meaning you would have to revise after seeing the animals fight. **Peaceful** is the only such word among the five choices.

Example 4: A two-blank logic-based question

The following question requires you to know the meanings of the words, know how the words are used in context, and understand the logic of a rather complicated sentence.

Although its publicity has been ---- , the film itself is intelligent, well-acted, handsomely produced, and altogether ---- .

(A) tasteless..respectable
(B) extensive..moderate
(C) sophisticated..amateur
(D) risqué..crude
(E) perfect..spectacular

The correct answer is (A).

Explanation:

The first thing to notice about this sentence is that it has two parts or clauses. The first clause begins with *Although*, the second clause begins with *the film*.

The logic of the sentence is determined by the way the two clauses relate to each other. The two parts have contrasting or conflicting meanings. Why? Because one of the clauses begins with *Although*. The word *Although* is used to introduce an idea that conflicts with something else in the sentence: *Although* something is true, something else that you would expect to be true is not.

The answer is *tasteless..respectable*. You would not expect a film with *tasteless publicity* to be *altogether respectable*. But the introductory word *Although* tells you that you should expect the unexpected.

Strategies

Start out by reading the entire sentence saying *blank* for the blank(s). This gives you an overall sense of the meaning of the sentence and helps you figure out how the parts of the sentence relate to each other.

Always begin by trying to pin down the standard dictionary definitions of the words in the sentence and the answers. To answer Sentence Completion questions, you usually don't have to know a nonstandard meaning of a word.

Introductory and transitional words are extremely important. They can be the key to figuring out the logic of a sentence. They tell you how the parts of the sentence relate to each other. Consider the following common introductory and transitional words: *but*, *although*, *however*, *yet*, *even though*. These words indicate that the two parts of the sentence will contradict or be in contrast with each other. There are many other introductory and transitional words that you should watch for when working on Sentence Completion questions. *Always* read the sentences carefully and don't ignore any of the details.

Some of the most difficult Sentence Completion questions contain negatives, which can make it hard to follow the logic of the sentences. Negatives in two clauses of a sentence can be even more of a challenge:

> According to Burgess, a novelist **should not** preach,
> for sermonizing **has no place** in good fiction.

A negative appears in each clause of this sentence. The transitional word "for" indicates that the second part of the sentence will explain the first.

Figure out what sort of word(s) should fill the blank(s) before looking at the choices, then look for a choice that is similar to the one(s) you thought up. For many one-blank questions, especially the easier ones, you'll find the word you thought of among the choices. Other times, a close synonym for your word will be one of the choices.

Try answering the following Sentence Completion question without looking at the choices.

> Once Murphy left home for good, he wrote no letters to his worried mother; he did not, therefore, live up to her picture of him as her ---- son.

The transitional word **therefore** indicates that the information in the second part of the sentence is a direct, logical result of the information in the first part. What words might fit in the blank?

________________ ________________

________________ ________________

The second part of the sentence includes a negative **(he did not...live up to her picture...)**, so the blank must be a positive term. Words like **perfect**, **sweet**, **respectful**, **devoted** — all could fit in the blank. Now, look at the actual choices:

(A) misunderstood
(B) elusive
(C) destructive
(D) persuasive
(E) dutiful

(E) **dutiful** is the only choice that is even close to the ones suggested. (E) is the correct answer.

You can also try this technique with two-blank questions. You are less likely to come up with as close a word match, but it will help you get a feel for the meaning and logic of the sentence.

With two-blank questions, try eliminating some answers based on just one blank. If one word in an answer doesn't make sense in the sentence, then you can reject the entire choice.

Try approaching two-blank questions like this:

- Work with one of the blanks alone. Eliminate any choices in which the word doesn't make sense.
- Work on the other blank alone. Eliminate any choices in which that

word doesn't make sense. If only one choice is left, that is the correct answer. If more than one choice remains, go to the next step.

- Work on both blanks together only for the remaining choices.
- Always read the complete sentence with both words in place to make sure your choice makes sense.

Example 4, discussed previously, shows how this approach works. The first blank is not tightly controlled by the words immediately around it. The first word depends on the word in the second blank. So start with the second blank.

The second blank is part of a list that includes **intelligent**, **well-acted**, **handsomely produced**, and ______________ . The word **and** indicates that the last word in the list (the blank) should be a positive word, in general agreement with the others. With that in mind, examine the second words in the choices:

intelligent, well-acted...and altogether respectable
intelligent, well-acted...and altogether moderate
~~**intelligent, well-acted...and altogether amateur**~~
~~**intelligent, well-acted...and altogether crude**~~
intelligent, well-acted...and altogether spectacular

Amateur and **crude** are definitely not complimentary. No matter what the rest of the sentence says, neither of these words makes sense in the second blank. So you can eliminate the answers that contain **amateur** and **crude**. With two choices eliminated, the question becomes much easier to deal with.

Remember that the instructions for all the verbal questions ask you to choose the *best* answer. One choice may seem to make sense, but it still might not be the *best* of the five choices. Unless you read all the choices, you may select only the *second best* and thus lose points.

Check your choice by reading the entire sentence with the answer you have selected in place to make sure the sentence makes sense. This step is extremely important, especially if you have used shortcuts to eliminate choices.

Choice (A) is correct because **respectable** and **tasteless** contrast with each other. Such a contrast is logically consistent because of the "although" construction of the sentence.

Sample Questions

1 A judgment made before all the facts are known must be called ----.

(A) harsh
(B) deliberate
(C) sensible
(D) premature
(E) fair

2 Despite their ---- proportions, the murals of Diego Rivera give his Mexican compatriots the sense that their history is ---- and human in scale, not remote and larger than life.

(A) monumental..accessible
(B) focused..prolonged
(C) vast..ancient
(D) realistic..extraneous
(E) narrow..overwhelming

3 The research is so ---- that it leaves no part of the issue unexamined.

(A) comprehensive
(B) rewarding
(C) sporadic
(D) economical
(E) problematical

4 A dictatorship ---- its citizens to be docile and finds it expedient to make outcasts of those who do not ----.

(A) forces..rebel
(B) expects..disobey
(C) requires..conform
(D) allows..withdraw
(E) forbids..agree

5 Alice Walker's prize-winning novel exemplifies the strength of first-person narratives; the protagonist tells her own story so effectively that any additional commentary would be ----.

(A) subjective
(B) eloquent
(C) superfluous
(D) incontrovertible
(E) impervious

6 The Supreme Court's reversal of its previous ruling on the issue of states' rights ---- its reputation for ----.

(A) sustained..infallibility
(B) compromised..consistency
(C) bolstered..doggedness
(D) aggravated..inflexibility
(E) dispelled..vacillation

Answers and Explanations

1 A judgment made before all the facts are known must be called ---- .

(A) harsh
(B) deliberate
(C) sensible
(D) premature
(E) fair

Difficulty level: Easy

The correct answer is (D).

Explanation:

Getting the correct answer to this question depends almost entirely on your knowing the definitions of the five words you must choose from. Which of the choices describes a judgment made before *all the facts are known*? Such a judgment, by definition, is not deliberate, and the sentence doesn't tell us whether the judgment was *harsh* or lenient, *sensible* or dumb, *fair* or unfair. *Premature* means hasty or early. It fits the blank perfectly.

Know your vocabulary. Think carefully about the meanings of the words in the answer choices.

2 Despite their ---- proportions, the murals of Diego Rivera give his Mexican compatriots the sense that their history is ---- and human in scale, not remote and larger than life.

(A) monumental..accessible
(B) focused..prolonged
(C) vast..ancient
(D) realistic..extraneous
(E) narrow..overwhelming

Difficulty level: Medium

The correct answer is (A).

Explanation:

The keys to this sentence are the word *Despite*, the words *human in scale*, and the words *not remote and larger than life*. The word filling the first blank has to be one that would relate closely to something that seems *larger than life*. The word filling the second blank has to fit with *human in scale*. If you focus on just one of the two blanks, you will be able to eliminate several choices before you even think about the other blank.

Tip:

Watch for key introductory and transitional words that determine how the parts of the sentence relate to each other. Then try answering two-blank questions one blank at a time. If you can eliminate one word in a choice, the entire choice can be ruled out.

3 The research is so ---- that it leaves no part of the issue unexamined.

(A) comprehensive
(B) rewarding
(C) sporadic
(D) economical
(E) problematical

Difficulty level: Medium

The correct answer is (A).

Explanation:

Try filling in the blank without reading the answer choices. What kind of words would fit? Words like *complete*, *thorough*, or *extensive* could all fit. Now look at the answer choices. *Comprehensive* is very similar to the words suggested, and none of the other choices fits at all.

Tip:

Try thinking about the logic of the sentence without looking at the choices. Then look for the choice that has a similar meaning to the words you thought up.

4 A dictatorship ---- its citizens to be docile and finds it expedient to make outcasts of those who do not ---- .

(A) forces..rebel
(B) expects..disobey
(C) requires..conform
(D) allows..withdraw
(E) forbids..agree

Difficulty level: Easy

The correct answer is (C).

Explanation:

Answering this question depends in part on your knowledge of vocabulary. You have to know what the words *dictatorship*, *docile*, and *expedient* mean. You also have to watch out for key words such as *not*.

Tip:

Think carefully about the standard dictionary definitions of the important words in the sentence. And remember that small words such as *not* can make a big difference. When you pick your answer, read the entire sentence with the blank(s) filled in to be sure that it makes sense.

5 Alice Walker's prize-winning novel exemplifies the strength of first-person narratives; the protagonist tells her own story so effectively that any additional commentary would be ---- .

(A) subjective
(B) eloquent
(C) superfluous
(D) incontrovertible
(E) impervious

Difficulty level: Medium

The correct answer is (C).

Explanation:

Words like *prize-winning*, *strength*, and *effectively* tell you that the writer thinks Alice Walker's novel is well written. So would *additional commentary* be necessary or unnecessary? Once you've figured out that it is unnecessary, you can look for an answer with a similar meaning. That way, you may be able to answer the question more quickly, since you won't have to plug in each choice one by one to see if it makes any sense.

Tip:

Think about the meaning of the sentence before you look at the choices. Get a sense of what you're looking for *before* you start looking.

6 The Supreme Court's reversal of its previous ruling on the issue of states' rights ---- its reputation for ---- .

(A) sustained..infallibility
(B) compromised..consistency
(C) bolstered..doggedness
(D) aggravated..inflexibility
(E) dispelled..vacillation

Difficulty level: Hard

The correct answer is (B).

Explanation:

Getting the correct answer to this question depends in large part on your knowledge of the meanings of the words offered as choices. You have to know the definitions of the words before you can try the choices one by one to arrive at the correct pair.

You also need to think about the central idea in the sentence: the court's *reversal* blank its *reputation* for blank. The logic is complicated and the vocabulary in the choices is hard; but, if you stick with it, you'll figure out that only (B) makes sense.

Tip:

When you read the sentence to yourself, substitute the word *blank* for each blank. Try to figure out what the sentence is saying before you start plugging in the choices.

Recap: Tips for Sentence Completion Questions

1. Learn the directions ahead of time.
2. Answer all the easy questions you can before moving on to the harder ones.
3. Read the sentence, substituting the word *blank* for each blank.
4. Always begin by trying to pin down the dictionary definitions of the key words in the sentence and the answer choices.
5. Watch for the key introductory and transitional words. These determine how the parts of the sentence relate to each other. Also watch carefully for negatives.
6. Try figuring out words to fill in the blank or blanks without looking at the answers. Then look for the choice that is similar to the one you thought up.
7. Try answering two-blank questions one blank at a time. If you can eliminate one word in an answer, the entire choice can be eliminated.
8. Always check all the answer choices before making a final decision. A choice may seem okay, but still not be the best answer. Make sure that the answer you select is the best one.
9. Check your answer to make sure it makes sense by reading the entire sentence with your choice in place.
10. Eliminate answers that you know are wrong and guess from those remaining.

Practice Questions and Answer Key

Each sentence below has one or two blanks, each blank indicating that something has been omitted. Beneath the sentence are five words or sets of words labeled A through E. Choose the word or set of words that, when inserted in the sentence, best fits the meaning of the sentence as a whole.

Example:

Medieval kingdoms did not become constitutional republics overnight; on the contrary, the change was ----.

(A) unpopular
(B) unexpected
(C) advantageous
(D) sufficient
(E) gradual Ⓐ Ⓑ Ⓒ Ⓓ ●

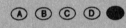

1 In many cases, the formerly ---- origins of diseases have now been identified through modern scientific techniques.

(A) insightful
(B) mysterious
(C) cruel
(D) notable
(E) useful

2 Freeing embedded fossils from rock has become less ---- for paleontologists, who now have tiny vibrating drills capable of working with great speed and delicacy.

(A) exploratory
(B) conclusive
(C) tedious
(D) respected
(E) demeaning

3 Many people find Stanley Jordan's music not only entertaining but also ---- ; listening to it helps them to relax and to ---- the tensions they feel at the end of a trying day.

(A) soothing..heighten
(B) therapeutic..alleviate
(C) sweet..underscore
(D) exhausting..relieve
(E) interesting..activate

4 Marine biologist Sylvia Earle makes a career of expanding the limits of deep-sea mobility, making hitherto-impossible tasks ---- through the new technology designed by her company.

(A) famous
(B) feasible
(c) fantastic
(D) controversial
(E) captivating

5 Two anomalies regarding her character are apparent: she is unfailingly ---- yet bursting with ambition, and she is truly ---- but unable to evoke reciprocal warmth in those with whom she works.

(A) aspiring..generous
(B) mercenary..impartial
(c) impulsive..resolute
(D) persistent..reserved
(E) humble..compassionate

6 In many parts of East Africa at that time, wild animals were so ---- that it was almost impossible for a photographer to approach close enough to film them.

(A) rare
(B) large
(C) wary
(D) numerous
(E) unsightly

7 The unflattering reviews that his latest recording received were ---- by his fans, who believe that everything he performs is a triumph of artistic ---- .

(A) dismissed..creativity
(B) hailed..responsibility
(C) suppressed..self-promotion
(D) accepted..genius
(E) regretted..pretension

8 The board members, accustomed to the luxury of being chauffeured to corporate meetings in company limousines, were predictably ---- when they learned that this service had been ---- .

(A) satisfied..annulled
(B) stymied..extended
(C) displeased..upheld
(D) disgruntled..suspended
(E) concerned..provided

9 Misrepresentative graphs and drawings ---- the real data and encourage readers to accept ---- arguments.

(A) obscure..legitimate
(B) distort..spurious
(C) illustrate..controversial
(D) complement..unresolved
(E) replace..esteemed

10 Conservative historians who represent a traditional account as ---- because of its age may be guilty of taking on trust what they should have ---- in a conscientious fashion.

(A) ancient..established
(B) false..reiterated
(C) mythical..fabricated
(D) accurate..examined
(E) suspicious..challenged

11 The art of Milet Andrejevic often presents us with an idyllic vision that is subtly ---- by more sinister elements, as if suggesting the ---- beauty of our surroundings.

(A) enhanced..pristine
(B) invaded..flawed
(C) altered..unmarred
(D) redeemed..hallowed
(E) devastated..bland

12 State commissioner Ming Hsu expected that her Commission on International Trade would not merely ---- the future effects of foreign competition on local businesses but would also offer practical strategies for successfully resisting such competition.

(A) counteract
(B) intensify
(C) imagine
(D) forecast
(E) excuse

13 Since many teachers today draw on material from a variety of sources, disciplines, and ideologies for their lessons, their approach could best be called ---- .

(A) eclectic
(B) simplistic
(C) invidious
(D) impromptu
(E) dogmatic

14 Unprecedented turmoil in the usually thriving nation has made the formerly ---- investors leery of any further involvement.

(A) pessimistic
(B) cautious
(C) clandestine
(D) reticent
(E) sanguine

15 Despite its apparent ---- , much of early Greek philosophical thought was actually marked by a kind of unconscious dogmatism that led to ---- assertions.

(A) liberality..doctrinaire
(B) independence..autonomous
(C) intransigence..authoritative
(D) fundamentalism..arrogant
(E) legitimacy..ambiguous

Answer Key

	Correct Answer	Difficulty
1.	B	E
2.	C	E
3.	B	E
4.	B	M
5.	E	M
6.	C	M
7.	A	M
8.	D	M
9.	B	M
10.	D	M
11.	B	H
12.	D	H
13.	A	H
14.	E	H
15.	A	H

Chapter 6

Analogy Questions

Analogies are vocabulary questions, but they require more than just knowing the definitions of words. Analogies ask you to figure out the relationships between pairs of words. They challenge you to think about why it makes sense to put two words together. So, you have to know the definitions of words, but you also have to know how the words are used.

Learn the directions ahead of time. Save yourself valuable time by knowing the directions before the day of the test. In the box below is an example of the kind of question you'll encounter, and the directions for Analogies.

Each question below consists of a related pair of words or phrases, followed by five pairs of words or phrases labeled A through E. Select the pair that best expresses a relationship similar to that expressed in the original pair.

Example:

CRUMB:BREAD::
(A) ounce:unit
(B) splinter:wood
(C) water:bucket
(D) twine:rope
(E) cream:butter

The correct answer is (B).

Explanation:

To answer Analogy questions, you must first figure out the relationship between the two words in CAPITAL LETTERS. Then look for the pair of words among the answers that has the same relationship.

In the sample, the words in capital letters are CRUMB and BREAD. What is the relationship between these two words? *A CRUMB is a very small piece that falls off or breaks off of a piece of BREAD.*

What makes (B) splinter:wood the right answer? *A splinter is a very small piece that breaks off or splits away from a piece of wood.* You can use almost the very same words to describe the

relationships between CRUMB and BREAD, on the one hand, and *splinter* and *wood*, on the other. That is what makes the relationships *analogous*, what makes them similar.

None of the relationships between the two words in the other choices is similar to the relationship between CRUMB and BREAD:

- An **ounce** is a type of **unit**; it is not a small piece of a **unit**.
- **Water** can be carried in a **bucket**; it is not a piece of a **bucket**.
- **Twine** is thinner and less strong than **rope**, but it is not a small piece that breaks off of a **rope**.
- **Cream** is what **butter** is made from, but cream is not a small piece of **butter**.

Strategies

With Analogies, you are looking for similar *relationships*, not similar meanings. Analogy questions *do not* ask you to look for words that have the same meaning as the word in capital letters.

In the preceding example, (B) is the correct answer because the relationship between **splinter** and **wood** is similar to the relationship between CRUMB and BREAD. The word CRUMB does not mean the same thing as the word **splinter**, and the word BREAD does not have the same meaning as the word **wood**.

The explanation of the preceding example gives you two clues: first, you can express the relationship between the two words in capital letters in a sentence that explains how they are related. Second, you can express the relationship between the two words in the correct answer by using almost the *same sentence* and substituting the words in the answer for the words in capitals.

To answer Analogy questions, start by making up a "test sentence" that explains how the two words in capital letters are related. Then try the words from each answer in your test sentence to see which pair makes the most sense.

Here's a question to practice on.

ALBUM:PHOTOGRAPHS::
(A) trial:briefs
(B) board:directors
(C) meeting:agendas
(D) scrapbook:clippings
(E) checkbook:money

Make up a sentence that expresses the relationship between the two words in capital letters. That sentence will become your test sentence for the answers.

An ALBUM is a place for saving PHOTOGRAPHS.
A ____________ is a place for saving____________ .

Try the words in each choice in your test sentence and eliminate any choices that don't make sense. The pair that makes the most sense in the test sentence is the correct answer.

(A) A **trial** is a place for saving **briefs**.
(B) A **board** is a place for saving **directors**.
(C) A **meeting** is a place for saving **agendas**.
(D) A **scrapbook** is a place for saving **clippings**.
(E) A **checkbook** is a place for saving **money**.

Only choice (D) makes sense. It's analogous to the words in capital letters.

Establish Relationships

To practice establishing relationships, write out a relationship for each pair of words below. Be as precise as possible. If you can think of more than one relationship between a pair of words, write down both relationships. (Use a dictionary for words you don't know.)

Pairs	Sentence Showing Relationship
1. mansion:house	________________
2. actor:stage	________________
3. tailor-made:suit	________________
4. miser:stingy	________________
5. patriotic:country	________________
6. composer:music	________________
7. minnow:fish	________________
8. herd:elephant	________________
9. head:helmet	________________
10. tractor:farm	________________
11. school:fish	________________
12. hospital:doctor	________________
13. carpenter:saw	________________
14. bulldozer:construction	________________
15. bold:foolhardy	________________
16. flock:bird	________________
17. runner:sled	________________
18. elegy:mournful	________________
19. teacher:school	________________

20. Now make a sentence establishing the relationship for

    surgeon:scalpel ________________________

    ____

    Which word pair above has the same relationship as the relationship expressed by **surgeon:scalpel?** ________________

Be Flexible

If you don't get a single correct answer right away, you'll have to revise your test sentence. Many English words have more than one meaning. And pairs of words can have more than one relationship. So you may have to try a couple of test sentences before you find one that gives you a single correct answer. Some test sentences will state a relationship that is so broad or general that more than one answer makes sense. Other test sentences may be so narrow or specific that none of the choices fit.

Practice is the key here. You may have to try several test sentences before you find one that gives you a single correct answer. Don't worry about writing style when making up your test sentences. You're just trying to state the relationship between the pair of words in a way that will help you choose the correct answer. And you don't get any points for making up grammatically correct test sentences. You get points for choosing correct answers. The sentences are only a technique. Once you make up a test sentence, you still have to think about how the choices work in it.

Analogy questions use words consistently. If you can't tell how a word in capital letters is being used (if it is a word that can represent more than one part of speech), look at the choices. The words in the choices can sometimes help you make sense of the two words in capital letters.

Comparing individual words. Don't be distracted by the relationships between individual words in the choices and individual words in capital letters. Remember that you are looking for analogous relationships between *pairs* of words.

Reversing word order. It's okay to reverse the order of the words in capital letters when you make up your test sentence. But if you do, remember to reverse the order of the words in the choices, too, when you try them in your test sentence.

Handling abstract questions. Although abstract words may be more challenging than concrete words, the same strategies are applicable to answering both kinds of Analogy questions. Identify the relationship between the two words, then express that relationship in a test sentence. Finally, use the test sentence to identify the correct answer.

Eliminate Wrong Choices and Guess. If you don't know the correct answer, eliminate any choices that you know are wrong and guess from those remaining.

Sample Questions

1 ACT:PLAY::
(A) song:music
(B) rhyme:poem
(C) page:novel
(D) chapter:book
(E) scenery:performance

Your test sentence:

Your answer:

2 BOLD:FOOLHARDY::
(A) lively:enthusiastic
(B) natural:synthetic
(C) generous:spendthrift
(D) wise:thoughtful
(E) creative:childlike

Your test sentence:

Your answer:

3 CHILL:COLD::
(A) parch:dry
(B) crush:soft
(C) freeze:white
(D) feed:hungry
(E) scrub:hard

Your test sentence:

Your answer:

4 LAWYER:CLIENT::
(A) doctor:surgeon
(B) admiral:sailor
(C) judge:defendant
(D) musician:audience
(E) tutor:student

Your test sentence:

Your answer:

5 IRON:BLACKSMITH::
(A) gold:miser
(B) clay:potter
(C) food:gourmet
(D) steel:industrialist
(E) silver:miner

Your test sentence:

Your answer:

6 ILLOGICAL:CONFUSION::
(A) profound:laughter
(B) revolting:sympathy
(C) astounding:amazement
(D) obscure:contrast
(E) deliberate:vitality

Your test sentence:

Your answer:

Answers and Explanations

1 ACT:PLAY::

(A) song:music
(B) rhyme:poem
(C) page:novel
(D) chapter:book
(E) scenery:performance

The correct answer is (D).

Test sentence:

A PLAY is divided into ACTs.
A __________ is divided into __________ s.

Explanation:

Your first test sentence may have stated a more general relationship, such as an ACT is *part of* a PLAY. Unfortunately, more than one choice would be correct in that sentence. The test sentence above reverses the order of the words, making the sentence more precise and making the correct answer easier to find. Be sure to reverse the words in the choices when trying them in your test sentence. The content of a PLAY is divided into ACTs, just as the content of a BOOK is divided into CHAPTERs. Your test sentence must be precise and detailed enough to leave only one correct answer.

If more than one answer makes sense in your test sentence, revise your sentence so it states a more specific relationship.

2 BOLD:FOOLHARDY::

(A) lively:enthusiastic

(B) natural:synthetic

(C) generous:spendthrift

(D) wise:thoughtful

(E) creative:childlike

The correct answer is (C).

Test sentence:

To be overly BOLD is to be FOOLHARDY.

To be overly __________ is to be __________ .

Explanation:

The relationship between BOLD and FOOLHARDY expresses a positive quality turning into a negative quality. Even though these terms are abstract, the basic approach is still the same: establish the relationship between the capitalized words in a test sentence and then try each of the choices in the test sentence until you figure out which choice fits best.

Whether the words are hard or easy, abstract or concrete, solve analogies by establishing the relationship between the words in capitals first and then looking for a similar or parallel relationship in the choices.

3 CHILL:COLD::

(A) parch:dry

(B) crush:soft

(C) freeze:white

(D) feed:hungry

(E) scrub:hard

The correct answer is (A).

Test sentence:

To CHILL something is to make it COLD.

To __________ something is to make it __________ .

Explanation:

The word CHILL can be used as several different parts of speech. It can be used as a verb (as it is in the test sentence), as an adjective (a CHILL wind), or as a noun (I caught a CHILL).

In this question, if you used the word CHILL as anything but a verb, your test sentence wouldn't work for any of the answer choices. If you're unsure of how to state the relationship between the words in capital letters, try working your way through the choices to establish relationships.

Tip:

Pay attention to the way you are using the words in capital letters in your test sentence. They should be used the same way (be the same parts of speech) as the words in the choices.

4 LAWYER:CLIENT::

(A) doctor:surgeon
(B) admiral:sailor
(C) judge:defendant
(D) musician:audience
(E) tutor:student

The correct answer is (E).

Test sentence:

A LAWYER is hired to help a CLIENT.

A __________ is hired to help a __________ .

Explanation:

Some students get distracted by the relationships between the individual words in the answers and the individual words in capital letters. There is a close relationship between a *judge* and a LAWYER, but the relationship between a *judge* and a *defendant* is not similar to the relationship between a LAWYER and a CLIENT.

Of course, tutors mostly teach (which lawyers do only rarely) and lawyers represent their clients in courtrooms (which tutors never do). Every analogy has some dissimilarities as well as similarities. The correct answer is the one that "best expresses" a similar relationship with the pair in capital letters.

Tip:

Remember that you are looking for analogous relationships between pairs of words. Don't be distracted by individual words in the choices that have relationships to individual words in capital letters.

5 IRON:BLACKSMITH::

(A) gold:miser
(B) clay:potter
(C) food:gourmet
(D) steel:industrialist
(E) silver:miner

The correct answer is (B).

Test sentence:

A BLACKSMITH shapes things out of IRON.

A ________ shapes things out of ________ .

Explanation:

You may initially have expressed the relationship with the test sentence a BLACKSMITH *deals with* IRON, but *deals with* is a very general statement and would not have eliminated many choices. The phrase *shapes things out of* is more precise because it specifies what the BLACKSMITH does with IRON.

You might also have thought of the sentence a BLACKSMITH *hammers* IRON. But *hammers* is too specific. It is only one of the things that the BLACKSMITH does while working with IRON. None of the choices would have worked using *hammers* as the key to the relationship.

Tip:

Be flexible when establishing relationships. If your first test sentence yields no possible answers, try a different or more general approach. If it yields several possible answers, try a more specific approach. And remember: it's okay to switch the order of the words in capitals when you make up your test sentence, but make sure that you also switch the order of the words in the answer choices when you test them.

6 ILLOGICAL:CONFUSION::
(A) profound:laughter
(B) revolting:sympathy
(C) astounding:amazement
(D) obscure:contrast
(E) deliberate:vitality

The correct answer is (C).

Test sentence:

If something is ILLOGICAL, it leads to CONFUSION.

If something is __________ , it leads to __________ .

Explanation:

CONFUSION is usually thought of as negative or undesirable, and amazement is more positive. But the dissimilarity between these words doesn't matter as long as the *relationship* between the words in capitals is parallel to the *relationship* between the words in the correct answer.

In Analogy questions, always look for similar *relationships* between words, NOT for similar meanings or similar connotations of words.

Recap: Tips for Analogy Questions

1. Learn the directions ahead of time.
2. Answer all the easy questions you can before moving on to the harder ones.
3. Look for *analogous* relationships between pairs of words, *not* for words that have *similar* meanings.
4. Learn the basic approach to Analogy questions.
   - State the relationship between the pair of words in capital letters as a sentence.
   - Try the pair of words in each choice in your test sentence, one at a time.
   - Eliminate choices that don't make sense.
   - If necessary, revise your test sentence until you can identify a single correct answer.
5. Be flexible. Words can have more than one meaning, and pairs of words can have different relationships. So you may have to try a few test sentences to find the right relationship.
6. Analogy questions use parts of speech consistently. If you can't tell how a word in capital letters is being used (if it is a word that can represent more than one part of speech), check the choices. The words in capital letters will be used in the same way as the words in the choices.
7. If you reverse the order of the words in capital letters when you make up your test sentence, remember to reverse the order of the words when you try the choices in your test sentence.
8. Eliminate choices that you know are wrong and guess from those remaining.

Practice Questions and Answer Key

Each question below consists of a related pair of words or phrases, followed by five pairs of words or phrases labeled A through E. Select the pair that best expresses a relationship similar to that expressed in the original pair.

Example:

CRUMB: BREAD ::
(A) ounce: unit
(B) splinter: wood
(C) water: bucket
(D) twine: rope
(E) cream: butter 

1 RIB CAGE: LUNGS ::
(A) skull: brain
(B) appendix: organ
(C) sock: foot
(D) skeleton: body
(E) hair: scalp

2 SELF-PORTRAIT: PAINTER ::
(A) soliloquy: actor
(B) interpretation: reader
(C) autobiography: writer
(D) manuscript: editor
(E) philosophy: thinker

3 BRITTLE: FRACTURE ::
(A) transparent: see
(B) fluid: melt
(C) perpetual: stop
(D) flammable: burn
(E) immobile: move

4 GYMNASIUM: EXERCISE ::
(A) birthday: celebrate
(B) building: construct
(C) store: shop
(D) disease: diagnose
(E) army: discharge

5 COMPASS: NAVIGATION ::
(A) physician: disease
(B) pilot: flight
(C) clock: dial
(D) camera: photography
(E) map: area

6 DAPPLED: SPOTS ::
(A) delicious: spices
(B) bleached: colors
(C) striped: lines
(D) rhymed: words
(E) squeaky: sounds

7 QUIBBLE: CRITICISM ::
(A) sermon: duty
(B) jeer: respect
(C) source: information
(D) tiff: quarrel
(E) scandal: disgrace

8 ETHICS: MORALITY ::
(A) premise: induction
(B) jurisprudence: law
(C) logic: error
(D) taboo: custom
(E) proof: generalization

9 GLOWER: ANGER ::
(A) sneer: contempt
(B) grin: expression
(C) fidget: movement
(D) console: grief
(E) slander: accusation

10 MELODIOUS: HEARD ::
(A) actual: witnessed
(B) legible: read
(C) mislaid: recovered
(D) pictorial: illustrated
(E) savory: eaten

11 EQUALIZE: PARITY ::
(A) coalesce: unity
(B) vary: frequency
(C) forestall: convenience
(D) synchronize: permanence
(E) normalize: individuality

12 ABERRATION: STANDARD ::
(A) censorship: news
(B) statement: policy
(C) detour: route
(D) rumor: gossip
(E) encore: performance

Answer Key

	Correct Answer	Difficulty
1.	A	E
2.	C	E
3.	D	E
4.	C	E
5.	D	E
6.	C	M
7.	D	M
8.	B	M
9.	A	M
10.	E	H
11.	A	H
12.	C	H

Chapter 7

Critical Reading Questions

Success in answering Critical Reading questions depends on your ability to understand and make sense of the information in a passage. It does not depend on any previous knowledge you may have about the subject.

- Each SAT test contains Critical Reading passages taken from different fields: the humanities, social sciences, and natural sciences.
- Passages vary in style and can include narrative, argumentative, and/or expository elements. Each test also contains a pair of related passages presented as one reading selection. One of the two passages supports, opposes, or in some other way complements the point of view expressed in the other.
- Each reading passage (or pair of related passages) is followed by a set of questions.

Like a lot of college-level reading, the passages will be thoughtful and sophisticated discussions of important issues, ideas, and events. The following kinds of questions may be asked about a passage.

Extended Reasoning Questions

You have to read actively to synthesize and analyze information and to evaluate the author's assumptions and techniques. You should be able to follow the logic of the passage and to recognize points that would strengthen or weaken the author's argument. Extended reasoning questions require you to:

- make inferences
- fill in gaps
- see implications
- relate parts of the text to each other or to the whole
- follow the logic of an argument
- identify cause and effect
- recognize consistency or inconsistency in the text
- interpret the purpose of rhetorical devices
- compare or contrast arguments

These questions also ask about the overall theme or meaning of the passage and about the purpose, attitude, or tone of the speaker.

Vocabulary-in-Context Questions

These questions ask you to infer the meanings of words from their context in the reading passage. Sometimes you need to know precisely how a fairly common but abstract word is used in the passage. Most questions will ask you to select the correct meaning of a word with multiple definitions as it is used in the passage.

Literal Comprehension Questions

You need to understand significant information presented in the passage. These questions assess a skill that is important for success in college, namely, reading to acquire information.

Strategies

Details in a passage are there because they mean something. And those details determine the answers to some of the Critical Reading questions.

The answers come from the passage. Every single answer to the Critical Reading questions can be found in or directly inferred from the passage. So be sure to read the passages carefully. If the author mentions that it's a rainy day, he or she has probably done so for a reason. The author did not have to talk about the weather at all. Rainy days suggest a certain mood, or reflect certain feelings, or set up certain situations—slippery roads, for instance—that the author wants you to know about or feel.

Every word counts. The same goes for words describing people, events, and things. If someone's face is described as *handsome* or *scarred*, if an event is *surprising*, or a word is *whispered* or *shouted* or *spoken with a smile*, pay attention. Details like these are mentioned to give you an understanding of what the author wants you to feel or think.

When you are faced with a question about the mood or tone of a passage, or when you are asked about the author's attitude or intent or whether the author might agree or disagree with a statement, you have to think about the details the author has provided.

Mark the passages or make short notes. It may help you to mark important sections or words or sentences. But be careful that you don't mark too much. The idea of marking the passage is to help you find information quickly. If you have underlined or marked three-quarters of it, your marks won't help.

Some students jot a short note — a few words at most — in the margin that summarizes what a paragraph or key sentence is about. Just be careful not to spend more time marking the passage than you will save. And remember, you get points for answering the questions, not for marking your test booklet.

Read the questions and answers carefully. Most Critical Reading questions require three things: you have to think about what the question is asking, you have to look back at the passage for information that will help you with the question, then you have to think again about how you can use the information to answer the question correctly. Unless you read the question carefully, you won't know what to think about, and you won't know where to look in the passage.

An answer choice can be true and still be wrong. The correct choice is the one that best answers the question, not any choice that makes a true statement. A choice may express something that is perfectly true and still be the wrong choice. The only way you're going to keep from being caught by a choice that is true but wrong is to make sure you read the passage, the questions, and the answer choices carefully.

The passage must support your answer. There should always be information or details in the passage that provide support for your answer — specific words, phrases, and/or sentences that help to prove your choice is correct. Remember that Critical Reading questions depend on the information in the passage and your ability to *interpret* it correctly. Even with the inference, tone, and attitude questions — the ones in which you have to do some "reading between the lines" to figure out the answers — you can find evidence in the passage supporting the correct choice.

Try eliminating choices. Compare each choice to the passage and you'll find that some choices can be eliminated as definitely wrong. Then it should be easier to choose the correct answer from the remaining choices.

Double-check the other choices. When you have made your choice, read quickly (again) through the other choices to make sure there isn't a better one.

Pace yourself. You will spend a lot of time reading a passage before you're ready to answer even one question. So take the time to answer as many questions as you can about each passage before you move on to another.

- Jump around within a set of questions to find the ones you can answer quickly, but don't jump from passage to passage.
- Don't leave a reading passage until you are sure you have answered all the questions you can. If you return to the passage later, you'll probably have to reread it.

Go back to any questions you skipped. When you've gone through all the questions on a passage, go back and review any you left out or weren't sure of. Sometimes information you picked up while thinking about one question will help you answer another.

Pick your topic. Some verbal sections contain more than one reading passage. Students often find it easier to read about familiar topics or topics that they find interesting. So if you have a choice, you may want to look for a passage that deals with a familiar or especially interesting subject to work on first. If you skip a passage and set of questions, be sure that you don't lose your place on the answer sheet.

Note: All passages contain numbered lines. When a question refers to a particular line or lines in the passage, it will often be helpful to go back and read the appropriate line(s) before answering the question.

Should You Read the Passage First or the Questions First?

1. Is the subject of the passage interesting to you or something that you know about? If the answer to this question is yes, you should probably read the passage carefully and critically before you read the questions; that is, you should follow the author's logic, paying attention to details. Then answer the questions, going back to the passage when appropriate.

   If you do not find the passage accessible or particularly interesting, you might want to read the questions before you read the passage to get a sense of what to look for. But if the content of the passage is familiar, looking at the questions first might be a waste of time. Try both methods when working through sample or practice questions to see if one approach is more helpful than the other.

2. If you have trouble following the author's argument, you may want to skip the passage and come back to it later if you have time. But, once the time allowed for a section has ended, you may not return to that section again.

3. Are you running out of testing time? If yes, it may be best to skim the passage quickly, then read the questions and refer back to the passage when appropriate.

Extended Reasoning Questions

Extended reasoning questions ask you to draw conclusions from the information in the passage. The answers to these questions will not be directly stated in the passage but can be inferred from it. Questions that contain words like *probably*, *apparently*, *seems*, or *suggests* or phrases like *it can be inferred*...and *the author implies*...are extended reasoning questions.

The Difference Between Facts, Assumptions, and Inferences

Facts

Facts are statements that are known to be true and that can be demonstrated to be true. For example:

> There are 12 inches in a foot.
>
> It is against the law to drive above the speed limit.

Assumptions

Assumptions are suppositions or propositions that authors make to reach their conclusions. Often they are not explicitly stated. To read critically, you must be able to recognize unstated assumptions the author has made because these assumptions may be accurate or inaccurate, at least from your viewpoint. Identify some of the underlying assumptions in the following examples:

> The principal has promised a big victory dance after the championship game next week.
>
> Let's have a picnic tomorrow.
>
> Reducing the workforce will increase the profits.

Inferences

Inferences are conclusions that you reach based on what has been stated in the reading passage. To infer is to arrive at a conclusion through reasoning, to understand what the statements imply.

Example:

The problem of junk mail has grown to epidemic proportions. I've counted no fewer than 616 pieces of junk mail in my mail box in a given year! Not only is the sheer magnitude appalling, but the antics of these "post-office pirates" are equally disturbing. For example, one enterprising salesman promised me prizes ranging from a car to a transistor radio if I would drive 200 miles to look at a piece of property. I wrote this con artist and told him I'd come if he paid for the gas, but I never heard from him.

The author's description of junk mail is probably based on:

(A) personal experience
(B) research and statistics
(C) newspaper articles
(D) hearsay
(E) interviews

The author never explicitly states the source of the information, but all the examples are taken from the author's own life. Phrases such as *"I've counted...my mail box," "promised me prizes," "I wrote this con artist,"* and *"I never heard from him"* all indicate that the author's opinions are based on personal experience.

Logic, Style, and Tone

Many Critical Reading questions will ask you about the way the author develops and presents the ideas in the passage. Some questions will ask you to assess the mood or attitude of the author. They also may ask you to assess the reactions that may be expected from the reader.

In well-written material, the writer uses both style and tone to express what he or she has to say and to try to influence the reader. Recognizing the author's intent, whether it is to tell an exciting story, to express enjoyment, or to start a revolution, is an important part of reading.

Vocabulary-in-Context Questions

Some Critical Reading questions will ask about the meaning of a word as it is used in the passage. When a word has several meanings, a vocabulary-in-context question won't necessarily use the most common meaning.

Even if you don't know the word, you can sometimes figure it out from the passage and the answers. This is why the questions are called *vocabulary-in-context*. The context in which the word is used determines its meaning. You can also use the context to figure out the meaning of words you're not sure of.

Vocabulary-in-context questions usually take less time to answer than other types of Critical Reading questions. Usually, you can answer them by reading only a sentence or two around the word, without reading the entire passage.

When answering vocabulary-in-context questions, keep the following in mind:

- One word can have several meanings.
- Questions asking for the meaning of a word or phrase refer to the meaning in the context in which the word or phrase is being used.
- It helps to go back to the passage and reread the context in which the word is used. Be sure to read enough of the context to thoroughly understand the meaning of the word.
- The answer choices will often include other meanings of the word.

Literal Comprehension Questions

This type of question assesses how well you read to acquire information. Here are some strategies to help you successfully answer comprehension questions:

- Locate the place in the passage where the detail is discussed; reread enough of the text to find the answer. Even if you know something about the subject of the passage, remember to answer the question based on what is stated or implied in the passage.

- Recognize different ways of stating the same fact or idea. Sometimes the phrasing of the question is different from the wording in the passage.
- Underline key words or important information in the question and the passage.
- Cross out incorrect responses as you eliminate them. Remember, you may write anywhere in your test book.
- Read questions carefully, looking for words such as *except*, *not*, and *only*, and for other words that describe exactly what you are asked to do with the information.
- Make sure you can defend your answer choice by referring to words or phrases within the passage that support it.

Questions Involving Two Passages

At least one of the reading selections will involve a pair of passages. The two passages will have a common theme or subject. One of the passages will oppose, support, or in some way relate to the other. If one of the paired passages seems easier or more interesting than the other, you may want to start with that one and answer the questions specific to it first. Then go back and wrestle with the questions specific to the other passage and with the questions that refer to both passages.

In most cases, you'll find that the questions are grouped: first, questions about Passage 1, then questions about Passage 2, finally questions comparing the two passages.

When a question asks you to compare two passages, don't try to remember everything from both passages. Take each choice one at a time. Review the relevant parts of each passage before you select your answer.

If a question asks you to identify something that is true in *both* passages, it is often easier to start by eliminating choices that are *not* true for one of the passages.

Don't be fooled by a choice that is true for one passage but not for the other.

Key Words and Phrases

The following words and phrases are frequently used in reading passage questions. Learn to look for them and be sure you understand their meaning when you are answering test questions.

WHEN YOU SEE THIS...	REMEMBER THAT...
according to the author **according to the passage**	You must answer the question in terms of the statements, assumptions, or inferences that the author is making, even if you disagree with what the author has stated. The question is designed to see if you understand what the author has written.
best	This is an important word in test questions because it usually asks you to find the most suitable or acceptable of the answer choices. This means that even though you may find a response that seems to fit, you still need to look at the rest of the responses in order to be sure that you have selected the *best* one. Sometimes you may think none of the answers is particularly good, but you must pick the one that is *best.*
chiefly	This means "above the rest," "mostly," "mainly, but not exclusively." When you see *chiefly*, you will probably be looking for the most central element or most important explanation of something.
except	A question with *except* usually asks you to identify something that does not belong with the other choices. When you see this word at the end of a question, you will probably be looking for the one choice that is an incorrect response to the question.
(the author) **implies** (it can be) **inferred** (the author) **suggests**	These terms ask you to come to a conclusion that is suggested by the information in the passage but not directly stated by the author. You must be careful that your inference is indeed based on the material in the passage and not solely on your own ideas or opinions.
least	Opposite of *most, chiefly.*
mainly	Most importantly, or *chiefly.*
most	Frequently used as a qualifier, as in *most* likely, *most* frequently, *most* reasonable. A qualifier recognizes that there are exceptions to *most* situations and tries to allow for those exceptions.

WHEN YOU SEE THIS...	REMEMBER THAT...
only	Only means "just the one." "This is the *only*...for me." It also can indicate a restriction, as in "You can go *only* after you wash the car."
primarily	Most importantly, or *chiefly*.
sometimes	This is another qualifier. The following list reflects the decrease in the number of times that something might happen: **always** ↓ **frequently** ↓ **sometimes** ↓ **rarely** ↓ **never** Think of some other words that describe how often something happens, and compare them with the list. Be sure to consider carefully the impact of these words when they appear in Critical Reading questions or answer choices.

Sample Questions

Sample directions and a sample pair of passages and questions are followed by discussions of the correct answers and some hints.

The two passages below are followed by questions based on their content and the relationship between the two passages. Answer the questions on the basis of what is *stated* or *implied* in the passages and in any introductory material that may be provided.

In Passage 1, the author presents his view of the early years of the silent film industry. In Passage 2, the author draws on her experiences as a mime to generalize about her art. (A mime is a performer who, without speaking, entertains through gesture, facial expression, and movement.)

Passage 1

Talk to those people who first saw films when they were silent, and they will tell you the experience was magic. The silent film had extraordinary powers to draw members of an audience into the story, and an equally potent capacity to make their imaginations work. It required the audience to become engaged—to supply voices and sound effects. The audience was the final, creative contributor to the process of making a film.

The finest films of the silent era depended on two elements that we can seldom provide today—a large and receptive audience and a well-orchestrated score. For the audience, the fusion of picture and live music added up to more than the sum of the respective parts.

The one word that sums up the attitude of the silent filmmakers is *enthusiasm*, conveyed most strongly before formulas took shape and when there was more room for experimentation. This enthusiastic uncertainty often resulted in such accidental discoveries as new camera or editing techniques. Some films experimented with players; the 1915 film *Regeneration*, for example, by using real gangsters and streetwalkers, provided startling local color. Other films, particularly those of Thomas Ince, provided tragic endings as often as films by other companies supplied happy ones.

Unfortunately, the vast majority of silent films survive today in inferior prints that no longer reflect the care that the original technicians put into them. The modern versions of silent films may appear jerky and flickery, but the vast picture palaces did not attract four to six thousand people a night by giving them eyestrain. A silent film depended on its visuals; as soon as you degrade those, you lose elements that go far beyond the image on the surface. The acting in silents was often very subtle, very restrained, despite legends to the contrary.

Passage 2

Mime opens up a new world to the beholder, but it does so insidiously, not by purposely injecting points of interest in the manner of a tour guide. Audiences are not unlike visitors to a foreign land who discover that the modes, manners, and thoughts of its inhabitants are not meaningless oddities, but are sensible in context.

I remember once when an audience seemed perplexed at what I was doing. At first, I tried to gain a more immediate response by using slight exaggerations. I soon realized that these actions had nothing to do with the audience's understanding of the character. What I had believed to be a failure of the audience to respond in the manner I expected was, in fact, only their concentration on what I was doing; they were enjoying a gradual awakening—a slow transference of their understanding from their own time and place to one that appeared so unexpectedly before their eyes. This was evidenced by their growing response to succeeding numbers.

Mime is an elusive art, as its expression is entirely dependent on the ability of the performer to imagine a character and to re-create that character for each performance. As a mime, I am a physical medium, the instrument upon which the figures of my imagination play their dance of life. The individuals in my audience also have responsibilities—they must be alert collaborators. They cannot sit back, mindlessly complacent, and wait to have their emotions titillated by mesmeric musical sounds or visual rhythms or acrobatic feats, or by words that tell them what to think. Mime is an art that, paradoxically, appeals both to those who respond instinctively to entertainment and to those whose appreciation is more analytical and complex. Between these extremes lie those audiences conditioned to resist any collaboration with what is played before them and these the mime must seduce despite themselves. There is only one way to attack those reluctant minds—take them unaware! They will be delighted at an unexpected pleasure.

1 The author of Passage 1 uses the phrase "enthusiastic uncertainty" in line 17 to suggest that the filmmakers were

(A) excited to be experimenting in a new field
(B) delighted at the opportunity to study new technology
(C) optimistic in spite of the obstacles that faced them
(D) eager to challenge existing conventions
(E) eager to please but unsure of what the public wanted

2 In lines 19-24, *Regeneration* and the films of Thomas Ince are presented as examples of

(A) formulaic and uninspired silent films
(B) profitable successes of a flourishing industry
(C) suspenseful action films drawing large audiences
(D) daring applications of an artistic philosophy
(E) unusual products of a readiness to experiment

3 In context, the reference to "eyestrain" (line 30) conveys a sense of

(A) irony regarding the incompetence of silent film technicians
(B) regret that modern viewers are unable to see high quality prints of silent films
(C) resentment that the popularity of picture palaces has waned in recent years
(D) pleasure in remembering a grandeur that has passed
(E) amazement at the superior quality of modern film technology

4 In line 34, "legends" most nearly means

(A) ancient folklore
(B) obscure symbols
(C) history lessons
(D) famous people
(E) common misconceptions

5 The author of Passage 2 most likely considers the contrast of mime artist and tour guide appropriate because both

(A) are concerned with conveying factual information
(B) employ artistic techniques to communicate their knowledge
(C) determine whether others enter a strange place
(D) shape the way others perceive a new situation
(E) explore new means of self-expression

6 In lines 41-52, the author most likely describes a specific experience in order to

(A) dispel some misconceptions about what a mime is like
(B) show how challenging the career of a mime can be
(C) portray the intensity required to see the audience's point of view
(D) explain how unpredictable mime performances can be
(E) indicate the adjustments an audience must make in watching mime

7 In lines 60-63, the author's description of techniques used in the types of performances is

(A) disparaging
(B) astonished
(C) sorrowful
(D) indulgent
(E) sentimental

8 Both passages are primarily concerned with the subject of

(A) shocking special effects
(B) varied dramatic styles
(C) visual elements in dramatic performances
(D) audience resistance to theatrical performances
(E) nostalgia for earlier forms of entertainment

9 The incident described in lines 41-52 shows the author of Passage 2 to be similar to the silent filmmakers of Passage 1 in the way she

(A) required very few props
(B) used subtle technical skills to convey universal truths
(C) learned through trial and error
(D) combined narration with visual effects
(E) earned a loyal audience of followers

10 What additional information would reduce the apparent similarity between these two art forms?

(A) Silent film audiences were also accustomed to vaudeville and theatrical presentations.
(B) Silent films could show newsworthy events as well as dramatic entertainment.
(C) Dialogue in the form of captions was integrated into silent films.
(D) Theaters running silent films gave many musicians steady jobs.
(E) Individual characters created for silent films became famous in their own right.

11 Both passages mention which of the following as being important to the artistic success of the dramatic forms they describe?

(A) Effective fusion of disparate dramatic elements
(B) Slightly exaggerated characterization
(C) Incorporation of realistic details
(D) Large audiences
(E) Audience involvement

Answers and Explanations

1 The author of Passage 1 uses the phrase "enthusiastic uncertainty" in line 17 to suggest that the filmmakers were

(A) excited to be experimenting in a new field
(B) delighted at the opportunity to study new technology
(C) optimistic in spite of the obstacles that faced them
(D) eager to challenge existing conventions
(E) eager to please but unsure of what the public wanted

Difficulty level: Hard

The correct answer is (A).

Explanation:

Look at the beginning of the third paragraph of Passage 1. The filmmakers were *enthusiastic* about a new kind of art form in which they could experiment. And experimentation led to *accidental discoveries* (line 18), which suggests *uncertainty*.

Choice (B) is wrong because the filmmakers were delighted to use the new technology rather than to study it.

Choice (C) can be eliminated because the passage does not talk about **obstacles** faced by the filmmakers.

Choice (D) is specifically contradicted by line 16, which refers to these filmmakers as working **before formulas took shape**. The word **formulas** in this context means the same thing as **conventions**.

Choice (E) is not correct because the **uncertainty** of the filmmakers was related to the new technology and how to use it, not to **what the public wanted**.

Read each choice carefully and compare what it says to the information in the passage.

2 In lines 19-24, *Regeneration* and the films of Thomas Ince are presented as examples of

(A) formulaic and uninspired silent films
(B) profitable successes of a flourishing industry
(C) suspenseful action films drawing large audiences
(D) daring applications of an artistic philosophy
(E) unusual products of a readiness to experiment

Difficulty level: Hard

The correct answer is (E).

Explanation:

The author's argument in the third paragraph is that there was lots of *room for experimentation* (line 17) in the silent film industry. Both *Regeneration* and Ince's films are specifically mentioned as examples of that readiness to experiment.

Choice (A) is directly contradicted in two ways by the information in the passage. First, line 16 says that the filmmakers worked **before formulas took shape**, so their work could not be **formulaic**. Second, the author refers to ***Regeneration*** as having some **startling** effects and indicates that the endings of Ince's films were different from other films of the time. So it would not be correct to describe these films as **uninspired**.

Choices (B), (C), and (D) are wrong because the author does not argue that these films were **profitable**, **suspenseful**, or **applications of an artistic philosophy**. He argues that they are examples of a willingness to **experiment**.

Tip:

As you consider the choices, think of the words, phrases, and sentences in the passage that relate to the question you are answering. Be aware of how the ideas in the passage are presented. What is the author's point? How does the author explain and support important points?

3 In context, the reference to "eyestrain" (line 30) conveys a sense of

(A) irony regarding the incompetence of silent film technicians
(B) regret that modern viewers are unable to see high-quality prints of silent films
(C) resentment that the popularity of picture palaces has waned in recent years
(D) pleasure in remembering a grandeur that has passed
(E) amazement at the superior quality of modern film technology

Difficulty level: Medium

The correct answer is (B).

Explanation:

The author draws a distinction between the way silent films look when viewed today —*jerky and flickery* (line 28) — and the way they looked when they were originally shown. He implies that thousands of people would not have come to the movie houses if the pictures had given them *eyestrain*. The author indicates that the perception of silent films today is unfortunate. This feeling can be described as regret.

Choice (A) can be eliminated because there is no indication in the passage that silent film technicians were **incompetent**. The author even mentions **the care** taken by **the original technicians** (lines 26-27).

Both choices (C) and (D) are wrong because they do not answer this question. Remember, the question refers to the statement about **eyestrain**. The remark about eyestrain concerns the technical quality of the films, not the **popularity of picture palaces** or a **grandeur that has passed**.

Choice (E) is incorrect for two reasons. First, no sense of **amazement** is conveyed in the statement about eyestrain. Second, the author does not say that modern films are **superior** to silent films, only that the **prints** of silent films are **inferior** to what they once were (lines 25-26).

Try eliminating choices that you know are wrong. Rule out choices that don't answer the question being asked or that are contradicted by the information in the passage.

4 In line 34, "legends" most nearly means

(A) ancient folklore
(B) obscure symbols
(C) history lessons
(D) famous people
(E) common misconceptions

Difficulty level: Medium

The correct answer is (E).

Explanation:

A *legend* is an idea or story that has come down from the past. A secondary meaning of *legend* is anything made up rather than based on fact. Throughout the final paragraph of Passage 1, the author emphasizes that people today have the wrong idea about the visual quality of silent films. In the last sentence, the author states that the acting was *often very subtle* and *very restrained*, and then he adds, *despite legends to the contrary*. So, according to the author, silent film acting is today thought of as unsubtle and unrestrained, but that is a misconception, an idea not based on fact, a *legend*.

Choice (A) is the most common meaning of **legend**, but it doesn't make any sense here. There is no reference to or suggestion about **ancient folklore**.

Choice (B) has no support at all in the passage.

Choice (C) can be eliminated because the author does not refer to **history lessons** in this sentence, but to mistaken notions about the performances in silent films.

Choice (D) simply doesn't make sense. In line 34, the word **legends** refers to acting, not to **people**.

Tip:

This is a vocabulary-in-context question. Even if you don't know the meaning of the word, try to figure it out from the passage and the choices. Examine the context in which the word is used.

Think of some word(s) that would make sense in the sentence, then look at the answers to see if any choice is similar to the word(s) you thought of.

5 The author of Passage 2 most likely considers the contrast of mime artist and tour guide appropriate because both

(A) are concerned with conveying factual information
(B) employ artistic techniques to communicate their knowledge
(C) determine whether others enter a strange place
(D) shape the way others perceive a new situation
(E) explore new means of self-expression

Difficulty level: Hard

The correct answer is (D).

Explanation:

To answer this question, you have to find a choice that describes a similarity between the performances of a mime and the work of a tour guide. The author begins Passage 2 by saying that a mime *opens up a new world to the beholder*, but in a *manner* (or way) different from that of a tour guide. Thus the author assumes that contrasting the mime and the tour guide is appropriate because both of them *shape the way others perceive a new situation*.

Choice (A) may correctly describe a tour guide, but it doesn't fit the mime. Nowhere in the passage does the author say the mime conveys **factual information**.

Choice (B) is true for the mime but not for the tour guide.

Choice (C) is wrong because the author of Passage 2 contrasts how mimes and tour guides introduce others to **a new world**, not how they **determine** entrance to **a strange place**.

Choice (E) is incorrect because the author does not discuss **self-expression** as a tour guide's work, and because she indicates that, as a mime, she expresses a particular character, not her own personality.

Tip:

Pay close attention when authors make connections, comparisons, or contrasts. These parts of passages help you identify the authors' points of view and assumptions.

6 In lines 41-52, the author most likely describes a specific experience in order to

(A) dispel some misconceptions about what a mime is like
(B) show how challenging the career of a mime can be
(C) portray the intensity required to see the audience's point of view
(D) explain how unpredictable mime performances can be
(E) indicate the adjustments an audience must make in watching mime

Difficulty level: Medium

The correct answer is (E).

Explanation:

The correct answer must explain why the author described a particular experience in lines 41-52. The author's point is that she learned the audience was *enjoying a gradual awakening*. Only choice (E) indicates that the story shows the *adjustments* the audience had to make to appreciate her performance.

Choice (A) can be eliminated because the only **misconception** that is dispelled is the author's **misconception** about the audience.

Choice (B) is wrong because, while the story might suggest that mime is a **challenging career**, that is not the author's point in describing the experience.

Choice (C) can't be correct because there is no reference to **intensity** on the part of the mime.

Choice (D) is wrong because the emphasis of lines 41-52 is not on how **unpredictable** mime performance is but on what the author learned from her failure to understand the audience's initial reaction.

Tip:

Every word counts. When you're asked about the author's intent in describing something, you have to pay close attention to how the author uses details to explain, support, or challenge the point being made.

7 In lines 60-63, the author's description of techniques used in the types of performances is

(A) disparaging
(B) astonished
(C) sorrowful
(D) indulgent
(E) sentimental

Difficulty level: Easy

The correct answer is (A).

Explanation:

The sentence beginning in line 60 says that when viewing mime, the audience *cannot sit back, mindlessly complacent*. The author then says that other types of performances *titillate* audience emotions by *mesmeric musical sounds* or *acrobatic feats*. The author uses these kinds of words to belittle other techniques — her tone is *disparaging*.

Choices (B), (C), and (E) can be eliminated because no **astonishment**, **sorrow**, or **sentimentalism** is suggested in lines 60-63.

Choice (D) is almost the opposite of what the author means. She is not at all **indulgent** toward these other types of performance.

Tip:

To figure out the author's attitude or tone, or how the author feels about something, think about how the author uses language in the passage.

8 Both passages are primarily concerned with the subject of

(A) shocking special effects
(B) varied dramatic styles
(C) visual elements in dramatic performances
(D) audience resistance to theatrical performances
(E) nostalgia for earlier forms of entertainment

Difficulty level: Easy

The correct answer is (C).

Explanation:

This question asks you to think about *both* passages. Notice that the question asks you to look for the main subject or focus of the pair of passages, not simply to recognize that one passage is about silent film and the other about mime.

The discussion in Passage 1 is most concerned with the effectiveness of silent films for audiences of that era. The discussion in Passage 2 is most concerned with what makes a mime performance effective for the audience. The main subject for *both* passages is ways that a silent, visual form of entertainment affects an audience. Choice (C) is correct because it refers to performance in a visual art form.

Choice (A) can be eliminated because **shocking special effects** is not a main subject of either passage.

Choice (B) is wrong because, although **varied dramatic styles** (used by film performers and in mime) is briefly touched on in both passages, it is not the main subject of the *pair* of passages.

In choice (D), **audience resistance to theatrical performances** is too specific: both authors are making points about the overall role of audiences in the performance. Choice (D) is also incorrect because that topic is primarily addressed only in Passage 2.

Choice (E) can be eliminated because a tone of nostalgia appears only in Passage 1.

Tip:

This question involves a comparison of two reading passages. Review the relevant parts of *each* passage as you consider the choices.

9 The incident described in lines 41-52 shows the author of Passage 2 to be similar to the silent filmmakers of Passage 1 in the way she

(A) required very few props
(B) used subtle technical skills to convey universal truths
(C) learned through trial and error
(D) combined narration with visual effects
(E) earned a loyal audience of followers

Difficulty level: Hard

The correct answer is (C).

Explanation:

The question focuses on the story related in lines 41-52 and already examined in question 6. This question asks you to explain how that story shows that the mime is similar to silent filmmakers. So the correct answer has to express a point made about the mime in lines 41-52 that is also true for the filmmakers described in Passage 1. Lines 41-52 show the mime changing her performance when she found something that did not work. Passage 1 says that filmmakers learned through *experimentation* and *accidental discoveries*. So all of these people *learned through trial and error*.

Choices (A), (B), (D), and (E) are not correct answers because they don't include traits both *described in lines 41-52* and *shared with the filmmakers*.

Choice (A) is wrong because **props** aren't mentioned in either passage.

Choice (B) is wrong because **conveying universal truths** is not discussed in Passage 1.

Choice (D) is wrong because a mime performs without speaking or **narration**.

Choice (E) is wrong because Passage 1 describes loyal audiences but lines 41-52 do not.

Tip:

When a question following a pair of passages asks you to identify something that is common to both passages or true for both passages, eliminate any answer that is true for only one of the two passages.

10 What additional information would reduce the apparent similarity between these two art forms?

(A) Silent film audiences were also accustomed to vaudeville and theatrical presentations.

(B) Silent films could show newsworthy events as well as dramatic entertainment.

(C) Dialogue in the form of captions was integrated into silent films.
(D) Theaters running silent films gave many musicians steady jobs.
(E) Individual characters created for silent films became famous in their own right.

Difficulty level: Hard

The correct answer is (C).

Explanation:

This question asks you to do two things: first, figure out a similarity between silent films and mime; second, choose an answer with information that isn't found in either passage but would make mime performance and silent films seem *less* similar.

If you think about the art forms discussed in the two passages, you should realize that neither uses *speech*. And this is an important similarity. Silent films include music but not spoken words. As stated in the Introduction to the two passages, a mime entertains *without speaking*. Choice (C) adds the information that *dialogue* between characters was part of silent films. Characters "spoke" to each other even though audiences read captions instead of hearing spoken words. So silent film indirectly used speech and was different from mime, which relies on *gesture, facial expression, and movement*.

Choices (A), (B), (D), and (E) are wrong because they don't deal with the fundamental **similarity** between the two art forms — the absence of words. These may all be interesting things to know about silent film, but **vaudeville** performances, **newsworthy events**, **steady jobs** for musicians, and fame of **individual characters** have nothing to do with mime. None of these things is related to an apparent similarity between mime and silent films.

Tip:

This question asks you to think about the two reading passages together. Remember that you should also consider the information in the Introduction when you compare passages.

11 Both passages mention which of the following as being important to the artistic success of the dramatic forms they describe?

(A) Effective fusion of disparate dramatic elements
(B) Slightly exaggerated characterization
(C) Incorporation of realistic details
(D) Large audiences
(E) Audience involvement

Difficulty level: Medium

The correct answer is (E).

Explanation:

Passage 1 very clearly states in lines 5-8 that audience involvement was important to the success of silent films. In lines 58-60 of Passage 2, the author makes a similarly strong statement about how important it is for the audience to be involved in mime performance.

Choices (A)-(D) are wrong because they don't refer to ideas mentioned in *both* passages as **important to the artistic success of the dramatic forms**. Choice (A) can be eliminated because Passage 1 talks about the **fusion** of pictures and music, but Passage 2 is not concerned at all with **disparate dramatic elements**.

Choice (B) refers to something mentioned in Passage 2 (line 43), but it is *not* something important to the success of a mime performance. And Passage 1 says that the **acting in silents was often very subtle, very restrained** (lines 33-34), which is the opposite of **exaggerated**.

Choice (C) is mentioned only in Passage 1 (lines 20-22), and not as an element **important to the artistic success** of silent films in general.

Choice (D) is not correct because the author of Passage 1 says that silent films did enjoy **large audiences**, but he doesn't say that **large audiences** were critical to the **artistic success** of the films. Passage 2 doesn't mention the size of the audiences at all.

When comparing two passages, focus on the specific subject of the question. Don't try to remember everything from both passages. Refer to the passages as you work your way through the five choices.

Recap: Tips for Critical Reading Questions

1. Learn the directions.
2. Questions DO NOT go from easy to hard.
3. The information you need to answer each question *is in the passage(s)*. All questions ask you to base your answer on what you read in the passages, introductions, and (sometimes) footnotes.
4. Every word counts. Details in a passage help you understand how the author wants you to feel or think.
5. Try marking up the passages or making short notes in the sample test and practice questions in this book.
6. Reading the questions and answers carefully is as important as reading the passage carefully.
7. An answer can be true and still be the wrong answer to a particular question.
8. There should always be information in the passage(s) that supports your choice — specific words, phrases, and/or sentences that help to prove your choice is correct.
9. If you're not sure of the correct answer, try eliminating choices and guess.
10. When you have made your choice, double-check the other choices to make sure there isn't a better one.
11. For some passages, you might want to read the questions before you read the passage so you get a sense of what to look for. If the content of the passage is familiar, looking at the questions before you read the passage might be a waste of time. So try both methods when you take the sample test and do the practice questions in this book to see if one approach is more helpful than the other.
12. Don't get bogged down on difficult questions. You might want to skim a set of questions and start by answering those you feel sure of. Then concentrate on the harder questions. Don't skip between sets of reading questions, because when you return to a passage you'll probably have to read it again.
13. When you have gone through all the questions associated with a passage, go back and review any you left out or weren't sure about.
14. If a verbal section contains more than one reading passage, you may want to look for one that deals with a familiar or especially interesting topic to work on first. If you skip a set of questions, however, be sure to fill in your answer sheet correctly.

A Final Note on Critical Reading Questions

There's no shortcut to doing well on Critical Reading questions. The best way to improve your reading skills is to practice — not just with specific passages and multiple-choice test questions but with books, magazines, essays, and newspapers that include complex ideas, challenging vocabulary, and subjects that make you think.

There are some things to keep in mind as you tackle the actual test questions. The most important is always to go back to the passages and look for the specific words, phrases, sentences, and ideas that either support or contradict each choice.

You may not have time to go back to the passage for every answer to every question. If you remember enough from what you have read to answer a question quickly and confidently, you should do so, and then go on to the next question. But the source for the answers is the passages. And when you're practicing for the test, it's a good idea to go back to the passage after answering a question and prove to yourself that your choice is right and the other choices are wrong. This will help you sharpen your reading and reasoning skills and give you practice in using the information in the passages to figure out the correct answers.

Practice Questions and Answer Key

The passage below is followed by questions based on its content. Answer the questions on the basis of what is *stated* or *implied* in the passage and in any introductory material that may be provided.

Questions 1-6 are based on the following passage.

The following passage is an excerpt from a book written by two female historians about professional women who began their careers in science in the late nineteenth and early twentieth centuries.

The strong efforts to gain equality for women in the scientific workplace began to show results in the last quarter of the twentieth century; women have secured positions as research scientists and won recognition and promotion within their fields. Though the modern struggle for equality in scientific fields is the same in many ways as it was in the early part of the century, it is also different. The women who first began undertaking careers in science had little support from any part of the society in which they lived. This vanguard had to struggle alone against the social conditioning they had received as women members of that society and against the male-dominated scientific community.

Women scientific researchers made a seemingly auspicious beginning. In the first quarter of the twentieth century, some women scientists who engaged in research worked at the most prestigious institutes of the period and enjoyed more career mobility than women researchers would experience again for several decades. Florence Sabin, an anatomist at the Rockefeller Institute of Medical Research noted for her research on the lymphatic system, is one important example. This encouraging beginning, however, was not to be followed by other successes for many decades. To have maintained an active role in research institutions, women would have had to share some of the decision-making power: they needed to be part of hiring, promotion, and funding decisions. Unfortunately, these early women scientists were excluded from the power structure of scientific research. As a result, they found it almost impossible to provide opportunities for a younger set of female colleagues seeking employment in a research setting, to foster their productivity and facilitate their career mobility, and eventually to allow them access to the top ranks.

Even those with very high professional aspirations accepted subordinate status as assistants if doing so seemed necessary to gain access to research positions—and too often these were the only positions offered them in their chosen careers. Time and again they pulled back from offering any real resistance or challenge to the organizational structure that barred their advancement. But we must remember that these women scientists were few in number, their participation in decision-making positions was virtually nil, and their political clout was minimal. Thus they could easily become highly visible targets for elimination from the staff, especially if their behavior was judged in the least imprudent.

Women's awareness that they were unequal colleagues, included in professional settings only on the sufferance of male colleagues, who held the positions of power, conflicted with their belief in meritocracy. They wanted to believe that achieving persons would be welcomed for their abilities and contributions. Yet they were surrounded by evidence to the contrary. An assistant professor of zoology observed that the men who were heads of departments were insistent on having other men in the department; they told her that women ought to be satisfied teaching high school. She relates that, during her ten years in the department, men were given at least six positions that she was qualified for and wanted desperately, but for which she was not even considered because she was a woman.

1 The primary purpose of the passage is to

(A) explain a situation
(B) refute an argument
(C) propose a change
(D) predict an outcome
(E) honor an achievement

2 The passage as a whole suggests that "career mobility" (lines 20-21 and 38) means the

(A) freedom to work on projects that one is most interested in
(B) freedom to publish research findings no matter how controversial they are
(C) ability to obtain funding to travel to important professional meetings
(D) ability to find a job in any part of the country
(E) ability to advance in one's chosen field

3 The statement that women could be eliminated from their jobs if their behavior was "the least imprudent" (line 54) suggests primarily that they

(A) were more likely than their male colleagues to be rebellious
(B) participated in the creation of the standards by which the performance of researchers was judged
(C) could gain advancement if they avoided political confrontations about their rights as women
(D) were judged by a standard different from the one used to judge their male colleagues
(E) were as critical of their colleagues as their colleagues were of them

4 The last paragraph of the passage suggests that for the majority of women scientists, the "belief in meritocracy" (lines 58-59) was

(A) justified, considering the opportunities available to them
(B) fortunate because it provided them with attainable goals
(C) inconsistent with the fact that they were discriminated against on the job
(D) understandable in that the concept had worked for the previous generation of women scientists
(E) trend-setting in that their views soon received universal acceptance

5 The example of the assistant professor of zoology (lines 62-71) serves primarily to indicate the

(A) extent of male bias against women in scientific fields at a particular time
(B) results of a woman's challenging male dominance in the early part of this century
(C) reasons for women's right to equal treatment
(D) inability of men and women to work together in an academic setting
(E) early attempts of women to achieve a share of scientific awards

6 All of the following questions can be explicitly answered on the basis of the passage EXCEPT:

(A) What conditions did women scientists find it necessary to struggle against in the first quarter of the twentieth century?
(B) What specific steps were taken in the early part of the twentieth century to help women gain equality in the scientific workplace?
(c) What changes in the organization of the scientific community would have enhanced the position of women scientists as the twentieth century advanced?
(D) What were the views of some women scientific researchers on the subject of meritocracy?
(E) What degree of success was attained by the generation of women scientists who followed those who came into prominence earlier in the twentieth century?

Answer Key

	Correct Answer	Difficulty
1.	A	M
2.	E	M
3.	D	M
4.	C	M
5.	A	M
6.	B	M

Chapter 8

Verbal Practice

The following questions are meant to give you a chance to practice the test-taking skills and strategies you've developed so far. Use them to try out different hints and ways of approaching questions before you take the practice tests in the last section of this book. Keep in mind that this chapter is intended to give you practice with the different types of questions, so it isn't arranged the way the questions will actually appear on the SAT.

Sentence Completions

Each sentence below has one or two blanks, each blank indicating that something has been omitted. Beneath the sentence are five lettered words or sets of words labeled A through E. Choose the word or set of words that, when inserted in the sentence, best fits the meaning of the sentence as a whole.

Example:

Medieval kingdoms did not become constitutional republics overnight; on the contrary, the change was – – – – .

(A) unpopular
(B) unexpected
(C) advantageous
(D) sufficient
(E) gradual

Ⓐ Ⓑ Ⓒ Ⓓ ●

1 Investigation of the epidemic involved determining what was – – – – about the people who were affected, what made them differ from those who remained well.

(A) chronic
(B) unique
(C) fortunate
(D) misunderstood
(E) historical

2 Because management – – – – the fact that employees find it difficult to work alertly at repetitious tasks, it sponsors numerous projects to – – – – enthusiasm for the job.

(A) recognizes..generate
(B) disproves..create
(C) respects..quench
(D) controls..regulate
(E) surmises..suspend

3 They did their best to avoid getting embroiled in the quarrel, preferring to maintain their – – – – as long as possible.

(A) consciousness
(B) suspense
(C) interest
(D) decisiveness
(E) neutrality

4 The strong affinity of these wild sheep for mountains is not – – – – : mountain slopes represent – – – – because they effectively limit the ability of less agile predators to pursue the sheep.

(A) useful..peril
(B) accidental..security
(C) instinctive..attainment
(D) restrained..nourishment
(E) surprising..inferiority

5 Even those who do not – – – – Robinson's views – – – – him as a candidate who has courageously refused to compromise his convictions.

(A) shrink from..condemn
(B) profit from..dismiss
(C) concur with..recognize
(D) disagree with..envision
(E) dissent from..remember

6 The alarm voiced by the committee investigating the accident had a ---- effect, for its dire predictions motivated people to take precautions that ---- an ecological disaster.

(A) trivial..prompted
(B) salutary..averted
(C) conciliatory..supported
(D) beneficial..exacerbated
(E) perverse..vanquished

7 At the age of forty-five, with a worldwide reputation and an as yet unbroken string of notable successes to her credit, Carson was at the ---- of her career.

(A) paradigm
(B) zenith
(C) fiasco
(D) periphery
(E) inception

8 The fact that they cherished religious objects more than most of their other possessions ---- the ---- role of religion in their lives.

(A) demonstrates..crucial
(B) obliterates..vital
(C) limits..daily
(D) concerns..informal
(E) denotes..varying

9 Mary Cassatt, an Impressionist painter, was the epitome of the ---- American: a native of Philadelphia who lived most of her life in Paris.

(A) conservative
(B) provincial
(C) benevolent
(D) prophetic
(E) expatriate

10 In the nineteenth century many literary critics saw themselves as stern, authoritarian figures defending society against the ---- of those ---- beings called authors.

(A) depravities..wayward
(B) atrocities..exemplary
(C) merits..ineffectual
(D) kudos..antagonistic
(E) indictments..secretive

Analogies

Each question below consists of a related pair of words or phrases, followed by five pairs of words or phrases labeled A through E. Select the pair that best expresses a relationship similar to that expressed in the original pair.

Example:

CRUMB:BREAD::
(A) ounce:unit
(B) splinter:wood
(C) water:bucket
(D) twine:rope
(E) cream:butter

 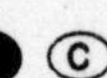 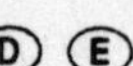

1 NEEDLE:KNITTING::

(A) finger:sewing
(B) sign:painting
(C) throat:singing
(D) hurdle:running
(E) chisel:carving

2 SUBMERGE:WATER::

(A) parch:soil
(B) bury:earth
(C) suffocate:air
(D) disperse:gas
(E) extinguish:fire

3 TALON:HAWK::

(A) horn:bull
(B) fang:snake
(C) claw:tiger
(D) tail:monkey
(E) shell:tortoise

4 ACRE:LAND::

(A) distance:space
(B) speed:movement
(C) gallon:liquid
(D) degree:thermometer
(E) year:birthday

5 COMPATRIOTS:COUNTRY::

(A) transients:home
(B) kinsfolk:family
(C) competitors:team
(D) performers:audience
(E) figureheads:government

6 INFURIATE:DISPLEASE::

(A) release:drop
(B) oppress:swelter
(C) drench:moisten
(D) stir:respond
(E) conceive:imagine

7 STRATAGEM:OUTWIT::

(A) prototype:design
(B) variation:change
(C) decoy:lure
(D) riddle:solve
(E) charade:guess

8 WANDERLUST:TRAVEL::

(A) fantasy:indulge
(B) innocence:confess
(C) ignorance:know
(D) digression:speak
(E) avarice:acquire

9 DEFECTOR:CAUSE::

(A) counterfeiter:money
(B) deserter:army
(C) critic:book
(D) advertiser:sale
(E) intruder:meeting

10 TACIT:WORDS::

(A) visible:scenes
(B) inevitable:facts
(C) colorful:hues
(D) suspicious:clues
(E) unanimous:disagreements

Critical Reading

Each passage below is followed by questions based on its content. Answer the questions following the passage on the basis of what is *stated* or *implied* in that passage and in any introductory material that may be provided.

Fear of communism swept through the United States in the years following the Russian Revolution of 1917. Several states passed espionage acts that restricted political discussion, and radicals of all descriptions were rounded up in so-called Red Raids conducted by the attorney general's office. Some were convicted and imprisoned; others were deported. This was the background of a trial in Chicago involving twenty men charged under Illinois's espionage statute with advocating the violent overthrow of the government. The charge rested on the fact that all the defendants were members of the newly formed Communist Labor party.

The accused in the case were represented by Clarence Darrow, one of the foremost defense attorneys in the country. Throughout his career, Darrow had defended the poor and the despised against exploitation and prejudice. He defended the rights of labor unions, for example, at a time when many sought to outlaw the strike, and he was resolute in defending constitutional freedoms. The following are excerpts from Darrow's summation to the jury.

Members of the Jury . . . . If you want to convict these twenty men, then do it. I ask no consideration on behalf of any one of them. They are no better than any other twenty men or women; they are no better than the millions down through the ages who have been prosecuted and convicted in cases like this. And if it is necessary for my clients to show that America is like all the rest, if it is necessary that my clients shall go to prison to show it, then let them go. They can afford it if you members of the jury can; make no mistake about that. . . .

The State says my clients "dare to criticize the Constitution." Yet this police officer (who the State says is a fine, right-living person) twice violated the federal Constitution while a prosecuting attorney was standing by. They entered Mr. Owen's home without a search warrant. They overhauled his papers. They found a flag, a red one, which he had the same right to have in his house that you have to keep a green one, or a yellow one, or any other color, and the officer impudently rolled it up and put another flag on the wall, nailed it there. By what right was that done? What about this kind of patriotism that violates the Constitution? Has it come to pass in this country that officers of the law can trample on constitutional rights and then excuse it in a court of justice? . . .

Most of what has been presented to this jury to stir up feeling in your souls has not the slightest bearing on proving conspiracy in this case. Take Mr. Lloyd's speech in Milwaukee. It had nothing to do with conspiracy. Whether the speech was a joke or was serious, I will not attempt to discuss. But I will say that if it was serious it was as mild as a summer's shower compared with many of the statements of those who are responsible for working conditions in this country. We have heard from people in high places that those individuals who express sympathy with labor should be stood up against a wall and shot. We have heard people of position declare that individuals who criticize the actions of those who are getting rich should be put in a cement ship with leaden sails and sent out to sea. Every violent appeal that could be conceived by the brain has been used by the powerful and the strong. I repeat, Mr. Lloyd's speech was gentle in comparison. . . .

My clients are condemned because they say in their platform that, while they vote, they believe the ballot is secondary to education and organization. Counsel suggests that those who get something they did not vote for are sinners, but I suspect you the jury know full well that my clients are right. Most of you have an eight-hour day. Did you get it by any vote you ever cast? No. It came about because workers laid down their tools and said we will no longer work until we get an eight-hour day. That is how they got the twelve-hour day, the ten-hour day, and the eight-hour day—not by voting but by laying down their tools. Then when it was over and the victory won . . . then the politicians, in order to get the labor vote, passed legislation creating an eight-hour day. That is how things changed; victory preceded law. . . .

You have been told that if you acquit these defendants you will be despised because you will endorse everything they believe. But I am not here to defend my clients' opinions. I am here to defend their right to express their opinions. I ask you, then, to decide this case upon the facts as you have heard them, in light of the law as you understand it, in light of the history of our country, whose institutions you and I are bound to protect.

1 Which best captures the meaning of the word "consideration" in line 23?

(A) Leniency
(B) Contemplation
(C) Due respect
(D) Reasoned judgment
(E) Legal rights

2 By "They can afford it if you members of the jury can" (lines 30-31), Darrow means that

(A) no harm will come to the defendants if they are convicted in this case
(B) the jurors will be severely criticized by the press if they

convict the defendants

(C) the defendants are indifferent about the outcome of the trial

(D) the verdict of the jury has financial implications for all of the people involved in the trial

(E) a verdict of guilty would be a potential threat to everyone's rights

3 Lines 32-45 suggest that the case against Owen would have been dismissed if the judge had interpreted the Constitution in which of the following ways?

(A) Defendants must have their rights read to them when they are arrested.
(B) Giving false testimony in court is a crime.
(C) Evidence gained by illegal means is not admissible in court.
(D) No one can be tried twice for the same crime.
(E) Defendants cannot be forced to give incriminating evidence against themselves.

4 In line 47, the word "bearing" most nearly means

(A) connection
(B) posture
(C) endurance
(D) location
(E) resemblance

5 In lines 46-62, Darrow's defense rests mainly on convincing the jury that

(A) a double standard is being employed
(B) the prosecution's evidence is untrustworthy
(C) the defendants share mainstream American values
(D) labor unions have the right to strike
(E) the defendants should be tried by a federal rather than a state court

6 The information in lines 46-62 suggests that the prosecution treated Mr. Lloyd's speech primarily as

(A) sarcasm to be resented
(B) propaganda to be ridiculed
(C) criticism to be answered
(D) a threat to be feared
(E) a bad joke to be dismissed

7 Darrow accuses "people in high places" (lines 54-55) of

(A) conspiring to murder members of the Communist party
(B) encouraging violence against critics of wealthy business owners
(C) pressuring members of the jury to convict the defendants
(D) advocating cruel and unusual punishment for criminals
(E) insulting the public's intelligence by making foolish suggestions

8 The word "education" (line 65) is a reference to the need for

(A) establishing schools to teach the philosophy of the Communist Labor party
(B) making workers aware of their economic and political rights
(C) teaching factory owners about the needs of laborers
(D) creating opportunities for on-the-job training in business
(E) helping workers to continue their schooling

9 The statement "victory preceded law" (line 77) refers to the fact that

(A) social reform took place only after labor unions organized support for their political candidates
(B) politicians need to win the support of labor unions if they are to be elected
(C) politicians can introduce legislative reform only if they are elected to office
(D) politicians did not initiate improved working conditions but legalized them after they were in place
(E) politicians have shown that they are more interested in winning elections than in legislative reform

10 Judging from lines 78-80, the jury had apparently been told that finding the defendants innocent would be the same as

(A) denying the importance of the Constitution
(B) giving people the right to strike
(C) encouraging passive resistance
(D) inhibiting free speech
(E) supporting communist doctrine

11 In order for Darrow to win the case, it would be most crucial that the jurors possess

(A) a thorough understanding of legal procedures and terminology
(B) a thorough understanding of the principles and beliefs of the Communist Labor party
(C) sympathy for labor's rights to safe and comfortable working conditions
(D) the ability to separate the views of the defendants from the rights of the defendants
(E) the courage to act in the best interests of the nation's economy

Answer Key

Sentence Completions	Analogies	Critical Reading
1. B	1. E	1. A
2. A	2. B	2. E
3. E	3. C	3. C
4. B	4. C	4. A
5. C	5. B	5. A
6. B	6. C	6. D
7. B	7. C	7. B
8. A	8. E	8. B
9. E	9. B	9. D
10. A	10. E	10. E
		11. D

Chapter 9

About Mathematics Questions

Math Reference Information

Reference information is included in the math test. You may find these facts and formulas helpful in answering some of the questions on the test. Don't let the Reference Information give you a false sense of security. It isn't going to tell you how to solve math problems. To do well on the math test, you have to be comfortable working with these facts and formulas. If you haven't had practice using them before the test, you will have a hard time using them efficiently during the test.

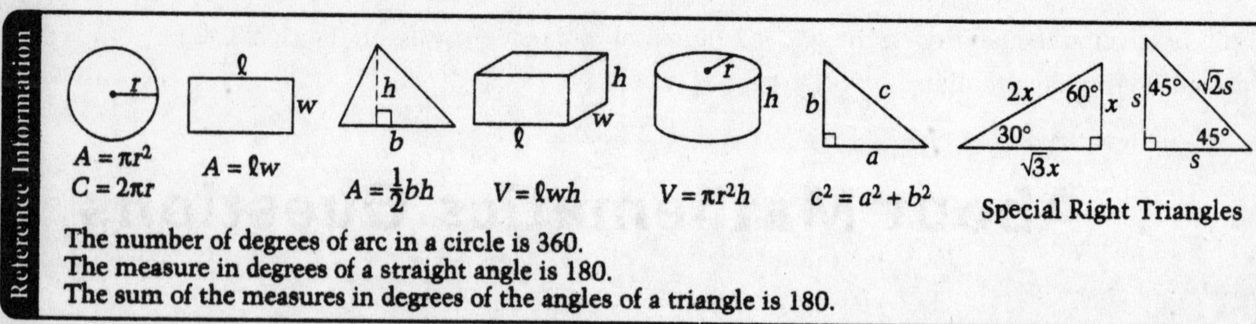

Types of Questions

Three types of mathematics questions appear on the SAT:

- Five-Choice Multiple-Choice questions
- Quantitative Comparison questions
- Student-Produced Response questions (with no answer choices)

The questions emphasize mathematical reasoning, evaluating how well you can think through mathematics problems.

The test requires that you know some specific math concepts and have learned some math skills, but it's intended to evaluate how well you can use what you know to solve problems.

Five-Choice Multiple-Choice Questions

Here's an example of a multiple-choice question with five choices:

If $2x + 2x + 2x = 12$, what is the value of $2x - 1$?

(A) 2
(B) 3
(C) 4
(D) 5
(E) 6

The correct answer is (B).

Tips for answering specific kinds of Five-Choice Multiple-Choice questions are presented in Chapter 12.

Quantitative Comparison Questions

Quantitative Comparison questions are quite different from regular Five-Choice Multiple-Choice questions. Instead of presenting a problem and asking you to figure out the answer, Quantitative Comparison questions give you two quantities and ask you to compare them.

You'll be given one quantity on the left in Column A, and one quantity on the right in Column B. You have to figure out whether:

- The quantity in Column A is greater.
- The quantity in Column B is greater.
- The quantities are equal.
- You cannot determine which is greater from the information given.

Here are the directions you'll see on the test.

Directions for Quantitative Comparison Questions

Questions 1-15 each consist of two quantities in boxes, one in Column A and one in Column B. You are to compare the two quantities and on the answer sheet fill in oval

A if the quantity in Column A is greater;
B if the quantity in Column B is greater;
C if the two quantities are equal;
D if the relationship cannot be determined from the information given.

AN E RESPONSE WILL NOT BE SCORED.

Notes:

1. In some questions, information is given about one or both of the quantities to be compared. In such cases, the given information is centered above the two columns and is not boxed.
2. In a given question, a symbol that appears in both columns represents the same thing in Column A as it does in Column B.
3. Letters such as x, n, and k stand for real numbers.

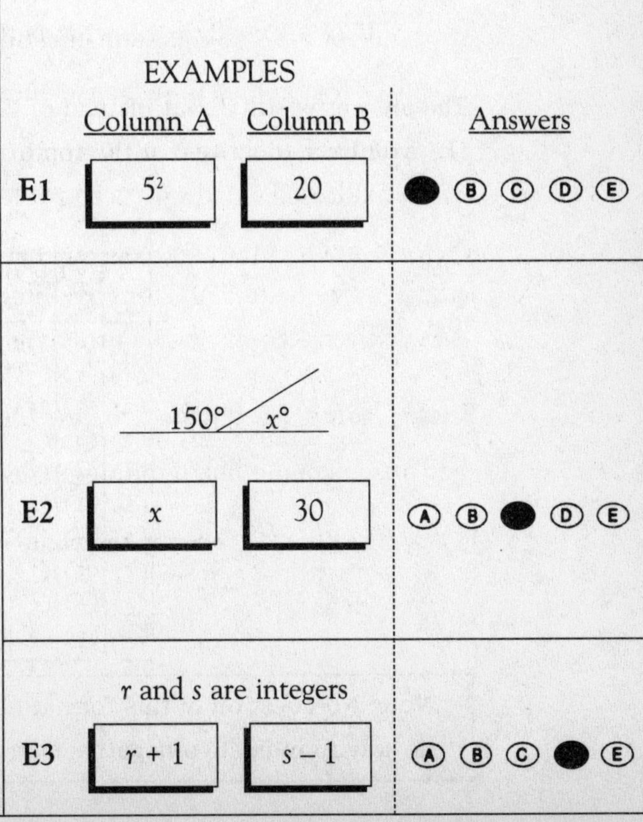

All you are asked to do is make a comparison between two quantities. Frequently, you don't have to finish your calculations or determine an exact answer. You just have to know enough about the quantities to determine which one is greater. For example:

Column A	Column B
34 + 43 + 58	36 + 43 + 58

You don't have to add up all the numbers to compare these two quantities. You can eliminate numbers 43 and 58, which appear in both columns. Now your comparison is much easier to make.

The correct answer is (B).

Specific tips on Quantitative Comparison questions are presented in Chapter 13.

Student-Produced Response Questions

Student-produced response questions are not multiple choice. You must figure out the correct answer and grid it on the answer sheet.

Student-produced response, or Grid-in, questions are solved just like any other math problems. Here's the same question presented in the discussion of Five-Choice Multiple-Choice questions, but as a Grid-in question.

If $2x + 2x + 2x = 12$, what is the value of $2x - 1$?

The answer is still 3, but instead of filling in Choice (A), (B), (C), (D), or (E), you have to write 3 at the top of the grid and fill in 3 below.

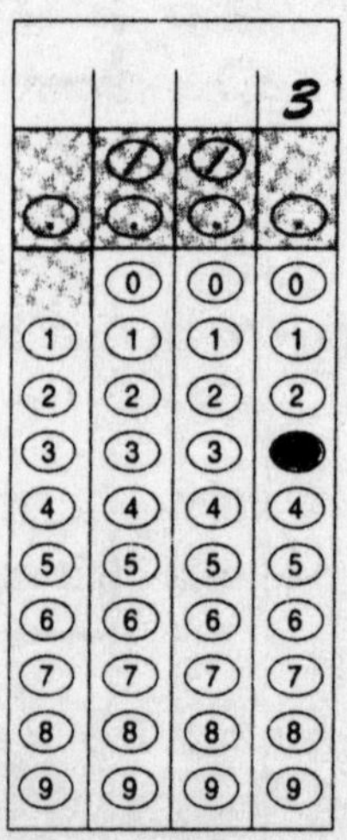

Note: No question in this format has a negative answer since there is no way to indicate a negative sign in the grid.

One of the most important rules to remember about Grid-in questions is that **only answers entered on the grid are scored. Your handwritten answer at the top of the grid is not scored.** However, writing your answer at the top of the grid may help you avoid gridding errors.

Specific tips for completing the grids are presented in Chapter 14.

General Math Tips

Learn the directions ahead of time. The directions for the Quantitative Comparison questions are unusual. Memorize all four answer choices before the test to save time. Also, learn how to complete the grids for Student-Produced Response questions (see Chapter 14).

Questions are arranged from easy to hard. The questions on the SAT are organized from easy to hard. This means that within a group of questions, for example Quantitative Comparisons, the easier ones come first and the questions get more difficult as you move along. If you find that the questions of one type are getting too difficult, quickly read through the rest of the questions in that group to see if there are others you can answer. Then go on to the next group of questions in that section.

Don't spend too much time on any one question. All questions are worth the same number of points. So if you can't answer a question without spending a long time figuring it out, go on to the next one. You may have time to come back to it later.

Don't lose points to carelessness. No matter how frustrated you are, don't pass over questions without at least reading through them. And be sure to consider all the choices in each question. You could lose points on easy questions through careless errors. Take each question as it comes and avoid careless mistakes:

1. Answer the question asked. For example, if the question asks for the area of a shaded region, don't answer with the unshaded area.
2. Check that your answer makes sense. Is a discount higher than the original price? Is the average age of a high school student 56 years old?
3. Check your work from the beginning. If you can, use a *different* method from the one you used to get the answer. If you use the same method, you may make the same mistake twice.

Work the problems in your test booklet. You will not receive credit for anything written in the booklet but you will be able to check your work easily later:

- Draw figures to help you think through problems that involve geometric shapes, segment lengths, distances, proportions, sizes, etc.
- Mark key information on graphs and add information to drawings and diagrams as you figure.
- Mark each question that you don't answer so that you can easily go back to it later.
- When working on a question, put a line through each choice as you eliminate it.

Eliminate choices. If you don't know the correct answer to a question, try eliminating wrong choices. It's sometimes easier to find the wrong answers than the correct one. On some questions, you can eliminate all the choices until you have only the one correct answer left. In other cases, eliminating choices can help you think your way through to the correct answer.

Guess when you can eliminate at least one answer choice. On multiple-choice questions, if you can eliminate even one answer you increase your chances of getting a question right. With each correct answer you gain one point; if you leave the answer blank you get no points; if your answer is wrong you only lose 1/4 of a point.

Strategies for Finding the Right Answer

Ask yourself the following questions before solving each problem:

1. What is the question asking?
2. What do I know?

Once you've answered these questions, make sure to:

- Answer the question asked.
- Check that your answer makes sense.
- Check your work from the beginning. If you can, use a *different* method from the one you used to get the answer. If you use the same method, you may make the same mistake twice.

If you can't figure out how to approach a problem, the form of the answer choices may give you a hint. It may also help you to try solving difficult problems either by substituting numbers or by plugging in the answer choices to backsolve a question.

Substitute Numbers. Some questions use variables (indicated by letters) to represent the values you are asked to consider. You can make the problem more concrete by substituting numbers for the variables. For example, consider the following quantitative comparison question:

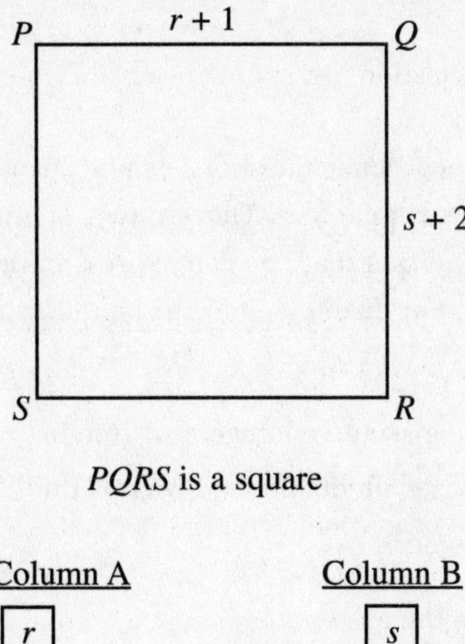

PQRS is a square

Column A	Column B
r	s

Substitute: Think about what you are given and what you know. You are given a square and you know the sides are equal:

- Suppose the length of each side of the square is 10.
- Then r must be 9 and s must be 8.
- So, r is greater than s.
- Now you know the answer cannot be B or C because you have found Column A to be greater in at least one case.
- At this point, it is easy to see that r has to be one more than s. The correct answer is A.
- A direct way to solve this problem is to set $r + 1$ equal to $s + 2$. Then, $r = s + 1$, which tells you that $r > s$.

Tip: Substituting Numbers

- Use common sense when picking numbers to substitute.
- Substitute numbers that are easy to work with.
- Make sure you check the special cases: 0, 1, at least one number between 0 and 1, a number or numbers greater than 1, and a few negative numbers.

Plug in the answer choices. Some questions can be answered by working backwards from the answer choices. This strategy is often useful when the question includes a condition that you can express in the form of a formula — even a verbal one. For example, look at the following multiple-choice question:

> If the product of three consecutive integers written in increasing order equals the middle integer, what is the LEAST of the three integers?
>
> (A) 2
> (B) 1
> (C) 0
> (D) -1
> (E) -2

Plugging in: Use the answer choices to figure out which choice satisfies the conditions of the question:

- Can the answer be (A)? If so, then it must be true that $2 \times 3 \times 4 = 3$ (the middle integer). Clearly, this is NOT TRUE.
- Ask yourself the same question for the other choices.
- When you get to choice (D), the consecutive integers are -1, 0, and 1. The product of these three integers is 0, which is the middle integer.
- The correct answer is (D) .

Tip: Plugging in Answer Choices

When plugging in the answer choices to see which one works, start with choice (C). If the choices are numbers, they are usually listed in order from lowest to highest value, or highest to lowest. So, if (C) turns out to be too high, you don't have to try out the larger numbers and if (C) is too low, you don't have to try out the smaller numbers.

Recap: Tips on General Mathematics Reasoning Questions

1. Familiarize yourself with the Reference Information.
2. Study the concepts and skills in Chapter 11, "Mathematics Review."
3. Make notes in your test booklet:
   - Draw figures to help you think through problems with geometric shapes, distances, proportions, etc.
   - Write out calculations to check later.
   - When a question contains a figure, note any measurements or values you calculate right on the figure in the test booklet.
4. If you have time to check your work, redo your calculations in a different way from the way you did them the first time.
5. Use the answer choices to your advantage:
   - If you can't figure out how to approach a problem, the form of the answer choices may give you a hint.
   - If you aren't sure of the answer, try to eliminate some choices so you can make an educated guess.
6. Try solving easy problems with variables by substituting numbers.
7. Consider plugging in answer choices to help you find the right answer. It's often helpful to start with choice C.
8. If it seems like you have a lot of calculating to do, there may be a short-cut.
9. If you're told that a figure is not drawn to scale, lengths and angles may not be shown accurately.
10. Number lines and graphs are generally drawn accurately.
11. When faced with special symbols, don't panic. Read the definition carefully and use it as your instruction for working out the answer.
12. Some seemingly difficult questions are really just a series of easy questions. Take the solution one step at a time.

Chapter 10

Calculators

Calculators are Recommended

It is recommended that you bring a calculator to use on the mathematics sections of the SAT. Research shows that students who use calculators on the SAT do slightly better than students who do not. Using a calculator helps ensure that you won't miss a question because of computational error.

Although math scores may improve on average with the use of calculators, there is no way of generalizing about the effect of calculator use on an individual student's score.

Bring Your Own Calculator

You are expected to provide your own calculator. You may use almost any of the following calculators:

- four-function,
- scientific, or
- graphing.

However, you may NOT use any of the following:

- pocket organizers,
- "hand-held" minicomputers or laptop computers,
- electronic writing pads or pen-input devices,
- calculators with typewriter-style keypads (known as "QWERTY"),
- calculators with paper tape or printers,
- calculators that "talk" or make unusual noise, or
- calculators that require an electrical outlet.

Calculator Tips

1. Bring a calculator with you when you take the SAT, even if you're not sure if you will use it. Calculators will not be available at the test center.
2. If you don't use a calculator regularly, practice on the calculator you plan to use before the test.
3. All questions on the test can be answered without a calculator. No questions will require complicated or tedious calculations.
4. Don't buy an expensive, sophisticated calculator just to take the test. You'll only need basic functions. We allow more sophisticated calculators so people who already have them don't have to buy a new one.
5. Don't try to use a calculator on every question. Before you start using the calculator, think through how you will solve each problem, and then decide whether to use the calculator.
6. Use common sense. The calculator is meant to aid you in problem solving, not to get in the way.
7. It may help to do scratchwork in the test booklet in order to get your thoughts down on paper before you use your calculator.
8. Make sure your calculator is in good working order and that the batteries (if needed) are fresh. If you calculator fails during the test, you'll need to complete the test without it.

Chapter 11

Mathematics Review

Concepts You Need to Know

There are four broad categories of problems in the math test: Arithmetic, Algebra, Geometry, and Miscellaneous.

The following table lists the basic skills and concepts with which you need to be familiar in each of the four categories. Remember, "be familiar with" means that you understand them and can apply them to a variety of math problems.

Arithmetic
• Problem solving that involves simple addition, subtraction, multiplication, and division • Conceptual understanding of arithmetic operations with fractions • Averages (arithmetic mean), median, and mode • Properties of integers: odd and even numbers, prime numbers, positive and negative integers, factors, divisibility, and multiples • Word problems involving such concepts as rate/time/distance, percents, averages • Number line: order, betweenness, and consecutive numbers • Ratio and proportion ***Not included*** • Tedious or long computations

Algebra
• Operations involving signed numbers • Word problems: translating verbal statements into algebraic expressions • Substitution • Simplifying algebraic expressions • Elementary factoring • Solving algebraic equations and inequalities • Manipulation of positive integer exponents and roots • Simple quadratic equations ***Not included*** • Complicated manipulations with radicals and roots • Solving quadratic equations that require the use of the quadratic formula • Exponents that are NOT whole numbers

Geometry
• Properties of parallel and perpendicular lines • Angle relationships—vertical angles and angles in geometric figures • Properties of triangles: right, isosceles, and equilateral; 30°-60°-90° and other "special" right triangles; total of interior angles; Pythagorean theorem; similarity • Properties of polygons: perimeter, area, angle measures • Properties of circles: circumference, area, radius, diameter • Solids: volume, surface area • Simple coordinate geometry, including slope, coordinates of points ***Not included*** • Formal geometric proofs • Volumes other than rectangular solids and those given in the reference material or in individual questions

Miscellaneous
• Probability • Data interpretation • Counting and ordering problems • Special symbols • Logical analysis

Arithmetic

Properties of Integers

You will need to know the following information for a number of questions on the math test:

- Integers include positive whole numbers, their negatives, and zero (0).

  –3, –2, –1, 0, 1, 2, 3, 4

- Integers extend indefinitely in both negative and positive directions.
- Integers *do not* include fractions or decimals.

  The following are negative integers:

  –4, –3, –2, –1

  The following are positive integers:

  1, 2, 3, 4

  The integer zero (0) is neither positive nor negative.

Odd Numbers

–5, –3, –1, 1, 3, 5

Even Numbers

–4, –2, 0, 2, 4

The integer zero (0) is an even number.

Consecutive Integers

Integers that follow in sequence, where the positive difference between two successive integers is 1, are consecutive integers.

$$-1, 0, 1, 2, 3$$
$$1001, 1002, 1003, 1004$$
$$-14, -13, -12, -11$$

The following is a general mathematical notation for representing consecutive integers:

$n, n + 1, n + 2, n + 3 \ldots$, where n is any integer.

Prime Numbers

A prime number is any number that has exactly two whole number factors — itself and the number 1. The number 1 itself *is not* prime.

Prime numbers include:

2, 3, 5, 7, 11, 13, 17, 19

Addition of Integers

even	+	even	=	even
odd	+	odd	=	even
odd	+	even	=	odd

Multiplication of Integers

even	×	even	=	even
odd	×	odd	=	odd
odd	×	even	=	even

Number Lines

A number line is used to geometrically represent the relationships between numbers: integers, fractions, and/or decimals.

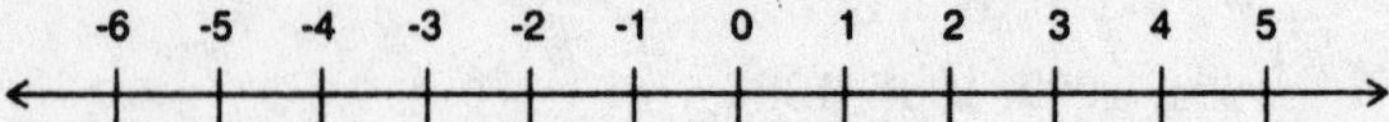

- Numbers on a number line always increase as you move to the right.
- Negative numbers are always shown with a negative sign (–). The plus sign (+) is usually not shown.
- Number lines are drawn to scale. You will be expected to make reasonable approximations of positions between labeled points on the line.

Number-line questions generally require you to figure out the relationships among numbers placed on the line. Number-line questions may ask:

- Where a number should be placed in relation to other numbers;
- The differences between two numbers;
- The lengths and the ratios of the lengths of line segments represented on the number line.

Sample Question

Here is a sample number-line question:

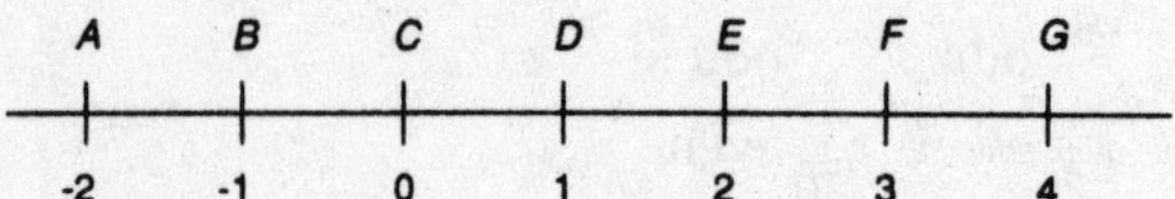

On the number line above, the ratio of the length of AC to the length of AG is equal to the ratio of the length of CD to the length of which of the following?

(A) *AD*
(B) *BD*
(C) *CG*
(D) *DF*
(E) *EG*

In this question, the number line is used to determine lengths: $AC = 2$, $AG = 6$, $CD = 1$. Once you have these lengths, the question becomes a ratio and proportion problem.

- The ratio of AC to AG is 2 to 6.
- AC is to AG as CD is to what?
- $\frac{2}{6} = \frac{1}{x}$
- $x = 3$

Now you have to go back to the number line to find the segment that has the length of 3. The answer is (A).

Tip:

The distances between tick marks on a number line *do not* have to be measured in whole units.

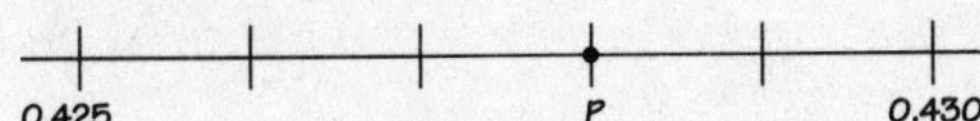

The number line shown above is from a question that appeared on the SAT. The question requires that you figure out the coordinate of point *P*.

The units of measure are *thousandths*. (The distance between adjacent tick marks is .001.) Point *P* is at 0.428 on this number line.

Squares and Square Roots

Squares of Integers

Although you can always figure them out with paper and pencil or with your calculator, it's helpful if you know or at least can recognize the squares of integers between –12 and 12. Here they are:

x	1	2	3	4	5	6	7	8	9	10	11	12
x^2	1	4	9	16	25	36	49	64	81	100	121	144

x	−1	−2	−3	−4	−5	−6	−7	−8	−9	−10	−11	−12
x^2	1	4	9	16	25	36	49	64	81	100	121	144

Your knowledge of common squares and square roots may speed up your solution to some math problems. The most common types of problems for which this knowledge will help you will be those involving:

- Factoring and/or simplifying expressions;
- Problems involving the Pythagorean theorem ($a^2 + b^2 = c^2$);
- Areas of circles or squares.

Squares of Fractions

Remember that if a positive fraction whose value is less than 1 is squared, the result is always *smaller* than the original fraction:

$$\text{If } 0 < n < 1$$

$$\text{Then } n^2 < n.$$

Try it.

What are the values of the following fractions?

$$\left(\frac{2}{3}\right)^2$$

$$\left(\frac{1}{8}\right)^2$$

The answers are 4/9 and 1/64, respectively. Each of these is less in value than the original fraction. For example, 4/9 < 2/3.

Fractions

You should know how to do basic operations with fractions:

- Adding, subtracting, multiplying, and dividing fractions;
- Reducing to lowest terms;
- Finding the least common denominator;
- Expressing a value as a mixed number ($2\frac{1}{3}$) and as an improper fraction ($\frac{7}{3}$);
- Working with complex fractions — ones that have fractions in their numerators or denominators.

Decimal Fraction Equivalents

You may have to work with decimal/fraction equivalents. That is, you may have to be able to recognize common fractions as decimals and vice versa.

To change any fraction to a decimal, divide the denominator into the numerator.

Although you can figure out the decimal equivalent of any fraction (a calculator will help here), you'll be doing yourself a favor if you know the following:

Fraction	$\frac{1}{4}$	$\frac{1}{3}$	$\frac{1}{2}$	$\frac{2}{3}$	$\frac{3}{4}$
Decimal	0.25	0.3333*	0.5	0.6666*	0.75

* These fractions don't convert to terminating decimals — the 3 and 6 repeat indefinitely.

Factors, Multiples, and Remainders

In most math tests, you'll find several questions that require you to understand and work with these three related concepts.

Factors

The factors of a number are integers that can be divided into the number without any remainders.

For instance, consider the number 24:

The numbers 24, 12, 8, 6, 4, 3, 2, and 1 are all factors of the number 24.

Common Factors — Common factors are factors that two numbers have in common. For instance, 3 is a common factor of 6 and 15.

Prime Factors — Prime factors are the factors of a number that are prime numbers. That is, the prime factors of a number cannot be further divided into factors.

The prime factors of the number 24 are: 2 and 3.

The term "divisible by" means divisible by *without any remainder* or *with a remainder of zero*. For instance, 12 is divisible by 4 because 12 divided by 4 is 3 with a remainder of 0. Twelve is not divisible by 5 because 12 divided by 5 is 2 with a remainder of 2.

Multiples

The multiples of any given number are those numbers that can be divided by that given number *without a remainder*.

For instance: 16, 24, 32, 40, and 48 are all multiples of 8. They are also multiples of 2 and 4. Remember: The multiples of any number will always be multiples of all the factors of that number.

For instance:

- 30, 45, 60, and 75 are all multiples of the number 15.
- Two factors of 15 are the numbers 3 and 5.
- That means that 30, 45, 60, and 75 are all multiples of 3 and 5.

Sample Questions

Example 1:

What is the *least* positive integer divisible by the numbers 2, 3, 4, and 5?

- To find *any* number that is divisible by several other numbers, multiply those numbers together. You could multiply 2 × 3 × 4 × 5 and the result would be divisible by all those factors.
- But the question asks for the *least* positive number divisible by all four. To find that, you have to eliminate any extra factors.
- Any number divisible by 4 will also be divisible by 2. So you can eliminate 2 from your initial multiplication. If you multiply 3 × 4 × 5, you will get a smaller number than if you multiply 2 × 3 × 4 × 5. And the number will still be divisible by 2.
- Because the remaining factors (3, 4, and 5) have no common factor, the result of 3 × 4 × 5 will give you the answer.

Example 2:

Which of the following could be the remainders when four consecutive positive integers are each divided by 3?

(A) 1,2,3,1
(B) 1,2,3,4
(C) 0,1,2,3
(D) 0,1,2,0
(E) 0,2,3,0

Remember, the question asks only for the remainders.

- When you divide *any* positive integer by 3, the remainder must be less than or equal to 2.
- All the choices except (D) include remainders greater than 2. So (D) is the correct answer.

Averages

The word "average" can refer to several different measures.

- Arithmetic mean
- Median
- Mode

Arithmetic Mean

Arithmetic mean is what is usually thought of when talking about averages. If you want to know the arithmetic mean of a list of values, the formula is:

$$\frac{\textit{The sum of a list of values}}{\textit{The number of values in the list}}$$

For example, if there are three children, aged 6, 7, and 11, the arithmetic mean of their ages is:

$$\frac{6 + 7 + 11}{3}$$

or 8 years.

Median

The median is the middle value of a list. To find the median, place the values in ascending (or descending) order and select the middle value.

For instance:

What is the median of the following values?

1, 2, 667, 4, 19, 309, 44, 6, 200

- Place the values in ascending order:

  1, 2, 4, 6, 19, 44, 200, 309, 667

- Select the value in the middle.
- There are nine values listed. The middle value is the fifth.
- The median of these values is 19.

The Median of a List with an Even Number of Values

When the number of values in a list is an even number, the median is the average (arithmetic mean) of the two middle values. For example, the median of 3, 7, 10, 20 is $\frac{7+10}{2} = 8.5$

Mode

The mode of a list of values is the value or values that appear the greatest number of times.

In the list used to illustrate the median, there was no mode, because all the values appeared just once. But consider the following list:

1, 5, 5, 7, 276, 4, 100, 276, 89, 4, 276, 1, 8

- The number 276 appears three times, which is more times than any other number appears.
- The **mode** of this list is 276.

Multiple Modes

It is possible to have more than one mode in a list of numbers:

1, 5, 5, 7, 276, 4, 10004, 89, 4, 276, 1, 8

In the list above, there are four modes: 1, 4, 5, and 276.

Weighted Average

A weighted average is the average of two or more groups in which there are more members in one group than there are in another. For instance:

> 15 members of a class had an average (arithmetic mean) SAT math score of 500. The remaining 10 members of the class had an average of 550. What is the average score of the entire class?

You can't simply take the average of 500 and 550 because there are more students with 500s than with 550s. The correct average has to be weighted toward the group with the greater number.

To find a weighted average, multiply each individual average by its weighting factor. The weighting factor is the number of values that correspond to a particular average. In this problem, you multiply each average by the number of students that corresponds to that average. Then you divide by the total number of students involved:

$$\frac{(500 \times 15) + (550 \times 10)}{25} = 520$$

So the average score for the entire class is 520.

A Calculator may help you find the answer to this question more quickly.

Average of Algebraic Expressions

Algebraic expressions can be averaged in the same way as any other values:

What is the average (arithmetic mean) of $3x + 1$ and $x - 3$?

There are two expressions, $3x + 1$ and $x - 3$, to be averaged. Take the sum of the values and divide by the number of values:

$$\frac{1}{2}[(3x + 1) + (x - 3)]$$

$$= \frac{(4x - 2)}{2}$$

$$= 2x - 1$$

Using Averages to Find Missing Numbers

You can use simple algebra in the basic average formula to find missing values when the average is given:

- The basic average formula is:

$$\frac{\textit{The sum of a list of values}}{\textit{The number of values in the list}}$$

- If you have the average and the number of values, you can figure out the sum of the values:

(average) (number of values) = sum of values

Sample Question

Try putting this knowledge to work with a typical question on averages:

The average (arithmetic mean) of a list of 10 numbers is 15. If one of the numbers is removed, the average of the remaining numbers is 14. What is the value of the number that was removed?

- You know the average and the number of values in the list, so you can figure out the sum of all values in the list.
- The difference between the sum before you remove the number and after you remove the number will give you the value of the number you removed.
- The sum of all the values when you start out is the average times the number of values: $10 \times 15 = 150$.
- The sum of the values after you remove a number is $9 \times 14 = 126$.
- The difference between the sums is $150 - 126 = 24$.
- You only removed one number, so the value of that number is 24.

Ratio and Proportion

Ratio

A ratio expresses a mathematical relationship between two quantities. Specifically, a ratio is a quotient of those quantities. The following are all relationships that can be expressed as ratios:

- My serving of pizza is $\frac{1}{4}$ of the whole pie.
- There are twice as many chocolate cookies as vanilla cookies in the cookie jar.
- My brother earns $5 for each $6 I earn.

These ratios can be expressed in several different ways. They can be stated in words:

- The ratio of my serving of pizza to the whole pie is one to four.
- The ratio of chocolate to vanilla cookies is two to one.
- The ratio of my brother's earnings to mine is five to six.

They can be expressed as fractions:

- $\frac{1}{4}$
- $\frac{2}{1}$
- $\frac{5}{6}$

Or they can be expressed with a colon (:) as follows:

- 1:4
- 2:1
- 5:6

Sample Question

The weight of the tea in a box of 100 identical tea bags is 8 ounces. What is the weight, in ounces, of the tea in 3 tea bags?

Start by setting up two ratios. A proportion is two ratios set equal to each other.

- The ratio of 3 tea bags to all of the tea bags is 3 to 100 ($\frac{3}{100}$).
- Let x equal the weight, in ounces, of the tea in 3 tea bags.
- The ratio of the weight of 3 tea bags to the total weight of the tea is x ounces to 8 ounces ($\frac{x}{8}$).

The relationship between x ounces and 8 ounces is equal to the relationship between 3 and 100:

$$\frac{x}{8} = \frac{3}{100}$$

$$100x = 24$$

$$x = \frac{24}{100} \text{ or } .24$$

Sample Question

You may find questions that involve ratios in any of the following situations:

- Lengths of line segments;
- Sizes of angles;
- Areas and perimeters;
- Rate/time/distance;
- Numbers on a number line.

You may be asked to combine ratios with other mathematical concepts. For instance:

> The ratio of the length of a rectangular floor to its width is 3:2. If the length of the floor is 12 meters, what is the perimeter of the floor, in meters?

The ratio of the length to the width of the rectangle is 3:2, so set that ratio equal to the ratio of the actual measures of the sides of the rectangle:

$$\frac{3}{2} = \frac{length}{width}$$

$$\frac{3}{2} = \frac{12}{x}$$

$$3x = 24$$

$$x = 8 \text{ (the width)}$$

Now that you have the width of the rectangle, it is easy to find the perimeter: 2(length + width). The perimeter is 40 meters.

Algebra

Many math questions require a knowledge of algebra, so the basics of algebra should be second nature to you. You have to be able to manipulate and solve a simple equation for an unknown, simplify and evaluate algebraic expressions, and use algebraic concepts in problem-solving situations.

Factoring

The types of factoring included on the math test are:

- Difference of two squares:

$$a^2 - b^2 = (a + b)(a - b)$$

- Finding common factors, as in:

$$x^2 + 2x = x(x + 2)$$

$$2x + 4y = 2(x + 2y)$$

- Factoring quadratics:

$$x^2 - 3x - 4 = (x - 4)(x + 1)$$

$$x^2 + 2x + 1 = (x + 1)(x + 1) = (x + 1)^2$$

You are not likely to find a question instructing you to "factor the following expression." You may see questions that ask you to evaluate or compare expressions that require factoring. For instance, here is a Quantitative Comparison question:

Column A **Column B**

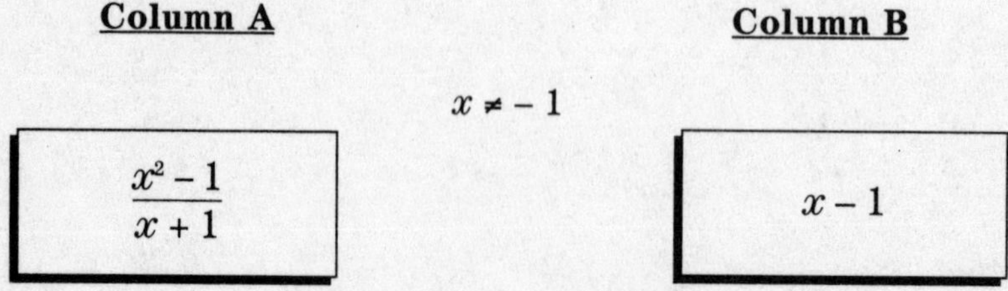

The numerator of the expression in Column A can be factored:

$$x^2 - 1$$

$$= (x + 1)(x - 1)$$

The $(x + 1)(x - 1)$ cancels with the $(x + 1)$ in the denominator, leaving the factor $(x - 1)$. So the two quantities — the one in Column A and the one in Column B — are equal.

Exponents

Three Points to Remember

1. When multiplying expressions with the same base, *add* the exponents:

$$a^2 \cdot a^5$$
$$= (a \cdot a)(a \cdot a \cdot a \cdot a \cdot a)$$
$$= a^7$$

2. When dividing expressions with the same base, subtract exponents:

$$\frac{r^5}{r^3} = \frac{r \cdot r \cdot \cancel{r} \cdot \cancel{r} \cdot \cancel{r}}{\cancel{r} \cdot \cancel{r} \cdot \cancel{r}} = r^2$$

3. When raising one power to another power, *multiply* the exponents:

$$(n^3)^6 = n^{18}$$

Solving Equations

Most of the equations that you will need to solve are linear equations. Equations that are not linear can usually be solved by factoring or by inspection.

Working With "Unsolvable" Equations

At first, some equations may look like they can't be solved. You will find that although you can't solve the equation, you can answer the question. For instance:

If $a + b = 5$, what is the value of $2a + 2b$?

You can't solve the equation $a + b = 5$ for either a or b. But you can answer the question:

- The question doesn't ask for the value of a or b. It asks for the value of the entire quantity $(2a + 2b)$.
- $2a + 2b$ can be factored:

  $2a + 2b = 2(a + b)$
- $a + b = 5$

You are asked what 2 times $a + b$ is. That's 2 times 5, or 10.

Solving for One Variable in Terms of Another

You may be asked to solve for one variable in terms of another. Again, you're not going to be able to find a specific, numerical value for all of the variables.

For example:

If $3x + y = z$, what is x in terms of y and z?

You aren't asked what x equals. You are asked to manipulate the expression so that you can isolate x (put it by itself) on one side of the equation. That equation will tell you what x is in terms of the other variables:

- $3x + y = z$
- Subtract y from each side of the equation.

  $3x = z - y$
- Divide both sides by 3 to get the value of x.

  $x = \frac{(z - y)}{3}$

The value of x in terms of y and z is $\frac{(z - y)}{3}$.

Direct Translations of Mathematical Terms

Many word problems require that you translate the verbal description of a mathematical fact or relationship into mathematical terms.

Always read the word problem carefully and double-check that you have translated it exactly.

A number is 3 times the quantity $(4x + 6)$ translates to $3(4x + 6)$

A number y decreased by 60 translates to $y - 60$

5 less than a number k translates to $k - 5$

A number that is x less than 5 translates to $5 - x$

20 divided by n is $\frac{20}{n}$

20 divided into a number y is $\frac{y}{20}$

See the Word Problem tips in this chapter.

Be especially careful with subtraction and division because the order of these operations is important.

$5 - 3$ is not the same as $3 - 5$.

Inequalities

An inequality is a statement that two values are *not* equal, or that one value is greater than or equal to or less than or equal to another. Inequalities are shown by four signs:

- Greater than: $>$
- Greater than or equal to: $\geq$
- Less than: $<$
- Less than or equal to: $\leq$

Most of the time, you can work with simple inequalities in exactly the same way you work with equalities.

Consider the following:

$$2x + 1 > 11$$

If this were an equation, it would be pretty easy to solve:

$$2x + 1 = 11$$
$$2x = 11 - 1$$
$$2x = 10$$
$$x = 5$$

You can use a similar process to solve inequalities:

$$2x + 1 > 11$$
$$2x > 11 - 1$$
$$2x > 10$$
$$x > 5$$

Tip:

Remember that multiplying or dividing both sides of an inequality by a negative number reverses the direction of the inequality:

If $-x < 3$, then $x > -3$.

Number Sequences

A number sequence is a sequence of numbers that follows a specific pattern. For instance, the sequence

$$3, 7, 11, 15, \ldots$$

follows the pattern, **add 4**. That is, each term in the sequence is 4 more than the one before it. The three dots (. . .) indicate that this sequence goes on forever.

Not all sequences go on indefinitely. The sequence

$$1, 3, 5, \ldots, 21, 23$$

contains odd numbers only up to 23, where the sequence ends. The three dots in the middle indicate that the sequence continues according to the pattern as shown, but it ends with the number 23.

The math test *does not* usually ask you to figure out the rule for determining the numbers in a sequence. When a number sequence is used in a question, you will usually be told what the rule is.

Number sequence questions might ask you for:

- The sum of certain numbers in the sequence;
- The average of certain numbers in the sequence;
- The value of a specific number in the sequence.

Word Problems

Some math questions are presented as word problems. They require you to apply math skills to everyday situations. With word problems you have to:

- Read and interpret what is being asked.
- Determine what information you are given.
- Determine what information you need to know.
- Decide what mathematical skills or formulas you need to apply to find the answer.
- Work out the answer.
- Double-check to make sure the answer makes sense.

Tips on Solving Word Problems

Translate as You Read

As you read word problems, translate the words into mathematical expressions:

- When you read **Jane has three dollars more than Tom**, translate $J = T + 3$.

- When you read **the average (arithmetic mean) of the weights of three children is 80 pounds**, translate to $(a + b + c)/3 = 80$.
- When you read **Jane buys one clown fish and two guppies for $3.00**, translate $c + 2g = \$3.00$.

When you've finished reading the problem, you will have already translated it into mathematical expressions. The following table will help you with some of the more common phrases and mathematical translations:

Words	Operation	Translation
Is, was, has:	=	
Jane's son is as old as Tom's daughter.	=	$S = D$ or $J = T$
More than, older than, farther than, greater than, sum of:	+	Addition
Jane has 2 more dollars than Tom.	+	$J = 2 + T$ or $J = T + 2$
Tom ran 10 miles farther than Jane.		$T = 10 + J$ or $T = J + 10$
The sum of two integers is 36.		$x + y = 36$
Less than, difference, younger than, fewer:	–	Subtraction
Tom has 5 fewer marbles than twice the number Jane has.	–	$T = 2J - 5$ (Don't make the "$5 - 2J$" mistake!)
The difference between Tom's height and Jane's height is 22 centimeters.		$T - J = 22$ (or maybe $J - T = 22$)
Of:	×	Multiplication
20% of Tom's socks are red.	%	$R = .2 \times T$
Jane ate 3/4 of the candy.		$J = 3/4 \times C$
For, per:	ratio	Division
Jane won 3 games for every 2 that Tom won.	÷	$J/T = 3/2$
50 miles per hour		50 miles/hour
2 bleeps per revolution		2 bleeps/revolution

Sample Questions

Figuring out these problems takes more than just knowing a bunch of math formulas. You have to think about what math skills and tools you will apply to the questions in order to reason your way through to the correct answer.

1. The price of a sweater went up 20% since last year. If last year's price was x, what is this year's price in terms of x?

   - Last year's price = 100% of x
   - This year's price is 100% of x plus 20% of x. $(100/100)x + (20/100)x = 1.2x$

2. One year ago an average restaurant meal cost $12.00. Today, the average restaurant meal costs $15.00. By what percent has the cost of the meal increased?

You can figure percent increase by taking the difference in prices first and then expressing it as a percentage of the original price:

$15 – $12 = $3 difference.

What percentage of the original price is $3?

$$\left(\frac{x}{100}\right) 12 = 3$$

$$\frac{x}{100} = \frac{3}{12}$$

$$12x = 300$$

$$x = 25\%$$

Or you can figure what percent the new price is of the old price:

15 is what percent of 12?

$$15 = \left(\frac{x}{100}\right) 12$$

$$\frac{15}{12} = \frac{x}{100}$$

$$x = 125\%$$

This tells you what percent the current price ($15) is of the old price ($12). But the question asks for the percent increase. So you have to subtract 100 percent from 125 percent.

$$125 - 100 = 25\% \text{ increase}$$

3. The average height of 4 members of a 6-person volleyball team is 175 cm. What does the average height in centimeters of the other 2 players have to be if the average height of the entire team equals 180 cm?

Start with the formula for the average:

$$\frac{\textit{sum of values}}{\textit{number of values}} = \textit{average}$$

Use what you know to find out the sum of the heights of the 4 members whose average is 175 cm.

$$\frac{\textit{sum}}{4} = 175$$

$$\textit{sum} = 4(175) = 700$$

The average of all 6 players is 180 cm.

$$\text{Average of 6} = \frac{(\textit{sum of } 4 + \textit{sum of } 2)}{6}$$

$$180 = \frac{(700 + \textit{sum of } 2)}{6}$$

$$1080 = 700 + \textit{sum of } 2$$

$$1080 - 700 = \textit{sum of } 2$$

$$380 = \textit{sum of } 2$$

What is the average of the heights of the 2 players?

$$\text{Average} = \frac{\textit{sum}}{\textit{number of players}}$$

$$\text{Average} = \frac{380}{2} = 190 \text{ cm.}$$

4. A car traveling at an average rate of 55 kilometers per hour made a trip in 6 hours. If it had traveled at an average rate of 50 kilometers per hour, the trip would have taken how many <u>minutes</u> longer?

 - How long was the trip?

   Distance = rate × time

   Distance = 55 kph × 6 hours

   Distance = 330 km.

 - How long does the 330-kilometer trip take if the car is traveling at 50 kilometers per hour?

   $\text{Time} = \dfrac{\textit{distance}}{\textit{rate}}$

   $\text{Time} = \dfrac{330}{50}$

   $\text{Time} = 6\,\dfrac{3}{5}$ hours

 - What does the question ask?

   The difference <u>in minutes</u> between the two trips.

   $\text{Difference} = \dfrac{3}{5}$ hour

   Difference = ? minutes

   $\dfrac{3}{5} = \dfrac{x}{60}$

   $5x = 180$

   $x = 36$ minutes

Geometry

The geometry questions focus on your ability to recognize and use the special properties of many geometric figures. You will find questions requiring you to know about:

- Triangles, in general;
- Special triangles — right triangles, isosceles, and equilateral triangles;
- Rectangles, squares, and other polygons;
- Areas and perimeters of simple figures;
- The angles formed by intersecting lines, and angles involving parallel and perpendicular lines;
- Area, circumference, and arc degrees in a circle.

Triangles

Equilateral Triangles

The three sides of an equilateral triangle (a, b, c) are equal in length. The three angles (x, y, z) are also equal and they each measure 60 degrees ($x = y = z = 60$).

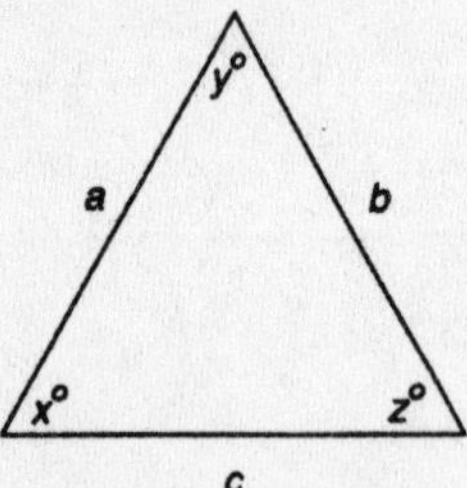

Isosceles Triangles

An isosceles triangle is a triangle with two sides of equal length ($m = n$). The angles opposite the equal sides are also equal ($x = y$).

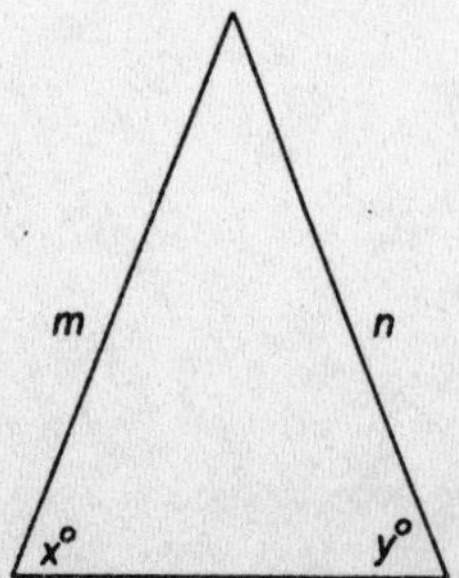

Right Triangles and the Pythagorean Theorem

You can get a lot of information from figures that contain right triangles. And this information frequently involves the Pythagorean theorem:

> The square of the hypotenuse of a right triangle is equal to the sum of the squares of the other two sides.

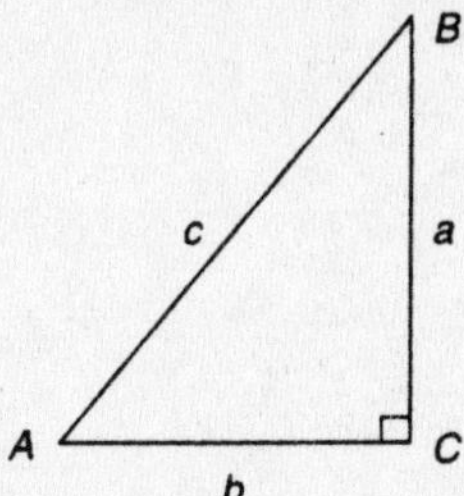

The hypotenuse is the longest side of the triangle and is opposite the right angle. The other two sides are usually referred to as legs. In the figure above:

- AB is the hypotenuse with length c.
- BC and AC are the two legs with lengths a and b, respectively.
- The Pythagorean theorem leads to the equation:

$$a^2 + b^2 = c^2$$

30°-60°-90° Right Triangles

The lengths of the sides of a 30°-60°-90° triangle are in the ratio of $1{:}\sqrt{3}{:}2$, as shown in the figure:

- Short leg = x
- Long leg = $x\sqrt{3}$
- Hypotenuse = $2x$

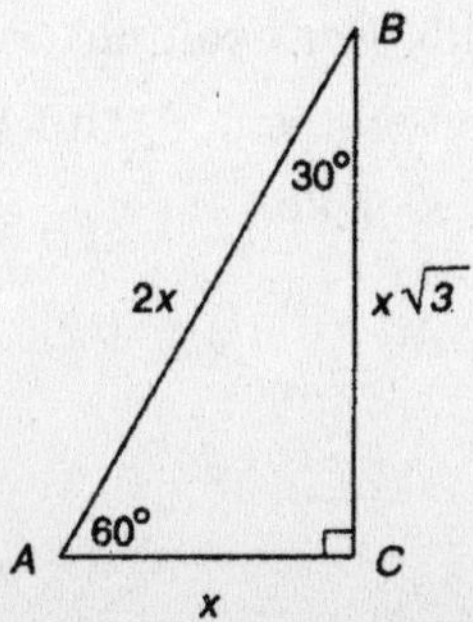

If you know the lengths of any two sides, the Pythagorean theorem will help you to find the length of the third.

For instance, if you know the length of the short leg is 1 and the length of the hypotenuse is 2, then the theorem gives you the length of the longer leg:

$$c^2 = a^2 + b^2$$

$$c = 2, b = 1$$

$$2^2 = a^2 + 1$$

$$4 = a^2 + 1$$

$$3 = a^2$$

$$\sqrt{3} = a$$

45°-45°-90° Triangle

The lengths of the sides of a 45°-45°-90° triangle are in the ratio of 1:1:$\sqrt{2}$, as shown in the figure below. To verify this ratio when the equal sides are of length 1, apply the Pythagorean theorem to find the length of the hypotenuse:

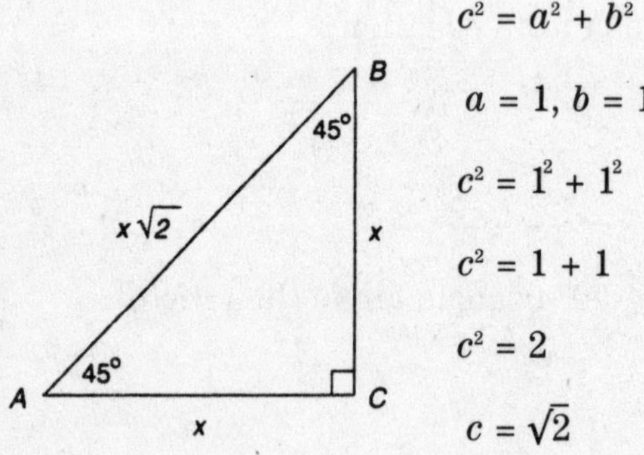

$$c^2 = a^2 + b^2$$

$$a = 1, b = 1$$

$$c^2 = 1^2 + 1^2$$

$$c^2 = 1 + 1$$

$$c^2 = 2$$

$$c = \sqrt{2}$$

3-4-5 Triangle

The sides of a 3-4-5 right triangle are in the ratio of 3:4:5. For example, in the figure below, if $x = 2$, the sides of the triangle have lengths 6, 8, and 10. The Pythagorean theorem is easy to verify for this example:

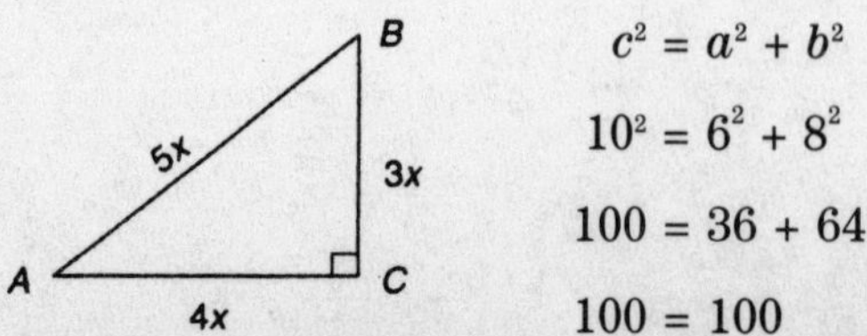

$$c^2 = a^2 + b^2$$

$$10^2 = 6^2 + 8^2$$

$$100 = 36 + 64$$

$$100 = 100$$

Quadrilaterals, Lines, and Angles

In some special quadrilaterals — parallelograms, rectangles, and squares — there are relationships among the angles and sides that can help you solve geometry problems.

Parallelograms

In a parallelogram, the opposite angles are equal and the opposite sides are of equal length.

Angles *BAD* and *BCD* are equal; and angles *ABC* and *ADC* are equal. $AB = CD$ and $AD = BC$.

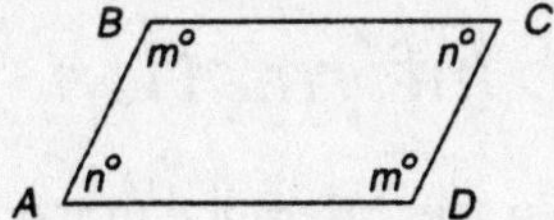

Rectangles

A rectangle is a special case of a parallelogram. In rectangles, all the angles are right angles.

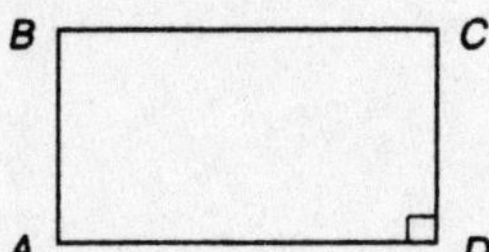

Squares

A square is a special case of a rectangle in which all the sides are equal.

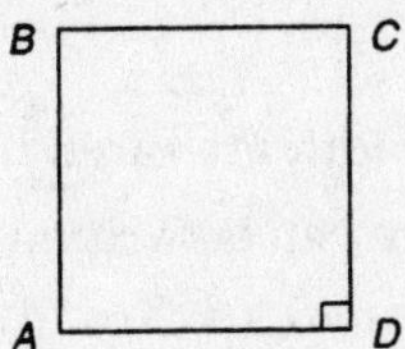

Notice that if you know the length of any side of a square, you also know the length of the diagonal.

The diagonal makes two 45°-45°-90° triangles with the sides of the square. So you can figure out the length of the sides from the length of the diagonal or the length of the diagonal from the length of a side.

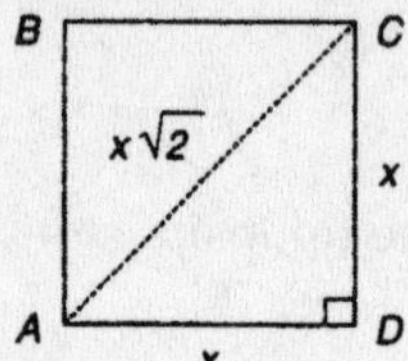

Tip: Remember the Reference Information

Formulas for areas of common figures are given in the reference material that is printed in the test booklet.

Areas and Perimeters

Rectangles and Squares

The formula for the area of any rectangle is:

$$\text{Area} = \text{length} \times \text{width}$$

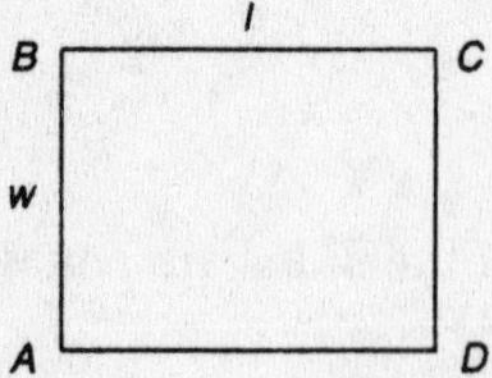

Because all sides of a square are equal, the length and width are often both referred to as the length of a side, s. So the area of a square can be written as:

$$\text{Area} = s^2$$

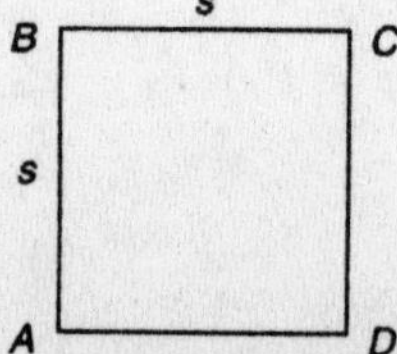

Perimeters of Rectangles and Squares — The perimeter of a simple closed figure is the length all the way around the figure. Because the opposite sides of rectangles are equal, the formula for the perimeter of a rectangle is:

Perimeter of rectangle = 2(length + width) = $2(l + w)$

The same is true for any parallelogram. For a square, it's even easier. Because all four sides of a square are equal, the perimeter of a square is:

Perimeter of a square = 4(length of any side) = $4s$

Area of Triangles

The area of a triangle is:

$$A = \left(\frac{1}{2}\right)bh$$

- b is thc base
- h is the height, a perpendicular line drawn from a vertex of the triangle to the base.

Tip:

You can start with any vertex of the triangle. The side opposite the vertex you choose becomes the base and the perpendicular line from that vertex to the base becomes the height. For instance, the area of the triangle in the figure could be calculated using point A as the vertex instead of point B.

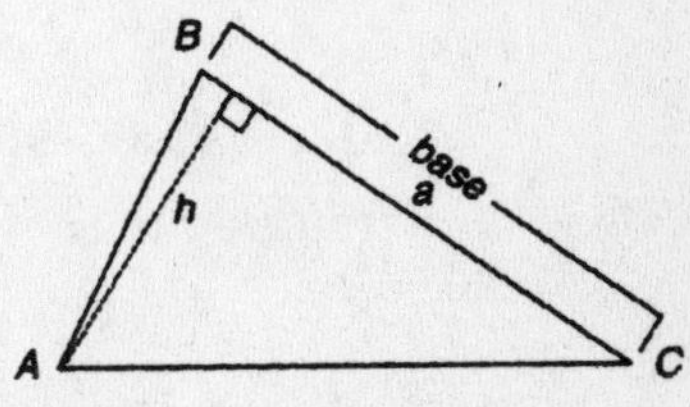

Area of Parallelograms

To find the area of a parallelogram, you "square up" the slanted side of the parallelogram by dropping a perpendicular — line *BE* in the figure shown below. This makes a right triangle *ABE*.

If you take this triangle away from the parallelogram and add it to the other side (triangle *DCF*) you have a rectangle with the same area as the original parallelogram.

The area of the rectangle is length × width.

The width of this rectangle is the same as the height of the parallelogram. So the formula for the area of a parallelogram is:

Area = length × height

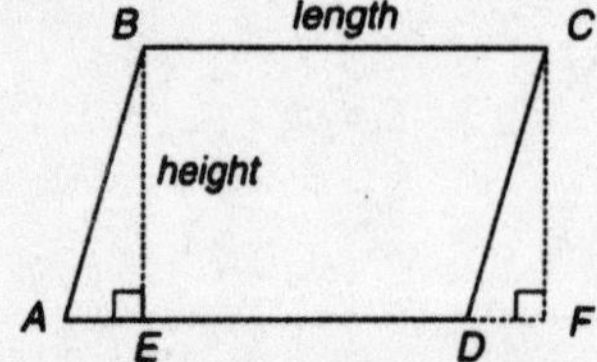

Other Polygons

Occasionally, a math question will ask you to work with polygons other than triangles and quadrilaterals. Here are a few things to remember about other polygons.

Angles in a Polygon

You can figure out the total number of degrees in the interior angles of most polygons by dividing the polygon into triangles:

- From any vertex, divide the polygon into as many nonoverlapping triangles as possible. Use only straight lines. Make sure that all the space inside the polygon is divided into triangles.
- Count the triangles. In this figure, there are four triangles.
- There is a total of 180° in the angles of each triangle, so multiply the number of triangles by 180. The product will be the sum of the angles in the polygon (720° in the hexagon shown below).

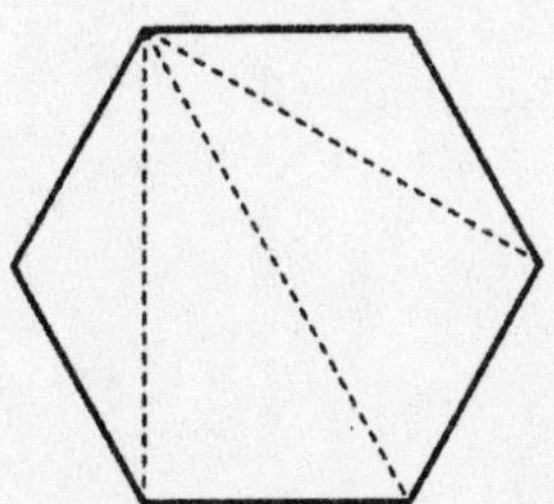

Sample Question

In the figure shown below, lengths *AB*, *BD*, and *CD* are all $3\sqrt{2}$ units long. Angles *BAD* and *BCD* are both 45°. What is the perimeter of *ABCD*? What is the area of *ABCD*?

You are asked for the perimeter and the area of the figure. For the perimeter you will need to know the lengths of sides *BC* and *AD*. For the area you will also need to know the height.

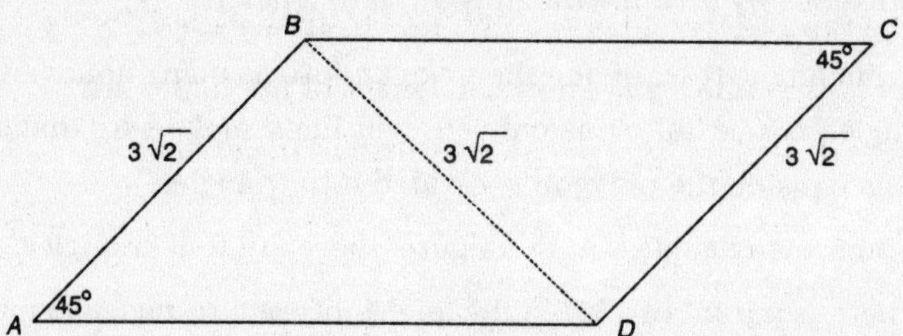

Perimeter

- You are given the lengths of 3 line segments, all of which are the same: $3\sqrt{2}$.
- You are given two angles, both of which are the same: 45°.
- *ABD* is a triangle with two equal sides.
- *BCD* is a triangle with two equal sides.
- So, they are both isosceles triangles.
- Angle *BCD* is 45°, so angle *CBD* has to equal 45°, since angles opposite equal sides are equal.
- The same is true for angles *ADB* and *DAB*, which both equal 45°.
- Both triangles are 45°-45°-90° triangles.
- You can figure out the lengths of *AD* and *BC* by the Pythagorean theorem:

$$AD^2 = (3\sqrt{2})^2 + (3\sqrt{2})^2 = 36, \text{ so } AD = 6$$

- Do the same for the length of *BC* to find that $BC = 6$.
- You can now add up the lengths of the sides to get the perimeter:

$$2(6+3\sqrt{2}) = 12 + 6\sqrt{2}.$$

Area

- *ABCD* is a parallelogram. You know this because both sets of opposite sides are equal: $AB = CD$ and $AD = BC$.
- That means that you can use the formula for the area of a parallelogram: area = length × height.
- To find the height, drop a perpendicular from *B*.
- That creates another 45°-45°-90° triangle whose hypotenuse is *AB*.
- The ratio of the sides of a 45°-45°-90° triangle is $1:1:\sqrt{2}$.
- From that ratio, you know the height of the figure is 3.
- With the height, you can then calculate the area: $3 \times 6 = 18$.

If you label everything you figure out as you go along, you will end up with a figure that looks like the one below.

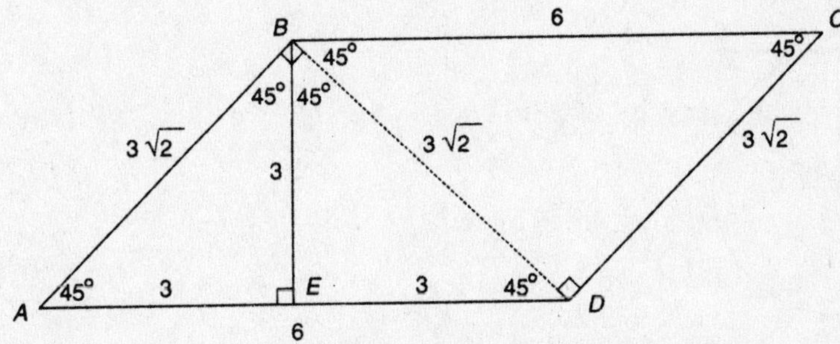

Circles

Diameter

The diameter of a circle is a line segment that passes through the center and has its endpoints on the circle. All diameters of the same circle have equal lengths.

Radius

The radius of a circle is a line segment extending from the center of the circle to a point on the circle. In the figure shown below, *OB* and *OA* are radii.

All radii of the same circle have equal lengths, and the radius is half the diameter. In the figure, the length of *OB* equals the length of *OA*.

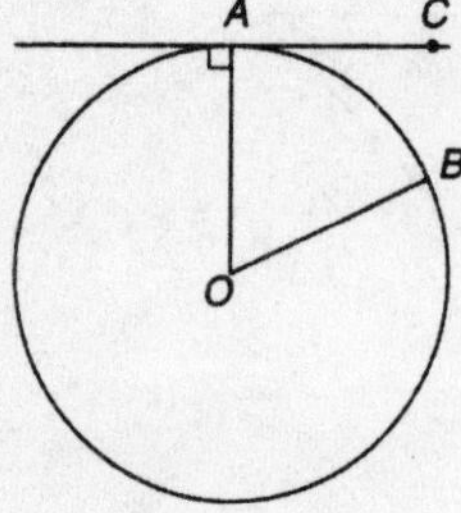

Arc

An arc is a part of a circle. In the figure above, *AB* is an arc. An arc can be measured in degrees or in units of length.

If you form an angle by drawing radii from the ends of the arc to the center of the circle, the number of degrees in the arc (arc *AB* in the figure) equals the number of degrees in the angle formed by the two radii at the center of the circle ($\angle AOB$).

Tangent to a Circle

A tangent to a circle is a line that touches the circle at only one point. In the figure, line *AC* is a tangent.

Circumference

The circumference is the distance around a circle, and it is equal to π times the diameter d (or π times twice the radius r).

$$\text{Circumference} = \pi d$$
$$\text{Circumference} = 2\pi r$$

If the diameter is 16, the circumference is 16π. If the radius is 3, the circumference is $2(3)\pi$ or 6π.

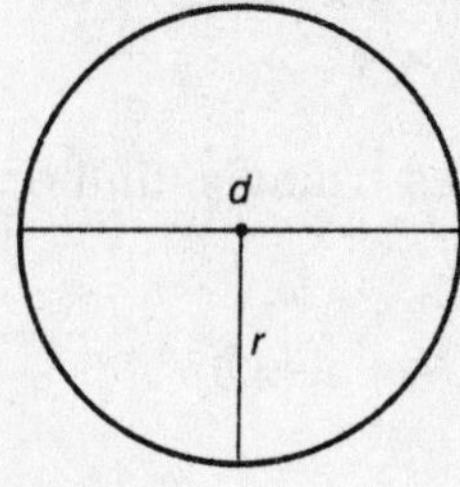

Area

The area of a circle is equal to π times the square of the radius.

$$\text{Area} = \pi r^2$$

Sample Question

In the figure shown below, A is the center of a circle whose area is 25π. B and C are points on the circle. Angle ACB is 45°. What is the length of line segment BC?

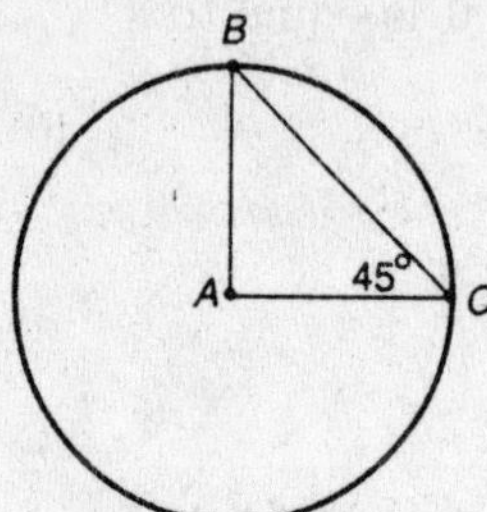

- Point A is the center of the circle.
- That makes both line segments AB and AC radii, which means that they are of equal length.
- Because AB and AC are equal, ΔABC is an isosceles triangle, and one angle opposite one of the equal sides is 45°.
- That means the angle opposite the other equal side is also 45°.
- The remaining angle is 90°.
- The area of the circle is 25π.
- The formula for the area of a circle is πr^2. You can use that formula to figure out the length of the radius, r.
- That length, r, is also the length of the legs of the triangle whose hypotenuse (BC) is the length you are trying to figure out.

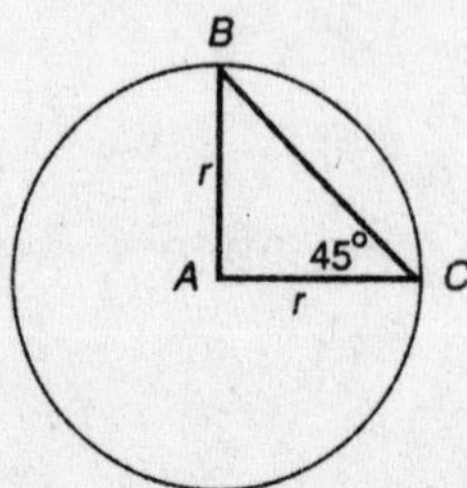

What is the value of r?

$$\text{Area} = \pi r^2$$

$$\text{Area} = 25\pi$$

$$r^2 = 25$$

$$r = 5$$

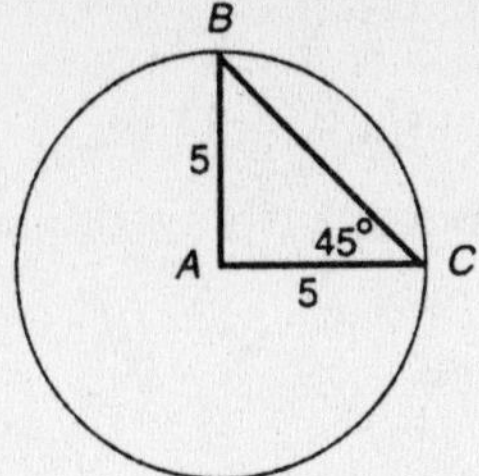

Figuring out the final answer to the problem is a simple matter of working through the Pythagorean theorem or remembering that the ratio of the sides of 45°-45°-90° triangles is $1:1:\sqrt{2}$. The answer is $5\sqrt{2}$.

Miscellaneous Math Questions

Most math questions fall into the three broad areas of arithmetic, algebra, and geometry. Some questions, however, do not fall neatly into one of these areas. Miscellaneous questions on the math test cover areas such as:

- Data interpretation;
- Counting and ordering problems;
- Special symbols;
- Logical analysis;
- Probability.

Data Interpretation

Your primary task in these questions is to interpret information in graphs, tables, or charts, and then compare quantities, recognize trends and changes in the data, or perform calculations based on the information you have found.

A question on a graph like the one shown below might require you to identify specific pieces of information (data), compare data from different parts of the graph, and manipulate the data.

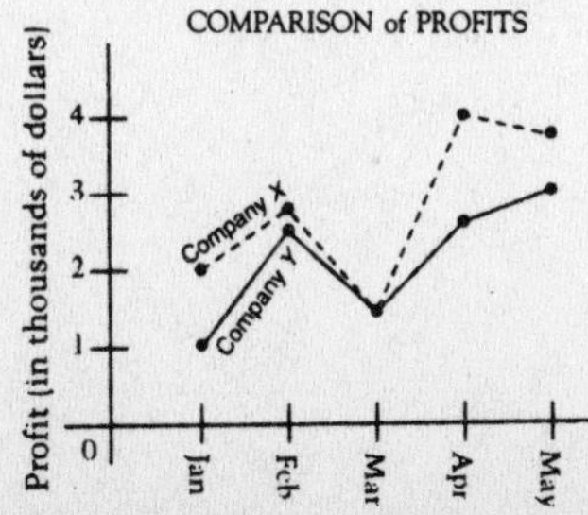

When working with data interpretation questions, you have to:

- Look at the graph, table, or chart to make sure you understand it. Make sure you know what type of information is being displayed.
- Read the question carefully.

With data interpretation questions — graphs, charts, and tables — always make sure you understand the information being presented:

- Read the labels.
- Make sure you know the units.
- Make sure you understand what is happening to the data as you move through the table, graph, or chart.

The graph below shows profits over time. The higher the point on the vertical axis, the greater the profits. (Each tick mark on the vertical axis is another $1,000.) As you move to the right along the horizontal axis, months are passing.

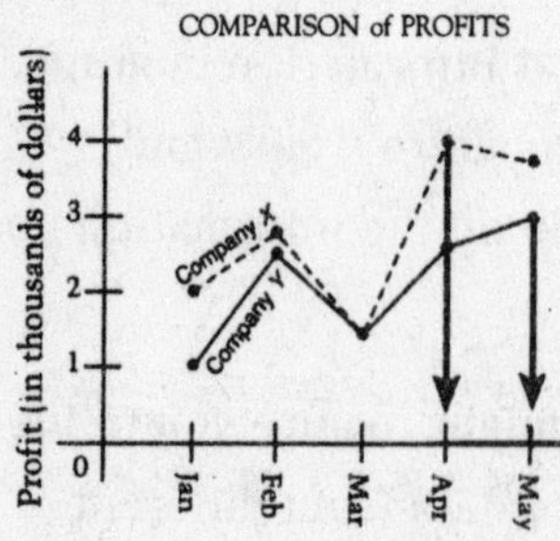

Sample Questions

1. In what month or months did each company make the greatest profit?

Follow the line labeled Company X to its highest point. Then check the month at the bottom of the graph. Follow the same procedure for Company Y.

For Company X, the greatest profit was made in April.

For Company Y, the greatest profit was made in May.

2. Between which two consecutive months did each company show the greatest increase in profit?

The increase (or decrease) in profit is shown by the steepness or "slope" of the graph.

For Company X, it's easy to see that the biggest jump occurred between March and April.

For Company Y, you have to be a little more careful. The biggest increase in profits occurred between January and February. You know this because the slope of the line connecting January and February is the steepest. The increase between January and February is about $1,500, which is greater than the increase for any other pair of consecutive months.

3. In what month did the profits of the two companies show the greatest difference?

To figure this out, you have to compare one company to the other, month by month. The month in which the dots are farthest apart is the one in which there is the greatest difference between the two companies. The distance between the two graph points is greatest in April.

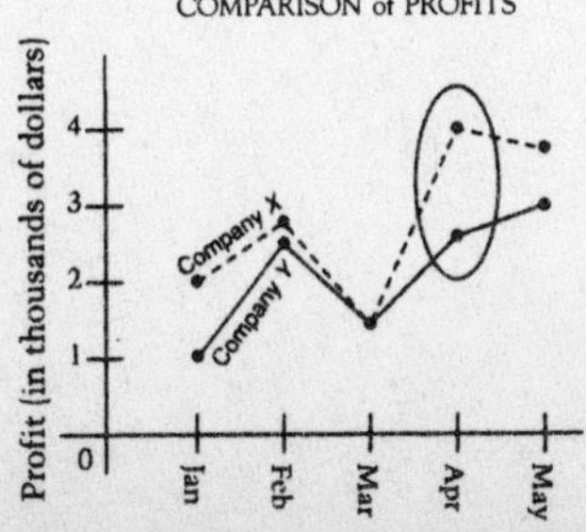

4. If the rate of increase or decrease for each company continues for the next six months at the same rate shown between April and May, which company would have higher profits at the end of that time?

This question is asking you to look at the graph and project changes in the future. To project changes, extend the lines between April and May for each company. The lines cross pretty quickly—well before six more months have passed. So the answer is that Company *Y* would be doing better in six months if the rates of change from month to month stay the same as they were between April and May.

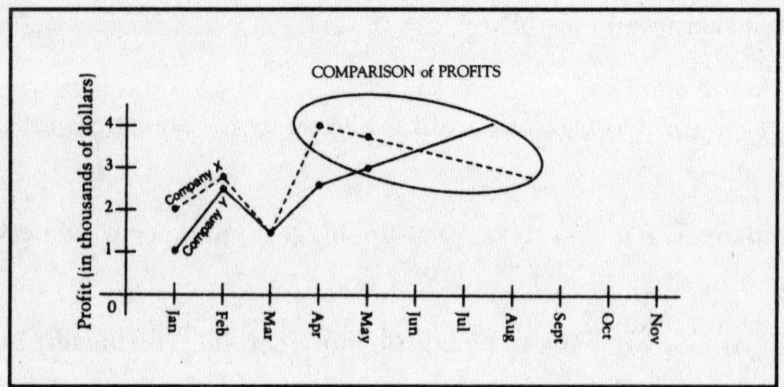

From Graph to Table — The same information presented in the profit chart could be presented in a profit table, which might look something like this:

Profit (in dollars)

	Jan.	Feb.	Mar.	Apr.	May
Company *X*	2,000	2,750	1,500	4,000	3,750
Company *Y*	1,000	2,500	1,500	2,500	3,000

With a table it's a little harder to make the comparisons and see the trends. But the table is much more precise. The graph does not show the exact numbers the way the table does.

Counting and Ordering Problems

Counting and ordering problems involve figuring out how many ways you can select or arrange members of groups, such as letters of the alphabet, numbers, or menu selections.

Fundamental Counting Principle

The fundamental counting principle is the principle by which you figure out how many possibilities there are for selecting members of a group:

If one event can happen in *n* ways, and a second event can happen in *m* ways, the total ways in which the two events can happen is *n* times *m*.

For example:

On a restaurant menu, there are three appetizers and four main courses. How many different dinners can be ordered if each dinner consists of one appetizer and one main course?

- The first event is the choice of appetizer, and there are three choices available.
- The second event is the choice of main course, and there are four main courses.
- The total number of different dinners is therefore, $3 \times 4 = 12$.

This idea can be extended to more than two events:

If you had two choices for beverage added to your choices for appetizer and main course, you would multiply the total by 2: $2 \times 3 \times 4 = 24$.

If you also had three choices for dessert, you would multiply by 3: $3 \times 2 \times 3 \times 4 = 72$.

For example:

A security system uses a four-letter password, but no letter can be used more than once. How many possible passwords are there?

- For the first letter, there are 26 possible choices — one for each letter of the alphabet.
- Because you cannot reuse any letters, there are only 25 choices for the second letter (26 minus the letter used in the first letter of the password).
- There are only 24 choices for the third letter, and only 23 choices for the fourth.

The total number of passwords will be $26 \times 25 \times 24 \times 23$.

Special Symbols

To test your ability to learn and apply mathematical concepts, a special symbol is sometimes introduced and defined.

These symbols generally have unusual looking signs (☆, *, §) so you won't confuse them with standard mathematical symbols.

The key to these questions is to make sure that you read the definition carefully.

A typical special symbol question might look something like this:

Let 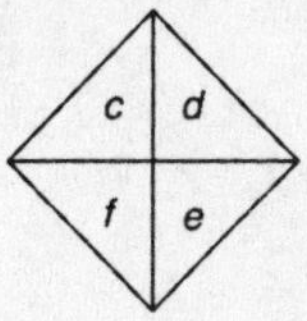 c d / f e $= ce - df$,

where c, d, e, and f are integers.

What is the value of 2 3 / 4 1 ?

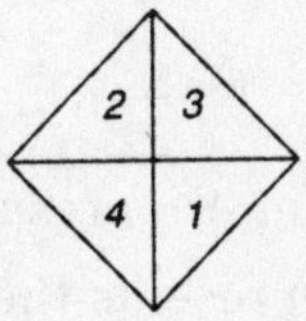

To answer this question, substitute the numbers according to the definition:

- Substitute 2 for c, 3 for d, 4 for f, and 1 for e. 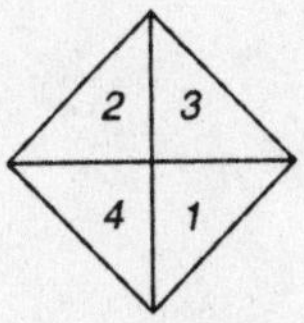
- 2 3 / 4 1 $= (2)\ (1) - (3)\ (4) = -10$

Some questions will ask you to apply the definition of the symbol to more complicated situations. For instance:

- You may be asked to compare two values, each of which requires the use of the symbol.
- You may be asked to evaluate an expression that involves multiplying, dividing, adding, squaring, or subtracting terms that involve the symbol.

- You could be asked to solve an equation that involves the use of the symbol.
- You may find a special symbol as part of a Quantitative Comparison question.

Logical Analysis

Some math questions emphasize logical thinking. You have to figure out how to draw conclusions from a set of facts.

Here's an example:

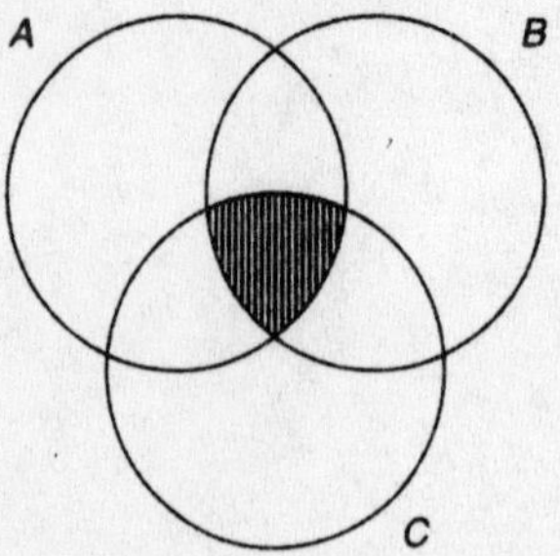

In the figure above, circular region A represents the set of all numbers of the form $2m$, circular region B represents the set of all numbers of the form n^2, and circular region C represents the set of all numbers of the form 10^k, where m, n, and k are positive integers. Which of the following numbers belongs in the set represented by the shaded region?

(A) 2
(B) 4
(C) 10
(D) 25
(E) 100

Answering this question correctly depends on understanding the logic of the figure:

- The question is asking about the shaded region.
- The shaded region is part of *all* of the circles.
- Therefore, any numbers in the shaded region have to obey the rules for *all* the circles:

The rule for A: The numbers must be of the form $2m$, which means that they must all be even numbers.

And the rule for B: the numbers must be of the form n^2, which means that they must all be perfect squares.

And the rule for C: the numbers must also be of the form 10^k, which means they have to be some whole-number power of 10 (10, 100, 1,000, 10,000, etc.).

- When you realize that the numbers in the shaded area must obey *all* the individual rules, you have figured out the logic of the question, and the answer is easy. The only choice that obeys *all* the rules is (E).

Chapter 12

Five-Choice Multiple-Choice Questions

The SAT includes 35 Five-Choice Multiple-Choice questions. The questions test the content areas reviewed in Chapter 11: arithmetic, algebra, geometry, data interpretation, etc. None of the problems require the use of a calculator, but you may find it helpful. Practice using the calculator you plan to take to the test on the sample questions in this chapter.

Strategies

Ask yourself the following questions before solving each problem:

1. What is the question asking?
2. What do I know?

Once you've answered these questions, make sure to:

- Answer the question asked.
- Check that your answer makes sense.
- Check your work from the beginning. If you can, use a *different* method from the one you used to get the answer. If you use the same method, you may make the same mistake twice.

Work the Problems in Your Test Booklet

You will not receive credit for anything written in the booklet but you will be able to check your work later:

- Draw figures to help you think through problems that involve geometric shapes, segment lengths, distances, proportions, sizes, etc.
- Mark key information on graphs and add information to drawings and diagrams as you figure.
- Mark each question that you don't answer so that you can easily go back to it later.
- When working on a question, put a line through each choice you eliminate.

Substitute Numbers

Some questions use variables (indicated by letters) to represent the values you are asked to consider. You can make the problem more concrete by substituting numbers for the variables:

- Use common sense when picking numbers to substitute.
- Substitute numbers that are easy to work with.
- Make sure you check the special cases: 0, 1, at least one number between 0 and 1, a number or numbers greater than 1, and a few negative numbers.

Plug in the Answer Choices

Sometimes you can find the correct answer by working backwards. Try plugging in the answer choices to see which one works. When plugging in the answer choices, start with choice (C). If the choices are numbers, they are usually listed in order from lowest to highest value, or highest to lowest. So, if (C) turns out to be too high, you may not have to try out the larger numbers. And if (C) is too low, you don't have to try out the smaller numbers.

Guess When You Can Eliminate at Least One Answer Choice

On multiple-choice questions, if you can eliminate even one answer you increase your chances of getting a question right. With each correct answer you gain one point; if you leave the answer blank you get no points; if your answer is wrong you only lose 1/4 of a point.

Sample Questions

In this section solve each problem, using any available space on the page for scratchwork. Then decide which is the best of the choices given and fill in the corresponding oval on the answer sheet.

Notes:

(1) The use of a calculator is permitted. All numbers used are real numbers.

(2) Figures that accompany problems in this test are intended to provide information useful in solving the problems. They are drawn as accurately as possible EXCEPT when it is stated in a specific problem that the figure is not drawn to scale. All figures lie in a plane unless otherwise indicated.

Reference Information:

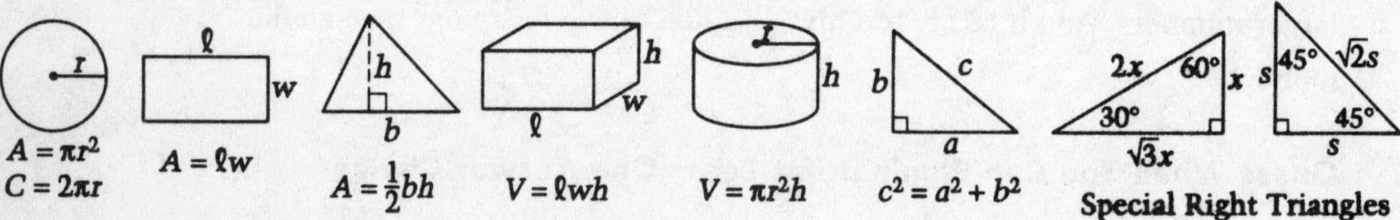

The number of degrees of arc in a circle is 360.
The measure in degrees of a straight angle is 180.
The sum of the measures in degrees of the angles of a triangle is 180.

1 $\frac{1}{2} \cdot \frac{2}{3} \cdot \frac{3}{4} \cdot \frac{4}{5} \cdot \frac{5}{6} \cdot \frac{6}{7} =$

(A) $\frac{1}{7}$

(B) $\frac{3}{7}$

(C) $\frac{21}{27}$

(D) $\frac{6}{7}$

(E) $\frac{7}{8}$

2 If $\frac{x}{3} = x^2$, the value of x can be which of the following?

I. $-\frac{1}{3}$

II. 0

III. $\frac{1}{3}$

(A) I only
(B) II only
(C) III only
(D) II and III only
(E) I, II, and III

3 All numbers divisible by both 4 and 15 are also divisible by which of the following?

(A) 6
(B) 8
(C) 18
(D) 24
(E) 45

4 If United States imports increased 20 percent and exports decreased 10 percent during a certain year, the ratio of imports to exports at the end of the year was how many times the ratio at the beginning of the year?

(A) $\frac{12}{11}$
(B) $\frac{4}{3}$
(C) $\frac{11}{8}$
(D) $\frac{3}{2}$
(E) 2

5

4 cm
6 cm

The figure above shows how a rectangular piece of paper is rolled to form a cylindrical tube. If it is assumed that the 4-centimeter sides of the rectangle meet with no overlap, what is the area, in square centimeters, of the base of the cylindrical tube?

(A) 16π
(B) 9π
(C) 4π
(D) $\frac{9}{\pi}$
(E) $\frac{4}{\pi}$

6 The odometer of a new automobile functions improperly and registers only 2 miles for every 3 miles driven. If the odometer indicates 48 miles, how many miles has the automobile actually been driven?

(A) 144
(B) 72
(C) 64
(D) 32
(E) 24

7

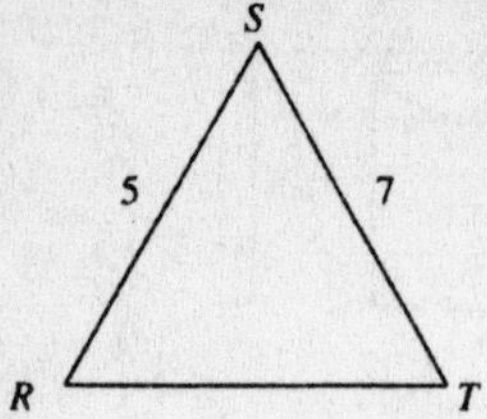

Note: Figure not drawn to scale.

If the perimeter of ΔRST above is 3 times the length of RS, then RT =

(A) 3
(B) 5
(C) 8
(D) 9
(E) 10

8 A, B, C, and D are points on a line, with D the midpoint of segment BC. The lengths of segments AB, AC, and BC are 10, 2, and 12, respectively. What is the length of segment AD?

(A) 2
(B) 4
(C) 6
(D) 10
(E) 12

9

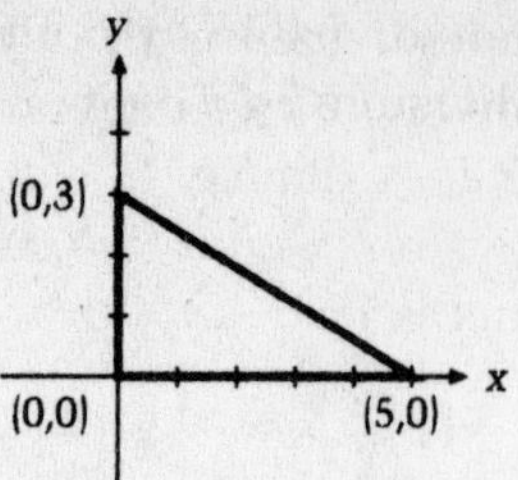

What is the area of the triangle in the figure above?

(A) 4.0
(B) 7.5
(C) 8.0
(D) 8.5
(E) 15.0

10

A = {3,6,9}
B = {5,7,9}
C = {7,8,9}

If three different numbers are selected, one from each of the sets shown above, what is the greatest sum that these three numbers could have?

(A) 22
(B) 23
(C) 24
(D) 25
(E) 27

11 Let the symbol ⓧ represent the number of different pairs of positive integers whose product is x. For example, ⑯ = 3, since there are 3 different pairs of positive integers whose product is 16:

$$16 \times 1,\ 8 \times 2, \text{ and } 4 \times 4$$

What does ㊱ equal?

(A) 5
(B) 6
(C) 8
(D) 10
(E) 12

12 Several people are standing in a straight line. Starting at one end of the line Bill is counted as the 5th person, and starting at the other end he is counted as the 12th person. How many people are in the line?

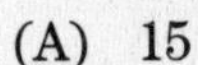

(A) 15
(B) 16
(C) 17
(D) 18
(E) 19

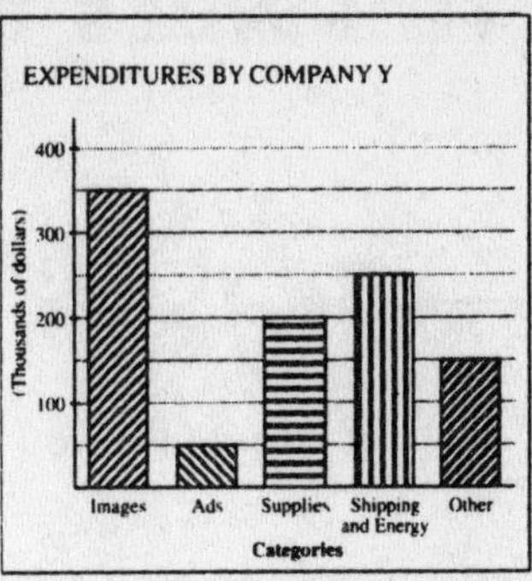

13 In the graph above, if the total expenditures by Company Y were $1,000,000, the shaded area of which of the following pie charts best represents the expenditures other than shipping and energy?

(A)
(B)
(C)
(D)
(E)

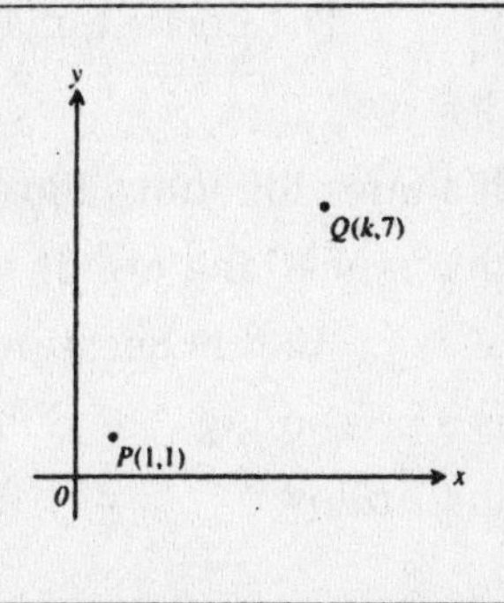

14 In the figure above, the slope of the line through points P and Q is $\frac{3}{2}$. What is the value of k?

(A) 4
(B) 5
(C) 6
(D) 7
(E) 8

Answers and Explanations

If it seems like you have a lot of calculating to do, look for a shortcut.

1 $\frac{1}{2} \cdot \frac{2}{3} \cdot \frac{3}{4} \cdot \frac{4}{5} \cdot \frac{5}{6} \cdot \frac{6}{7} =$

(A) $\frac{1}{7}$

(B) $\frac{3}{7}$

(C) $\frac{21}{27}$

(D) $\frac{6}{7}$

(E) $\frac{7}{8}$

Difficulty: Easy

The correct answer is (A).

If a question looks like it requires a lot of calculating, that's often a tip-off that something else is going on. There's usually a quick way to find the answer. In this question, all the fractions are being multiplied, so canceling is a possibility. The denominators cancel diagonally with the numerators that follow.

- The 2 from $\frac{1}{2}$ cancels with the 2 from $\frac{2}{3}$.
- The 3 from $\frac{2}{3}$ cancels with the 3 from $\frac{3}{4}$.
- And so on, right down to the equal sign.

$$\frac{1}{\cancel{2}} \cdot \frac{\cancel{2}}{\cancel{3}} \cdot \frac{\cancel{3}}{\cancel{4}} \cdot \frac{\cancel{4}}{\cancel{5}} \cdot \frac{\cancel{5}}{\cancel{6}} \cdot \frac{\cancel{6}}{7}$$

After you have canceled everything that can be canceled, you are left with the fraction $\frac{1}{7}$.

2 If $\frac{x}{3} = x^2$, the value of x can be which of the following?

I. $-\frac{1}{3}$

II. 0

III. $\frac{1}{3}$

(A) I only
(B) II only
(C) III only
(D) II and III only
(E) I, II, and III

Difficulty: Hard

The correct answer is (D).

Tip:

When checking the values of expressions, remember the rules for multiplying positive and negative numbers:

(+)(+) = (+)

(−)(+) = (−)

(−)(−) = (+)

This means that the square of any nonzero number will be positive.

Question 2 uses what is referred to as the Roman numeral answer format. This format is used in both math and Critical Reading questions. The way to approach these is to work on each Roman numeral as a separate true/false question. Once you have decided (and marked) each Roman numeral as true or false, it's easy to find the correct answer.

Roman Numeral I: Can the Value of x Be $-\frac{1}{3}$?

You could test this answer by substituting $-\frac{1}{3}$ for x in the equation and seeing whether the result is true. But you can also reason this question out without substituting numbers:

- x^2 has to be a positive number, because any nonzero number squared is positive.
- If x were negative, $\frac{x}{3}$ would be negative.
- So $\frac{x}{3}$ is negative and x^2 is positive.
- Therefore, x cannot be $-\frac{1}{3}$.

Mark Roman numeral I with an "F" for false.

Roman Numeral II: Can the Value of x Be 0?

This is a very easy substitution to make:

$$\frac{x}{3} = x^2$$
$$\frac{0}{3} = 0^2 = 0$$

Roman numeral II is true, so mark it with a "T" for true.

Roman Numeral III: Can the Value of x Be $\frac{1}{3}$?

Substitute $\frac{1}{3}$ for x:

If $x = \frac{1}{3}, \frac{x}{3} = \frac{1}{9}$.

Also, $x^2 = \left(\frac{1}{3}\right)^2 = \frac{1}{9}$.

Roman numeral III is true, so mark it with a "T" for true.

Check the Answers:

You now know whether each of the Roman numeral statements is true or false:

I is false.

II is true.

III is true.

Find the answer that says only II and III are true, choice (D).

Tip:

Remember the approach to Roman numeral format answers:

- **Take each Roman numeral statement as a separate true/false question.**
- **Mark each Roman numeral with a "T" for True or an "F" for False as you evaluate it.**
- **Look for the answer that matches your "T"s and "F"s.**

3 All numbers divisible by both 4 and 15 are also divisible by which of the following?

(A) 6
(B) 8
(C) 18
(D) 24
(E) 45

Difficulty: Medium

The correct answer is (A).

Tip:

"Divisible by" means that the remainder is zero after the division.

For example, 8 is divisible by 4, but it is not divisible by 3.

One way to solve this problem is to first find a number that is divisible by both 4 and 15. One such number is 60. Now check each choice to see if 60 is divisible by that choice. 60 is divisible by choice (A) but is not divisible by any of the other choices. The answer must be (A).

Tip:

When the arithmetic is simple and you understand what the question is asking, it's okay to find the answer by:

- *checking each choice*
- *eliminating choices*

In more complicated problems, this can take more time than finding a solution through mathematical reasoning.

4 If United States imports increased 20 percent and exports decreased 10 percent during a certain year, the ratio of imports to exports at the end of the year was how many times the ratio at the beginning of the year?

(A) $\frac{12}{11}$

(B) $\frac{4}{3}$

(C) $\frac{11}{8}$

(D) $\frac{3}{2}$

(E) 2

Difficulty: Hard

The correct answer is (B).

Express What You Know in Mathematical Terms

- State the ratio of imports to exports as $\frac{I}{E}$.
- At the end of the year, imports were up by 20%. So the change in imports can be expressed as 100% of beginning year imports *plus* 20%:

$$100\% + 20\% = 120\%$$

- At the end of the year, exports were down by 10%. So the change in exports can be expressed as 100% of beginning year exports *minus* 10%:

$$100\% - 10\% = 90\%$$

- Express the ratio of imports to exports at the end of the year:

$$\frac{I}{E} = \frac{120\%}{90\%}$$

Cancel the %s and reduce the fraction.

$$\frac{120\%}{90\%}$$

$$= \frac{12}{9}$$

$$= \frac{4}{3}$$

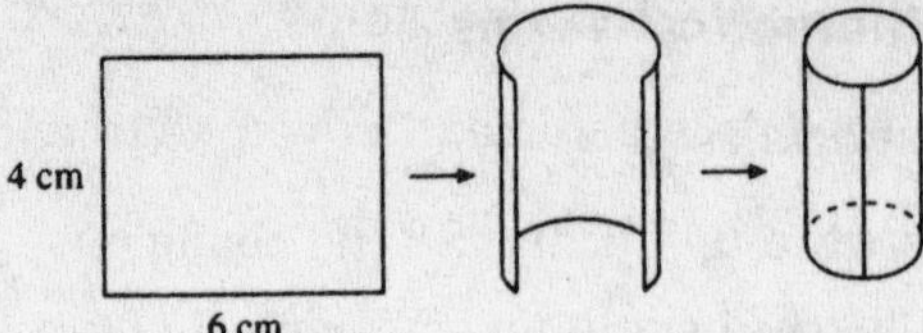

5 The figure above shows how a rectangular piece of paper is rolled to form a cylindrical tube. If it is assumed that the 4-centimeter sides of the rectangle meet with no overlap, what is the area, in square centimeters, of the base of the cylindrical tube?

(A) 16π
(B) 9π
(C) 4π
(D) $\frac{9}{\pi}$
(E) $\frac{4}{\pi}$

Difficulty: Hard

The correct answer is (D).

Label diagrams and figures with the information you have. This often reveals key information that you need to answer the question.

What Do You Know?

- You know the *circumference* of the circle.
- Label the middle and right-hand figures in the diagram.

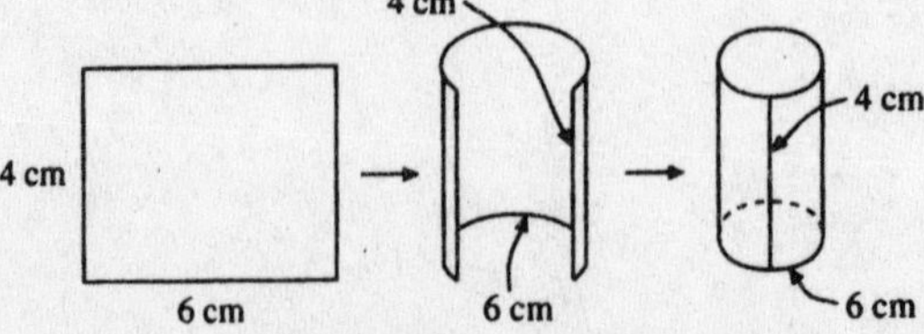

Notice that the 4-centimeter sides meet to form the seam in the cylinder and the 6-centimeter sides curl around to become the top and bottom of the cylinder.

- So the circumference of the circle is 6 centimeters.

Are There Any Formulas That Will Solve the Problem?

The question has now become a rather simple one. You know the circumference of the circle, and you have to figure out the area.

- There is no single formula to calculate the area, but you can get there in two steps:

  Relate the radius to the circumference by the formula:

  $$\text{Circumference} = 2\pi r$$

  Relate the area to the radius by the formula:

  $$\text{Area} = \pi r^2$$

- You know the circumference, so start there and work toward the area. The radius (r) is the common term in the two formulas so start by solving for r.

Apply the Formula to Get the Answer

$$\text{Circumference} = 2\pi r$$

$$6 = 2\pi r$$

$$\pi r = 3$$

$$r = \frac{3}{\pi}$$

- Now use the value for r in the formula for the area.

$$\text{A} = \pi r^2$$

$$r = \frac{3}{\pi}$$

$$\text{A} = \pi\left(\frac{3}{\pi}\right)^2$$

$$\text{A} = \pi\left(\frac{9}{\pi^2}\right)$$

$$\text{A} = \frac{9}{\pi}$$

6 The odometer of a new automobile functions improperly and registers only 2 miles for every 3 miles driven. If the odometer indicates 48 miles, how many miles has the automobile actually been driven?

(A) 144
(B) 72
(C) 64
(D) 32
(E) 24

Difficulty: Medium

The correct answer is (B).

In this problem you are told that the odometer registers only 2 miles for every 3 miles driven. So the ratio of miles registered to miles driven is 2 to 3 or $\frac{2}{3}$. This can be expressed as

$$\frac{\textit{odometer reading}}{\textit{actual miles}} = \frac{2}{3}$$

If the odometer indicates 48 miles, the actual miles can be found using the above relationship as follows:

$$\frac{48}{x} = \frac{2}{3}$$
$$2x = 144$$
$$x = 72$$

So if the odometer indicates 48 miles, the actual number of miles driven is 72.

How to Avoid Errors When Working with Proportions

The most important thing with proportions is to be consistent in the way you set them up. If you mix up the terms, you won't get the correct answer. For instance, if you put the registered mileage in the numerator of one ratio but the actual mileage in the numerator of the other ratio, you will come up with a wrong answer:

$$\frac{3}{2} = \frac{48}{x}$$
$$3x = 96$$
$$x = \frac{96}{3} = 32 \text{ miles}$$ ***Wrong!***

Make a "Does-It-Make-Sense?" Check

When you arrive at an answer to a word problem, check to see whether it makes sense. The question states that the actual mileage is greater than the registered mileage. So the actual mileage has to be a number *larger* than 48.

Your check should warn you not to choose the incorrect answer (D) 32 that was obtained by setting up the wrong proportion.

Tip:

A quick "make-sense" check before you start working on a question can help you eliminate some of the answers right away. If you realize that the actual mileage has to be greater than the registered mileage, you can eliminate answers D and E immediately.

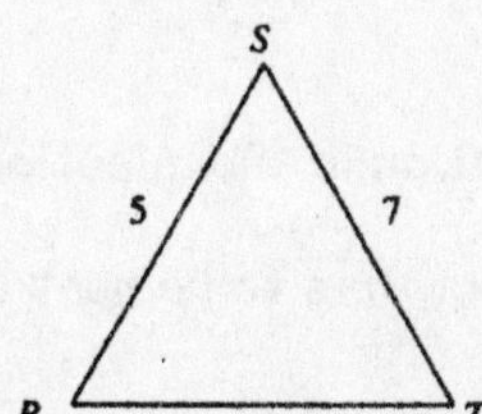

Note: Figure not drawn to scale.

7 If the perimeter of ΔRST above is 3 times the length of RS, then RT =

(A) 3
(B) 5
(C) 8
(D) 9
(E) 10

Difficulty: Easy

The correct answer is (A).

"Note: Figure not drawn to scale" means that the points and angles are in their relative positions, but the lengths of the sides and the sizes of the angles may not be as pictured.

What Do You Know?

- The perimeter of the triangle is the sum of the lengths of the 3 sides.
- The question states that the perimeter is 3 times the length of *RS*.
- *RS* is 5 units long.
- *ST* is 7 units long.

Express the Problem Using an Equation

- The perimeter is equal to 3 times the length of *RS*.
- That means that the perimeter is 3 times 5 or 15.
- So $5 + 7 + RT = 15$

  $RT = 3$

It's always a good idea to draw the lines and figures that are described in a question if a figure is not given.

Make sure that what you draw fits the information in the question.

Don't worry about how pretty the figure is. It only has to be neat enough for you to work with it.

8 *A*, *B*, *C*, and *D* are points on a line, with *D* the midpoint of segment *BC*. The lengths of segments *AB*, *AC*, and *BC* are 10, 2, and 12 respectively. What is the length of segment *AD*?

(A) 2
(B) 4
(C) 6
(D) 10
(E) 12

Difficulty: Medium

The correct answer is (B).

The key to this question lies in *not* jumping to incorrect conclusions. The question names the points on a line. It gives you a variety of information about the points. The one thing it *does not* do is tell you the order in which the points fall.

Many students assume that the order of the points is *A*, then *B*, then *C*, then *D*. As you will see, if you try to locate the points in this order, you will be unable to answer the question.

What Is the Question Asking?

The question asks for the length of line segment *AD*. In order to find this length, you have to establish the relative positions of the four points on the line.

What Do You Know?

Try to draw the figure. You might be tempted to locate point A first. Unfortunately, you don't have enough information about *A*, yet, to place it.

- You can place *B*, *C*, and *D* because *D* is the midpoint of *BC*.

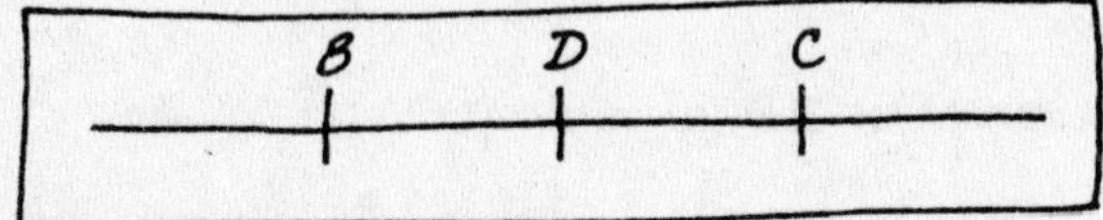

- You know the lengths of three of the line segments:

$AB = 10$
$AC = 2$
$BC = 12$

- Because you know where *BC* is, you can label the length of *BC*.

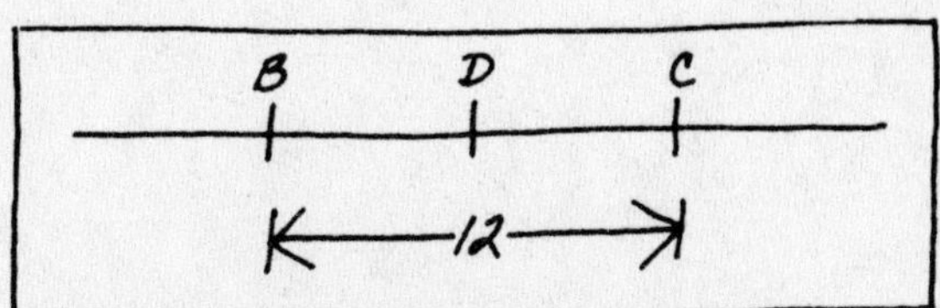

Build the Figure, Adding What You Know and What You Can Figure Out

Because *D* is the midpoint of *BC*, you know that *BD* and *DC* are each 6 units long.

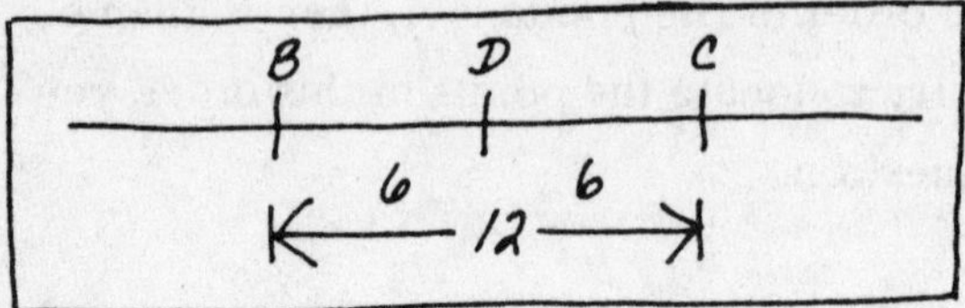

Where can you place point *A*?

It has to be 2 units from *C*, because *AC* = 2.

It also has to be 10 units from *B*, because *AB* = 10.

So the only location for *A* is between *B* and *C*, but closer to *C*.

- Place point *A* and mark the distances.

It is now an easy matter to figure out the answer to the question:

- *DC* is 6 units.
- *A* is 2 units closer to *D* than *C*, so *AD* is 4 units.

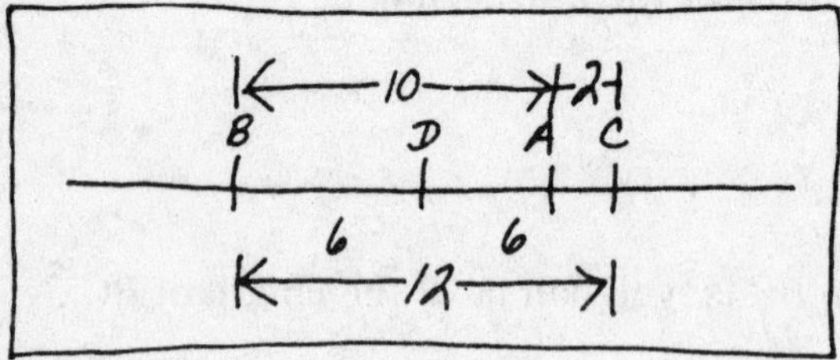

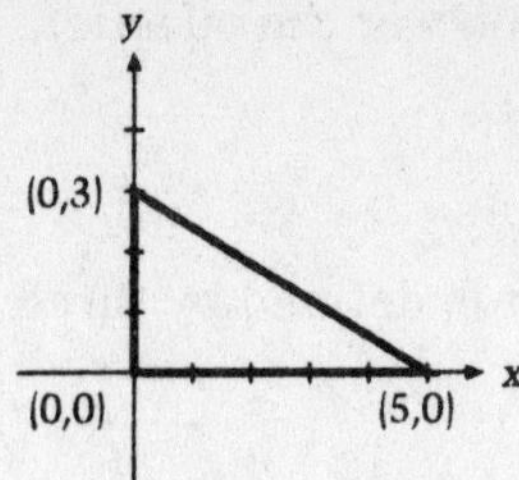

9 What is the area of the triangle in the figure above?

(A) 4.0
(B) 7.5
(C) 8.0
(D) 8.5
(E) 15.0

Difficulty: Medium

The correct answer is (B).

Tip:

The coordinate system provides essential information for solving this problem.

Your knowledge of the coordinate system can give you information about lengths and angles, such as:

- **Whether lines are parallel, perpendicular, or neither;**
- **Whether figures are squares, special triangles, etc.;**
- **How long line segments are;**
- **Whether angles are right angles or other special angles.**

The figure provides all the information you need to answer the question.

What Is the Question Asking?

You are asked to figure out the area of a triangle that is defined by three points on a coordinate plane.

What Do You Know?

- The triangle in the figure is a right triangle with the right angle at the lower left.
- Because it is a right triangle, its base and height are the two sides that form the right angle.
- The area of a triangle is $\frac{1}{2}bh$.
- The base of the triangle extends from point (0,0) to point (5,0). So it is 5 units long.
- The height of the triangle extends from point (0,0) to point (0,3). So it is 3 units long.

$$\begin{aligned}\text{Area} &= \frac{1}{2}bh \\ &= \frac{1}{2}(3)(5) \\ &= \frac{1}{2}(15) \\ &= 7.5\end{aligned}$$

Tip:

If you are presented with a math question that shows the grid lines of a graph, you may rely on the accuracy of those lines.

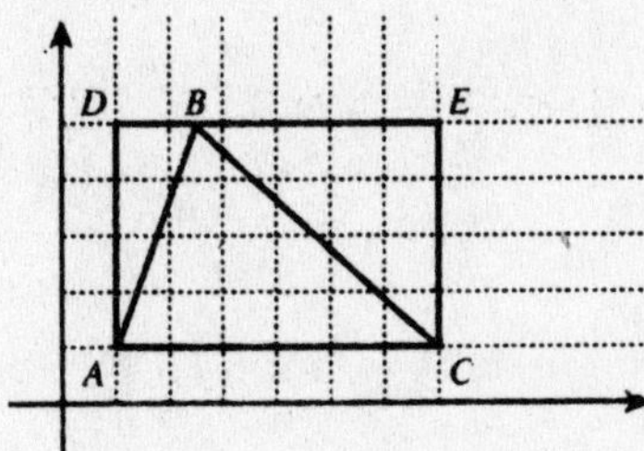

You can use the grid on the graph above to determine the following information:

- *AC* is 6 units long.
- *ADEC* is a rectangle.
- Side *AD* is 4 units long.
- The height of the triangle *ABC* is the same as the width of the rectangle (*ADEC*). So the height of the triangle is 4 units.
- The area of the triangle is $\frac{1}{2}$ the area of the rectangle.
- The area of a rectangle = width × length = $AD \times AC = 4 \times 6 = 24$ square units.
- The area of the triangle = $\frac{1}{2}$ (base × height) = $\frac{1}{2}(AC \times AD)$ = $\frac{1}{2}(6 \times 4) = 12$ square units.

A = {3,6,9}

B = {5,7,9}

C = {7,8,9}

10 Three different numbers are selected, one from each of the sets shown above, what is the greatest sum that these three numbers could have?

(A) 22
(B) 23
(C) 24
(D) 25
(E) 27

Difficulty: Medium

The correct answer is (C).

This question challenges your ability to reason with numbers. In other words, it is more a question of logic than of arithmetic.

What Is the Question Asking?

The question asks what is the largest sum you can get if you choose one number from each set and add those numbers together. There's a catch, however. Each number you select must be different. So you *cannot* take the largest number, 9, from each set, add the nines together, and come up with choice (E) 27.

What Do You Know?

- 9 is the largest number in each set.
- You can only take one number 9. This means that you will have to take the second largest number from two of the sets.

Make Your Selections

- The second largest number in set A is 6, which is smaller than the second largest number in sets B and C. So select 9 from set A.
- The other two choices are now easy. Take the largest numbers available from sets B and C.
- The greatest sum is 9 + 7 + 8 = 24.

11 Let the symbol ⓧ represent the number of different pairs of positive integers whose product is x. For example, ⑯ = 3, since there are 3 different pairs of positive integers whose product is 16:

$$16 \times 1,\ 8 \times 2, \text{ and } 4 \times 4$$

What does ㊱ equal?

(A) 5
(B) 6
(C) 8
(D) 10
(E) 12

Difficulty: Easy

The correct answer is (A).

Most SAT math tests have at least one question involving a newly defined symbol. Sometimes there will be an easy question, like this one, followed by a more difficult one in which you might have to use the new symbol in an equation.

To answer these questions, you have to read the definition of the special symbol carefully and follow the instructions. *It is not expected that you have ever seen the new symbol before.*

The question asks you to figure out how many pairs of positive integers can be multiplied together to give you the number in the circle.

Put the Special Symbol to Work

- To figure out ㊱, list the pairs of positive integers whose product is 36:

  1×36
  2×18
  3×12
  4×9
  6×6

- Count up the pairs. The answer is 5.

Tip:

When you're faced with a special symbol, read the definition carefully and use it as your instruction for working out the answer.

12 Several people are standing in a straight line. Starting at one end of the line Bill is counted as the 5th person, and starting at the other end he is counted as the 12th person. How many people are in the line?

(A) 15
(B) 16
(C) 17
(D) 18
(E) 19

Difficulty: Easy

The correct answer is (B).

You can answer this question by careful reasoning, or you can draw it out and count. Either way, be careful that you don't leave Bill out or count him twice.

What Do You Know?

- Bill is the 5th person from one end of the line.
- Bill is the 12th person from the other end.

Using Logic to Solve the Problem

- If Bill is the 5th person from one end of the line, there are 4 people (not counting Bill) between him and that end of the line.
- If Bill is the 12th person from the other end of the line, there are 11 people (not counting Bill) between him and that end of the line.
- 4 people between Bill and one end, plus 11 people between Bill and the other end, add up to 15 people. Then you have to add Bill. So there are 16 people in line.

Tip:

Problems like this one focus on your ability to reason logically.

There's nothing wrong with drawing a figure using dots to represent the people in line. Just make sure that you follow the instructions carefully when you draw your figure.

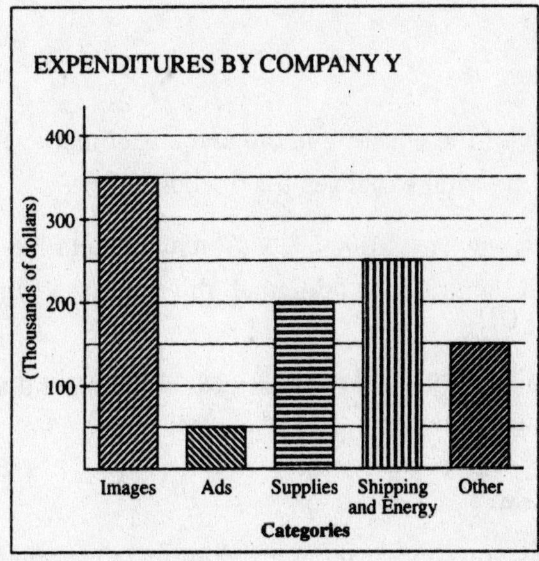

13 In the graph above, if the total expenditures by Company Y were $1,000,000, the shaded area of which of the following pie charts best represents the expenditures other than shipping and energy?

(A) 

(B) 

(C) 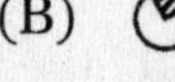

(D) 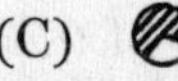

(E) 

Difficulty: Medium

The correct answer is (D).

In this question you have to interpret information from one type of graph (bar graph) and translate that information into another type of graph (pie chart).

Questions that involve interpreting data presented on graphs or in tables will be common on the SAT.

What Is the Question Asking?

The question asks you to identify the pie chart that shows all of Company Y's expenses *other than* shipping and energy. That *other than* is important. It's easy to overlook.

What Do You Know?

All you need to know to answer the question is the amount of money spent on shipping and energy and the total expenses for the company.

- You are given the total expenses: \$1,000,000. (You also could have figured that total out from the graph by adding all the expenses from the individual categories.)
- The graph will show you that the expenditures for shipping and energy amount to \$250,000.

Translating the Information

- The question really asks you to identify approximately what fraction of the total costs *did not* go for shipping and energy. Although the question does not ask this specifically, the pie charts in the answer choices show fractions of the whole. So that's the way you will have to express the information you have.
- Shipping and energy expenses amount to \$250,000 of the \$1,000,000 of total expenses.
- Shipping and energy cost $\frac{\$250,000}{\$1,000,000}$ or $\frac{1}{4}$ of the total.
- That means that the answer is (B) because the pie chart in (B) shows about $\frac{1}{4}$ of the total, right? . . . WRONG!!!!
- Remember, the question asks which pie chart "best represents expenditures *other than* shipping and energy?"
- If $\frac{1}{4}$ goes for shipping and energy, that leaves $\frac{3}{4}$ for other things.

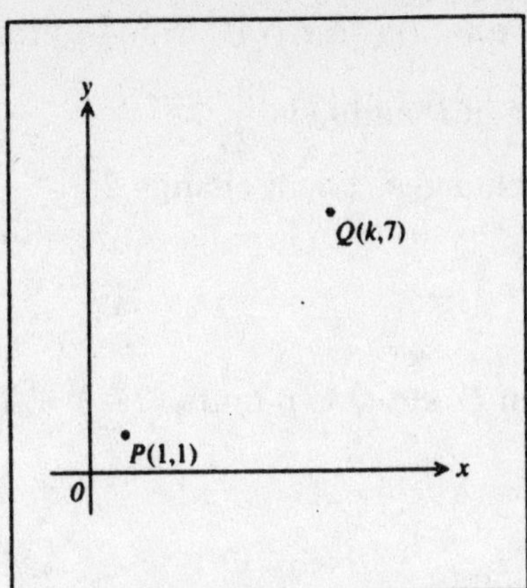

14 In the figure above, the slope of the line through points P and Q is $\frac{3}{2}$. What is the value of k?

(A) 4
(B) 5
(C) 6
(D) 7
(E) 8

Difficulty: This question was written for this book.
We do not know the difficulty.

The correct answer is (B).

Your ability to answer this question depends on your knowing and being able to apply the definition of "slope."

The **slope** of a line in the xy-coordinate plane is:

$$\frac{\text{the change in } y \text{ between any two points on the line}}{\text{the change in } x \text{ between the same points on the line}}$$

The question asks for the value of k, which is the x coordinate of point Q.

What Do You Know?

- The slope of the line that goes between P and Q is $\frac{3}{2}$.
- That means for every 3 units that y changes, x will change 2.
- The coordinates of P are (1,1).
- The coordinates of Q are (k,7).
- The change in the value of y between P and Q is 6 units ($7 - 1 = 6$).

Apply What You Know

- y changes 6 units between the two points.
- That means that x will change 4 units, since for every 3 units that y changes, x changes 2 units.
- The x coordinate of point P is 1.
- The x coordinate of point Q will be $1 + 4 = 5$.

Recap: Tips on Five-Choice Multiple-Choice Questions

1. Use a calculator you are familiar with.
2. Answer the question that is asked.
3. Check to make sure that your answer makes sense.
4. On questions you find difficult, try substituting numbers for variables or try plugging in the answers to backsolve the problem.
5. On Roman numeral format questions, consider each Roman numeral statement as a separate true-false question.
6. Translate word problems as you go.
7. When you don't know the answer, eliminate incorrect answer choices and guess.

Chapter 13

Quantitative Comparison Questions

The SAT includes 15 Quantitative Comparison questions. They do not necessarily require that you figure out a specific value or answer. Rather, you must determine which of two quantities has the greater value.

Here's how they work:

- Each Quantitative Comparison question shows two quantities to be compared — one in the left column (Column A) and one in the right column (Column B). Some may also have additional information that you'll find centered above the quantities to be compared.
- Your job is to determine which quantity, if either, has the greater value.

You choose the letter that indicates the correct relationship between the two quantities being compared.

Strategies

You don't always have to finish your calculations or determine an exact answer. You just have to know enough about the quantities to determine which is greater.

Memorize the directions and answer choices. The four answer choices are printed at the top of each page of every Quantitative Comparison section, but you can save time if you memorize them:

(A) if the Column A quantity is greater;
(B) if the Column B quantity is greater;
(C) if they are equal;
(D) if you cannot tell from the information given.

If any two of the relationships (A), (B), or (C) can be true for a particular Quantitative Comparison question, then the answer to that question is (D).

Think of the columns as a balanced scale. You are trying to figure out which side of the scale is heavier. Before you make your measurement, you can eliminate any quantities that are the same on both sides of the scale. In other words, look for ways to simplify expressions and remove equal quantities from both columns before you make your comparison.

Substitute numbers. Some questions use variables (indicated by letters) to represent the values you are asked to consider. You can make the problem more concrete by substituting numbers for the variables.

- Use common sense when picking numbers to substitute.
- Substitute numbers that are easy to work with.
- Make sure you check the special cases: 0, 1, at least one number between 0 and 1, a number or numbers greater than 1, and a few negative numbers.

Sample Questions

Directions for Quantitative Comparison Questions

Questions 15-20 each consist of two quantities in boxes, one in Column A and one in Column B. You are to compare the two quantities and on the answer sheet fill in oval

A if the quantity in Column A is greater;
B if the quantity in Column B is greater;
C if the two quantities are equal;
D if the relationship cannot be determined from the information given.

AN E RESPONSE WILL NOT BE SCORED.

Notes:

1. In some questions, information is given about one or both of the quantities to be compared. In such cases, the given information is centered above the two columns and is not boxed.
2. In a given question, a symbol that appears in both columns represents the same thing in Column A as it does in Column B.
3. Letters such as x, n, and k stand for real numbers.

EXAMPLES

	Column A	Column B	Answers
E1	5^2	20	● Ⓑ Ⓒ Ⓓ Ⓔ
	(a straight line, with angles of 150° and $x°$)		
E2	x	30	Ⓐ Ⓑ ● Ⓓ Ⓔ
	r and s are integers		
E3	$r + 1$	$s - 1$	Ⓐ Ⓑ Ⓒ ● Ⓔ

Special note: On the actual test, directions to Quantitative Comparison questions are summarized at the top of every page containing Quantitative Comparisons.

Column A / Column B

$$23 + 16 + 57 + x = 108$$
$$23 + 16 + 27 + y = 108$$

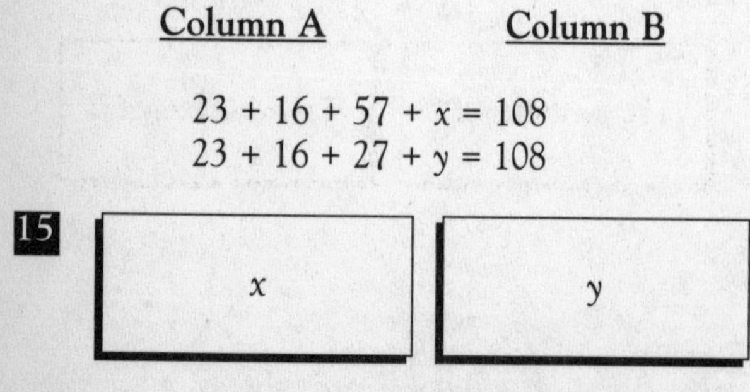

Column A / Column B

$$y^2 = x$$
$$y > 0$$

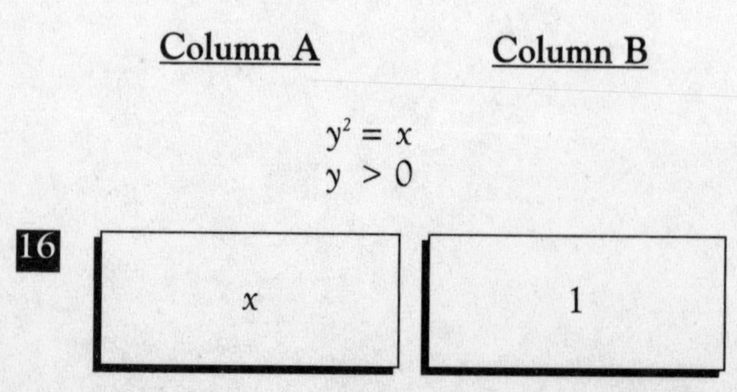

SUMMARY DIRECTIONS FOR COMPARISON QUESTIONS

Answer: A if the quantity in Column A is greater;
B if the quantity in Column B is greater;
C if the two quantities are equal;
D if the relationship cannot be determined from the information given.

	Column A	Column B

A fair six-sided die with faces numbered 1 through 6 is to be rolled twice.

17	The probability of obtaining a 6 on the top face on the first roll and 5 on the top face of the second roll	The probability of obtaining a 5 on the top face on both the first and second rolls

In ΔABC, side AB has length 6 and side BC has length 4.

18	The length of side AC	8

	Column A	Column B

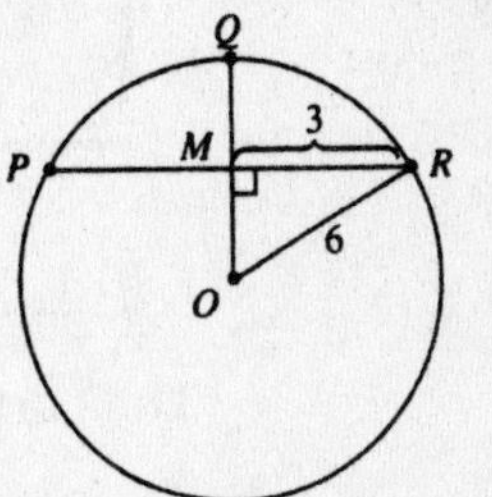

Note: Figure not drawn to scale.
P, Q, and R are points on the circle with center O. PR and OQ are line segments.

19	The length of OM	The length of MQ

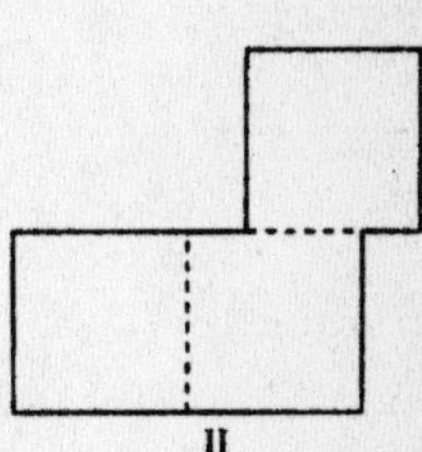

Six squares of equal size form the figures above.

20	The perimeter of I	The perimeter of II

Answers and Explanations

Column A **Column B**

$$23 + 16 + 57 + x = 108$$

$$23 + 16 + 27 + y = 108$$

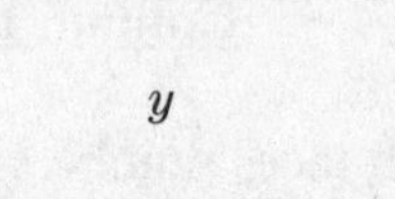

Difficulty: Easy

The correct answer is (B).

What Do You Know?

- The two equations contain some common terms. The only differences are in the two terms just before the equal sign.
- In both equations, the expressions on the left side of the equal sign add up to the same number.
- The numbers that are common to the two expressions will have no effect on which variable has the greater value, so you can eliminate 23 and 16.

$$57 + x = 27 + y$$

- Which has to be greater, x or y, in order for this equation to be true?
- Because y is added to a smaller number, y has to be greater.

By estimating and comparing, you can frequently establish which quantity is greater without figuring out the value of either quantity.

Column A	Column B

$$y^2 = x$$
$$y > 0$$

16 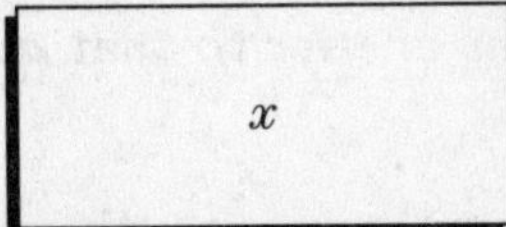

1

Difficulty: Medium

The correct answer is (D).

To answer this question, you can sample a few values for y, but you must make sure that you sample a variety of values.

Tip:

When you are substituting values to answer a Quantitative Comparison question, make sure you check the special cases:

- **0**
- **1**
- **at least one number between 0 and 1**
- **a number or numbers greater than 1**
- **negative numbers**

Substituting Values

Because y is greater than 0, you don't have to worry about 0 or negative values. But when you raise numbers to powers, fractions and the number 1 act differently from numbers greater than 1.

Tip:

If any two of the answers (A), (B), or (C) can be true for particular values in a Quantitative Comparison question, then the answer to that question is (D).

So you need to sample:

The number 1;

A number between 0 and 1;

A number greater than 1.

Try $y = 1$.

$$y^2 = x$$
$$1^2 = x$$
$$1 = x$$

Try a value of y between 0 and 1, such as $\frac{1}{2}$.

$$y^2 = x$$
$$\left(\frac{1}{2}\right)^2 = x$$
$$\frac{1}{4} = x$$

We've found two possible values of x (1 and $\frac{1}{4}$). In the first case, the quantity in Column A ($x = 1$) is equal to the quantity in Column B. In the second case, the quantity in Column A ($x = \frac{1}{4}$) is less than the quantity in Column B. So you cannot tell and the answer is (D).

Column A	Column B

A fair six-sided die with faces numbered 1 through 6 is to be rolled twice.

17

The probability of obtaining a 6 on the top face on the first roll and 5 on the top face of the second roll	The probability of obtaining a 5 on the top face on both the first and second rolls

Difficulty: Medium

Answer: C

You are given that a fair die is to be rolled twice. This means that on each roll of each of the six numbered faces is equally likely to be the top face. For example, the face numbered 3 is just as likely to be the top face as the face numbered 4. The probability that any specific number will appear on the top die is $\frac{1}{6}$.

- In Column A, the probability of obtaining a 6 on the first roll and a 5 on the second roll is $\frac{1}{6} \times \frac{1}{6} = \frac{1}{36}$.
- In Column B, the probability of obtaining a 5 on the first roll and another 5 on the second roll is also $\frac{1}{6} \times \frac{1}{6} = \frac{1}{36}$.

Therefore, the two quantities are equal.

Caution: In this question, you are given the order in which the numbered faces appear. If in Column A you had been asked for "The probability of obtaining a 6 on the top face of one roll and a 5 on the top face of the other roll," the answer would be different. Why? Because there are *two* equally likely ways to succeed: a 6 on the first roll and a 5 on the second, or a 5 on the first roll and a 6 on the second. Each of these two outcomes has a probability of $\frac{1}{36}$. Therefore, in this case, the quantity in Column A would equal $\frac{2}{36}$.

Column A	**Column B**

In ΔABC, side AB has length 6 and side BC has length 4.

18	The length of side AC	8

The correct answer is (D).

There are two related properties of triangles that you should remember. The length of any one side must be less than the sum of the lengths of the other two sides. And the length of any one side must be greater than the difference between the lengths of the other two sides.

If you remember these properties, the answer to this question is easy:

- The sum of lengths AB and BC is 6 + 4 or 10. So side AC has to be less than 10.
- The difference between lengths AB and BC is 6 – 4 or 2. So AC must be greater than 2.
- The length of AC can be greater than 8, equal to 8, or less than 8. In other words, you cannot tell which quantity (Column A or Column B) is greater.

The sum of the lengths of any two sides of a triangle is always greater than the length of the third side.

Column A **Column B**

19

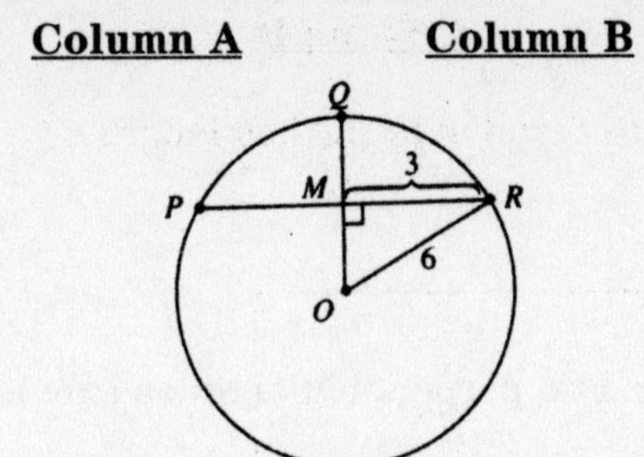

Note: Figure not drawn to scale.
P, *Q*, and *R* are points on the circle with center *O*.
PR and *OQ* are the line segments.

The length of *OM*	The length of *MQ*

Difficulty: Hard

The correct answer is (A).

What Do You Know?

- *O* is the center of the circle. Therefore, *OR* is a radius of the circle with a length of 6.
- *OQ* is a line segment that starts from the center and extends to the edge of the circle. So it is also a radius with a length of 6.
- Angle *OMR* is a right angle. Therefore, triangle *OMR* is a right triangle.

What Lengths Do You Need to Find?

- *OQ* has a length of 6.
- *OM* is a side of right triangle (*OMR*). And you know the length of the other side and of the hypotenuse.
- Therefore, you can find the length of *OM* by using the Pythagorean theorem.

Apply the Theorem

The Pythagorean theorem:

$$a^2 + b^2 = c^2$$

Where:

a and b are the lengths of the two perpendicular sides (the legs) of a right triangle.

c is the length of the hypotenuse.

In the triangle in Question 19

The two legs are OM and MR

$MR = 3$

The hypotenuse OR is 6.

Substitute these numbers into the Pythagorean theorem:

$$a^2 + b^2 = c^2$$

$$3^2 + (OM)^2 = 6^2$$

$$9 + (OM)^2 = 36$$

$$(OM)^2 = 27$$

$$OM = \sqrt{27}$$

Compare the Lengths

- $OM = \sqrt{27}$, which is a little more than 5.
- $MQ = 6 - OM$
- $MQ = 6 - \sqrt{27}$
- You don't have to figure out the exact lengths. If OM is more than 5, MQ has to be less than 1. So OM is longer than MQ.

Tip:

The Reference section of the math test booklet gives the properties of some special triangles. Because the hypotenuse (6) is twice the shorter leg (3) you know the ratio of the sides of the right triangle in this question is 1: $\sqrt{3}$: 2. Then you can figure out that $OM = 3\sqrt{3}$, so $OM > MQ$.

You will probably find that if you are not familiar with most of the information in the Reference section before you take the test, you will have a hard time using it efficiently during the test.

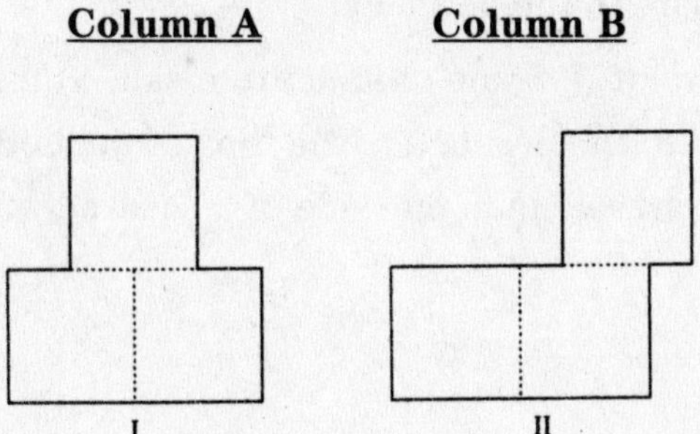

Six squares of equal size form the figures above.

20

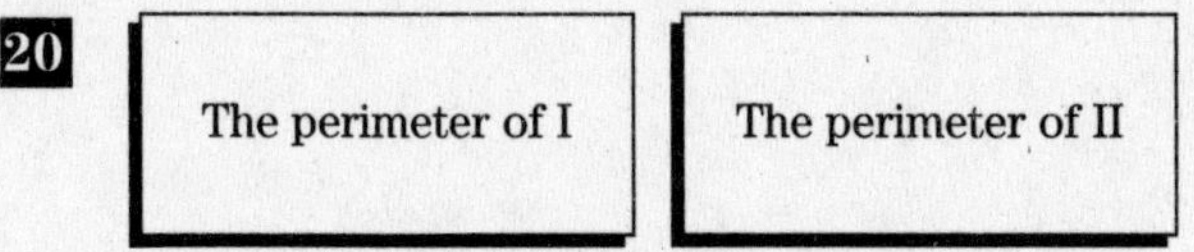

Difficulty: Medium

The correct answer is (B).

Explanation:

If you know the definition of perimeter, you should be able to figure out the answer to this question just by looking at the figures.

What Do You Know?

- Three squares make up each figure, and all the squares are of equal size.
- The perimeter of a figure is equal to the sum of the lengths of its sides, not the sides of the individual squares that make up the figure. The perimeters *do not* include any of the dotted lines.
- The lengths of the bottoms of both figures are equal. So your focus should be on what's happening where the top square and the top of the bottom squares meet.
- Look at the top square of I. Its entire bottom side overlaps with the upper sides of the lower squares, so its bottom side *does not* add to the perimeter. The tops of the bottom squares in I add to a length equal to one side of a square to the perimeter.
- Now look at the top square of II. Some of its bottom side—the part that sticks out—does add to the perimeter. The tops of the bottom squares in II add a length greater than one side of a square to the perimeter.
- Therefore, the perimeter of II is greater.

Recap: Tips on Quantitative Comparison Questions

1. With Quantitative Comparison questions, frequently you don't have to finish your calculations or determine an exact answer. You just have to know enough about the quantities to determine which one is greater.
2. Memorize the four answer choices for Quantitative Comparison questions.
3. If any two of the answers (A), (B), or (C) can be true for a particular Quantitative Comparison question, then the answer to that question is (D).
4. Think of the columns as a balanced scale. You are trying to figure out which side of the scale is heavier, so eliminate any quantities that are the same on both sides of the scale.
5. Try evaluating the quantities by substituting values for variables. Just remember:
   - Make sure you check above the columns for any information about what the values can be.
   - When substituting values to answer a Quantitative Comparison question, make sure you check the special cases: 0, 1, at least one number between 0 and 1, a number or numbers greater than 1, and negative numbers.

Chapter 14

Student-Produced Response Questions

The SAT includes 10 Student-Produced Response or Grid-in questions. These questions require the same math skills and reasoning abilities as the other two types of math questions. Many Grid-in questions are similar to Five-Choice Multiple-Choice questions except that no answers are provided. You must, therefore, work out the problem yourself and enter your answer onto a special math grid. Use the sample grids on page 222 to practice gridding techniques.

Strategies and Guidelines for Completing the Grid

You should be familiar with the guidelines for answering and gridding Student-Produced Response questions. Knowing the rules before the test will save you time and tension.

Calculators May Help Here

If a Grid-in problem requires you to calculate the answer, you should be careful to check your work because you will not get feedback from multiple-choice options. Without answer choices to choose from, you may make careless mistakes. For that reason, it is a good idea to use a calculator on this section to avoid unnecessary errors.

Practicing with the Grid

You should practice completing the grids before the test. Although it is not necessary to write your answer in the boxes above the grid, it is suggested that you do so to avoid gridding errors. Remember that only the gridded answers will be scored. Be careful to mark no more than one oval in any column. Because answer sheets are machine-scored, you will receive credit only if the ovals are filled in correctly.

Positive Numbers and Zero Only

The grid can only hold four places and only accommodate positive numbers and zero. It is not possible to grid a negative number of any type. If you obtain a negative answer for a Grid-in question, you will know that you have made a mistake. REWORK the problem.

Place Answer in Any Column

Do not worry about which column to begin writing the answer. As long as the answer is gridded completely, you will receive credit. For example, 156 can be gridded as shown below; both answers are correct.

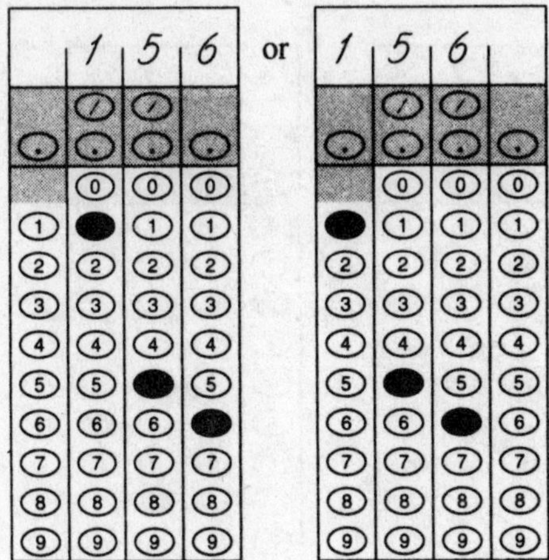

Integers

You can grid one-, two-, three-, or four-digit positive integers or zero as follows.

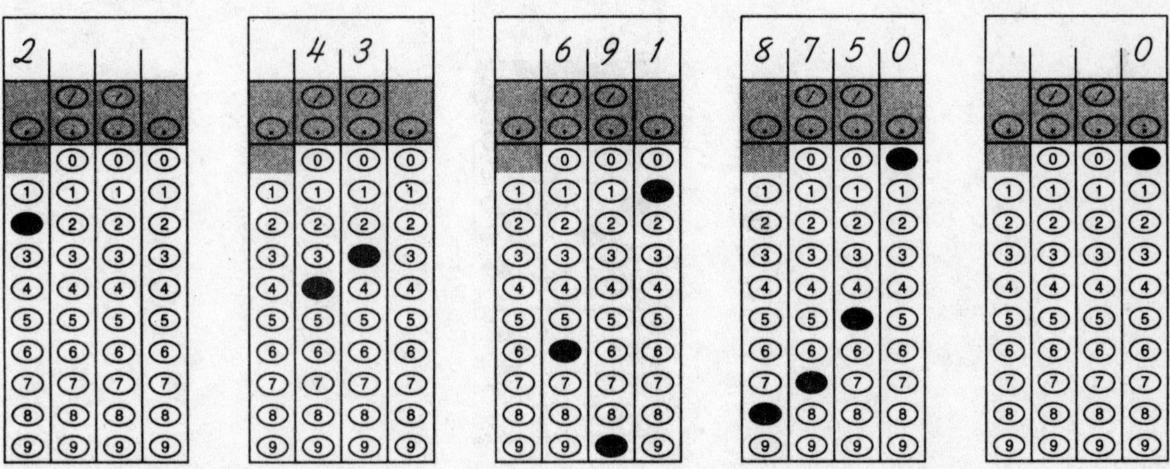

Decimals and Fractions

The grids include decimal points (.) and fraction lines (/) so that you can enter answers both in decimal and fraction form. Unless a problem indicates otherwise, you can grid your answer as a decimal or a fraction.

Decimal Points

Do not grid zeros before decimal points.

No Mixed Numbers

You can grid both proper and improper fractions. However, it is not possible to grid mixed numbers. If your answer is a mixed number, convert it to an improper fraction or to a decimal. For example, if you get the answer $2\frac{3}{4}$, grid 11/4 or 2.75, as shown.

The fraction line appears in the first shaded row of ovals.

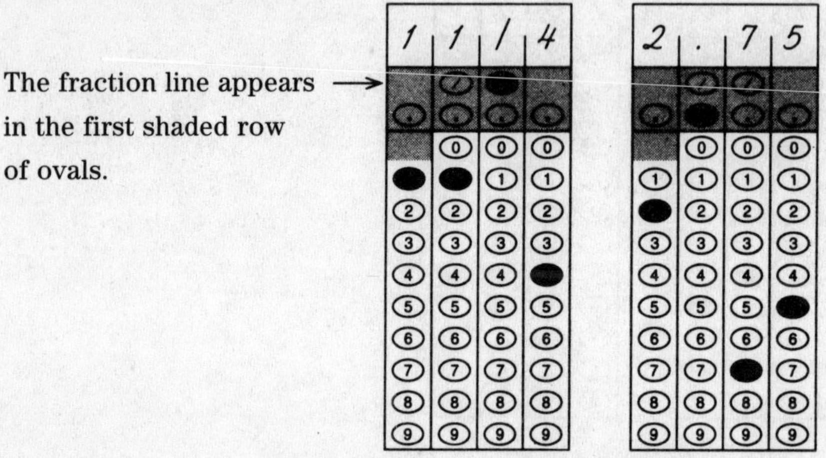

If you grid $2\frac{3}{4}$, the scoring machine will read the answer as $\frac{23}{4}$, which is wrong.

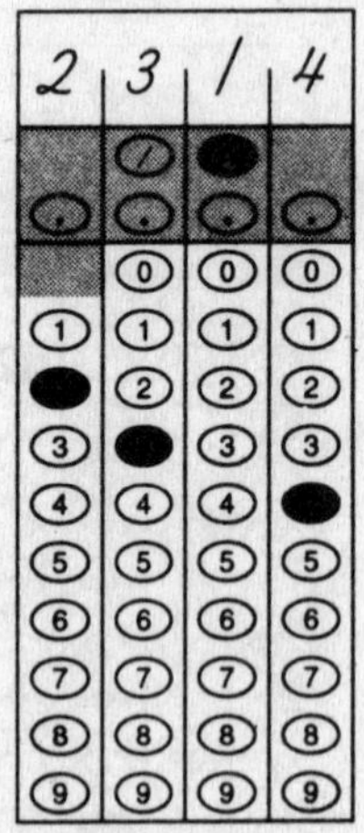

Repeating Decimals

If the answer you are gridding is a repeating decimal, you must grid the most accurate possible decimal. The easiest way to follow the rule for repeating decimals is to completely fill the grid with the answer.

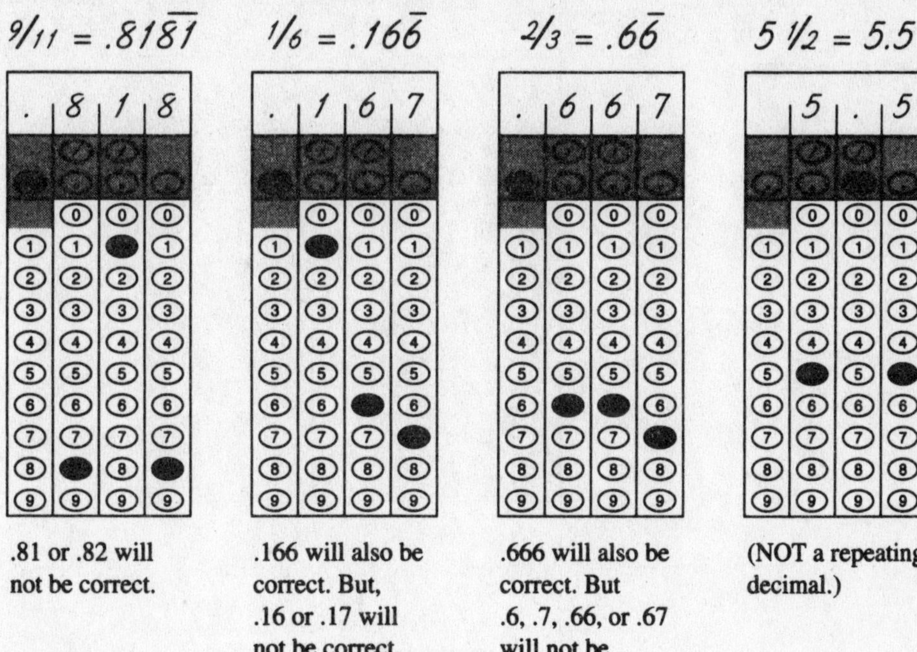

.81 or .82 will not be correct.

.166 will also be correct. But, .16 or .17 will not be correct.

.666 will also be correct. But .6, .7, .66, or .67 will not be.

(NOT a repeating decimal.)

Multiple Answers

Some of the Grid-in questions may have more than one correct answer. These questions may say something like, "What is one possible value of x?" This wording indicates that there may be more than one value of x that is correct. Under these circumstances, simply choose one of the possible answers to grid on your answer sheet.

No Penalty for Wrong Answers

Unlike multiple-choice questions, no points are subtracted for wrong answers on Grid-in questions. You can feel comfortable gridding whatever answer you get without fear that it may subtract from your final score if it is wrong.

IMPORTANT

Remember that only the answer entered on the grid, and not the answer handwritten at the top of the grid, is scored. You must decide whether to first write your answer in at the top of the grid and then transfer it to the grid, or to transfer your answer directly from notes in your test booklet, or in your head, to the grid. You might practice both approaches and see which one works best for you. You want to make sure you enter your answer correctly. While it might be more time-consuming to first write your answer in at the top of the grid, you may find this approach helps you avoid errors.

Sample Questions

21 In a restaurant where the sales tax on a \$4.00 lunch is \$0.24, what will be the sales tax due, in dollars, on a \$15.00 dinner? (Disregard the \$ sign when gridding your answer. For example, if the answer is \$1.37, grid 1.37.)

22 A team has won 60 percent of the 20 games it has played so far this season. If the team plays a total of 50 games all season and wins 80 percent of the remaining games, how many games will the team win for the entire season?

23 If n is a two-digit number that can be expressed as the product of two consecutive <u>even</u> integers, what is one possible value of n?

24 If the ratio of a to b is $\frac{7}{3}$, what is the value of the ratio of $2a$ to b?

25 If the population of a town doubles every 10 years, the population in the year $X + 100$ will be how many times the population in the year X?

26

Number of Donuts	Total Price
1	\$ 0.40
Box of 6	\$ 1.89
Box of 12	\$ 3.59

According to the information in the table above, what would be the least amount of money needed, in dollars, to purchase exactly 21 donuts? (Disregard the \$ sign when gridding your answer. For example, if the answer is \$1.37, grid 1.37.)

27 If $\frac{x}{2} = y$ and $2y = y$, what is the value of x?

28

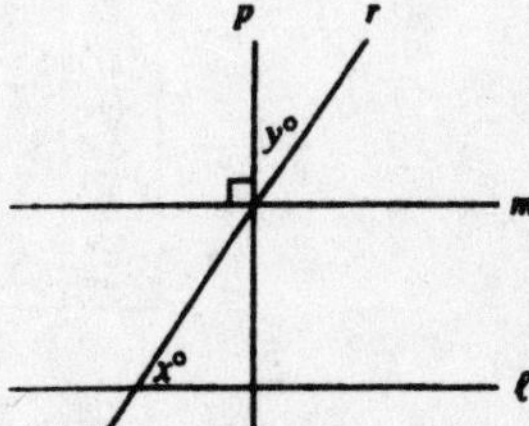

Note: Figure not drawn to scale.
In the figure above, line m is parallel to line l and is perpendicular to line p. If $x = y$, what is the value of x?

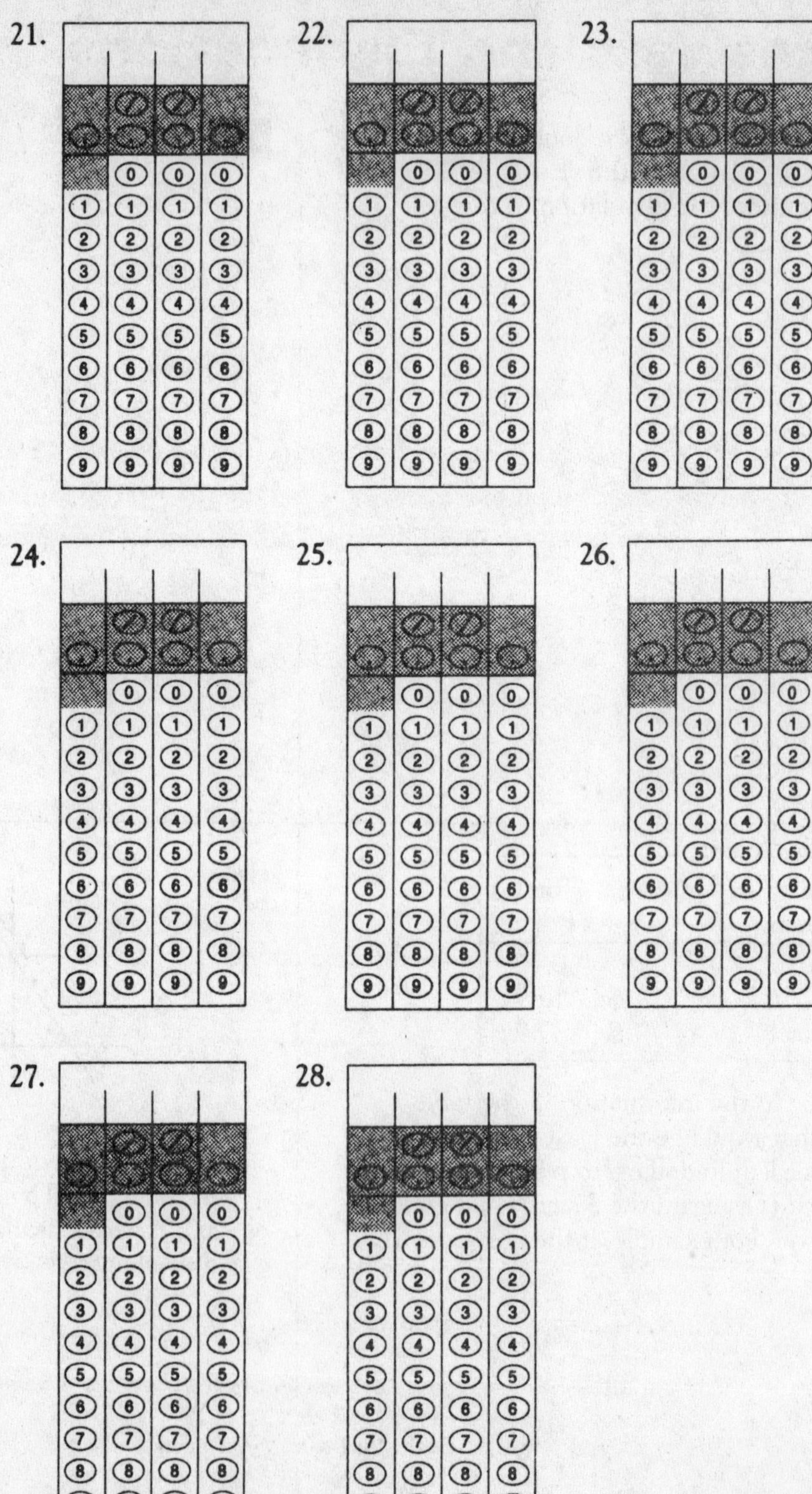
21.
22.
23.
24.
25.
26.
27.
28.

Answers and Explanations

21 In a restaurant where the sales tax on a $4.00 lunch is $0.24, what will be the sales tax due, in dollars, on a $15.00 dinner? (Disregard the $ sign when gridding your answer. For example, if the answer is $1.37, grid 1.37.)

Difficulty: Easy

The correct answer is .90 or .9.

One way to solve this problem is to determine the tax on each $1.00 and then multiply this amount by 15 to get the tax on $15.00. The tax on a $4.00 lunch is $0.24. Then the tax on $1.00 would be one-fourth this amount, which is $0.06. So the tax on $15.00 would be 15 × .06 = .90 dollars.

Tip:

Do not grid zeros before the decimal point. For example, don't try to grid 0.90; just grid .90 or .9.

The question asks for the number of dollars, so 90 for 90 cents would be wrong.

Tip:

Some seemingly difficult questions are really just a series of easy questions.

- Take the question one step at a time.
- Think about what you need to know in order to answer the question.
- Use what you know to figure out what you need to know.
- Make sure your *final* answer answers the question that has been asked.

22 A team has won 60 percent of the 20 games it has played so far this season. If the team plays a total of 50 games all season and wins 80 percent of the remaining games, how many games will the team win for the entire season?

Difficulty: Medium

The correct answer is 36.

Express the Information in Mathematical Terms:

How many games has the team won so far?

60% of 20 games =

$\frac{60}{100} \times 20 = .6 \times 20 = 12$ games

How many games will the team win the rest of the season? The total number of games left is 50 – 20 = 30.

The team will win 80% of 30 games during the rest of the season.

$\frac{80}{100} \times 30 = .8 \times 30 = 24$ games

The total number of wins is: 12 + 24 = 36.

Grid in 36.

23 If n is a two-digit number that can be expressed as the product of two consecutive even integers, what is one possible value of n?

Difficulty: Medium

There are three acceptable correct answers: 24, 48, and 80. You only have to find one.

Explanation:

Although there are several values for n that will work, you only have to find one.

Follow the Instructions

- n is the product of two consecutive even integers. In other words, the question tells you to multiply consecutive even integers.
- n is also a two-digit number.

Try Some Values

Start with two small consecutive even integers, 2 and 4.

- $2 \times 4 = 8$
- 8 is not a two-digit number, so n cannot be 8.

Try the next two consecutive even integers, 4 and 6.

- $4 \times 6 = 24$
- 24 is a two-digit number.
- 24 is the product of two consecutive even integers.

24 is an acceptable value for n. Grid in 24.

Other Correct Answers

The other possible values are 48 (6×8) and 80 (8×10). You can grid in *any one* of these three values and get credit for answering the question correctly.

Some questions have more than one correct answer.

You can grid any *one* of the correct answers and you will get full credit.

24 If the ratio of a to b is $\frac{7}{3}$, what is the value of the ratio of $2a$ to b?

Difficulty: Easy

The correct answer is $\frac{14}{3}$.

The question is easy as long as you know the definition of ratio. It is included in the sample section to show you how to grid the answer.

Express the Ratio

The ratio of a to b can be written as $\frac{a}{b}$.

The ratio of a to b is $\frac{7}{3}$, which can be expressed as $\frac{a}{b} = \frac{7}{3}$.

If $\frac{a}{b} = \frac{7}{3}$

then $\frac{2a}{b} = 2\left(\frac{a}{b}\right) = 2\left(\frac{7}{3}\right) = \frac{14}{3}$.

Grid in the answer $\frac{14}{3}$.

Tip: On Gridding

$\frac{14}{3}$ cannot be gridded as $4\frac{2}{3}$. The grid-reading system cannot tell the difference between $4\frac{2}{3}$ and $\frac{42}{3}$. Also, if you change $\frac{14}{3}$ to a decimal, either 4.66 or 4.67 is an acceptable answer.

25 If the population of a town doubles every 10 years, the population in the year $X + 100$ will be how many times the population in the year X?

Difficulty: Hard

The correct answer is 1,024.

Express the Population Growth in Mathematical Terms

Each time the population doubles, multiply it by 2. Let p represent the population in year X.

- In 10 years the population increases from p to $2p$.
- In 10 more years it increases to $2(2p)$.
- In 10 more years it increases to $2[2(2p)]$ and so on for 100 years.

This repeated doubling can be expressed by using powers of 2:

- Another way to express $2(2)$ is 2^2.
- So a population of $2(2p) = (2^2)p$.
- In 10 more years the population is $2(2^2)p$ or $(2^3)p$.
- In 10 more years the population is $2(2^3)p$ or $(2^4)p$, etc.

How Many Growth Cycles Are There?

- The population doubles (is raised to another power of 2) every 10 years.
- This goes on for 100 years.
- So there are $\frac{100}{10} = 10$ cycles.
- The population increases 2^{10} times what it was in year X.

Figure Out the Answer

You can multiply ten 2s, but this invites error. You may want to use your calculator to find 2^{10}. Some calculators have an exponent key that allows you to find y^x directly. If your calculator does not have this feature, you can still quickly get the value of 2^{10} on your calculator as follows.

$2^5 = 2 \times 2 \times 2 \times 2 \times 2 = 32$

$2^{10} = 2^5 \times 2^5 = 32 \times 32 = 1{,}024.$

Grid in the answer, 1,024.

On some questions a calculator can help speed up getting the answer.

Number of Donuts	Total Price
1	$ 0.40
Box of 6	$ 1.89
Box of 12	$ 3.59

According to the information in the table above, what would be the *least* amount of money needed, in dollars, to purchase exactly 21 donuts? (Disregard the $ sign when gridding your answer. For example, if the answer is $1.37, grid 1.37.)

Difficulty: Medium

The correct answer is $6.68.

What Do You Know?

- You can save money by purchasing donuts by the box. A box of 6 donuts costs $1.89, but 6 individual donuts cost $2.40.
- You can save more money by purchasing the larger box. A box of 12 donuts costs $3.59, but 2 boxes of 6 donuts cost 2($1.89) = $3.78.
- The question says you have to buy exactly 21 donuts.

Use Your Head

You want to buy as few individual donuts as you can.

You want to buy as many donuts in large boxes as you can. You cannot buy 2 boxes of 12, because that would put you over the 21-donut limit. So start with 1 box of 12 donuts.

- Mark down 12 donuts, so you can keep track as you add more donuts.
- Mark down $3.59, so you can keep track as you spend more money.

You have 12 donuts, so there are 9 left to buy. You can save money by buying a box of 6 donuts.

- Add 6 to your donut total.
- Add $1.89 to your money total.

You now have 18 donuts, which means you will have to buy 3 individual donuts.

- Add 3 to your donut total. You now have exactly 21 donuts.
- Add 3 × $.40 = $1.20 to your money total.
- Add up the dollar figures: $3.59 + $1.89 + $1.20 = $6.68

Grid in 6.68. Remember to disregard the $ sign.

> **Note:** Do not grid 668 without the decimal mark—it will be interpreted as $668!

When you're working out an answer, jot down your calculations in the space provided in your test booklet.

27 If $\frac{x}{2} = y$ and $2y = y$, what is the value of x?

Difficulty: Medium

The correct answer is 0.

This is another question that takes some reasoning in addition to some simple mathematical manipulation.

Look at the Equations

The second equation may look a little unusual to you:

$$2y = y$$

If $2y = y$ then $y = 0$. Therefore:

$$\frac{x}{2} = 0$$

$$x = 0$$

Grid in the answer, 0.

Tip: On Gridding

To grid zero, just enter 0 in a single column (*any* column where 0 appears). Leave the other three columns blank.

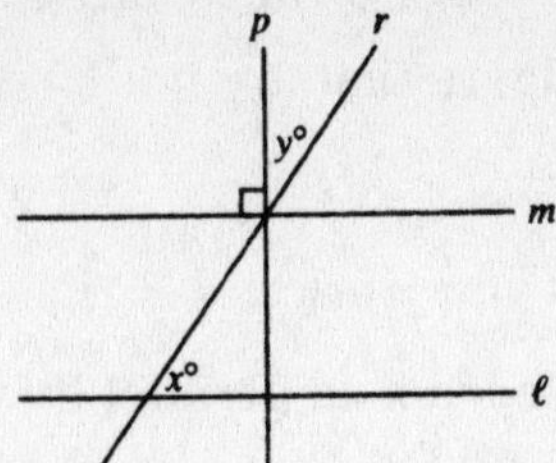

Note: Figure not drawn to scale.

28 In the figure above, line m is parallel to line l and is perpendicular to line p. If $x = y$, what is the value of x?

Difficulty: Medium

The correct answer is 45.

Tip:

Look for special properties that may help you answer the question. If it is about angles, look for special properties of angles. If it is about areas, look for special properties of areas.

Special properties that help you translate between different kinds of measurements can be especially useful.

For instance:

- If you know two sides of a triangle are of equal length, then you know that the measures of the angles opposite those two sides are equal.
- If you know two segments are radii of the same circle, you know that they are of equal length.

This question requires that you use your knowledge of lines, angles, and triangles to calculate values for parts of the figure that are not labeled. As you work on the question, remember:

- It's helpful to label parts of the figure as you work.
- Use your knowledge of special properties such as parallel lines, vertical angles, and special types of triangles.

What Do You Know?

- Lines l and m are parallel.
- Line p is perpendicular to line m.
- $x = y$.

Write relevant facts (angles, lengths of sides) on the figure as you pick up more information.

What Can You Figure Out From the Figure?

You can use the parallel lines in the figure to label another angle that is equal to $x°$, since corresponding angles are congruent.

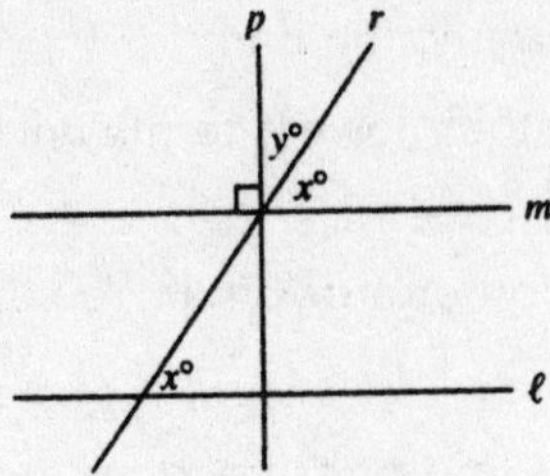

Since line p is perpendicular to line m, $x° + y° = 90°$. You are told that $x = y$. Therefore,

$$x° + x° = 90°$$

$$2x = 90$$

$$x = 45$$

Grid the answer, 45. Disregard the degree sign (°).

Recap: Tips on Grid-in Questions

1. The slash mark (/) is used to indicate a fraction bar.
2. You don't have to reduce fractions to their lowest terms unless your answer will not fit in the grid.
3. You may express an answer as a fraction or a decimal: You can grid $\frac{1}{2}$ as 1/2 or .5.
4. Mixed numbers **must** be expressed as improper fractions: You must express $1\frac{3}{5}$ as 8/5. The grid-reading system cannot distiguish between 1 3/5 and 13/5.
5. Grid as much of a repeating decimal as will fit in the grid. You may need to round a repeating decimal, but round only the last digit: grid $\frac{2}{3}$ as 2/3 or .666 or .667. Do not grid the value $\frac{2}{3}$ as .67 or .66.
6. Since you don't have choices provided to help avoid careless errors on Grid-in questions:
   - Carefully check your calculations.
   - Always double-check your answers. Make sure the answer you enter makes sense.
7. Make sure you have gridded your answer accurately and according to all the Grid-in rules.
8. Practice a few Grid-in questions with a variety of answer types—whole numbers, fractions, and decimals. Get familiar with the mechanics of gridding.
9. Some Grid-in questions have more than one correct answer. You can grid any one of the correct answers and get full credit for the question.
10. To grid zero, just enter 0 in a single column (any column where 0 appears).

Chapter 15

Mathematics Practice

The following questions are meant to give you a chance to practice the test-taking skills and strategies you've developed so far. Use them to try out different tips and ways of approaching questions before you take the practice tests in the last section of this book. Keep in mind that this chapter is intended to give you practice with the different types of questions, so it isn't arranged the way the questions will actually appear on the SAT.

Five-Choice Multiple-Choice Questions

Reference Information

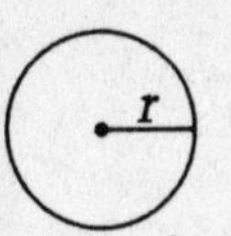

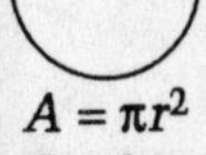

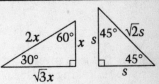

$A = \pi r^2$
$C = 2\pi r$

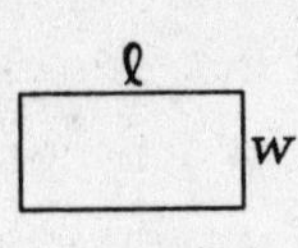

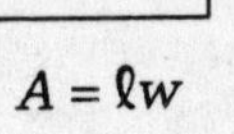

$A = \ell w$

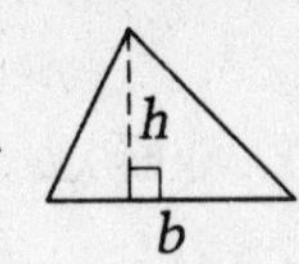

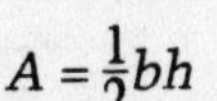

$A = \frac{1}{2}bh$

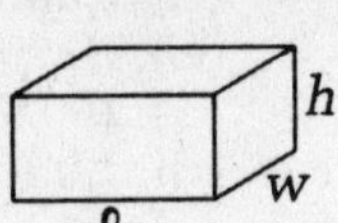

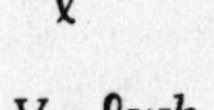

$V = \ell wh$

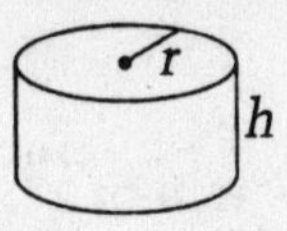

$V = \pi r^2 h$

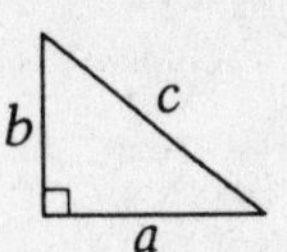

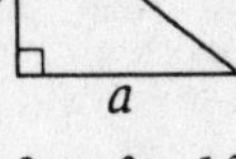

$c^2 = a^2 + b^2$

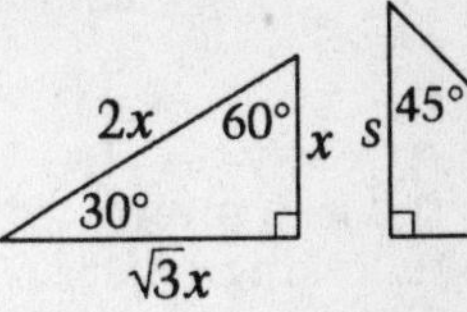

Special Right Triangles

The number of degrees of arc in a circle is 360.
The measure in degrees of a straight angle is 180.
The sum of the measures in degrees of the angles of a triangle is 180.

1 On the number line above, what number is the coordinate of point R ?

(A) $-1\frac{3}{4}$

(B) $-1\frac{1}{4}$

(C) $-\frac{3}{4}$

(D) $-\frac{1}{3}$

(E) $-\frac{1}{4}$

2 If a certain number is doubled and the result is increased by 7, the number obtained is 19. What is the original number?

(A) 2.5
(B) 6
(C) 13
(D) 16.5
(E) 24

Tangent Line: touches shape only once.

Right angle to center of circles

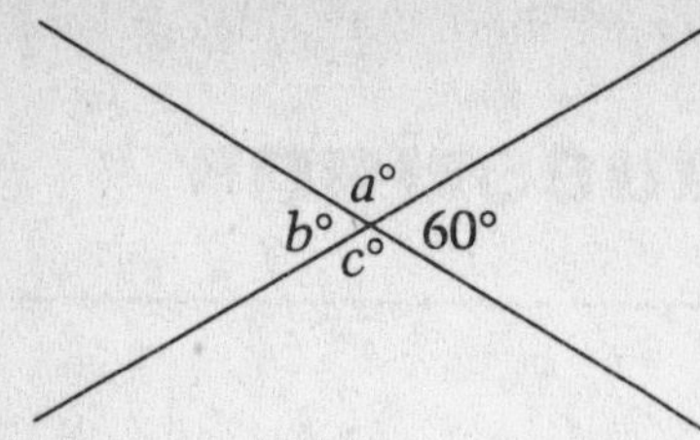

3 For the two intersecting lines above, which of the following must be true?

I. $a > c$
II. $a = 2b$
III. $a + 60 = b + c$

(A) I only
(B) II only
(C) I and II only
(D) II and III only
(E) I, II, and III

4 Three consecutive integers are listed in increasing order. If their sum is 102, what is the second integer in the list?

(A) 28
(B) 29
(C) 33
(D) 34
(E) 35

5 If 10,000 microns = 1 centimeter and 100,000,000 angstrom units = 1 centimeter, how many angstrom units equal 1 micron?

(A) 0.000000000001
(B) 0.0001
(C) 10,000
(D) 100,000
(E) 1,000,000,000,000

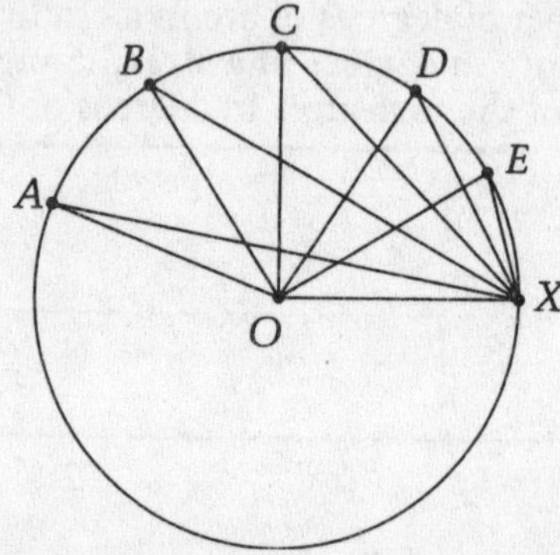

6 In the figure above, OX is a radius of the circle with center O. Which of the following triangles has the least area?

(A) ΔAOX
(B) ΔBOX
(C) ΔCOX
(D) ΔDOX
(E) ΔEOX

7 If the product of five integers is negative, then, at most, how many of the five integers could be negative?

(A) One
(B) Two
(C) Three
(D) Four
(E) Five

8 If $x - 7 = 2y$ and $x = 5 + 3y$, what is the value of y?

(A) -5
(B) -2
(C) 2
(D) 5
(E) 12

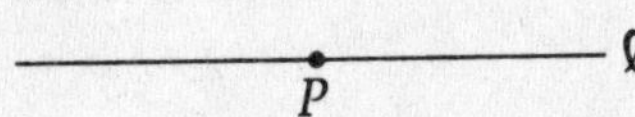

9 In the figure above, if two points S and T are to be placed on line ℓ on opposite sides of point P so that $2SP = PT$, what will be the value of $\frac{ST}{PT}$?

(A) $\frac{2}{1}$
(B) $\frac{3}{2}$
(C) $\frac{2}{3}$
(D) $\frac{1}{2}$
(E) $\frac{1}{3}$

10 There are g gallons of paint available to paint a house. After n gallons have been used, then in terms of g and n, what percent of the paint has not been used?

(A) $\frac{100n}{g}\%$
(B) $\frac{g}{100n}\%$
(C) $\frac{100g}{n}\%$
(D) $\frac{g}{100(g-n)}\%$
(E) $\frac{100(g-n)}{g}\%$

11 If x is an integer and $2 < x < 7$, how many different triangles are there with sides of lengths 2, 7, and x?

(A) One
(B) Two
(C) Three
(D) Four
(E) Five

12 If $a > b$ and $a(b - a) = 0$, which of the following must be true?

I. $a = 0$
II. $b < 0$
III. $a - b > 0$

(A) I only
(B) II only
(C) III only
(D) I and II only
(E) I, II, and III

Quantitative Comparison Questions

Reference Information

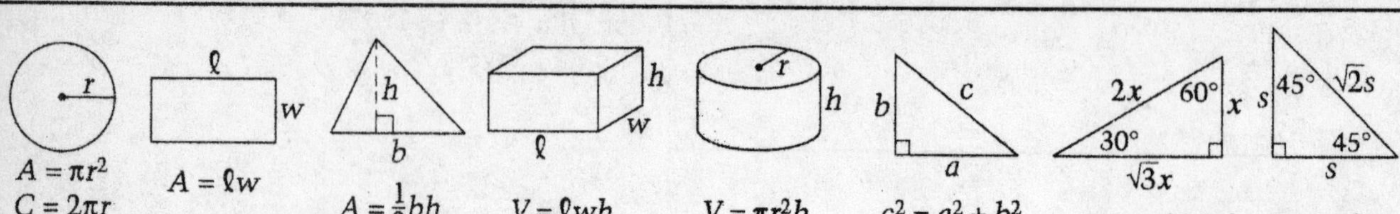

The number of degrees of arc in a circle is 360.
The measure in degrees of a straight angle is 180.
The sum of the measures in degrees of the angles of a triangle is 180.

Directions for Quantitative Comparison Questions

Questions 1-10 each consist of two quantities in boxes, one in Column A and one in Column B. You are to compare the two quantities and on the answer sheet fill in oval

A if the quantity in Column A is greater;
B if the quantity in Column B is greater;
C if the two quantities are equal;
D if the relationship cannot be determined from the information given:

AN E RESPONSE WILL NOT BE SCORED.

Notes:

1. In some questions, information is given about one or both of the quantities to be compared. In such cases, the given information is centered above the two columns and is not boxed.
2. In a given question, a symbol that appears in both columns represents the same thing in Column A as it does in Column B.
3. Letters such as x, n, and k stand for real numbers.

EXAMPLES

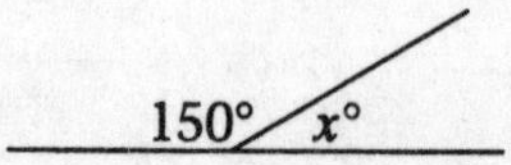

	Column A	Column B	Answers
E1	5^2	20	● Ⓑ Ⓒ Ⓓ
	(figure: straight line with angles 150° and $x°$)		
E2	x	30	Ⓐ Ⓑ ● Ⓓ
	r and s are integers.		
E3	$r+1$	$s-1$	Ⓐ Ⓑ Ⓒ ●

SUMMARY DIRECTIONS FOR COMPARISON QUESTIONS

Answer: A if the quantity in Column A is greater;
B if the quantity in Column B is greater;
C if the two quantities are equal;
D if the relationship cannot be determined from the information given.

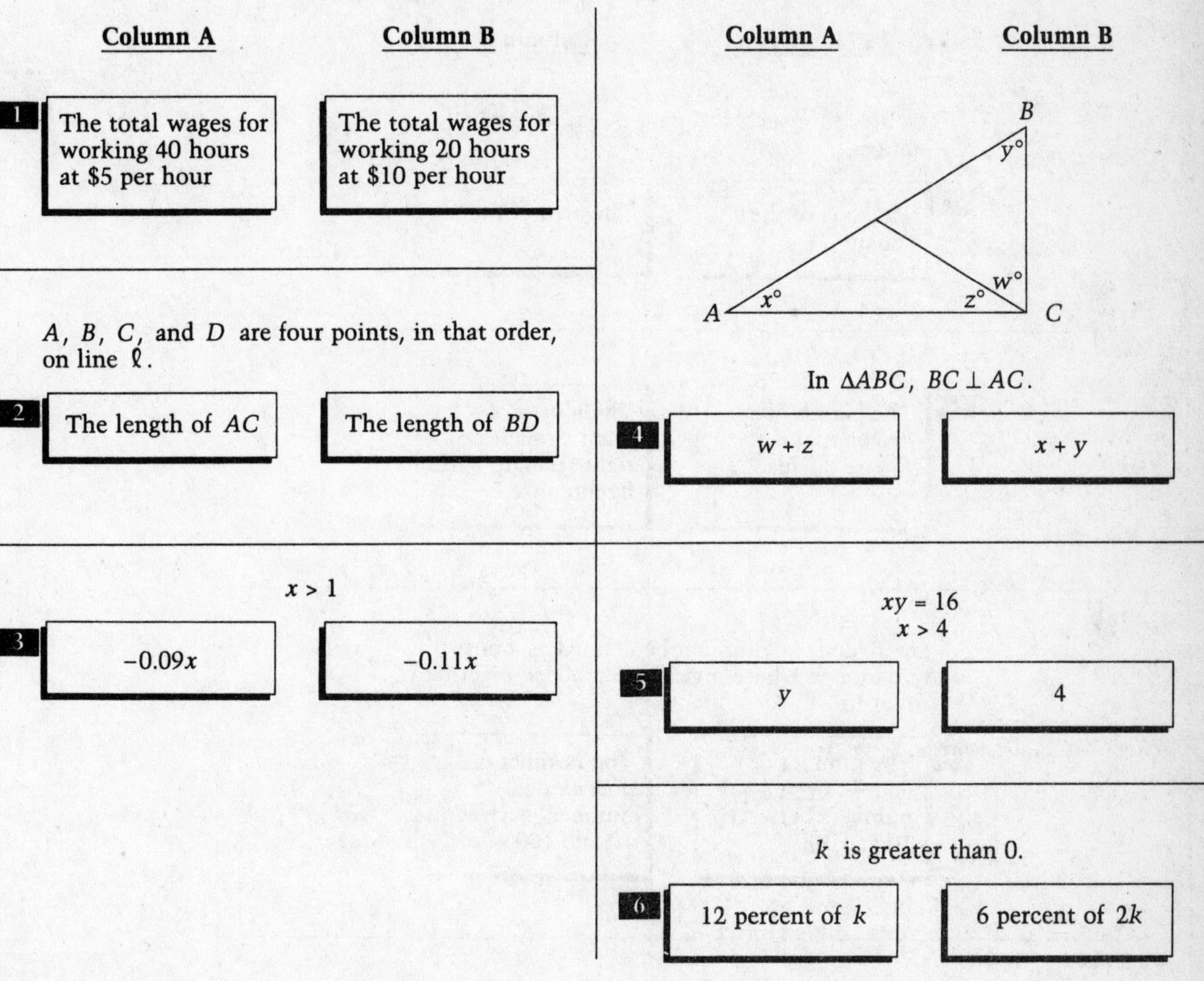

	Column A	Column B
1	The total wages for working 40 hours at \$5 per hour	The total wages for working 20 hours at \$10 per hour

A, B, C, and D are four points, in that order, on line ℓ.

	Column A	Column B
2	The length of AC	The length of BD

$x > 1$

	Column A	Column B
3	$-0.09x$	$-0.11x$

In ΔABC, $BC \perp AC$.

	Column A	Column B
4	$w + z$	$x + y$

$xy = 16$
$x > 4$

	Column A	Column B
5	y	4

k is greater than 0.

	Column A	Column B
6	12 percent of k	6 percent of $2k$

SUMMARY DIRECTIONS FOR COMPARISON QUESTIONS

Answer: A if the quantity in Column A is greater;
B if the quantity in Column B is greater;
C if the two quantities are equal;
D if the relationship cannot be determined from the information given.

	Column A	Column B

A circle intersects a square in exactly two points.

	Column A	Column B
7	The area of the square	The area of the circle

	Column A	Column B
8	The length of a diagonal of a square of side 2	The length of a leg of an isosceles right triangle with hypotenuse 2

Let a "dodeka" number be defined as a positive integer whose digits, when added together, equal 12.

	Column A	Column B
9	The number of dodeka <u>even</u> numbers between 10 and 100	The number of dodeka <u>odd</u> numbers between 10 and 100

---

a and b are nonzero integers.

	Column A	Column B
10	$(a + b)^2$	$(a^2 + b^2)$

Student-Produced Response Questions

Directions for Student-Produced Response Questions

Each of the remaining 6 questions requires you to solve the problem and enter your answer by marking the ovals in the special grid, as shown in the examples below.

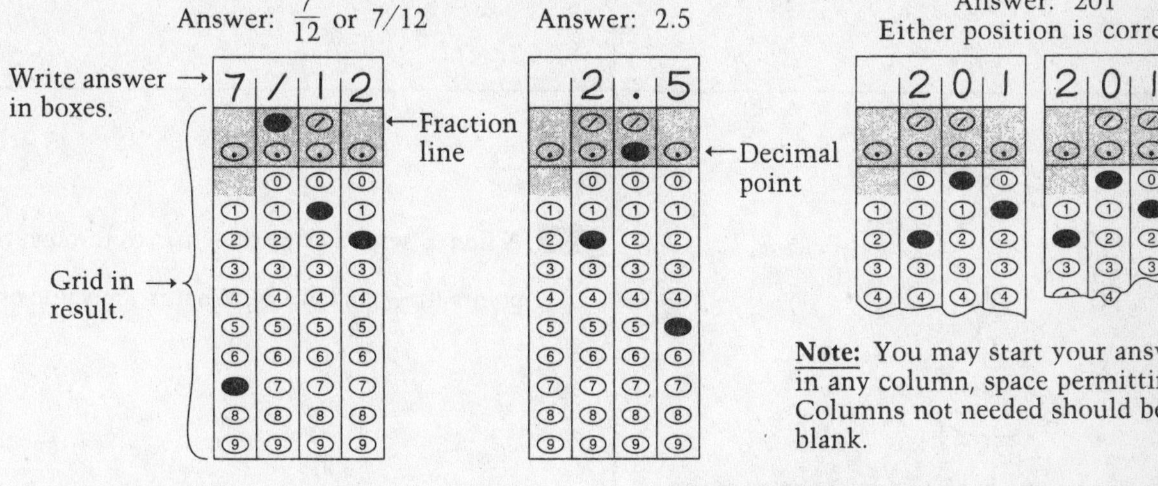

Note: You may start your answers in any column, space permitting. Columns not needed should be left blank.

- Mark no more than one oval in any column.
- Because the answer sheet will be machine-scored, **you will receive credit only if the ovals are filled in correctly.**
- Although not required, it is suggested that you write your answer in the boxes at the top of the columns to help you fill in the ovals accurately.
- Some problems may have more than one correct answer. In such cases, grid only one answer.
- No question has a negative answer.
- **Mixed numbers** such as $2\frac{1}{2}$ must be gridded as 2.5 or 5/2. (If 2 1 / 2 is gridded, it will be interpreted as $\frac{21}{2}$, not $2\frac{1}{2}$.)
- Decimal Accuracy: If you obtain a decimal answer, **enter the most accurate value the grid will accommodate.** For example, if you obtain an answer such as 0.6666 . . . , you should record the result as .666 or .667. **Less accurate values such as .66 or .67 are not acceptable.**

Acceptable ways to grid $\frac{2}{3} = .6666\ldots$

2/3   .666   .667

1 In 2 weeks, 550 cartons of juice were sold in the school cafeteria. At this rate, how many cartons of juice would one expect to be sold in 5 weeks?

2 For what integer value of x is $3x + 5 > 11$ and $x - 3 < 1$?

3 The number 0.008 is equivalent to the ratio of 8 to what number?

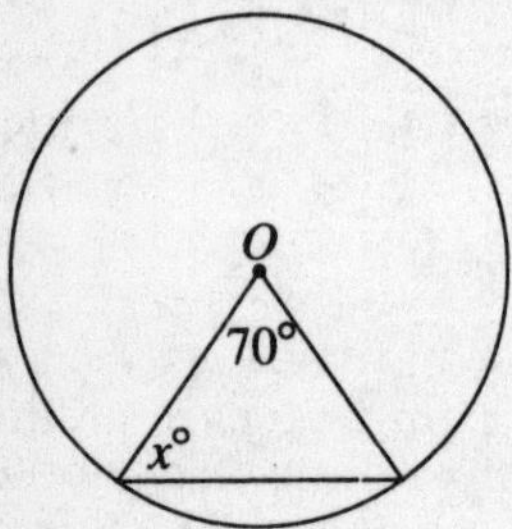

4 In the figure above, if O is the center of the circle, what is the value of x ?

5 The average (arithmetic mean) of 4 numbers is greater than 7 and less than 11. What is one possible number that could be the sum of these 4 numbers?

6 A line ℓ with a slope of $\frac{1}{4}$ passes through the points $(0, \frac{1}{2})$ and $(4, y)$. What is the value of y ?

Answer Key

Five-Choice Multiple Choice		Quantitative Comparisons		Grid-ins	
1.	C	1.	C	1.	1375
2.	B	2.	D	2.	3
3.	D	3.	A	3.	1000
4.	D	4.	C	4.	55
5.	C	5.	B	5.	28<x<44
6.	A	6.	C	6.	3/2 or 1.5
7.	E	7.	D		
8.	C	8.	A		
9.	B	9.	B		
10.	E	10.	D		
11.	A				
12.	E				

Chapter 16

About the PSAT/NMSQT

Introduction

The PSAT/NMSQT (Preliminary SAT/National Merit Scholarship Qualifying Test) gives you firsthand practice for the SAT I: Reasoning Test and the SAT II: Writing Test. It also gives you a chance to qualify for scholarships sponsored by the National Merit Scholarship Corporation. The PSAT/NMSQT measures the critical reading, math problem-solving, and writing skills that you've been developing throughout your life.

The PSAT/NMSQT is administered by high schools in October. Talk to your school counselor about how to sign up for the PSAT/NMSQT. Many sophomores and juniors take the test to get as much practice as possible, but only test scores from your junior year are used to award scholarships. Ask in your guidance office for a copy of the *PSAT/NMSQT Student Bulletin*; it includes a complete practice test.

Take the PSAT/NMSQT So You Can...

- Compare yourself with other college-bound students around the country.
- Find out what the SAT is like. (The PSAT/NMSQT includes actual verbal and math questions from the SAT.)
- Assess your verbal, math, and writing skills.
- Forecast your scores on the SAT I: Reasoning Test and SAT II: Writing Test.
- Qualify for scholarships sponsored by the National Merit Scholarship Corporation.
- Participate in the *Student Search Service* to get mail from colleges. See pages 9-10.

Types of Questions

The PSAT/NMSQT includes the six types of verbal and math questions on the SAT as well as three types of writing skills questions:

Verbal	No.	Math	No.
Sentence Completions	13	Five-Choice Multiple Choice	20
Analogies	13	Quantitative Comparisons	12
Critical Reading	26	Grid-ins	8
Total	52	Total	40

Writing Skills	No.
Identifying Sentence Errors	19
Improving Sentences	14
Improving Paragraphs	6
Total	39

Timing

The PSAT/NMSQT requires 2 hours and 10 minutes and includes 5 sections:

- Two 25-minute verbal sections
- Two 25-minute math sections
- One 30-minute writing skills section

Scoring

PSAT/NMSQT scores are reported on a scale of 20 to 80.

Your PSAT/NMSQT score report is full of information to help you get ready academically for college and testwise for the SAT. PSAT/NMSQT scores indicate how ready you are for college-level work. But the score report also offers information about your test-taking skills and some details about your academic preparation. The score report gives you:

- Three separate PSAT/NMSQT scores for verbal, math, and writing skills;
- Score ranges;
- Percentiles;
- Selection Index used by the National Merit Scholarship Corporation to determine scholarship eligibility (sum of the three scores: V + M + W);

- Question-by-question feedback;
- Your estimated SAT I: Reasoning Test scores (verbal and math);
- Your estimated SAT II: Writing score;
- Eligibility criteria and status for National Merit Scholarships;
- Guidance information to help in college and career planning.

Preparing for the PSAT/NMSQT

Use all of the test-taking tips and strategies described in this book for the SAT and make sure you are familiar with the information in Chapter 2: "Test-Taking Strategies." Understand the differences between the PSAT/NMSQT and the SAT; familiarize yourself with all the question types and their directions before the test. Give special attention to the writing skills directions and sample questions presented in this chapter because they do not appear on the SAT or elsewhere in this book.

Tip: General Tips for the PSAT/NMSQT

1. Know the directions for each kind of question.
2. Expect easy questions at the beginning of each group of questions.
3. Answer as many easy questions as you can, because all questions are worth the same number of points.
4. Read all the answer choices for multiple-choice questions.
5. Do scratchwork in the test booklet.
6. Work steadily.
7. Take a calculator that you are comfortable using.
8. Practice and have a thorough understanding of how to complete math grids.
9. Stay relaxed.

Verbal and Math Preparation

The six types of verbal and math questions on the PSAT/NMSQT are the same as on the SAT, so here's what you'll need to do to prepare:

- Review the verbal and math chapters in this book.
- Go through the math review section carefully. If it is close to exam time, concentrate on the math skills and concepts that you've studied but may need to review. If you have time before the test, start learning some of the unfamiliar skills and concepts.
- Practice applying the tips and strategies on the sample tests.

Writing Skills Preparation

The writing skills section of the PSAT/NMSQT includes the three types of multiple-choice questions that appear on the SAT II: Writing Test:

- Identifying Sentence Errors
- Improving Sentences
- Improving Paragraphs

These questions measure your ability to express ideas effectively in standard written English, to recognize faults in usage and structure, and to use language with sensitivity to meaning. Test questions do not ask you to define or use grammatical terms and do not test spelling or capitalization.

- Save valuable time by learning the directions beforehand.
- Try answering the following sample questions before looking at the correct choice.
- Study the explanations for each example. Make sure that you understand what the question is asking.
- If you cannot find the correct answer, eliminate the choice or choices that you know are wrong and guess from the remaining answers.

Four Characteristics of Effective Writing

Some writing skills questions require students to recognize when a sentence has no errors. Other questions focus on common problems associated with the following four characteristics of effective writing.

Characteristics and Their Associated Problems	Illustrations
1. Being Consistent	
Sequence of tenses	After he broke his arm, he is home for two weeks.
Shift of pronoun person	If one is tense, they should try to relax.
Parallelism	She skis, plays tennis, and flying hang gliders.
Noun number agreement	Ann and Sarah want to be a pilot.
Subject-verb agreement	There is eight people on shore.
2. Expressing Ideas Logically	
Coordination and subordination	Nancy has a rash, and she is probably allergic to something.
Logical comparison	Harry grew more vegetables than his neighbor's garden.
Modification and word order	Barking loudly, the tree had the dog's leash wrapped around it.
3. Being Clear and Precise	
Ambiguous and vague pronouns	In the newspaper they say that few people voted.
Diction	He circumvented the globe on his trip.
Wordiness	There are many problems in the contemporary world in which we live.
Missing subject	If your car is parked here while not eating in the restaurant, it will be towed away.
Weak passive verbs	When you bake a cake, the oven should be preheated.
4. Following Conventions	
Adjective and adverb confusion	His friends agree that he drives too reckless.
Double negative	Manuel has scarcely no free time.
Pronoun case	He sat between you and I at the stadium.
Idiom	Natalie had a different opinion towards her.
Comparison of modifiers	Of the sixteen executives, Meg makes more money.
Sentence fragment	Fred having to go home early.
Comma splice or fused sentence	Shawna enjoys crossword puzzles, she works on one every day.

Sample Writing Skills Questions with Explanations

Identifying Sentence Errors

Directions: The following sentences test your knowledge of grammar, usage, word choice, and idiom.

Some sentences are correct.

No sentence contains more than one error.

You will find that the error, if there is one, is underlined and lettered. Elements of the sentence that are not underlined will not be changed. In choosing answers, follow the requirements of standard written English.

If there is an error, select the one underlined part that must be changed to make the sentence correct and fill in the corresponding oval on your answer sheet.

If there is no error, fill in oval E.

1 The bright (A) fiberglass sculptures of Luis Jimenez has received (B) critical acclaim not only (C) in his home state, New Mexico, but also in (D) New York. No error (E)

Explanation:

The problem with this sentence lies in (B): the subject of the sentence, "sculptures," is plural and requires the plural verb "have received." The other choices are all correct. The word "bright" in choice (A) is used properly as an adjective, and in (C), "not only" is part of the combination "not only . . . but also." The preposition in (D), "in," begins a phrase that effectively parallels the preceding phrase "in his home state." The best answer, then, is (B). The correct sentence reads: The bright fiberglass sculptures of Luis Jimenez have received critical acclaim not only in his home state, New Mexico, but also in New York.

2 Even with a calculator, you must have a
A
basic understanding of mathematics if
B
one expects to solve complex problems
C
correctly. No error
D E

Explanation:

The answer here is (C). The first part of the sentence addresses "you." Since this pronoun is not underlined it cannot be changed, and subsequent pronouns must also use the second person. In (C), the third-person pronoun "one" is used incorrectly; choice (C) should be worded "you expect." The other choices are all appropriate. Choice (A) introduces the conditional relationship set forth in the rest of the sentence, (B) appropriately uses the preposition "of" with "understanding," and the adverb "correctly" in (D) modifies the verb "solve." The correct sentence reads: Even with a calculator, you must have a basic understanding of mathematics if you expect to solve complex problems correctly.

3 People who dislike cats sometimes criticize
A
them for being aloof and independent;
B
people who are fond of cats often admire
C
them for the same qualities. No error
D E

Explanation:

All of the underlined choices in this sentence are appropriate. The word "sometimes" in (A) properly modifies the verb "criticize." In (B), "being" is the verbal form that fits idiomatically with the phrase "criticize . . . for." The preposition "of" in (C) is appropriate to use after "fond." In (D), the proper plural pronoun, "them," is used to refer to "cats," and "for" is the correct preposition to use with the verb "admire." Since all of the underlined parts of this sentence are correct, the best answer is (E), "No error."

4 The decision that <u>has just been</u> (A) <u>agreed with</u> (B) by the committee members should serve as a basis <u>for their</u> (C) work in the <u>years to come</u> (D). <u>No error</u> (E)

Explanation:

The error is the preposition used in choice (B). In the context of this sentence, the correct idiomatic expression is "agreed to" rather than "agreed with." In (A), the verb phrase is acceptable; in (C) "for" appropriately completes the expression "basis for," and "their" properly refers to the plural noun "members." Choice (D) properly expresses the time reference in the sentence. The correct sentence reads: The decision that has just been agreed to by the committee members should serve as a basis for their work in the years to come.

Tip: Tips on Identifying Sentence Errors

1. Read the entire sentence carefully but quickly.
2. Look at choices (A) to (D) to see whether anything needs to be changed to make the sentence correct.
3. Don't waste time searching for errors. Mark (E), <u>No error</u>, on your answer sheet if you believe the sentence is correct as written.
4. Move quickly through questions about Identifying Sentence Errors. The other kinds of questions (Improving Sentences and Improving Paragraphs) will probably take more time.
5. Mark questions that seem hard for you and return to them later.

Improving Sentences

Directions: In each of the following sentences, some part or all of the sentence is underlined. Below each sentence you will find five ways of phrasing the underlined part. Select the answer that produces the most effective sentence, one that is clear and exact, without awkwardness or ambiguity, and fill in the corresponding oval on your answer sheet. In choosing answers, follow the requirements of standard written English. Choose the answer that best expresses the meaning of the original sentence.

Answer (A) is always the same as the underlined part. Choose answer (A) if you think the original sentence needs no revision.

1 Alice Walker, one of America's best-known writers, she has published both poetry and prose.

(A) writers, she has published
(B) writers, has published
(C) writers, and publishing
(D) writers since publishing
(E) writers when she published

Explanation:

In this sentence, "Alice Walker" is clearly the person who has "published" poetry and prose. Choice (A), then, is incorrect because the pronoun "she" is redundant. Simply dropping "she" will correct this problem; therefore, (B) is the answer: Alice Walker, one of America's best-known writers, has published both poetry and prose. Choices (C), (D), and (E) are incorrect because they do not contain verb forms that produce grammatically complete sentences.

2 Consumers are beginning to take notice of electric cars because they are quiet, cause no air pollution, and gasoline is not used.

(A) cause no air pollution, and gasoline is not used
(B) air pollution is not caused, and gasoline is not used
(C) cause no air pollution, and use no gasoline
(D) causing no air pollution and using no gasoline
(E) air pollution is not caused, and no gasoline is used

Explanation:

Here, you must recognize that parts of a series separated by commas should parallel each other. In the original sentence and choice (A), the first two items in the series ("are quiet" and "cause") take the plural subject "they" and use active verbs, but the third item ("gasoline is not used") introduces a new subject and the passive voice. To follow the structure set forth by the phrase "they are quiet," the words "cause" and "use"— which also take "they" as their subject — should be used. Choice (C), then, is the answer: Consumers are beginning to take notice of electric cars because they are quiet, cause no air pollution, and use no gasoline. Choices (B), (D), and (E) do not follow this parallel structure and so are incorrect.

3 The convenience and availability of watercolor paint <u>account for its popularity</u> with amateur artists.

(A) account for its popularity
(B) account for their popularity
(C) accounts for its popularity
(D) is why it is popular
(E) are a reason for its popularity

Explanation:

This sentence requires you to pay close attention to the plural subject. The original sentence is correct, so the answer is (A). The other choices introduce errors into the sentence. In (B), the verb "account" correctly refers back to the plural subject "convenience and availability," but the plural pronoun "their" is incorrect — what is popular is "watercolor paint," not "convenience and availability." In (C) and (D), the verb is singular rather than plural, and in (E) the singular noun "reason" does not agree with the plural subject.

Tip: Tips on Improving Sentences

1. Read the entire sentence carefully but quickly. Note the underlined portion because that is the portion that may have to be revised.
2. Remember that the portion with no underline stays the same.
3. Mark choice (A) if the underlined portion seems correct. Check the other choices quickly to make sure that (A) is really the best choice.
4. Think of how you would revise the underlined portion if it seems wrong. Look for your revision among the choices given.
5. Replace the underlined portion of the sentence with choices (B) to (E) if you don't find your revision. Concentrate on the choices that seem clear and exact when you read them.
6. Mark questions that seem hard for you and return to them later.

Improving Paragraphs

Directions: The following passage is an early draft of an essay. Some parts of the passage need to be rewritten. Read the passage and select the best answers for the questions that follow. Some questions are about particular sentences or parts of sentences and ask you to improve sentence structure and word choice. Other questions refer to parts of the essay or the entire essay and ask you to consider organization and development. In making your decisions, follow the conventions of standard written English. After you have chosen your answer, fill in the corresponding oval on your answer sheet.

Questions 1-6 are based on the following essay, which is a response to an assignment to write about an economic issue facing the United States today.

(1) *Recently a group of workers from a clothing factory in my home-town picketed peacefully in front of a department store.*

(2) *They carried signs, and passing shoppers were urged by them to buy products that were made in the United States.* (3) *A newspaper article suggested that they were wrong.* (4) *It pointed out that nearly all stores now sell goods that are not made in this country.* (5) *However, I would argue that the demonstrators are right, consumers should think about the effect they can have on industries here in the United States.*

(6) *Consumers have the right to buy whatever they want.* (7) *They should consider the effects of their choices.* (8) *In the last several years, hundreds of thousands of workers in United States industries have lost their jobs.* (9) *They represent billions of dollars of lost wages and taxes.*

(10) *Consumers should know that consumer goods that are not made in the United States contribute to the loss of jobs in many different American industries and businesses.* (11) *Buying goods made in the United States means investing in our future.*

(12) *Without government subsidies, our industries only have the American consumer to help them compete in the world market and therefore guarantee jobs for hundreds of thousands of workers in the United States.*

1 In context, which is the best version of the underlined portion of sentence 2 (reproduced below)?

They carried signs, and passing shoppers were urged by them to buy products that were made in the United States.

(A) (As it is now)
(B) They carry signs and urge passing shoppers
(C) Carrying signs and urging passing shoppers, the workers asked them
(D) The workers carried signs that urged the passing shoppers
(E) These signs urged passing shoppers

Tip:

Keep in mind that the revised sentence must make sense in the context of the passage as a whole.

Explanation:

In question 1, the pronoun "them" in the underlined part of the sentence is unclear because it could refer to either "signs" or "workers." The underlined phrase also presents an unnecessary shift from the active voice ("They carried signs") to the passive voice ("passing shoppers were urged by them"). Choice (A), then, is incorrect. In (B), the present-tense verbs "carry" and "urge" are inconsistent with the past tense used in the rest of the paragraph. Choice (C) is wordy and contains another unclear reference to "them." The most logical revision is choice (D), which makes it clear that the workers used signs to urge the shoppers. Choice (E), while grammatically correct, is incorrect because the phrase "These signs" does not refer to anything mentioned previously. The correct sentence reads: The workers carried signs that urged the passing shoppers to buy products that were made in the United States.

2 In context, which is the best way to revise and combine the underlined portions of sentences 3 and 4 (reproduced below)?

A newspaper article suggested that they were wrong. It pointed out that nearly all stores now sell goods that are not made in this country.

(A) A newspaper article suggested that the demonstrators were wrong, pointing out
(B) They were wrong, a newspaper article suggested, it pointed out that
(C) Suggesting that they are wrong, in a newspaper article it says
(D) The newspaper article suggests that the shoppers were wrong,
(E) In the newspaper article was the suggestion that they were wrong and

Explanation:

Question 2 asks you to connect two related sentences. Choice (A) is the correct answer. Choice (B) improperly connects two complete sentences with a comma. In (C) and (E), the pronoun "they" is ambiguous and could refer to either "workers" or "shoppers." Another problem in (C) is the ambiguous "it." Choice (D) changes the meaning of the original sentences by using the definite article "the" and the present-tense verb "suggests." The correct sentence reads: A newspaper article suggested that the demonstrators were wrong, pointing out that nearly all stores now sell goods that are not made in this country.

3 In context, which is the best version of the underlined portions of sentences 6 and 7 (reproduced below)?

Consumers have the right to buy whatever they want. They should consider the effects of their choices.

(A) (As it is now)
(B) Consumers certainly have the right to buy whatever they want, but they should consider
(C) Consumers certainly have the right to buy whatever they want, regardless of
(D) Although consumers have the right to buy whatever they want, they also consider
(E) Apparently, consumers have the right to buy whatever they want. If only they would consider

Tip:

When combining sentences, make sure that the relationship between the two sentences is clear.

Explanation:

Your answer to question 3 must take into account the meaning of sentences 6 and 7 in the context of the passage. Choice (A), the original version, is choppy and does not convey the logical relationship between the two ideas. The best version of the sentence is (B), which emphasizes the correlation between a purchase and its effects: Consumers certainly have the right to buy whatever they want, but they should consider the effects of their choices. The other choices are all incorrect in context: the word "regardless" in (C), the word "also" in (D), and the word "Apparently" in (E) all improperly alter the meaning of the sentences.

4 Which of the following best replaces the word "They" in sentence 9?

(A) The consumers
(B) These lost jobs
(C) The industries
(D) Those arguments
(E) The United States

Explanation:

In sentence 9 the word or idea to which "They" refers is unclear. This sentence needs to be revised to specify what represents "billions of dollars." By looking back to sentence 8, you can see that "they" in sentence 9 refers to "their jobs." The answer to this question, then, is choice (B). The revised sentence reads: These lost jobs represent billions of dollars of lost wages and taxes.

5 Which sentence would be most appropriate to follow sentence 12?

(A) I see now that the demonstrators were right.
(B) Consumers have rights, too.
(C) In conclusion, we have no one else to blame.
(D) The next time you go shopping, think of the workers and their families in your community.
(E) We, the American consumers, must find out how to invest in our industries.

Explanation:

Question 5 asks you to select the best concluding sentence for the essay, and so requires you to consider the argument and development of the entire passage. The correct answer is (D). It relates logically to the main idea of the essay, which is an appeal to consumers to "consider the effects of their choices" (sentence 7). Choice (A) would be out of place at the end of the second paragraph since sentence 5 has already stated that the "demonstrators are right." Choice (B) contradicts the passage's main focus on workers. Choice (C) does not logically follow sentence 12 because there is nothing leading to the conclusion that "we have no one else to blame." Choice (E) is inappropriate because the passage already reveals how consumers can invest in domestic industries by buying their products.

6 Including a paragraph on which of the following would most strengthen the writer's argument?

(A) The effect of strikes in industry
(B) A comparison of working conditions in the United States and elsewhere in the world
(C) Quotations from the newspaper article referred to in sentence 3
(D) Buying patterns of different groups of consumers
(E) The impact that the closing of a factory has had on a particular community

Explanation:

Question 6 asks you to consider what paragraph added to the original essay would make it more convincing. To answer this question you must realize that sentence 5, the last sentence of the first paragraph, summarizes the writer's main point, that "consumers should think about the effect they can have on industries here in the United States." Logically, the writer's argument would be most strengthened by demonstrating the effect that consumers *do* have on industries in the United States. Choice (E) supports the writer's argument because it describes what happens when consumers do not buy domestic goods. Choices (A) through (D), while related to the main idea to varying degrees, do not directly reinforce it. The best answer, then, is (E).

Tip: Tips on Improving Paragraphs

1. Read the entire essay quickly to determine its overall meaning. The essay is meant to be a draft, so don't be surprised if you notice errors. Don't linger over those errors.
2. Make sure that your answer about a particular sentence or sentences makes sense in the context of the passage as a whole.
3. Choose the best answer from among the choices given, even if you can imagine another correct response.
4. Mark questions that seem hard for you and return to them later.

Writing Skills Practice & Answer Key

Identifying Sentence Errors

Directions: The following sentences test your knowledge of grammar, usage, word choices, and idioms.

Some sentences are correct.

No sentence contains more than one error.

You will find that the error, if there is one, is underlined and lettered. Elements of the sentence that are not underlined will not be changed. In choosing answers, follow the requirements of standard written English.

If there is an error, select the one underlined part that must be changed to make the sentence correct and fill in the corresponding oval on your answer sheet.

If there is no error, select E.

1 Air pollution caused by industrial fumes has been studied (A) for years, but (B) only recently has (C) the harmful effects of noise pollution become (D) known. No error (E)

2 No matter (A) how cautious (B) snowmobiles are (C) driven, they are capable of damaging (D) the land over which they travel. No error (E)

3 The starling is such a (A) pest in rural areas that it has become (B) necessary to find ways (C) of controlling the growth of their (D) population. No error (E)

4 Maude Adams, after her spectacular triumph as (A) the original Peter Pan, went about (B) heavy veiled (C) and was accessible to only a handful (D) of intimate friends. No error (E)

5 All states impose severe penalties on
A B
drivers who do not stop when
he or she is involved in accidents.
C D
No error
E

6 If one is interested in learning
A B
even more about Zora Neale Hurston,
C
you should read Robert Hemenway's
D
biography. No error
E

7 If he had begun earlier, he might have
A B
succeeded in finishing the
C
extremely complex project before the
D
deadline. No error
E

8 In the early twentieth century, new
thinking about symbolism and the
A
unconscious were greatly inspired by
B C
the writings of Sigmund Freud
D
and Carl Jung. No error
E

Improving Sentences

Directions: In each of the following sentences, some part or all of the sentence is underlined. Below each sentence you will find five ways of phrasing the underlined part. Select the answer that produces the most effective sentence, one that is clear and exact, and is without awkwardness or ambiguity, and fill in the corresponding oval on your answer sheet. In choosing answers, follow the requirements of standard written English. Choose the answer that best expresses the meaning of the original sentence.

Answer (A) is always the same as the underlined part. Choose answer (A) if you think the original sentence needs no revision.

1 Anita liked to watch television, of which she found the science programs especially fascinating.

(A) television, of which she found the science programs especially fascinating
(B) television; she found the science programs especially fascinating
(C) television, and it was especially the science programs that were of fascination
(D) television; the fascination of the science programs especially
(E) television, especially fascinating to her were the science programs

2 Although gale force winds often pass through the Eiffel Tower, causing it to sway no more than four inches.

(A) causing it to sway no more
(B) and yet it sways no more
(C) they do not cause it to sway more
(D) and they do not cause it to sway
(E) yet causing it to sway no more

3 Underestimating its value, breakfast is a meal many people skip.

(A) Underestimating its value, breakfast is a meal many people skip.
(B) Breakfast is skipped by many people because of their underestimating its value.
(C) Many people, underestimating the value of breakfast, and skipping it.
(D) Many people skip breakfast because they underestimate its value.
(E) A meal skipped by many people underestimating its value is breakfast.

4 Certain shipwrecks have a particular fascination for those people which have a belief in finding the treasure in them.

(A) which have a belief in finding the treasure in them
(B) that belief there is treasure to be found in them
(C) who believe they hold treasure and that they can find it
(D) who believe that there is treasure to be found in them
(E) who believe about treasure to be found in them

5 Many of the instruments used in early operations of the United States Army Signal Corps were adaptations of equipment used by the Plains Indians, particularly that of the heliograph.

(A) Corps were adaptations of equipment used by the Plains Indians, particularly that of the heliograph
(B) Corps, there were adaptations of equipment used by the Plains Indians, particularly the heliograph
(C) Corps, and in particular the heliograph, was an adaptation of equipment used by the Plains Indians
(D) Corps, and in particular the heliograph, were adaptations of equipment used by the Plains Indians
(E) Corps being adaptations, the heliograph in particular, of those used by Plains Indians

6 Marie and Pierre Curie discovered radium but refused to patent the process they used nor otherwise profiting from the commercial exploitation of radium.

(A) used nor otherwise profiting
(B) had used nor otherwise did they profit
(C) have used or otherwise to have profited
(D) used or otherwise profited
(E) had used or otherwise to profit

7 Many drivers violate traffic laws knowingly and openly, in other respects they are law-abiding citizens, however.

(A) Many drivers violate traffic laws knowingly and openly, in other respects they are law-abiding citizens, however.
(B) Many drivers who are otherwise law-abiding citizens violate traffic laws knowingly and openly.
(C) Many drivers violate traffic laws knowingly and openly and are otherwise law-abiding citizens.
(D) Although otherwise law-abiding citizens, many drivers, however, violate traffic laws knowingly and openly.
(E) Many drivers which violate traffic laws knowingly and openly are in other respects law-abiding citizens.

8 The revolt against Victorianism was perhaps even more marked in poetry than either fiction or drama.

(A) either fiction or drama
(B) either fiction or in drama
(C) either in fiction or drama
(D) in either fiction or drama
(E) in either fiction or in drama

Improving Paragraphs

Directions: The following passage is an early draft of an essay. Some parts of the passage need to be rewritten.

Read the passage and answer the questions that follow. Some questions are about particular sentences or parts of sentences and ask you to improve sentence structure and word choice. Other questions refer to parts of the essay or the entire essay and ask you to consider organization and development. In making your decisions, follow the conventions of standard written English. After you have chosen your answer, fill in the corresponding oval on your answer sheet.

Questions 1–6 refer to the following passage.

(1) *I have just read an excellent book called "Having Our Say: The Delany Sisters' First 100 Years."* (2) *Usually I do not enjoy autobiographies.* (3) *I could hardly put this one down.* (4) *It is about Sadie Delany, who is 103 years old, and her "little" sister Bessie, she is 101.*

(5) *The sisters grew up in North Carolina in times that were not easy for African Americans.* (6) *Around 1916 they moved to New York City and went to Columbia University at their father's urging.* (7) *He tells them, "You are college material.* (8) *And if you don't go, shame on you!"* (9) *Sadie became a teacher and Bessie a dentist.* (10) *The second Black woman dentist in New York.*

(11) *They lived through an incredible amount of history.* (12) *For instance, Bessie participated in civil rights marches and protests in New York for decades, starting in the 1920s.* (13) *Imagine having people like Paul Robeson over to dinner!*

(14) *One aspect of the book that I especially liked was its humor; though Sadie is not as irreverent as Bessie, both are full of wisecracks.* (15) *The Delany sisters seem livelier than many twenty year olds.* (16) *They care deeply about what is going on around them—and they laugh at things whenever possible.*

1 What is the best way to deal with sentence 3?

(A) Leave it as it is.
(B) Connect it to sentence 2 with the word "but."
(C) Place it before sentence 2.
(D) Change "this one" to "this autobiography."
(E) Omit it.

2 In context, which is the best version of "*He tells them*" in sentence 7?

(A) (As it is now)
(B) Their father tells them,
(C) This is because he tells them,
(D) He had told them,
(E) His suggestion was:

3 Which phrase, if inserted at the beginning of sentence 10 (reproduced below), best fits the context?

The second Black woman dentist in New York.

(A) Thus she was only
(B) However, she was
(C) Later, Bessie became
(D) In fact, she became
(E) And actually

4 Which of the following sentences is best to insert between sentences 12 and 13?

(A) The two sisters also knew many famous figures personally.
(B) Sadie usually did not march, but protested by other means.
(C) Many young people seem to think this did not begin until the 1960s.
(D) The last hundred years have seen many changes in civil rights laws.
(E) Paul Robeson was a prominent singer, actor, and political activist.

5 In context, what is the best way to deal with sentence 14?

(A) Move it to the beginning of the first paragraph.
(B) Move it to the beginning of the second paragraph.
(C) Start a new sentence after "irreverent" and delete "though."
(D) Connect it to sentence 15 with a comma.
(E) Follow it with an example.

6 Which of the following, if placed after sentence 16, would be the most effective concluding sentence for the essay?

(A) They eat healthy food and do yoga every day.
(B) Therefore, it is no small thing to survive past age 100.
(C) This book is a remarkable story made even better by the way it is told.
(D) Finally, young people should definitely communicate with their elders.
(E) Much as I enjoyed the rest of the book, the final chapter is my favorite.

Answer Key

Identifying Sentence Errors	Improving Sentences	Improving Paragraphs
1. C	1. B	1. B
2. B	2. C	2. D
3. D	3. D	3. D
4. C	4. D	4. A
5. C	5. D	5. E
6. D	6. E	6. C
7. E	7. B	
8. B	8. D	

Chapter 17

10 Complete, Real SATs with Answer Keys

Taking the Practice Tests

The practice tests that follow include 10 real editions of the SAT. Each edition of the SAT includes only six of the seven sections that the test contains. The equating sections have been omitted because they contain questions that may be used in future editions of the SAT and do not count toward the scores. You'll get the most out of the practice tests by taking them under conditions as close as possible to those of the real tests.

- When taking one of the sample tests, you'll need $2\frac{1}{2}$ hours to complete it.
- Sit at a desk or table cleared of any other papers or books. You should have the calculator on hand that you plan to take with you to the test. Other items such as dictionaries, books, or notes will not be allowed.
- Have a kitchen timer or clock in front of you for timing yourself on the sections.
- Tear out the practice answer sheet located just before each practice test and fill it in just as you will on the day of the test.
- Once you finish a practice test, use the answer key, scoring instructions, and worksheet following it to calculate your scores.

10 SAT Practice Tests

SAT I: Reasoning Test

Saturday, March 1994

YOUR NAME (PRINT) ______________________________
LAST FIRST MI

TEST CENTER ______________________________
NUMBER NAME OF TEST CENTER ROOM NUMBER

SAT® I: Reasoning Test — General Directions

Timing

- You will have three hours to work on this test.
- There are five 30-minute sections and two 15-minute sections.
- You may work on only one section at a time.
- The supervisor will tell you when to begin and end each section.
- If you finish a section before time is called, check your work on that section. You may NOT turn to any other section.
- Work as rapidly as you can without losing accuracy. Don't waste time on questions that seem too difficult for you.

Marking Answers

- Carefully mark only one answer for each question.
- Make sure each mark is dark and completely fills the oval.
- Do not make any stray marks on your answer sheet.
- If you erase, do so completely. Incomplete erasures may be scored as intended answers.
- Use only the answer spaces that correspond to the question numbers.
- For questions with only four answer choices, an answer marked in oval E will not be scored.
- Use the test book for scratchwork, but you will not receive credit for anything written there.
- You may not transfer answers to your answer sheet or fill in ovals after time has been called.
- You may not fold or remove pages or portions of a page from this book, or take the book or answer sheet from the testing room.

Scoring

- For each correct answer, you receive one point.
- For questions you omit, you receive no points.
- For a wrong answer to a multiple-choice question, you lose a fraction of a point.
  - ► If you can eliminate one or more of the answer choices as wrong, however, you increase your chances of choosing the correct answer and earning one point.
  - ► If you can't eliminate any choice, move on. You can return to the question later if there is time.
- For a wrong answer to a math question that is not multiple-choice, you don't lose any points.

The passages for this test have been adapted from published material. The ideas contained in them do not necessarily represent the opinions of the College Board or Educational Testing Service.

IMPORTANT: The codes below are unique to your test book. Copy them on your answer sheet in boxes 8 and 9 and fill in the corresponding ovals exactly as shown.

8. Form Code

A	A	0	0	0
B	B	1	1	1
C	C	2	2	2
D	D	3	3	3
E	E	4	4	4
F	F	5	5	5
G	G	6	6	6
H	H	7	7	7
I	I	8	8	8
J	J	9	9	9
K	K			
L	L			
M	M			
N	N			
O	O			
P	P			
Q	Q			
R	R			
S	S			
T	T			
U	U			
V	V			
W	W			
X	X			
Y	Y			
Z	Z			

9. Test Form

DO NOT OPEN THIS BOOK UNTIL THE SUPERVISOR TELLS YOU TO DO SO.

Use a No. 2 pencil only. Be sure each mark is dark and completely fills the intended oval. Completely erase any errors or stray marks.

1. Your Name

First 4 letters of Last Name | First init. | Mid. init.

A B C D E F G H I J K L M N O P Q R S T U V W X Y Z

2. Your Name: (Print) Last First M.I.

I agree to the conditions on the back of the SAT I test book.

Signature: Date: / /

Home Address: (Print) Number and Street

City State Zip Code

Center: (Print) City State Center Number

IMPORTANT: Fill in items 8 and 9 exactly as shown on the back of test book.

8. Form Code

(Copy and grid as on back of test book.)

3. Date of Birth

Month	Day	Year
Jan.		
Feb.		
Mar.	0 0	0 0
Apr.	1 1	1 1
May	2 2	2 2
June	3 3	3 3
July	4	4 4
Aug.	5	5 5
Sept.	6	6 6
Oct.	7	7 7
Nov.	8	8 8
Dec.	9	9

4. Social Security Number

0 1 2 3 4 5 6 7 8 9

5. Sex

Female Male

6. Registration Number

(Copy from Admission Ticket.)

0 1 2 3 4 5 6 7 8 9

7. Test Book Serial Number

(Copy from front of test book.)

0 1 2 3 4 5 6 7 8 9

FOR ETS USE ONLY

9. Test Form

(Copy from back of test book.)

Start with number 1 for each new section. If a section has fewer questions than answer spaces, leave the extra answer spaces blank.

SECTION 1

1–40 (A) (B) (C) (D) (E)

SECTION 2

1–40 (A) (B) (C) (D) (E)

Q2778-06/2 CHW98324 11027 • 09132 • TF129M17.5eX I.N. 207158
1 2 3 4

Use a No. 2 pencil only. Be sure each mark is dark and completely fills the intended oval. Completely erase any errors or stray marks.

Start with number 1 for each new section. If a section has fewer questions than answer spaces, leave the extra answer spaces blank.

SECTION 3

1 Ⓐ Ⓑ Ⓒ Ⓓ Ⓔ
2 Ⓐ Ⓑ Ⓒ Ⓓ Ⓔ
3 Ⓐ Ⓑ Ⓒ Ⓓ Ⓔ
4 Ⓐ Ⓑ Ⓒ Ⓓ Ⓔ
5 Ⓐ Ⓑ Ⓒ Ⓓ Ⓔ
6 Ⓐ Ⓑ Ⓒ Ⓓ Ⓔ
7 Ⓐ Ⓑ Ⓒ Ⓓ Ⓔ
8 Ⓐ Ⓑ Ⓒ Ⓓ Ⓔ
9 Ⓐ Ⓑ Ⓒ Ⓓ Ⓔ
10 Ⓐ Ⓑ Ⓒ Ⓓ Ⓔ
11 Ⓐ Ⓑ Ⓒ Ⓓ Ⓔ
12 Ⓐ Ⓑ Ⓒ Ⓓ Ⓔ
13 Ⓐ Ⓑ Ⓒ Ⓓ Ⓔ
14 Ⓐ Ⓑ Ⓒ Ⓓ Ⓔ
15 Ⓐ Ⓑ Ⓒ Ⓓ Ⓔ
16 Ⓐ Ⓑ Ⓒ Ⓓ Ⓔ
17 Ⓐ Ⓑ Ⓒ Ⓓ Ⓔ
18 Ⓐ Ⓑ Ⓒ Ⓓ Ⓔ
19 Ⓐ Ⓑ Ⓒ Ⓓ Ⓔ
20 Ⓐ Ⓑ Ⓒ Ⓓ Ⓔ
21 Ⓐ Ⓑ Ⓒ Ⓓ Ⓔ
22 Ⓐ Ⓑ Ⓒ Ⓓ Ⓔ
23 Ⓐ Ⓑ Ⓒ Ⓓ Ⓔ
24 Ⓐ Ⓑ Ⓒ Ⓓ Ⓔ
25 Ⓐ Ⓑ Ⓒ Ⓓ Ⓔ
26 Ⓐ Ⓑ Ⓒ Ⓓ Ⓔ
27 Ⓐ Ⓑ Ⓒ Ⓓ Ⓔ
28 Ⓐ Ⓑ Ⓒ Ⓓ Ⓔ
29 Ⓐ Ⓑ Ⓒ Ⓓ Ⓔ
30 Ⓐ Ⓑ Ⓒ Ⓓ Ⓔ
31 Ⓐ Ⓑ Ⓒ Ⓓ Ⓔ
32 Ⓐ Ⓑ Ⓒ Ⓓ Ⓔ
33 Ⓐ Ⓑ Ⓒ Ⓓ Ⓔ
34 Ⓐ Ⓑ Ⓒ Ⓓ Ⓔ
35 Ⓐ Ⓑ Ⓒ Ⓓ Ⓔ
36 Ⓐ Ⓑ Ⓒ Ⓓ Ⓔ
37 Ⓐ Ⓑ Ⓒ Ⓓ Ⓔ
38 Ⓐ Ⓑ Ⓒ Ⓓ Ⓔ
39 Ⓐ Ⓑ Ⓒ Ⓓ Ⓔ
40 Ⓐ Ⓑ Ⓒ Ⓓ Ⓔ

If section 3 of your test book contains math questions that are not multiple-choice, continue to item 16 below. Otherwise, continue to item 16 above.

ONLY ANSWERS ENTERED IN THE OVALS IN EACH GRID AREA WILL BE SCORED.
YOU WILL NOT RECEIVE CREDIT FOR ANYTHING WRITTEN IN THE BOXES ABOVE THE OVALS.

16 17 18 19 20

21 22 23 24 25

Each grid: / / in columns 2–3; . in all four columns; 0 in columns 2–4; 1 2 3 4 5 6 7 8 9 in all four columns.

BE SURE TO ERASE ANY ERRORS OR STRAY MARKS COMPLETELY.

DO NOT WRITE IN THIS AREA.

0

PLEASE PRINT YOUR INITIALS

First	Middle	Last

Use a No. 2 pencil only. Be sure each mark is dark and completely fills the intended oval. Completely erase any errors or stray marks.

Start with number 1 for each new section. If a section has fewer questions than answer spaces, leave the extra answer spaces blank.

SECTION 4

1 (A) (B) (C) (D) (E)
2 (A) (B) (C) (D) (E)
3 (A) (B) (C) (D) (E)
4 (A) (B) (C) (D) (E)
5 (A) (B) (C) (D) (E)
6 (A) (B) (C) (D) (E)
7 (A) (B) (C) (D) (E)
8 (A) (B) (C) (D) (E)
9 (A) (B) (C) (D) (E)
10 (A) (B) (C) (D) (E)
11 (A) (B) (C) (D) (E)
12 (A) (B) (C) (D) (E)
13 (A) (B) (C) (D) (E)
14 (A) (B) (C) (D) (E)
15 (A) (B) (C) (D) (E)
16 (A) (B) (C) (D) (E)
17 (A) (B) (C) (D) (E)
18 (A) (B) (C) (D) (E)
19 (A) (B) (C) (D) (E)
20 (A) (B) (C) (D) (E)
21 (A) (B) (C) (D) (E)
22 (A) (B) (C) (D) (E)
23 (A) (B) (C) (D) (E)
24 (A) (B) (C) (D) (E)
25 (A) (B) (C) (D) (E)
26 (A) (B) (C) (D) (E)
27 (A) (B) (C) (D) (E)
28 (A) (B) (C) (D) (E)
29 (A) (B) (C) (D) (E)
30 (A) (B) (C) (D) (E)
31 (A) (B) (C) (D) (E)
32 (A) (B) (C) (D) (E)
33 (A) (B) (C) (D) (E)
34 (A) (B) (C) (D) (E)
35 (A) (B) (C) (D) (E)
36 (A) (B) (C) (D) (E)
37 (A) (B) (C) (D) (E)
38 (A) (B) (C) (D) (E)
39 (A) (B) (C) (D) (E)
40 (A) (B) (C) (D) (E)

If section 4 of your test book contains math questions that are not multiple-choice, continue to item 16 below. Otherwise, continue to item 16 above.

ONLY ANSWERS ENTERED IN THE OVALS IN EACH GRID AREA WILL BE SCORED.
YOU WILL NOT RECEIVE CREDIT FOR ANYTHING WRITTEN IN THE BOXES ABOVE THE OVALS.

16 17 18 19 20 21 22 23 24 25

(Each grid: / / ; . . . . ; 0 0 0 ; 1 1 1 1 ; 2 2 2 2 ; 3 3 3 3 ; 4 4 4 4 ; 5 5 5 5 ; 6 6 6 6 ; 7 7 7 7 ; 8 8 8 8 ; 9 9 9 9)

BE SURE TO ERASE ANY ERRORS OR STRAY MARKS COMPLETELY.

DO NOT WRITE IN THIS AREA.

0

PLEASE PRINT YOUR INITIALS

First Middle Last

Use a No. 2 pencil only. Be sure each mark is dark and completely fills the intended oval. Completely erase any errors or stray marks.

Start with number 1 for each new section. If a section has fewer questions than answer spaces, leave the extra answer spaces blank.

SECTION 5

1 A B C D E	11 A B C D E	21 A B C D E	31 A B C D E
2 A B C D E	12 A B C D E	22 A B C D E	32 A B C D E
3 A B C D E	13 A B C D E	23 A B C D E	33 A B C D E
4 A B C D E	14 A B C D E	24 A B C D E	34 A B C D E
5 A B C D E	15 A B C D E	25 A B C D E	35 A B C D E
6 A B C D E	16 A B C D E	26 A B C D E	36 A B C D E
7 A B C D E	17 A B C D E	27 A B C D E	37 A B C D E
8 A B C D E	18 A B C D E	28 A B C D E	38 A B C D E
9 A B C D E	19 A B C D E	29 A B C D E	39 A B C D E
10 A B C D E	20 A B C D E	30 A B C D E	40 A B C D E

SECTION 6

1 A B C D E	6 A B C D E	11 A B C D E	16 A B C D E
2 A B C D E	7 A B C D E	12 A B C D E	17 A B C D E
3 A B C D E	8 A B C D E	13 A B C D E	18 A B C D E
4 A B C D E	9 A B C D E	14 A B C D E	19 A B C D E
5 A B C D E	10 A B C D E	15 A B C D E	20 A B C D E

SECTION 7

1 A B C D E	6 A B C D E	11 A B C D E	16 A B C D E
2 A B C D E	7 A B C D E	12 A B C D E	17 A B C D E
3 A B C D E	8 A B C D E	13 A B C D E	18 A B C D E
4 A B C D E	9 A B C D E	14 A B C D E	19 A B C D E
5 A B C D E	10 A B C D E	15 A B C D E	20 A B C D E

CERTIFICATION STATEMENT

Copy the statement below (do not print) and sign your name as you would an official document.

I hereby agree to the conditions set forth in the Registration Bulletin and certify that I am the person whose name and address appear on this answer sheet.

____

____

____

Signature: ______________________ Date: ______________

Section 1 1 1 1 1 1 1

Time—30 Minutes 25 Questions	**In this section solve each problem, using any available space on the page for scratchwork. Then decide which is the best of the choices given and fill in the corresponding oval on the answer sheet.**

Notes:

1. The use of a calculator is permitted. All numbers used are real numbers.
2. Figures that accompany problems in this test are intended to provide information useful in solving the problems. They are drawn as accurately as possible EXCEPT when it is stated in a specific problem that the figure is not drawn to scale. All figures lie in a plane unless otherwise indicated.

Reference Information

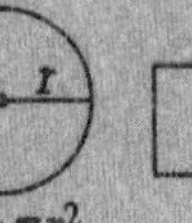
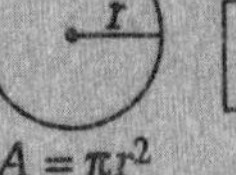
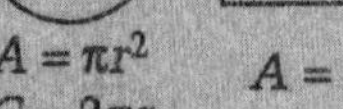

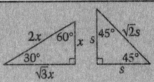

$A = \pi r^2$
$C = 2\pi r$

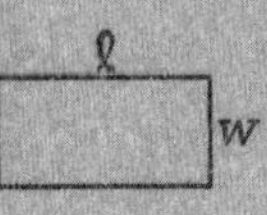

$A = \ell w$

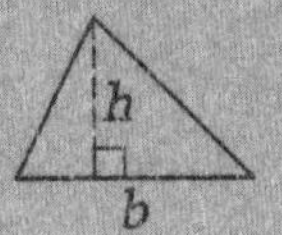

$A = \frac{1}{2}bh$

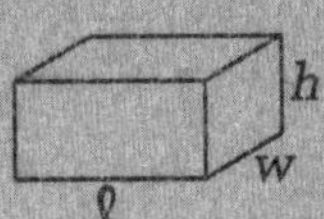

$V = \ell wh$

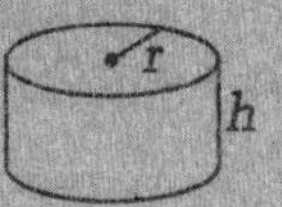

$V = \pi r^2 h$

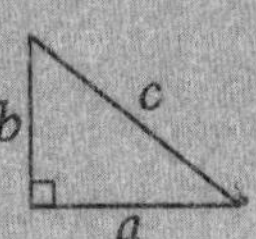

$c^2 = a^2 + b^2$

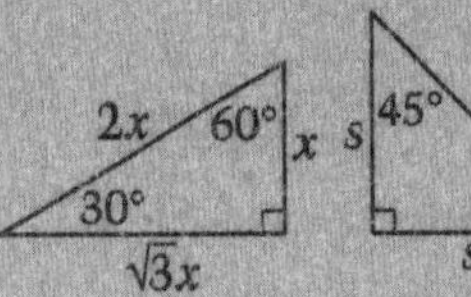

Special Right Triangles

The number of degrees of arc in a circle is 360.
The measure in degrees of a straight angle is 180.
The sum of the measures in degrees of the angles of a triangle is 180.

1. How many bottles, each holding 8 fluid ounces, are needed to hold 3 quarts of cider? (1 quart = 32 fluid ounces)

(A) 8
(B) 12
(C) 14
(D) 16
(E) 18

2. If $x + 7$ is an even integer, then x could be which of the following?

(A) −2
(B) −1
(C) 0
(D) 2
(E) 4

3. If $(n + 3)(9 - 5) = 16$, then $n =$

(A) 1
(B) 4
(C) 7
(D) 9
(E) 15

GO ON TO THE NEXT PAGE

$$\frac{4}{n}, \frac{5}{n}, \frac{7}{n}$$

4 If each of the fractions above is in its simplest reduced form, which of the following could be the value of n ?

(A) 24
(B) 25
(C) 26
(D) 27
(E) 28

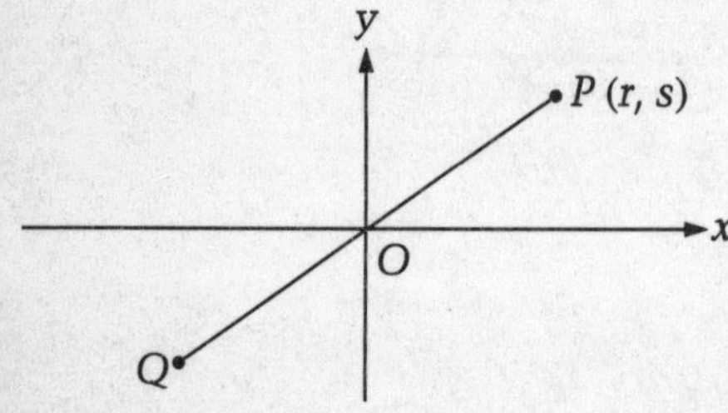

5 In the figure above, if PQ is a line segment and $PO = OQ$, what are the coordinates of point Q ?

(A) (s, r)
(B) $(s, -r)$
(C) $(-s, -r)$
(D) $(-r, s)$
(E) $(-r, -s)$

6 A certain building has 2,600 square feet of surface that needs to be painted. If 1 gallon of paint will cover 250 square feet, what is the least whole number of gallons that must be purchased in order to have enough paint to apply one coat to the surface? (Assume that only whole gallons of paint can be purchased.)

(A) 5
(B) 10
(C) 11
(D) 15
(E) 110

7 The number p is 4 more than 3 times the number r. The sum of p and r is 10. Which of the following pairs of equations could be used to find the values of p and r ?

(A) $p = 3r + 4$
$p + r = 10$

(B) $p = 3r + 4$
$pr = 10$

(C) $p = 3(r + 4)$
$p + r = 10$

(D) $p + 4 = 3r$
$p + r = 10$

(E) $p + 4 = 3r$
$pr = 10$

GO ON TO THE NEXT PAGE

8 Let a "k-triple" be defined as $(\frac{k}{2}, k, \frac{3}{2}k)$ for some number k. Which of the following is a k-triple?

(A) (0, 5, 10)
(B) $(4\frac{1}{2}, 5, 6\frac{1}{2})$
(C) (25, 50, 75)
(D) (250, 500, 1000)
(E) (450, 500, 650)

9 If the vertices of a square are at (–3, 4), (3, 4), (3, –2), and (–3, –2), what is the area of the square?

(A) 12
(B) 16
(C) 24
(D) 25
(E) 36

10 When a certain rectangle is divided in half, two squares are formed. If each of these squares has perimeter 48, what is the perimeter of the original rectangle?

(A) 96
(B) 72
(C) 36
(D) 24
(E) 12

11 If a ball is thrown straight up at a certain speed, its height h, in feet, after t seconds is given by the formula $h = 40t - 16t^2$. How many feet high will the ball be one second after it is thrown?

(A) 12
(B) 16
(C) 24
(D) 32
(E) 40

12 Which of the following sets of numbers has the property that the product of any two numbers in the set is also a number in the set?

I. The set of even integers
II. The set of prime numbers
III. The set of positive numbers

(A) I only
(B) II only
(C) I and III only
(D) II and III only
(E) I, II, and III

GO ON TO THE NEXT PAGE

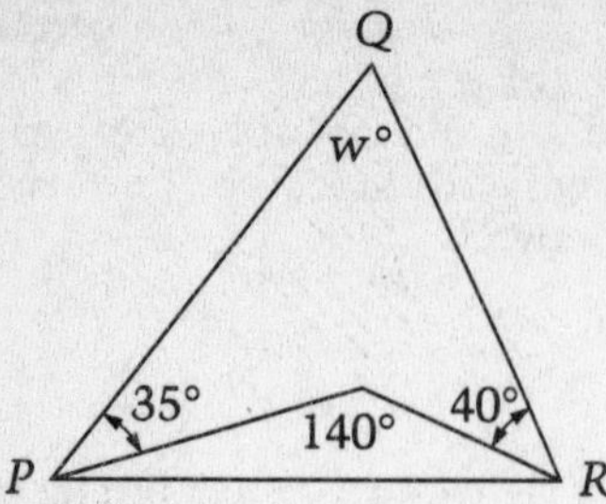

13 In ΔPQR above, $w =$

(A) 50
(B) 55
(C) 60
(D) 65
(E) 75

14 A class of 30 girls and 40 boys sponsored a hayride. If 60 percent of the girls and 25 percent of the boys went on the ride, what percent of the class went on the ride?

(A) 30%
(B) 35%
(C) 40%
(D) 50%
(E) 70%

15 If $x = yz$, which of the following must be equal to xy?

(A) yz

(B) yz^2

(C) y^2z

(D) $\frac{x}{y}$

(E) $\frac{z}{x}$

16 Which of the following operations has the same effect as dividing by $\frac{4}{3}$ and then multiplying by $\frac{2}{3}$?

(A) Multiplying by $\frac{1}{2}$

(B) Multiplying by 2

(C) Dividing by $\frac{1}{2}$

(D) Dividing by 3

(E) Dividing by 4

GO ON TO THE NEXT PAGE

17 The average (arithmetic mean) of a, b, s, and t is 6 and the average of s and t is 3. What is the average of a and b ?

(A) 3

(B) $\frac{9}{2}$

(C) 6

(D) 9

(E) 12

18 During a sale at a music store, if a customer buys one tape at full price, the customer is given a 50 percent discount on a second tape of equal or lesser value. If Linda buys two tapes that have full prices of \$15 and \$10, by what percent is the total cost of the two tapes reduced during this sale?

(A) 5%
(B) 20%
(C) 25%
(D) 30%
(E) 50%

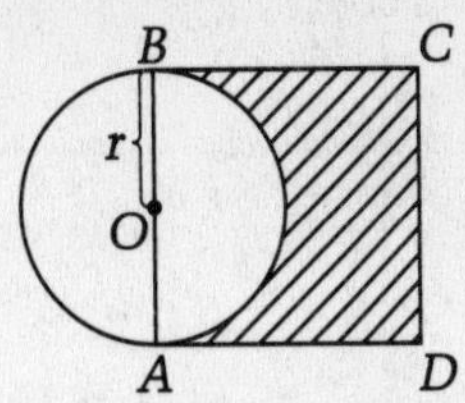

19 In the figure above, AB is a diameter of the circle with center O and $ABCD$ is a square. What is the area of the shaded region in terms of r ?

(A) $\pi(r^2 - 4)$

(B) $\pi(4 - \pi)$

(C) $r^2(\pi - 2)$

(D) $r^2(4 - \frac{\pi}{2})$

(E) $r^2(2 - \frac{\pi}{2})$

20 If the sum of 4 consecutive integers is f, then, in terms of f, what is the least of these integers?

(A) $\frac{f}{4}$

(B) $\frac{f-2}{4}$

(C) $\frac{f-3}{4}$

(D) $\frac{f-4}{4}$

(E) $\frac{f-6}{4}$

GO ON TO THE NEXT PAGE

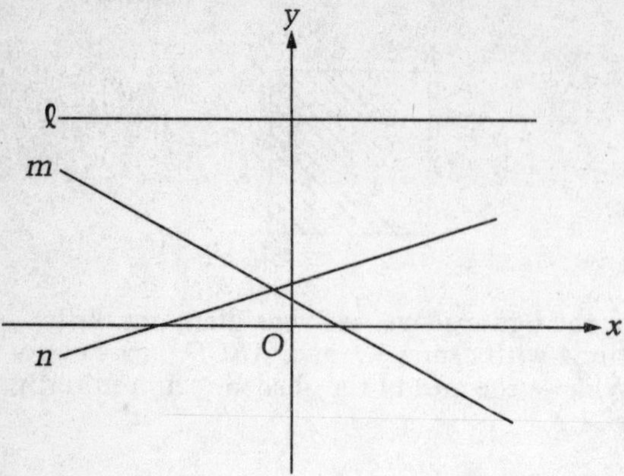

21 In the figure above, lines ℓ, m, and n have slopes r, s, and t, respectively. Which of the following is a correct ordering of these slopes?

(A) $r < s < t$
(B) $r < t < s$
(C) $s < r < t$
(D) $s < t < r$
(E) $t < s < r$

22 In the equation $S = 3\pi r^2$, if the value of r is doubled, then the value of S is multiplied by

(A) $\frac{1}{2}$

(B) 2

(C) 3

(D) 4

(E) 8

23 Excluding rest stops, it took Juanita a total of 10 hours to hike from the base of a mountain to the top and back down again by the same path. If while hiking she averaged 2 kilometers per hour going up and 3 kilometers per hour coming down, how many kilometers was it from the base to the top of the mountain?

(A) 8
(B) 10
(C) 12
(D) 20
(E) 24

24 If $-1 < x < 0$, which of the following statements must be true?

(A) $x < x^2 < x^3$
(B) $x < x^3 < x^2$
(C) $x^2 < x < x^3$
(D) $x^2 < x^3 < x$
(E) $x^3 < x < x^2$

25 One side of a triangle has length 6 and a second side has length 7. Which of the following could be the area of this triangle?

I. 13
II. 21
III. 24

(A) I only
(B) II only
(C) III only
(D) I and II only
(E) I, II, and III

IF YOU FINISH BEFORE TIME IS CALLED, YOU MAY CHECK YOUR WORK ON THIS SECTION ONLY. DO NOT TURN TO ANY OTHER SECTION IN THE TEST.

Section 2 2 2 2 2 2

Time—30 Minutes
35 Questions

For each question in this section, select the best answer from among the choices given and fill in the corresponding oval on the answer sheet.

Each sentence below has one or two blanks, each blank indicating that something has been omitted. Beneath the sentence are five words or sets of words labeled A through E. Choose the word or set of words that, when inserted in the sentence, best fits the meaning of the sentence as a whole.

Example:

Medieval kingdoms did not become constitutional republics overnight; on the contrary, the change was ----.

(A) unpopular
(B) unexpected
(C) advantageous
(D) sufficient
(E) gradual

1 The spacecraft has two ---- sets of electronic components; if one fails, its duplicate will still function.

(A) divergent (B) identical (C) simulated (D) mutual (E) prohibitive

2 Only if business continues to expand can it ---- enough new jobs to make up for those that will be ---- by automation.

(A) produce. .required
(B) invent. .introduced
(C) create. .eliminated
(D) repeal. .reduced
(E) formulate. .engendered

3 Trinkets intended to have only ---- appeal can exist virtually forever in landfills because of the ---- of some plastics.

(A) arbitrary. .scarcity
(B) theoretical. .resilience
(C) ephemeral. .durability
(D) obsessive. .fragility
(E) impetuous. .cheapness

4 Despite years of poverty and ----, the poet Ruth Pitter produced work that is now ---- by a range of literary critics.

(A) security. .hailed
(B) depression. .criticized
(C) celebrity. .publicized
(D) inactivity. .undermined
(E) adversity. .acclaimed

5 Teachers are, in effect, encouraging ---- when they fail to enforce rules governing the time allowed to students for completion of their assignments.

(A) conformity (B) procrastination (C) impartiality (D) scholarship (E) plagiarism

6 Although surfing is often ---- as merely a modern pastime, it is actually ---- practice, invented long ago by the Hawaiians to maneuver through the surf.

(A) touted. .a universal
(B) depicted. .an impractical
(C) incorporated. .a leisurely
(D) overestimated. .a high-spirited
(E) dismissed. .a time-honored

7 Fungus beetles are quite ----: they seldom move more than the few yards between fungi, their primary food.

(A) pugnacious (B) sedentary (C) gregarious (D) capricious (E) carnivorous

8 Many linguists believe that our ability to learn language is at least in part ----, that it is somehow woven into our genetic makeup.

(A) innate (B) accidental (C) empirical (D) transitory (E) incremental

9 An apparently gratuitous gesture, whether it is spiteful or solicitous, arouses our suspicion, while a gesture recognized to be ---- gives no reason for surprise.

(A) warranted (B) dubious (C) affected (D) benevolent (E) rancorous

10 The student's feelings about presenting the commencement address were ----; although visibly happy to have been chosen, he was nonetheless ---- about speaking in public.

(A) positive. .insecure
(B) euphoric. .hopeful
(C) unknown. .modest
(D) ambivalent. .anxious
(E) restrained. .confident

GO ON TO THE NEXT PAGE

2 2 2 2 2 2 2 2

Each question below consists of a related pair of words or phrases, followed by five pairs of words or phrases labeled A through E. Select the pair that best expresses a relationship similar to that expressed in the original pair.

Example:

CRUMB : BREAD ::
(A) ounce : unit
(B) splinter : wood
(C) water : bucket
(D) twine : rope
(E) cream : butter

11 RECUPERATE : SURGERY ::
(A) restore : furniture
(B) cleanse : alcohol
(C) cure : illness
(D) revive : faint
(E) hospitalize : patient

12 SKETCH : ARTIST ::
(A) secret : confidant
(B) palette : painter
(C) cell : prisoner
(D) draft : writer
(E) chisel : sculptor

13 YEARN : LONGING ::
(A) beware : danger
(B) rush : patience
(C) enjoy : pleasure
(D) suppress : rage
(E) sleep : insomnia

14 FREIGHT : TRUCK ::
(A) goods : warehouse
(B) customers : store
(C) stevedores : ship
(D) engine : train
(E) passengers : bus

15 CHAT : CONVERSE ::
(A) allege : deny
(B) halt : traverse
(C) purchase : rent
(D) study : learn
(E) browse : read

16 COLLAGE : IMAGES ::
(A) medley : songs
(B) book : volumes
(C) survey : lands
(D) collection : lists
(E) assembly : bills

17 ABASH : EMBARRASSMENT ::
(A) dislike : hypocrisy
(B) pretend : imagination
(C) annoy : irritation
(D) suspect : illegality
(E) demolish : renovation

18 TERRESTRIAL : LAND ::
(A) vegetarian : plants
(B) predatory : animal
(C) nocturnal : day
(D) arid : desert
(E) aquatic : water

19 TRIAL : JURY ::
(A) dispute : arbiter
(B) poll : contestant
(C) championship : spectator
(D) conference : speaker
(E) match : competitor

20 WEDDING : MARRIAGE ::
(A) birthday : cake
(B) coronation : reign
(C) graduation : diploma
(D) promotion : job
(E) decoration : bravery

21 SALVE : WOUND ::
(A) utter : apology
(B) exploit : weakness
(C) mollify : anger
(D) squander : opportunity
(E) emulate : achievement

22 REFUGEE : ASYLUM ::
(A) astronaut : capsule
(B) perfectionist : frustration
(C) consumer : impulse
(D) opportunist : advantage
(E) director : stage

23 MYSTIFY : UNDERSTANDING ::
(A) nip : maturation
(B) insure : disaster
(C) rearrange : order
(D) intensify : endurance
(E) reciprocate : interchange

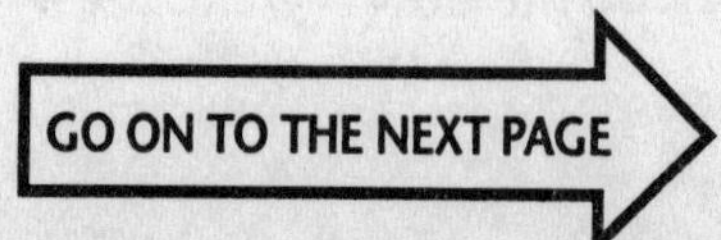

The passage below is followed by questions based on its content. Answer the questions on the basis of what is stated or implied in the passage and in any introductory material that may be provided.

Questions 24-35 are based on the following passage.

During the 1830's, Parisians began to refer to artistic individuals who pursued unconventional life-styles as Bohemians. The Bohemian world—Bohemia—fascinated members of the bourgeoisie, the conventional and materialistic middle class of French society.

"Bohemia, bordered on the North by hope, work and gaiety; on the South by necessity and courage; on the West and East by slander and the hospital."

Henry Murger (1822-1861)

For its nineteenth-century discoverers and explorers, Bohemia was an identifiable country with visible inhabitants, but one not marked on any map. To trace its frontiers was to cross constantly back and forth between reality and fantasy.

Explorers recognized Bohemia by certain signs: art, youth, socially defiant behavior, the vagabond life-style. To Henry Murger, the most influential mapper, Bohemia was the realm of young artists struggling to surmount the barriers poverty erected against their vocations, "all those who, driven by an unstinting sense of calling, enter into art with no other means of existence than art itself." They lived in Bohemia because they could not—or not yet—establish their citizenship anywhere else. Ambitious, dedicated, but without means and unrecognized, they had to turn life itself into an art: "Their everyday existence is a work of genius."

Yet even Murger admitted that not all Bohemians were future artists. Other reporters did not think even the majority were future artists. To that sharp-eyed social anatomist Balzac*, Bohemia was more simply the country of youth. All the most talented and promising young people lived in it, those in their twenties who had not yet made their names but who were destined eventually to lead their nation. "In fact all kinds of ability, of talent, are represented there. It is a microcosm. If the emperor of Russia bought up Bohemia for twenty million—assuming it were willing to take leave of the boulevard pavements—and transferred it to Odessa, in a year Odessa would be Paris." In its genius for life, Balzac's Bohemia resembled Murger's. "Bohemia has nothing and lives from what it has. Hope is its religion, faith in itself its code, charity is all it has for a budget."

Artists and the young were not alone in their ability to make more of life than objective conditions seemed to permit. Some who were called Bohemians did so in more murky and mysterious ways, in the darker corners of society. "By Bohemians," a well-known theater owner of the 1840's declared, "I understand that class of individuals whose existence is a problem, social condition a myth, fortune an enigma, who are located nowhere and who one encounters everywhere! Rich today, famished tomorrow, ready to live honestly if they can and some other way if they can't." The nature of these Bohemians was less easy to specify than either Murger's or Balzac's definitions. They might be unrecognized geniuses or swindlers. The designation "Bohemian" located them in a twilight zone between ingenuity and criminality.

These alternative images of Bohemia are ones we still recognize when we use the term: more recent incarnations like the Beat Generation of the 1950's or the hippiedom of the 1960's contained these real or potential elements, too. Artistic, youthful, unattached, inventive, or suspect, Bohemian styles are recurring features of modern life. Have they not always existed in Western society? In a way, yes: wandering medieval poets and eighteenth-century literary hacks also exhibited features of Bohemians. But written references to Bohemia as a special, identifiable kind of life appear initially in the nineteenth century. It was in the France of the 1830's and 1840's that the terms "Bohemia," "*La Bohème*," and "Bohemian" first appeared in this sense. The new vocabulary played on the common French word for gypsy—*bohémien*—which erroneously identified the province of Bohemia, part of old Czechoslovakia, as the gypsies' place of origin.

From the start, Bohemianism took shape by contrast with the image with which it was commonly paired: bourgeois life. The opposition is so well established and comes so easily to mind that it may mislead us, for it implies a form of

GO ON TO THE NEXT PAGE

separation and an intensity of hostility often belied by experience. Bohemia has always exercised a powerful attraction on many solid bourgeois, matched by the deeply bourgeois instincts and aspirations of numerous Bohemians. This mysterious convergence sometimes leads to accusations of insincerity, even dishonesty: "Scratch a Bohemian, find a bourgeois." But the quality revealed by scraping away that false appearance of opposition is seldom hypocrisy. Like positive and negative magnetic poles, Bohemian and bourgeois were—and are—parts of a single field: they imply, require, and attract each other.

*French novelist (1799-1850)

24 The passage is best described as

(A) a refutation of an ancient misconception
(B) a definition of a concept
(C) a discussion of one historical era
(D) a catalog of nineteenth-century biases
(E) an example of a class struggle

25 In the quotation at the beginning of the passage (lines 1-3), Bohemia is presented in terms of

(A) an extended metaphor
(B) a complex argument
(C) geographic distances
(D) a logical paradox
(E) popular legend

26 Murger's Bohemians would differ most from the bourgeois in that Bohemians

(A) are motivated by strong artistic impulses
(B) are primarily political reactionaries
(C) have higher social status than the bourgeois
(D) prefer to live off inherited wealth and the generosity of friends
(E) prefer an anarchic social order to a stable one

27 In line 17, Murger uses the word "unstinting" to emphasize the Bohemians'

(A) desire for wealth
(B) power to assimilate bourgeois ideals
(C) reservations about society
(D) dedication to their goals
(E) generous nature

28 The quotation in lines 23-24 ("Their . . . genius") can best be interpreted to mean that the Bohemians

(A) are lucky to be alive
(B) are highly successful achievers
(C) are spirited and creative in spite of meager resources
(D) live at the expense of the bourgeois
(E) live chiefly by deceit, theft, and violation of accepted social codes

29 The quotations from Murger suggest that he viewed the Bohemians with

(A) reserve and suspicion
(B) benevolence yet perplexity
(C) amusement and superiority
(D) timidity and fear
(E) interest and admiration

30 In contrast to Murger's Bohemia, Balzac's Bohemia was composed of

(A) young artists struggling in poverty
(B) young bourgeois playing with a new social role
(C) the criminal as well as the genuine
(D) talented artists working together
(E) talented youths seeking to build their futures

31 In line 44, "objective" most nearly means

(A) unassuming
(B) fair
(C) intentional
(D) material
(E) detached

GO ON TO THE NEXT PAGE

32 The quotation in lines 47-55 most probably reflects the point of view of

(A) the gypsies
(B) Murger
(C) Balzac
(D) some Bohemians
(E) some bourgeois

33 Which statement best summarizes the point made in lines 61-71 ?

(A) Bohemians have always been subjected to suspicion and scorn.
(B) The Bohemian is an inescapable feature of urban society.
(C) Bohemianism, as a way of life, is not unique to the nineteenth century.
(D) Eighteenth-century Bohemia was similar to nineteenth-century Bohemia.
(E) The province of Bohemia was home to aspiring young artists.

34 The statement in lines 92-93 ("Scratch . . . bourgeois") is best interpreted as conveying

(A) skepticism about the Bohemians' commitment to their life-style
(B) a desire to study the Bohemian life-style
(C) distrust of both the Bohemian and the bourgeois worlds
(D) a lack of appreciation of the arts
(E) envy of the artist's uncomplicated life-style

35 Which statement best summarizes the author's argument in the last paragraph?

(A) Bohemians were purposely misleading in their actions.
(B) Bohemians received considerable financial support from bourgeois customers.
(C) Bohemians and bourgeois were more similar than is often realized.
(D) Bourgeois were oblivious to the struggles of Bohemians.
(E) Bourgeois and Bohemians inherited the same cultural traditions from their ancestors.

IF YOU FINISH BEFORE TIME IS CALLED, YOU MAY CHECK YOUR WORK ON THIS SECTION ONLY. DO NOT TURN TO ANY OTHER SECTION IN THE TEST. **STOP**

Section 3 3 3 3 3 3 3

Time—30 Minutes 25 Questions	**This section contains two types of questions. You have 30 minutes to complete both types. You may use any available space for scratchwork.**

Notes:

1. The use of a calculator is permitted. All numbers used are real numbers.
2. Figures that accompany problems in this test are intended to provide information useful in solving the problems. They are drawn as accurately as possible EXCEPT when it is stated in a specific problem that the figure is not drawn to scale. All figures lie in a plane unless otherwise indicated.

Reference Information

$A = \pi r^2$, $C = 2\pi r$; $A = \ell w$; $A = \frac{1}{2}bh$; $V = \ell wh$; $V = \pi r^2 h$; $c^2 = a^2 + b^2$

Special Right Triangles: $2x$, $60°$, x, $30°$, $\sqrt{3}x$; s, $45°$, $\sqrt{2}s$, $45°$, s

The number of degrees of arc in a circle is 360.
The measure in degrees of a straight angle is 180.
The sum of the measures in degrees of the angles of a triangle is 180.

Directions for Quantitative Comparison Questions

Questions 1-15 each consist of two quantities in boxes, one in Column A and one in Column B. You are to compare the two quantities and on the answer sheet fill in oval

A if the quantity in Column A is greater;
B if the quantity in Column B is greater;
C if the two quantities are equal;
D if the relationship cannot be determined from the information given.

AN E RESPONSE WILL NOT BE SCORED.

Notes:

1. In some questions, information is given about one or both of the quantities to be compared. In such cases, the given information is centered above the two columns and is not boxed.
2. In a given question, a symbol that appears in both columns represents the same thing in Column A as it does in Column B.
3. Letters such as x, n, and k stand for real numbers.

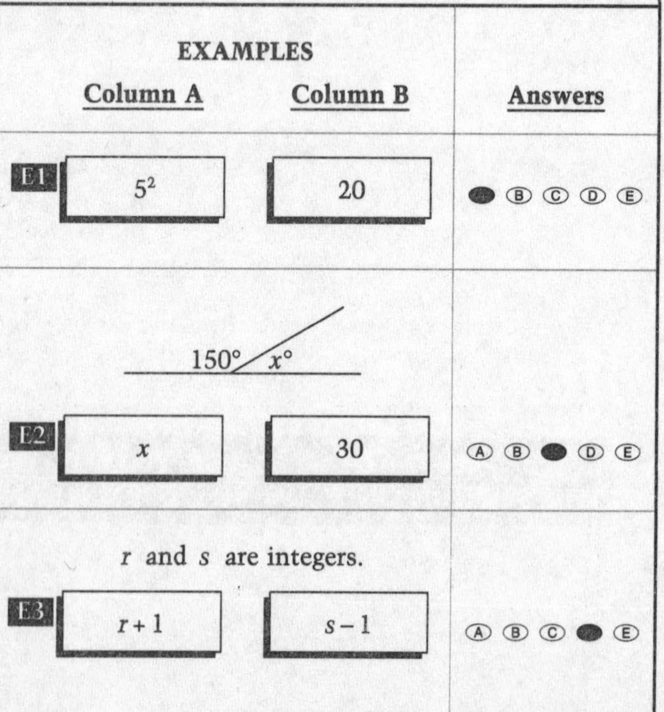

EXAMPLES

	Column A	Column B	Answers
E1	5^2	20	● Ⓑ Ⓒ Ⓓ Ⓔ
	150° x°		
E2	x	30	Ⓐ Ⓑ ● Ⓓ Ⓔ
	r and s are integers.		
E3	$r + 1$	$s - 1$	Ⓐ Ⓑ Ⓒ ● Ⓔ

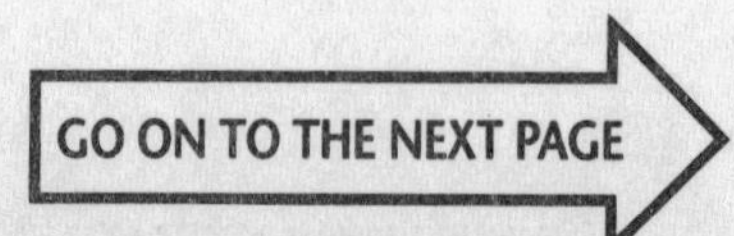

3 3 3 3 3 3 3 3 3

SUMMARY DIRECTIONS FOR COMPARISON QUESTIONS

Answer: A if the quantity in Column A is greater;
B if the quantity in Column B is greater;
C if the two quantities are equal;
D if the relationship cannot be determined from the information given.

	Column A	Column B
1	$\frac{3}{2} - \frac{1}{2}$	$\frac{7}{8} - \frac{1}{8}$

$rs = 0$

	Column A	Column B
2	r	0

$x^3 = y$

	Column A	Column B
3	x^6	y^2

	Column A	Column B
4	The circumference of a circle with radius 2	The sum of the circumferences of two circles, each with radius 1

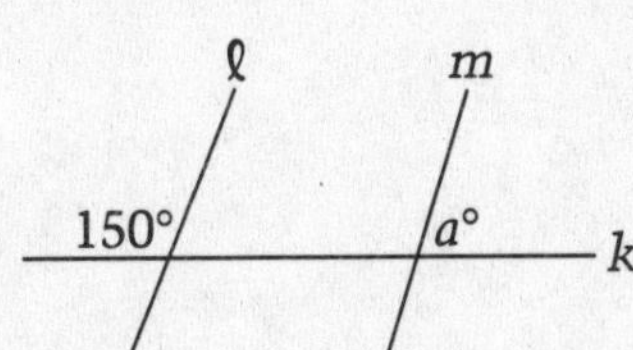

Note: Figure not drawn to scale.

$\ell \parallel m$

	Column A	Column B
5	$5a$	150

The average (arithmetic mean) of f and g is greater than the average of f and h.

	Column A	Column B
6	h	g

$t + v = 76$
$t \neq 5$

	Column A	Column B
7	v	71

For all positive integers a and b, let $\overline{a\rfloor b}$ be defined as $\overline{a\rfloor b} = ab - (a + b)$.

	Column A	Column B
8	$\overline{5\rfloor 2}$	$\overline{2\rfloor 5}$

	Column A	Column B
9	The perimeter of a rectangle with area 10	The perimeter of a rectangle with area 12

GO ON TO THE NEXT PAGE

SUMMARY DIRECTIONS FOR COMPARISON QUESTIONS

Answer: A if the quantity in Column A is greater;
B if the quantity in Column B is greater;
C if the two quantities are equal;
D if the relationship cannot be determined from the information given.

	Column A	Column B
	$r + 3 > 5$	
10	$r + 2$	4
	$6x - 2y < 0$	
11	x	0

Set T consists of all of the 3-digit numbers greater than 450 that contain the digits 2, 4, and 5 with no digit repeated.

	Column A	Column B
12	The number of 3-digit numbers in set T	4

Points A and B lie on a circle. Line segment AB does not pass through the center of the circle. The length of line segment AB is 16.

	Column A	Column B
13	The circumference of the circle	16π

$$\frac{x}{3} = \frac{y}{6}$$

	Column A	Column B
14	$\frac{x+1}{3}$	$\frac{y+1}{6}$

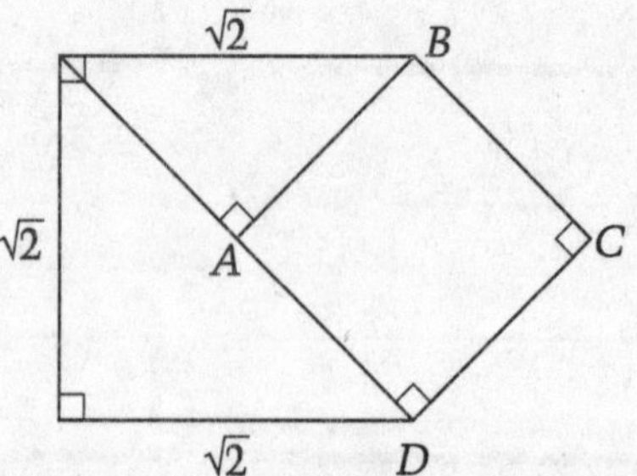

	Column A	Column B
15	The area of square $ABCD$	$\sqrt{2}$

GO ON TO THE NEXT PAGE

Directions for Student-Produced Response Questions

Each of the remaining 10 questions requires you to solve the problem and enter your answer by marking the ovals in the special grid, as shown in the examples below.

Answer: $\frac{7}{12}$ or 7/12 — Write answer in boxes. (7 / 1 2) — Fraction line — Grid in result.

Answer: 2.5 — (2 . 5) — Decimal point

Answer: 201 — Either position is correct. (2 0 1 | 2 0 1)

Note: You may start your answers in any column, space permitting. Columns not needed should be left blank.

- Mark no more than one oval in any column.
- Because the answer sheet will be machine-scored, **you will receive credit only if the ovals are filled in correctly.**
- Although not required, it is suggested that you write your answer in the boxes at the top of the columns to help you fill in the ovals accurately.
- Some problems may have more than one correct answer. In such cases, grid only one answer.
- No question has a negative answer.
- **Mixed numbers** such as $2\frac{1}{2}$ must be gridded as 2.5 or 5/2. (If 2 1 / 2 is gridded, it will be interpreted as $\frac{21}{2}$, not $2\frac{1}{2}$.)

- **Decimal Accuracy:** If you obtain a decimal answer, **enter the most accurate value the grid will accommodate.** For example, if you obtain an answer such as 0.6666 . . . , you should record the result as .666 or .667. **Less accurate values such as .66 or .67 are not acceptable.**

Acceptable ways to grid $\frac{2}{3}$ = .6666 . . .

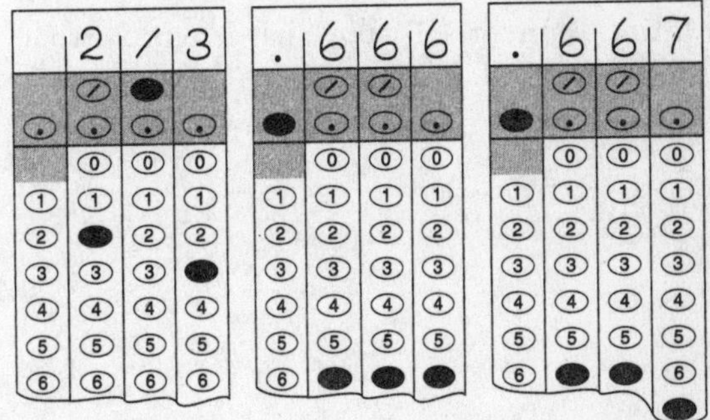

50° 2x° ℓ

16 In the figure above, what is the value of x ?

17 If $(x+2)^2 = 25$ and $x > 0$, what is the value of x^2 ?

GO ON TO THE NEXT PAGE

TRACK MEET AMONG SCHOOLS A, B, AND C

	First Place (5 points)	Second Place (3 points)	Third Place (1 point)
Event I	A		
Event II	A	B	
Event III		C	

18 A partially completed scorecard for a track meet is shown above. Schools A, B, and C each entered one person in each of the three events and there were no ties. What is one possible total score for School C? (Assume that all points are awarded in each event.)

R —— $6k$ —— S —— $4k$ —— T

19 If line segment RT above has length 5, what is the value of k?

$$\begin{array}{r} 7 \\ 4 \\ x \\ y \\ +\ 5 \\ \hline 32 \end{array} \qquad \begin{array}{r} 7 \\ 4 \\ x \\ z \\ +\ 5 \\ \hline 52 \end{array}$$

20 In the correctly worked addition problems above, what is the value of $z - y$?

21 Assume that $\frac{1}{4}$ quart of lemonade concentrate is mixed with $1\frac{3}{4}$ quarts of water to make lemonade for 4 people. How many quarts of lemonade concentrate are needed to make lemonade at the same strength for 14 people?

GO ON TO THE NEXT PAGE

22 Let $k \phi j$ be defined as the sum of all integers between k and j. For example, $5 \phi 9 = 6 + 7 + 8 = 21$. What is the value of $(80 \phi 110) - (81 \phi 109)$?

23 In 1980 the ratio of male students to female students at Frost College was 2 males to 3 females. Since then, the enrollment of male students in the college has increased by 400 and the enrollment of female students has remained the same. The ratio of males to females is currently 1 to 1. How many students are currently enrolled at Frost College?

24 A triangle has a base of length 13 and the other two sides are equal in length. If the lengths of the sides of the triangle are integers, what is the shortest possible length of a side?

25 In a stack of six cards, each card is labeled with a different integer 0 through 5. If two cards are selected at random without replacement, what is the probability that their sum will be 3 ?

IF YOU FINISH BEFORE TIME IS CALLED, YOU MAY CHECK YOUR WORK ON THIS SECTION ONLY. DO NOT TURN TO ANY OTHER SECTION IN THE TEST.

Section 4 4 4 4 4

Time—30 Minutes
30 Questions

For each question in this section, select the best answer from among the choices given and fill in the corresponding oval on the answer sheet.

Each sentence below has one or two blanks, each blank indicating that something has been omitted. Beneath the sentence are five words or sets of words labeled A through E. Choose the word or set of words that, when inserted in the sentence, best fits the meaning of the sentence as a whole.

Example:

Medieval kingdoms did not become constitutional republics overnight; on the contrary, the change was ----.

(A) unpopular
(B) unexpected
(C) advantageous
(D) sufficient
(E) gradual

1 Fearing excessive publicity, the patient refused to discuss her situation without a promise of ---- from the interviewer.

(A) empathy (B) abstinence
(C) attribution (D) confidentiality
(E) candor

2 Ed's great skills as a basketball player ---- his ---- stature, enabling him to compete successfully against much taller opponents.

(A) reveal. .gargantuan
(B) emphasize. .modest
(C) detract from. .lofty
(D) compensate for. .diminutive
(E) contrast with. .towering

3 The biologist's discovery was truly ----: it occurred not because of any new thinking or diligent effort but because he mistakenly left a few test tubes out of the refrigerator overnight.

(A) assiduous (B) insightful (C) fortuitous
(D) exemplary (E) ominous

4 Alice Walker's *The Temple of My Familiar*, far from being a tight, ---- narrative, is instead ---- novel that roams freely and imaginatively over a half-million years.

(A) traditional. .a chronological
(B) provocative. .an insensitive
(C) forceful. .a concise
(D) focused. .an expansive
(E) circuitous. .a discursive

5 In sharp contrast to the previous night's revelry, the wedding was ---- affair.

(A) a fervent
(B) a dignified
(C) a chaotic
(D) an ingenious
(E) a jubilant

6 The theory of the ---- of cultures argues that all societies with highly developed technologies will evolve similar social institutions.

(A) isolation
(B) aesthetics
(C) convergence
(D) fragmentation
(E) longevity

7 Both by ---- and by gender, American painter Mary Cassatt was an ----, because her artistic peers were French men.

(A) background. .amateur
(B) citizenship. .intellectual
(C) nationality. .anomaly
(D) style. .advocate
(E) skill. .expert

8 She told the conference that, far from having to be ---- subjects of an ---- technology, human beings can actually control the system to improve their collective future.

(A) loyal. .inconsequential
(B) passive. .ungovernable
(C) diligent. .experimental
(D) reluctant. .impeccable
(E) zealous. .incompatible

9 Like a charlatan, Harry tried to ---- the audience with ---- evidence.

(A) confuse. .cogent
(B) persuade. .incontrovertible
(C) dupe. .spurious
(D) educate. .devious
(E) enthrall. .substantiated

GO ON TO THE NEXT PAGE

Each question below consists of a related pair of words or phrases, followed by five pairs of words or phrases labeled A through E. Select the pair that best expresses a relationship similar to that expressed in the original pair.

Example:

CRUMB : BREAD ::
(A) ounce : unit
(B) splinter : wood
(C) water : bucket
(D) twine : rope
(E) cream : butter

10 ACTOR : CAST ::
(A) musician : orchestra
(B) singer : song
(C) lecturer : class
(D) congregation : church
(E) proofreader : text

11 BORDER : COUNTRY ::
(A) current : river
(B) water : lake
(C) waves : sea
(D) horizon : sunset
(E) shore : ocean

12 CATALOG : SHOPPER ::
(A) contract : lawyer
(B) schedule : worker
(C) menu : diner
(D) article : author
(E) bank : teller

13 VOLATILE : VAPORIZE ::
(A) translucent : illuminate
(B) brittle : bend
(C) frigid : chill
(D) ponderous : lift
(E) soluble : dissolve

14 BUTTRESS : SUPPORT ::
(A) encore : applause
(B) ornament : decoration
(C) choreography : dance
(D) prayer : religion
(E) thesis : evidence

15 ICONOCLAST : ORTHODOXY ::
(A) scientist : theory
(B) impostor : identity
(C) libertarian : tyranny
(D) conformist : expectation
(E) soldier : combat

GO ON TO THE NEXT PAGE

Each passage below is followed by questions based on its content. Answer the questions on the basis of what is stated or implied in the passage and in any introductory material that may be provided.

Questions 16-22 are based on the following passage.

This passage is from a book written by a Chinese American woman about Chinese American women writers.

The question of one's identity is at the same time a simple and very complex issue. Is one to be identified by one's race, nationality, sex, place of birth, place of death, place of longest residence, occupation, class, relationships to others, personality traits, size, age, interests, religion, astrological sign, salary, by how one perceives oneself, by how one is perceived by others? When born to parents of different races or nationalities, or when born in one country, reared in another, and finally settled in a third, one cannot give a simple answer to the question of racial or national identity. When one is born female in a world dominated by males of two different races, further complications ensue.

At what point does an immigrant become an American? How does one identify one's nationality if one has moved about the world a great deal? Mai-Mai Sze, for example, was born in China to Chinese parents, taken to England as a young child, cared for by an Irish nanny, sent to a private high school and college in the United States, to a painting school in France, and now lives in New York City. Another example is Diana Chang, whose mother was Eurasian (of Irish and Chinese ancestry) and whose father was Chinese; she was born in New York City, taken to China as an infant, reared in the International Sector in Shanghai where she attended American schools, then brought back to the United States for high school and college. In the early 1970's, scholars included her work in anthologies of Asian American literature but also castigated her for the lack of ethnic pride and themes in her novels.

To complicate further the question of identity, not only are parentage and geographical factors significant, but external or social factors impinge as well. That recent immigrants feel a sense of alienation and strangeness in a new country is to be expected, but when American-born Chinese Americans, from families many generations in the United States, are asked where they learned such good English, they too are made to feel foreign and alien. The "double consciousness" with which W. E. B. Du Bois characterized the African American—"this sense of always looking at one's self through the eyes of others, of measuring one's soul by the tape of a world that looks on in amused contempt and pity"—equally characterizes Chinese Americans. However, if they should go to the People's Republic of China, they would soon realize, by their unfamiliarity with conditions and customs and by the reactions of the Chinese to them, how American they are. As Lindo Jong tells her daughter in Amy Tan's *The Joy Luck Club*, "When you go to China . . . you don't even need to open your mouth. They already know you are an outsider. . . . They know just watching the way you walk, the way you carry your face. They know you do not belong."

Thus, the feeling of being between worlds, totally at home nowhere, is at the core of all the writers in this study and, consequently, of the books they write.

16 The passage serves primarily to

(A) inform the reader of the conflicting senses of identity experienced by Chinese American and other multicultural writers
(B) encourage Chinese American writers to write more fully about the variety of cultural experiences they have had
(C) inform Chinese American writers about writers from other cultures who have experienced conflicts similar to theirs
(D) praise the talent and resourcefulness of contemporary Chinese American women writers
(E) refute those who criticize Chinese American literature for its multicultural perspective

17 The author refers to the life of Mai-Mai Sze (lines 18-23) chiefly to illustrate the

(A) difficulty of determining one's identity after many relocations
(B) beneficial effects of a multiethnic heritage
(C) influence of social rank on the perception of ethnic identity
(D) advantages of wide experiences on an author's creativity
(E) disruptive effects on a family caused by extensive travel

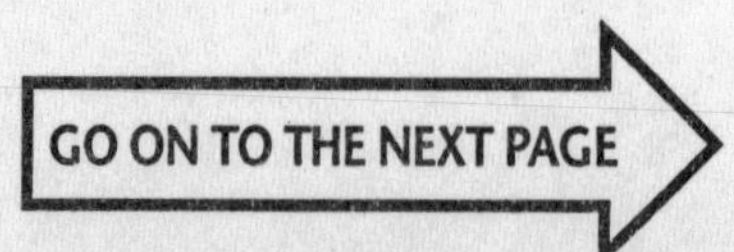

18 The discussion of Diana Chang's life (lines 23-33) suggests that she was

(A) unfamiliar with the culture of the United States
(B) isolated from other writers
(C) concerned with developing an unusual style
(D) unwilling to identify solely with any one cultural background
(E) trying to influence a small group of specialized readers

19 Which does the author consider the best example of the "external or social factors" mentioned in line 36 ?

(A) The ability to speak several languages
(B) The number of friends one has
(C) The political climate of the country in which one resides
(D) The number of countries one has lived in
(E) The assumptions other people make about one's identity

20 In line 36, "impinge" means

(A) enlarge
(B) contribute
(C) resolve
(D) fall apart
(E) fix firmly

21 The author's views (lines 34-59) about Chinese American identity can best be summarized as which of the following?

(A) Chinese Americans are as curious about their United States heritage as they are about their Chinese heritage.
(B) Chinese Americans have made contributions to both Chinese and United States literature.
(C) Chinese Americans are perceived as foreigners in both the People's Republic of China and the United States.
(D) Chinese Americans are viewed as role models by new immigrants to the United States from the People's Republic of China.
(E) Chinese Americans find their dual heritage an advantage in their writing careers.

22 The quotation (lines 55-59) from *The Joy Luck Club* emphasizes the point that American-born Chinese Americans

(A) would have difficulty understanding the sense of separation felt by their relatives who emigrated
(B) should travel to China to learn about their heritage
(C) would feel alienated in their ancestors' homeland of China
(D) need to communicate with their relatives in China
(E) tend to idealize life in China

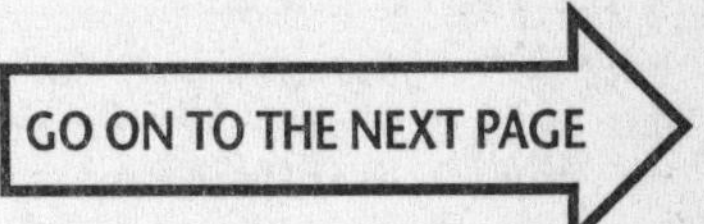

Questions 23-30 are based on the following passage.

The following passage is from a discussion of various ways that living creatures have been classified over the years.

The world can be classified in different ways, depending on one's interests and principles of classification. The classifications (also known as taxonomies) in turn determine which comparisons seem natural or unnatural, which literal or analogical. For example, it has been common to classify living creatures into three distinct groups—plants, animals, and humans. According to this classification, human beings are not a special kind of animal, nor animals a special kind of plant. Thus any comparisons between the three groups are strictly analogical. Reasoning from inheritance in garden peas to inheritance in fruit flies, and from these two species to inheritance in human beings, is sheer poetic metaphor.

Another mode of classifying living creatures is commonly attributed to Aristotle. Instead of treating plants, animals, and humans as distinct groups, they are nested. All living creatures possess a vegetative soul that enables them to grow and metabolize. Of these, some also have a sensory soul that enables them to sense their environments and move. One species also has a rational soul that is capable of true understanding. Thus, human beings are a special sort of animal, and animals are a special sort of plant. Given this classification, reasoning from human beings to all other species with respect to the attributes of the vegetative soul is legitimate, reasoning from human beings to other animals with respect to the attributes of the sensory soul is also legitimate, but reasoning from the rational characteristics of the human species to any other species is merely analogical. According to both classifications, the human species is unique. In the first, it has a kingdom all to itself; in the second, it stands at the pinnacle of the taxonomic hierarchy.

Homo sapiens is unique. All species are. But this sort of uniqueness is not enough for many (probably most) people, philosophers included. For some reason, it is very important that the species to which we belong be uniquely unique. It is of utmost importance that the human species be insulated from all other species with respect to how we explain certain qualities. Human beings clearly are capable of developing and learning languages. For some reason, it is very important that the waggle dance performed by bees* not count as a genuine language. I have never been able to understand why. I happen to think that the waggle dance differs from human languages to such a degree that little is gained by terming them both "languages," but even if "language" is so defined that the waggle dance slips in, bees still remain bees. It is equally important to some that no other species use tools. No matter how ingenious other species get in the manipulation of objects in their environment, it is absolutely essential that nothing they do count as "tool use." I, however, fail to see what difference it makes whether any of these devices such as probes and anvils, etc. are really tools. All the species involved remain distinct biological species no matter what decisions are made. Similar observations hold for rationality and anything a computer might do.

*After finding food, a bee returns to the hive and indicates, through an elaborate sequence of movements, the location of the food to other members of the hive.

23 According to the author, what is most responsible for influencing our perception of a comparison between species?

(A) The behavior of the organisms in their natural environment
(B) The organizational scheme imposed on the living world by researchers and philosophers
(C) The style of language used by scientists in presenting their research
(D) The sophistication of the communication between organisms
(E) The magnitude of hierarchical distance between a species and *Homo sapiens*

24 Which of the following is NOT possible within an Aristotelian classification scheme?

(A) Two species that are alike in having sensory souls but differ in that one lacks a rational soul
(B) Two species that are alike in having vegetative souls but differ in that only one has a sensory soul
(C) A species having a vegetative soul while lacking sensory and rational souls
(D) A species having vegetative and rational souls while lacking a sensory soul
(E) A species having vegetative and sensory souls while lacking a rational soul

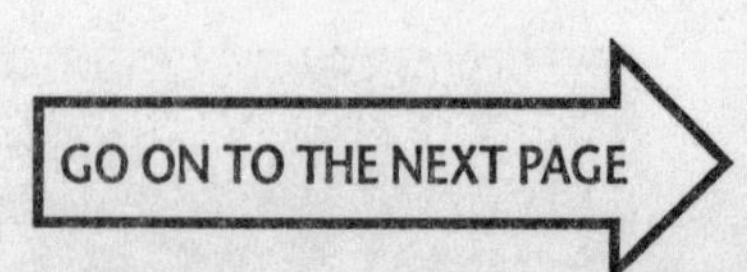

25 Which of the following comparisons would be "legitimate" for all living organisms according to the Aristotelian scheme described in paragraph two?

I. Comparisons based on the vegetative soul
II. Comparisons based on the sensory soul
III. Comparisons based on the rational soul

(A) I only
(B) II only
(C) III only
(D) II and III only
(E) I, II, and III

26 If the author had wished to explain why "most" people (line 40) feel the way they do, the explanation would have probably focused on the

(A) reality of distinct biological species
(B) most recent advances in biological research
(C) behavioral similarities between *Homo sapiens* and other species
(D) role of language in the development of technology
(E) lack of objectivity in the classification of *Homo sapiens*

27 The author uses the words "For some reason" in lines 40-41 to express

(A) rage
(B) disapproval
(C) despair
(D) sympathy
(E) uncertainty

28 Which best summarizes the idea of "uniquely unique" (line 42)?

(A) We are unique in the same way that all other species are unique.
(B) We are defined by attributes that we alone possess and that are qualitatively different from those of other species.
(C) We are, by virtue of our elevated rank, insulated from many of the problems of survival faced by less sophisticated species.
(D) Our awareness of our uniqueness defines us as a rational species.
(E) Our apparently unique status is an unintended by-product of classification systems.

29 In line 44, "insulated from" means

(A) warmed by
(B) covered with
(C) barred from
(D) segregated from
(E) protected from

30 In the third paragraph, the author criticizes those who believe that

(A) the similarities between *Homo sapiens* and other species are more significant than their differences
(B) the differences between *Homo sapiens* and other animals are those of degree, not kind
(C) *Homo sapiens* and animals belong to separate and distinct divisions of the living world
(D) *Homo sapiens* and animals have the ability to control their environment
(E) *Homo sapiens* and other organisms can be arranged in Aristotelian nested groups

IF YOU FINISH BEFORE TIME IS CALLED, YOU MAY CHECK YOUR WORK ON THIS SECTION ONLY. DO NOT TURN TO ANY OTHER SECTION IN THE TEST. **STOP**

Section 5 5

Time—15 Minutes
13 Questions

For each question in this section, select the best answer from among the choices given and fill in the corresponding oval on the answer sheet.

The two passages below are followed by questions based on their content and on the relationship between the two passages. Answer the questions on the basis of what is stated or implied in the passages and in any introductory material that may be provided.

Questions 1-13 are based on the following passages.

These passages present two perspectives of the prairie, the grasslands that covered much of the central plains of the United States during the nineteenth century. In Passage 1, a young English journalist writes about his visit to the prairie on a sight-seeing tour in the 1840's. In Passage 2, an American writer describes the area near his childhood home of the early 1870's.

Passage 1

We came upon the Prairie at sunset. It would be difficult to say why, or how—though it was possibly from having heard and read so much about it—but the effect on me was disappointment. Towards the setting sun, there lay stretched out before my view a vast expanse of level ground, unbroken (save by one thin line of trees, which scarcely amounted to a scratch upon the great blank) until it met the glowing sky, wherein it seemed to dip, mingling with its rich colors and mellowing in its distant blue. There it lay, a tranquil sea or lake without water, if such a simile be admissible, with the day going down upon it: a few birds wheeling here and there, solitude and silence reigning paramount around. But the grass was not yet high; there were bare black patches on the ground and the few wild flowers that the eye could see were poor and scanty. Great as the picture was, its very flatness and extent, which left nothing to the imagination, tamed it down and cramped its interest. I felt little of that sense of freedom and exhilaration that the open landscape of a Scottish moor, or even the rolling hills of our English downlands, inspires. It was lonely and wild, but oppressive in its barren monotony. I felt that in traversing the Prairies, I could never abandon myself to the scene, forgetful of all else, as I should instinctively were heather moorland beneath my feet. On the Prairie I should often glance towards the distant and frequently receding line of the horizon, and wish it gained and passed. It is not a scene to be forgotten, but it is scarcely one, I think (at all events, as I saw it), to remember with much pleasure or to covet the looking-on again, in after years.

Passage 2

In herding the cattle on horseback, we children came to know all the open prairie round about and found it very beautiful. On the uplands a short, light-green grass grew, intermixed with various resinous weeds, while in the lowland grazing grounds luxuriant patches of blue joint, wild oats, and other tall forage plants waved in the wind. Along the streams, cattails and tiger lilies nodded above thick mats of wide-bladed marsh grass. Almost without realizing it, I came to know the character of every weed, every flower, every living thing big enough to be seen from the back of a horse.

Nothing could be more generous, more joyous, than these natural meadows in summer. The flash and ripple and glimmer of the tall sunflowers, the chirp and gurgle of red-winged blackbirds swaying on the willow, the meadowlarks piping from grassy bogs, the peep of the prairie chick and the wailing call of plover on the flowery green slopes of the uplands made it all an ecstatic world to me. It was a wide world with a big, big sky that gave alluring hints of the still more glorious unknown wilderness beyond.

Sometimes we wandered away to the meadows along the creek, gathering bouquets of pinks, sweet william, tiger lilies, and lady's slippers. The sun flamed across the splendid serial waves of the grasses and the perfumes of a hundred spicy plants rose in the shimmering midday air. At such times the mere joy of living filled our hearts with wordless satisfaction.

On a long ridge to the north and west, the soil, too wet and cold to cultivate easily, remained

GO ON TO THE NEXT PAGE

unplowed for several years. Scattered over these clay lands stood small wooded groves that we called "tow-heads." They stood out like islands in the waving seas of grasses. Against these dark-green masses, breakers of blue joint radiantly rolled. To the east ran the river; plum trees and crabapples bloomed along its banks. In June immense crops of wild strawberries appeared in the natural meadows. Their delicious odor rose to us as we rode our way, tempting us to dismount.

On the bare upland ridges lay huge antlers, bleached and bare, in countless numbers, telling of the herds of elk and bison that had once fed in these vast savannas. On sunny April days the mother fox lay out with her young on southward-sloping swells. Often we met a prairie wolf, finding in it the spirit of the wilderness. To us it seemed that just over the next long swell toward the sunset the shaggy brown bison still fed in myriads, and in our hearts was a longing to ride away into the "sunset regions" of our pioneer songs.

1 In creating an impression of the prairie for the reader, the author of Passage 1 makes use of

(A) reference to geological processes
(B) description of its inhabitants
(C) evocation of different but equally attractive areas
(D) comparison with other landscapes
(E) contrast to imaginary places

2 In line 13, the author includes the detail of "a few birds" primarily to emphasize the

(A) loneliness of the scene
(B) strangeness of the wildlife
(C) lateness of the evening
(D) dominance of the sky
(E) infertility of the land

3 In line 20, "tamed" most nearly means

(A) composed
(B) trained
(C) subdued
(D) captured
(E) befriended

4 In line 26, "abandon myself" most nearly means

(A) dismiss as worthless
(B) isolate from all others
(C) overlook unintentionally
(D) retreat completely
(E) become absorbed in

5 The author of Passage 1 qualifies his judgment of the prairie by

(A) pointing out his own subjectivity
(B) commenting on his lack of imagination
(C) mentioning his physical fatigue
(D) apologizing for his prejudices against the landscape
(E) indicating his psychological agitation

6 In line 66, "mere" most nearly means

(A) tiny
(B) trivial
(C) simple
(D) direct
(E) questionable

7 In Passage 2, the author's references to things beyond his direct experience (lines 57-59 and lines 86-91) indicate the

(A) unexpected dangers of life on the unsettled prairie
(B) psychological interweaving of imagination and the natural scene
(C) exaggerated sense of mystery that is natural to children
(D) predominant influence of sight in experiencing a place
(E) permanence of the loss of the old life of the prairie

8 In line 74, "masses" metaphorically compares the tow-heads to

(A) ships on a stormy ocean
(B) birds on a pond
(C) reefs submerged by rising waters
(D) islands amidst the surf
(E) islands engulfed by a river

GO ON TO THE NEXT PAGE

9 One aspect of Passage 2 that might make it difficult to appreciate is the author's apparent assumption that readers will

(A) have seen nineteenth-century paintings or photographs of the prairie
(B) connect accounts of specific prairie towns with their own experiences of the prairie
(C) be able to visualize the plants and the animals that are named
(D) recognize the references to particular pioneer songs
(E) understand the children's associations with the flowers that they gathered

10 The contrast between the two descriptions of the prairie is essentially one between

(A) misfortune and prosperity
(B) homesickness and anticipation
(C) resignation and joy
(D) bleakness and richness
(E) exhaustion and energy

11 In both passages, the authors liken the prairie to

(A) a desert
(B) an island
(C) a barren wilderness
(D) a large animal
(E) a body of water

12 Both authors indicate that the experience of a beautiful landscape involves

(A) artistic production
(B) detached observation of appearances
(C) emotional turmoil
(D) stimulation of the imagination
(E) fanciful reconstruction of bygone times

13 The contrast between the two passages reflects primarily the biases of a

(A) grown man and a little boy
(B) journalist and a writer of fiction
(C) passing visitor and a local resident
(D) native of Europe and a native of the United States
(E) weary tourist and an energetic farm worker

IF YOU FINISH BEFORE TIME IS CALLED, YOU MAY CHECK YOUR WORK ON THIS SECTION ONLY. DO NOT TURN TO ANY OTHER SECTION IN THE TEST. **STOP**

Section 6  

Time—15 Minutes 10 Questions	**In this section solve each problem, using any available space on the page for scratchwork. Then decide which is the best of the choices given and fill in the corresponding oval on the answer sheet.**

Notes:

1. The use of a calculator is permitted. All numbers used are real numbers.
2. Figures that accompany problems in this test are intended to provide information useful in solving the problems. They are drawn as accurately as possible EXCEPT when it is stated in a specific problem that the figure is not drawn to scale. All figures lie in a plane unless otherwise indicated.

Reference Information

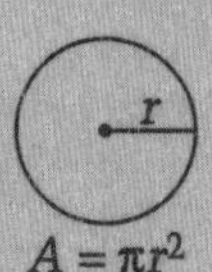
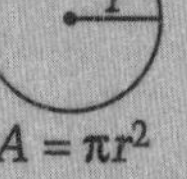
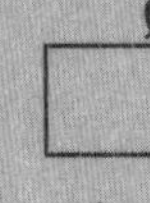
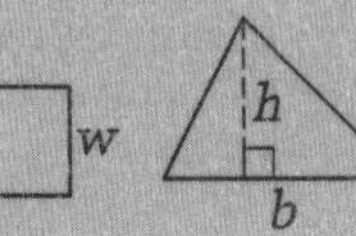
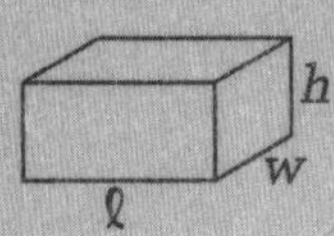

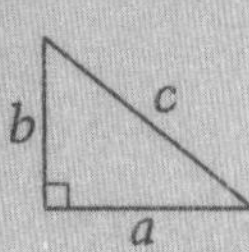
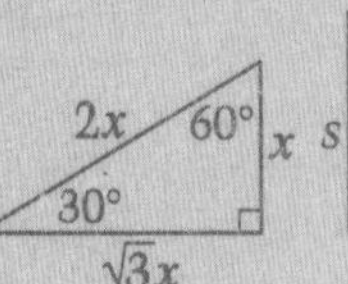

$A = \pi r^2$, $C = 2\pi r$; $A = \ell w$; $A = \frac{1}{2}bh$; $V = \ell wh$; $V = \pi r^2 h$; $c^2 = a^2 + b^2$; Special Right Triangles

The number of degrees of arc in a circle is 360.
The measure in degrees of a straight angle is 180.
The sum of the measures in degrees of the angles of a triangle is 180.

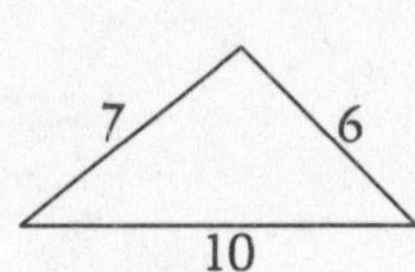

1 If the triangles shown above have the same perimeter, what is the value of x ?

(A) 5
(B) 6
(C) 7
(D) 8
(E) 9

$$\begin{array}{r} \square 5 \\ \square 6 \\ \square 7 \\ +\ \square 8 \\ \hline 146 \end{array}$$

2 In the correctly worked addition problem above, each $\square$ represents the same digit. What is the value of $\square$?

(A) 3
(B) 4
(C) 6
(D) 8
(E) 10

GO ON TO THE NEXT PAGE

Figure I

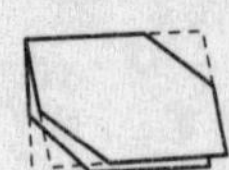

Figure II

3 A rectangular piece of paper is folded in half as shown in Figure I above. If two opposite corners of the folded paper are cut off as shown in Figure II, which of the following is the design of the paper when unfolded?

(A)

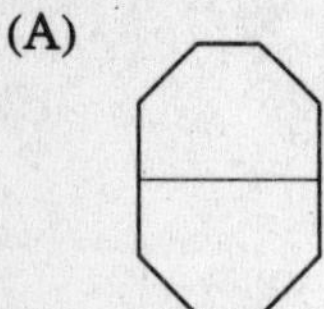

(B)

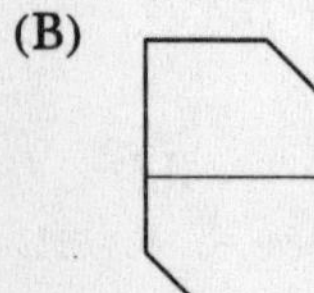

(C)

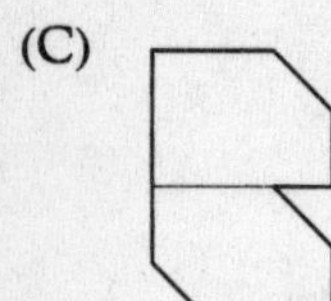

(D)

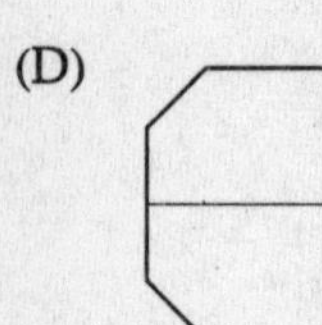

(E)

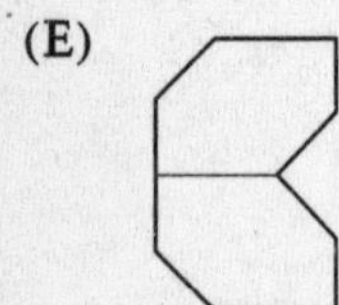

Speed (in miles per hour)	Thinking Distance (in feet)	Braking Distance (in feet)
20	20	20
30	30	45
40	40	80
50	50	125
60	60	180

4 The table above can be used to calculate the distance required to stop a car traveling at a given speed by adding the thinking distance and the braking distance. How many more feet does it take to stop a car traveling at 50 miles per hour than at 20 miles per hour?

(A) 75
(B) 105
(C) 135
(D) 165
(E) 175

GO ON TO THE NEXT PAGE

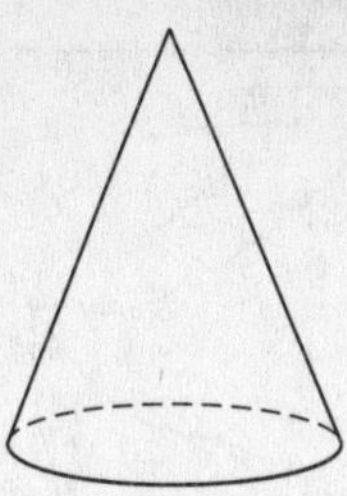

Note: Figure not drawn to scale.

5 The height of the solid cone above is 18 inches and the radius of the base is 8 inches. A cut parallel to the circular base is made completely through the cone so that one of the two resulting solids is a smaller cone. If the radius of the base of the small cone is 2 inches, what is the height of the small cone, in inches?

(A) 2.5
(B) 4.0
(C) 4.5
(D) 9.0
(E) 12.0

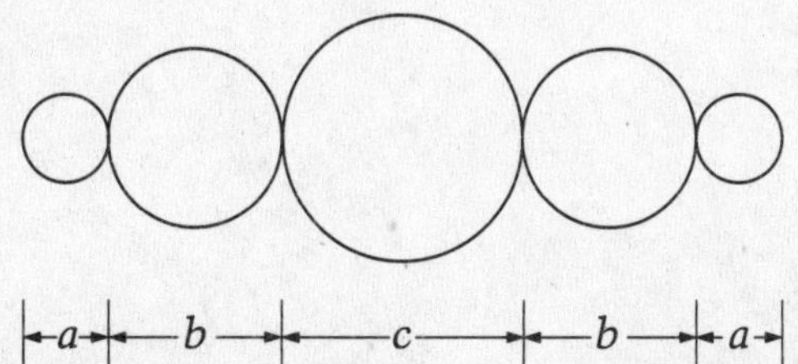

6 The figure above shows a pattern of beads with integer diameter lengths a, b, and c centimeters. This five-bead pattern is to be repeated without variation to make one complete necklace. If $a : b : c = 1 : 2 : 3$, which of the following could be the total length of the beads on the necklace?

(A) 56 cm
(B) 57 cm
(C) 60 cm
(D) 63 cm
(E) 64 cm

NUMBER OF MILES TRAVELED TO WORK BY EMPLOYEES OF COMPANY *X*

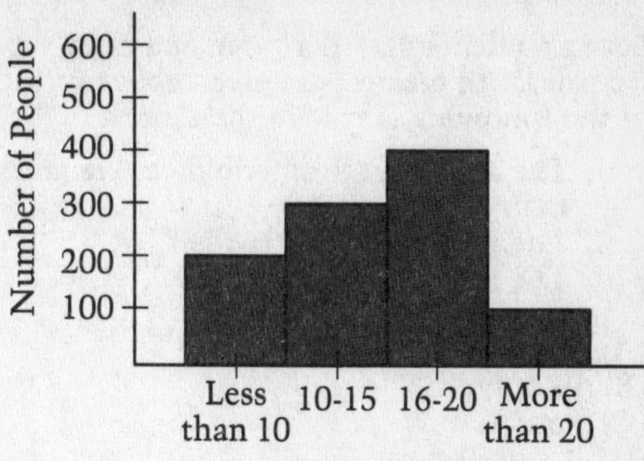

7 According to the graph above, which of the following is the closest approximation to the percent of employees of Company X who travel at least 16 miles to work?

(A) 25%
(B) 30%
(C) 40%
(D) 50%
(E) 60%

GO ON TO THE NEXT PAGE

20, 30, 50, 70, 80, 80, 90

8 Seven students played a game and their scores from least to greatest are given above. Which of the following is true of the scores?

I. The average (arithmetic mean) is greater than 70.
II. The median is greater than 70.
III. The mode is greater than 70.

(A) None
(B) III only
(C) I and II only
(D) II and III only
(E) I, II, and III

9 P is the set of positive factors of 20 and Q is the set of positive factors of 12. If x is a member of set P and y is a member of set Q, what is the greatest possible value of $x - y$?

(A) 4
(B) 8
(C) 14
(D) 19
(E) 20

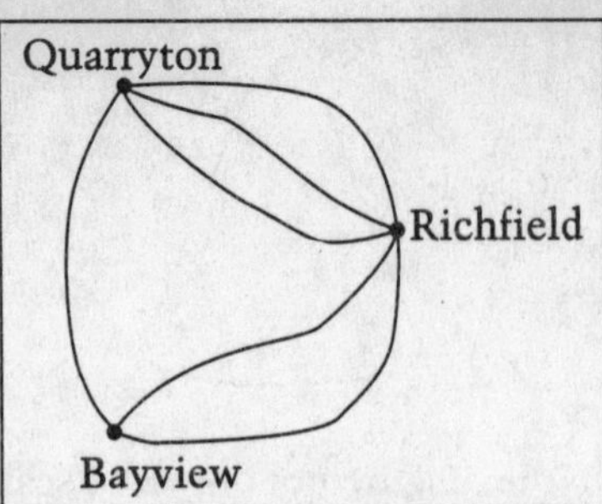

10 The figure above shows all roads between Quarryton, Richfield, and Bayview. Martina is traveling from Quarryton to Bayview and back. How many different ways could she make the round-trip, going through Richfield exactly once on a round-trip and not traveling any section of road more than once on a round-trip?

(A) 5
(B) 6
(C) 10
(D) 12
(E) 16

IF YOU FINISH BEFORE TIME IS CALLED, YOU MAY CHECK YOUR WORK ON THIS SECTION ONLY. DO NOT TURN TO ANY OTHER SECTION IN THE TEST. **STOP**

SAT I: Reasoning Test Answer Key
Saturday, March 1994

VERBAL

Section 2

Five-choice Questions

	COR. ANS.	DIFF. LEV.
1.	B	1
2.	C	1
3.	C	2
4.	E	2
5.	B	2
6.	E	3
7.	B	3
8.	A	3
9.	A	5
10.	D	5
11.	D	3
12.	D	2
13.	C	2
14.	E	3
15.	E	3
16.	A	3
17.	C	3
18.	E	3
19.	A	3
20.	B	4
21.	C	4
22.	D	5
23.	A	5
24.	B	5
25.	A	4
26.	A	2
27.	D	2
28.	C	3
29.	E	2
30.	E	3
31.	D	4
32.	E	5
33.	C	4
34.	A	4
35.	C	3

______ no. correct

______ no. incorrect

Section 4

Five-choice Questions

	COR. ANS.	DIFF. LEV.
1.	D	1
2.	D	2
3.	C	3
4.	D	3
5.	B	4
6.	C	4
7.	C	3
8.	B	4
9.	C	5
10.	A	1
11.	E	1
12.	C	3
13.	E	3
14.	B	4
15.	C	5
16.	A	2
17.	A	1
18.	D	2
19.	E	2
20.	B	1
21.	C	2
22.	C	1
23.	B	4
24.	D	4
25.	A	4
26.	E	5
27.	B	4
28.	B	3
29.	D	2
30.	C	4

______ no. correct

______ no. incorrect

Section 5

Five-choice Questions

	COR. ANS.	DIFF. LEV.
1.	D	3
2.	A	1
3.	C	2
4.	E	3
5.	A	3
6.	C	1
7.	B	4
8.	D	3
9.	C	3
10.	D	4
11.	E	3
12.	D	3
13.	C	4

______ no. correct

______ no. incorrect

MATHEMATICAL

Section 1

Five-choice Questions

	COR. ANS.	DIFF. LEV.
1.	B	1
2.	B	1
3.	A	1
4.	D	2
5.	E	2
6.	C	2
7.	A	2
8.	C	3
9.	E	3
10.	B	3
11.	C	2
12.	C	3
13.	D	3
14.	C	3
15.	C	4
16.	A	3
17.	D	3
18.	B	3
19.	D	4
20.	E	3
21.	C	4
22.	D	4
23.	C	4
24.	B	5
25.	D	5

______ no. correct

______ no. incorrect

Section 3

Four-choice Questions

	COR. ANS.	DIFF. LEV.
1.	A	1
2.	D	2
3.	C	2
4.	C	2
5.	C	3
6.	B	2
7.	D	2
8.	C	3
9.	D	5
10.	A	3
11.	D	3
12.	B	3
13.	A	4
14.	A	4
15.	B	4

______ no. correct

______ no. incorrect

Section 6

Five-choice Questions

	COR. ANS.	DIFF. LEV.
1.	A	1
2.	A	1
3.	E	2
4.	C	2
5.	C	3
6.	D	3
7.	D	4
8.	B	4
9.	D	4
10.	D	5

______ no. correct

______ no. incorrect

Section 3

Student-produced Response Questions

	COR. ANS.	DIFF. LEV.
16.	65	1
17.	9	3
18.	5 or 7	2
19.	1/2 or .5	2
20.	20	3
21.	7/8 or .875	3
22.	190	3
23.	2400	3
24.	7	4
25.	2/15 or .133	5

______ no. correct (16-25)

NOTE:
Difficulty levels are estimates of question difficulty for a recent group of college-bound seniors. Difficulty levels range from 1 (easiest) to 5 (hardest). A specified number of questions of each difficulty level is required for each edition of the SAT I. While there will be some variation from edition to edition, the specified number of questions of each level of difficulty is as follows:

	Difficulty Level	Number of Questions: Verbal	Math
(easiest)	1	8	6
	2	16	12
	3	30	24
	4	16	12
(hardest)	5	8	6
	Total	78	60

The Scoring Process

Machine-scoring is done in three steps:

- *Scanning.* Your answer sheet is "read" by a scanning machine and the oval you filled in for each question is recorded on a computer tape.
- *Scoring.* The computer compares the oval filled in for each question with the correct response. Each correct answer receives one point; omitted questions do not count toward your score. For each wrong answer to the multiple-choice questions, a fraction of a point is subtracted to correct for random guessing. For questions with five answer choices, one-fourth of a point is subtracted for each wrong response; for questions with four answer choices, one-third of a point is subtracted for each wrong response. The SAT I verbal test has 78 questions with five answer choices each. If, for example, a student has 44 right, 32 wrong, and 2 omitted, the resulting raw score is determined as follows:

$$44 \text{ right} - \frac{32 \text{ wrong}}{4} = 44 - 8 = 36 \text{ raw score points}$$

Obtaining raw scores frequently involves the rounding of fractional numbers to the nearest whole number. For example, a raw score of 36.25 is rounded to 36, the nearest whole number. A raw score of 36.50 is rounded upward to 37.

- *Converting to reported scaled score.* Raw test scores are then placed on the College Board scale of 200 to 800 through a process that adjusts scores to account for minor differences in difficulty among different editions of the test. This process, known as equating, is performed so that a student's reported score is not affected by the edition of the test taken nor by the abilities of the group with whom the student takes the test. As a result of placing SAT I scores on the College Board scale, scores earned by students at different times can be compared.

How to Score the Practice Test

SAT I Verbal Sections 2, 4, and 5

Step A: Count the number of correct answers for Section 2 and record the number in the space provided on the worksheet on the next page. Then do the same for the incorrect answers. (Do not count omitted answers.) To determine subtotal A, use the formula:

$$\text{number correct} - \frac{\text{number incorrect}}{4} = \text{subtotal A}$$

Step B: Count the number of correct answers and the number of incorrect answers for *Section 4* and record the number in the space provided on the worksheet. To determine subtotal B, use the formula:

$$\text{number correct} - \frac{\text{number incorrect}}{4} = \text{subtotal B}$$

Step C: Count the number of correct answers and the number of incorrect answers for *Section 5* and record the number in the space provided on the worksheet. To determine subtotal C, use the formula:

$$\text{number correct} - \frac{\text{number incorrect}}{4} = \text{subtotal C}$$

Step D: To obtain D, add subtotal A, subtotal B, and subtotal C, keeping any decimals. Enter the resulting figure on the worksheet.

Step E: To obtain E, your raw verbal score, round D to the nearest whole number. (For example, any number from 44.50 to 45.49 rounds to 45.) Enter the resulting figure on the worksheet.

Step F: To find your SAT verbal score, look up the total raw verbal score you obtained in step E in the conversion table. Enter this figure on the worksheet.

SAT I Mathematical Sections 1, 3, and 6

Step A: Count the number of correct answers and the number of incorrect answers for *Section 1* and record the numbers in the spaces provided on the worksheet. To determine subtotal A, use the formula:

$$\text{number correct} - \frac{\text{number incorrect}}{4} = \text{subtotal A}$$

Step B: Count the number of correct answers and the number of incorrect answers for the *four-choice quantitative comparison questions (questions 1 through 15) in Section 3* and record the number in the space provided on the worksheet. Note: Do not count any E responses to questions 1 through 15 as correct or incorrect. Because these four-choice questions have no E answer choices, E responses to these questions are treated as omits. To determine subtotal B, use the formula:

$$\text{number correct} - \frac{\text{number incorrect}}{3} = \text{subtotal B}$$

Step C: Count the number of correct answers for the student-produced response questions *(questions 16 through 25) in Section 3* and record the number in the space provided on the worksheet. This is subtotal C.

Step D: Count the number of correct answers and the number of incorrect answers for *Section 6* and record the number in the space provided on the worksheet. To determine subtotal D, use the formula:

$$\text{number correct} - \frac{\text{number incorrect}}{4} = \text{subtotal D}$$

Step E: To obtain E, add subtotal A, subtotal B, subtotal C, and subtotal D, keeping any decimals. Enter the resulting figure on the worksheet.

Step F: To obtain F, your raw mathematical score, round E to the nearest whole number. (For example, any number from 44.50 to 45.49 rounds to 45.) Enter the resulting figure on the worksheet.

Step G: To find your SAT I mathematical score, look up the total raw mathematical score you obtained in step F in the conversion table. Enter this figure on the worksheet.

SAT I Scoring Worksheet

SAT I Verbal Sections

A. Section 2:	______ no. correct	− (______ no. incorrect	÷ 4) =	______ subtotal A
B. Section 4:	______ no. correct	− (______ no. incorrect	÷ 4) =	______ subtotal B
C. Section 5:	______ no. correct	− (______ no. incorrect	÷ 4) =	______ subtotal C
D. Total unrounded raw score (Total A + B + C)				______ D
E. Total rounded raw score (Rounded to nearest whole number)				______ E
F. SAT I verbal reported scaled score (Use the appropriate conversion table)				[ ] SAT I verbal score

SAT I Mathematical Sections

A. Section 1:	______ no. correct	− (______ no. incorrect	÷ 4) =	______ subtotal A
B. Section 3: Questions 1-15 (quantitative comparison)	______ no. correct	− (______ no. incorrect	÷ 3) =	______ subtotal B
C. Section 3: Questions 16-25 (student-produced response)	______ no. correct		=	______ subtotal C
D. Section 6:	______ no. correct	− (______ no. incorrect	÷ 4) =	______ subtotal D
E. Total unrounded raw score (Total A + B + C + D)				______ E
F. Total rounded raw score (Rounded to nearest whole number)				______ F
G. SAT I mathematical reported scaled score (Use the appropriate conversion table)				[ ] SAT I mathematical score

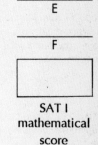

Score Conversion Table
SAT I: Reasoning Test
Saturday, March 1994
Recentered Scale

Raw Score	Verbal Scaled Score	Math Scaled Score	Raw Score	Verbal Scaled Score	Math Scaled Score
78	800		36	500	560
77	800		35	500	550
76	800		34	490	540
75	800		33	480	540
74	800		32	480	530
73	780		31	470	520
72	770		30	470	520
71	760		29	460	510
70	740		28	450	510
69	730		27	450	500
68	720		26	440	490
67	710		25	440	490
66	700		24	430	480
65	700		23	420	470
64	690		22	420	470
63	680		21	410	460
62	670		20	400	460
61	660		19	400	450
60	650	800	18	390	440
59	650	800	17	380	440
58	640	780	16	370	430
57	630	760	15	370	420
56	630	740	14	360	420
55	620	720	13	350	410
54	610	710	12	340	400
53	610	700	11	330	390
52	600	690	10	330	380
51	590	680	9	320	380
50	590	670	8	310	370
49	580	660	7	300	360
48	570	650	6	290	350
47	570	640	5	280	330
46	560	630	4	270	320
45	560	620	3	260	310
44	550	610	2	240	300
43	540	610	1	230	280
42	540	600	0	210	260
41	530	590	−1	200	240
40	530	580	−2	200	230
39	520	580	−3 and below	200	200
38	510	570			
37	510	560			

This table is for use only with this test.

SAT I: Reasoning Test

Saturday, November 1994

YOUR NAME (PRINT) ______ LAST ______ FIRST ______ MI

TEST CENTER ______ NUMBER ______ NAME OF TEST CENTER ______ ROOM NUMBER

SAT® I: Reasoning Test — General Directions

Timing

- You will have three hours to work on this test.
- There are five 30-minute sections and two 15-minute sections.
- You may work on only one section at a time.
- The supervisor will tell you when to begin and end each section.
- If you finish a section before time is called, check your work on that section. You may NOT turn to any other section.
- Work as rapidly as you can without losing accuracy. Don't waste time on questions that seem too difficult for you.

Marking Answers

- Carefully mark only one answer for each question.
- Make sure each mark is dark and completely fills the oval.
- Do not make any stray marks on your answer sheet.
- If you erase, do so completely. Incomplete erasures may be scored as intended answers.
- Use only the answer spaces that correspond to the question numbers.
- For questions with only four answer choices, an answer marked in oval E will not be scored.
- Use the test book for scratchwork, but you will not receive credit for anything written there.
- You may not transfer answers to your answer sheet or fill in ovals after time has been called.
- You may not fold or remove pages or portions of a page from this book, or take the book or answer sheet from the testing room.

Scoring

- For each correct answer, you receive one point.
- For questions you omit, you receive no points.
- For a wrong answer to a multiple-choice question, you lose a fraction of a point.
  - ► If you can eliminate one or more of the answer choices as wrong, however, you increase your chances of choosing the correct answer and earning one point.
  - ► If you can't eliminate any choice, move on. You can return to the question later if there is time.
- For a wrong answer to a math question that is not multiple-choice, you don't lose any points.

The passages for this test have been adapted from published material. The ideas contained in them do not necessarily represent the opinions of the College Board or Educational Testing Service.

IMPORTANT: The codes below are unique to your test book. Copy them on your answer sheet in boxes 8 and 9 and fill in the corresponding ovals exactly as shown.

8. Form Code

A	A	0	0	0
B	B	1	1	1
C	C	2	2	2
D	D	3	3	3
E	E	4	4	4
F	F	5	5	5
G	G	6	6	6
H	H	7	7	7
I	I	8	8	8
J	J	9	9	9
K	K			
L	L			
M	M			
N	N			
O	O			
P	P			
Q	Q			
R	R			
S	S			
T	T			
U	U			
V	V			
W	W			
X	X			
Y	Y			
Z	Z			

9. Test Form

DO NOT OPEN THIS BOOK UNTIL THE SUPERVISOR TELLS YOU TO DO SO.

THE COLLEGE BOARD — SAT I   Page 1

Use a No. 2 pencil only. Be sure each mark is dark and completely fills the intended oval. Completely erase any errors or stray marks.

1. Your Name

First 4 letters of Last Name	First init.	Mid. init.
A–Z	A–Z	A–Z

2.
Your Name: ______________________________
(Print) Last First M.I.

I agree to the conditions on the back of the SAT I test book.

Signature: ______________________ Date: ___/___/___

Home Address: ______________________________
(Print) Number and Street

____
City State Zip Code

Center: ______________________________
(Print) City State Center Number

IMPORTANT: Fill in items 8 and 9 exactly as shown on the back of test book.

3. Date of Birth

Month	Day	Year
Jan.	0–3	0–9
Feb.	0–9	0–9
Mar.		
Apr.		
May		
June		
July		
Aug.		
Sept.		
Oct.		
Nov.		
Dec.		

4. Social Security Number

(9 columns, 0–9)

5. Sex

Female ◯ Male ◯

6. Registration Number

(Copy from Admission Ticket.)

(7 columns, 0–9)

7. Test Book Serial Number

(Copy from front of test book.)

(6 columns, 0–9)

8. Form Code

(Copy and grid as on back of test book.)

(2 columns A–Z, 3 columns 0–9)

FOR ETS USE ONLY

9. Test Form

(Copy from back of test book.)

Start with number 1 for each new section. If a section has fewer questions than answer spaces, leave the extra answer spaces blank.

SECTION 1

1 A B C D E	11 A B C D E	21 A B C D E	31 A B C D E
2 A B C D E	12 A B C D E	22 A B C D E	32 A B C D E
3 A B C D E	13 A B C D E	23 A B C D E	33 A B C D E
4 A B C D E	14 A B C D E	24 A B C D E	34 A B C D E
5 A B C D E	15 A B C D E	25 A B C D E	35 A B C D E
6 A B C D E	16 A B C D E	26 A B C D E	36 A B C D E
7 A B C D E	17 A B C D E	27 A B C D E	37 A B C D E
8 A B C D E	18 A B C D E	28 A B C D E	38 A B C D E
9 A B C D E	19 A B C D E	29 A B C D E	39 A B C D E
10 A B C D E	20 A B C D E	30 A B C D E	40 A B C D E

SECTION 2

1 A B C D E	11 A B C D E	21 A B C D E	31 A B C D E
2 A B C D E	12 A B C D E	22 A B C D E	32 A B C D E
3 A B C D E	13 A B C D E	23 A B C D E	33 A B C D E
4 A B C D E	14 A B C D E	24 A B C D E	34 A B C D E
5 A B C D E	15 A B C D E	25 A B C D E	35 A B C D E
6 A B C D E	16 A B C D E	26 A B C D E	36 A B C D E
7 A B C D E	17 A B C D E	27 A B C D E	37 A B C D E
8 A B C D E	18 A B C D E	28 A B C D E	38 A B C D E
9 A B C D E	19 A B C D E	29 A B C D E	39 A B C D E
10 A B C D E	20 A B C D E	30 A B C D E	40 A B C D E

Q2778-06/2 CHW98324 11027 • 09132 • TF129M17.5eX I.N. 207158
1 2 3 4

Use a No. 2 pencil only. Be sure each mark is dark and completely fills the intended oval. Completely erase any errors or stray marks.

Start with number 1 for each new section. If a section has fewer questions than answer spaces, leave the extra answer spaces blank.

SECTION 3

1 (A) (B) (C) (D) (E)
2 (A) (B) (C) (D) (E)
3 (A) (B) (C) (D) (E)
4 (A) (B) (C) (D) (E)
5 (A) (B) (C) (D) (E)
6 (A) (B) (C) (D) (E)
7 (A) (B) (C) (D) (E)
8 (A) (B) (C) (D) (E)
9 (A) (B) (C) (D) (E)
10 (A) (B) (C) (D) (E)
11 (A) (B) (C) (D) (E)
12 (A) (B) (C) (D) (E)
13 (A) (B) (C) (D) (E)
14 (A) (B) (C) (D) (E)
15 (A) (B) (C) (D) (E)

16 (A) (B) (C) (D) (E)
17 (A) (B) (C) (D) (E)
18 (A) (B) (C) (D) (E)
19 (A) (B) (C) (D) (E)
20 (A) (B) (C) (D) (E)
21 (A) (B) (C) (D) (E)
22 (A) (B) (C) (D) (E)
23 (A) (B) (C) (D) (E)
24 (A) (B) (C) (D) (E)
25 (A) (B) (C) (D) (E)
26 (A) (B) (C) (D) (E)
27 (A) (B) (C) (D) (E)
28 (A) (B) (C) (D) (E)
29 (A) (B) (C) (D) (E)
30 (A) (B) (C) (D) (E)

31 (A) (B) (C) (D) (E)
32 (A) (B) (C) (D) (E)
33 (A) (B) (C) (D) (E)
34 (A) (B) (C) (D) (E)
35 (A) (B) (C) (D) (E)
36 (A) (B) (C) (D) (E)
37 (A) (B) (C) (D) (E)
38 (A) (B) (C) (D) (E)
39 (A) (B) (C) (D) (E)
40 (A) (B) (C) (D) (E)

If section 3 of your test book contains math questions that are not multiple-choice, continue to item 16 below. Otherwise, continue to item 16 above.

ONLY ANSWERS ENTERED IN THE OVALS IN EACH GRID AREA WILL BE SCORED. YOU WILL NOT RECEIVE CREDIT FOR ANYTHING WRITTEN IN THE BOXES ABOVE THE OVALS.

16 17 18 19 20

21 22 23 24 25

(Each grid: / / ; . . . . ; 0 0 0 ; 1–9 in each of four columns)

BE SURE TO ERASE ANY ERRORS OR STRAY MARKS COMPLETELY.

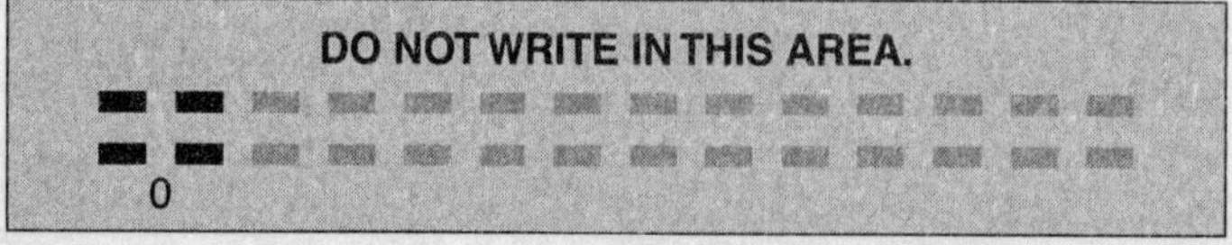

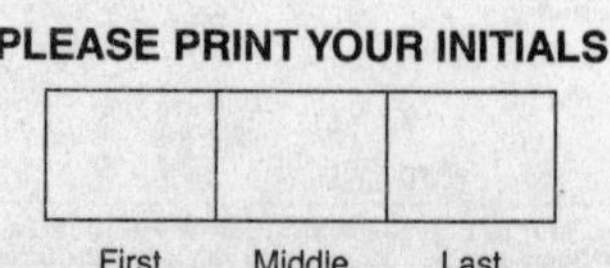

Use a No. 2 pencil only. Be sure each mark is dark and completely fills the intended oval. Completely erase any errors or stray marks.

Start with number 1 for each new section. If a section has fewer questions than answer spaces, leave the extra answer spaces blank.

SECTION 4

1 (A) (B) (C) (D) (E)
2 (A) (B) (C) (D) (E)
3 (A) (B) (C) (D) (E)
4 (A) (B) (C) (D) (E)
5 (A) (B) (C) (D) (E)
6 (A) (B) (C) (D) (E)
7 (A) (B) (C) (D) (E)
8 (A) (B) (C) (D) (E)
9 (A) (B) (C) (D) (E)
10 (A) (B) (C) (D) (E)
11 (A) (B) (C) (D) (E)
12 (A) (B) (C) (D) (E)
13 (A) (B) (C) (D) (E)
14 (A) (B) (C) (D) (E)
15 (A) (B) (C) (D) (E)
16 (A) (B) (C) (D) (E)
17 (A) (B) (C) (D) (E)
18 (A) (B) (C) (D) (E)
19 (A) (B) (C) (D) (E)
20 (A) (B) (C) (D) (E)
21 (A) (B) (C) (D) (E)
22 (A) (B) (C) (D) (E)
23 (A) (B) (C) (D) (E)
24 (A) (B) (C) (D) (E)
25 (A) (B) (C) (D) (E)
26 (A) (B) (C) (D) (E)
27 (A) (B) (C) (D) (E)
28 (A) (B) (C) (D) (E)
29 (A) (B) (C) (D) (E)
30 (A) (B) (C) (D) (E)
31 (A) (B) (C) (D) (E)
32 (A) (B) (C) (D) (E)
33 (A) (B) (C) (D) (E)
34 (A) (B) (C) (D) (E)
35 (A) (B) (C) (D) (E)
36 (A) (B) (C) (D) (E)
37 (A) (B) (C) (D) (E)
38 (A) (B) (C) (D) (E)
39 (A) (B) (C) (D) (E)
40 (A) (B) (C) (D) (E)

If section 4 of your test book contains math questions that are not multiple-choice, continue to item 16 below. Otherwise, continue to item 16 above.

ONLY ANSWERS ENTERED IN THE OVALS IN EACH GRID AREA WILL BE SCORED.
YOU WILL NOT RECEIVE CREDIT FOR ANYTHING WRITTEN IN THE BOXES ABOVE THE OVALS.

16 17 18 19 20

21 22 23 24 25

BE SURE TO ERASE ANY ERRORS OR STRAY MARKS COMPLETELY.

DO NOT WRITE IN THIS AREA.

0

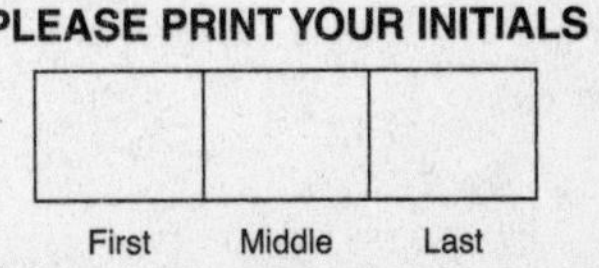

THE COLLEGE BOARD – SAT I **Page 4**

Use a No. 2 pencil only. Be sure each mark is dark and completely fills the intended oval. Completely erase any errors or stray marks.

Start with number 1 for each new section. If a section has fewer questions than answer spaces, leave the extra answer spaces blank.

SECTION 5

1 Ⓐ Ⓑ Ⓒ Ⓓ Ⓔ	11 Ⓐ Ⓑ Ⓒ Ⓓ Ⓔ	21 Ⓐ Ⓑ Ⓒ Ⓓ Ⓔ	31 Ⓐ Ⓑ Ⓒ Ⓓ Ⓔ
2 Ⓐ Ⓑ Ⓒ Ⓓ Ⓔ	12 Ⓐ Ⓑ Ⓒ Ⓓ Ⓔ	22 Ⓐ Ⓑ Ⓒ Ⓓ Ⓔ	32 Ⓐ Ⓑ Ⓒ Ⓓ Ⓔ
3 Ⓐ Ⓑ Ⓒ Ⓓ Ⓔ	13 Ⓐ Ⓑ Ⓒ Ⓓ Ⓔ	23 Ⓐ Ⓑ Ⓒ Ⓓ Ⓔ	33 Ⓐ Ⓑ Ⓒ Ⓓ Ⓔ
4 Ⓐ Ⓑ Ⓒ Ⓓ Ⓔ	14 Ⓐ Ⓑ Ⓒ Ⓓ Ⓔ	24 Ⓐ Ⓑ Ⓒ Ⓓ Ⓔ	34 Ⓐ Ⓑ Ⓒ Ⓓ Ⓔ
5 Ⓐ Ⓑ Ⓒ Ⓓ Ⓔ	15 Ⓐ Ⓑ Ⓒ Ⓓ Ⓔ	25 Ⓐ Ⓑ Ⓒ Ⓓ Ⓔ	35 Ⓐ Ⓑ Ⓒ Ⓓ Ⓔ
6 Ⓐ Ⓑ Ⓒ Ⓓ Ⓔ	16 Ⓐ Ⓑ Ⓒ Ⓓ Ⓔ	26 Ⓐ Ⓑ Ⓒ Ⓓ Ⓔ	36 Ⓐ Ⓑ Ⓒ Ⓓ Ⓔ
7 Ⓐ Ⓑ Ⓒ Ⓓ Ⓔ	17 Ⓐ Ⓑ Ⓒ Ⓓ Ⓔ	27 Ⓐ Ⓑ Ⓒ Ⓓ Ⓔ	37 Ⓐ Ⓑ Ⓒ Ⓓ Ⓔ
8 Ⓐ Ⓑ Ⓒ Ⓓ Ⓔ	18 Ⓐ Ⓑ Ⓒ Ⓓ Ⓔ	28 Ⓐ Ⓑ Ⓒ Ⓓ Ⓔ	38 Ⓐ Ⓑ Ⓒ Ⓓ Ⓔ
9 Ⓐ Ⓑ Ⓒ Ⓓ Ⓔ	19 Ⓐ Ⓑ Ⓒ Ⓓ Ⓔ	29 Ⓐ Ⓑ Ⓒ Ⓓ Ⓔ	39 Ⓐ Ⓑ Ⓒ Ⓓ Ⓔ
10 Ⓐ Ⓑ Ⓒ Ⓓ Ⓔ	20 Ⓐ Ⓑ Ⓒ Ⓓ Ⓔ	30 Ⓐ Ⓑ Ⓒ Ⓓ Ⓔ	40 Ⓐ Ⓑ Ⓒ Ⓓ Ⓔ

SECTION 6

1 Ⓐ Ⓑ Ⓒ Ⓓ Ⓔ	6 Ⓐ Ⓑ Ⓒ Ⓓ Ⓔ	11 Ⓐ Ⓑ Ⓒ Ⓓ Ⓔ	16 Ⓐ Ⓑ Ⓒ Ⓓ Ⓔ
2 Ⓐ Ⓑ Ⓒ Ⓓ Ⓔ	7 Ⓐ Ⓑ Ⓒ Ⓓ Ⓔ	12 Ⓐ Ⓑ Ⓒ Ⓓ Ⓔ	17 Ⓐ Ⓑ Ⓒ Ⓓ Ⓔ
3 Ⓐ Ⓑ Ⓒ Ⓓ Ⓔ	8 Ⓐ Ⓑ Ⓒ Ⓓ Ⓔ	13 Ⓐ Ⓑ Ⓒ Ⓓ Ⓔ	18 Ⓐ Ⓑ Ⓒ Ⓓ Ⓔ
4 Ⓐ Ⓑ Ⓒ Ⓓ Ⓔ	9 Ⓐ Ⓑ Ⓒ Ⓓ Ⓔ	14 Ⓐ Ⓑ Ⓒ Ⓓ Ⓔ	19 Ⓐ Ⓑ Ⓒ Ⓓ Ⓔ
5 Ⓐ Ⓑ Ⓒ Ⓓ Ⓔ	10 Ⓐ Ⓑ Ⓒ Ⓓ Ⓔ	15 Ⓐ Ⓑ Ⓒ Ⓓ Ⓔ	20 Ⓐ Ⓑ Ⓒ Ⓓ Ⓔ

SECTION 7

1 Ⓐ Ⓑ Ⓒ Ⓓ Ⓔ	6 Ⓐ Ⓑ Ⓒ Ⓓ Ⓔ	11 Ⓐ Ⓑ Ⓒ Ⓓ Ⓔ	16 Ⓐ Ⓑ Ⓒ Ⓓ Ⓔ
2 Ⓐ Ⓑ Ⓒ Ⓓ Ⓔ	7 Ⓐ Ⓑ Ⓒ Ⓓ Ⓔ	12 Ⓐ Ⓑ Ⓒ Ⓓ Ⓔ	17 Ⓐ Ⓑ Ⓒ Ⓓ Ⓔ
3 Ⓐ Ⓑ Ⓒ Ⓓ Ⓔ	8 Ⓐ Ⓑ Ⓒ Ⓓ Ⓔ	13 Ⓐ Ⓑ Ⓒ Ⓓ Ⓔ	18 Ⓐ Ⓑ Ⓒ Ⓓ Ⓔ
4 Ⓐ Ⓑ Ⓒ Ⓓ Ⓔ	9 Ⓐ Ⓑ Ⓒ Ⓓ Ⓔ	14 Ⓐ Ⓑ Ⓒ Ⓓ Ⓔ	19 Ⓐ Ⓑ Ⓒ Ⓓ Ⓔ
5 Ⓐ Ⓑ Ⓒ Ⓓ Ⓔ	10 Ⓐ Ⓑ Ⓒ Ⓓ Ⓔ	15 Ⓐ Ⓑ Ⓒ Ⓓ Ⓔ	20 Ⓐ Ⓑ Ⓒ Ⓓ Ⓔ

CERTIFICATION STATEMENT

Copy the statement below (do not print) and sign your name as you would an official document.

I hereby agree to the conditions set forth in the Registration Bulletin and certify that I am the person whose name and address appear on this answer sheet.

____

____

____

Signature: ________________________ Date: ____________

Section 1 1 1 1 1 1 1

Time—30 Minutes
25 Questions

In this section solve each problem, using any available space on the page for scratchwork. Then decide which is the best of the choices given and fill in the corresponding oval on the answer sheet.

Notes:

1. The use of a calculator is permitted. All numbers used are real numbers.
2. Figures that accompany problems in this test are intended to provide information useful in solving the problems. They are drawn as accurately as possible EXCEPT when it is stated in a specific problem that the figure is not drawn to scale. All figures lie in a plane unless otherwise indicated.

Reference Information

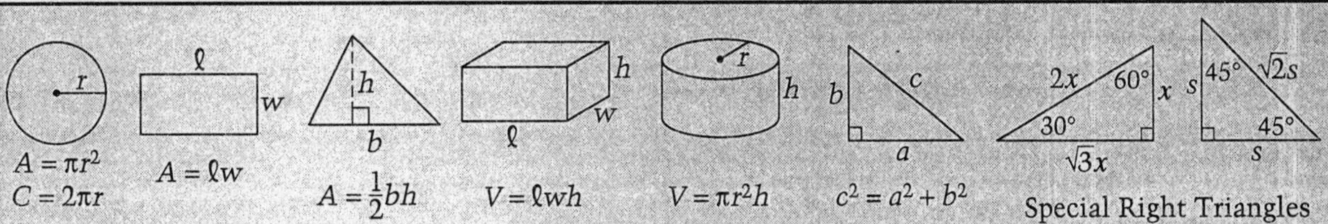

The number of degrees of arc in a circle is 360.
The measure in degrees of a straight angle is 180.
The sum of the measures in degrees of the angles of a triangle is 180.

1 If $(x - 5) + 5 = 12$, what is the value of x?

(A) 2
(B) 7
(C) 12
(D) 17
(E) 22

2 Which of the following numbers has the digit 8 in the hundredths place?

(A) 0.008
(B) 0.080
(C) 0.800
(D) 80.0
(E) 800.0

3 If $2x + y = 5$, what is the value of $4x + 2y$?

(A) 5
(B) 8
(C) 10
(D) 15
(E) 20

4 Gene and JoAnn each bought some Ink-O pens and an ink eraser. Gene paid \$1.75 for 3 pens and 1 eraser. JoAnn paid \$1.25 for 2 pens and 1 eraser. What is the price of one of the pens?

(A) \$0.10
(B) \$0.15
(C) \$0.25
(D) \$0.50
(E) \$0.60

GO ON TO THE NEXT PAGE

NUMBER OF COLLEGES AND UNIVERSITIES IN NEW ENGLAND BY STATE

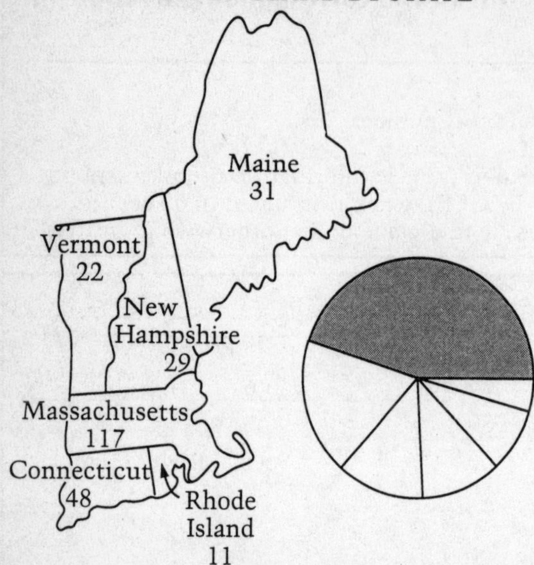

5 If the data in the map above were represented in the unlabeled circle graph, which of the following states would be represented by the shaded sector?

(A) Connecticut
(B) Massachusetts
(C) Vermont
(D) New Hampshire
(E) Maine

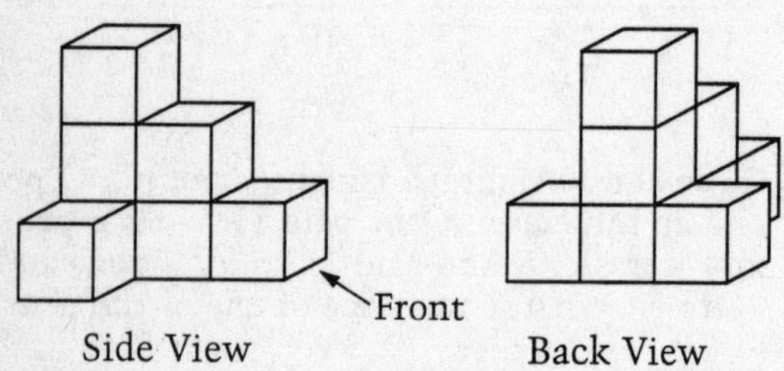

6 The figure above shows two views of a solid that is constructed from cubes of the same size. How many cubes are needed to construct the solid?

(A) Eleven
(B) Ten
(C) Nine
(D) Eight
(E) Seven

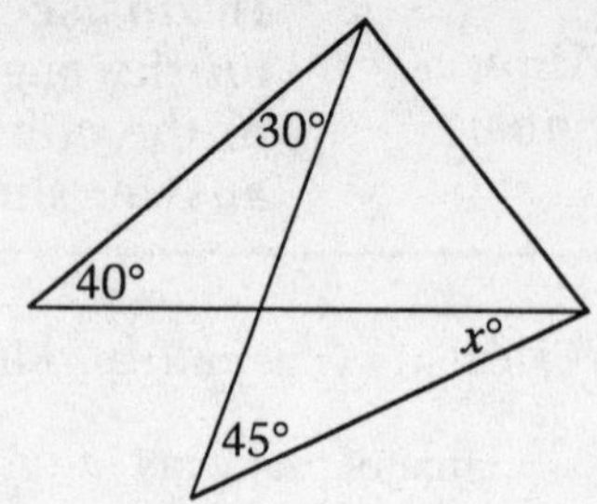

7 In the figure above, what is the value of x ?

(A) 65
(B) 45
(C) 40
(D) 30
(E) 25

8 If $4^{x+1} = 64$, what is the value of x ?

(A) 2
(B) 3
(C) 4
(D) 5
(E) 6

9 Of the students in a certain homeroom, 9 are in the school play, 12 are in the orchestra, and 15 are in the choral group. If 5 students participate in exactly 2 of the 3 activities and all other students participate in only 1 activity, how many students are in the homeroom?

(A) 31
(B) 30
(C) 26
(D) 25
(E) 21

GO ON TO THE NEXT PAGE

10 If $y = \frac{x^2}{z}$ and $x \neq 0$, then $\frac{1}{x^2} =$

(A) yz

(B) $\frac{y}{z}$

(C) $\frac{z}{y}$

(D) $y - \frac{1}{z}$

(E) $\frac{1}{yz}$

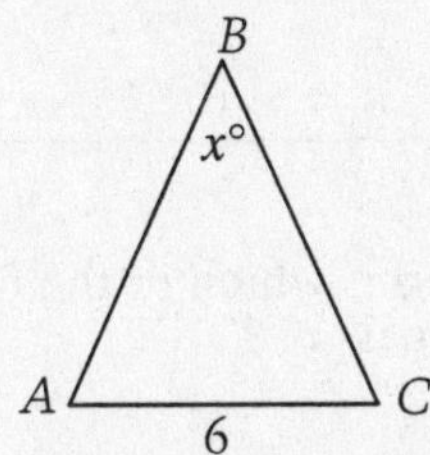

Note: Figure not drawn to scale.

11 In the figure above, $AB = BC$. If $x = 60$, then $AB =$

(A) 3

(B) 6

(C) $3\sqrt{2}$

(D) $3\sqrt{3}$

(E) $6\sqrt{3}$

12 What percent of 4 is 5 ?

(A) 75%
(B) 80%
(C) 125%
(D) 150%
(E) 180%

13 Through how many degrees does the minute hand of a clock turn from 3:10 p.m. to 3:25 p.m. of the same day?

(A) 15°
(B) 30°
(C) 45°
(D) 60°
(E) 90°

14 The length of a rectangle is 4 times the width. If the perimeter of the rectangle is 60, what is the width?

(A) 6
(B) 7.5
(C) 10
(D) 12
(E) 15

GO ON TO THE NEXT PAGE

15 If n is divided by 9, the remainder is 5. What is the remainder if $3n$ is divided by 9 ?

(A) 4
(B) 5
(C) 6
(D) 7
(E) 8

16 If $a \times b \times c = 72$, where a, b, and c are integers and $a > b > c > 1$, what is the greatest possible value of a ?

(A) 12
(B) 18
(C) 24
(D) 36
(E) 72

17 What is the slope of a line that passes through the origin and the point $(-2, -1)$?

(A) 2
(B) $\frac{1}{2}$
(C) 0
(D) $-\frac{1}{2}$
(E) -2

18 Julie has cats, fish, and frogs for pets. The number of frogs she has is 1 more than the number of cats, and the number of fish is 3 times the number of frogs. Of the following, which could be the total number of these pets?

(A) 15
(B) 16
(C) 17
(D) 18
(E) 19

19 If x is an integer, which of the following could NOT equal x^3 ?

(A) -8
(B) 0
(C) 1
(D) 16
(E) 27

20 If $x = 7 + y$ and $4x = 6 - 2y$, what is the value of x ?

(A) -4
(B) $-\frac{4}{3}$
(C) $-\frac{1}{6}$
(D) $\frac{10}{3}$
(E) 10

GO ON TO THE NEXT PAGE

CHESS CLUB MEMBERSHIP

Status	Number of Members Under 20 Years Old	Number of Members 20 Years or Older	Total
Number of Amateurs	4		9
Number of Professionals		8	11
Total	7	13	20

21 The incomplete table above categorizes the members of a chess club according to their age and status. During a tournament, each member of the club plays exactly one game with each of the other members. How many games of chess are played between amateurs 20 years or older and professionals under 20 years old during the tournament?

(A) 8
(B) 12
(C) 15
(D) 16
(E) 30

22 A bag contains a number of pieces of candy of which 78 are red, 24 are brown, and the remainder are yellow. If the probability of selecting a yellow piece of candy from this bag at random is $\frac{1}{3}$, how many yellow pieces of candy are in the bag?

(A) 34
(B) 51
(C) 54
(D) 102
(E) 306

GO ON TO THE NEXT PAGE

23 If $p = 4\left(\frac{x+y+z}{3}\right)$, then, in terms of p, what is the average (arithmetic mean) of x, y, and z ?

(A) $4p$

(B) $3p$

(C) $\frac{p}{3}$

(D) $\frac{p}{4}$

(E) $\frac{p}{12}$

24 If $n > 0$ and $9x^2 + kx + 36 = (3x + n)^2$ for all values of x, what is the value of $k - n$?

(A) 0
(B) 6
(C) 12
(D) 30
(E) 36

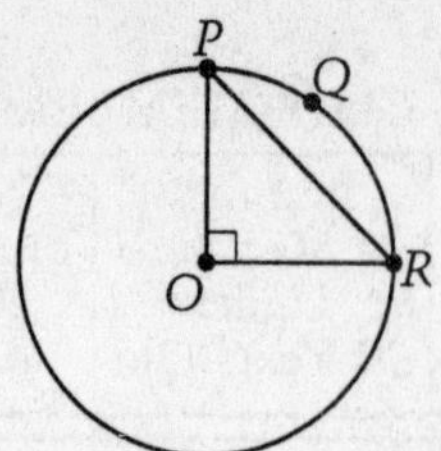

25 The circle in the figure above has center O. Which of the following measures for the figure would be sufficient by itself to determine the radius of the circle?

I. The length of arc PQR
II. The perimeter of $\triangle OPR$
III. The length of chord PR

(A) None
(B) I only
(C) II only
(D) III only
(E) I, II, and III

IF YOU FINISH BEFORE TIME IS CALLED, YOU MAY CHECK YOUR WORK ON THIS SECTION ONLY. DO NOT TURN TO ANY OTHER SECTION IN THE TEST. **STOP**

Section 2 2 2 2 2 2

**Time—30 Minutes
36 Questions**

For each question in this section, select the best answer from among the choices given and fill in the corresponding oval on the answer sheet.

Each sentence below has one or two blanks, each blank indicating that something has been omitted. Beneath the sentence are five words or sets of words labeled A through E. Choose the word or set of words that, when inserted in the sentence, best fits the meaning of the sentence as a whole.

Example:

Medieval kingdoms did not become constitutional republics overnight; on the contrary, the change was ----.

(A) unpopular
(B) unexpected
(C) advantageous
(D) sufficient
(E) gradual

1 Because his paintings represented the Midwest of the mid-1800's as a serene and settled landscape, Robert Duncanson ---- Easterners hesitant about moving westward that relocation was indeed ----.

(A) convinced. .ridiculous
(B) contradicted. .necessary
(C) reminded. .rash
(D) assured. .safe
(E) persuaded. .risky

2 Rachel Carson's book *Silent Spring*, which described a world made lifeless by the accumulation of hazardous pesticides, ---- a grass-roots campaign to ---- the indiscriminate use of such substances.

(A) catalyzed. .propagate
(B) protested. .limit
(C) conceived. .encourage
(D) inspired. .control
(E) allowed. .recommend

3 Florida Congresswoman Ileana Ros-Lehtinen chose to focus on how national issues affect her own ----, those voters she represents.

(A) opponents (B) constituents
(C) successors (D) mentors (E) colleagues

4 In a society that abhors ----, the nonconformist is persistently ----.

(A) creativity. .glorified
(B) rebelliousness. .suppressed
(C) insurgency. .heeded
(D) smugness. .persecuted
(E) stagnation. .denigrated

5 Instead of presenting a balanced view of both sides of the issue, the speaker became increasingly ----, insisting on the correctness of his position.

(A) inarticulate (B) dogmatic (C) elliptical
(D) tactful (E) ambiguous

6 Astronomers who suspected that the sunspot cycle is not eleven years long have been ---- by studies ---- their belief that the entire cycle is actually twice that long.

(A) vindicated. .confirming
(B) exonerated. .refuting
(C) discredited. .substantiating
(D) encouraged. .rejecting
(E) humiliated. .proving

7 He ---- the practices of aggressive autograph seekers, arguing that anyone distinguished enough to merit such ---- also deserved to be treated courteously.

(A) decried. .adulation
(B) defended. .adoration
(C) endorsed. .brusqueness
(D) ignored. .effrontery
(E) vilified. .disdain

8 Andrew has enrolled in a specialized culinary arts program as a way of indulging his ---- French cuisine.

(A) abstinence from (B) tenacity over
(C) distaste for (D) acquisition of
(E) predilection for

9 Someday technology may make door-to-door mail delivery seem ----, that is, as incongruous as pony express delivery would seem now.

(A) recursive (B) contemporaneous
(C) predictable (D) anachronistic
(E) revered

10 The novelist brings out the ---- of human beings time and time again by ---- their lives to the permanence of the vast landscape.

(A) absurdity. .relating
(B) transience. .likening
(C) evanescence. .contrasting
(D) complexity. .comparing
(E) uniqueness. .opposing

GO ON TO THE NEXT PAGE

Each question below consists of a related pair of words or phrases, followed by five pairs of words or phrases labeled A through E. Select the pair that best expresses a relationship similar to that expressed in the original pair.

Example:

CRUMB : BREAD ::
(A) ounce : unit
(B) splinter : wood
(C) water : bucket
(D) twine : rope
(E) cream : butter

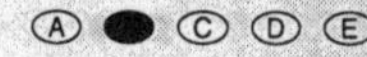

11 ERASER : PAGE ::
(A) mop : floor
(B) sponge : soap
(C) pen : ink
(D) nail : wall
(E) bleach : stain

12 GOGGLES : EYES ::
(A) belt : waist
(B) earrings : ears
(C) razor : hair
(D) gloves : cold
(E) helmet : head

13 PORTFOLIO : DOCUMENTS ::
(A) album : photographs
(B) government : policies
(C) drama : acts
(D) excavation : artifacts
(E) rhythm : drums

14 TENTACLES : OCTOPUS ::
(A) petals : flower
(B) tadpoles : frog
(C) claws : crab
(D) algae : seaweed
(E) quills : porcupine

15 TICKET : ADMISSION ::
(A) letter : salutation
(B) coupon : discount
(C) receipt : payment
(D) license : travel
(E) application : interview

16 PROFICIENCY : EXPERT ::
(A) recognition : winner
(B) victory : athlete
(C) passion : enthusiast
(D) appointment : official
(E) medicine : doctor

17 COSMETICS : EMBELLISH ::
(A) calculation : assess
(B) ornament : adorn
(C) painting : hang
(D) posture : improve
(E) dish : garnish

18 CARPING : CRITICIZE ::
(A) vain : admire
(B) obliging : help
(C) retiring : boast
(D) jealous : possess
(E) wary : surprise

19 RECLUSIVE : COMPANIONSHIP ::
(A) frugal : extravagance
(B) organized : structure
(C) pitiful : compassion
(D) provocative : anger
(E) moody : unhappiness

20 TACTILE : TOUCH ::
(A) musical : hearing
(B) audible : volume
(C) nasal : smell
(D) sensitive : feeling
(E) visible : sight

21 SORT : CRITERION ::
(A) shuffle : order
(B) train : competence
(C) rank : value
(D) divide : quantity
(E) poll : opinion

22 FORENSICS : ARGUMENTATION ::
(A) autopsy : death
(B) syntax : grammar
(C) jurisprudence : law
(D) archaeology : site
(E) etymology : dictionary

23 INTRANSIGENT : COMPROMISE ::
(A) permanent : stability
(B) dogged : surrender
(C) disorganized : chaos
(D) lonesome : friendship
(E) strenuous : exercise

GO ON TO THE NEXT PAGE

The passage below is followed by questions based on its content. Answer the questions on the basis of what is stated or implied in the passage and in any introductory material that may be provided.

Questions 24-36 are based on the following passage.

This excerpt is the beginning of a memoir, published in 1989, by a woman who emigrated with her family from Poland to Canada when she was a teenager.

It is April 1959, I'm standing at the railing of the Batory's upper deck, and I feel that my life is ending. I'm looking out at the crowd that has gathered on the shore to see the ship's departure from Gdynia—a crowd that, all of a sudden, is irrevocably on the other side—and I want to break out, run back, run toward the familiar excitement, the waving hands, the exclamations. We can't be leaving all this behind—but we are. I am thirteen years old, and we are emigrating. It's a notion of such crushing, definitive finality that to me it might as well mean the end of the world.

My sister, four years younger than I, is clutching my hand wordlessly; she hardly understands where we are, or what is happening to us. My parents are highly agitated; they had just been put through a body search by the customs police. Still, the officials weren't clever enough, or suspicious enough, to check my sister and me—lucky for us, since we are both carrying some silverware we were not allowed to take out of Poland in large pockets sewn onto our skirts especially for this purpose, and hidden under capacious sweaters.

When the brass band on the shore strikes up the jaunty mazurka rhythms of the Polish anthem, I am pierced by a youthful sorrow so powerful that I suddenly stop crying and try to hold still against the pain. I desperately want time to stop, to hold the ship still with the force of my will. I am suffering my first, severe attack of nostalgia, or *tesknota*—a word that adds to nostalgia the tonalities of sadness and longing. It is a feeling whose shades and degrees I'm destined to know intimately, but at this hovering moment, it comes upon me like a visitation from a whole new geography of emotions, an annunciation of how much an absence can hurt. Or a premonition of absence, because at this divide, I'm filled to the brim with what I'm about to lose—images of Cracow, which I loved as one loves a person, of the sunbaked villages where we had taken summer vacations, of the hours I spent poring over passages of music with my piano teacher, of conversations and escapades with friends. Looking ahead, I come across an enormous, cold blankness—a darkening, and erasure, of the imagination, as if a camera eye has snapped shut, or as if a heavy curtain has been pulled over the future. Of the place where we're going—Canada—I know nothing. There are vague outlines of half a continent, a sense of vast spaces and little habitation. When my parents were hiding in a branch-covered forest bunker during the war, my father had a book with him called *Canada Fragrant with Resin* which, in his horrible confinement, spoke to him of majestic wilderness, of animals roaming without being pursued, of freedom. That is partly why we are going there, rather than to Israel, where most of our Jewish friends have gone. But to me, the word "Canada" has ominous echoes of the "Sahara." No, my mind rejects the idea of being taken there, I don't want to be pried out of my childhood, my pleasures, my safety, my hopes for becoming a pianist. The Batory pulls away, the foghorn emits its lowing, shofar[1] sound, but my being is engaged in a stubborn refusal to move. My parents put their hands on my shoulders consolingly; for a moment, they allow themselves to acknowledge that there's pain in this departure, much as they wanted it.

Many years later, at a stylish party in New York, I met a woman who told me that she had an enchanted childhood. Her father was a highly positioned diplomat in an Asian country, and she had lived surrounded by sumptuous elegance. . . . No wonder, she said, that when this part of her life came to an end, at age thirteen, she felt she had been exiled from paradise, and had been searching for it ever since.

No wonder. But the wonder is what you can make a paradise out of. I told her that I grew up in a lumpen[2] apartment in Cracow, squeezed into three rudimentary rooms with four other people, surrounded by squabbles, dark political rumblings, memories of wartime suffering, and daily struggle for existence. And yet, when it came time to leave, I, too, felt I was being pushed out of the happy, safe enclosures of Eden.

[1] A trumpet made from a ram's horn and sounded in the synagogue on the Jewish High Holy Days

[2] Pertaining to dispossessed, often displaced, individuals who have been cut off from the socioeconomic class with which they would ordinarily have been identified

GO ON TO THE NEXT PAGE

24 This passage serves mainly to

(A) provide a detailed description of what the author loved most about her life in Poland
(B) recount the author's experience of leaving Cracow
(C) explain why the author's family chose to emigrate
(D) convey the author's resilience during times of great upheaval
(E) create a factual account of the author's family history

25 In lines 2-3, "I feel that my life is ending" most nearly reflects the author's

(A) overwhelming sense of the desperate life that she and her family have led
(B) sad realization that she is leaving a familiar life
(C) unsettling premonition that she will not survive the voyage to Canada
(D) severe state of depression that may lead her to seek professional help
(E) irrational fear that she will be permanently separated from her family

26 In lines 5-6, the author's description of the crowd on the shore suggests that

(A) her family does not expect to find a warm welcome in Canada
(B) her relatives will not be able to visit her in Canada
(C) her family's friends have now turned against them
(D) she will find it difficult to communicate with her Polish friends
(E) the step she is taking is irreversible

27 The passage as a whole suggests that the author differs from her parents in that she

(A) has happier memories of Poland than her parents do
(B) is more sociable than they are
(C) feels no response to the rhythms of the Polish anthem
(D) has no desire to wave to the crowd on the shore
(E) is not old enough to comprehend what she is leaving behind

28 For the author, the experience of leaving Cracow can best be described as

(A) enlightening
(B) exhilarating
(C) annoying
(D) wrenching
(E) ennobling

29 In lines 17-19, the author's description of the customs police suggests that the author views them with

(A) alarm
(B) skepticism
(C) disrespect
(D) caution
(E) paranoia

30 In lines 29-37, the author indicates that "nostalgia" differs from "*tesknota*" in that

(A) *tesknota* cannot be explained in English
(B) *tesknota* denotes a gloomy, bittersweet yearning
(C) *tesknota* is a feeling that never ends
(D) nostalgia is a more painful emotion than *tesknota*
(E) nostalgia connotes a greater degree of desire than *tesknota*

31 By describing her feelings as having "shades and degrees" (line 33), the author suggests that

(A) she is allowing herself to grieve only a little at a time
(B) she is numb to the pain of her grief
(C) she is overwhelmed by her emotions
(D) her sadness is greatest at night
(E) her emotional state is multifaceted

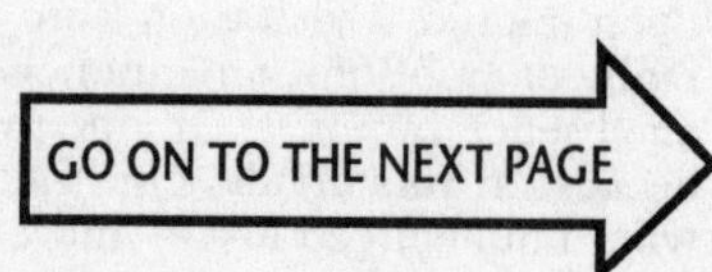

32 In lines 33-34, the phrase "I'm destined to know intimately" implies that the author

(A) cannot escape the path her father has chosen for the family
(B) believes that the future will bring many new emotional experiences
(C) will be deeply affected by the experience of emigrating
(D) must carefully analyze her conflicting emotional reactions
(E) has much to learn about the experience of emigrating

33 The author refers to the "camera eye" (line 46) and the "heavy curtain" (line 47) in order to suggest

(A) the difference between reality and art
(B) the importance of images to the human mind
(C) the difference between Poland and Canada
(D) her inability to overcome her fear of death
(E) her inability to imagine her future life

34 The description of the author as "engaged in a stubborn refusal to move" (lines 65-66) suggests her

(A) determination to claim her space on the crowded deck of the ship
(B) refusal to accept the change in her life
(C) wish to strike back at her parents for taking her away from Poland
(D) resolve not to become a Canadian citizen
(E) need to stay in close proximity to her family

35 In lines 66-69, the author suggests that her parents' comforting gesture indicates

(A) a recognition of feelings of distress over their departure
(B) their exhilaration and relief at the thought of personal freedom
(C) a great deal of ambivalence regarding their decision
(D) pain so great that they can feel no joy in their departure
(E) a complete loss of feeling due to the stressful events

36 The author mentions the anecdote about the person she met at a "stylish party in New York" (line 70) in order to

(A) prove that the author had become less childlike and more sophisticated
(B) demonstrate that the author's parents had become affluent in Canada
(C) describe how wealthy children are raised in Asian countries
(D) make an important point about childhood happiness
(E) show that the author had ultimately lived in the United States as well as in Canada

IF YOU FINISH BEFORE TIME IS CALLED, YOU MAY CHECK YOUR WORK ON THIS SECTION ONLY. DO NOT TURN TO ANY OTHER SECTION IN THE TEST. **STOP**

Section 3 3 3 3 3 3 3

Time—30 Minutes
25 Questions

This section contains two types of questions. You have 30 minutes to complete both types. You may use any available space for scratchwork.

Notes:

1. The use of a calculator is permitted. All numbers used are real numbers.
2. Figures that accompany problems in this test are intended to provide information useful in solving the problems. They are drawn as accurately as possible EXCEPT when it is stated in a specific problem that the figure is not drawn to scale. All figures lie in a plane unless otherwise indicated.

Reference Information

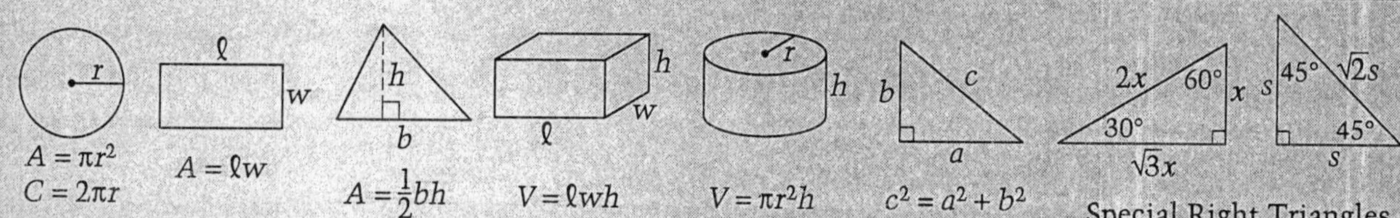

The number of degrees of arc in a circle is 360.
The measure in degrees of a straight angle is 180.
The sum of the measures in degrees of the angles of a triangle is 180.

Directions for Quantitative Comparison Questions

Questions 1-15 each consist of two quantities in boxes, one in Column A and one in Column B. You are to compare the two quantities and on the answer sheet fill in oval

A if the quantity in Column A is greater;
B if the quantity in Column B is greater;
C if the two quantities are equal;
D if the relationship cannot be determined from the information given.

AN E RESPONSE WILL NOT BE SCORED.

Notes:

1. In some questions, information is given about one or both of the quantities to be compared. In such cases, the given information is centered above the two columns and is not boxed.
2. In a given question, a symbol that appears in both columns represents the same thing in Column A as it does in Column B.
3. Letters such as x, n, and k stand for real numbers.

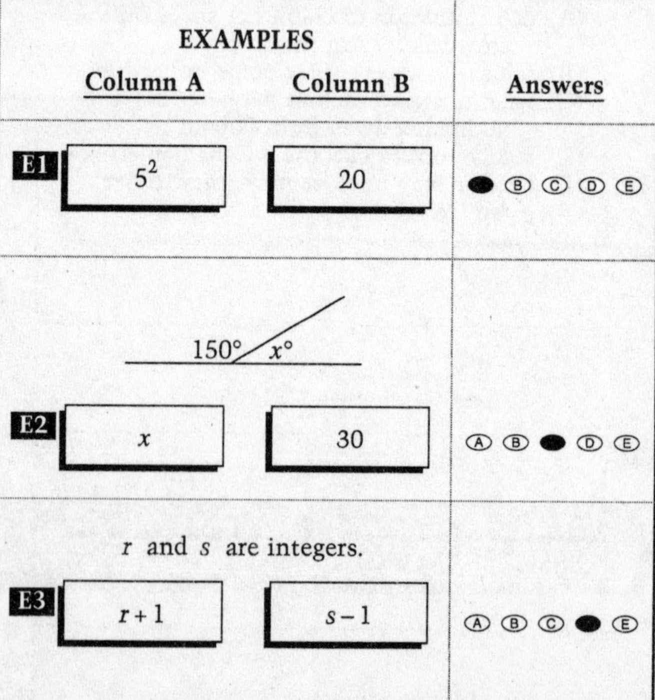

EXAMPLES
Column A
Column B
Answers
E1
5^2
20
150°
x°
E2
x
30
r and s are integers.
E3
r + 1
s − 1

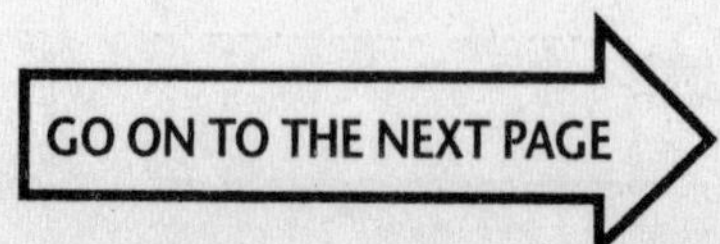

SUMMARY DIRECTIONS FOR COMPARISON QUESTIONS

Answer: A if the quantity in Column A is greater;
B if the quantity in Column B is greater;
C if the two quantities are equal;
D if the relationship cannot be determined from the information given.

	Column A	Column B
1	The average (arithmetic mean) of −3, 1, and 3	The average (arithmetic mean) of −3, 2, and 3

$x > y$
$y = z$

	Column A	Column B
2	x	z

The vertices of equilateral polygon $ABCDE$ lie on a circle.

	Column A	Column B
3	The length of arc ABC	The length of arc CDE

r and s are positive integers.

	Column A	Column B
4	$\frac{r}{r+s}$	$\frac{r+s}{r}$

Point P, with coordinates (x, y), is exactly 5 units from the origin.

	Column A	Column B
5	x	y

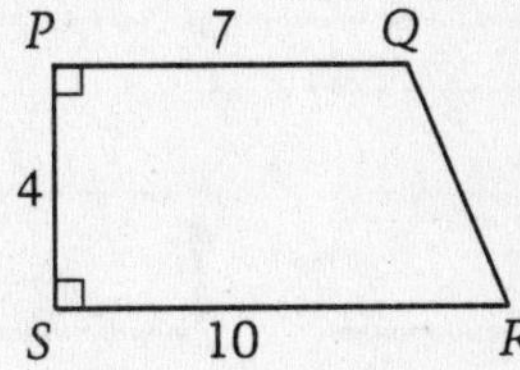

	Column A	Column B
6	The area of $PQRS$	30

Eggs cost x cents per dozen.
$(x > 0)$

	Column A	Column B
7	The cost of 60 eggs	$6x$ cents

$A = \{1, 2, 3\}$
$B = \{4, 5, 6, 7\}$

	Column A	Column B
8	The total number of ordered pairs (a, b) that can be formed where a is from set A and b is from set B	The total number of ordered pairs (b, a) that can be formed where b is from set B and a from set A

GO ON TO THE NEXT PAGE

SUMMARY DIRECTIONS FOR COMPARISON QUESTIONS

Answer: A if the quantity in Column A is greater;
B if the quantity in Column B is greater;
C if the two quantities are equal;
D if the relationship cannot be determined from the information given.

	Column A	Column B
	$z = \frac{x}{y}$	
9	z	y
	Square S and equilateral triangle T have equal areas.	
10	The length of a side of S	The length of a side of T
	The first number in a sequence of 10 numbers is 3.	
11	The sum of the 10 numbers in the sequence	30
	Machine M produces 27 cans in h hours. $0 < h < \frac{1}{2}$	
12	The number of cans machine M produces in 2 hours at this rate	54
	$x > 3$	
13	$3(3 - x)$	$x(3 - x)$
	$x + \frac{1}{7} = y$	
14	$y - 1$	$x - 1$
	$w > 0$	
15	w increased by 400 percent of w	$5w$

GO ON TO THE NEXT PAGE

Directions for Student-Produced Response Questions

Each of the remaining 10 questions requires you to solve the problem and enter your answer by marking the ovals in the special grid, as shown in the examples below.

Answer: $\frac{7}{12}$ or 7/12 — Write answer in boxes. → 7/12 ← Fraction line. Grid in result.

Answer: 2.5 — 2.5 ← Decimal point

Answer: 201 — Either position is correct. 201 | 201

Note: You may start your answers in any column, space permitting. Columns not needed should be left blank.

- Mark no more than one oval in any column.
- Because the answer sheet will be machine-scored, **you will receive credit only if the ovals are filled in correctly.**
- Although not required, it is suggested that you write your answer in the boxes at the top of the columns to help you fill in the ovals accurately.
- Some problems may have more than one correct answer. In such cases, grid only one answer.
- No question has a negative answer.
- **Mixed numbers** such as $2\frac{1}{2}$ must be gridded as 2.5 or 5/2. (If 21/2 is gridded, it will be interpreted as $\frac{21}{2}$, not $2\frac{1}{2}$.)
- Decimal Accuracy: If you obtain a decimal answer, **enter the most accurate value the grid will accommodate.** For example, if you obtain an answer such as 0.6666 . . . , you should record the result as .666 or .667. **Less accurate values such as .66 or .67 are not acceptable.**

Acceptable ways to grid $\frac{2}{3} = .6666\ldots$

2/3 | .666 | .667

16 Raul packed 144 bottles of soft drink in cartons of 6 bottles each and Julio packed 144 bottles of soft drink in cartons of 24 bottles each. How many more cartons did Raul use than Julio used?

17 On a certain map, a distance of 25 miles is represented by 1.0 centimeter. How many miles are represented by 3.3 centimeters on the map?

18 The sum of k and $k + 1$ is greater than 9 but less than 17. If k is an integer, what is one possible value of k ?

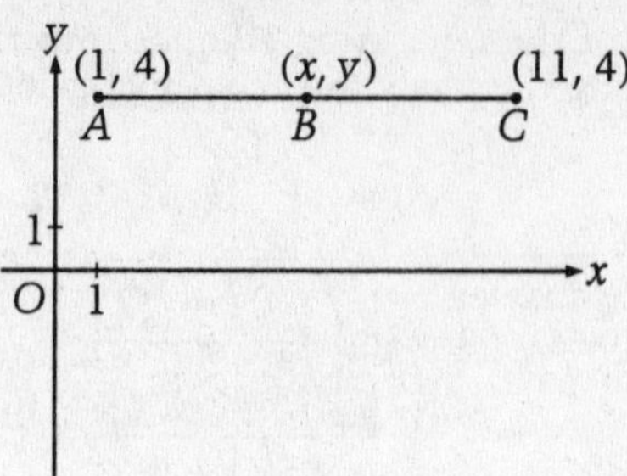

20 If $AB = BC$ in the figure above, what is the x-coordinate of point B ?

19

$$\begin{array}{r} 0.XY \\ +\ 0.YX \\ \hline 0.XX \end{array}$$

In the correctly worked addition problem above, X and Y are digits. What must the digit Y be?

21 For all nonnegative numbers a, let $\boxed{a}$ be defined by $\boxed{a} = \frac{\sqrt{a}}{3}$. If $\boxed{a} = 2$, what is the value of a ?

GO ON TO THE NEXT PAGE

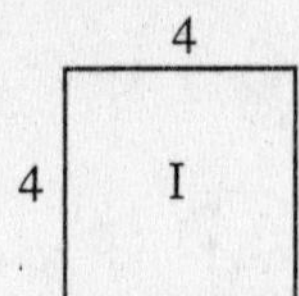

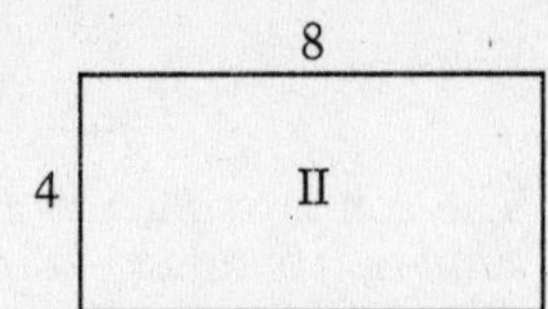

22 A rectangular solid has two faces the same size and shape as figure I above and four faces the same size and shape as figure II above. What is the volume of the solid?

23 How many of the first one hundred positive integers contain the digit 9 ?

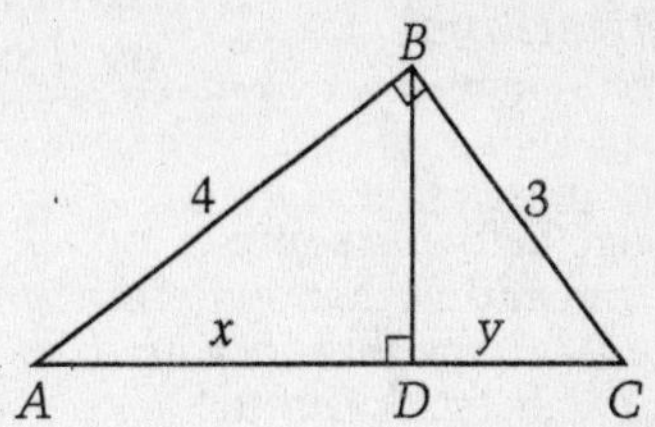

24 In right $\triangle ABC$ above, $\frac{y}{3} = \frac{3}{x + y}$. What is the value of y ?

25 For the numbers r, s, and t, the average (arithmetic mean) is twice the median. If $r < s < t$, $r = 0$, and $t = ns$, what is the value of n ?

IF YOU FINISH BEFORE TIME IS CALLED, YOU MAY CHECK YOUR WORK ON THIS SECTION ONLY. DO NOT TURN TO ANY OTHER SECTION IN THE TEST. **STOP**

Section 4 4 4 4 4

Time—30 Minutes
31 Questions

For each question in this section, select the best answer from among the choices given and fill in the corresponding oval on the answer sheet.

Each sentence below has one or two blanks, each blank indicating that something has been omitted. Beneath the sentence are five words or sets of words labeled A through E. Choose the word or set of words that, when inserted in the sentence, best fits the meaning of the sentence as a whole.

Example:

Medieval kingdoms did not become constitutional republics overnight; on the contrary, the change was ----.

(A) unpopular
(B) unexpected
(C) advantageous
(D) sufficient
(E) gradual

1 Some lizards display the characteristic of ----: if their tails are broken off during predatory encounters, the tails will eventually grow back.

(A) adaptation (B) mimicry (C) regeneration (D) aggression (E) mutability

2 The two travelers may have chosen ---- routes across the continent, but the starting point was the same for each.

(A) coinciding (B) direct (C) charted (D) divergent (E) intersecting

3 The author's use of copious detail, though intended to ---- the reader's appreciation of a tumultuous era, was instead regarded by many as a barrage of ---- information.

(A) excite. .illuminating
(B) reverse. .accurate
(C) curtail. .boring
(D) deepen. .trivial
(E) deter. .historical

4 Seemingly permeated by natural light, Rufino Tamayo's painting looks as if it had been created with ---- hues.

(A) luminous (B) florid (C) ominous (D) varnished (E) fading

5 The commissioner is an irreproachable public servant, trying to ---- integrity and honor to a department that, while not totally corrupt, has nonetheless been ---- by greed and corruption.

(A) deny. .overrun
(B) impute. .tainted
(C) attribute. .purified
(D) entrust. .invigorated
(E) restore. .undermined

6 Emily Dickinson was ---- poet, making few concessions to ordinary grammar or to conventions of meter and rhyme.

(A) a sensitive (B) an imitative (C) an idiosyncratic (D) a realistic (E) a decorous

7 Conflicting standards for allowable radiation levels in foods made ---- appraisals of the damage to crops following the reactor meltdown extremely difficult.

(A) reliable (B) private (C) intrusive (D) conscious (E) inflated

8 In earlier ages, a dilettante was someone who delighted in the arts; the term had none of the ---- connotations of superficiality that it has today and, in fact, was considered ----.

(A) implicit. .disreputable
(B) romantic. .threatening
(C) patronizing. .complimentary
(D) irritating. .presumptuous
(E) entertaining. .prestigious

9 The historian noted irony in the fact that developments considered ---- by people of that era are now viewed as having been ----.

(A) inspirational. .impetuous
(B) bizarre. .irrational
(C) intuitive. .uncertain
(D) actual. .grandiose
(E) improbable. .inevitable

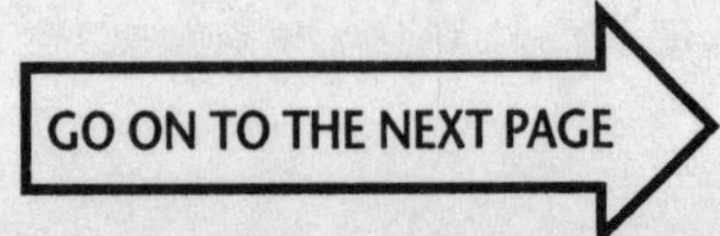

Each question below consists of a related pair of words or phrases, followed by five pairs of words or phrases labeled A through E. Select the pair that best expresses a relationship similar to that expressed in the original pair.

Example:

CRUMB : BREAD ::
(A) ounce : unit
(B) splinter : wood
(C) water : bucket
(D) twine : rope
(E) cream : butter

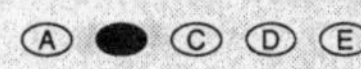

10 CURRENT : ELECTRICITY ::
(A) gauge : measurement
(B) forge : metal
(C) beam : light
(D) ripple : lake
(E) curve : circle

11 EMBROIDERY : CLOTH ::
(A) bracelet : jewelry
(B) mural : wall
(C) tattoo : design
(D) paint : color
(E) flower : vase

12 WAITER : DINER ::
(A) ballerina : dancer
(B) clerk : customer
(C) nurse : orderly
(D) juror : judge
(E) captain : teammate

13 KERNEL : NUT ::
(A) yolk : egg
(B) grape : raisin
(C) flour : bread
(D) soil : seed
(E) thorn : stem

14 NIGHTMARE : DREAM ::
(A) semaphore : signal
(B) dread : expectation
(C) lure : trap
(D) fear : victim
(E) frustration : confusion

15 COGENT : PERSUASIVENESS ::
(A) pardoned : blame
(B) staid : manner
(C) tactful : awkwardness
(D) conceited : reputation
(E) lucid : clarity

GO ON TO THE NEXT PAGE

Each passage below is followed by questions based on its content. Answer the questions on the basis of what is stated or implied in each passage and in any introductory material that may be provided.

Questions 16-20 are based on the following passage.

This excerpt discusses the relationship between plants and their environments.

Why do some desert plants grow tall and thin like organ pipes? Why do most trees in the tropics keep their leaves year round? Why in the Arctic tundra are there no trees at all? After many years without convincing general answers, we now know much about what sets the fashion in plant design.

Using terminology more characteristic of a thermal engineer than of a botanist, we can think of plants as mechanisms that must balance their heat budgets. A plant by day is staked out under the Sun with no way of sheltering itself. All day long it absorbs heat. If it did not lose as much heat as it gained, then eventually it would die. Plants get rid of their heat by warming the air around them, by evaporating water, and by radiating heat to the atmosphere and the cold, black reaches of space. Each plant must balance its heat budget so that its temperature is tolerable for the processes of life.

Plants in the Arctic tundra lie close to the ground in the thin layer of still air that clings there. A foot or two above the ground are the winds of Arctic cold. Tundra plants absorb heat from the Sun and tend to warm up; they probably balance most of their heat budgets by radiating heat to space, but also by warming the still air that is trapped among them. As long as Arctic plants are close to the ground, they can balance their heat budgets. But if they should stretch up as a tree does, they would lift their working parts, their leaves, into the streaming Arctic winds. Then it is likely that the plants could not absorb enough heat from the Sun to avoid being cooled below a critical temperature. Your heat budget does not balance if you stand tall in the Arctic.

Such thinking also helps explain other characteristics of plant design. A desert plant faces the opposite problem from that of an Arctic plant — the danger of overheating. It is short of water and so cannot cool itself by evaporation without dehydrating. The familiar sticklike shape of desert plants represents one of the solutions to this problem: the shape exposes the smallest possible surface to incoming solar radiation and provides the largest possible surface from which the plant can radiate heat. In tropical rain forests, by way of contrast, the scorching Sun is not a problem for plants because there is sufficient water.

This working model allows us to connect the general characteristics of the forms of plants in different habitats with factors such as temperature, availability of water, and presence or absence of seasonal differences. Our Earth is covered with a patchwork quilt of meteorological conditions, and the patterns of this patchwork are faithfully reflected by the plants.

16 The passage primarily focuses on which of the following characteristics of plants?

(A) Their ability to grow equally well in all environments
(B) Their effects on the Earth's atmosphere
(C) Their ability to store water for dry periods
(D) Their fundamental similarity of shape
(E) Their ability to balance heat intake and output

17 Which of the following could best be substituted for the words "sets the fashion in" (line 6) without changing the intended meaning?

(A) improves the appearance of
(B) accounts for the uniformity of
(C) defines acceptable standards for
(D) determines the general characteristics of
(E) reduces the heat budgets of

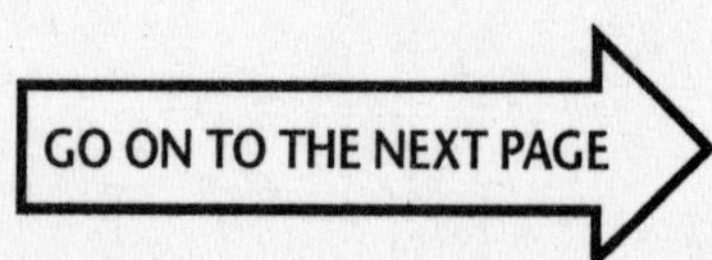

18 According to the passage, which of the following is most responsible for preventing trees from growing tall in the Arctic?

(A) The hard, frozen ground
(B) The small amount of available sunshine
(C) The cold, destructive winds
(D) The large amount of snow that falls each year
(E) The absence of seasonal differences in temperature

19 The author suggests that the "sticklike shape of desert plants" (lines 41-42) can be attributed to the

(A) inability of the plants to radiate heat to the air around them
(B) presence of irregular seasonal differences in the desert
(C) large surface area that the plants must expose to the Sun
(D) absence of winds strong enough to knock down tall, thin plants
(E) extreme heat and aridity of the habitat

20 The contrast mentioned in lines 46-48 specifically concerns the

(A) availability of moisture
(B) scorching heat of the Sun
(C) seasonal differences in temperature
(D) variety of plant species
(E) heat radiated by plants to the atmosphere

GO ON TO THE NEXT PAGE

Questions 21-31 are based on the following passage.

This passage is from a book by an African American woman who is a law professor.

This semester I have been teaching a course entitled Women and Notions of Property. I have been focusing on the ways in which gender affects individuals' perspectives—gender in this instance having less to do with the biology of male and female than with the language of power relations, of dominance and submission, of assertion and deference, of big and little. An example of the stories we discuss is the following, used to illustrate the rhetoric of power relations, whose examination, I tell my students, is at the heart of the course.

Walking down Fifth Avenue in New York not long ago, I came up behind a couple and their young son. The child, about four or five years old, had evidently been complaining about big dogs. The mother was saying, "But why are you afraid of big dogs?" "Because they're big," he responded with eminent good sense. "But what's the difference between a big dog and a little dog?" the father persisted. "They're *big*," said the child. "But there's really no difference," said the mother, pointing to a large, slavering wolfhound with narrow eyes and the calculated amble of a gangster, and then to a beribboned Pekingese the size of a roller skate, who was flouncing along just ahead of us all, in that little fox-trotty step that keeps Pekingeses from ever being taken seriously. "See?" said the father. "If you look really closely you'll see there's no difference at all. They're all just dogs."

And I thought: Talk about a static, unyielding, totally uncompromising point of reference. These people must be lawyers. Where else do people learn so well the idiocies of High Objectivity? How else do people learn to capitulate so uncritically to a norm that refuses to allow for difference? How else do grown-ups sink so deeply into the authoritarianism of their own world view that they can universalize their relative bigness so completely as to obliterate the viewpoint of their child's relative smallness? (To say nothing of the viewpoint of the slavering wolfhound, from whose own narrow perspective I dare say the little boy must have looked exactly like a lamb chop.)

I use this story in my class because I think it illustrates a paradigm of thought by which children are taught not to see what they see; by which African Americans are reassured that there is no real inequality in the world, just their own bad dreams; and by which women are taught not to experience what they experience, in deference to men's ways of knowing. The story also illustrates the possibility of a collective perspective or social positioning that would give rise to a claim for the legal interests of groups. In a historical moment when individual rights have become the basis for any remedy, too often group interests are defeated by, for example, finding the one four year old who has wrestled whole packs of wolfhounds fearlessly to the ground; using that individual experience to attack the validity of there ever being any generalizable fear of wolfhounds by four year olds; and then recasting the general group experience as a fragmented series of specific, isolated events rather than a pervasive social phenomenon ("You have every right to think that that wolfhound has the ability to bite off your head, but that's just your point of view").

My students, most of whom signed up expecting to experience that crisp, refreshing, clear-headed sensation that "thinking like a lawyer" purportedly endows, are confused by this and all the stories I tell them in my class on Women and Notions of Property. They are confused enough by the idea of property alone, overwhelmed by the thought of dogs and women as academic subjects, and paralyzed by the idea that property, ownership, and rights might have a gender and that gender might be a matter of words.

21 In lines 2-8, the author describes "gender" primarily in terms of

(A) early childhood experience
(B) genetics and hormonal chemistry
(C) the distribution of power in relationships
(D) the influence of role models on personality formation
(E) the varying social conventions in different cultures

22 In line 19, "eminent" most nearly means

(A) famed
(B) exalted
(C) protruding
(D) influential
(E) obvious

GO ON TO THE NEXT PAGE

23 The description of the two dogs in lines 23-28 serves primarily to

(A) defuse a tense situation with humor
(B) discredit what the parents are saying
(C) emphasize the dogs' resemblance to their owners
(D) suggest that dogs are more sensible than humans
(E) illustrate a legal concept regarding pet ownership

24 In line 24, "calculated" most nearly means

(A) scheming
(B) predetermined
(C) deliberate
(D) predictable
(E) estimated

25 The author uses the term "authoritarianism" in line 39 in order to

(A) link habits of thought with political repression
(B) ridicule the parents in the story by using comically exaggerated terms
(C) criticize the harsh teaching methods used in law schools
(D) show that the attitude represented by the parents is unconstitutional
(E) allude to parental roles in societies of the past

26 The author describes the wolfhound's viewpoint (lines 42-45) in order to

(A) refute those who disapprove of storytelling as a teaching tool
(B) introduce an example of desirable objectivity
(C) suggest that it is similar to the parents' viewpoint
(D) show that viewpoints are not always predictable
(E) lend credence to the child's point of view

27 The "paradigm of thought" in lines 46-53 may be described as one that disposes people toward

(A) cooperating with one another for the common good
(B) discussing family problems frankly and openly
(C) resorting to violence when thwarted
(D) discounting their own experiences
(E) suing others over trivial matters

28 The process of defeating group interests described in lines 56-69 is one in which

(A) an exception is made to look like a general rule
(B) a logical flaw in the group's arguments is attacked
(C) a crucial legal term is used in a misleading way
(D) statistical evidence is distorted to the opposition's advantage
(E) personal arguments are used to discredit group leaders

29 The author presents the idea of wrestling "whole packs of wolfhounds" (line 60) as an example of

(A) an argument that no lawyer would find plausible
(B) an event so unusual as to be irrelevant
(C) something that only a child would attempt
(D) a morally reprehensible act
(E) an easier task than studying law

30 In lines 66-69, the "right" is characterized as

(A) central to the concept of democracy
(B) probably not attainable without a constitutional amendment
(C) something that is hardly worth having
(D) something that powerful groups are reluctant to give up
(E) something that most people are not aware that they have

31 The final paragraph suggests that the author probably believes that a law professor's main duty is to

(A) make a highly technical subject exciting to students
(B) jar students out of unexamined assumptions about the study of law
(C) emphasize the importance of clear legal writing
(D) encourage more students from disadvantaged groups to become lawyers
(E) train students in the practical skills they will need in the courtroom

IF YOU FINISH BEFORE TIME IS CALLED, YOU MAY CHECK YOUR WORK ON THIS SECTION ONLY. DO NOT TURN TO ANY OTHER SECTION IN THE TEST. **STOP**

Section 6 6 6 6

Time—15 Minutes
10 Questions

In this section solve each problem, using any available space on the page for scratchwork. Then decide which is the best of the choices given and fill in the corresponding oval on the answer sheet.

Notes:

1. The use of a calculator is permitted. All numbers used are real numbers.
2. Figures that accompany problems in this test are intended to provide information useful in solving the problems. They are drawn as accurately as possible EXCEPT when it is stated in a specific problem that the figure is not drawn to scale. All figures lie in a plane unless otherwise indicated.

Reference Information

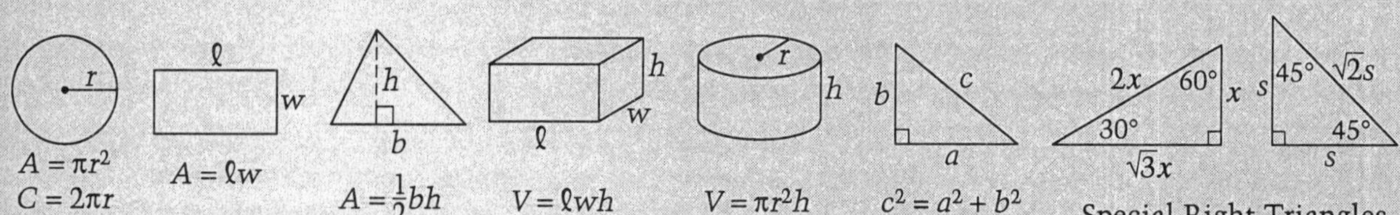

$A = \pi r^2$
$C = 2\pi r$

$A = \ell w$

$A = \frac{1}{2}bh$

$V = \ell wh$

$V = \pi r^2 h$

$c^2 = a^2 + b^2$

Special Right Triangles

The number of degrees of arc in a circle is 360.
The measure in degrees of a straight angle is 180.
The sum of the measures in degrees of the angles of a triangle is 180.

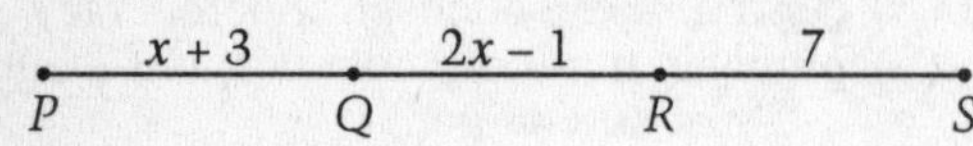

1 In the figure above, what is the length of PS in terms of x?

(A) $x + 2$
(B) $x + 9$
(C) $2x + 2$
(D) $3x + 9$
(E) $3x + 11$

2 Brenda received pledges from 30 people for a 50-mile bike-a-thon. If Brenda rode 50 miles and each person gave \$0.10 for each mile she rode, which of the following gives the total dollar amount of money Brenda collected?

(A) $30 \times 50 \times 0.10$
(B) $30 \times 50 + 0.10$
(C) $50 \times 0.10 + 30$
(D) $50 + 30 \times 0.10$
(E) $30 + 50 + 0.10$

GO ON TO THE NEXT PAGE

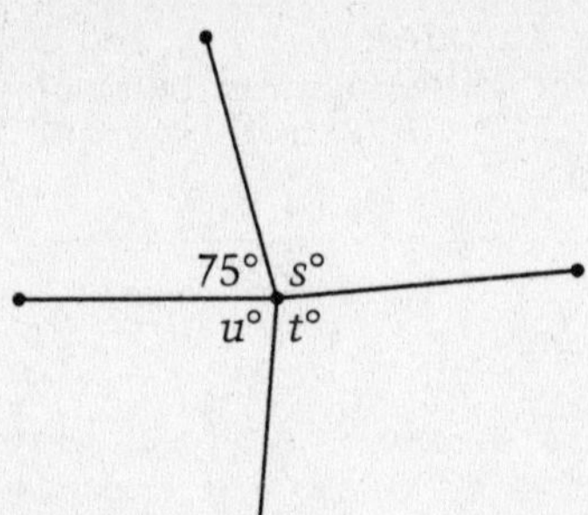

3 In the figure above, what is the value of $s + t + u$?

(A) 105
(B) 115
(C) 225
(D) 285
(E) 295

---

4 On a report, the typing begins $\frac{3}{4}$ inch from the left edge of the paper and ends $1\frac{1}{2}$ inches from the right edge. If the width of the paper is $8\frac{1}{2}$ inches, how many inches per line is used for typing?

(A) $7\frac{3}{4}$

(B) $7\frac{1}{2}$

(C) 7

(D) $6\frac{1}{2}$

(E) $6\frac{1}{4}$

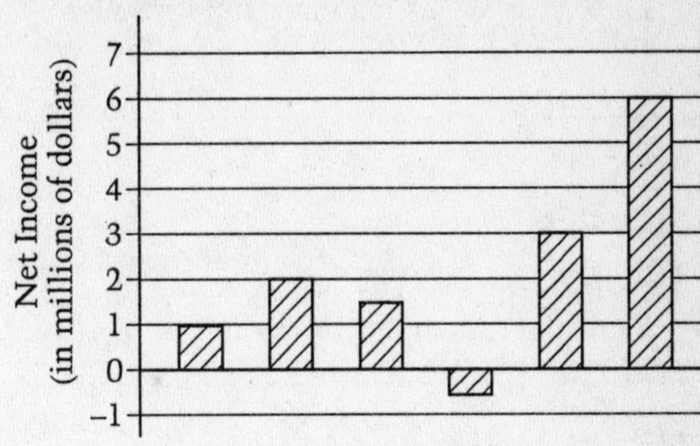

5 According to the graph above, Company X showed the greatest change in net income between which two consecutive years?

(A) 1985 and 1986
(B) 1986 and 1987
(C) 1987 and 1988
(D) 1988 and 1989
(E) 1989 and 1990

GO ON TO THE NEXT PAGE

6 If $r = as^4$ and $s = bt^3$, which of the following is a correct expression for r in terms of $a, b,$ and t?

(A) abt^{12}
(B) ab^4t^7
(C) ab^4t^{12}
(D) $a^4b^4t^7$
(E) $a^4b^4t^{12}$

7 What is the area of a right triangle whose perimeter is 36 and whose sides are x, $x + 3$, and $x + 6$?

(A) 27
(B) 54
(C) 81
(D) 108
(E) 135

8 If p and r are integers, $p \neq 0$, and $p = -r$, which of the following must be true?

(A) $p < r$
(B) $p > r$
(C) $p + r < 0$
(D) $p - r < 0$
(E) $pr < 0$

GO ON TO THE NEXT PAGE

9 One number is 3 times another number, and their sum is –10. What is the lesser of the two numbers?

(A) –2.5
(B) –3.0
(C) –5.5
(D) –7.0
(E) –7.5

Digit of N	Digit of Ⓝ
0	1
1	2
2	3
3	4
4	5
5	6
6	7
7	8
8	9
9	0

10 For any positive integer N, the symbol Ⓝ represents the number obtained when every digit of N, <u>except</u> the leftmost digit, is replaced by its corresponding digit in the second column of the table above. For which of the following is Ⓝ less than N?

(A) $N = 349$
(B) $N = 394$
(C) $N = 487$
(D) $N = 934$
(E) $N = 984$

IF YOU FINISH BEFORE TIME IS CALLED, YOU MAY CHECK YOUR WORK ON THIS SECTION ONLY. DO NOT TURN TO ANY OTHER SECTION IN THE TEST. **STOP**

Section 7 7

Time—15 Minutes
11 Questions

For each question in this section, select the best answer from among the choices given and fill in the corresponding oval on the answer sheet.

The two passages below are followed by questions based on their content and on the relationship between the two passages. Answer the questions on the basis of what is stated or implied in the passages and in any introductory material that may be provided.

Questions 1-11 are based on the following pair of passages.

Robinson Crusoe, *a novel first published in England in 1719, was written by Daniel Defoe. It relates the story of Crusoe's successful efforts to make a tolerable existence for himself after being shipwrecked alone on an apparently uninhabited island. The passages below are adapted from two twentieth-century commentaries by Ian Watt and James Sutherland on the novel's main character.*

Passage 1—Ian Watt (1957)

That Robinson Crusoe is an embodiment of economic individualism hardly needs demonstration. All of Defoe's heroes and heroines pursue money, and they pursue it very methodically. Crusoe's bookkeeping conscience, indeed, has established an effective priority over all of his other thoughts and emotions. The various forms of traditional group relationship—family, village, a sense of nationality—all are weakened, as are the competing claims of noneconomic individual achievement and enjoyment, ranging from spiritual salvation to the pleasures of recreation. For the most part, the main characters in Defoe's works either have no family or, like Crusoe, leave it at an early age never to return. Not too much importance can be attached to this fact, since adventure stories demand the absence of conventional social ties. Still, Robinson Crusoe does have a home and family, and he leaves them for the classic reason of economic individualism—that it is necessary to better his condition. "Something fatal in that propension of nature" calls him to the sea and adventure, and against "settling to business" in the station to which he is born—and this despite the elaborate praise that his father heaps upon that condition. Leaving home, improving the lot one was born to, is a vital feature of the individualist pattern of life.

Crusoe is not a mere footloose adventurer, and his travels, like his freedom from social ties, are merely somewhat extreme cases of tendencies that are normal in modern society as a whole since, by making the pursuit of gain a primary motive, economic individualism has much increased the mobility of the individual. More specifically, the story of Robinson Crusoe is based on some of the many volumes recounting the exploits of those voyagers who in the sixteenth and seventeenth centuries had assisted the development of capitalism. Defoe's story, then, expresses some of the most important tendencies of the life of his time, and it is this that sets his hero apart from most other travelers in literature. Robinson Crusoe is not, like Ulysses, an unwilling voyager trying to get back to his family and his native land: profit is Crusoe's only vocation, and the whole world is his territory.

Passage 2—James Sutherland (1971)

To Ian Watt, Robinson Crusoe is a characteristic embodiment of economic individualism. "Profit," he assures us, "is Crusoe's only vocation," and "only money—fortune in its modern sense—is a proper cause of deep feeling." Watt therefore claims that Crusoe's motive for disobeying his father and leaving home was to better his economic condition, and that the argument between Crusoe and his parents in the early pages of the book is really a debate "not about filial duty or religion, but about whether going or staying is likely to be the most advantageous course materially: both sides accept the economic motive as primary." We certainly cannot afford to ignore those passages in which Crusoe attributes his misfortunes to an evil influence that drove him into "projects and undertakings beyond my reach, such as are indeed often the ruin of the best heads in business." But

GO ON TO THE NEXT PAGE

surely the emphasis is not on the economic motive as such, but on the willingness to gamble and seek for quick profits beyond what "the nature of the thing permitted." Crusoe's father wished him to take up the law as a profession, and if Crusoe had done so, he would likely have become a very wealthy man indeed. Crusoe's failure to accept his father's choice for him illustrates not economic individualism so much as Crusoe's lack of economic prudence, indifference to a calm and normal bourgeois life, and love of travel.

Unless we are to say—and we have no right to say it—that Crusoe did not know himself, profit hardly seems to have been his "only vocation." Instead, we are presented with a man who was driven (like so many contemporary Englishmen whom Defoe either admired or was fascinated by) by a kind of compulsion to wander footloose about the world. As if to leave no doubt about his restless desire to travel, Crusoe contrasts himself with his business partner, the very pattern of the economic motive and of what a merchant ought to be, who would have been quite happy "to have gone like a carrier's horse, always to the same inn, backward and forward, provided he could, as he called it, find his account in it." Crusoe, on the other hand, was like a rambling boy who never wanted to see again what he had already seen. "My eye," he tells us, "was never satisfied with seeing, was still more desirous of wand'ring and seeing."

1 The first paragraph of Passage 1 (lines 1-28) primarily explores the contrast between

(A) economics and religion
(B) business and adventure
(C) family responsibilities and service to one's country
(D) Crusoe's sense of duty and his desire for pleasure
(E) economic individualism and group-oriented behavior

2 Watt refers to "spiritual salvation" (lines 11-12) as an example of

(A) something in which Crusoe seemed to show relatively little interest
(B) the ultimate goal in life for most of Defoe's contemporaries
(C) an important difference in priorities between Crusoe and his father
(D) something that Defoe believed was incompatible with the pursuit of pleasure
(E) a crucial value that Crusoe's family failed to pass on to him

3 Which statement about Crusoe is most consistent with the information in Passage 1 ?

(A) He left home because his father forced him to do so.
(B) He single-mindedly pursued financial gain.
(C) He was driven to seek pleasure through world travel.
(D) He had a highly developed sense of morality.
(E) He was economically imprudent to a fault.

4 In line 86, "pattern" most nearly means

(A) configuration
(B) duplicate
(C) decoration
(D) perfection
(E) model

5 It can be inferred that Crusoe's business partner was "like a carrier's horse" (line 89) in that the partner was

(A) satisfied with a life of routine
(B) descended from ancestors who were both noble and strong
(C) strong enough to bear any burden
(D) stubborn in refusing to change
(E) loyal to Crusoe to a degree of near servility

6 In context, the phrase "find his account in it" (line 91) can best be interpreted to mean

(A) be exposed to new experiences
(B) make a reasonable profit
(C) seek adventure around the world
(D) become popular and well known
(E) acquire great power and responsibility

GO ON TO THE NEXT PAGE

7 Crusoe's self-assessment quoted at the end of Passage 2 (lines 94-96) serves primarily to

(A) reveal that Crusoe did not know himself as well as he thought he did
(B) suggest that vision entails more than merely seeing
(C) suggest that, though boylike, Crusoe was more like Ulysses than Watt acknowledges
(D) provide support for Sutherland's view of Crusoe
(E) introduce one of Crusoe's traits

8 Both passages indicate that Crusoe's father was

(A) similar to the parents of main characters in other works by Defoe
(B) confident that his son would succeed in whatever field he chose
(C) in favor of more prudent behavior by his son
(D) opposed to the business partners chosen by his son
(E) proud of his son's ability to survive comfortably after being shipwrecked

9 In both passages, Crusoe's attitude toward the idea of "settling to business" (lines 23-24) like his father is described as

(A) eager anticipation
(B) conventional acceptance
(C) confused uncertainty
(D) moral suspicion
(E) innate opposition

10 The authors of the two passages would apparently agree that Crusoe was

(A) motivated only by personal financial gain
(B) profoundly unaware of his basic nature and calling in life
(C) commendable in his devotion to his family and his business partners
(D) willing to take risks while traveling
(E) responsible for whatever misfortunes befell him in life

11 The primary focus of this pair of passages is

(A) earlier commentaries on Defoe's *Robinson Crusoe*
(B) the exact nature of the flaws in Crusoe's character
(C) the style and structure of *Robinson Crusoe*
(D) Defoe's positive portrayal of greed
(E) Crusoe's motivation for leaving home and traveling abroad

IF YOU FINISH BEFORE TIME IS CALLED, YOU MAY CHECK YOUR WORK ON THIS SECTION ONLY. DO NOT TURN TO ANY OTHER SECTION IN THE TEST. **STOP**

SAT I: Reasoning Test Answer Key
Saturday, November 1994

VERBAL

Section 2

Five-choice Questions

	COR. ANS.	DIFF. LEV.
1.	D	2
2.	D	2
3.	B	3
4.	B	3
5.	B	4
6.	A	3
7.	A	4
8.	E	3
9.	D	4
10.	C	5
11.	A	2
12.	E	1
13.	A	1
14.	C	3
15.	B	3
16.	C	3
17.	B	3
18.	B	4
19.	A	3
20.	E	4
21.	C	4
22.	C	5
23.	B	5
24.	B	3
25.	B	1
26.	E	2
27.	A	2
28.	D	3
29.	C	4
30.	B	3
31.	E	4
32.	C	3
33.	E	2
34.	B	2
35.	A	3
36.	D	3

______ no. correct

______ no. incorrect

Section 4

Five-choice Questions

	COR. ANS.	DIFF. LEV.
1.	C	2
2.	D	2
3.	D	3
4.	A	3
5.	E	3
6.	C	3
7.	A	3
8.	C	3
9.	E	4
10.	C	2
11.	B	2
12.	B	3
13.	A	3
14.	B	4
15.	E	5
16.	E	2
17.	D	2
18.	C	1
19.	E	3
20.	A	2
21.	C	3
22.	E	2
23.	B	3
24.	C	5
25.	A	5
26.	E	3
27.	D	3
28.	A	4
29.	B	3
30.	C	5
31.	B	3

______ no. correct

______ no. incorrect

Section 7

Five-choice Questions

	COR. ANS.	DIFF. LEV.
1.	E	3
2.	A	4
3.	B	3
4.	E	3
5.	A	2
6.	B	3
7.	D	4
8.	C	3
9.	E	3
10.	D	5
11.	E	3

______ no. correct

______ no. incorrect

MATHEMATICAL

Section 1

Five-choice Questions

	COR. ANS.	DIFF. LEV.
1.	C	1
2.	B	1
3.	C	1
4.	D	1
5.	B	1
6.	D	1
7.	E	2
8.	A	2
9.	A	3
10.	E	3
11.	B	3
12.	C	3
13.	E	3
14.	A	3
15.	C	3
16.	A	3
17.	B	3
18.	E	3
19.	D	4
20.	D	3
21.	C	4
22.	B	4
23.	D	4
24.	D	5
25.	E	5

______ no. correct

______ no. incorrect

Section 3

Four-choice Questions

	COR. ANS.	DIFF. LEV.
1.	B	1
2.	A	1
3.	C	2
4.	B	3
5.	D	2
6.	A	3
7.	B	3
8.	C	2
9.	D	3
10.	B	4
11.	D	4
12.	A	3
13.	A	3
14.	A	3
15.	C	5

______ no. correct

______ no. incorrect

Section 6

Five-choice Questions

	COR. ANS.	DIFF. LEV.
1.	D	1
2.	A	1
3.	D	2
4.	E	2
5.	D	2
6.	C	3
7.	B	3
8.	E	4
9.	E	5
10.	B	4

______ no. correct

______ no. incorrect

Section 3

Student-produced Response Questions

	COR. ANS.	DIFF. LEV.
16.	18	1
17.	82.5	2
18.	5, 6 or 7	2
19.	0	1
20.	6	2
21.	36	3
22.	128	3
23.	19	4
24.	1.8 or 9/5	4
25.	5	4

______ no. correct (16-25)

Note: Difficulty levels are estimates of question difficulty for a recent group of college-bound seniors. Difficulty levels range from 1 (easiest) to 5 (hardest)

The Scoring Process

Machine-scoring is done in three steps:

- *Scanning.* Your answer sheet is "read" by a scanning machine and the oval you filled in for each question is recorded on a computer tape.
- *Scoring.* The computer compares the oval filled in for each question with the correct response. Each correct answer receives one point; omitted questions do not count toward your score. For each wrong answer to the multiple-choice questions, a fraction of a point is subtracted to correct for random guessing. For questions with five answer choices, one-fourth of a point is subtracted for each wrong response; for questions with four answer choices, one-third of a point is subtracted for each wrong response. The SAT I verbal test has 78 questions with five answer choices each. If, for example, a student has 44 right, 32 wrong, and 2 omitted, the resulting raw score is determined as follows:

$$44 \text{ right} - \frac{32 \text{ wrong}}{4} = 44 - 8 = 36 \text{ raw score points}$$

Obtaining raw scores frequently involves the rounding of fractional numbers to the nearest whole number. For example, a raw score of 36.25 is rounded to 36, the nearest whole number. A raw score of 36.50 is rounded upward to 37.

- *Converting to reported scaled score.* Raw test scores are then placed on the College Board scale of 200 to 800 through a process that adjusts scores to account for minor differences in difficulty among different editions of the test. This process, known as equating, is performed so that a student's reported score is not affected by the edition of the test taken nor by the abilities of the group with whom the student takes the test. As a result of placing SAT I scores on the College Board scale, scores earned by students at different times can be compared.

How to Score the Practice Test

SAT I Verbal Sections 2, 4, and 7

Step A: Count the number of correct answers for *Section 2* and record the number in the space provided on the worksheet on the next page. Then do the same for the incorrect answers. (Do not count omitted answers.) To determine subtotal A, use the formula:

$$\text{number correct} - \frac{\text{number incorrect}}{4} = \text{subtotal A}$$

Step B: Count the number of correct answers and the number of incorrect answers for *Section 4* and record the number in the space provided on the worksheet. To determine subtotal B, use the formula:

$$\text{number correct} - \frac{\text{number incorrect}}{4} = \text{subtotal B}$$

Step C: Count the number of correct answers and the number of incorrect answers for *Section 7* and record the number in the space provided on the worksheet. To determine subtotal C, use the formula:

$$\text{number correct} - \frac{\text{number incorrect}}{4} = \text{subtotal C}$$

Step D: To obtain D, add subtotal A, subtotal B, and subtotal C, keeping any decimals. Enter the resulting figure on the worksheet.

Step E: To obtain E, your raw verbal score, round D to the nearest whole number. (For example, any number from 44.50 to 45.49 rounds to 45.) Enter the resulting figure on the worksheet.

Step F: To find your SAT I verbal score, look up the total raw verbal score you obtained in step E in the conversion table. Enter this figure on the worksheet.

SAT I Mathematical Sections 1, 3, and 6

Step A: Count the number of correct answers and the number of incorrect answers for *Section 1* and record the numbers in the spaces provided on the worksheet. To determine subtotal A, use the formula:

$$\text{number correct} - \frac{\text{number incorrect}}{4} = \text{subtotal A}$$

Step B: Count the number of correct answers and the number of incorrect answers for the *four-choice quantitative comparison questions (questions 1 through 15) in Section 3* and record the number in the space provided on the worksheet. Note: Do not count any E responses to questions 1 through 15 as correct or incorrect. Because these four-choice questions have no E answer choices, E responses to these questions are treated as omits. To determine subtotal B, use the formula:

$$\text{number correct} - \frac{\text{number incorrect}}{3} = \text{subtotal B}$$

Step C: Count the number of correct answers for the student-produced response questions *(questions 16 through 25) in Section 3* and record the number in the space provided on the worksheet. This is subtotal C.

Step D: Count the number of correct answers and the number of incorrect answers for *Section 6* and record the number in the space provided on the worksheet. To determine subtotal D, use the formula:

$$\text{number correct} - \frac{\text{number incorrect}}{4} = \text{subtotal D}$$

Step E: To obtain E, add subtotal A, subtotal B, subtotal C, and subtotal D, keeping any decimals. Enter the resulting figure on the worksheet.

Step F: To obtain F, your raw mathematical score, round E to the nearest whole number. (For example, any number from 44.50 to 45.49 rounds to 45.) Enter the resulting figure on the worksheet.

Step G: To find your SAT I mathematical score, look up the total raw mathematical score you obtained in step F in the conversion table. Enter this figure on the worksheet.

SAT I Scoring Worksheet

SAT I Verbal Sections

A. Section 2:	________ no. correct	− (________ no. incorrect	÷ 4) =	________ subtotal A
B. Section 4:	________ no. correct	− (________ no. incorrect	÷ 4) =	________ subtotal B
C. Section 7:	________ no. correct	− (________ no. incorrect	÷ 4) =	________ subtotal C
D. Total unrounded raw score (Total A + B + C)				________ D
E. Total rounded raw score (Rounded to nearest whole number)				________ E
F. SAT I verbal reported scaled score (Use the conversion table)				☐ SAT I verbal score

SAT I Mathematical Sections

A. Section 1:	________ no. correct	− (________ no. incorrect	÷ 4) =	________ subtotal A
B. Section 3: Questions 1-15 (quantitative comparison)	________ no. correct	− (________ no. incorrect	÷ 3) =	________ subtotal B
C. Section 3: Questions 16-25 (student-produced response)	________ no. correct		=	________ subtotal C
D. Section 6:	________ no. correct	− (________ no. incorrect	÷ 4) =	________ subtotal D
E. Total unrounded raw score (Total A + B + C + D)				________ E
F. Total rounded raw score (Rounded to nearest whole number)				________ F
G. SAT I mathematical reported scaled score (Use the conversion table)				☐ SAT I mathematical score

Score Conversion Table
SAT I: Reasoning Test
Saturday, November 1994
Recentered Scale

Raw Score	Verbal Scaled Score	Math Scaled Score	Raw Score	Verbal Scaled Score	Math Scaled Score
78	800		37	510	560
77	800		36	510	550
76	800		35	500	540
75	800		34	500	540
74	790		33	490	530
73	780		32	480	520
72	760		31	480	520
71	750		30	470	510
70	740		29	470	500
69	730		28	460	500
68	720		27	460	490
67	710		26	450	480
66	700		25	440	480
65	690		24	440	470
64	680		23	430	460
63	670		22	430	460
62	660		21	420	450
61	660		20	410	440
60	650	800	19	410	430
59	640	790	18	400	430
58	630	770	17	390	420
57	630	750	16	390	410
56	620	730	15	380	410
55	610	720	14	370	400
54	610	700	13	360	390
53	600	690	12	360	380
52	600	680	11	350	370
51	590	670	10	340	370
50	580	660	9	330	360
49	580	650	8	320	350
48	570	640	7	310	340
47	570	640	6	300	320
46	560	630	5	290	310
45	560	620	4	280	300
44	550	610	3	270	280
43	540	600	2	260	270
42	540	600	1	240	250
41	530	590	0	230	230
40	530	580	-1	220	210
39	520	570	-2	200	200
38	520	570	and below		

This table is for use only with this test.

SAT I: Reasoning Test

Saturday, November 1995

YOUR NAME (PRINT) ______________________________
LAST FIRST MI

TEST CENTER ______________________________
NUMBER NAME OF TEST CENTER ROOM NUMBER

SAT® I: Reasoning Test — General Directions

Timing

- You will have three hours to work on this test.
- There are five 30-minute sections and two 15-minute sections.
- You may work on only one section at a time.
- The supervisor will tell you when to begin and end each section.
- If you finish a section before time is called, check your work on that section. You may NOT turn to any other section.
- Work as rapidly as you can without losing accuracy. Don't waste time on questions that seem too difficult for you.

Marking Answers

- Carefully mark only one answer for each question.
- Make sure each mark is dark and completely fills the oval.
- Do not make any stray marks on your answer sheet.
- If you erase, do so completely. Incomplete erasures may be scored as intended answers.
- Use only the answer spaces that correspond to the question numbers.
- For questions with only four answer choices, an answer marked in oval E will not be scored.
- Use the test book for scratchwork, but you will not receive credit for anything written there.
- You may not transfer answers to your answer sheet or fill in ovals after time has been called.
- You may not fold or remove pages or portions of a page from this book, or take the book or answer sheet from the testing room.

Scoring

- For each correct answer, you receive one point.
- For questions you omit, you receive no points.
- For a wrong answer to a multiple-choice question, you lose a fraction of a point.
  - ► If you can eliminate one or more of the answer choices as wrong, however, you increase your chances of choosing the correct answer and earning one point.
  - ► If you can't eliminate any choice, move on. You can return to the question later if there is time.
- For a wrong answer to a math question that is not multiple-choice, you don't lose any points.

The passages for this test have been adapted from published material. The ideas contained in them do not necessarily represent the opinions of the College Board or Educational Testing Service.

IMPORTANT: The codes below are unique to your test book. Copy them on your answer sheet in boxes 8 and 9 and fill in the corresponding ovals exactly as shown.

8. Form Code

A	A	0	0	0
B	B	1	1	1
C	C	2	2	2
D	D	3	3	3
E	E	4	4	4
F	F	5	5	5
G	G	6	6	6
H	H	7	7	7
I	I	8	8	8
J	J	9	9	9
K	K			
L	L			
M	M			
N	N			
O	O			
P	P			
Q	Q			
R	R			
S	S			
T	T			
U	U			
V	V			
W	W			
X	X			
Y	Y			
Z	Z			

9. Test Form

DO NOT OPEN THIS BOOK UNTIL THE SUPERVISOR TELLS YOU TO DO SO.

THE COLLEGE BOARD — SAT I **Page 1**

Use a No. 2 pencil only. Be sure each mark is dark and completely fills the intended oval. Completely erase any errors or stray marks.

1. Your Name

First 4 letters of Last Name | First init. | Mid. init.

A B C D E F G H I J K L M N O P Q R S T U V W X Y Z

2.
Your Name: (Print) ______ Last ______ First ______ M.I.

I agree to the conditions on the back of the SAT I test book.

Signature: ______ Date: ___/___/___

Home Address: (Print) ______ Number and Street

______ City ______ State ______ Zip Code

Center: (Print) ______ City ______ State ______ Center Number

IMPORTANT: Fill in items 8 and 9 exactly as shown on the back of test book.

8. Form Code

(Copy and grid as on back of test book.)

A–Z | 0–9

3. Date of Birth

Month	Day	Year
Jan.	0 1 2 3	0–9
Feb.	0–9	0–9
Mar.		
Apr.		
May		
June		
July		
Aug.		
Sept.		
Oct.		
Nov.		
Dec.		

4. Social Security Number

0 1 2 3 4 5 6 7 8 9

5. Sex

Female Male

6. Registration Number

(Copy from Admission Ticket.)

0 1 2 3 4 5 6 7 8 9

7. Test Book Serial Number

(Copy from front of test book.)

0 1 2 3 4 5 6 7 8 9

FOR ETS USE ONLY

9. Test Form

(Copy from back of test book.)

Start with number 1 for each new section. If a section has fewer questions than answer spaces, leave the extra answer spaces blank.

SECTION 1

1–40 Ⓐ Ⓑ Ⓒ Ⓓ Ⓔ

SECTION 2

1–40 Ⓐ Ⓑ Ⓒ Ⓓ Ⓔ

Q2778-06/2 CHW98324 11027 • 09132 • TF129M17.5eX I.N. 207158
1 2 3 4

Use a No. 2 pencil only. Be sure each mark is dark and completely fills the intended oval. Completely erase any errors or stray marks.

Start with number 1 for each new section. If a section has fewer questions than answer spaces, leave the extra answer spaces blank.

SECTION 3

1 (A) (B) (C) (D) (E)
2 (A) (B) (C) (D) (E)
3 (A) (B) (C) (D) (E)
4 (A) (B) (C) (D) (E)
5 (A) (B) (C) (D) (E)
6 (A) (B) (C) (D) (E)
7 (A) (B) (C) (D) (E)
8 (A) (B) (C) (D) (E)
9 (A) (B) (C) (D) (E)
10 (A) (B) (C) (D) (E)
11 (A) (B) (C) (D) (E)
12 (A) (B) (C) (D) (E)
13 (A) (B) (C) (D) (E)
14 (A) (B) (C) (D) (E)
15 (A) (B) (C) (D) (E)
16 (A) (B) (C) (D) (E)
17 (A) (B) (C) (D) (E)
18 (A) (B) (C) (D) (E)
19 (A) (B) (C) (D) (E)
20 (A) (B) (C) (D) (E)
21 (A) (B) (C) (D) (E)
22 (A) (B) (C) (D) (E)
23 (A) (B) (C) (D) (E)
24 (A) (B) (C) (D) (E)
25 (A) (B) (C) (D) (E)
26 (A) (B) (C) (D) (E)
27 (A) (B) (C) (D) (E)
28 (A) (B) (C) (D) (E)
29 (A) (B) (C) (D) (E)
30 (A) (B) (C) (D) (E)
31 (A) (B) (C) (D) (E)
32 (A) (B) (C) (D) (E)
33 (A) (B) (C) (D) (E)
34 (A) (B) (C) (D) (E)
35 (A) (B) (C) (D) (E)
36 (A) (B) (C) (D) (E)
37 (A) (B) (C) (D) (E)
38 (A) (B) (C) (D) (E)
39 (A) (B) (C) (D) (E)
40 (A) (B) (C) (D) (E)

If section 3 of your test book contains math questions that are not multiple-choice, continue to item 16 below. Otherwise, continue to item 16 above.

ONLY ANSWERS ENTERED IN THE OVALS IN EACH GRID AREA WILL BE SCORED.
YOU WILL NOT RECEIVE CREDIT FOR ANYTHING WRITTEN IN THE BOXES ABOVE THE OVALS.

16 17 18 19 20 21 22 23 24 25

(each grid: / / ; . . . . ; 0 0 0 ; 1 1 1 1 ; 2 2 2 2 ; 3 3 3 3 ; 4 4 4 4 ; 5 5 5 5 ; 6 6 6 6 ; 7 7 7 7 ; 8 8 8 8 ; 9 9 9 9)

BE SURE TO ERASE ANY ERRORS OR STRAY MARKS COMPLETELY.

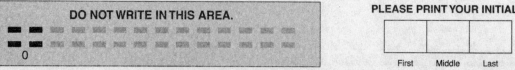

DO NOT WRITE IN THIS AREA.

0

PLEASE PRINT YOUR INITIALS

First	Middle	Last

Use a No. 2 pencil only. Be sure each mark is dark and completely fills the intended oval. Completely erase any errors or stray marks.

Start with number 1 for each new section. If a section has fewer questions than answer spaces, leave the extra answer spaces blank.

SECTION 4

1 Ⓐ Ⓑ Ⓒ Ⓓ Ⓔ
2 Ⓐ Ⓑ Ⓒ Ⓓ Ⓔ
3 Ⓐ Ⓑ Ⓒ Ⓓ Ⓔ
4 Ⓐ Ⓑ Ⓒ Ⓓ Ⓔ
5 Ⓐ Ⓑ Ⓒ Ⓓ Ⓔ
6 Ⓐ Ⓑ Ⓒ Ⓓ Ⓔ
7 Ⓐ Ⓑ Ⓒ Ⓓ Ⓔ
8 Ⓐ Ⓑ Ⓒ Ⓓ Ⓔ
9 Ⓐ Ⓑ Ⓒ Ⓓ Ⓔ
10 Ⓐ Ⓑ Ⓒ Ⓓ Ⓔ
11 Ⓐ Ⓑ Ⓒ Ⓓ Ⓔ
12 Ⓐ Ⓑ Ⓒ Ⓓ Ⓔ
13 Ⓐ Ⓑ Ⓒ Ⓓ Ⓔ
14 Ⓐ Ⓑ Ⓒ Ⓓ Ⓔ
15 Ⓐ Ⓑ Ⓒ Ⓓ Ⓔ
16 Ⓐ Ⓑ Ⓒ Ⓓ Ⓔ
17 Ⓐ Ⓑ Ⓒ Ⓓ Ⓔ
18 Ⓐ Ⓑ Ⓒ Ⓓ Ⓔ
19 Ⓐ Ⓑ Ⓒ Ⓓ Ⓔ
20 Ⓐ Ⓑ Ⓒ Ⓓ Ⓔ
21 Ⓐ Ⓑ Ⓒ Ⓓ Ⓔ
22 Ⓐ Ⓑ Ⓒ Ⓓ Ⓔ
23 Ⓐ Ⓑ Ⓒ Ⓓ Ⓔ
24 Ⓐ Ⓑ Ⓒ Ⓓ Ⓔ
25 Ⓐ Ⓑ Ⓒ Ⓓ Ⓔ
26 Ⓐ Ⓑ Ⓒ Ⓓ Ⓔ
27 Ⓐ Ⓑ Ⓒ Ⓓ Ⓔ
28 Ⓐ Ⓑ Ⓒ Ⓓ Ⓔ
29 Ⓐ Ⓑ Ⓒ Ⓓ Ⓔ
30 Ⓐ Ⓑ Ⓒ Ⓓ Ⓔ
31 Ⓐ Ⓑ Ⓒ Ⓓ Ⓔ
32 Ⓐ Ⓑ Ⓒ Ⓓ Ⓔ
33 Ⓐ Ⓑ Ⓒ Ⓓ Ⓔ
34 Ⓐ Ⓑ Ⓒ Ⓓ Ⓔ
35 Ⓐ Ⓑ Ⓒ Ⓓ Ⓔ
36 Ⓐ Ⓑ Ⓒ Ⓓ Ⓔ
37 Ⓐ Ⓑ Ⓒ Ⓓ Ⓔ
38 Ⓐ Ⓑ Ⓒ Ⓓ Ⓔ
39 Ⓐ Ⓑ Ⓒ Ⓓ Ⓔ
40 Ⓐ Ⓑ Ⓒ Ⓓ Ⓔ

If section 4 of your test book contains math questions that are not multiple-choice, continue to item 16 below. Otherwise, continue to item 16 above.

ONLY ANSWERS ENTERED IN THE OVALS IN EACH GRID AREA WILL BE SCORED.
YOU WILL NOT RECEIVE CREDIT FOR ANYTHING WRITTEN IN THE BOXES ABOVE THE OVALS.

16 17 18 19 20 21 22 23 24 25

	/	/	
.	.	.	.
	0	0	0
1	1	1	1
2	2	2	2
3	3	3	3
4	4	4	4
5	5	5	5
6	6	6	6
7	7	7	7
8	8	8	8
9	9	9	9

BE SURE TO ERASE ANY ERRORS OR STRAY MARKS COMPLETELY.

DO NOT WRITE IN THIS AREA.

0

PLEASE PRINT YOUR INITIALS

First	Middle	Last

Page 4

Use a No. 2 pencil only. Be sure each mark is dark and completely fills the intended oval. Completely erase any errors or stray marks.

Start with number 1 for each new section. If a section has fewer questions than answer spaces, leave the extra answer spaces blank.

SECTION 5

1	A	B	C	D	E	11	A	B	C	D	E	21	A	B	C	D	E	31	A	B	C	D	E
2	A	B	C	D	E	12	A	B	C	D	E	22	A	B	C	D	E	32	A	B	C	D	E
3	A	B	C	D	E	13	A	B	C	D	E	23	A	B	C	D	E	33	A	B	C	D	E
4	A	B	C	D	E	14	A	B	C	D	E	24	A	B	C	D	E	34	A	B	C	D	E
5	A	B	C	D	E	15	A	B	C	D	E	25	A	B	C	D	E	35	A	B	C	D	E
6	A	B	C	D	E	16	A	B	C	D	E	26	A	B	C	D	E	36	A	B	C	D	E
7	A	B	C	D	E	17	A	B	C	D	E	27	A	B	C	D	E	37	A	B	C	D	E
8	A	B	C	D	E	18	A	B	C	D	E	28	A	B	C	D	E	38	A	B	C	D	E
9	A	B	C	D	E	19	A	B	C	D	E	29	A	B	C	D	E	39	A	B	C	D	E
10	A	B	C	D	E	20	A	B	C	D	E	30	A	B	C	D	E	40	A	B	C	D	E

SECTION 6

1	A	B	C	D	E	6	A	B	C	D	E	11	A	B	C	D	E	16	A	B	C	D	E
2	A	B	C	D	E	7	A	B	C	D	E	12	A	B	C	D	E	17	A	B	C	D	E
3	A	B	C	D	E	8	A	B	C	D	E	13	A	B	C	D	E	18	A	B	C	D	E
4	A	B	C	D	E	9	A	B	C	D	E	14	A	B	C	D	E	19	A	B	C	D	E
5	A	B	C	D	E	10	A	B	C	D	E	15	A	B	C	D	E	20	A	B	C	D	E

SECTION 7

1	A	B	C	D	E	6	A	B	C	D	E	11	A	B	C	D	E	16	A	B	C	D	E
2	A	B	C	D	E	7	A	B	C	D	E	12	A	B	C	D	E	17	A	B	C	D	E
3	A	B	C	D	E	8	A	B	C	D	E	13	A	B	C	D	E	18	A	B	C	D	E
4	A	B	C	D	E	9	A	B	C	D	E	14	A	B	C	D	E	19	A	B	C	D	E
5	A	B	C	D	E	10	A	B	C	D	E	15	A	B	C	D	E	20	A	B	C	D	E

CERTIFICATION STATEMENT

Copy the statement below (do not print) and sign your name as you would an official document.

I hereby agree to the conditions set forth in the Registration Bulletin and certify that I am the person whose name and address appear on this answer sheet.

Signature: ______________________ Date: ____________

Section 1 1 1 1 1 1 1

Time—30 Minutes
35 Questions

For each question in this section, select the best answer from among the choices given and fill in the corresponding oval on the answer sheet.

Each sentence below has one or two blanks, each blank indicating that something has been omitted. Beneath the sentence are five words or sets of words labeled A through E. Choose the word or set of words that, when inserted in the sentence, best fits the meaning of the sentence as a whole.

Example:

Medieval kingdoms did not become constitutional republics overnight; on the contrary, the change was ----.

(A) unpopular
(B) unexpected
(C) advantageous
(D) sufficient
(E) gradual 

1. Although Christa Wolf was one of East Germany's most famous authors, her works were often ---- and, therefore, often unavailable.

(A) suppressed (B) revised (C) imitated (D) tolerated (E) analyzed

2. A few of the people on the island may live ----, but most have no hope of ---- even the basic amenities of life.

(A) poorly. .enjoying
(B) pretentiously. .yielding
(C) responsibly. .acquiring
(D) lavishly. .attaining
(E) simply. .missing

3. The new pluralism in art ---- a great variety of styles and points of view while denying ---- to any single approach.

(A) ignores. .originality
(B) distorts. .probability
(C) espouses. .embellishment
(D) undermines. .secrecy
(E) accommodates. .dominance

4. Interest in the origin of life is ----; all cultures and societies have narratives about creation.

(A) distant (B) mythical (C) universal (D) debatable (E) superficial

5. The number of African American inventors from the 1600's to the late 1800's will never be ----, since their work was often ---- by others.

(A) seen. .reintegrated
(B) determined. .expropriated
(C) withheld. .trivialized
(D) disclosed. .uncensored
(E) archived. .marketed

6. Housewares and bookbindings by designer Josef Hoffmann exemplify a range of styles, from simple and austere to ---- and opulent.

(A) basic (B) efficient (C) severe (D) florid (E) straightforward

7. Although the personality that emerges from May Sarton's autobiography seems unmistakably ----, the journals for which she became famous described her ---- life in a sparsely populated area.

(A) complex. .intricate
(B) celebrated. .humorous
(C) affable. .solitary
(D) stoic. .isolated
(E) scholarly. .intellectual

8. Negotiators predicted an early end to the strike, but the reporters were ---- because both sides refused to compromise.

(A) cordial (B) dubious (C) benevolent (D) biased (E) prophetic

9. He was always ---- in performing his tasks, waiting until the last moment to finish them.

(A) dilatory (B) incompetent (C) extroverted (D) surreptitious (E) obtrusive

10. In effect, the Voting Rights Act of 1965 ---- African Americans in the southern United States by outlawing restrictions that had barred them from voting.

(A) inspired (B) promulgated (C) enfranchised (D) preserved (E) proliferated

GO ON TO THE NEXT PAGE

Each question below consists of a related pair of words or phrases, followed by five pairs of words or phrases labeled A through E. Select the pair that best expresses a relationship similar to that expressed in the original pair.

Example:

CRUMB : BREAD ::
(A) ounce : unit
(B) splinter : wood
(C) water : bucket
(D) twine : rope
(E) cream : butter

11 DROUGHT : RAIN ::
(A) desert : sun
(B) hurricane : wind
(C) epidemic : disease
(D) volcano : lava
(E) famine : nourishment

12 ANTIBIOTIC : INFECTION ::
(A) thermometer : fever
(B) anesthesia : surgery
(C) vaccine : inoculation
(D) antiseptic : alcohol
(E) antidote : poisoning

13 HUMIDIFIER : MOISTURE ::
(A) iron : wrinkle
(B) candle : wax
(C) tub : liquid
(D) furnace : heat
(E) chimney : smoke

14 CONDOLENCE : MOURNER ::
(A) secret : stranger
(B) loan : borrower
(C) rescue : knight
(D) congratulation : victor
(E) record : athlete

15 PETAL : FLOWER ::
(A) oak : tree
(B) staple : paper
(C) sprout : seed
(D) tooth : comb
(E) tide : beach

16 RUTHLESS : COMPASSION ::
(A) theatrical : emotion
(B) naïve : sophistication
(C) scrupulous : propriety
(D) self-righteous : indignation
(E) formidable : awe

17 EMOLLIENT : SOFTEN ::
(A) oil : lubricate
(B) disinfectant : contaminate
(C) concrete : harden
(D) storm : thunder
(E) steam : evaporate

18 CAPTION : CARTOON ::
(A) byline : newspaper
(B) laughter : comedy
(C) subtitle : film
(D) translation : paraphrase
(E) billboard : road

19 BERATE : CRITICIZE ::
(A) goad : urge
(B) accuse : apologize
(C) regret : remember
(D) betray : follow
(E) evaluate : praise

20 PERCEPTIVE : DISCERN ::
(A) determined : hesitate
(B) authoritarian : heed
(C) persistent : persevere
(D) abandoned : neglect
(E) restrained : rebel

21 EMULATE : PERSON ::
(A) admire : reputation
(B) obey : leader
(C) cooperate : partner
(D) mimic : gesture
(E) mock : sarcasm

22 INCUMBENT : OFFICE ::
(A) politician : campaign
(B) tenant : dwelling
(C) jailer : cell
(D) secretary : desk
(E) retiree : service

23 CONUNDRUM : PERPLEX ::
(A) theory : refute
(B) explanation : suffice
(C) blueprint : construct
(D) entertainment : divert
(E) expedition : discover

GO ON TO THE NEXT PAGE

The passage below is followed by questions based on its content. Answer the questions on the basis of what is stated or implied in the passage and in any introductory material that may be provided.

Questions 24-35 are based on the following passage.

The following selection is taken from the autobiography of a Hispanic American writer.

In fourth grade I embarked upon a grandiose reading program. "Give me the names of important books," I would say to startled teachers. They soon found out that I had in mind "adult books." I ignored their suggestion of anything I suspected was written for children. And whatever I read, I read for extra credit. Each time I finished a book, I reported the achievement to a teacher and basked in the praise my effort earned. Despite my best efforts, however, there seemed to be more and more books I needed to read. At the library I would literally tremble as I came upon whole shelves of books I hadn't read. So I read and I read and I read. Librarians who initially frowned when I checked out the maximum ten books at a time started saving books they thought I might like. Teachers would say to the rest of the class, "I only wish that the rest of you took reading as seriously as Richard obviously does."

But at home I would hear my mother, who was not an educated woman, wondering, "What do you see in your books?" (Was reading a hobby like her knitting? Was so much reading even healthy for a boy? Was it a sign of "brains"? Or was it just a convenient excuse for not helping around the house on Saturday mornings?) Always, "What do you see?"

What did I see in my books? I had the idea that they were crucial for my academic success, though I couldn't have said exactly how or why. In the sixth grade I simply concluded that what gave a book its value was some major idea or theme it contained. If that core essence could be mined and memorized, I would become learned like my teachers. I decided to record in a notebook the themes of the books that I read. After reading *Robinson Crusoe*, I wrote that its theme was "the value of learning to live by oneself." When I completed *Wuthering Heights*, I noted the danger of "letting emotions get out of control." Rereading these brief moralistic appraisals usually left me disheartened. I couldn't believe that they were really the source of reading's value. But for many more years, they constituted the only means I had of describing to myself the educational value of books.

In spite of my earnestness, I found reading a pleasurable activity. I came to enjoy the lonely good company of books. Early on weekday mornings, I'd read in my bed. I'd feel a mysterious comfort then, reading in the dawn quiet. On weekends I'd go to the public library to read, surrounded by old men and women. Or, if the weather was fine, I would take my books to the park and read in the shade of a tree.

I also had favorite writers. But often those writers I enjoyed most I was least able to value. When I read William Saroyan's *The Human Comedy*, I was immediately pleased by the narrator's warmth and the charm of his story. But as quickly I became suspicious. A book so enjoyable to read couldn't be very "important." Another summer I determined to read all the novels of Dickens. Reading his fat novels, I loved the feeling I got—after the first hundred pages—of being at home in a fictional world where I knew the names of the characters and cared about what was going to happen to them. And it bothered me that I was forced away at the conclusion, when the fiction closed tight, like a fortune-teller's fist—the futures of all the major characters neatly resolved. I never knew how to take such feelings seriously, however. Nor did I suspect that these experiences could be part of a novel's meaning. Still, there were pleasures to sustain me after I'd finished my books. Carrying a volume back to the library, I would be pleased by its weight. I'd run my fingers along the edges of the pages and marvel at the breadth of my achievement. Around my room, growing stacks of paperback books reinforced my assurance.

I entered high school having read hundreds of books. My habit of reading made me a confident speaker and writer of English and in various ways, books brought me academic success as I hoped they would. But I was not a good reader. Merely bookish, I lacked a point of view when I read. Rather, I read in order to acquire a point of view. I vacuumed books for epigrams, scraps of information, ideas, themes—anything to fill the hollow within me and make me feel educated. When one of my teachers suggested to his drowsy tenth-grade English class that a person could not have a "complicated idea" until that person had read at least two thousand books, I heard the remark without detecting either its irony or its very complicated truth.

The reading passages in this test are brief excerpts or adaptations of excerpts from published material. The ideas contained in them do not necessarily represent the opinions of the College Board or Educational Testing Service. To make the text suitable for testing purposes, we may in some cases have altered the style, contents, or point of view of the original.

GO ON TO THE NEXT PAGE

24 The author uses the phrase "embarked upon" (line 1) to emphasize which of the following?

(A) The transient nature of the fictional world
(B) His commitment to an exploration of the world of books
(C) His realization that literature can change one's outlook
(D) The fear he feels about leaving the familiar world of his parents
(E) His sense of isolation from his classmates

25 The author initially believed "important books" (lines 2-3) to be books that

(A) did not contain any references to children
(B) had been praised by critics
(C) were recommended by his mother
(D) were directed toward a mature audience
(E) were written by renowned authors

26 The author would "literally tremble" (line 12) at the library because he

(A) did not know which books were important
(B) was intimidated by the librarians
(C) felt a personal connection to all the authors represented there
(D) was worried that he would never be able to read all the books
(E) was excited by the idea of being allowed to borrow books

27 The author's purpose in mentioning that some of the librarians "frowned" (line 14) is most likely to

(A) indicate that his reading project was met with some skepticism at first
(B) imply that they thought children should not check out books written for adults
(C) suggest that what he was doing was wrong
(D) explain why he was so frightened at the library
(E) characterize librarians who favor intellectual children

28 The mother's attitude toward the boy's interest in reading (lines 20-27) can be best described as

(A) exasperation
(B) indignation
(C) perplexity
(D) sympathy
(E) admiration

29 In line 33, "mined" most nearly means

(A) followed
(B) dug out
(C) entrenched
(D) tunneled
(E) blown up

30 The author states that he was "disheartened" (line 42) because

(A) he was unable to find books that were of lasting value
(B) the tragic themes of the books he was reading were depressing to him
(C) his ability to write descriptions was lagging behind his reading ability
(D) his teachers were not giving him as much encouragement as he needed
(E) his desire for meaning was not being met by the themes that he wrote down

31 The fourth paragraph (lines 47-55) describes the author as

(A) comfortable only in the company of fellow scholars
(B) dissatisfied with the rate at which his reading progressed
(C) happy with his books despite his isolation from others
(D) lonely because he often had no other children around him
(E) determined to get outside and enjoy nature

GO ON TO THE NEXT PAGE

32 The author uses the phrase "the fiction closed tight" (lines 69-70) in order to

(A) demonstrate that the endings of the novels were not believable
(B) blur the distinction between fictional works and real life
(C) indicate how impenetrable some of the novels were
(D) criticize the artificiality of Dickens' characters
(E) show his unhappiness at having to part with a fictional world

33 In line 75 "sustain" most nearly means

(A) defend
(B) support
(C) endure
(D) prolong
(E) ratify

34 The author uses the phrase "the breadth of my achievement" (lines 78-79) primarily in order to suggest that

(A) he was confusing quantity with quality
(B) the books he had read varied widely in difficulty
(C) he should have been prouder of himself than he was
(D) he believes every child should read as much as possible
(E) no one else knew how much he was reading

35 The author implies that "a good reader" (line 85) is one who

(A) engages in a structured reading program
(B) reads constantly and widely
(C) reads with a critical perspective
(D) makes lists of books to be read
(E) can summarize a book's theme simply and concisely

IF YOU FINISH BEFORE TIME IS CALLED, YOU MAY CHECK YOUR WORK ON THIS SECTION ONLY. DO NOT TURN TO ANY OTHER SECTION IN THE TEST. **STOP**

Section 2 2 2 2 2 2

Time—30 Minutes
25 Questions

In this section solve each problem, using any available space on the page for scratchwork. Then decide which is the best of the choices given and fill in the corresponding oval on the answer sheet.

Notes:

1. The use of a calculator is permitted. All numbers used are real numbers.

2. Figures that accompany problems in this test are intended to provide information useful in solving the problems. They are drawn as accurately as possible EXCEPT when it is stated in a specific problem that the figure is not drawn to scale. All figures lie in a plane unless otherwise indicated.

Reference Information

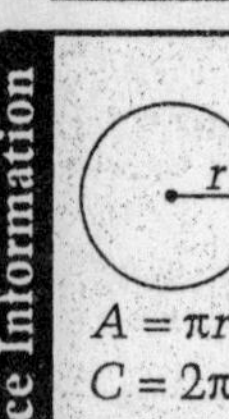

$A = \pi r^2$
$C = 2\pi r$

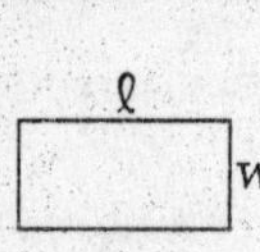

$A = \ell w$

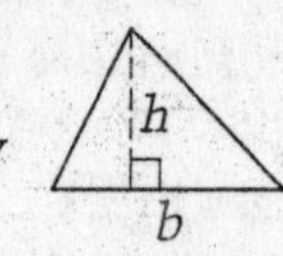

$A = \frac{1}{2}bh$

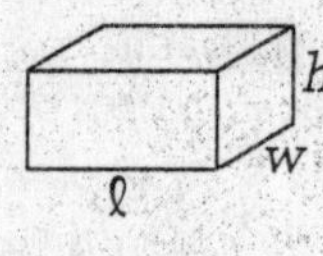

$V = \ell wh$

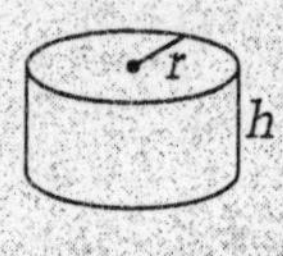

$V = \pi r^2 h$

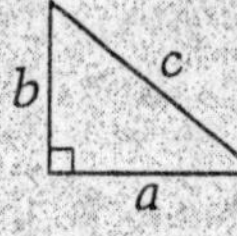

$c^2 = a^2 + b^2$

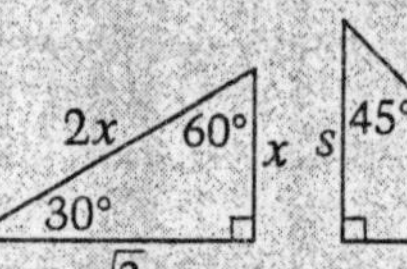

Special Right Triangles

The number of degrees of arc in a circle is 360.
The measure in degrees of a straight angle is 180.
The sum of the measures in degrees of the angles of a triangle is 180.

1 If $2x + y = 7$ and $y = 5x$, then $x =$

(A) $\frac{1}{7}$

(B) $\frac{5}{7}$

(C) 1

(D) $\frac{7}{5}$

(E) 7

2 If it takes Sam 6 hours working at a constant rate to complete his science project, what part of the project is completed in 2 hours?

(A) $\frac{1}{12}$

(B) $\frac{1}{8}$

(C) $\frac{1}{6}$

(D) $\frac{1}{4}$

(E) $\frac{1}{3}$

3 Three lines intersect in the figure above. What is the value of $x + y$?

(A) 170
(B) 160
(C) 150
(D) 140
(E) 120

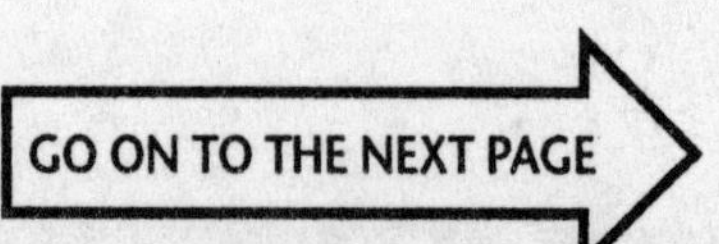

4 If $2p + 5 = 20$, then $2p - 5 =$

(A) 0
(B) 5
(C) 10
(D) 15
(E) 25

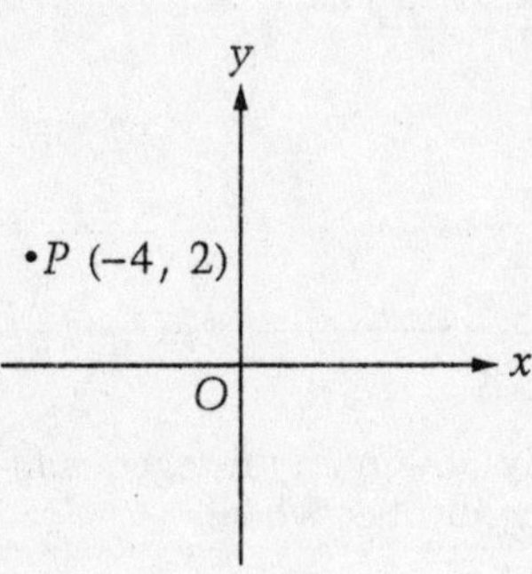

5 In the figure above, a line is to be drawn through point P so that it never crosses the x-axis. Through which of the following points must the line pass?

(A) (4, 2)
(B) (4, −2)
(C) (2, 4)
(D) (2, −4)
(E) (−4, −2)

6 The ratio of 8 to 3 is equal to the ratio of 24 to what number?

(A) 8
(B) 9
(C) 19
(D) 29
(E) 64

7 What number decreased by 6 equals 3 times the number?

(A) −3

(B) −1

(C) $-\frac{2}{3}$

(D) $\frac{2}{3}$

(E) 3

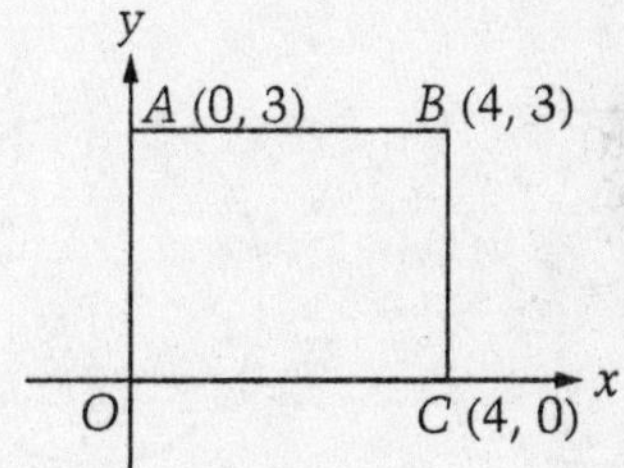

8 What is the area of rectangle $OABC$ in the figure above?

(A) 7
(B) 9
(C) 12
(D) 14
(E) 16

9 The distance from Town A to Town B is 5 miles and the distance from Town B to Town C is 4 miles. Which of the following could NOT be the distance, in miles, from Town A to Town C ?

(A) 1
(B) 4
(C) 8
(D) 9
(E) 10

GO ON TO THE NEXT PAGE

Questions 10-12 refer to the following information.

Alissa makes a number wheel to represent the integers from 0 through 99, inclusive. The short hand points to the tens digit, and the long hand points to the units digit.

For example, the number wheel above shows 07, which we would write as 7.

+

10 Which of the following represents the sum of the two integers represented on the two number wheels above?

(A)
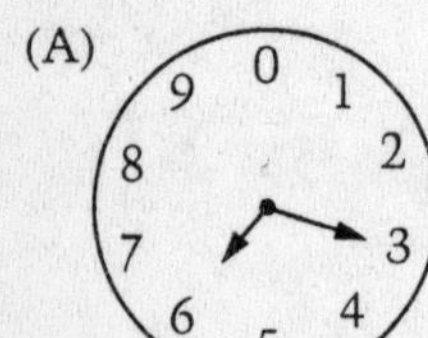

(B)
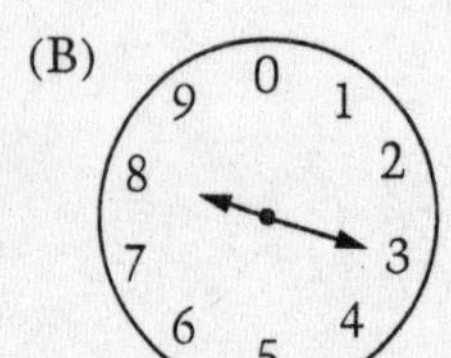

(C)
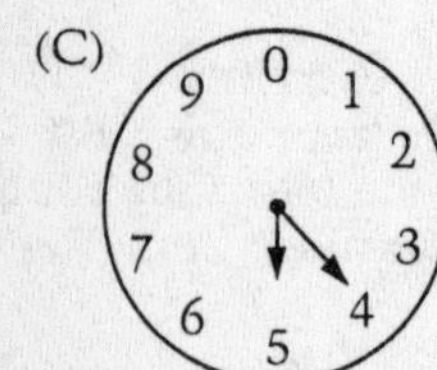

(D)
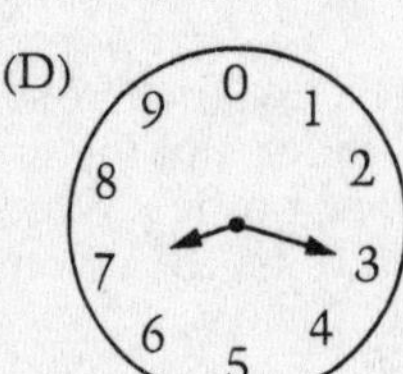

(E)
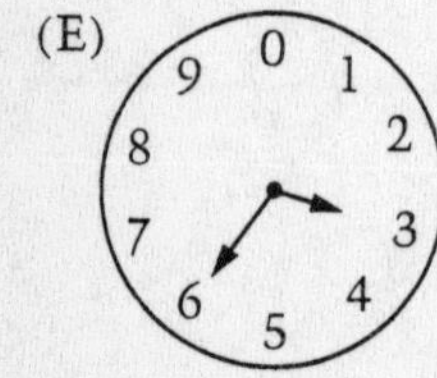

11 Which of the following is the next greater prime number after the prime number represented above?

(A) 15
(B) 17
(C) 33
(D) 37
(E) 41

12 Exactly how many integers can be represented on this number wheel?

(A) 91
(B) 98
(C) 99
(D) 100
(E) 101

13 Exactly $\frac{1}{2}$ yard of ribbon is needed to make a certain bow. Which of the following lengths of ribbon could be used to make the bow with the least amount remaining?

(A) $\frac{2}{5}$ yd

(B) $\frac{3}{5}$ yd

(C) $\frac{3}{4}$ yd

(D) $\frac{1}{3}$ yd

(E) $\frac{2}{3}$ yd

GO ON TO THE NEXT PAGE

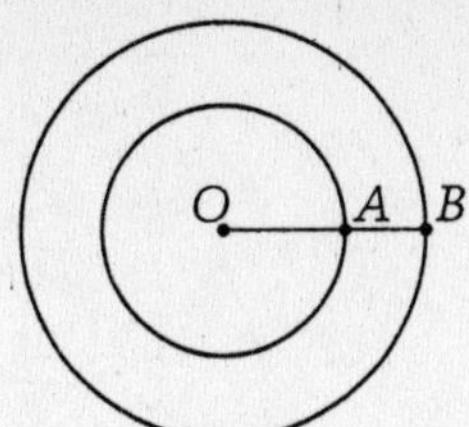

14 In the figure above, both circles have their centers at point O, and point A lies on segment OB. If $OA = 3$ and $AB = 2$, what is the ratio of the circumference of the smaller circle to the circumference of the larger circle?

(A) $\frac{2}{3}$

(B) $\frac{3}{5}$

(C) $\frac{9}{16}$

(D) $\frac{1}{2}$

(E) $\frac{4}{9}$

---

15 The total weight of Bill and his son Tommy is 250 pounds. If Bill's weight is 10 pounds more than 3 times Tommy's, what is Tommy's weight in pounds?

(A) 40
(B) 50
(C) 60
(D) 80
(E) 90

---

16 Set I contains six consecutive integers. Set J contains all integers that result from adding 3 to each of the integers in set I and also contains all integers that result from subtracting 3 from each of the integers in set I. How many more integers are there in set J than in set I?

(A) 0
(B) 2
(C) 3
(D) 6
(E) 9

---

17 If $s \neq 0$, then $\frac{1}{\frac{6}{2s}} =$

(A) $\frac{1}{3s}$

(B) $\frac{3}{s}$

(C) $\frac{s}{3}$

(D) $\frac{3s}{2}$

(E) $3s$

GO ON TO THE NEXT PAGE

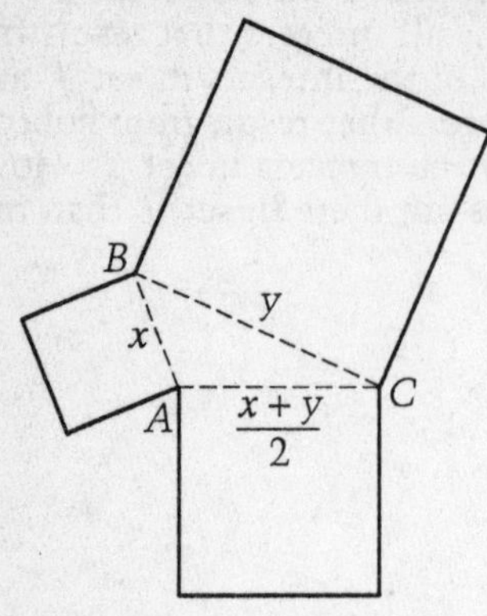

18 In the figure above, triangle ABC has sides of lengths x, y, and $\frac{x + y}{2}$. On each side, a square is constructed as shown. What is the sum of the lengths of the sides of the resulting 9-sided figure, in terms of x and y?

(A) $\frac{9x + 9y}{2}$

(B) $\frac{7x + 7y}{2}$

(C) $\frac{3x + 3y}{2}$

(D) $5x + 5y$

(E) $4x + 4y$

19 If x is an integer and $\frac{x + 7}{2}$ is an integer, which of the following must be true?

I. x is odd.

II. x is a multiple of 7.

III. $\frac{x + 5}{2}$ is an integer.

(A) I only
(B) II only
(C) III only
(D) I and II
(E) I and III

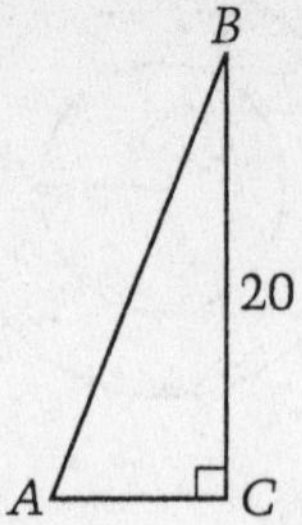

Note: Figure not drawn to scale.

20 If the area of the triangle in the figure above is 100, what is the length of side AB?

(A) $10\sqrt{3}$ (approximately 17.32)

(B) $10\sqrt{5}$ (approximately 22.36)

(C) 20

(D) 24

(E) 25

21 If $(x + 3)(x + 5) - (x - 4)(x - 2) = 0$, then $x =$

(A) -2

(B) $-\frac{1}{2}$

(C) 0

(D) $\frac{1}{2}$

(E) 2

GO ON TO THE NEXT PAGE

22 If $x < y$, which of the following must be true?

(A) $x^2 < y^2$
(B) $-y < -x$
(C) $x^2 < xy$
(D) $xy < y^2$
(E) $2x < y$

23 The first term of a sequence is -3 and every term after the first is 5 more than the term immediately preceding it. What is the value of the 101st term?

(A) 505
(B) 502
(C) 500
(D) 497
(E) 492

24 In a certain club, the median age of the members is 11. Which of the following must be true?

I. The oldest member in the club is at least 1 year older than the youngest.
II. If there is a 10 year old in the club, there is also a 12 year old.
III. The mode of the members' ages is 11.

(A) None
(B) I only
(C) II only
(D) III only
(E) II and III

25 In a certain shop, items were put in a showcase and assigned prices for January. Each month after that, the price was 10 percent less than the price for the previous month. If the price of an item was p dollars for January, what was the price for April?

(A) $0.4p$
(B) $0.6p$
(C) $0.6561p$
(D) $0.7p$
(E) $0.729p$

IF YOU FINISH BEFORE TIME IS CALLED, YOU MAY CHECK YOUR WORK ON THIS SECTION ONLY. DO NOT TURN TO ANY OTHER SECTION IN THE TEST. **STOP**

Section 3 3 3 3 3 3 3

Time — 30 Minutes
30 Questions

For each question in this section, select the best answer from among the choices given and fill in the corresponding oval on the answer sheet.

Each sentence below has one or two blanks, each blank indicating that something has been omitted. Beneath the sentence are five words or sets of words labeled A through E. Choose the word or set of words that, when inserted in the sentence, best fits the meaning of the sentence as a whole.

Example:

Medieval kingdoms did not become constitutional republics overnight; on the contrary, the change was ----.

(A) unpopular
(B) unexpected
(C) advantageous
(D) sufficient
(E) gradual 

1 The usually ---- Mr. Henderson shocked his associates by reacting violently to the insignificant and moderate comments of his critic.

(A) demanding (B) inarticulate (C) aggressive (D) persuasive (E) composed

2 Disappointingly, the researchers' failure was a direct result of their ----; we had not expected that their focus would be so indistinct.

(A) egoism (B) irreverence (C) relevance (D) vagueness (E) hindsight

3 Although her restaurant already has a large and devoted following, Magda tries to expand her ---- by offering special promotions.

(A) clientele (B) investments (C) coverage (D) staffing (E) liability

4 By showing such a large shaded area, this map of wildlife distribution encourages the ---- that certain species living in isolated spots are actually ----.

(A) misconception. .widespread
(B) impression. .remote
(C) illusion. .extant
(D) notion. .carnivorous
(E) sense. .feral

5 The author portrays research psychologists not as disruptive ---- in the field of psychotherapy, but as effective ---- working ultimately toward the same ends as the psychotherapists.

(A) proponents. .opponents
(B) antagonists. .pundits
(C) interlocutors. .surrogates
(D) meddlers. .usurpers
(E) intruders. .collaborators

6 Despite their ---- backgrounds, those who fought for women's right to vote successfully overcame their differences in a ---- effort.

(A) incompatible. .divisive
(B) disparate. .united
(C) distinguished. .futile
(D) eccentric. .prosaic
(E) comparable. .joint

7 The candidate recognized that his attempt to build a broad base of support had been ----, but he was still ---- by the magnitude of his defeat.

(A) obstinate. .elated
(B) insightful. .impenitent
(C) persuasive. .exultant
(D) thwarted. .discomfited
(E) successful. .satisfied

8 Although it is not ----, Clara Rodriguez' book on Puerto Rican life is especially useful because the supply of books on the subject is so ----.

(A) intense. .vast
(B) obsolete. .outdated
(C) ostentatious. .varied
(D) comprehensive. .meager
(E) contemporary. .plentiful

9 Wave direction, apparently the primary ---- used by young turtles to navigate in water, is later ---- by their orientation to magnetic fields.

(A) mechanism. .confused
(B) vestige. .propagated
(C) restraint. .complemented
(D) agent. .propelled
(E) cue. .supplanted

GO ON TO THE NEXT PAGE

Each question below consists of a related pair of words or phrases, followed by five pairs of words or phrases labeled A through E. Select the pair that best expresses a relationship similar to that expressed in the original pair.

Example:

CRUMB : BREAD ::
(A) ounce : unit
(B) splinter : wood
(C) water : bucket
(D) twine : rope
(E) cream : butter

10 MUSEUM : EXHIBIT ::
(A) studio : painter
(B) library : research
(C) theater : performance
(D) picture : frame
(E) orchestra : conductor

11 LENS : GLASS ::
(A) well : water
(B) saw : wood
(C) sweater : wool
(D) fuel : fire
(E) ink : paper

12 ARENA : CONFLICT ::
(A) mirage : reality
(B) forum : discussion
(C) asylum : pursuit
(D) utopia : place
(E) amphitheater : stage

13 ARABLE : CULTIVATION ::
(A) exploited : protection
(B) healthy : medication
(C) insular : discovery
(D) productive : surplus
(E) navigable : sailing

14 REFURBISH : WORN ::
(A) revive : exhausted
(B) reward : outstanding
(C) resume : interrupted
(D) replace : stolen
(E) repaint : glossy

15 DEFEND : UNTENABLE ::
(A) escape : unfettered
(B) judge : punitive
(C) modify : invariable
(D) flourish : vigorous
(E) protect : dangerous

GO ON TO THE NEXT PAGE

Each passage below is followed by questions based on its content. Answer the questions on the basis of what is stated or implied in each passage and in any introductory material that may be provided.

Questions 16-20 are based on the following passage.

The following passage is adapted from an essay on women and writing by a noted contemporary American poet.

As I tried to understand my dual roles of writer and mother, I realized that most, if not all, human lives are full of fantasy—passive daydreaming that need not be acted on. But to write poetry or fiction, or even to think well, is not to fantasize, or even to put fantasies on paper. For a poem to coalesce, for a character or an action to take shape, there has to be an imaginative transformation of reality that is in no way passive. And a certain freedom of the mind is needed—freedom to press on, to enter the currents of your thought like a glider pilot, knowing that your motion can be sustained, that the buoyancy of your attention will not be suddenly snatched away. Moreover, if the imagination is to transcend and transform experience, it has to question, to challenge, to conceive of alternatives, perhaps to the very life you are living at that moment. You have to be free to play around with the notion that day might be night, love might be hate; nothing can be too sacred for the imagination to turn into its opposite or to call experimentally by another name. For writing is renaming. Now, to be maternally with small children all day in the old way, to be with a man in the old way of marriage, requires a holding back, a putting aside of that imaginative activity, and demands instead a kind of conservatism. I want to make it clear that I am not saying that in order to write well, or think well, it is necessary to become unavailable to others, or to become a devouring ego. This has been the myth of the masculine artist and thinker, and I do not accept it. But to be a female human being trying to fulfill traditional female functions in a traditional way is in direct conflict with the subversive function of the imagination. The word "traditional" is important here. There must be ways, and we will be finding out more and more about them, in which the energy of creation and the energy of relation can be united. But in those years I always felt the conflict as a failure of love in myself. I had thought I was choosing a full life: the life available to most men, in which sexuality, work, and parenthood could coexist. But I felt, at twenty-nine, guilt toward the people closest to me, and guilty toward my own being. I wanted, then, more than anything, the one thing of which there was never enough: time to think, time to write.

16 The passage is primarily concerned with the

(A) different ways a writer uses imagination
(B) variety of roles a woman has during her lifetime
(C) contrasting theories of writing that are held today
(D) tendency for authors to confuse the real and the imaginary
(E) tension between traditional female roles and a writer's needs

17 The author's statement that "writing is renaming" (line 22) suggests a conviction that writing involves

(A) gaining a large vocabulary of traditional definitions
(B) safeguarding language from change through misuse
(C) realizing that definitions are more important than perceptions
(D) transforming ideas in an active and creative manner
(E) overcoming the desire to use contradictory examples

18 The author's attitude toward those who believe a writer must become a "devouring ego" (line 30) in order to write well is one of

(A) reluctant agreement
(B) confused ambivalence
(C) casual indifference
(D) emphatic disapproval
(E) personal abhorrence

19 The author suggests that, in the future, women writers who are caring for small children will have the opportunity to

(A) join two tasks into a single effort that requires little attention
(B) integrate two pursuits in a way that enhances both experiences
(C) identify two roles as a means of choosing one role over the other
(D) articulate two impulses that have become indistinguishable
(E) obtain the formal training necessary to accomplish two goals

20 According to the passage, which of the following is a necessary prerequisite to writing well?

(A) Opportunities for the imagination to function actively
(B) Freedom to read widely among great writers of the past
(C) Shaping thoughts through disciplined study
(D) Complete withdrawal into the self
(E) Desire for literary continuity

GO ON TO THE NEXT PAGE

Questions 21-30 are based on the following passage.

The following passage was adapted from an account by two scientists about the emergence of genetics, the science of inherited traits.

You have seen them in movies: scientists who are infallible and coldly objective—little more than animated computers in white lab coats. They take measurements and record results as if the collection of data were the sole object of their lives. The assumption: If one gathers enough facts about something, the relationships between those facts will spontaneously reveal themselves.

Nonsense!

The myth of the infallible scientist evaporates when one thinks of the number of great ideas in science whose originators were correct in general but wrong in detail. The English physicist John Dalton (1766-1844) gets credit for modern atomic theory, but his mathematical formulas for calculating atomic weights were incorrect. The Polish astronomer Copernicus, who corrected Ptolemy's ancient concept of an Earth-centered universe, nevertheless was mistaken in the particulars of the planets' orbits.

Luck, too, has played a determining role in scientific discovery. The French chemist Pasteur demonstrated that life does not arise spontaneously from air. But it may have been luck that he happened to use an easy-to-kill yeast and not the hay bacillus that another, long-forgotten, investigator had chosen for the same experiment. We now know that hay bacillus is heat-resistant and grows even after the boiling that killed Pasteur's yeast. If Pasteur had used the hay bacillus, his "proof" would not have materialized.

Gregor Mendel, the founder of modern genetics, epitomizes the humanness of the scientist. Plant hybridization intrigued and puzzled Mendel, an Augustinian monk with some training in mathematics and the natural sciences. He had read in the professional literature that crosses between certain species regularly yielded many hybrids with identical traits; but when hybrids were crossed, all kinds of strange new combinations of traits cropped up. The principle of inheritance, if there was one, was elusive.

Mendel had the basic idea that there might be simple mathematical relationships among plants in different generations. To pursue this hypothesis, he decided to establish experimental plots in the monastery garden at Brünn, raise a number of varieties of peas, interbreed them, count and classify the offspring of each generation, and see whether any reliable mathematical ratios could be deduced.

After many years of meticulously growing, harvesting, and counting pea plants, Mendel thought he had something worth talking about. So, in 1865, he appeared before the Brünn Society for the Study of Natural Science, reported on his research, and postulated what have since come to be called the Mendelian laws. Society members listened politely but, insofar as anybody knows, asked few questions and engaged in little discussion. It may even be that, as he proceeded, a certain suspicion emerged out of the embarrassed silence. After all, Mendel lacked a degree and had published no research. Now, if Pasteur had advanced this idea . . .

Mendel's assertion that separate and distinct "elements" of inheritance must exist, despite the fact that he couldn't produce any, was close to asking the society to accept something on faith. There was no evidence for Mendel's hypothesis other than his computations; and his wildly unconventional application of algebra to botany made it difficult for his listeners to understand that those computations *were* the evidence.

Mendel undoubtedly died without knowing that his findings on peas had indeed illuminated a well-nigh universal pattern. Luck had been with him in his choice of which particular traits to study. We now know that groups of genes do not always act independently. Often they are linked, their effect being to transmit a "package" of traits. Knowing nothing about genes, let alone the phenomenon of linkage, Mendel was spared failure because the traits that he chose to follow were each controlled separately.* The probability of making such a happy choice in random picks is only about 1 in 163!

*Some scientists believe that Mendel actually did have some idea of linkage and did choose traits purposefully.

21 The word "Nonsense!" (line 9) conveys the extent to which the authors

(A) object to the tendency of scientists to rely on existing data
(B) reject the way in which scientists are portrayed in the media
(C) are amused at the accidental nature of some scientific findings
(D) oppose the glorification of certain scientists at the expense of others
(E) realize the necessity of objectivity in research

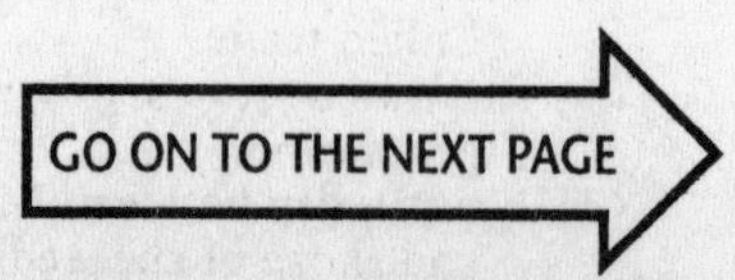

22 The authors cite the example of Copernicus (lines 16-20) to substantiate which of the following claims?

(A) The achievements of scientists are not always recognized.
(B) Scientific progress depends on a variety of factors.
(C) Scientists often suffer from professional jealousy and competition.
(D) Noted scientists are not always wholly accurate in their theories.
(E) A scientist may stumble on an important truth accidentally.

23 The term "humanness" (line 33) as it is applied to Mendel refers to

(A) the tendency to rely excessively on emotion
(B) an interest in improving the human condition through scientific research
(C) an attitude of forgiveness toward those who underrated him
(D) a combination of intellect, intuition, and good fortune
(E) a talent for persevering in the face of opposition

24 In the passage, Pasteur's use of a certain yeast is comparable to

(A) a previous investigator's use of the hay bacillus
(B) Dalton's discovery of atomic weights
(C) Mendel's choice of traits to study
(D) Copernicus' study of the universe
(E) Mendel's use of mathematical ratios

25 In lines 61-63, the authors imply that in comparison to Mendel, Pasteur

(A) was a more proficient researcher
(B) based his theories on more extensive investigations
(C) possessed a more impressive professional reputation
(D) was more meticulous in his observations
(E) devoted more energy to promoting his scientific ideas

26 The "universal pattern" (line 75) refers to

(A) the initial skepticism with which new ideas are received
(B) a tendency of botanists to resist purely theoretical proof
(C) the way peas tend to exhibit the quality of linked traits
(D) the way traits usually reappear in succeeding generations
(E) a similarity between Mendel's experiments and those of succeeding geneticists

27 The word "happy" (line 84) most nearly means

(A) joyful
(B) fortunate
(C) willing
(D) dazed
(E) pleasing

28 The passage suggests that Mendel's contemporaries assumed that valid biological theories

(A) are often proposed by inexperienced researchers
(B) cannot be based on mathematical proof alone
(C) must be supported by years of careful research
(D) often represent a departure from established practice
(E) must be circulated to a wide audience

29 The passage suggests that Mendel's experiments succeeded because

(A) Mendel was able to convince his colleagues to support his research
(B) Mendel discovered flaws in his research design and corrected them
(C) Mendel had a thorough understanding of the concept of linked traits
(D) the scientific community finally understood the connection between mathematical computations and heredity
(E) the traits in peas happen to reappear in a distinct and predictable way

30 As described in the passage, the experiences of Mendel are most like those of

(A) Albert Einstein, who fled Nazi Germany to become the most famous physicist of this century
(B) Pierre Curie, whose career as a chemist was cut short by a tragic accident
(C) Barbara McClintock, whose theories about inherited traits in corn were not understood or accepted until long after she had advanced them
(D) Leonardo da Vinci, whose numerous attempts to make a successful flying machine resulted in failure
(E) James Watson and Francis Crick, who competed with other teams of scientists in the race to unravel the genetic code

IF YOU FINISH BEFORE TIME IS CALLED, YOU MAY CHECK YOUR WORK ON THIS SECTION ONLY. DO NOT TURN TO ANY OTHER SECTION IN THE TEST. **STOP**

Section 4 4 4 4 4

Time—30 Minutes
25 Questions

This section contains two types of questions. You have 30 minutes to complete both types. You may use any available space for scratchwork.

Notes:

1. The use of a calculator is permitted. All numbers used are real numbers.
2. Figures that accompany problems in this test are intended to provide information useful in solving the problems. They are drawn as accurately as possible EXCEPT when it is stated in a specific problem that the figure is not drawn to scale. All figures lie in a plane unless otherwise indicated.

Reference Information

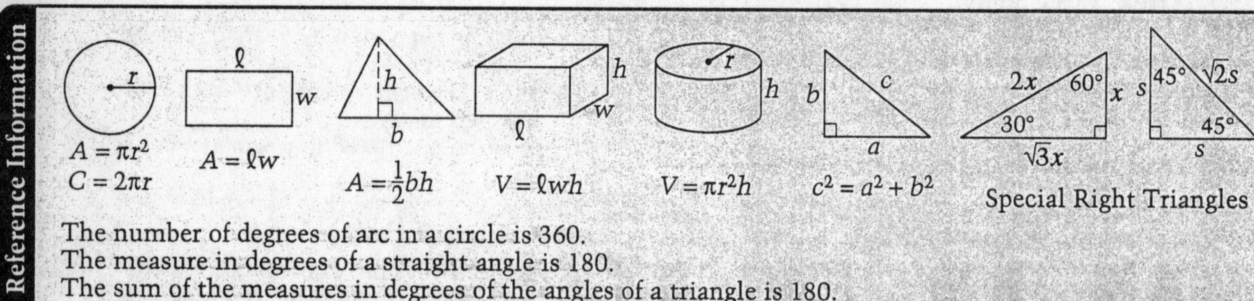

The number of degrees of arc in a circle is 360.
The measure in degrees of a straight angle is 180.
The sum of the measures in degrees of the angles of a triangle is 180.

Directions for Quantitative Comparison Questions

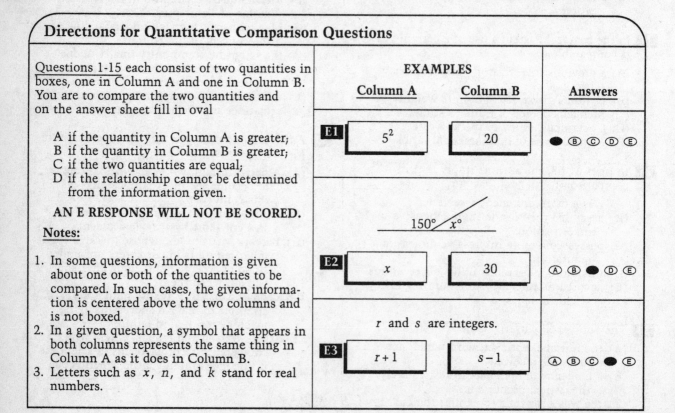

Questions 1-15 each consist of two quantities in boxes, one in Column A and one in Column B. You are to compare the two quantities and on the answer sheet fill in oval

A if the quantity in Column A is greater;
B if the quantity in Column B is greater;
C if the two quantities are equal;
D if the relationship cannot be determined from the information given.

AN E RESPONSE WILL NOT BE SCORED.

Notes:

1. In some questions, information is given about one or both of the quantities to be compared. In such cases, the given information is centered above the two columns and is not boxed.
2. In a given question, a symbol that appears in both columns represents the same thing in Column A as it does in Column B.
3. Letters such as x, n, and k stand for real numbers.

EXAMPLES

	Column A	Column B	Answers
E1	5^2	20	● Ⓑ Ⓒ Ⓓ Ⓔ
	(figure: 150°, $x°$)		
E2	x	30	Ⓐ Ⓑ ● Ⓓ Ⓔ
	r and s are integers.		
E3	$r+1$	$s-1$	Ⓐ Ⓑ Ⓒ ● Ⓔ

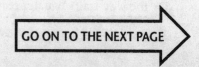

GO ON TO THE NEXT PAGE

4 4 4 4 4 4

SUMMARY DIRECTIONS FOR COMPARISON QUESTIONS

Answer: A if the quantity in Column A is greater;
B if the quantity in Column B is greater;
C if the two quantities are equal;
D if the relationship cannot be determined from the information given.

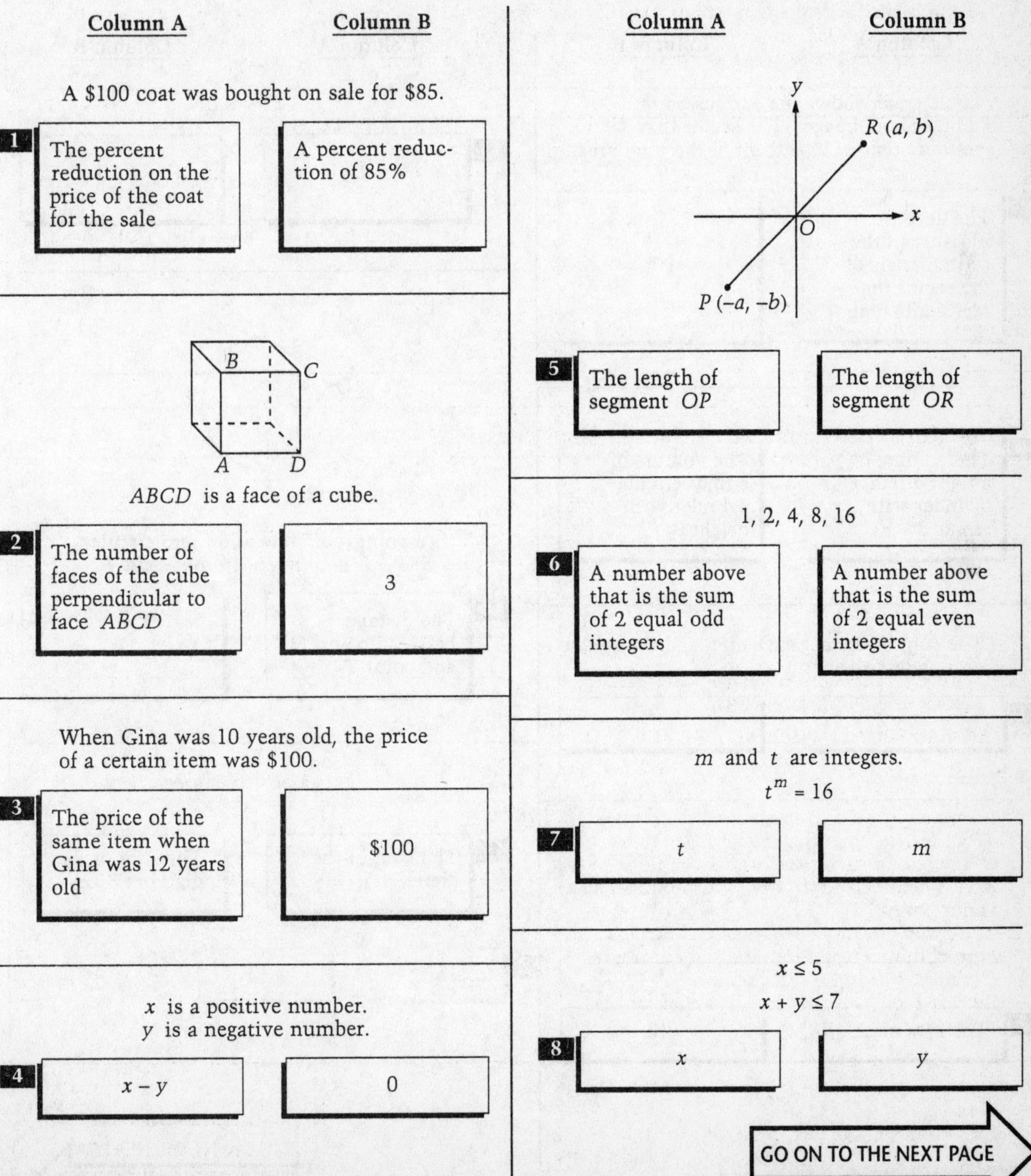

	Column A	Column B

A \$100 coat was bought on sale for \$85.

	Column A	Column B
1	The percent reduction on the price of the coat for the sale	A percent reduction of 85%

$ABCD$ is a face of a cube.

	Column A	Column B
2	The number of faces of the cube perpendicular to face $ABCD$	3

When Gina was 10 years old, the price of a certain item was \$100.

	Column A	Column B
3	The price of the same item when Gina was 12 years old	\$100

x is a positive number.
y is a negative number.

	Column A	Column B
4	$x - y$	0

	Column A	Column B
5	The length of segment OP	The length of segment OR

1, 2, 4, 8, 16

	Column A	Column B
6	A number above that is the sum of 2 equal odd integers	A number above that is the sum of 2 equal even integers

m and t are integers.

$t^m = 16$

	Column A	Column B
7	t	m

$x \leq 5$

$x + y \leq 7$

	Column A	Column B
8	x	y

GO ON TO THE NEXT PAGE

SUMMARY DIRECTIONS FOR COMPARISON QUESTIONS

Answer: A if the quantity in Column A is greater;
B if the quantity in Column B is greater;
C if the two quantities are equal;
D if the relationship cannot be determined from the information given.

	Column A	Column B

A circle graph shows the various parts of a household budget. The sector that represents rent is 25 percent of the total area.

	Column A	Column B
9	The degree measure of the central angle of the sector that represents rent	90°
10	The volume of a right circular cylinder with radius 3	The volume of a right circular cylinder with height 3

The sum of the negative of t and the square of s is less than 2.

	Column A	Column B
11	$t + 2$	s^2

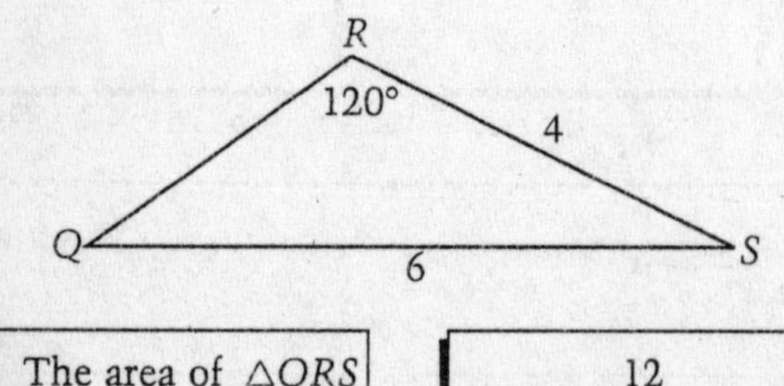

	Column A	Column B
12	The area of $\triangle QRS$	12

$f > g > 0$

	Column A	Column B
13	$\frac{f+1}{f}$	$\frac{g+1}{g}$

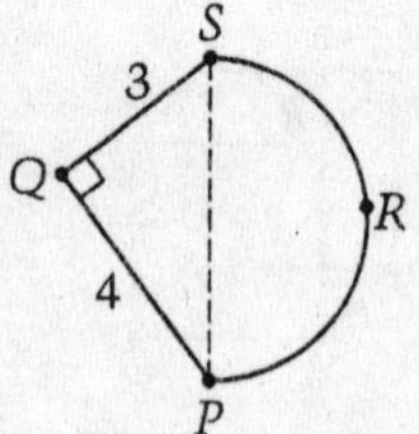

T is a point (not shown) on semicircular arc SRP. T is different from S and P.

	Column A	Column B
14	The distance between point Q and point T	3

k is a positive integer.
$v = 10 \times k$

	Column A	Column B
15	The sum of the digits of k	The sum of the digits of v

GO ON TO THE NEXT PAGE

Directions for Student-Produced Response Questions

Each of the remaining 10 questions requires you to solve the problem and enter your answer by marking the ovals in the special grid, as shown in the examples below.

Answer: $\frac{7}{12}$ or 7/12

Write answer → in boxes.

Fraction line

Grid in → result.

Answer: 2.5

Decimal point

Answer: 201
Either position is correct.

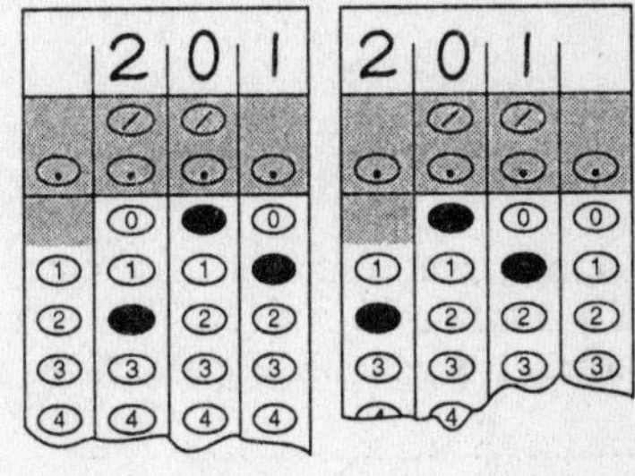

Note: You may start your answers in any column, space permitting. Columns not needed should be left blank.

- Mark no more than one oval in any column.
- Because the answer sheet will be machine-scored, **you will receive credit only if the ovals are filled in correctly.**
- Although not required, it is suggested that you write your answer in the boxes at the top of the columns to help you fill in the ovals accurately.
- Some problems may have more than one correct answer. In such cases, grid only one answer.
- No question has a negative answer.
- **Mixed numbers** such as $2\frac{1}{2}$ must be gridded as 2.5 or 5/2. (If 2|1|/|2 is gridded, it will be interpreted as $\frac{21}{2}$, not $2\frac{1}{2}$.)

- **Decimal Accuracy:** If you obtain a decimal answer, **enter the most accurate value the grid will accommodate.** For example, if you obtain an answer such as 0.6666 . . . , you should record the result as .666 or .667. **Less accurate values such as .66 or .67 are not acceptable.**

Acceptable ways to grid $\frac{2}{3}$ = .6666 . . .

2/3 | .666 | .667

16 If $\begin{smallmatrix} a & b \\ c & d \end{smallmatrix}$ (diamond) is defined by $\begin{smallmatrix} a & b \\ c & d \end{smallmatrix} = ad + bc$,

what is the value of $\begin{smallmatrix} 2 & 3 \\ 6 & 4 \end{smallmatrix}$?

17 A recipe calls for $7\frac{1}{3}$ tablespoons of milk. This amount is equivalent to how many teaspoons of milk? (3 teaspoons = 1 tablespoon)

GO ON TO THE NEXT PAGE

18 If $0.92x = 9.2$, what is the value of $\frac{1}{x}$?

Note: Figure not drawn to scale.

19 In the triangle above, x and y are integers. If $35 < y < 40$, what is one possible value of x ?

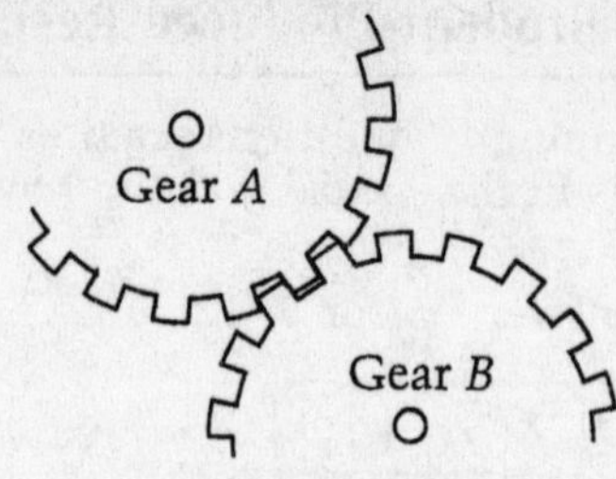

Note: Figure not drawn to scale.

20 The figure above shows parts of two circular gears whose teeth interlock when the gears turn. Gear A has 72 teeth and gear B has 48 teeth. How many complete revolutions does gear A make when gear B makes 9 complete revolutions?

21 If the sum of two numbers is 2 and their difference is 1, what is their product?

GO ON TO THE NEXT PAGE

22 If $27^{15} = 3^y$, what is the value of y?

23 If the perimeter of a rectangle is 10 times the width of the rectangle, then the length of the rectangle is how many times the width?

24 There are 120 red marbles and 80 blue marbles in a bag that contains 200 marbles. If only blue marbles are to be added to the bag so that the probability of randomly drawing a blue marble from the bag becomes $\frac{2}{3}$, how many blue marbles must be added to the bag?

25 The average (arithmetic mean) of 5 positive integers is 350. Two of the integers are 99 and 102 and the other integers are greater than 102. If all 5 integers are different, what is the greatest possible value for any of the 5 integers?

IF YOU FINISH BEFORE TIME IS CALLED, YOU MAY CHECK YOUR WORK ON THIS SECTION ONLY. DO NOT TURN TO ANY OTHER SECTION IN THE TEST. **STOP**

Section 6 6 6 6

Time—15 Minutes
13 Questions

For each question in this section, select the best answer from among the choices given and fill in the corresponding oval on the answer sheet.

The two passages below are followed by questions based on their content and on the relationship between the two passages. Answer the questions on the basis of what is stated or implied in the passages and in any introductory material that may be provided.

Questions 1-13 refer to the following passages.

These two passages reflect two different views of the values and integrity of journalism. Passage 1 is from a 1990 account of the origins of investigative journalism and "muckraking." Passage 2 was written in the 1920's by a noted satirist famous for voicing strong opinions.

Passage 1

Since the lineage of investigative journalism is most directly traceable to the Progressive era of the early 1900's, it is not surprising that the President of the United States at the time was among the first to articulate its political dimensions. Theodore Roosevelt called investigative reporters "muckrakers," after a character from John Bunyan's *Pilgrim's Progress* who humbly cleaned "the filth off the floor." Despite the misgivings implied by the comparison, Roosevelt saw the muckrakers as "often indispensable to the well-being of society":

> There are in the body politic, economic and social, many and grave evils, and there is urgent necessity for the sternest war upon them. There should be relentless exposure of and attack upon every evil man, whether politician or businessman.

Roosevelt recognized the value-laden character of investigative journalism. He perceived correctly that investigative reporters are committed to unearthing *wrongdoing*. For these journalists, disclosures of morally outrageous conduct maximize the opportunity for the forces of "good" to recognize and do battle with the forces of "evil."

So, the current folklore surrounding investigative reporting closely resembles the American ideal of popular democracy. Vigilant journalists bring wrongdoing to public attention. An informed citizenry responds by demanding reforms from their elected representatives. Policymakers respond in turn by taking corrective action. Partly a product of its muckraking roots, this idealized perspective is also an outgrowth of the commonly perceived effects of exposés published in the early 1970's. The most celebrated of these exposés were the news stories that linked top White House officials to Watergate crimes.* These stories were widely held responsible for the public's loss of confidence in the Nixon administration, ultimately forcing the President's resignation.

Investigative journalists *intend* to provoke outrage in their reports of malfeasance. Their work is validated when citizens respond by demanding change from their leaders. By bringing problems to public attention, the "journalists of outrage" attempt to alter societal agendas.

*The burglarizing of the Democratic party headquarters at the Watergate complex and other crimes committed during the 1972 presidential elections

Passage 2

What ails newspapers in the United States is the fact that their gigantic commercial development compels them to appeal to larger and larger masses of undifferentiated people and that the truth is the commodity that the masses of undifferentiated people cannot be induced to buy. The dominant citizen of democratic society, despite a superficial appearance of intelligence, is really quite incapable of anything resembling reasoning.

So, the problem before a modern newspaper, hard pressed by the need of carrying on a thoroughly wholesome business, is that of enlisting the interest of these masses of people, and by interest, of course, I do not mean their mere listless attention, but their active emotional cooperation. Unless a newspaper can manage to arouse these people's *feelings* it might just as well not have at them at all, for their feelings are the essential part of them, and it is out of their feelings that they dredge up their obscure loyalties and aversions. Well, and how are their feelings to be stirred up? At bottom, the business is quite simple. First scare them—and then reassure them. First get people into a panic with a bugaboo—and then go to the rescue, gallantly and uproariously, with a stuffed club to lay it. First fake 'em—and then fake 'em again.

GO ON TO THE NEXT PAGE

Insofar as our public gazettes have any serious business at all, it is the business of snouting out and exhibiting new and startling horrors, atrocities, impending calamities, tyrannies, villainies, enormities, mortal perils, jeopardies, outrages, catastrophes—first snouting out and exhibiting them, and then magnificently circumventing and disposing of them. The first part is easy. It is almost unheard of for the mob to disbelieve in a new bugaboo. As soon as the hideous form is unveiled it begins to quake and cry out: the reservoir of its primary fears is always ready to run over. And the second part is not much more difficult. The one thing demanded of the remedy is that it be simple, more or less familiar, easy to comprehend, that it make no draft upon the higher cerebral centers—that it avoid leading the shy and delicate intelligence of the mob into strange and hence painful fields of speculation. All healthy journalism in America—healthy in the sense that it flourishes spontaneously and needs no outside aid—is based firmly upon just such an invention and scotching of bugaboos. And so is all politics. Whatever stands above that fundamental imposture is an artificiality. Intelligent and honest journalism and politics—these things, in a democratic society, have no legitimate place. They are, when they are encountered, exotic curiosities, pale and clammy orchids, half-fabulous beasts in cages.

1 Passage 1 suggests that Roosevelt's choice of name for investigative reporters reflects his belief that

(A) they were irresponsible about checking the accuracy of their reporting
(B) their writing style was unrefined and colloquial
(C) they were motivated by greed and desire for fame
(D) they were unsung and underpaid
(E) they did unpleasant but necessary work

2 The terms "folklore" (line 26) and "idealized perspective" (line 33) suggest that the author of Passage 1 would agree with which statement?

(A) Democracy and journalism are incompatible.
(B) Investigative journalism depends on creating a false villain.
(C) Many people have a romanticized conception of the role of journalists.
(D) Readers are easily swayed by appeals to their patriotism.
(E) People seldom believe what they read in newspapers.

3 The author of Passage 1 refers to the report on the "Watergate crimes" (line 38) primarily as an example of

(A) a story covered better by television than by print media
(B) editorial pandering to an ignorant public
(C) journalism that had a tangible effect on politics
(D) a flagrant abuse of the freedom of the press
(E) the subversion of legitimate political power

4 In the last paragraph of Passage 1 (lines 42-47), the author is

(A) showing how investigative reporting has broken with its past tradition
(B) acknowledging that reporters are not merely trying to impart information
(C) disparaging those who believe that meaningful reform is possible
(D) expressing sympathy for victims of overzealous reportage
(E) citing an exception to the generalization mentioned by Roosevelt

5 The brand of journalism discussed in Passage 1 is based on the assumption that

(A) public awareness of injustice is necessary for change to occur
(B) newspapers are read chiefly for information that will help people to get ahead
(C) most people take for granted that politicians are corrupt
(D) most people are suspicious of whistleblowers
(E) most people's beliefs are inconsistent with their actions

6 In line 53, "dominant" most nearly means

(A) compelling
(B) influential
(C) headstrong
(D) typical
(E) superior

GO ON TO THE NEXT PAGE

7 The tactics described in lines 69-73 convey the

(A) main difference between reporters' and editors' attitudes toward the public
(B) immense difficulty involved in solving society's problems
(C) physical danger that occasionally awaits reporters
(D) extent to which journalism relies on manipulation
(E) reason why newspapers are so seldom profitable

8 In the last sentence of Passage 2, the author mentions orchids and beasts in order to

(A) give an example of sensationalism in newspaper reporting
(B) suggest something so unusual as to be bizarre
(C) indicate a preference for fiction over news
(D) chide newspapers for dealing with excessively morbid subjects
(E) cite exceptions that disprove the previous sentence

9 Both passages indicate that a fundamental ingredient in the success of a newspaper is

(A) financial assistance from the government
(B) a thirst for truth
(C) commercial development
(D) reporters of great integrity
(E) an engaged readership

10 The author of Passage 2 would most likely respond to the journalists' view in Passage 1 of the battle between the forces of "good" and "evil" (lines 24-25) by

(A) praising the journalists' idealism
(B) mocking the journalists' naïveté
(C) admiring the journalists' wit
(D) arguing that good and evil are not easily defined
(E) offering exceptions to the general rule

11 Unlike Passage 2, Passage 1 assumes that newspapers generally

(A) cater to a thoughtful, responsible citizenry
(B) rely on an obedient and docile public for assent
(C) are compromised by the advertising that supports them
(D) are read by only an elite minority of subscribers
(E) require close supervision by government censors

12 Both authors' discussions assume that the public

(A) ignores the press more often than not
(B) will react when prompted by the press
(C) is indifferent to corruption
(D) has a higher degree of literacy than is found in most other countries
(E) is well-informed and astute in its political choices

13 The two authors would most likely agree with which statement?

(A) Newspapers are a powerful means of getting the public's attention.
(B) Journalism is an important force for good.
(C) Competition between newspapers tends to improve the coverage of news.
(D) Most investigative journalism is actually driven by the profit motive.
(E) A knowledge of history is more important to a journalist than is a talent for writing.

IF YOU FINISH BEFORE TIME IS CALLED, YOU MAY CHECK YOUR WORK ON THIS SECTION ONLY. DO NOT TURN TO ANY OTHER SECTION IN THE TEST. **STOP**

Section 7 7

Time—15 Minutes 10 Questions	**In this section solve each problem, using any available space on the page for scratchwork. Then decide which is the best of the choices given and fill in the corresponding oval on the answer sheet.**

Notes:

1. The use of a calculator is permitted. All numbers used are real numbers.
2. Figures that accompany problems in this test are intended to provide information useful in solving the problems. They are drawn as accurately as possible EXCEPT when it is stated in a specific problem that the figure is not drawn to scale. All figures lie in a plane unless otherwise indicated.

Reference Information

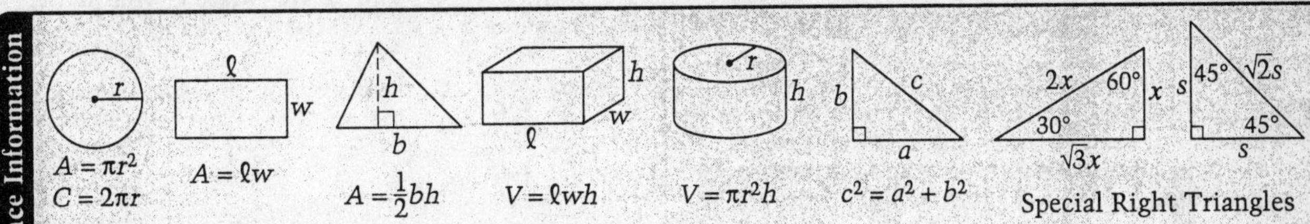

The number of degrees of arc in a circle is 360.
The measure in degrees of a straight angle is 180.
The sum of the measures in degrees of the angles of a triangle is 180.

1 If $x^2 = y^3$ and $x = 8$, what is the value of y?

(A) 2
(B) 4
(C) 5
(D) 6
(E) 12

2 Stickers are 4 for \$0.80 (including tax) and trading cards are 3 for \$1.05 (including tax). What is Kim's change from \$5.00 if she buys 8 stickers and 6 trading cards at these prices?

(A) \$0.30
(B) \$1.00
(C) \$1.30
(D) \$3.70
(E) \$4.00

GO ON TO THE NEXT PAGE

3 C is the midpoint of line segment AB, and D and E are the midpoints of line segments AC and CB, respectively. If the length of DE is 8, what is the length of AB ?

(A) 4
(B) 8
(C) 12
(D) 16
(E) 32

4 Carla has 2 more than 3 times the number of cassette tapes that Jules has. If C represents the number of Carla's tapes and if J represents the number of Jules's tapes, which of the following is a correct expression relating C and J ?

(A) $C = 2J + 3$
(B) $C = 2(J + 3)$
(C) $C = 3J - 2$
(D) $C = 3J + 2$
(E) $C = 3(J + 2)$

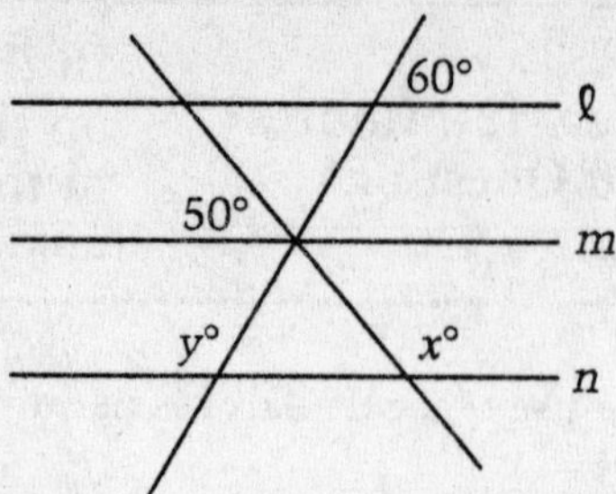

5 In the figure above, five lines intersect as shown. If lines ℓ, m, and n are parallel, what is the value of $x + y$?

(A) 210
(B) 220
(C) 230
(D) 240
(E) 250

GO ON TO THE NEXT PAGE

Questions 6-7 refer to the following table.

PROJECTED SALES FOR GAME Q

Price of Game Q	Projected Number of Games Sold
$50	50,000
$30	100,000
$10	150,000

6 Based on the projections, how much more money would be received from sales of game Q when the price is $30 than when the price is $50?

(A) $50,000
(B) $100,000
(C) $500,000
(D) $1,000,000
(E) $2,750,000

---

7 Which of the following graphs best represents the relationship between the price of game Q and the projected number of games sold, as indicated by the table?

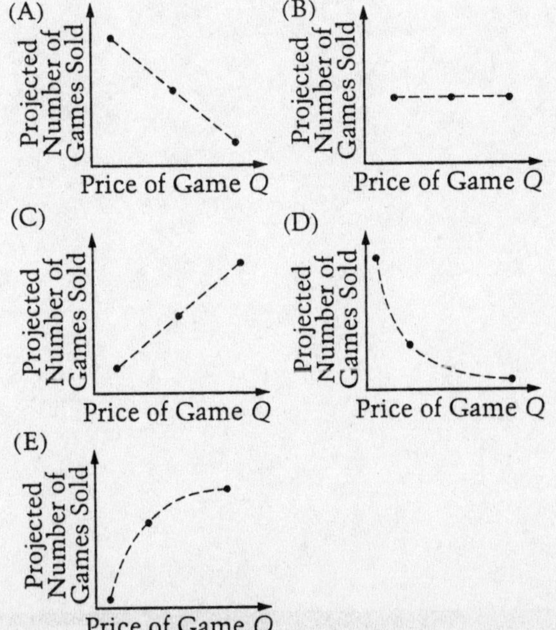

8 In the repeating decimal

$$0.\overline{12468} = 0.1246812468\ldots,$$

where the digits 12468 repeat, which digit is in the 4,000th place to the right of the decimal point?

(A) 1
(B) 2
(C) 4
(D) 6
(E) 8

GO ON TO THE NEXT PAGE

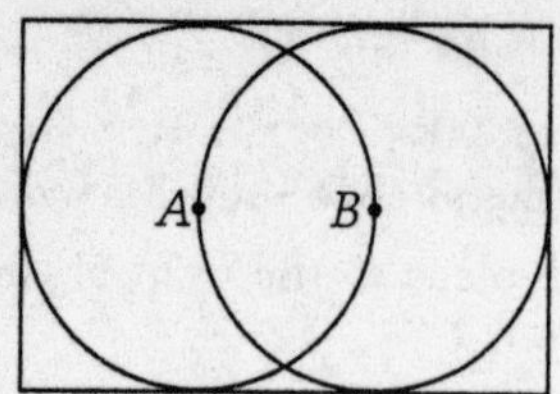

9 In the figure above, A and B are the centers of the two circles. If each circle has area 10, what is the area of the rectangle?

(A) 20

(B) $20 - \frac{10}{\pi}$

(C) $\frac{40}{\pi}$

(D) $\frac{50}{\pi}$

(E) $\frac{60}{\pi}$

10 There are 3 roads from Plattsville to Ocean Heights and 4 roads from Ocean Heights to Bay Cove. If Martina drives from Plattsville to Bay Cove and back, passes through Ocean Heights in both directions, and does not travel any road twice, how many different routes for the trip are possible?

(A) 72
(B) 36
(C) 24
(D) 18
(E) 12

Passage on genetics; Section 3

IF YOU FINISH BEFORE TIME IS CALLED, YOU MAY CHECK YOUR WORK ON THIS SECTION ONLY. DO NOT TURN TO ANY OTHER SECTION IN THE TEST. **STOP**

SAT I: Reasoning Test Answer Key
Saturday, November 1995

VERBAL

Section 1 — Five-choice Questions

COR. ANS.	DIFF. LEV.
1. A	1
2. D	2
3. E	3
4. C	3
5. B	3
6. D	3
7. C	4
8. B	3
9. A	5
10. C	5
11. E	1
12. E	2
13. D	2
14. D	2
15. D	3
16. B	3
17. A	3
18. C	3
19. A	4
20. C	4
21. D	5
22. B	5
23. D	5
24. B	1
25. D	2
26. D	2
27. A	2
28. C	3
29. B	3
30. E	3
31. C	1
32. E	3
33. B	4
34. A	4
35. C	3

no. correct

no. incorrect

Section 3 — Five-choice Questions

COR. ANS.	DIFF. LEV.
1. E	2
2. D	3
3. A	3
4. A	3
5. E	3
6. B	3
7. D	3
8. D	3
9. E	5
10. C	2
11. C	2
12. B	2
13. E	4
14. A	3
15. C	5
16. E	3
17. D	2
18. D	4
19. B	3
20. A	2
21. B	3
22. D	1
23. D	3
24. C	4
25. C	3
26. D	4
27. B	2
28. B	4
29. E	4
30. C	3

no. correct

no. incorrect

Section 6 — Five-choice Questions

COR. ANS.	DIFF. LEV.
1. E	3
2. C	5
3. C	2
4. B	3
5. A	3
6. D	4
7. D	2
8. B	5
9. E	4
10. B	4
11. A	4
12. B	2
13. A	2

no. correct

no. incorrect

MATHEMATICAL

Section 2 — Five-choice Questions

COR. ANS.	DIFF. LEV.
1. C	1
2. E	1
3. C	1
4. C	2
5. A	2
6. B	2
7. A	2
8. C	2
9. E	3
10. D	1
11. D	3
12. D	3
13. B	3
14. B	3
15. C	3
16. D	3
17. C	3
18. A	3
19. E	3
20. B	3
21. B	3
22. B	5
23. D	5
24. A	4
25. E	5

no. correct

no. incorrect

Section 4 — Four-choice Questions

COR. ANS.	DIFF. LEV.
1. B	3
2. A	2
3. D	2
4. A	3
5. C	1
6. B	2
7. D	3
8. D	3
9. C	3
10. D	3
11. A	4
12. B	5
13. B	4
14. A	3
15. C	4

no. correct

no. incorrect

Section 7 — Five-choice Questions

COR. ANS.	DIFF. LEV.
1. B	1
2. C	1
3. D	2
4. D	1
5. E	3
6. C	3
7. A	3
8. E	4
9. E	5
10. A	5

no. correct

no. incorrect

Section 4 — Student-produced Response Questions

COR. ANS.	DIFF. LEV.
16. 26	1
17. 22	2
18. .1 or 1/10	2
19. 102,104,106 or 108	3
20. 6	3
21. 3/4 or .75	3
22. 45	3
23. 4	3
24. 160	4
25. 1342	4

no. correct (16-25)

NOTE: Difficulty levels are estimates of question difficulty for a recent group of college-bound seniors. Difficulty levels range from 1 (easiest) to 5 (hardest).

The Scoring Process

Machine-scoring is done in three steps:

- *Scanning.* Your answer sheet is "read" by a scanning machine and the oval you filled in for each question is recorded on a computer tape.
- *Scoring.* The computer compares the oval filled in for each question with the correct response. Each correct answer receives one point; omitted questions do not count toward your score. For each wrong answer to the multiple-choice questions, a fraction of a point is subtracted to correct for random guessing. For questions with five answer choices, one-fourth of a point is subtracted for each wrong response; for questions with four answer choices, one-third of a point is subtracted for each wrong response. The SAT I verbal test has 78 questions with five answer choices each. If, for example, a student has 44 right, 32 wrong, and 2 omitted, the resulting raw score is determined as follows:

$$44 \text{ right} - \frac{32 \text{ wrong}}{4} = 44 - 8 = 36 \text{ raw score points}$$

Obtaining raw scores frequently involves the rounding of fractional numbers to the nearest whole number. For example a raw score of 36.25 is rounded to 36, the nearest whole number. A raw score of 36.50 is rounded upward to 37.

- *Converting to reported scaled score.* Raw test scores are then placed on the College Board scale of 200 to 800 through a process that adjusts scores to account for minor differences in difficulty among different editions of the test. This process, known as equating, is performed so that a student's reported score is not affected by the edition of the test taken nor by the abilities of the group with whom the student takes the test. As a result of placing SAT I scores on the College Board scale, scores earned by students at different times can be compared. For example, an SAT I verbal score of 400 on a test taken at one administration indicates the same level of developed verbal ability as a 400 score obtained on a different edition of the test taken at another time.

How to Score the Test

SAT I Verbal Sections 1, 3, and 6

Step A: Count the number of correct answers for *Section 1* and record the number in the space provided on the worksheet on the next page. Then do the same for the incorrect answers. (Do not count omitted answers.) To determine subtotal A, use the formula:

$$\text{number correct} - \frac{\text{number incorrect}}{4} = \text{subtotal A}$$

Step B: Count the number of correct answers and the number of incorrect answers for *Section 3* and record the number in the space provided on the worksheet. To determine subtotal B, use the formula:

$$\text{number correct} - \frac{\text{number incorrect}}{4} = \text{subtotal B}$$

Step C: Count the number of correct answers and the number of incorrect answers for *Section 6* and record the number in the space provided on the worksheet. To determine subtotal C, use the formula:

$$\text{number correct} - \frac{\text{number incorrect}}{4} = \text{subtotal C}$$

Step D: To obtain D, add subtotal A, subtotal B, and subtotal C, keeping any decimals. Enter the resulting figure on the worksheet.

Step E: To obtain E, your raw verbal score, round D to the nearest whole number. (For example, any number from 44.50 to 45.49 rounds to 45.) Enter the resulting figure on the worksheet.

Step F: To find your SAT 1 verbal score, look up the total raw verbal score you obtained in step E in the appropriate conversion table. Enter this figure on the worksheet.

SAT I Mathematical Sections 2, 4, and 7

Step A: Count the number of correct answers and the number of incorrect answers for *Section 2* and record the numbers in the spaces provided on the worksheet. To determine subtotal A use the formula:

$$\text{number correct} - \frac{\text{number incorrect}}{4} = \text{subtotal A}$$

Step B: Count the number of correct answers and the number of incorrect answers for the *four-choice quantitative comparison questions (questions 1 through 15) in Section 4* and record the number in the space provided on the worksheet. Note: Do not count any E responses to questions 1 through 15 as correct or incorrect. Because these four-choice questions have no E answer choices, E responses to these questions are treated as omits. To determine subtotal B, use the formula:

$$\text{number correct} - \frac{\text{number incorrect}}{3} = \text{subtotal B}$$

Step C: Count the number of correct answers for the student-produced response questions *(questions 16 through 25) in Section 4* and record the number in the space provided on the worksheet. This is subtotal C.

Step D: Count the number of correct answers and the number of incorrect answers for *Section 7* and record the number in the space provided on the worksheet. To determine subtotal D, use the formula:

$$\text{number correct} - \frac{\text{number incorrect}}{4} = \text{subtotal D}$$

Step E: To obtain E, add subtotal A, subtotal B, subtotal C, and subtotal D, keeping any decimals. Enter the resulting figure on the worksheet.

Step F: To obtain F, your raw mathematical score, round E to the nearest whole number. (For example, any number from 44.50 to 45.49 rounds to 45.) Enter the resulting figure on the worksheet.

Step G: To find your SAT 1 mathematical score, look up the total raw mathematical score you obtained in step F in the appropriate conversion table. Enter this figure on the worksheet.

SAT I Scoring Worksheet

SAT I Verbal Sections

A. Section 1: ________ − (________ ÷ 4) = ________
no. correct no. incorrect subtotal A

B. Section 3: ________ − (________ ÷ 4) = ________
no. correct no. incorrect subtotal B

C. Section 6: ________ − (________ ÷ 4) = ________
no. correct no. incorrect subtotal C

D. Total unrounded raw score (Total A + B + C) ________ D

E. Total rounded raw score (Rounded to nearest whole number) ________ E

F. **SAT 1 verbal reported scaled score (See the appropriate conversion table)** [ ] SAT I verbal score

SAT I Mathematical Sections

A. Section 2: ________ − (________ ÷ 4) = ________
no. correct no. incorrect subtotal A

B. Section 4: Questions 1-15 (quantitative comparison) ________ − (________ ÷ 3) = ________
no. correct no. incorrect subtotal B

C. Section 4: Questions 16-25 (student-produced response) ________ = ________
no. correct subtotal C

D. Section 7: ________ − (________ ÷ 4) = ________
no. correct no. incorrect subtotal D

E. Total unrounded raw score (Total A + B + C + D) ________ E

F. Total rounded raw score (Rounded to nearest whole number) ________ F

G. **SAT 1 mathematical reported scaled score (See the appropriate conversion table)** [ ] SAT I mathematical score

Score Conversion Table
SAT I: Reasoning Test
Saturday, November 1995
Recentered Scale

Raw Score	Verbal Scaled Score	Math Scaled Score	Raw Score	Verbal Scaled Score	Math Scaled Score
78	800		37	510	560
77	800		36	510	560
76	800		35	500	550
75	780		34	490	540
74	770		33	490	530
73	750		32	480	530
72	740		31	480	520
71	730		30	470	510
70	720		29	470	510
69	710		28	460	500
68	700		27	450	490
67	690		26	450	490
66	680		25	440	480
65	680		24	440	470
64	670		23	430	470
63	660		22	420	460
62	660		21	420	460
61	650		20	410	450
60	640	800	19	410	440
59	640	790	18	400	440
58	630	770	17	390	430
57	620	750	16	390	420
56	620	730	15	380	420
55	610	720	14	370	410
54	610	710	13	370	400
53	600	700	12	360	400
52	600	690	11	350	390
51	590	680	10	340	380
50	580	670	9	340	370
49	580	660	8	330	360
48	570	650	7	320	350
47	570	640	6	310	340
46	560	630	5	300	330
45	560	630	4	290	320
44	550	620	3	280	300
43	540	610	2	270	290
42	540	600	1	260	270
41	530	590	0	240	260
40	530	590	-1	230	240
39	520	580	-2	210	220
38	520	570	-3 and below	200	200

This table is for use only with this test.

SAT I: Reasoning Test

Sunday, May 1996

YOUR NAME (PRINT) ______________________________
LAST FIRST MI

TEST CENTER ______________________________
NUMBER NAME OF TEST CENTER ROOM NUMBER

SAT® I: Reasoning Test — General Directions

Timing

- You will have three hours to work on this test.
- There are five 30-minute sections and two 15-minute sections.
- You may work on only one section at a time.
- The supervisor will tell you when to begin and end each section.
- If you finish a section before time is called, check your work on that section. You may NOT turn to any other section.
- Work as rapidly as you can without losing accuracy. Don't waste time on questions that seem too difficult for you.

Marking Answers

- Carefully mark only one answer for each question.
- Make sure each mark is dark and completely fills the oval.
- Do not make any stray marks on your answer sheet.
- If you erase, do so completely. Incomplete erasures may be scored as intended answers.
- Use only the answer spaces that correspond to the question numbers.
- For questions with only four answer choices, an answer marked in oval E will not be scored.
- Use the test book for scratchwork, but you will not receive credit for anything written there.
- You may not transfer answers to your answer sheet or fill in ovals after time has been called.
- You may not fold or remove pages or portions of a page from this book, or take the book or answer sheet from the testing room.

Scoring

- For each correct answer, you receive one point.
- For questions you omit, you receive no points.
- For a wrong answer to a multiple-choice question, you lose a fraction of a point.
  - ► If you can eliminate one or more of the answer choices as wrong, however, you increase your chances of choosing the correct answer and earning one point.
  - ► If you can't eliminate any choice, move on. You can return to the question later if there is time.
- For a wrong answer to a math question that is not multiple-choice, you don't lose any points.

The passages for this test have been adapted from published material. The ideas contained in them do not necessarily represent the opinions of the College Board or Educational Testing Service.

IMPORTANT: The codes below are unique to your test book. Copy them on your answer sheet in boxes 8 and 9 and fill in the corresponding ovals exactly as shown.

8. Form Code

Ⓐ	Ⓐ	⓪	⓪	⓪
Ⓑ	Ⓑ	①	①	①
Ⓒ	Ⓒ	②	②	②
Ⓓ	Ⓓ	③	③	③
Ⓔ	Ⓔ	④	④	④
Ⓕ	Ⓕ	⑤	⑤	⑤
Ⓖ	Ⓖ	⑥	⑥	⑥
Ⓗ	Ⓗ	⑦	⑦	⑦
Ⓘ	Ⓘ	⑧	⑧	⑧
Ⓙ	Ⓙ	⑨	⑨	⑨
Ⓚ	Ⓚ			
Ⓛ	Ⓛ			
Ⓜ	Ⓜ			
Ⓝ	Ⓝ			
Ⓞ	Ⓞ			
Ⓟ	Ⓟ			
Ⓠ	Ⓠ			
Ⓡ	Ⓡ			
Ⓢ	Ⓢ			
Ⓣ	Ⓣ			
Ⓤ	Ⓤ			
Ⓥ	Ⓥ			
Ⓦ	Ⓦ			
Ⓧ	Ⓧ			
Ⓨ	Ⓨ			
Ⓩ	Ⓩ			

9. Test Form

DO NOT OPEN THIS BOOK UNTIL THE SUPERVISOR TELLS YOU TO DO SO.

THE COLLEGE BOARD — SAT I   Page 1

Use a No. 2 pencil only. Be sure each mark is dark and completely fills the intended oval. Completely erase any errors or stray marks.

1. Your Name

First 4 letters of Last Name | First init. | Mid. init.

2. Your Name: (Print) ______ Last ______ First ______ M.I.

I agree to the conditions on the back of the SAT I test book.

Signature: ______ Date: ___/___/___

Home Address: (Print) ______ Number and Street

______ City ______ State ______ Zip Code

Center: (Print) ______ City ______ State ______ Center Number

IMPORTANT: Fill in items 8 and 9 exactly as shown on the back of test book.

8. Form Code

(Copy and grid as on back of test book.)

3. Date of Birth

Month | Day | Year

Jan. Feb. Mar. Apr. May June July Aug. Sept. Oct. Nov. Dec.

4. Social Security Number

5. Sex

Female   Male

6. Registration Number

(Copy from Admission Ticket.)

7. Test Book Serial Number

(Copy from front of test book.)

FOR ETS USE ONLY

9. Test Form

(Copy from back of test book.)

Start with number 1 for each new section. If a section has fewer questions than answer spaces, leave the extra answer spaces blank.

SECTION 1

1–40 Ⓐ Ⓑ Ⓒ Ⓓ Ⓔ

SECTION 2

1–40 Ⓐ Ⓑ Ⓒ Ⓓ Ⓔ

Q2778-06/2 CHW98324 11027 • 09132 • TF129M17.5eX
1 2 3 4
I.N. 207158

Use a No. 2 pencil only. Be sure each mark is dark and completely fills the intended oval. Completely erase any errors or stray marks.

Start with number 1 for each new section. If a section has fewer questions than answer spaces, leave the extra answer spaces blank.

SECTION 3

1–40 Ⓐ Ⓑ Ⓒ Ⓓ Ⓔ

If section 3 of your test book contains math questions that are not multiple-choice, continue to item 16 below. Otherwise, continue to item 16 above.

ONLY ANSWERS ENTERED IN THE OVALS IN EACH GRID AREA WILL BE SCORED.
YOU WILL NOT RECEIVE CREDIT FOR ANYTHING WRITTEN IN THE BOXES ABOVE THE OVALS.

16 17 18 19 20

21 22 23 24 25

BE SURE TO ERASE ANY ERRORS OR STRAY MARKS COMPLETELY.

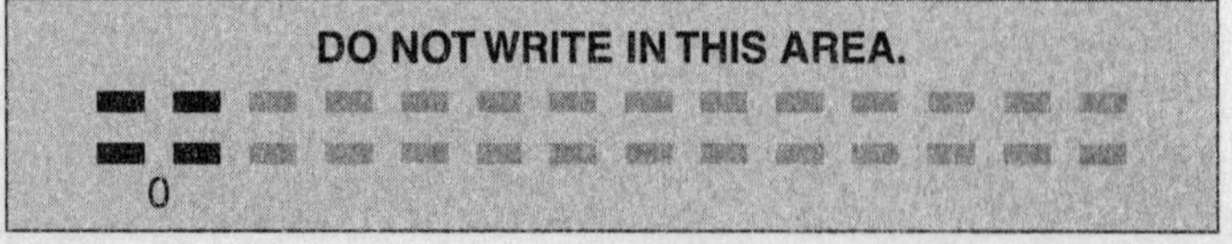

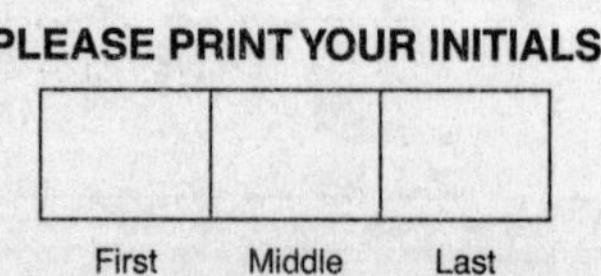

Use a No. 2 pencil only. Be sure each mark is dark and completely fills the intended oval. Completely erase any errors or stray marks.

Start with number 1 for each new section. If a section has fewer questions than answer spaces, leave the extra answer spaces blank.

SECTION 4

1 Ⓐ Ⓑ Ⓒ Ⓓ Ⓔ
2 Ⓐ Ⓑ Ⓒ Ⓓ Ⓔ
3 Ⓐ Ⓑ Ⓒ Ⓓ Ⓔ
4 Ⓐ Ⓑ Ⓒ Ⓓ Ⓔ
5 Ⓐ Ⓑ Ⓒ Ⓓ Ⓔ
6 Ⓐ Ⓑ Ⓒ Ⓓ Ⓔ
7 Ⓐ Ⓑ Ⓒ Ⓓ Ⓔ
8 Ⓐ Ⓑ Ⓒ Ⓓ Ⓔ
9 Ⓐ Ⓑ Ⓒ Ⓓ Ⓔ
10 Ⓐ Ⓑ Ⓒ Ⓓ Ⓔ
11 Ⓐ Ⓑ Ⓒ Ⓓ Ⓔ
12 Ⓐ Ⓑ Ⓒ Ⓓ Ⓔ
13 Ⓐ Ⓑ Ⓒ Ⓓ Ⓔ
14 Ⓐ Ⓑ Ⓒ Ⓓ Ⓔ
15 Ⓐ Ⓑ Ⓒ Ⓓ Ⓔ
16 Ⓐ Ⓑ Ⓒ Ⓓ Ⓔ
17 Ⓐ Ⓑ Ⓒ Ⓓ Ⓔ
18 Ⓐ Ⓑ Ⓒ Ⓓ Ⓔ
19 Ⓐ Ⓑ Ⓒ Ⓓ Ⓔ
20 Ⓐ Ⓑ Ⓒ Ⓓ Ⓔ
21 Ⓐ Ⓑ Ⓒ Ⓓ Ⓔ
22 Ⓐ Ⓑ Ⓒ Ⓓ Ⓔ
23 Ⓐ Ⓑ Ⓒ Ⓓ Ⓔ
24 Ⓐ Ⓑ Ⓒ Ⓓ Ⓔ
25 Ⓐ Ⓑ Ⓒ Ⓓ Ⓔ
26 Ⓐ Ⓑ Ⓒ Ⓓ Ⓔ
27 Ⓐ Ⓑ Ⓒ Ⓓ Ⓔ
28 Ⓐ Ⓑ Ⓒ Ⓓ Ⓔ
29 Ⓐ Ⓑ Ⓒ Ⓓ Ⓔ
30 Ⓐ Ⓑ Ⓒ Ⓓ Ⓔ
31 Ⓐ Ⓑ Ⓒ Ⓓ Ⓔ
32 Ⓐ Ⓑ Ⓒ Ⓓ Ⓔ
33 Ⓐ Ⓑ Ⓒ Ⓓ Ⓔ
34 Ⓐ Ⓑ Ⓒ Ⓓ Ⓔ
35 Ⓐ Ⓑ Ⓒ Ⓓ Ⓔ
36 Ⓐ Ⓑ Ⓒ Ⓓ Ⓔ
37 Ⓐ Ⓑ Ⓒ Ⓓ Ⓔ
38 Ⓐ Ⓑ Ⓒ Ⓓ Ⓔ
39 Ⓐ Ⓑ Ⓒ Ⓓ Ⓔ
40 Ⓐ Ⓑ Ⓒ Ⓓ Ⓔ

If section 4 of your test book contains math questions that are not multiple-choice, continue to item 16 below. Otherwise, continue to item 16 above.

ONLY ANSWERS ENTERED IN THE OVALS IN EACH GRID AREA WILL BE SCORED.
YOU WILL NOT RECEIVE CREDIT FOR ANYTHING WRITTEN IN THE BOXES ABOVE THE OVALS.

16 17 18 19 20

21 22 23 24 25

(Each grid: / / ; . . . . ; 0 0 0 ; 1 1 1 1 ; 2 2 2 2 ; 3 3 3 3 ; 4 4 4 4 ; 5 5 5 5 ; 6 6 6 6 ; 7 7 7 7 ; 8 8 8 8 ; 9 9 9 9)

BE SURE TO ERASE ANY ERRORS OR STRAY MARKS COMPLETELY.

DO NOT WRITE IN THIS AREA.

0

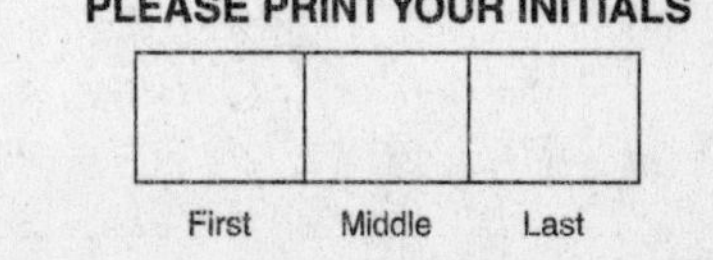

THE COLLEGE BOARD — SAT I **Page 4**

Use a No. 2 pencil only. Be sure each mark is dark and completely fills the intended oval. Completely erase any errors or stray marks.

Start with number 1 for each new section. If a section has fewer questions than answer spaces, leave the extra answer spaces blank.

SECTION 5

1 (A) (B) (C) (D) (E)	11 (A) (B) (C) (D) (E)	21 (A) (B) (C) (D) (E)	31 (A) (B) (C) (D) (E)
2 (A) (B) (C) (D) (E)	12 (A) (B) (C) (D) (E)	22 (A) (B) (C) (D) (E)	32 (A) (B) (C) (D) (E)
3 (A) (B) (C) (D) (E)	13 (A) (B) (C) (D) (E)	23 (A) (B) (C) (D) (E)	33 (A) (B) (C) (D) (E)
4 (A) (B) (C) (D) (E)	14 (A) (B) (C) (D) (E)	24 (A) (B) (C) (D) (E)	34 (A) (B) (C) (D) (E)
5 (A) (B) (C) (D) (E)	15 (A) (B) (C) (D) (E)	25 (A) (B) (C) (D) (E)	35 (A) (B) (C) (D) (E)
6 (A) (B) (C) (D) (E)	16 (A) (B) (C) (D) (E)	26 (A) (B) (C) (D) (E)	36 (A) (B) (C) (D) (E)
7 (A) (B) (C) (D) (E)	17 (A) (B) (C) (D) (E)	27 (A) (B) (C) (D) (E)	37 (A) (B) (C) (D) (E)
8 (A) (B) (C) (D) (E)	18 (A) (B) (C) (D) (E)	28 (A) (B) (C) (D) (E)	38 (A) (B) (C) (D) (E)
9 (A) (B) (C) (D) (E)	19 (A) (B) (C) (D) (E)	29 (A) (B) (C) (D) (E)	39 (A) (B) (C) (D) (E)
10 (A) (B) (C) (D) (E)	20 (A) (B) (C) (D) (E)	30 (A) (B) (C) (D) (E)	40 (A) (B) (C) (D) (E)

SECTION 6

1 (A) (B) (C) (D) (E)	6 (A) (B) (C) (D) (E)	11 (A) (B) (C) (D) (E)	16 (A) (B) (C) (D) (E)
2 (A) (B) (C) (D) (E)	7 (A) (B) (C) (D) (E)	12 (A) (B) (C) (D) (E)	17 (A) (B) (C) (D) (E)
3 (A) (B) (C) (D) (E)	8 (A) (B) (C) (D) (E)	13 (A) (B) (C) (D) (E)	18 (A) (B) (C) (D) (E)
4 (A) (B) (C) (D) (E)	9 (A) (B) (C) (D) (E)	14 (A) (B) (C) (D) (E)	19 (A) (B) (C) (D) (E)
5 (A) (B) (C) (D) (E)	10 (A) (B) (C) (D) (E)	15 (A) (B) (C) (D) (E)	20 (A) (B) (C) (D) (E)

SECTION 7

1 (A) (B) (C) (D) (E)	6 (A) (B) (C) (D) (E)	11 (A) (B) (C) (D) (E)	16 (A) (B) (C) (D) (E)
2 (A) (B) (C) (D) (E)	7 (A) (B) (C) (D) (E)	12 (A) (B) (C) (D) (E)	17 (A) (B) (C) (D) (E)
3 (A) (B) (C) (D) (E)	8 (A) (B) (C) (D) (E)	13 (A) (B) (C) (D) (E)	18 (A) (B) (C) (D) (E)
4 (A) (B) (C) (D) (E)	9 (A) (B) (C) (D) (E)	14 (A) (B) (C) (D) (E)	19 (A) (B) (C) (D) (E)
5 (A) (B) (C) (D) (E)	10 (A) (B) (C) (D) (E)	15 (A) (B) (C) (D) (E)	20 (A) (B) (C) (D) (E)

CERTIFICATION STATEMENT

Copy the statement below (do not print) and sign your name as you would an official document.

I hereby agree to the conditions set forth in the Registration Bulletin and certify that I am the person whose name and address appear on this answer sheet.

____

____

____

Signature: ________________________ Date: ____________

Section 1 1 1 1 1 1 1

Time—30 Minutes
25 Questions

In this section solve each problem, using any available space on the page for scratchwork. Then decide which is the best of the choices given and fill in the corresponding oval on the answer sheet.

Notes:

1. The use of a calculator is permitted. All numbers used are real numbers.
2. Figures that accompany problems in this test are intended to provide information useful in solving the problems. They are drawn as accurately as possible EXCEPT when it is stated in a specific problem that the figure is not drawn to scale. All figures lie in a plane unless otherwise indicated.

Reference Information

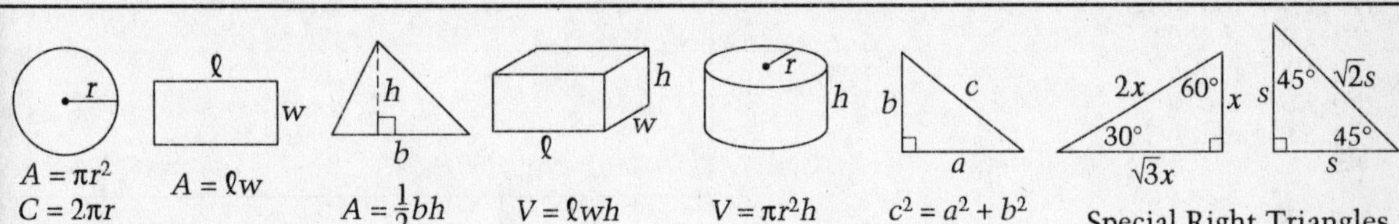

$A = \pi r^2$
$C = 2\pi r$ $\quad A = \ell w \quad A = \frac{1}{2}bh \quad V = \ell wh \quad V = \pi r^2 h \quad c^2 = a^2 + b^2$ Special Right Triangles

The number of degrees of arc in a circle is 360.
The measure in degrees of a straight angle is 180.
The sum of the measures in degrees of the angles of a triangle is 180.

1 If an object travels at 2 feet per minute, how many feet does it travel in a half hour?

(A) 1
(B) $2\frac{1}{2}$
(C) 10
(D) 30
(E) 60

2 Mona just bought a book from a bookstore that sells only biographies and novels. Which of the following must be true?

(A) The book is a novel.
(B) The book is a biography.
(C) The book is not a dictionary.
(D) The book is not a humorous novel.
(E) The book is not a biography of John Adams.

3 Ben spends \$1.95 for lunch at school each day. He wants to estimate the amount he will spend for lunch during the month of May, which has 22 school days. Which of the following will give him the best estimate?

(A) \$1.00 × 20
(B) \$1.50 × 20
(C) \$2.00 × 20
(D) \$1.50 × 25
(E) \$2.00 × 30

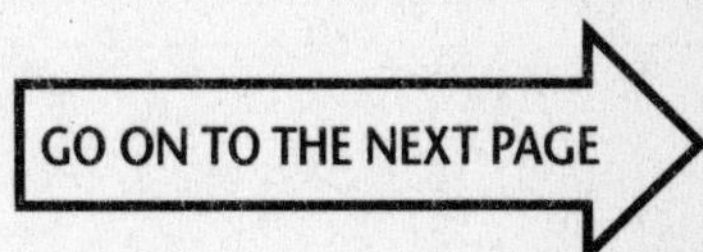

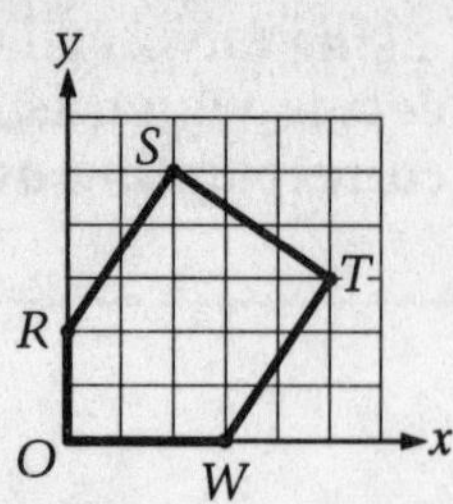

4 In the figure above, which two sides of polygon $ORSTW$ have the same slope?

(A) OR and OW
(B) OW and ST
(C) RS and ST
(D) RS and WT
(E) ST and WT

5 If n is an even integer greater than 2, what is the next greater even integer in terms of n?

(A) $n + 1$
(B) $n + 2$
(C) $n + 3$
(D) $2n$
(E) n^2

6 A piece of wire x feet in length is cut into exactly 6 pieces, each 2 feet 4 inches in length. What is the value of x? (1 foot = 12 inches)

(A) $12\frac{1}{3}$
(B) $12\frac{1}{2}$
(C) 13
(D) $13\frac{1}{2}$
(E) 14

7 Of the following numbers, which is <u>least</u>?

(A) $1 + \frac{1}{3}$
(B) $1 - \frac{1}{3}$
(C) $\frac{1}{3} - 1$
(D) $1 \times \frac{1}{3}$
(E) $1 \div \frac{1}{3}$

{2, 5, 6, 7, 10}

8 How many different pairs of unequal numbers can be chosen from the set above so that their sum is greater than 10 ? (Do not consider a pair such as 5, 2 to be different from 2, 5.)

(A) 7
(B) 10
(C) 14
(D) 32
(E) 60

GO ON TO THE NEXT PAGE

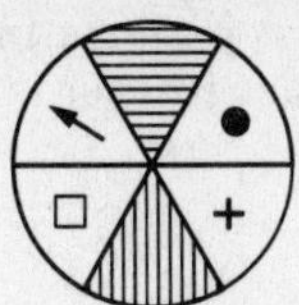

9 In the figure above, the three diameters divide the circle into six equal regions. If the circle is rotated 120° in a clockwise direction in its plane, which of the following represents the resulting circle?

(A)

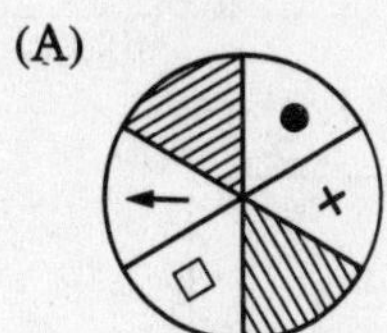

(B)

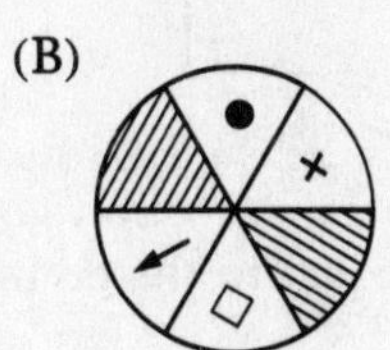

(C)

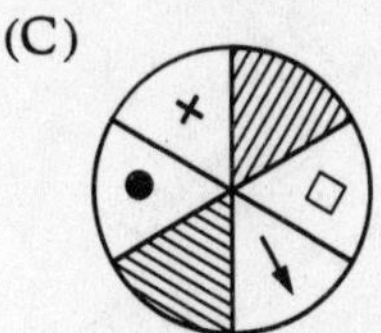

(D)

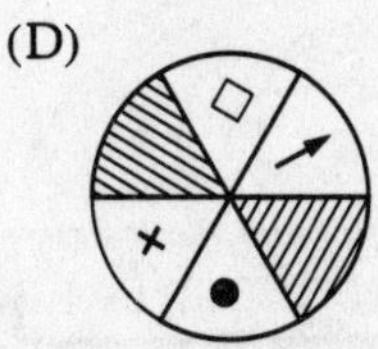

(E)

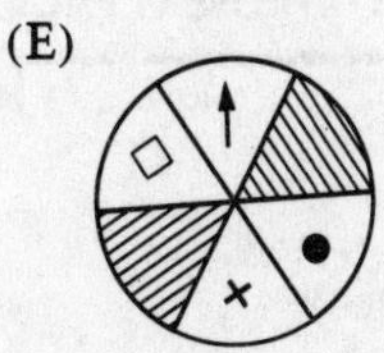

10 From 1 p.m. to 5 p.m. on Monday, a group of photographers will be taking individual pictures of 600 students. If it takes 2 minutes to take each student's picture, how many photographers are needed?

(A) Two
(B) Three
(C) Four
(D) Five
(E) Fifteen

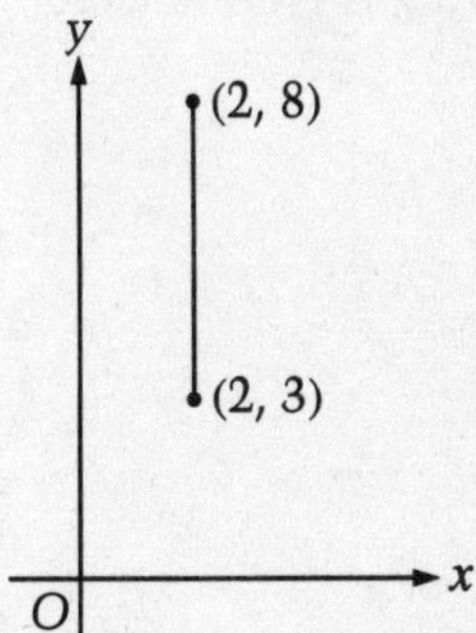

11 In the figure above, the line segment joining the points (2, 3) and (2, 8) forms one side of a square. Which of the following could be the coordinates of another vertex of that square?

(A) (−2, 5)
(B) (−2, 3)
(C) (5, 2)
(D) (7, 2)
(E) (7, 8)

GO ON TO THE NEXT PAGE

12 Three business partners are to share profits of $24,000 in the ratio 5 : 4 : 3. What is the amount of the least share?

(A) $1,200
(B) $3,000
(C) $6,000
(D) $8,000
(E) $10,000

13 If p is a prime number greater than 3, which of the following is NOT a factor of $6p$?

(A) p^2
(B) $6p$
(C) $3p$
(D) $2p$
(E) 3

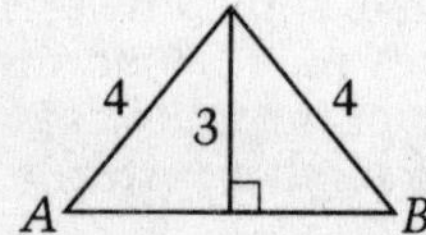

14 In the figure above, what is the length of AB ?

(A) 5
(B) 7
(C) $2\sqrt{7}$ (approximately 5.29)
(D) $4\sqrt{2}$ (approximately 5.66)
(E) $4\sqrt{3}$ (approximately 6.93)

15 What is the least possible integer for which 20 percent of that integer is greater than 1.2 ?

(A) 2
(B) 3
(C) 4
(D) 6
(E) 7

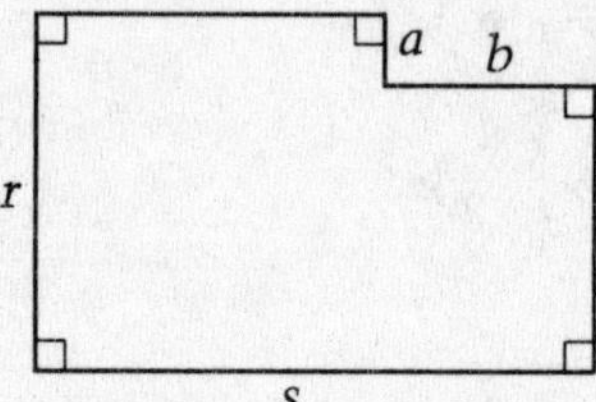

16 Which of the following is equal to the perimeter of the figure above?

(A) $r + s + a + b$
(B) $2r + s + (a + b)$
(C) $2(r + s) - (a + b)$
(D) $2(r + s) + (a + b)$
(E) $2(r + s)$

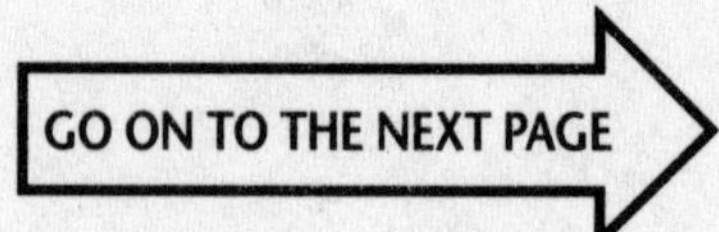

17 If $y = 1 + \frac{1}{x}$ and $x > 1$, then y could equal

(A) $\frac{1}{7}$

(B) $\frac{5}{7}$

(C) $\frac{9}{7}$

(D) $\frac{15}{7}$

(E) $\frac{19}{7}$

18 Five distinct points lie in a plane such that 3 of the points are on line ℓ and 3 of the points are on a different line, m. What is the total number of lines that can be drawn so that each line passes through exactly 2 of these 5 points?

(A) Two
(B) Four
(C) Five
(D) Six
(E) Ten

Add 3 to x.
Divide this sum by 4.
Subtract 2 from this quotient.

19 Which of the following is the result obtained by performing the operations described above?

(A) $\frac{x-5}{4}$

(B) $\frac{x+1}{4}$

(C) $\frac{x+3}{2}$

(D) $\frac{3x-8}{4}$

(E) $\frac{x+1}{2}$

20 If the ratio of q to r is 4 to 5, which of the following could be true?

(A) $q = 0, \ r = \frac{4}{5}$

(B) $q = 2, \ r = \frac{5}{2}$

(C) $q = 5, \ r = 6$

(D) $q = 15, \ r = 12$

(E) $q = 16, \ r = 25$

GO ON TO THE NEXT PAGE

21 Which of the following gives the number of revolutions that a tire with diameter x meters will make in traveling a distance of y kilometers without slipping? (1 kilometer = 1,000 meters)

(A) $\frac{1,000y}{\pi x}$

(B) $\frac{1,000}{\pi xy}$

(C) $\frac{500}{\pi x}$

(D) $\frac{y}{1,000\pi x}$

(E) $\frac{\pi x}{1,000y}$

1, 2, 1, −1, −2, . . .

22 The first five terms of a sequence are shown above. After the second term, each term can be obtained by subtracting from the previous term the term before that. For example, the third term can be obtained by subtracting the first term from the second term. What is the sum of the first 36 terms of the sequence?

(A) 0
(B) 4
(C) 12
(D) 24
(E) 30

23 If $n > 1$ and each of the three integers n, $n + 2$, and $n + 4$ is a prime number, then the set of three such numbers is called a "prime triple." There are how many different prime triples?

(A) None
(B) One
(C) Two
(D) Three
(E) More than three

24 If j and k are integers and $j + k = 2j + 4$, which of the following must be true?

I. j is even.
II. k is even.
III. $k - j$ is even.

(A) None
(B) I only
(C) II only
(D) III only
(E) I, II, and III

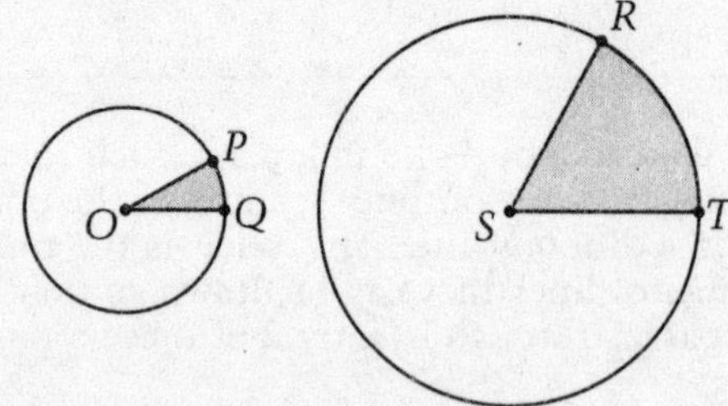

25 In the figure above, the radius of the circle with center S is twice the radius of the circle with center O and the measure of $\angle RST$ is twice that of $\angle POQ$. If the area of the shaded region of circle O is 3, what is the area of the shaded region of circle S?

(A) 24

(B) 12

(C) 6

(D) 3

(E) $\frac{3}{2}$

IF YOU FINISH BEFORE TIME IS CALLED, YOU MAY CHECK YOUR WORK ON THIS SECTION ONLY. DO NOT TURN TO ANY OTHER SECTION IN THE TEST. **STOP**

Section 2 2 2 2 2 2

Time — 30 Minutes
30 Questions

For each question in this section, select the best answer from among the choices given and fill in the corresponding oval on the answer sheet.

Each sentence below has one or two blanks, each blank indicating that something has been omitted. Beneath the sentence are five words or sets of words labeled A through E. Choose the word or set of words that, when inserted in the sentence, <u>best</u> fits the meaning of the sentence as a whole.

Example:

Medieval kingdoms did not become constitutional republics overnight; on the contrary, the change was ----.

(A) unpopular
(B) unexpected
(C) advantageous
(D) sufficient
(E) gradual

1 The unification of Upper and Lower Egypt around 3000 B.C. acted as a catalyst, ---- a flowering of Egyptian culture.

(A) triggering (B) describing (C) suspending (D) polarizing (E) symbolizing

2 If his works had been regarded merely as those of a fool, he might have met with only ---- , not with violent enmity and strict censorship.

(A) brutality (B) loathing (C) rebellion (D) ridicule (E) execution

3 Recent evidence that a special brain cell is critical to memory is so ---- that scientists are ---- their theories of how the brain stores information to include the role of this cell.

(A) pervasive. .reproducing
(B) perplexing. .formulating
(C) obscure. .confirming
(D) extreme. .restoring
(E) compelling. .revising

4 The ---- act was ---- even to the perpetrator, who regretted his deed to the end of his life.

(A) vulgar. .unaffected
(B) heinous. .appalling
(C) vengeful. .acceptable
(D) timorous. .intrepid
(E) forgettable. .offensive

5 The observation that nurses treating patients with pellagra did not ---- the disease led epidemiologists to question the theory that pellagra is ----.

(A) risk. .deadly
(B) fear. .curable
(C) acknowledge. .common
(D) contract. .contagious
(E) battle. .preventable

6 The general view of gorillas as menacing, ferocious King Kongs was not successfully ---- until Dian Fossey's field studies in the 1960's showed gorillas to be peaceable, rather fainthearted creatures, unlikely to ---- humans.

(A) counteracted. .please
(B) enhanced. .murder
(C) verified. .attack
(D) dispelled. .captivate
(E) challenged. .threaten

7 The quotation attributing to the mayor the view that funds for police services should be cut was ----: it completely ---- the mayor's position that more police should be hired.

(A) inflammatory. .justified
(B) abbreviated. .curtailed
(C) meticulous. .misstated
(D) egregious. .underscored
(E) spurious. .misrepresented

8 A ---- is concerned not with whether a political program is liberal or conservative but with whether it will work.

(A) radical (B) utopian (C) pragmatist (D) partisan (E) reactionary

9 Thomas Jefferson's decision not to ---- lotteries was sanctioned by classical wisdom, which held that, far from being a ---- game, lots were a way of divining the future and of involving the gods in everyday affairs.

(A) expand. .sacred
(B) publicize. .vile
(C) condemn. .debased
(D) legalize. .standardized
(E) restrict. .useful

GO ON TO THE NEXT PAGE

Each question below consists of a related pair of words or phrases, followed by five pairs of words or phrases labeled A through E. Select the pair that best expresses a relationship similar to that expressed in the original pair.

Example:

CRUMB : BREAD ::
(A) ounce : unit
(B) splinter : wood
(C) water : bucket
(D) twine : rope
(E) cream : butter

Ⓐ ● Ⓒ Ⓓ Ⓔ

10 FLAP : WING ::
(A) speak : sound
(B) wave : hand
(C) whisper : word
(D) stub : toe
(E) sing : bird

11 POISON : TOXIC ::
(A) mixture : soluble
(B) sugar : sweet
(C) medicine : prescribed
(D) milk : bottled
(E) solid : liquid

12 DEDUCTION : RATIONAL ::
(A) hunch : intuitive
(B) ploy : spontaneous
(C) maxim : hackneyed
(D) hypothesis : tested
(E) daydream : bored

13 BEAUTY : AESTHETE ::
(A) pleasure : hedonist
(B) emotion : demagogue
(C) opinion : sympathizer
(D) seance : medium
(E) luxury : ascetic

14 FLIPPANCY : JOLLITY ::
(A) recognition : achievement
(B) practice : expertise
(C) camaraderie : combativeness
(D) insolence : pride
(E) politeness : behavior

15 INCANTATION : WORDS ::
(A) malediction : harm
(B) oration : formality
(C) talisman : object
(D) enchantment : happiness
(E) divination : future

GO ON TO THE NEXT PAGE

Each passage below is followed by questions based on its content. Answer the questions on the basis of what is stated or implied in each passage and in any introductory material that may be provided.

Questions 16-20 are based on the following passage.

The following passage is about Black American fiction and the Romantic literary tradition. The Romance novel is a literary form that took shape during the eighteenth and nineteenth centuries. Different from the sentimental, escapist writing often described as romantic, Romance novels focus on the heroic dimensions of life, using symbolism to express abstract ideas.

During the nineteenth century, the traditional Romance became an important mode of expression for many Black American writers. A frequent characteristic of Romantic writing is the use of historical material; Black writers have used this genre to transform an often harsh historical reality into an imagined world ruled by their own ethical vision. In transforming history into fiction, Romantic writers have given their work a mythic quality that deepens the significance of plot, character, and historical event.

Clotel, a novel written in 1853 by William Wells Brown, is an early example from this romantic tradition. *Clotel*'s heroes are idealized, fighting slavery through superhuman action, and are used to convey a complex political message. For Brown, the Black man or woman was destined to move toward spiritual perfection, but was being blocked by the dehumanizing effects of slavery. The conflict in *Clotel* is both an ongoing political one, between slaves and their owners, and a wider moral conflict between good and evil; the story is placed in both a historical context and the larger context of human ethical progress. The resolution is satisfyingly hopeful—a victory over obstacles.

More than a hundred years after Brown wrote, Black writers like Toni Morrison and David Bradley work in a very different historical context. Yet one of the major themes for these two writers, the investigation of relationships between North American and African culture, is as deeply historical as Brown's concern with slavery. Both Morrison and Bradley address the close relationships between myth and history by writing of people who undertake the archetypal quest for selfhood. Their characters are compelled to confront not only their own personal histories, but their cultural histories as well. Both of these writers also explore this cultural history stylistically, by experimenting with rhetorical devices traditionally identified with both African and Western experience, including the oral narrative and the mythological theme of the journey to the home of one's ancestors.

Reaching into the past has meant that spirituality, religion, and the supernatural play an important role in the work of both of these writers. Yet rather than mythologizing history, as some of their predecessors had done, these writers chose to explore the mythical aspects already present in African American culture. Both emphasize that religion for many contemporary Black Americans can be at the same time a reclamation of African philosophy and a reenvisioning of the Judeo-Christian tradition; religion is for these writers the source of a conviction that knowledge of one's ancestors is crucial to self-knowledge. By developing these ancient themes, Morrison and Bradley have considerably expanded the boundaries of the Romantic tradition in which they have worked.

16 Which of the following titles best summarizes the content of the passage?

(A) A Return to Romance: The Contemporary Revival of a Nineteenth-Century Tradition
(B) The Role of Plot and Character in the Black American Literary Tradition
(C) Oral Narrative and Religion in the Romantic Fiction of Black American Novelists
(D) Moral Conflict in Literature: Slavery and the Black American Novelist
(E) History and the Romantic Tradition in Black American Fiction

17 It can be inferred from the passage that by describing the characters in Brown's *Clotel* as "idealized" (line 14), the author means that they

(A) believe themselves to be more virtuous than they actually are
(B) are not particularly realistic but represent attitudes admired by Brown
(C) represent the kind of person Brown would have liked to be
(D) are as close to being perfectly described as fictional characters can be
(E) are blind to the real problems that prevent them from succeeding

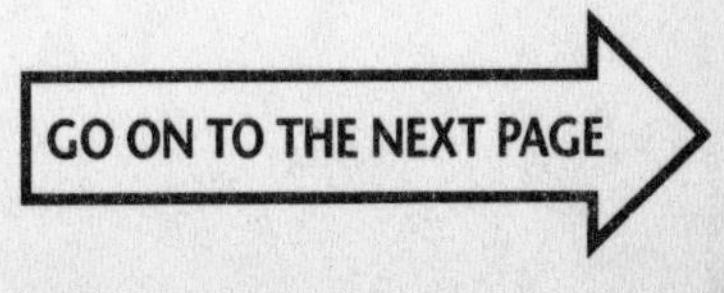

18 The "quest for selfhood" (line 35) undertaken by Morrison's and Bradley's characters is best described as an effort to

(A) come closer to the spiritual perfection described in Romantic fiction
(B) learn to describe their personal experiences through traditional storytelling
(C) understand themselves in terms of both their personal and their cultural pasts
(D) investigate the mythical and spiritual characteristics of their predecessors
(E) assert their own attitudes and ideas, especially when they differ from those of their ancestors

19 By stating that Morrison and Bradley explore history "stylistically" (line 39), the author means that they

(A) believe that style is the most important element in their fiction
(B) use a variety of fashionable techniques
(C) researched their own families before writing about their characters' ancestors
(D) use traditional forms of expression in writing current fiction
(E) use words and phrases from ancient languages to make their novels more authentic

20 Which of the following best describes the structure of the author's discussion in this passage?

(A) Examination of the aspects of Brown's work that led to important later developments in Black Romantic literature
(B) Description of first the advantages and then the disadvantages of the use of Romance in Black fiction
(C) Use of early and recent examples to demonstrate both change and continuity in Black Romantic fiction
(D) Use of comparison to demonstrate that contemporary Black Romantic fiction is superior to that of the nineteenth century
(E) Discussion of the work of three authors in order to develop a general definition of the Romantic literary genre

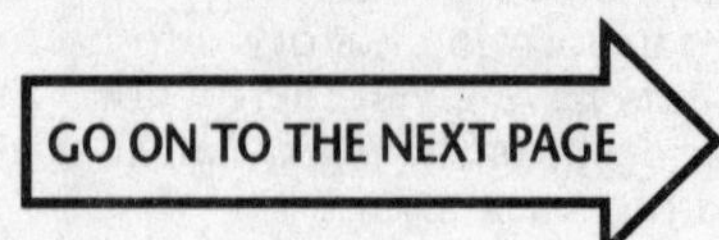

Questions 21-30 are based on the following passage.

The following excerpt from a novel focuses on a single photograph of a father and son taken in 1942 by a family friend.

Even without the shadow that partially obscures the child's face, it would be difficult to read much into its full anonymous curves. The sun is directly overhead, so that the cap's brim shadows most of his face. Only the eyebrows, cheeks, and nose catch the sun directly, making them appear touched with the dead white of clown's paint. This, in turn, may lead us to see more sadness in the eyes than is really there, as though they have been baffled witnesses to some violent tableau. The chin is tucked downward so that the eyes must glance up to greet the camera, giving to the entire figure a quality of uncertainty, of barely contained fear. Even the timorous lip-trembling half-smile contributes to this effect. But perhaps he is only uncomfortable. The folds in his plaid jacket and trousers suggest they are made of wool, and the cap is certainly of camel's hair. Yet the full-leafed trees and shrubbery visible in the photograph suggest midsummer, and with the sun overhead, the wincing look on the child's round face may be the result of coarse wool chafing his skin. At any rate, he seems uncomfortable and shy, with feet pigeon-toed awkwardly together. The single detail that argues against this impression is that he has hooked his thumbs into the pockets of his jacket, and his surprisingly long, lean fingers lend the gesture a note of adult confidence, even of swagger. These hands, which will later be much admired, are thus unconsciously arranged in a posture that will become habitual. There is another photograph, taken a quarter-century later, in which the hands are identically arranged, thumbs hooked into the pockets of a midnight-blue tuxedo jacket. And yet, taken in its entirety, there is little enough visible in the child's picture to provoke narration. Indeed, the cap, the chubby, boyish face, the sagging jacket, the wrinkled trousers are assembled into an almost anonymous image of a well-fed, modestly well-dressed little boy. Those who knew his son at the same age would have seen an astonishing similarity to the child who poses here, but the son is not born until nearly two decades after this photograph is made.

"Stand just there, by your father," Juanita says. The boy moves stiffly to the left, never taking his eyes from the camera in her hands. "Closer, now." He inches his left foot out, and brings his right up to join it. Then he ducks his head to avoid the stabbing rays of the sun, but still keeps his eyes firmly fixed on the camera, as though it is the only presence here besides himself, its twinkling eye his trusty guardian. Suddenly his slight body stiffens as a large hand is placed firmly between his shoulders. It feels immense, and he thinks it could crush his back as easily as it crumples an empty package of cigarettes. And now his own hands, which had hung loosely at his sides, feel weak and threatened. They will never possess the strength of the densely muscled, tightly tendoned hand that rests sinisterly on his back. He fears that as he grows they will remain weak and small, never capable of seizing with carefully aligned thumbs the leather-wrapped handle of a golf club, of grasping the butts of revolvers, the ivory steering wheel of an automobile, the wooden T of lawnmower handles. Yet he cannot be ashamed of them, for they are sturdy enough, capable of holding open the pages of a book, of guiding pencils and crayons into recognizable approximations of houses and horses and dump trucks. Unsure though he is of their ultimate abilities, the child nonetheless takes premature joy in the work of hands, and cannot be ashamed of his own. Therefore, he brings them slightly forward, hooking his thumbs into his jacket pocket, and lightly curling his fingers down against the plaid of the fabric. The trembling that began in them when the man's large hand was placed between his shoulders is stilled now.

21 The opening two sentences (lines 1-5) introduce a sense of

(A) mystery
(B) malice
(C) intense emotion
(D) disillusionment
(E) youthful innocence

GO ON TO THE NEXT PAGE

22 The effect of the sentence beginning "But perhaps" (line 15) is to

(A) introduce the author's change of attitude from criticism of the boy to sympathy
(B) lighten the tone by revealing the humor in the situation
(C) suggest that the boy's expression is open to interpretation
(D) express an opinion that is not supported by the photograph
(E) furnish a clue to the author's identity and relationship to the boy

23 The description of the clothing in lines 16-22 contributes to a sense of the

(A) comical nature of the scene
(B) family's eccentricity
(C) family's extreme poverty
(D) boy's independent spirit
(E) boy's overall unease

24 As used in line 28, "a note" most nearly means

(A) an observation
(B) a brief record
(C) an element
(D) a message
(E) a comment

25 In the second paragraph, the father is portrayed as exemplifying

(A) virile competence
(B) sophisticated intellect
(C) courageous perseverance
(D) unpredictable irrationality
(E) paternal generosity

26 How does the second paragraph function in relation to the first paragraph?

(A) It reiterates comments in the first paragraph.
(B) It provides clarification of ambiguities in the first paragraph.
(C) It functions as an extension of an analogy begun in the first paragraph.
(D) It uses information from the first paragraph to make predictions.
(E) It provides a more abstract argument than does the first paragraph.

27 The author's reference to "his trusty guardian" (line 53) suggests that the

(A) child is obliged to find comfort in an inanimate object
(B) child is fascinated by sparkling images
(C) child respects Juanita more than he respects his father
(D) father is more reliable than he appears to be
(E) father has always considered his child's happiness before his own

28 Which aspect of the author's description emphasizes a major contrast in the passage?

(A) The boy's face
(B) The boy's cap
(C) The photographer
(D) The characters' hands
(E) The sun

29 The second paragraph suggests that the boy in the photograph apparently regards his father with

(A) embittered resentment
(B) indifferent dismissal
(C) cynical suspicion
(D) fearful respect
(E) proud possessiveness

30 Throughout the passage, the primary focus is on

(A) the implications of the boy's pose in the photograph
(B) reasons for the photograph's existence
(C) mysteries solved by evidence in the photograph
(D) the valuable memories evoked by old photographs
(E) speculations about the age of the boy in the photograph

IF YOU FINISH BEFORE TIME IS CALLED, YOU MAY CHECK YOUR WORK ON THIS SECTION ONLY. DO NOT TURN TO ANY OTHER SECTION IN THE TEST. **STOP**

Time—30 Minutes
25 Questions

This section contains two types of questions. You have 30 minutes to complete both types. You may use any available space for scratchwork.

Notes:

1. The use of a calculator is permitted. All numbers used are real numbers.
2. Figures that accompany problems in this test are intended to provide information useful in solving the problems. They are drawn as accurately as possible EXCEPT when it is stated in a specific problem that the figure is not drawn to scale. All figures lie in a plane unless otherwise indicated.

Reference Information

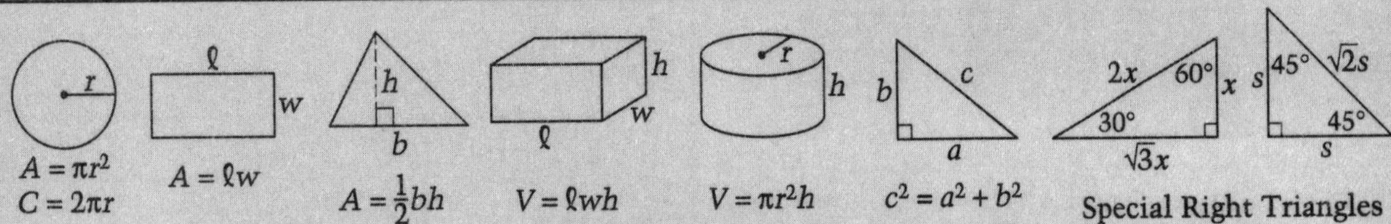

$A = \pi r^2$
$C = 2\pi r$
$A = \ell w$
$A = \frac{1}{2}bh$
$V = \ell wh$
$V = \pi r^2 h$
$c^2 = a^2 + b^2$
Special Right Triangles

The number of degrees of arc in a circle is 360.
The measure in degrees of a straight angle is 180.
The sum of the measures in degrees of the angles of a triangle is 180.

Directions for Quantitative Comparison Questions

Questions 1-15 each consist of two quantities in boxes, one in Column A and one in Column B. You are to compare the two quantities and on the answer sheet fill in oval

- A if the quantity in Column A is greater;
- B if the quantity in Column B is greater;
- C if the two quantities are equal;
- D if the relationship cannot be determined from the information given.

AN E RESPONSE WILL NOT BE SCORED.

Notes:

1. In some questions, information is given about one or both of the quantities to be compared. In such cases, the given information is centered above the two columns and is not boxed.
2. In a given question, a symbol that appears in both columns represents the same thing in Column A as it does in Column B.
3. Letters such as x, n, and k stand for real numbers.

EXAMPLES

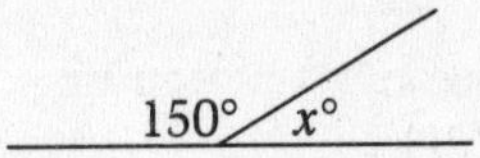

	Column A	Column B	Answers
E1	5^2	20	● Ⓑ Ⓒ Ⓓ Ⓔ
	(figure: 150° x°)		
E2	x	30	Ⓐ Ⓑ ● Ⓓ Ⓔ
	r and s are integers.		
E3	$r+1$	$s-1$	Ⓐ Ⓑ Ⓒ ● Ⓔ

GO ON TO THE NEXT PAGE

SUMMARY DIRECTIONS FOR COMPARISON QUESTIONS

Answer: A if the quantity in Column A is greater;
B if the quantity in Column B is greater;
C if the two quantities are equal;
D if the relationship cannot be determined from the information given.

	Column A	Column B
1	10 percent of 500	5

The number 34,759 is to be rounded to the nearest thousand.

	Column A	Column B
2	The digit in the thousands place of the rounded number	The digit in the hundreds place of the rounded number

A club sold a total of 200 candy bars, some at \$0.50 each and the rest at \$1.00 each.

	Column A	Column B
3	The total amount collected from the sale of the \$0.50 candy bars	The total amount collected from the sale of the \$1.00 candy bars

$a = 2$
$c = 3$

	Column A	Column B
4	$ab + 5$	$a(b + c)$

$x < 6 + y$

	Column A	Column B
5	x	y

The angles of a quadrilateral have measures 90°, 90°, 100°, and n°.

	Column A	Column B
6	n	90

$d > 1$

	Column A	Column B
7	$\frac{d}{d-1}$	1

Q
4
3
P
S

	Column A	Column B
8	The length of the curved path from point P to point S	5

Two sets of vertical angles are formed by two intersecting lines. The sum of the measures of one set of vertical angles is $2x$ and the sum of the measures of the other set is $2y$.

	Column A	Column B
9	x	y

GO ON TO THE NEXT PAGE

SUMMARY DIRECTIONS FOR COMPARISON QUESTIONS

Answer: A if the quantity in Column A is greater;
B if the quantity in Column B is greater;
C if the two quantities are equal;
D if the relationship cannot be determined from the information given.

Column A	Column B

Questions 10-11 refer to the following definition.

Let $\langle m, n\rangle$ be defined as the set of all integers between m and n, excluding m and n. For example, $\langle 0, 3.5\rangle = \{1, 2, 3\}$.

x is in $\langle 2, 6\rangle$.
y is in $\langle 6, 9\rangle$.

10\. 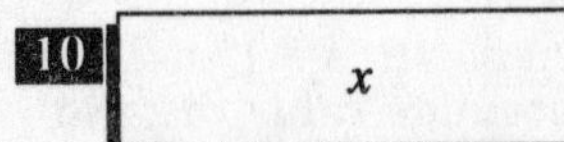 x  y

z is in $\langle\sqrt{5}, \pi\rangle$

11\. 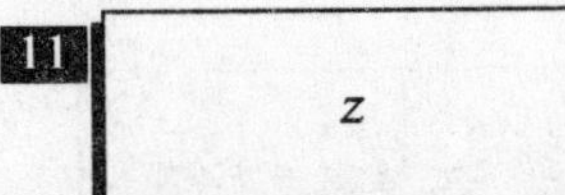 z 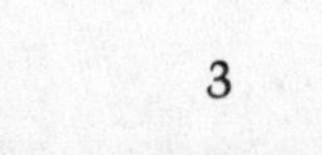 3

All of the members of Club M also belong to Club P. Club P has exactly 20 members.

12\. The number of members in Club M 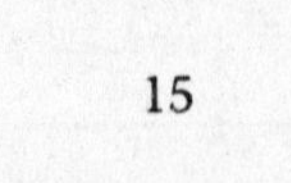 15

$s = a - b$
$t = b - c$
$u = c - a$

13\. $s + t + u$ | 0

Column A	Column B

x represents the sum of the first 20 positive integers.

y represents the sum of the first 10 positive integers.

14\.  $x - y$ | 100

SOYBEAN PRODUCTION IN STATE Z

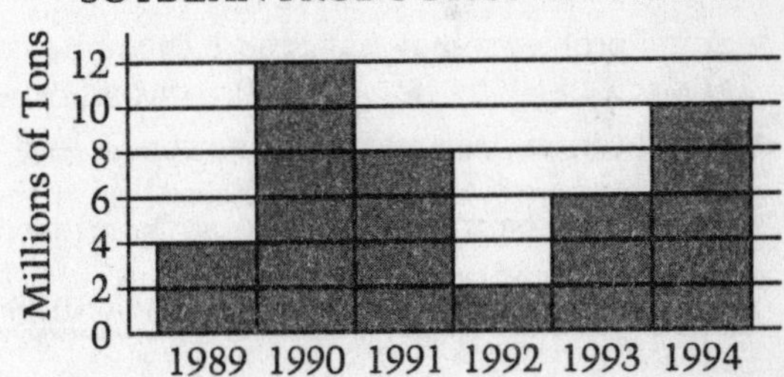

Soybean production decreased by x percent from 1990 to 1991 and increased by y percent from 1993 to 1994 in State Z.

15\. 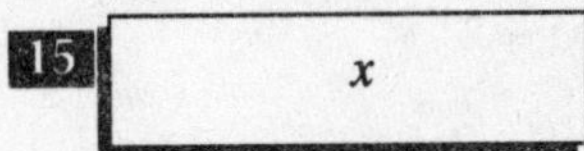 x | y

GO ON TO THE NEXT PAGE

Directions for Student-Produced Response Questions

Each of the remaining 10 questions requires you to solve the problem and enter your answer by marking the ovals in the special grid, as shown in the examples below.

Answer: $\frac{7}{12}$ or 7/12

Write answer in boxes. → 7 / 1 2

←Fraction line

Grid in result.

Answer: 2.5

2 . 5

←Decimal point

Answer: 201
Either position is correct.

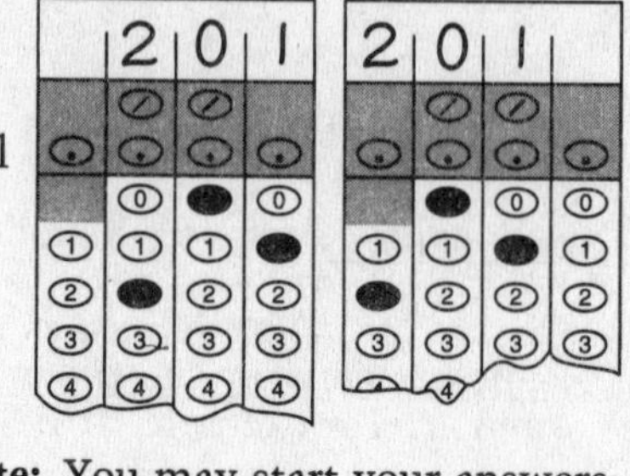

Note: You may start your answers in any column, space permitting. Columns not needed should be left blank.

- Mark no more than one oval in any column.
- Because the answer sheet will be machine-scored, **you will receive credit only if the ovals are filled in correctly.**
- Although not required, it is suggested that you write your answer in the boxes at the top of the columns to help you fill in the ovals accurately.
- Some problems may have more than one correct answer. In such cases, grid only one answer.
- No question has a negative answer.
- **Mixed numbers** such as $2\frac{1}{2}$ must be gridded as 2.5 or 5/2. (If 2 1 / 2 is gridded, it will be interpreted as $\frac{21}{2}$, not $2\frac{1}{2}$.)
- **Decimal Accuracy:** If you obtain a decimal answer, **enter the most accurate value the grid will accommodate.** For example, if you obtain an answer such as 0.6666 . . . , you should record the result as .666 or .667. **Less accurate values such as .66 or .67 are not acceptable.**

Acceptable ways to grid $\frac{2}{3} = .6666\ldots$

2 / 3 | . 6 6 6 | . 6 6 7

16 If $a > 1$ and $a^b a^4 = a^{12}$, what is the value of b?

17 If $s = \frac{1}{x}$ and $q = \frac{1}{y}$ and if $x = 2$ and $y = 3$, what is the value of $\frac{1}{s} + \frac{1}{q}$?

GO ON TO THE NEXT PAGE

18 The grand prize for winning a contest is \$10,000. After 28 percent of the prize is deducted for taxes, the winner receives the balance of the prize in annual payouts of equal amounts over a 3-year period. How many dollars will the prizewinner receive each year of the 3 years? (Disregard the \$ sign when gridding your answer.)

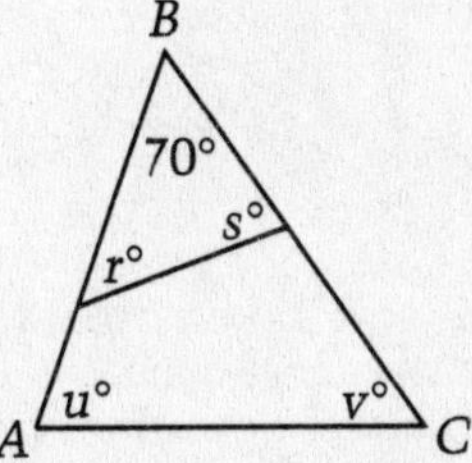

19 In $\triangle ABC$ above, what is the value of $r + s + u + v$?

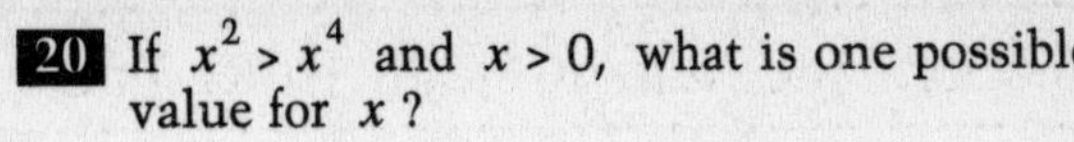

20 If $x^2 > x^4$ and $x > 0$, what is one possible value for x ?

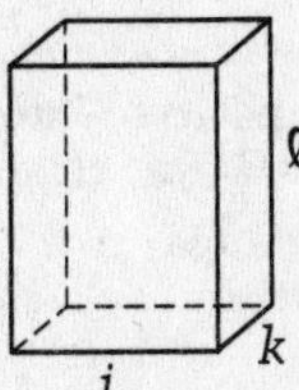

21 In the figure above, the area of the base of the rectangular box is 21 and the area of one of the faces is 30. Each of the dimensions j, k, and ℓ is an integer greater than 1. What is the volume of the rectangular box?

GO ON TO THE NEXT PAGE

$$\begin{array}{r} AB \\ +\,BA \\ \hline CD4 \end{array}$$

22 In the correctly worked addition problem above, each letter represents a different nonzero digit. What is one possible value of the two-digit number represented above as AB ?

23 If x and y are positive integers, $x + y < 15$, and $x > 5$, what is the greatest possible value of $x - y$?

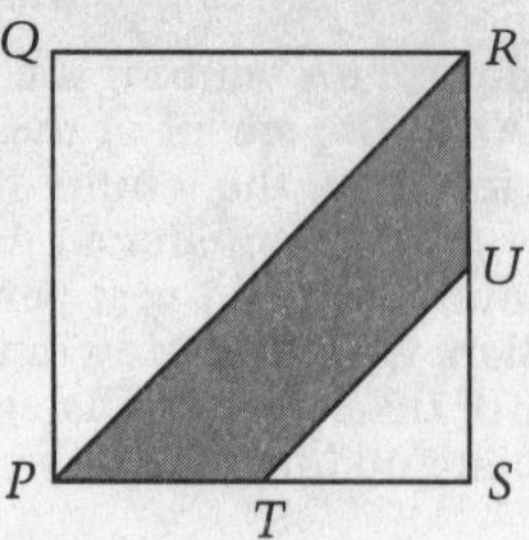

24 In square $PQRS$ above, $QR = 1$, $RU = US$, and $PT = TS$. What is the area of the shaded region?

25 A barrel contains only apples and oranges. There are twice as many apples as oranges. The apples are either red or yellow, and 4 times as many apples are red as are yellow. If one piece of fruit is to be drawn at random from the barrel, what is the probability that the piece drawn will be a yellow apple?

IF YOU FINISH BEFORE TIME IS CALLED, YOU MAY CHECK YOUR WORK ON THIS SECTION ONLY. DO NOT TURN TO ANY OTHER SECTION IN THE TEST.

Section 5 5

Time—30 Minutes
36 Questions

For each question in this section, select the best answer from among the choices given and fill in the corresponding oval on the answer sheet.

Each sentence below has one or two blanks, each blank indicating that something has been omitted. Beneath the sentence are five words or sets of words labeled A through E. Choose the word or set of words that, when inserted in the sentence, best fits the meaning of the sentence as a whole.

Example:

Medieval kingdoms did not become constitutional republics overnight; on the contrary, the change was ----.

(A) unpopular
(B) unexpected
(C) advantageous
(D) sufficient
(E) gradual

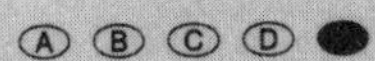

1 The visitor was of an ---- age: white-haired, but baby-faced, he might have been twenty-five or fifty.

(A) assiduous (B) unalterable (C) indecorous (D) indeterminate (E) extenuating

2 Unfortunately, for North American Indians the arrival of European settlers often meant ---- their lands, their ways of life, and even their very existence.

(A) a renewal of
(B) a respect for
(C) an assault on
(D) a retention of
(E) an idea of

3 Different species of mosquito conduct the essential activities of eating, growing, and reproducing in so many ways that no rule of mosquito behavior is without some ----.

(A) result (B) objectivity (C) exception (D) clarity (E) enforcement

4 Even more interesting than the completed masterpiece can be the ---- work of the artist: the first-draft manuscript, the initial pencil sketches, the symphony rehearsal.

(A) rough (B) intense (C) varied (D) thoughtless (E) atypical

5 Oceanographic research has shown that ridges on the ocean floor are not ---- features, but part of a 4,000-mile-long mountain range.

(A) conditional (B) unchanging (C) observable (D) definable (E) isolated

6 Although Jack and Mary Lynch are often ---- to strangers, they show only ---- to a pack of nearly extinct buffalo wolves, working seven days a week to help save the endangered species.

(A) gracious. .disdain
(B) rude. .exasperation
(C) gruff. .kindness
(D) agreeable. .gentleness
(E) condescending. .hostility

7 We need not be ---- about our performance thus far, but neither should we be ----: there is ample room for improvement.

(A) haughty. .generous
(B) lazy. .industrious
(C) apologetic. .smug
(D) opulent. .showy
(E) sympathetic. .crude

8 The art collection of the children's museum is quite ----, ranging from furniture to sculpture to finger painting.

(A) imaginary (B) repetitive (C) elusive (D) eclectic (E) circumscribed

9 By subsidizing small farms, the new government is hoping to ---- the flow of people into the cities and ---- farming.

(A) reverse. .incorporate
(B) arrest. .encourage
(C) boost. .initiate
(D) enhance. .regulate
(E) diminish. .prohibit

10 Despite Atlanta's large Black community, African American theater companies in that city are anything but ----; in fact, in 1993 there was only one, Jomandi Productions.

(A) legion (B) advantageous (C) bourgeois (D) nondescript (E) wily

GO ON TO THE NEXT PAGE

Each question below consists of a related pair of words or phrases, followed by five pairs of words or phrases labeled A through E. Select the pair that best expresses a relationship similar to that expressed in the original pair.

Example:

CRUMB : BREAD ::
(A) ounce : unit
(B) splinter : wood
(C) water : bucket
(D) twine : rope
(E) cream : butter

11 CAMERA : PHOTOGRAPHER ::
(A) house : architect
(B) sink : plumber
(C) studio : painter
(D) meat : butcher
(E) drill : dentist

12 FORMAT : NEWSPAPER ::
(A) binding : book
(B) design : building
(C) direction : sign
(D) market : commodity
(E) catalogue : library

13 DECIBEL : SOUND ::
(A) ingredient : food
(B) ruler : length
(C) calories : menu
(D) degree : temperature
(E) headphones : music

14 ARID : DRY ::
(A) glacial : cold
(B) coastal : tidal
(C) damp : muddy
(D) snowbound : polar
(E) shallow : deep

15 FISSION : ENERGY ::
(A) reaction : response
(B) distortion : image
(C) nutrient : growth
(D) evaporation : liquid
(E) combustion : heat

16 LOBBYIST : CAUSE ::
(A) legislator : voter
(B) clergy : congregation
(C) advertiser : product
(D) defendant : verdict
(E) consumer : goods

17 JOURNAL : ARTICLE ::
(A) dance : ballet
(B) magazine : cover
(C) set : scenery
(D) anthology : poem
(E) concert : orchestra

18 EMISSARY : REPRESENT ::
(A) draftee : enroll
(B) novice : train
(C) president : elect
(D) guard : protect
(E) comedian : laugh

19 POTENTATE : POWER ::
(A) broadcaster : news
(B) virtuoso : skill
(C) protégé : sponsorship
(D) maverick : group
(E) colleague : camaraderie

20 POSTSCRIPT : LETTER ::
(A) preamble : document
(B) footnote : reference
(C) epilogue : play
(D) signature : name
(E) index : page

21 IMPIOUS : REVERENCE ::
(A) profane : behavior
(B) paranoid : persecution
(C) contrite : offense
(D) superficial : depth
(E) contemptuous : scorn

22 DISINGENUOUS : CRAFTINESS ::
(A) ecstatic : contentment
(B) idolatrous : doubt
(C) narcissistic : appearance
(D) penitent : wrongdoing
(E) surreptitious : stealth

23 EXCULPATE : BLAME ::
(A) extricate : difficulty
(B) exemplify : illustration
(C) expedite : process
(D) divulge : secret
(E) bewilder : confusion

GO ON TO THE NEXT PAGE

The passage below is followed by questions based on its content. Answer the questions on the basis of what is stated or implied in the passage and in any introductory material that may be provided.

Questions 24-36 are based on the following passage.

The following passage is adapted from a book published in 1990. It is about unusual scientific enterprises that to some seemed impossible.

Gerald Feinberg, the Columbia University physicist, once went so far as to declare that "everything possible will eventually be accomplished." He didn't even think it would take very long for this to happen: "I am inclined to put two hundred years as an upper limit for the accomplishment of any possibility that we can imagine today."

Well, that of course left only the impossible as the one thing remaining for daring intellectual adventurers to whittle away at. Feinberg, for one, thought that they'd succeed even here. "Everything will be accomplished that does not violate known fundamental laws of science," he said, "as well as many things that do violate those laws."

So in no small numbers scientists tried to do the impossible. And how understandable this was. For what does the independent and inquiring mind hate more than being told that something just can't be done, pure and simple, by any agency at all, at any time, no matter what. Indeed, the whole concept of the impossible was something of an affront to creativity and advanced intelligence, which was why being told that something was impossible was an unparalleled stimulus for getting all sorts of people to try to accomplish it anyway, as witness all the attempts to build perpetual motion machines, antigravity generators, time-travel vehicles, and all the rest.

Besides, there was always the residual possibility that the naysayers would turn out to be wrong and the yeasayers right, and that one day the latter would reappear to laugh in your face. As one cryonicist* put it, "When you die, you're dead. When I die, I might come back. So who's the dummy?"

It was a point worth considering. How many times in the past had certain things been said to be impossible, only to have it turn out shortly thereafter that the item in question had already been done or soon would be. What greater cliché was there in the history of science than the comic litany of false it-couldn't-be-dones; the infamous case of Auguste Comte saying in 1844 that it would never be known what the stars were made of, followed in a few years by the spectroscope being applied to starlight to reveal the stars' chemical composition; or the case of Lord Rutherford, the man who discovered the structure of the atom, saying in 1933 that dreams of controlled nuclear fission were "moonshine."

And those weren't even the worst examples. No, the huffiest of all it-couldn't-be-done claims centered on the notion that human beings could actually fly, either at all, or across long distances, or to the moon, the stars, or wherever else. It was as if for unstated reasons human flight was something that couldn't be allowed to happen. "The demonstration that no possible combination of known substances, known forms of machinery and known forms of force, can be united in a practical machine by which man shall fly long distances through the air, seems to the writer as complete as it is possible for the demonstration of any physical fact to be." That was Simon Newcomb, the Johns Hopkins University mathematician and astronomer in 1906, three years after the Wright brothers actually flew.

There had been so many embarrassments of this type that about midcentury Arthur C. Clarke came out with a guideline for avoiding them, which he termed Clarke's Law: "When a distinguished but elderly scientist states that something is possible, he is almost certainly right. When he states that something is impossible, he is very probably wrong."

Still, one had to admit there were lots of things left that were really and truly impossible, even if it took some ingenuity in coming up with a proper list of examples. Such as: "A camel cannot pass through the eye of a needle." (Well, unless of course it was a very large needle.) Or: "It is impossible for a door to be simultaneously open and closed." (Well, unless of course it was a revolving door.)

Indeed, watertight examples of the really and truly impossible were so exceptionally hard to come by that paradigm cases turned out to be either trivial or absurd. "I know I will never play the piano like Vladimir Horowitz," offered Milton Rothman, a physicist, "no matter how hard I try." Or, from Scott Lankford, a mountaineer: "Everest on roller skates."

No one would bother trying to overcome those impossibilities, but off in the distance loomed some other, more metaphysically profound specimens. They beckoned like the Mount Everests of

GO ON TO THE NEXT PAGE

science: antigravity generators, faster-than-light travel, antimatter propulsion, space warps, time machines. There were physicists aplenty who took a look at these peaks and decided they had to climb them.

* Someone who believes in the possibility of freezing the dead and reanimating them at some later date when it is technically feasible to do so.

24 As used in line 5, the word "inclined" most nearly means

(A) headed upward
(B) deviated
(C) oblique
(D) prejudiced
(E) disposed

25 If the claim made by Feinberg in lines 11-14 should turn out to be true, which of the following must also be true?

(A) Science works by great leaps, not little steps.
(B) Scientists will work harder than they do today.
(C) Scientists' knowledge of fundamental laws is incomplete.
(D) The rate of scientific discovery will decrease.
(E) The definition of the impossible will remain constant.

26 The motivation ascribed to "no small numbers" (line 15) of scientists is most nearly analogous to that of

(A) treasure hunters who have recently found a map indicating the exact location of an extremely valuable treasure
(B) underdogs who have been told that they do not have a chance of beating the defending champions
(C) a police detective who works night and day to bring a dangerous criminal to justice
(D) a project director who oversees a project carefully to see that it comes in under budget
(E) a scientist who performs experiments to show that a rival's theory is not supported by the evidence

27 In what sense was the concept of the impossible an "affront" (line 21) ?

(A) It implied that previous scientific achievements were not very impressive.
(B) It suggested that the creativity of scientists was limited.
(C) It called into question the value of scientific research.
(D) It implied that scientists work for personal glory rather than for practical advantages.
(E) It blurred the distinction between science and religious belief.

28 The devices mentioned in lines 26-28 are cited as examples of

(A) projects that will be completed in the near future
(B) the kinds of things that can be considered only in science fiction
(C) devices that will enhance the well-being of humanity
(D) proof of the irresponsibility of leading scientists
(E) impossible projects that have generated much interest

29 The cryonicist's remarks (lines 33-35) depend on the notion that the cryonicist has

(A) everything to gain and nothing to lose
(B) a reasonable chance of remaining healthy for several years
(C) only one chance in life
(D) total confidence in technological progress
(E) greater intellectual powers than others

30 The author cites Lord Rutherford's accomplishment (lines 47-48) in order to show that

(A) even the most knowledgeable scientists are often too pessimistic
(B) many failed to see the negative aspects of nuclear technology
(C) Rutherford predicted future events more reliably than did Comte
(D) only those with technical expertise can predict future developments
(E) experts in one field should do research in that field only

GO ON TO THE NEXT PAGE

31 It can be inferred from the passage that the author considers Newcomb's comments (lines 57-64) more irresponsible than Comte's (lines 42-45) for which of the following reasons?

(A) Newcomb spoke on a subject in which he had almost no expertise.
(B) Newcomb made his assertions after the basic principle that suggested the contrary had been demonstrated.
(C) Newcomb was too willing to listen to those whose point of view was not sufficiently rigorous.
(D) Newcomb was disappointed not to be the first to announce the accomplishment of a feat previously thought impossible.
(E) Newcomb disagreed with those who had supported his views in the past.

32 The assumption in Clarke's Law (lines 71-74) is that

(A) if an experiment is repeated often enough it will prove or disprove a hypothesis to the extent that the results are identical in every case
(B) it is unlikely that those who have devoted their lives to the study of a particular science can imagine possibilities that run counter to their experience
(C) scientific discoveries grow not so much out of the lives and careers of individual scientists as out of the spirit of the age
(D) scientists who are embroiled in a controversy are less likely to make valid deductions than an impartial observer would be
(E) works of science fiction are often useful in predicting the future course of scientific progress

33 The parenthetical remarks in lines 79-82 serve to

(A) indicate why those who disagree with the author are in error
(B) support the author's position by citing authorities
(C) distance the author from controversial opinions
(D) point out problems with certain examples of the impossible
(E) prove that many arguments advanced earlier are sound

34 The implication of the author's comments in lines 83-86 is that

(A) scientists who focus on the impossible do not pay enough attention to details
(B) a scientist's notions of the impossible reveal the biases of the scientist's particular field
(C) in the past, things thought to be impossible have often turned out to be the next major scientific breakthrough
(D) the difficulty of finding examples supports the idea that most things thought to be impossible might be achieved
(E) people define as impossible things that they themselves find too difficult to be worth attempting

35 The reference to Mount Everest in lines 89-90 differs from that in lines 94-95 in that the first reference is an example of

(A) something easy to do, whereas the second reference is an example of something difficult
(B) goals that have been achieved in the past, whereas the second reference is an example of goals to be considered
(C) a tall mountain, whereas the second reference is an example of the tallest mountain
(D) an old-fashioned goal, whereas the second reference is an example of spiritual inspiration
(E) something outlandish, whereas the second reference is an example of a goal worth pursuing

36 Unlike the impossibilities mentioned in lines 86-90, those mentioned in lines 95-97 are

(A) considered worth attempting by some scientists
(B) now considered possible by most scientists
(C) absurd examples found only in science fiction
(D) without practical applications
(E) not really impossible, just prohibitively expensive

IF YOU FINISH BEFORE TIME IS CALLED, YOU MAY CHECK YOUR WORK ON THIS SECTION ONLY. DO NOT TURN TO ANY OTHER SECTION IN THE TEST. **STOP**

Time—15 Minutes
10 Questions

In this section solve each problem, using any available space on the page for scratchwork. Then decide which is the best of the choices given and fill in the corresponding oval on the answer sheet.

Notes:

1. The use of a calculator is permitted. All numbers used are real numbers.
2. Figures that accompany problems in this test are intended to provide information useful in solving the problems. They are drawn as accurately as possible EXCEPT when it is stated in a specific problem that the figure is not drawn to scale. All figures lie in a plane unless otherwise indicated.

Reference Information

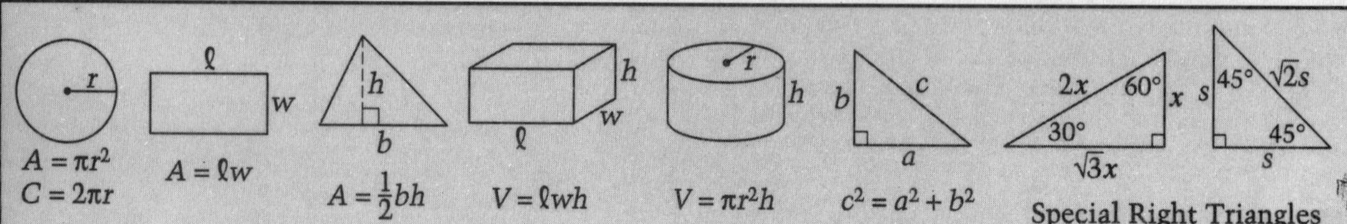

The number of degrees of arc in a circle is 360.
The measure in degrees of a straight angle is 180.
The sum of the measures in degrees of the angles of a triangle is 180.

1 If $a + 2a + 3a = 3b - 3$ and if $b = 1$, what is the value of a?

(A) 0
(B) $\frac{1}{6}$
(C) 1
(D) 3
(E) 6

TABLE OF APPROXIMATE CONVERSIONS

Number of Inches	5	10	x
Number of Centimeters	12.7	25.4	50.8

2 What is the value of x in the table above?

(A) 15
(B) 18
(C) 20
(D) 22
(E) 25

3 The product of two integers is between 102 and 115. Which of the following CANNOT be one of the integers?

(A) 5
(B) 10
(C) 12
(D) 15
(E) 20

Questions 4-5 refer to the following information.

Two companies charge different rates for painting lines on a road.

- Company X charges \$0.50 per foot of line painted and no base price.
- Company Y charges a base price of \$100.00 plus \$0.30 per foot of line painted.

4 Which of the following expressions gives the charge, in dollars, for painting f feet of line if Company X does the job?

(A) $0.20f$

(B) $0.50f$

(C) $f + 0.50$

(D) $0.20f + 100$

(E) $\frac{f}{0.50}$

5 Which of the following graphs could show the relation between the length of line painted and the charge if Company Y does the job?

(A)

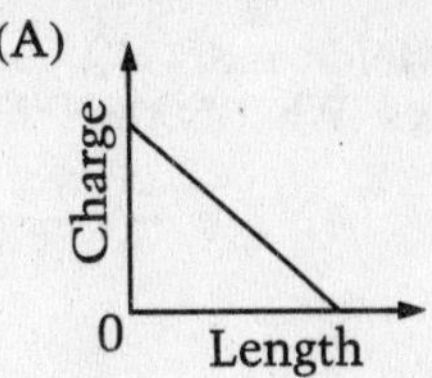

(B)

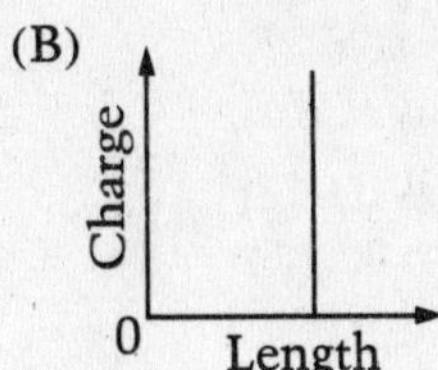

(C)

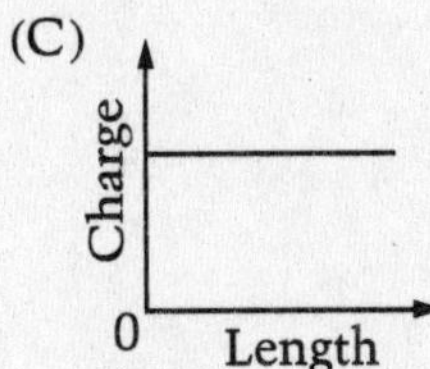

(D)

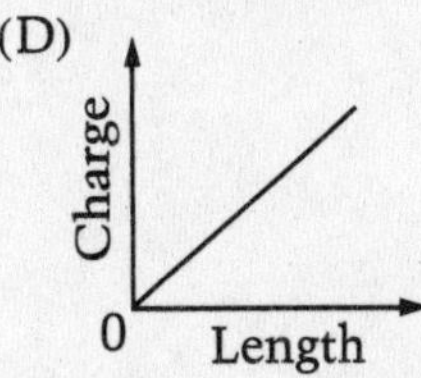

(E)

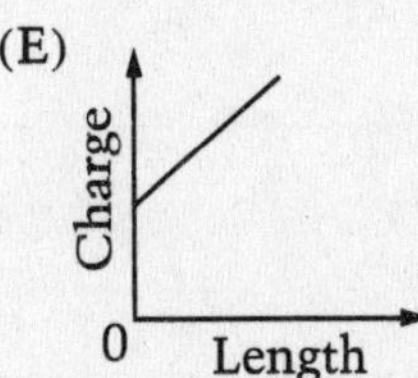

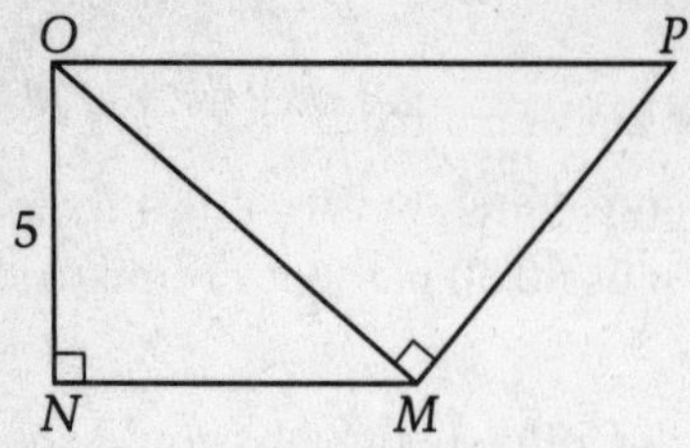

<u>Note:</u> Figure not drawn to scale.

6 In the figure above, *MNO* and *OPM* are isosceles right triangles. What is the length of *OP* ?

(A) 8
(B) 10
(C) $5\sqrt{3}$ (approximately 8.66)
(D) $7\sqrt{2}$ (approximately 9.90)
(E) $5\sqrt{5}$ (approximately 11.18)

7 If the average (arithmetic mean) of 5 consecutive even integers is n, what is the median of these 5 integers?

(A) 0
(B) 2
(C) n
(D) $n - 2$
(E) $n - 4$

8 If a and b are different positive integers and $5a + b = 32$, what is the sum of all possible values of a ?

(A) 6
(B) 11
(C) 15
(D) 18
(E) 21

GO ON TO THE NEXT PAGE

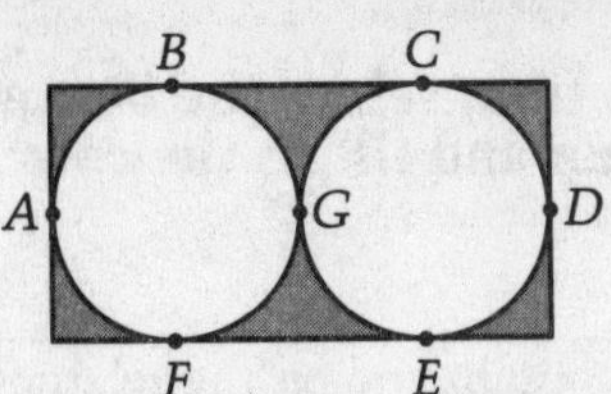

9 In the figure above, the circles touch each other and touch the sides of the rectangle at the lettered points shown. The radius of each circle is 1. Of the following, which is the best approximation of the area of the shaded region?

(A) 6
(B) 4
(C) 3
(D) 2
(E) 1

10 In the figure above, points P and T lie on line ℓ. How many different points on ℓ are twice as far from point T as from point P?

(A) None
(B) One
(C) Two
(D) Four
(E) More than four

IF YOU FINISH BEFORE TIME IS CALLED, YOU MAY CHECK YOUR WORK ON THIS SECTION ONLY. DO NOT TURN TO ANY OTHER SECTION IN THE TEST. **STOP**

Section 7

7

Time—15 Minutes
12 Questions

For each question in this section, select the best answer from among the choices given and fill in the corresponding oval on the answer sheet.

The two passages below are followed by questions based on their content and on the relationship between the two passages. Answer the questions on the basis of what is stated or implied in the passages and in any introductory material that may be provided.

Questions 1-12 are based on the following passages.

These passages, adapted from works by prominent twentieth-century British authors, are about Joan of Arc (c. 1412-1431), a young Frenchwoman who played a major role in the Hundred Years' War between France and England. She came to prominence when English forces occupied much of French territory.

Passage 1

The report of a supernatural visitant sent by God to save France, which inspired the French, clouded the minds and froze the energies of the English. The sense of awe, and even of fear, robbed them of their assurance. Upon Joan's invocation the spirit of victory changed sides, and the French began an offensive that never rested until the English invaders were driven out of France. She called for an immediate onslaught upon the besiegers, and herself led the storming parties against them. Wounded by an arrow, she plucked it out and returned to the charge. She mounted the scaling-ladders and was hurled half-stunned into the ditch. Prostrate on the ground, she commanded new efforts. "Forward, fellow countrymen!" she cried. "God has delivered them into our hands." One by one the English forts fell and their garrisons were slain. The siege was broken, and Orléans was saved. The English retired in good order, and the Maid[1] prudently restrained the citizens from pursuing them into the open country.

Despite her victories and her services to Charles VII, King of France, the attitude of both the Court and the Church toward Joan eventually began changing. It became clear that she served God rather than the Church,[2] and France rather than one particular political interest. Indeed, the whole conception of France seems to have sprung and radiated from her. Thus, the powerful particularist interests which had hitherto supported her were estranged.

Joan was captured by the Burgundians, a rival French faction of Orléans, and sold to the rejoicing English for a moderate sum. For a whole year her fate hung in the balance, while careless, ungrateful Charles lifted not a finger to save her. There is no record of any ransom being offered. History, however, has recorded the comment of an English soldier who witnessed her death at the stake. "We are lost," he said. "We have burnt a saint." All this proved true. Joan of Arc perished on May 29, 1431, and thereafter the tides of war flowed remorselessly against England.

Joan was a being so uplifted from the ordinary run of humankind that she finds no equal in a thousand years. The records of her trial present us with facts alive today through all the mists of time. Out of her own mouth can she be judged in each generation. She embodied the natural goodness and valour of the human race in unexampled perfection. Unconquerable courage, infinite compassion, the virtue of the simple, the wisdom of the just, shone forth in her. She glorifies as she freed the soil from which she sprang. All soldiers should read her story and ponder on the words and deeds of the true warrior, who in one single year, though untaught in technical arts, reveals in every situation the key of victory.

[1] Joan of Arc was known as the Maid of Orléans.

[2] The Roman Catholic church prior to the Reformation of the sixteenth century

Passage 2

Joan of Arc, a village girl from the Vosges, was born about 1412; burnt for heresy, witchcraft, and sorcery in 1431; but finally declared a saint by the Roman Catholic church in 1920. She is the most notable Warrior Saint in the Christian calendar, and the most unusual fish among the eccentric worthies of the Middle Ages. She was the pioneer of rational dressing for women, and dressed and fought and lived as men did.

Because she contrived to assert herself in all

GO ON TO THE NEXT PAGE

these ways with such force that she was famous throughout western Europe before she was out of her teens (indeed she never got out of them), it is hardly surprising that she was judicially burnt, ostensibly for a number of capital crimes that we no longer punish as such, but essentially for what we call unwomanly and insufferable presumption. At eighteen Joan's pretensions were beyond those of the proudest pope or the haughtiest emperor. She claimed to be the ambassador and plenipotentiary[3] of God. She patronized her own king and summoned the English king to repentance and obedience to her commands. She lectured, talked down, and overruled statesmen and prelates. She pooh-poohed the plans of generals, leading their troops to victory on plans of her own. She had an unbounded and quite unconcealed contempt for official opinion, judgment, and authority. Had she been a sage and monarch, her pretensions and proceedings would have been trying to the official mind. As her actual condition was pure upstart, there were only two opinions about her. One was that she was miraculous: the other, that she was unbearable.

[3] One who is given full power to act

1 Lines 10-16 portray Joan as

(A) rebellious
(B) courageous
(C) compassionate
(D) desperate
(E) fair

2 The word "retired" in line 18 most nearly means

(A) discarded
(B) recalled
(C) retreated
(D) slept peacefully
(E) ceased working

3 The sentence beginning "It became clear" (lines 24-26) indicates that Joan

(A) was more interested in military affairs than in religious or political ones
(B) preferred fighting for the underdog and lost interest once her side was winning
(C) had no particular loyalties, only vague and abstract ideas
(D) was devoted to God and country rather than to any religious or political institutions
(E) fought for religious reasons that had nothing to do with her allegiance to Charles VII

4 The statement by the English soldier in lines 38-39 serves primarily to

(A) explain the valorous behavior of the English in battle
(B) exemplify the awe Joan inspired in the English soldiers
(C) illustrate the affection the English really felt for Joan
(D) indicate the religious conviction behind the English cause
(E) provide the justification of Joan's later sainthood

5 The phrase "technical arts" (line 56) refers to

(A) military craft
(B) mechanical skills
(C) formal schooling
(D) practical affairs
(E) scientific knowledge

6 Which of the following best describes the approach of Passage 1 ?

(A) Straightforward, factual narration
(B) Analysis of a historical theory
(C) Comparison and contrast
(D) Colorful, dramatic description
(E) Criticism couched in sarcasm

7 Passage 2 views Joan's victories as stemming from her

(A) saintly behavior toward friend and foe alike
(B) natural goodness and essential simplicity
(C) threats to resort to witchcraft to frighten the enemy
(D) ability to command the respect of kings
(E) strength of personality and determination

8 The phrase "her actual condition was pure upstart" in line 88 indicates that Joan

(A) behaved spontaneously and optimistically
(B) defied conventional strategies of warfare
(C) was unaware of what was expected of her
(D) was not a member of the elite
(E) used illegal means to achieve her ends

GO ON TO THE NEXT PAGE

9 Both passages discuss which of the following regarding Joan?

(A) Her moral and ethical philosophy
(B) Her military background and training
(C) Her relationship to the Church and to the state
(D) The effect of her death on the outcome of the war
(E) The views that English subjects had of her

10 Which of the following questions is NOT explicitly answered by either passage?

(A) What was Joan charged with?
(B) Why did it take so long for Joan to be honored with sainthood?
(C) Where did Joan come from?
(D) What part did Joan personally play in the battle between the English and the French?
(E) How valuable was Joan to her country?

11 Both passages agree that Joan met with resistance primarily because of her

(A) attempt to undermine the Church and its teachings
(B) headstrong behavior and unwillingness to compromise
(C) petty squabbling with officials
(D) inability to continue to win military victories
(E) refusal to accept the typical female role of her time

12 Both passages suggest which of the following about the French and English monarchies?

(A) Both monarchies felt threatened by the power that Joan was able to command.
(B) The two monarchies were unable to settle their differences because of Joan's influence.
(C) Both monarchies were torn by internal strife.
(D) The English monarchy was more intent on waging war than was the French monarchy.
(E) Religion played a more significant role in the French monarchy than in that of the English.

IF YOU FINISH BEFORE TIME IS CALLED, YOU MAY CHECK YOUR WORK ON THIS SECTION ONLY. DO NOT TURN TO ANY OTHER SECTION IN THE TEST. **STOP**

SAT I: Reasoning Test Answer Key
Sunday, May 1996

VERBAL

Section 2

Five-choice Questions

	COR. ANS.	DIFF. LEV.
1.	A	2
2.	D	2
3.	E	2
4.	B	1
5.	D	3
6.	E	3
7.	E	4
8.	C	4
9.	C	5
10.	B	1
11.	B	2
12.	A	3
13.	A	5
14.	D	5
15.	C	5
16.	E	2
17.	B	3
18.	C	2
19.	D	4
20.	C	4
21.	A	3
22.	C	3
23.	E	3
24.	C	3
25.	A	5
26.	B	4
27.	A	3
28.	D	3
29.	D	3
30.	A	3

no. correct

no. incorrect

Section 5

Five-choice Questions

	COR. ANS.	DIFF. LEV.
1.	D	2
2.	C	2
3.	C	2
4.	A	3
5.	E	2
6.	C	2
7.	C	4
8.	D	4
9.	B	5
10.	A	5
11.	E	1
12.	B	1
13.	D	2
14.	A	3
15.	E	3
16.	C	3
17.	D	4
18.	D	3
19.	B	3
20.	C	4
21.	D	5
22.	E	5
23.	A	5
24.	E	5
25.	C	3
26.	B	3
27.	B	3
28.	E	3
29.	A	3
30.	A	2
31.	B	3
32.	B	4
33.	D	3
34.	D	5
35.	E	3
36.	A	3

no. correct

no. incorrect

Section 7

Five-choice Questions

	COR. ANS.	DIFF. LEV.
1.	B	1
2.	C	1
3.	D	1
4.	B	3
5.	A	2
6.	D	3
7.	E	2
8.	D	5
9.	C	4
10.	B	3
11.	B	4
12.	A	3

no. correct

no. incorrect

MATHEMATICAL

Section 1

Five-choice Questions

	COR. ANS.	DIFF. LEV.
1.	E	1
2.	C	1
3.	C	1
4.	D	1
5.	B	2
6.	E	2
7.	C	1
8.	A	2
9.	D	3
10.	D	2
11.	E	3
12.	C	3
13.	A	3
14.	C	3
15.	E	3
16.	E	5
17.	C	4
18.	B	4
19.	A	4
20.	B	4
21.	A	4
22.	A	3
23.	B	5
24.	D	5
25.	A	5

no. correct

no. incorrect

Section 3

Four-choice Questions

	COR. ANS.	DIFF. LEV.
1.	A	1
2.	A	2
3.	D	2
4.	B	3
5.	D	3
6.	B	3
7.	A	2
8.	A	3
9.	D	4
10.	B	3
11.	C	5
12.	D	4
13.	C	2
14.	A	3
15.	B	5

no. correct

no. incorrect

Section 3

Student-Produced Response Questions

	COR. ANS.	DIFF. LEV.
16.	8	2
17.	5	3
18.	2400	2
19.	220	3
20.	$0<x<1$	3
21.	210	3
22.	68 or 86	4
23.	12	4
24.	3/8 or .375	4
25.	2/15 or .133	5

no. correct (16-25)

Section 6

Five-choice Questions

	COR. ANS.	DIFF. LEV.
1.	A	1
2.	C	2
3.	E	3
4.	B	1
5.	E	3
6.	B	3
7.	C	3
8.	E	3
9.	D	3
10.	C	5

no. correct

no. incorrect

NOTE: Difficulty levels are estimates of question difficulty for a recent group of college-bound seniors. Difficulty levels range from 1 (easiest) to 5 (hardest).

The Scoring Process

Machine-scoring is done in three steps:

- *Scanning.* Your answer sheet is "read" by a scanning machine and the oval you filled in for each question is recorded on a computer tape.
- *Scoring.* The computer compares the oval filled in for each question with the correct response. Each correct answer receives one point; omitted questions do not count toward your score. For each wrong answer to the multiple-choice questions, a fraction of a point is subtracted to correct for random guessing. For questions with five answer choices, one-fourth of a point is subtracted for each wrong response; for questions with four answer choices, one-third of a point is subtracted for each wrong response. The SAT I verbal test has 78 questions with five answer choices each. If, for example, a student has 44 right, 32 wrong, and 2 omitted, the resulting raw score is determined as follows:

$$44 \text{ right} - \frac{32 \text{ wrong}}{4} = 44 - 8 = 36 \text{ raw score points}$$

Obtaining raw scores frequently involves the rounding of fractional numbers to the nearest whole number. For example, a raw score of 36.25 is rounded to 36, the nearest whole number. A raw score of 36.50 is rounded upward to 37.

- *Converting to reported scaled score.* Raw test scores are then placed on the College Board scale of 200 to 800 through a process that adjusts scores to account for minor differences in difficulty among different editions of the test. This process, known as equating, is performed so that a student's reported score is not affected by the edition of the test taken nor by the abilities of the group with whom the student takes the test. As a result of placing SAT I scores on the College Board scale, scores earned by students at different times can be compared.

How to Score the Practice Test

SAT I Verbal Sections 2, 5, and 7

Step A: Count the number of correct answers for Section 2 and record the number in the space provided on the worksheet on the next page. Then do the same for the incorrect answers. (Do not count omitted answers.) To determine subtotal A, use the formula:

$$\text{number correct} - \frac{\text{number incorrect}}{4} = \text{subtotal A}$$

Step B: Count the number of correct answers and the number of incorrect answers for *Section 5* and record the number in the space provided on the worksheet. To determine subtotal B, use the formula:

$$\text{number correct} - \frac{\text{number incorrect}}{4} = \text{subtotal B}$$

Step C: Count the number of correct answers and the number of incorrect answers for *Section 7* and record the number in the space provided on the worksheet. To determine subtotal C, use the formula:

$$\text{number correct} - \frac{\text{number incorrect}}{4} = \text{subtotal C}$$

Step D: To obtain D, add subtotal A, subtotal B, and subtotal C, keeping any decimals. Enter the resulting figure on the worksheet.

Step E: To obtain E, your raw verbal score, round D to the nearest whole number. (For example, any number from 44.50 to 45.49 rounds to 45.) Enter the resulting figure on the worksheet.

Step F: To find your SAT verbal score, look up the total raw verbal score you obtained in step E in the conversion table. Enter this figure on the worksheet.

SAT I Mathematical Sections 1, 3, and 6

Step A: Count the number of correct answers and the number of incorrect answers for *Section 1* and record the numbers in the spaces provided on the worksheet. To determine subtotal A, use the formula:

$$\text{number correct} - \frac{\text{number incorrect}}{4} = \text{subtotal A}$$

Step B: Count the number of correct answers and the number of incorrect answers for the *four-choice quantitative comparison questions (questions 1 through 15) in Section 3* and record the number in the space provided on the worksheet. Note: Do not count any E responses to questions 1 through 15 as correct or incorrect. Because these four-choice questions have no E answer choices, E responses to these questions are treated as omits. To determine subtotal B, use the formula:

$$\text{number correct} - \frac{\text{number incorrect}}{3} = \text{subtotal B}$$

Step C: Count the number of correct answers for the student-produced response questions *(questions 16 through 25) in Section 3* and record the number in the space provided on the worksheet. This is subtotal C.

Step D: Count the number of correct answers and the number of incorrect answers for *Section 6* and record the number in the space provided on the worksheet. To determine subtotal D, use the formula:

$$\text{number correct} - \frac{\text{number incorrect}}{4} = \text{subtotal D}$$

Step E: To obtain E, add subtotal A, subtotal B, subtotal C, and subtotal D, keeping any decimals. Enter the resulting figure on the worksheet.

Step F: To obtain F, your raw mathematical score, round E to the nearest whole number. (For example, any number from 44.50 to 45.49 rounds to 45.) Enter the resulting figure on the worksheet.

Step G: To find your SAT I mathematical score, look up the total raw mathematical score you obtained in step F in the conversion table. Enter this figure on the worksheet.

SAT I Scoring Worksheet

SAT I Verbal Sections

A. Section 2: ______ no. correct – (______ no. incorrect ÷ 4) = ______ subtotal A

B. Section 5: ______ no. correct – (______ no. incorrect ÷ 4) = ______ subtotal B

C. Section 7: ______ no. correct – (______ no. incorrect ÷ 4) = ______ subtotal C

D. Total unrounded raw score
(Total A + B + C) ______ D

E. Total rounded raw score
(Rounded to nearest whole number) ______ E

F. SAT I verbal reported scaled score
(Use the conversion table) [ ] SAT I verbal score

SAT I Mathematical Sections

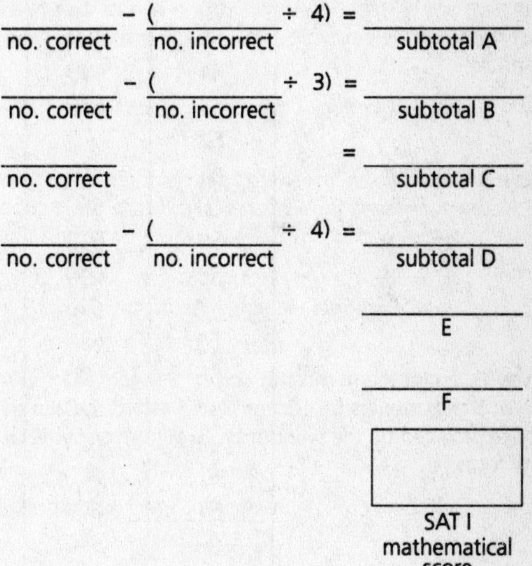

A. Section 1: ______ no. correct – (______ no. incorrect ÷ 4) = ______ subtotal A

B. Section 3:
Questions 1-15 (quantitative comparison) ______ no. correct – (______ no. incorrect ÷ 3) = ______ subtotal B

C. Section 3·
Questions 16-25 (student-produced response) ______ no. correct = ______ subtotal C

D. Section 6: ______ no. correct – (______ no. incorrect ÷ 4) = ______ subtotal D

E. Total unrounded raw score
(Total A + B + C + D) ______ E

F. Total rounded raw score
(Rounded to nearest whole number) ______ F

G. SAT I mathematical reported scaled score
(Use the conversion table) [ ] SAT I mathematical score

Score Conversion Table
SAT I: Reasoning Test
Sunday, May 1996
Recentered Scale

Raw Score	Verbal Scaled Score	Math Scaled Score	Raw Score	Verbal Scaled Score	Math Scaled Score
78	800		37	520	580
77	800		36	510	570
76	800		35	510	560
75	800		34	500	550
74	800		33	490	550
73	800		32	490	540
72	780		31	480	530
71	770		30	480	530
70	750		29	470	520
69	740		28	460	510
68	730		27	460	510
67	720		26	450	500
66	710		25	450	490
65	700		24	440	490
64	690		23	430	480
63	680		22	430	470
62	670		21	420	460
61	670		20	410	460
60	660	800	19	410	450
59	650	800	18	400	440
58	640	780	17	390	430
57	640	760	16	390	430
56	630	740	15	380	420
55	620	730	14	370	410
54	620	720	13	360	400
53	610	710	12	360	390
52	600	700	11	350	380
51	600	690	10	340	370
50	590	680	9	330	360
49	590	670	8	320	350
48	580	660	7	310	340
47	570	650	6	300	330
46	570	640	5	290	320
45	560	640	4	280	310
44	560	630	3	270	290
43	550	620	2	250	280
42	550	610	1	240	270
41	540	600	0	220	250
40	530	600	-1	200	240
39	530	590	-2	200	220
38	520	580	-3 and below	200	200

This table is for use only with this test.

SAT I: Reasoning Test

Saturday, November 1996

YOUR NAME (PRINT) ____

LAST FIRST MI

TEST CENTER ____

NUMBER NAME OF TEST CENTER ROOM NUMBER

SAT® I: Reasoning Test — General Directions

Timing

- You will have three hours to work on this test.
- There are five 30-minute sections and two 15-minute sections.
- You may work on only one section at a time.
- The supervisor will tell you when to begin and end each section.
- If you finish a section before time is called, check your work on that section. You may NOT turn to any other section.
- Work as rapidly as you can without losing accuracy. Don't waste time on questions that seem too difficult for you.

Marking Answers

- Carefully mark only one answer for each question.
- Make sure each mark is dark and completely fills the oval.
- Do not make any stray marks on your answer sheet.
- If you erase, do so completely. Incomplete erasures may be scored as intended answers.
- Use only the answer spaces that correspond to the question numbers.
- For questions with only four answer choices, an answer marked in oval E will not be scored.
- Use the test book for scratchwork, but you will not receive credit for anything written there.
- You may not transfer answers to your answer sheet or fill in ovals after time has been called.
- You may not fold or remove pages or portions of a page from this book, or take the book or answer sheet from the testing room.

Scoring

- For each correct answer, you receive one point.
- For questions you omit, you receive no points.
- For a wrong answer to a multiple-choice question, you lose a fraction of a point.
  - ► If you can eliminate one or more of the answer choices as wrong, however, you increase your chances of choosing the correct answer and earning one point.
  - ► If you can't eliminate any choice, move on. You can return to the question later if there is time.
- For a wrong answer to a math question that is not multiple-choice, you don't lose any points.

The passages for this test have been adapted from published material. The ideas contained in them do not necessarily represent the opinions of the College Board or Educational Testing Service.

IMPORTANT: The codes below are unique to your test book. Copy them on your answer sheet in boxes 8 and 9 and <u>fill in the corresponding ovals exactly as shown.</u>

8. Form Code

A	A	0	0	0
B	B	1	1	1
C	C	2	2	2
D	D	3	3	3
E	E	4	4	4
F	F	5	5	5
G	G	6	6	6
H	H	7	7	7
I	I	8	8	8
J	J	9	9	9
K	K			
L	L			
M	M			
N	N			
O	O			
P	P			
Q	Q			
R	R			
S	S			
T	T			
U	U			
V	V			
W	W			
X	X			
Y	Y			
Z	Z			

9. Test Form

DO NOT OPEN THIS BOOK UNTIL THE SUPERVISOR TELLS YOU TO DO SO.

THE COLLEGE BOARD — SAT I **Page 1**

Use a No. 2 pencil only. Be sure each mark is dark and completely fills the intended oval. Completely erase any errors or stray marks.

1. Your Name

First 4 letters of Last Name | First init. | Mid. init.

A B C D E F G H I J K L M N O P Q R S T U V W X Y Z

2.
Your Name: (Print) Last First M.I.

I agree to the conditions on the back of the SAT I test book.

Signature: Date: / /

Home Address: (Print) Number and Street

City State Zip Code

Center: (Print) City State Center Number

IMPORTANT: Fill in items 8 and 9 exactly as shown on the back of test book.

8. Form Code

(Copy and grid as on back of test book.)

3. Date of Birth

Month	Day	Year
Jan.		
Feb.		
Mar.	0 0	0 0
Apr.	1 1	1 1
May	2 2	2 2
June	3 3	3 3
July	4	4 4
Aug.	5	5 5
Sept.	6	6 6
Oct.	7	7 7
Nov.	8	8 8
Dec.	9	9

4. Social Security Number

5. Sex

Female Male

6. Registration Number

(Copy from Admission Ticket.)

7. Test Book Serial Number

(Copy from front of test book.)

FOR ETS USE ONLY

9. Test Form

(Copy from back of test book.)

Start with number 1 for each new section. If a section has fewer questions than answer spaces, leave the extra answer spaces blank.

SECTION 1

1 A B C D E	11 A B C D E	21 A B C D E	31 A B C D E
2 A B C D E	12 A B C D E	22 A B C D E	32 A B C D E
3 A B C D E	13 A B C D E	23 A B C D E	33 A B C D E
4 A B C D E	14 A B C D E	24 A B C D E	34 A B C D E
5 A B C D E	15 A B C D E	25 A B C D E	35 A B C D E
6 A B C D E	16 A B C D E	26 A B C D E	36 A B C D E
7 A B C D E	17 A B C D E	27 A B C D E	37 A B C D E
8 A B C D E	18 A B C D E	28 A B C D E	38 A B C D E
9 A B C D E	19 A B C D E	29 A B C D E	39 A B C D E
10 A B C D E	20 A B C D E	30 A B C D E	40 A B C D E

SECTION 2

1 A B C D E	11 A B C D E	21 A B C D E	31 A B C D E
2 A B C D E	12 A B C D E	22 A B C D E	32 A B C D E
3 A B C D E	13 A B C D E	23 A B C D E	33 A B C D E
4 A B C D E	14 A B C D E	24 A B C D E	34 A B C D E
5 A B C D E	15 A B C D E	25 A B C D E	35 A B C D E
6 A B C D E	16 A B C D E	26 A B C D E	36 A B C D E
7 A B C D E	17 A B C D E	27 A B C D E	37 A B C D E
8 A B C D E	18 A B C D E	28 A B C D E	38 A B C D E
9 A B C D E	19 A B C D E	29 A B C D E	39 A B C D E
10 A B C D E	20 A B C D E	30 A B C D E	40 A B C D E

Q2778-06/2 CHW98324 11027 • 09132 • TF129M17.5eX I.N. 207158

Use a No. 2 pencil only. Be sure each mark is dark and completely fills the intended oval. Completely erase any errors or stray marks.

Start with number 1 for each new section. If a section has fewer questions than answer spaces, leave the extra answer spaces blank.

SECTION 3

1 (A) (B) (C) (D) (E)
2 (A) (B) (C) (D) (E)
3 (A) (B) (C) (D) (E)
4 (A) (B) (C) (D) (E)
5 (A) (B) (C) (D) (E)
6 (A) (B) (C) (D) (E)
7 (A) (B) (C) (D) (E)
8 (A) (B) (C) (D) (E)
9 (A) (B) (C) (D) (E)
10 (A) (B) (C) (D) (E)
11 (A) (B) (C) (D) (E)
12 (A) (B) (C) (D) (E)
13 (A) (B) (C) (D) (E)
14 (A) (B) (C) (D) (E)
15 (A) (B) (C) (D) (E)
16 (A) (B) (C) (D) (E)
17 (A) (B) (C) (D) (E)
18 (A) (B) (C) (D) (E)
19 (A) (B) (C) (D) (E)
20 (A) (B) (C) (D) (E)
21 (A) (B) (C) (D) (E)
22 (A) (B) (C) (D) (E)
23 (A) (B) (C) (D) (E)
24 (A) (B) (C) (D) (E)
25 (A) (B) (C) (D) (E)
26 (A) (B) (C) (D) (E)
27 (A) (B) (C) (D) (E)
28 (A) (B) (C) (D) (E)
29 (A) (B) (C) (D) (E)
30 (A) (B) (C) (D) (E)
31 (A) (B) (C) (D) (E)
32 (A) (B) (C) (D) (E)
33 (A) (B) (C) (D) (E)
34 (A) (B) (C) (D) (E)
35 (A) (B) (C) (D) (E)
36 (A) (B) (C) (D) (E)
37 (A) (B) (C) (D) (E)
38 (A) (B) (C) (D) (E)
39 (A) (B) (C) (D) (E)
40 (A) (B) (C) (D) (E)

If section 3 of your test book contains math questions that are not multiple-choice, continue to item 16 below. Otherwise, continue to item 16 above.

ONLY ANSWERS ENTERED IN THE OVALS IN EACH GRID AREA WILL BE SCORED.
YOU WILL NOT RECEIVE CREDIT FOR ANYTHING WRITTEN IN THE BOXES ABOVE THE OVALS.

16 17 18 19 20 21 22 23 24 25

(each grid: / / ; . . . . ; 0 0 0 ; 1 1 1 1 ; 2 2 2 2 ; 3 3 3 3 ; 4 4 4 4 ; 5 5 5 5 ; 6 6 6 6 ; 7 7 7 7 ; 8 8 8 8 ; 9 9 9 9)

BE SURE TO ERASE ANY ERRORS OR STRAY MARKS COMPLETELY.

PLEASE PRINT YOUR INITIALS

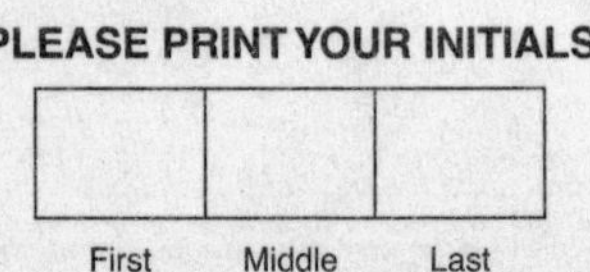

Use a No. 2 pencil only. Be sure each mark is dark and completely fills the intended oval. Completely erase any errors or stray marks.

Start with number 1 for each new section. If a section has fewer questions than answer spaces, leave the extra answer spaces blank.

SECTION 4

1 Ⓐ Ⓑ Ⓒ Ⓓ Ⓔ
2 Ⓐ Ⓑ Ⓒ Ⓓ Ⓔ
3 Ⓐ Ⓑ Ⓒ Ⓓ Ⓔ
4 Ⓐ Ⓑ Ⓒ Ⓓ Ⓔ
5 Ⓐ Ⓑ Ⓒ Ⓓ Ⓔ
6 Ⓐ Ⓑ Ⓒ Ⓓ Ⓔ
7 Ⓐ Ⓑ Ⓒ Ⓓ Ⓔ
8 Ⓐ Ⓑ Ⓒ Ⓓ Ⓔ
9 Ⓐ Ⓑ Ⓒ Ⓓ Ⓔ
10 Ⓐ Ⓑ Ⓒ Ⓓ Ⓔ
11 Ⓐ Ⓑ Ⓒ Ⓓ Ⓔ
12 Ⓐ Ⓑ Ⓒ Ⓓ Ⓔ
13 Ⓐ Ⓑ Ⓒ Ⓓ Ⓔ
14 Ⓐ Ⓑ Ⓒ Ⓓ Ⓔ
15 Ⓐ Ⓑ Ⓒ Ⓓ Ⓔ
16 Ⓐ Ⓑ Ⓒ Ⓓ Ⓔ
17 Ⓐ Ⓑ Ⓒ Ⓓ Ⓔ
18 Ⓐ Ⓑ Ⓒ Ⓓ Ⓔ
19 Ⓐ Ⓑ Ⓒ Ⓓ Ⓔ
20 Ⓐ Ⓑ Ⓒ Ⓓ Ⓔ
21 Ⓐ Ⓑ Ⓒ Ⓓ Ⓔ
22 Ⓐ Ⓑ Ⓒ Ⓓ Ⓔ
23 Ⓐ Ⓑ Ⓒ Ⓓ Ⓔ
24 Ⓐ Ⓑ Ⓒ Ⓓ Ⓔ
25 Ⓐ Ⓑ Ⓒ Ⓓ Ⓔ
26 Ⓐ Ⓑ Ⓒ Ⓓ Ⓔ
27 Ⓐ Ⓑ Ⓒ Ⓓ Ⓔ
28 Ⓐ Ⓑ Ⓒ Ⓓ Ⓔ
29 Ⓐ Ⓑ Ⓒ Ⓓ Ⓔ
30 Ⓐ Ⓑ Ⓒ Ⓓ Ⓔ
31 Ⓐ Ⓑ Ⓒ Ⓓ Ⓔ
32 Ⓐ Ⓑ Ⓒ Ⓓ Ⓔ
33 Ⓐ Ⓑ Ⓒ Ⓓ Ⓔ
34 Ⓐ Ⓑ Ⓒ Ⓓ Ⓔ
35 Ⓐ Ⓑ Ⓒ Ⓓ Ⓔ
36 Ⓐ Ⓑ Ⓒ Ⓓ Ⓔ
37 Ⓐ Ⓑ Ⓒ Ⓓ Ⓔ
38 Ⓐ Ⓑ Ⓒ Ⓓ Ⓔ
39 Ⓐ Ⓑ Ⓒ Ⓓ Ⓔ
40 Ⓐ Ⓑ Ⓒ Ⓓ Ⓔ

If section 4 of your test book contains math questions that are not multiple-choice, continue to item 16 below. Otherwise, continue to item 16 above.

ONLY ANSWERS ENTERED IN THE OVALS IN EACH GRID AREA WILL BE SCORED.
YOU WILL NOT RECEIVE CREDIT FOR ANYTHING WRITTEN IN THE BOXES ABOVE THE OVALS.

16 17 18 19 20

21 22 23 24 25

(Each grid: / / ; . . . . ; 0 0 0 ; 1 1 1 1 ; 2 2 2 2 ; 3 3 3 3 ; 4 4 4 4 ; 5 5 5 5 ; 6 6 6 6 ; 7 7 7 7 ; 8 8 8 8 ; 9 9 9 9)

BE SURE TO ERASE ANY ERRORS OR STRAY MARKS COMPLETELY.

DO NOT WRITE IN THIS AREA.

0

PLEASE PRINT YOUR INITIALS

First	Middle	Last

Use a No. 2 pencil only. Be sure each mark is dark and completely fills the intended oval. Completely erase any errors or stray marks.

Start with number 1 for each new section. If a section has fewer questions than answer spaces, leave the extra answer spaces blank.

SECTION 5

1 Ⓐ Ⓑ Ⓒ Ⓓ Ⓔ	11 Ⓐ Ⓑ Ⓒ Ⓓ Ⓔ	21 Ⓐ Ⓑ Ⓒ Ⓓ Ⓔ	31 Ⓐ Ⓑ Ⓒ Ⓓ Ⓔ
2 Ⓐ Ⓑ Ⓒ Ⓓ Ⓔ	12 Ⓐ Ⓑ Ⓒ Ⓓ Ⓔ	22 Ⓐ Ⓑ Ⓒ Ⓓ Ⓔ	32 Ⓐ Ⓑ Ⓒ Ⓓ Ⓔ
3 Ⓐ Ⓑ Ⓒ Ⓓ Ⓔ	13 Ⓐ Ⓑ Ⓒ Ⓓ Ⓔ	23 Ⓐ Ⓑ Ⓒ Ⓓ Ⓔ	33 Ⓐ Ⓑ Ⓒ Ⓓ Ⓔ
4 Ⓐ Ⓑ Ⓒ Ⓓ Ⓔ	14 Ⓐ Ⓑ Ⓒ Ⓓ Ⓔ	24 Ⓐ Ⓑ Ⓒ Ⓓ Ⓔ	34 Ⓐ Ⓑ Ⓒ Ⓓ Ⓔ
5 Ⓐ Ⓑ Ⓒ Ⓓ Ⓔ	15 Ⓐ Ⓑ Ⓒ Ⓓ Ⓔ	25 Ⓐ Ⓑ Ⓒ Ⓓ Ⓔ	35 Ⓐ Ⓑ Ⓒ Ⓓ Ⓔ
6 Ⓐ Ⓑ Ⓒ Ⓓ Ⓔ	16 Ⓐ Ⓑ Ⓒ Ⓓ Ⓔ	26 Ⓐ Ⓑ Ⓒ Ⓓ Ⓔ	36 Ⓐ Ⓑ Ⓒ Ⓓ Ⓔ
7 Ⓐ Ⓑ Ⓒ Ⓓ Ⓔ	17 Ⓐ Ⓑ Ⓒ Ⓓ Ⓔ	27 Ⓐ Ⓑ Ⓒ Ⓓ Ⓔ	37 Ⓐ Ⓑ Ⓒ Ⓓ Ⓔ
8 Ⓐ Ⓑ Ⓒ Ⓓ Ⓔ	18 Ⓐ Ⓑ Ⓒ Ⓓ Ⓔ	28 Ⓐ Ⓑ Ⓒ Ⓓ Ⓔ	38 Ⓐ Ⓑ Ⓒ Ⓓ Ⓔ
9 Ⓐ Ⓑ Ⓒ Ⓓ Ⓔ	19 Ⓐ Ⓑ Ⓒ Ⓓ Ⓔ	29 Ⓐ Ⓑ Ⓒ Ⓓ Ⓔ	39 Ⓐ Ⓑ Ⓒ Ⓓ Ⓔ
10 Ⓐ Ⓑ Ⓒ Ⓓ Ⓔ	20 Ⓐ Ⓑ Ⓒ Ⓓ Ⓔ	30 Ⓐ Ⓑ Ⓒ Ⓓ Ⓔ	40 Ⓐ Ⓑ Ⓒ Ⓓ Ⓔ

SECTION 6

1 Ⓐ Ⓑ Ⓒ Ⓓ Ⓔ	6 Ⓐ Ⓑ Ⓒ Ⓓ Ⓔ	11 Ⓐ Ⓑ Ⓒ Ⓓ Ⓔ	16 Ⓐ Ⓑ Ⓒ Ⓓ Ⓔ
2 Ⓐ Ⓑ Ⓒ Ⓓ Ⓔ	7 Ⓐ Ⓑ Ⓒ Ⓓ Ⓔ	12 Ⓐ Ⓑ Ⓒ Ⓓ Ⓔ	17 Ⓐ Ⓑ Ⓒ Ⓓ Ⓔ
3 Ⓐ Ⓑ Ⓒ Ⓓ Ⓔ	8 Ⓐ Ⓑ Ⓒ Ⓓ Ⓔ	13 Ⓐ Ⓑ Ⓒ Ⓓ Ⓔ	18 Ⓐ Ⓑ Ⓒ Ⓓ Ⓔ
4 Ⓐ Ⓑ Ⓒ Ⓓ Ⓔ	9 Ⓐ Ⓑ Ⓒ Ⓓ Ⓔ	14 Ⓐ Ⓑ Ⓒ Ⓓ Ⓔ	19 Ⓐ Ⓑ Ⓒ Ⓓ Ⓔ
5 Ⓐ Ⓑ Ⓒ Ⓓ Ⓔ	10 Ⓐ Ⓑ Ⓒ Ⓓ Ⓔ	15 Ⓐ Ⓑ Ⓒ Ⓓ Ⓔ	20 Ⓐ Ⓑ Ⓒ Ⓓ Ⓔ

SECTION 7

1 Ⓐ Ⓑ Ⓒ Ⓓ Ⓔ	6 Ⓐ Ⓑ Ⓒ Ⓓ Ⓔ	11 Ⓐ Ⓑ Ⓒ Ⓓ Ⓔ	16 Ⓐ Ⓑ Ⓒ Ⓓ Ⓔ
2 Ⓐ Ⓑ Ⓒ Ⓓ Ⓔ	7 Ⓐ Ⓑ Ⓒ Ⓓ Ⓔ	12 Ⓐ Ⓑ Ⓒ Ⓓ Ⓔ	17 Ⓐ Ⓑ Ⓒ Ⓓ Ⓔ
3 Ⓐ Ⓑ Ⓒ Ⓓ Ⓔ	8 Ⓐ Ⓑ Ⓒ Ⓓ Ⓔ	13 Ⓐ Ⓑ Ⓒ Ⓓ Ⓔ	18 Ⓐ Ⓑ Ⓒ Ⓓ Ⓔ
4 Ⓐ Ⓑ Ⓒ Ⓓ Ⓔ	9 Ⓐ Ⓑ Ⓒ Ⓓ Ⓔ	14 Ⓐ Ⓑ Ⓒ Ⓓ Ⓔ	19 Ⓐ Ⓑ Ⓒ Ⓓ Ⓔ
5 Ⓐ Ⓑ Ⓒ Ⓓ Ⓔ	10 Ⓐ Ⓑ Ⓒ Ⓓ Ⓔ	15 Ⓐ Ⓑ Ⓒ Ⓓ Ⓔ	20 Ⓐ Ⓑ Ⓒ Ⓓ Ⓔ

CERTIFICATION STATEMENT

Copy the statement below (do not print) and sign your name as you would an official document.

I hereby agree to the conditions set forth in the Registration Bulletin and certify that I am the person whose name and address appear on this answer sheet.

Signature: ______________________ Date: __________

Section 1 1 1 1 1 1 1

Time—30 Minutes
31 Questions

For each question in this section, select the best answer from among the choices given and fill in the corresponding oval on the answer sheet.

Each sentence below has one or two blanks, each blank indicating that something has been omitted. Beneath the sentence are five words or sets of words labeled A through E. Choose the word or set of words that, when inserted in the sentence, best fits the meaning of the sentence as a whole.

Example:

Medieval kingdoms did not become constitutional republics overnight; on the contrary, the change was ----.

(A) unpopular
(B) unexpected
(C) advantageous
(D) sufficient
(E) gradual

1 Many cultural historians believe that language has a ---- purpose: it serves not only as a means of communication but also as a means of defining culture.

(A) foreign (B) literary (C) false (D) dual (E) direct

2 In 1859 Black pioneer Clara Brown turned the unpromising conditions that had ---- many other settlers of the mining camp into a source of ---- by starting her own business.

(A) discouraged . . reconciliation
(B) defeated . . prosperity
(C) elevated . . happiness
(D) aided . . opportunity
(E) delayed . . unity

3 While the island country's dramatists typically use ---- settings and myths, their themes are not ---- their country alone; indeed, many plays are appreciated worldwide for their insightful treatment of common human issues.

(A) ancient . . condescending to
(B) modest . . concerned with
(C) native . . limited to
(D) ordinary . . lobbying for
(E) cosmopolitan . . indebted to

4 Far from ---- the old social inequities, the law ---- new ones by virtue of the loopholes it left for the wealthy.

(A) eradicating . . created
(B) jeopardizing . . corrected
(C) placating . . eliminated
(D) duplicating . . avoided
(E) corroborating . . anticipated

5 The use of gospel music in the modern production of the ancient Greek tragedy is effective, in spite of seeming ---- to critics interested only in historical accuracy.

(A) felicitous (B) inevitable (C) anachronistic (D) timeless (E) exemplary

6 It has been suggested that the detailed listings of animals, plants, and minerals by their usefulness to humans indicate the ---- of the ancient Mesopotamians.

(A) irrationality (B) humanity (C) temerity (D) serendipity (E) anthropocentrism

7 Buildings designed exclusively for strength and stability, structures for which only ---- considerations have been taken into account, are properly works of engineering, not true architecture.

(A) utilitarian (B) grandiose (C) imaginative (D) aesthetic (E) external

8 Many healing practices that doctors once derided as ---- have now been sanctioned by the medical community.

(A) benign (B) diagnostic (C) inefficacious (D) discretionary (E) therapeutic

9 Sometimes forgetting that rationality is only one part of a person's experience, Andrew takes an excessively ---- approach to life.

(A) cerebral (B) obdurate (C) sensitive (D) pretentious (E) enervated

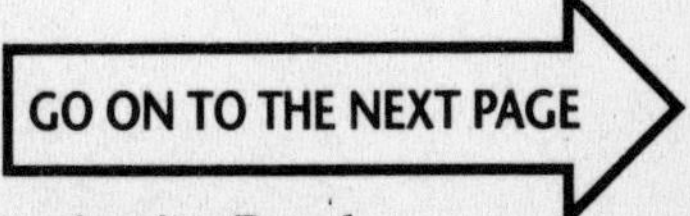

Each question below consists of a related pair of words or phrases, followed by five pairs of words or phrases labeled A through E. Select the pair that best expresses a relationship similar to that expressed in the original pair.

Example:

CRUMB : BREAD ::
(A) ounce : unit
(B) splinter : wood
(C) water : bucket
(D) twine : rope
(E) cream : butter

10 BRUISE : SKIN ::
(A) muscle : bone
(B) smudge : blemish
(C) rash : allergy
(D) layer : veneer
(E) stain : fabric

11 CARPENTER : WOODWORK ::
(A) guitarist : pick
(B) cook : heat
(C) sculptor : studio
(D) weaver : cloth
(E) potter : shape

12 WALK : SCURRY ::
(A) march : follow
(B) carouse : revel
(C) nap : sleep
(D) impress : notice
(E) jog : sprint

13 REGALE : ENTERTAIN ::
(A) extol : praise
(B) educate : learn
(C) beautify : refresh
(D) tempt : repel
(E) hide : secrete

14 RECYCLE : WASTE ::
(A) salvage : rescuer
(B) restate : emphasis
(C) recall : product
(D) reclaim : land
(E) irrigate : earth

15 FLORID : PROSE ::
(A) detailed : sketch
(B) melodious : music
(C) colorful : cliché
(D) tragic : play
(E) ornate : building

GO ON TO THE NEXT PAGE

Each passage below is followed by questions based on its content. Answer the questions on the basis of what is stated or implied in each passage and in any introductory material that may be provided.

Questions 16-21 are based on the following passage.

The excerpt below is from a memoir written by a Japanese American woman whose mother was born and raised in Japan. The memoir was first published in 1992.

Once, in a cross-cultural training manual, I came across a riddle. In Japan, a young man and woman meet and fall in love. They decide they would like to marry. The young man goes to his mother and describes the situation. "I will visit the girl's family," says the mother. "I will seek their approval." After some time, a meeting between mothers is arranged. The boy's mother goes to the girl's ancestral house. The girl's mother has prepared tea. The women talk about the fine spring weather: will this be a good year for cherry blossoms? The girl's mother serves a plate of fruit. Bananas are sliced and displayed in an exquisite design. Marriage never is mentioned. After the tea, the boy's mother goes home. "I am so sorry," she tells her son. "The other family has declined the match."

In the training manual, the following question was posed. How did the boy's mother know the marriage was unacceptable? That is easy, I thought when I read it. To a Japanese, the answer is obvious. Bananas do not go well with tea.

All of my life, I have been fluent in communicating through discordant fruit.

The Japanese raise their daughters differently than their sons. "*Gambatte!*" they exhort their sons. "Have courage, be like the carp, swim upstream!" "*Kiotsukete,*" they caution their daughters. "Be careful, be modest, keep safe."

My mother was raised in a world such as this, in a house of tradition and myth. And although she has traveled across continents, oceans, and time, although she considers herself a modern woman—a believer in the sunlight of science—it is a world that surrounds her still. Feudal Japan floats around my mother. Like an unwanted pool of ectoplasm, it quivers with supernatural might. It followed her into our American home and governed my girlhood life.

And so, I was shaped. In that feudal code, all females were silent and yielding. Even their possessions were accorded more rights than they. For, if mistreated, belongings were granted an annual holiday when they could spring into life and complain.

And so, I was haunted. If I left my clothes on the floor, or my bicycle in the rain; if I yanked on the comb with roughness; if it splintered and lost its teeth (and I did these things often and deliberately, trying to challenge their spell); then my misdeeds pursued me in dreams.

While other children were learning that in America you get what you ask for, I was being henpecked by inanimate objects. While other children were learning to speak their minds, I was locked in a losing struggle for dominance with my clothing, my toys, and my tools.

The objects meant me no harm; they meant to humble and educate me. "Ownership," they told me "means obligation, caretaking, reciprocity." And although I was a resistant student, in time I was trained. Well maintained, my possessions live long, useful, and mercifully quiet lives of service.

16 The "plate of fruit" (line 12) in the anecdote serves primarily as

(A) a sign that the young woman's mother is a generous host
(B) an example of the family's goodwill
(C) a symbol of affection
(D) a means of communication
(E) an opportunity to display good taste

17 In line 16, "declined" most nearly means

(A) grown less well
(B) refused to approve
(C) sloped sharply away
(D) fallen out of love
(E) been unable to understand

18 Which of the following most nearly expresses what the author means by being "fluent in communicating through discordant fruit" (lines 22-23) ?

(A) She has an aversion to certain foods.
(B) She is able to speak her mind clearly.
(C) She is able to adapt to the values of cultures other than her own.
(D) She understands various indirect forms of expression.
(E) She is sensitive to the feelings of others.

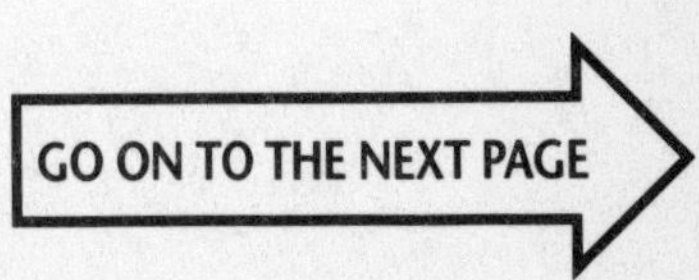

The reading passages in this test are brief excerpts or adaptations of excerpts from published material. The ideas contained in them do not necessarily represent the opinions of the College Board or Educational Testing Service. To make the text suitable for testing purposes, we may in some cases have altered the style, contents, or point of view of the original.

19 The distinction between "*Gambatte*" (line 25) and "*Kiotsukete*" (line 27) is the distinction between

(A) tradition and innovation
(B) passion and feeling
(C) age and youth
(D) intuition and wisdom
(E) perseverance and prudence

20 The carp is mentioned in line 26 as a symbol of

(A) food that the narrator likes
(B) the behavior expected of boys
(C) a traditional view of nature
(D) the link between humans and nature
(E) certain kinds of foolish behavior

21 The author implies that she felt different from other children because

(A) they seldom faced the hardships that she had to face every day
(B) she did not know how to take care of things as well as they did
(C) her mother was always criticizing her
(D) she felt guilty about rejecting the traditions of her parents
(E) she was discouraged from asserting herself

GO ON TO THE NEXT PAGE

Questions 22-31 are based on the following passage.

How "wild" can animals be after several generations in captivity? A nature writer who has traveled to zoos around the world discusses this subject in the excerpt below.

Many zoos in the United States have undergone radical changes in philosophy and design. All possible care is taken to reduce the stress of living in captivity. Cages and grounds are landscaped to make gorillas feel immersed in vegetation, as they would be in a Congo jungle. Zebras gaze across vistas arranged to appear (to zoo visitors, at least) nearly as broad as an African plain.

Yet, strolling past animals in zoo after zoo, I have noticed the signs of hobbled energy that has found no release — large cats pacing in a repetitive pattern, primates rocking for hours in one corner of a cage. These truncated movements are known as cage stereotypes, and usually these movements bring about no obvious physical or emotional effects in the captive animal. Many animal specialists believe they are more troubling to the people who watch than to the animals themselves. Such restlessness is an unpleasant reminder that — despite the careful interior decorating and clever optical illusions — zoo animals are prisoners, being kept in elaborate cells.

The rationale for breeding endangered animals in zoos is nevertheless compelling. Once a species falls below a certain number, it is beset by inbreeding* and other processes that nudge it closer and closer to extinction. If the animal also faces the whole-scale destruction of its habitat, its one hope for survival lies in being transplanted to some haven of safety, usually a cage. In serving as trusts for rare fauna, zoos have committed millions of dollars to caring for animals. Many zoo managers have given great consideration to the psychological health of the animals in their care. Yet the more I learned about animals bred in enclosures, the more I wondered how their sensibilities differed from those of animals raised to roam free.

In the wild, animals exist in a world of which we have little understanding. They may communicate with their kind through "languages" that are indecipherable by humans. A few studies suggest that some species perceive landscapes much differently than people do; for example, they may be keenly attuned to movement on the faces of mountains or across the broad span of grassy plains. Also, their social structures may be complex and integral to their well-being. Some scientists believe they may even develop cultural traditions that are key to the survival of populations.

But when an animal is confined, it lives within a vacuum. If it is accustomed to covering long distances in its searches for food, it grows lazy or bored. It can make no decisions for itself; its intelligence and wild skills atrophy from lack of use. It becomes, in a sense, one of society's charges, completely dependent on humans for nourishment and care.

How might an animal species be changed — subtly, imperceptibly — by spending several generations in a pen? I posed that question to the curator of birds at the San Diego Wild Animal Park, which is a breeding center for the endangered California condor. "I always have to chuckle when someone asks me that," the curator replied. "Evolution has shaped the behavior of the condor for hundreds of years. If you think I can change it in a couple of generations, you're giving me a lot of credit."

Recently the condor was reintroduced into the California desert — only a moment after its capture, in evolutionary terms. Perhaps the curator was right; perhaps the wild nature of the birds would emerge unscathed, although I was not convinced. But what of species that will spend decades or centuries in confinement before they are released?

*Inbreeding, which refers to the mating of offspring of the same parents, often amplifies any genetic weaknesses a species may have.

22 The primary purpose of the passage is to

(A) highlight the improvements in the conditions of American zoos
(B) examine behavioral traits of animals living in zoos
(C) prompt scientists to conduct more research on animal behavior
(D) raise concerns about the confinement of wild animals in zoos
(E) suggest alternative ways of protecting endangered species

23 On the whole, the author's attitude toward captive breeding is one of

(A) sympathy (B) puzzlement
(C) indifference (D) ambivalence
(E) disgust

24 The primary function of the second paragraph (lines 9-21) is to show that

(A) wild animals adapt to their cages by modifying their movements
(B) improvements in zoo design have not had the intended effects
(C) confined animals are not being seriously harmed
(D) zoos are designed with the reactions of spectators in mind
(E) people are overly sensitive to seeing animals in captivity

GO ON TO THE NEXT PAGE

25 One of the major implications of the passage is that

(A) animals bred in captivity are as likely to survive in the wild as are wild animals
(B) zoos do a disservice to animals by trying to entertain zoo visitors
(C) animal extinctions can mainly be attributed to human activity
(D) present methods of protecting animal populations may be flawed
(E) public concerns about the extinction of species have been exploited by the media

26 In the fourth paragraph (lines 37-48), the author's most important point is that animals in the wild

(A) perceive landscapes differently than do animals in captivity
(B) have modes of communicating that are very similar to those of humans
(C) are likely to live longer than animals kept in zoos
(D) depend on the care and support of others of their species
(E) may have highly developed sensibilities about which scientists know little

27 Which of the following best describes the relationship between the fourth paragraph (lines 37-48) and the fifth paragraph (lines 49-56) ?

(A) The fourth paragraph presents a question that is answered in the fifth paragraph.
(B) The fourth paragraph contains an assertion that is evaluated in the fifth paragraph.
(C) The fifth paragraph describes a contrast to the situation presented in the fourth paragraph.
(D) The fifth paragraph discusses the second part of the process described in the fourth paragraph.
(E) The fifth paragraph describes the cause of the situation discussed in the fourth paragraph.

28 In line 54, "charges" most nearly means

(A) costs
(B) responsibilities
(C) demands
(D) accusations
(E) attacks

29 The curator's primary point in lines 62-66 is that

(A) people's ideas about the power of humans to alter animal behavior are presumptuous
(B) scientists should strive to mimic natural selection processes more closely
(C) animals have little trouble adapting their behavior to captive environments
(D) animals have been surviving for years without the intervention of humans
(E) captive breeding is essential to the survival of animals

30 The author's attitude toward the curator's statement in lines 62-66 can best be described as

(A) ironic
(B) objective
(C) hopeless
(D) doubtful
(E) offended

31 It can be inferred from the passage that the author believes that wild animals

(A) should be removed from their natural habitats only in dire circumstances
(B) suffer few long-term consequences from changes in their habitat
(C) are pawns in a political battle over the protection of wildlife habitats
(D) provide an inadequate source of data for the experimental designs of captive breeding habitats
(E) fulfill the expectations of zoo visitors who hope to see animals behave as they would have before they were captured

IF YOU FINISH BEFORE TIME IS CALLED, YOU MAY CHECK YOUR WORK ON THIS SECTION ONLY. DO NOT TURN TO ANY OTHER SECTION IN THE TEST. **STOP**

Section 2

Time—30 Minutes 25 Questions	**In this section solve each problem, using any available space on the page for scratchwork. Then decide which is the best of the choices given and fill in the corresponding oval on the answer sheet.**

Notes:

1. The use of a calculator is permitted. All numbers used are real numbers.
2. Figures that accompany problems in this test are intended to provide information useful in solving the problems. They are drawn as accurately as possible EXCEPT when it is stated in a specific problem that the figure is not drawn to scale. All figures lie in a plane unless otherwise indicated.

Reference Information

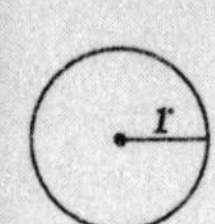

$A = \pi r^2$
$C = 2\pi r$

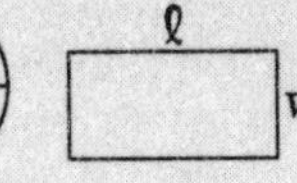

$A = \ell w$

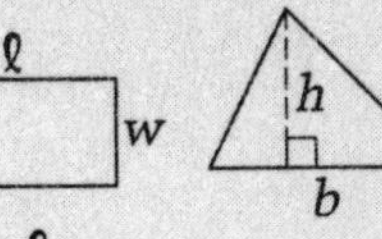

$A = \frac{1}{2}bh$

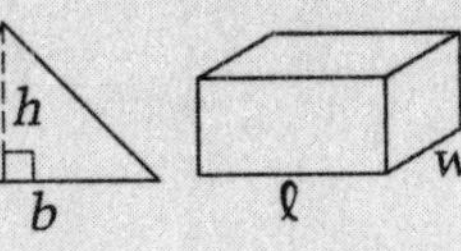

$V = \ell wh$

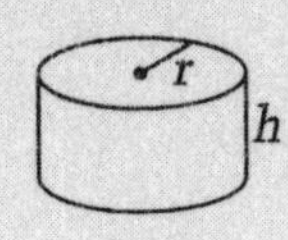

$V = \pi r^2 h$

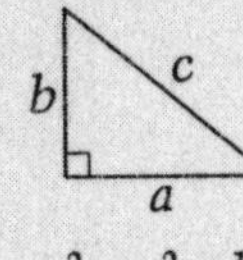

$c^2 = a^2 + b^2$

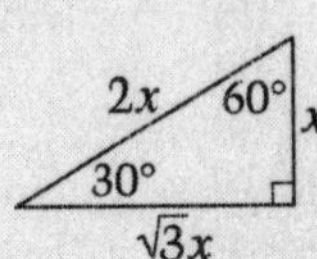

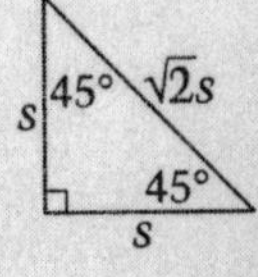

Special Right Triangles

The number of degrees of arc in a circle is 360.
The measure in degrees of a straight angle is 180.
The sum of the measures in degrees of the angles of a triangle is 180.

1 If $\frac{x}{9} = \frac{2}{3}$, then $x =$

(A) $\frac{8}{3}$
(B) 3
(C) 6
(D) 7
(E) $\frac{27}{2}$

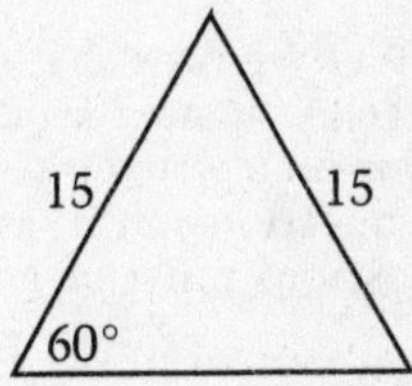

2 What is the perimeter of the triangle above?

(A) 30
(B) 45
(C) 47
(D) 50
(E) 55

GO ON TO THE NEXT PAGE

COMPACT-CAR PRODUCTION IN YEAR X

3 According to the chart above, Company A produced approximately how many more compact cars in year X than Company B did?

(A) 200,000
(B) 250,000
(C) 300,000
(D) 400,000
(E) 500,000

4 A certain state requires that an applicant for a driver's license answer at least 80 percent of the questions on a written test correctly. If the test has 30 questions on it, at least how many of these questions must be answered correctly?

(A) 20
(B) 21
(C) 22
(D) 23
(E) 24

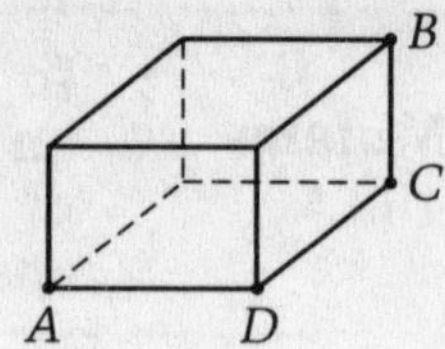

5 In the rectangular solid above, $AD = 6$, $CD = 8$, and $BC = \frac{1}{2}CD$. What is the volume of the solid?

(A) 18
(B) 144
(C) 192
(D) 208
(E) 384

6 For which of the following ordered pairs (s, t) is $s + t > 2$ and $s - t < -3$?

(A) $(3, 2)$

(B) $(2, 3)$

(C) $(1, 8)$

(D) $\left(\frac{1}{2}, \frac{3}{2}\right)$

(E) $(0, 3)$

GO ON TO THE NEXT PAGE

7 If $\frac{x}{y} = -1$, then $x + y =$

(A) 0
(B) 1
(C) x
(D) y
(E) $2x$

8 Yesterday Art earned $10.00 less than Bill, and today Art earned $7.50 more than Bill. Which of the following must be true about Art's total earnings for the two days compared to Bill's?

(A) Art earned $\frac{3}{4}$ of what Bill earned.

(B) Art earned $17.50 more than Bill.

(C) Art earned $2.50 more than Bill.

(D) Art earned $2.50 less than Bill.

(E) Art earned $17.50 less than Bill.

9 If $k^2 + 5 = 22$, then $k^2 - 5 =$

(A) 12
(B) 17
(C) 39
(D) 144
(E) 284

10 If a line ℓ is perpendicular to a segment AB at point E and $AE = EB$, how many points on line ℓ are the same distance from point A as from point B ?

(A) None
(B) One
(C) Two
(D) Three
(E) All points

11 If r, s, and t are integers greater than 1, where $rs = 15$ and $st = 33$, which of the following must be true?

(A) $t > r > s$
(B) $s > t > r$
(C) $s > r > t$
(D) $r > t > s$
(E) $r > s > t$

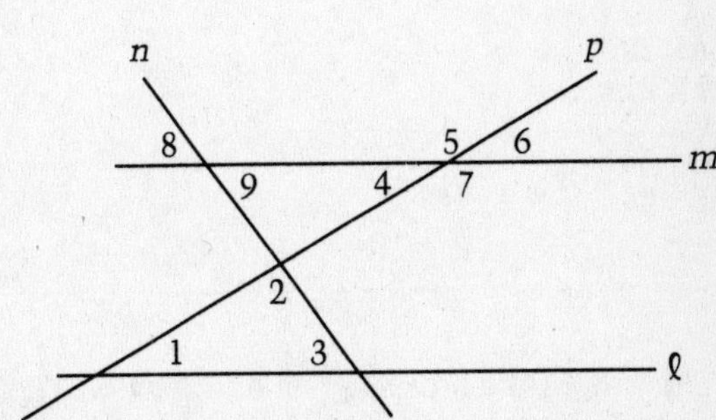

12 In the figure above, line ℓ is parallel to line m. Which of the following pairs of angles have equal measures?

I. 1 and 4
II. 3 and 8
III. 5 and 7

(A) I only
(B) I and II only
(C) I and III only
(D) II and III only
(E) I, II, and III

GO ON TO THE NEXT PAGE

13 A total of 60 advertisements were sold for a school yearbook. If 20 percent of the first 20 sold were in color, 40 percent of the next 30 sold were in color, and 80 percent of the last 10 sold were in color, what percent of the 60 advertisements were in color?

(A) 30%

(B) $33\frac{1}{3}\%$

(C) 40%

(D) $46\frac{2}{3}\%$

(E) 60%

---

14 Let $\left\langle \begin{smallmatrix} & b & \\ a & & c \\ & d & \end{smallmatrix} \right\rangle$ be defined for all numbers a, b, c, and d by $\left\langle \begin{smallmatrix} & b & \\ a & & c \\ & d & \end{smallmatrix} \right\rangle = ac - bd$. If

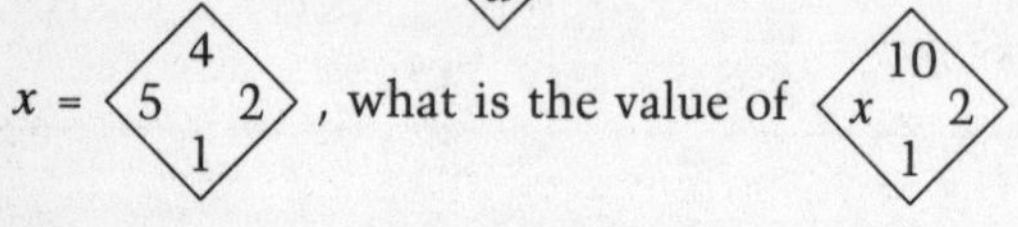

$x = \left\langle \begin{smallmatrix} & 4 & \\ 5 & & 2 \\ & 1 & \end{smallmatrix} \right\rangle$, what is the value of $\left\langle \begin{smallmatrix} & 10 & \\ x & & 2 \\ & 1 & \end{smallmatrix} \right\rangle$?

(A) 1
(B) 2
(C) 18
(D) 38
(E) 178

---

15 The sum of the integers t and w is 495. The units digit of t is 0. If t is divided by 10, the result is equal to w. What is the value of t ?

(A) 40
(B) 45
(C) 245
(D) 250
(E) 450

---

16 A certain college offers students two monthly options for local telephone service.

Option A: Unlimited number of local calls for \$20.00 per month

Option B: Basic charge of \$15.00 per month plus \$0.10 charge for each local call

What is the least number of local calls in a month for which option A is <u>less expensive</u> than option B ?

(A) 5
(B) 15
(C) 49
(D) 50
(E) 51

---

17 Points X and Y are the endpoints of a line segment, and the length of the segment is less than 25. There are five other points on the line segment, R, S, T, U, and V, which are located at distances of 1, 3, 6, 10, and 13, respectively, from point X. Which of the points could be the midpoint of XY ?

(A) R
(B) S
(C) T
(D) U
(E) V

GO ON TO THE NEXT PAGE

18 The positive difference between k and $\frac{1}{8}$ is the same as the positive difference between $\frac{1}{2}$ and $\frac{1}{3}$. Which of the following could be the value of k ?

(A) $\frac{1}{7}$

(B) $\frac{1}{6}$

(C) $\frac{7}{24}$

(D) $\frac{23}{24}$

(E) $\frac{4}{3}$

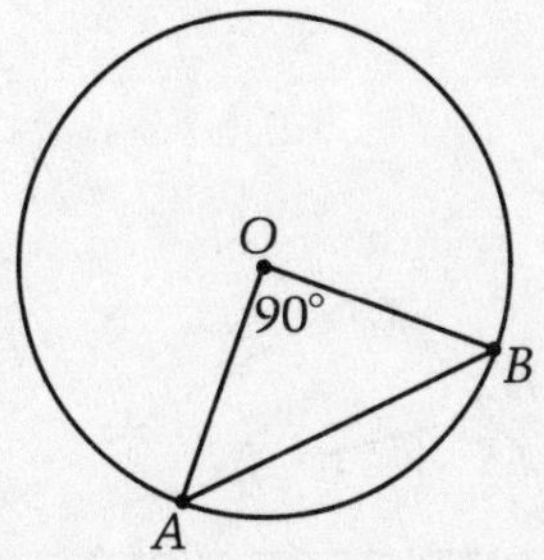

19 In the figure above, O is the center of the circle of radius 10. What is the area of $\triangle AOB$?

(A) 25

(B) 50

(C) $\frac{25}{2}\pi$

(D) 20π

(E) 25π

20 Five students are to be photographed for the school paper. They are to be arranged standing side by side in a single row with the tallest student in the center and the two shortest students on the ends. If no two students are the same height, how many different arrangements are possible?

(A) Two
(B) Four
(C) Five
(D) Six
(E) Ten

21 In a plane, two regions, S and T, are called "unlinked" if

(1) S has no points in common with T, and

(2) any line segment that can be drawn with both endpoints in S has no points in common with any line segment that can be drawn with both endpoints in T.

Which of the following shows a pair of regions that are unlinked?

(A)

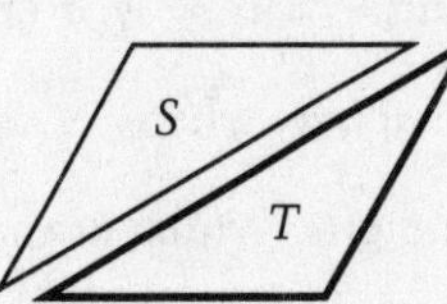

(B)

(C)

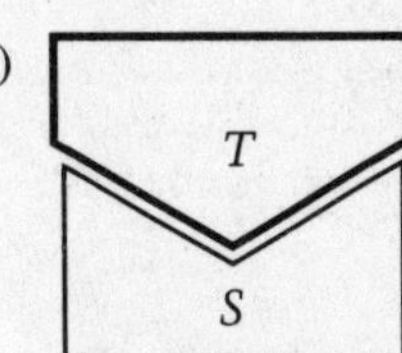

(D)

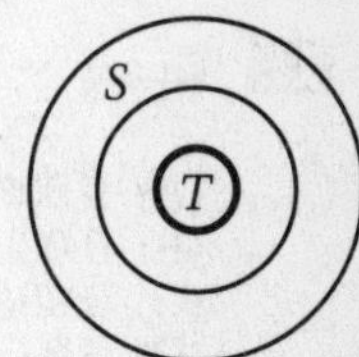

(E)

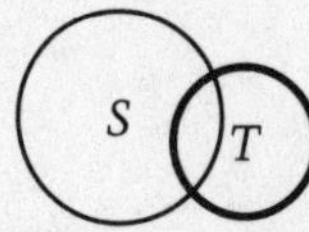

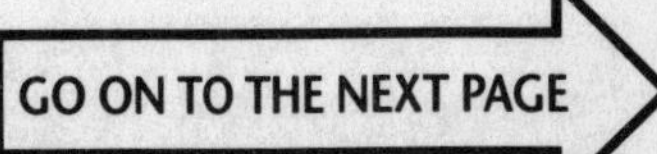
GO ON TO THE NEXT PAGE

22 A ball is dropped from 192 inches above level ground and after the third bounce it rises to a height of 24 inches. If the height to which the ball rises after each bounce is always the same fraction of the height reached on its previous bounce, what is this fraction?

(A) $\frac{1}{8}$

(B) $\frac{1}{4}$

(C) $\frac{1}{3}$

(D) $\frac{1}{2}$

(E) $\frac{2}{3}$

$$\frac{1}{x} = 0.0N$$

$$\frac{1}{y} = 0.00P$$

23 The fractions $\frac{1}{x}$ and $\frac{1}{y}$ can be written as decimals as shown above, where N and P represent different digits. Which of the following is equal to $\frac{1}{xy}$ if S equals N times P and S is a digit?

(A) $0.0000S$
(B) $0.000S$
(C) $0.00S$
(D) $0.0S$
(E) $0.S$

CENTRAL HIGH'S
FIELD HOCKEY RESULTS

Games Played in September

	Goals		Goals	Margin of Victory
Central	7	Northern	0	
Central	3	Westfield	1	
Central	3	Easton	2	
Central	5	Southern	1	
Central	2	Bayville	1	

24 Central High's field hockey team was undefeated in September, as shown in the table above. A team's margin of victory for a single game is defined as the number of goals it made minus the number of goals made by the losing team. What is the median of the missing values in the column labeled Margin of Victory?

(A) 1
(B) 2
(C) 3
(D) 4
(E) 5

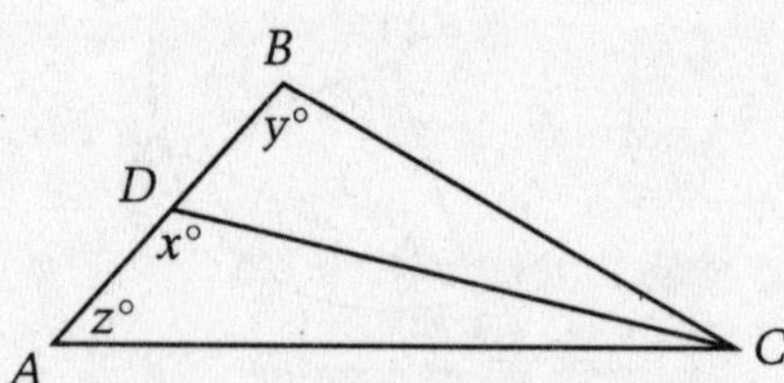

Note: Figure not drawn to scale.

25 In $\triangle ABC$ above, $AB = BC$ and CD bisects $\angle C$. If $y = \frac{1}{3}x$, then $z =$

(A) 40
(B) 60
(C) 64
(D) 72
(E) 80

IF YOU FINISH BEFORE TIME IS CALLED, YOU MAY CHECK YOUR WORK ON THIS SECTION ONLY. DO NOT TURN TO ANY OTHER SECTION IN THE TEST. **STOP**

Section 3 3 3 3 3 3 3

Time—30 Minutes
35 Questions

For each question in this section, select the best answer from among the choices given and fill in the corresponding oval on the answer sheet.

Each sentence below has one or two blanks, each blank indicating that something has been omitted. Beneath the sentence are five words or sets of words labeled A through E. Choose the word or set of words that, when inserted in the sentence, best fits the meaning of the sentence as a whole.

Example:

Medieval kingdoms did not become constitutional republics overnight; on the contrary, the change was ----.

(A) unpopular
(B) unexpected
(C) advantageous
(D) sufficient
(E) gradual

Ⓐ Ⓑ Ⓒ Ⓓ ●

1 For centuries, the coastline of Uruguay was regarded by European mariners as a ---- place, one seemingly devoid of inhabitants.

(A) conceivable (B) desolate (C) fallacious (D) prepossessing (E) discourteous

2 Chocolate connects us to the past, for despite modern ---- in food-processing technology, the steps necessary for transforming cocoa beans into chocolate have been ---- for nearly two centuries.

(A) developments . . varied
(B) setbacks . . constant
(C) failures . . inconsistent
(D) progress . . unstable
(E) advances . . unchanged

3 The landscape was truly ----, so arid that even the hardiest plants could not survive.

(A) lurid (B) parched (C) drubbed (D) verdant (E) variegated

4 Born ----, children will follow their natural inclination to explore their surroundings with a ---- that belies the random appearance of their play.

(A) innocent . . deviousness
(B) serious . . merriment
(C) curious . . purposefulness
(D) eager . . moderation
(E) aware . . casualness

5 Although English philosopher Anne Conway was ---- by her seventeenth-century contemporaries, she has through oversight been nearly ---- in recent times.

(A) revered . . forgotten
(B) censured . . venerated
(C) abandoned . . ignored
(D) imitated . . emulated
(E) pardoned . . absolved

6 While the ---- explorers faced risks courageously, they were not ----, choosing instead to avoid needless dangers.

(A) flagrant . . punctual
(B) intrepid . . foolhardy
(C) genial . . clandestine
(D) resolute . . amicable
(E) culpable . . irresponsible

7 Maxine Hong Kingston presents universal themes in the context of Chinese American culture; this has helped her achieve a literary ---- that is ----, yet speaks to the full range of human experience.

(A) success . . indistinct
(B) voice . . unique
(C) convention . . encompassing
(D) style . . comprehensive
(E) prominence . . general

8 The grief and sadness of parting and the sorrows that seem eternal are ---- by time, but they leave their scars.

(A) revived (B) magnified (C) nurtured (D) mitigated (E) concocted

9 The traditional process of producing an oil painting requires so many steps that it seems ---- to artists who prefer to work quickly.

(A) provocative (B) consummate (C) interminable (D) facile (E) prolific

10 Photography as an art form often seeks the ---- in its subjects, those qualities that cannot be expressed in words.

(A) ineffable (B) mundane (C) onerous (D) incisive (E) auspicious

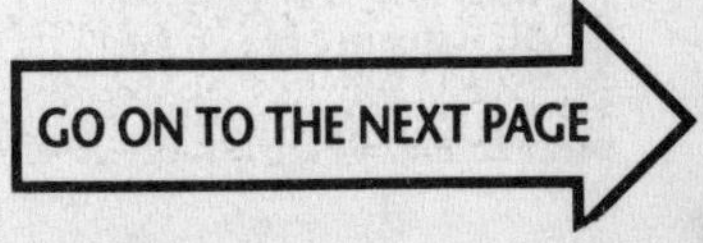

Each question below consists of a related pair of words or phrases, followed by five pairs of words or phrases labeled A through E. Select the pair that best expresses a relationship similar to that expressed in the original pair.

Example:

CRUMB : BREAD ::
(A) ounce : unit
(B) splinter : wood
(C) water : bucket
(D) twine : rope
(E) cream : butter 

11 STORY : BUILDING ::
(A) crust : sandwich
(B) shingle : roof
(C) data : file
(D) layer : cake
(E) root : plant

12 SPROUT : SEED ::
(A) pollinate : bee
(B) cure : disease
(C) stimulate : growth
(D) hatch : egg
(E) filter : impurity

13 DOORMAT : SHOES ::
(A) place mat : table
(B) napkin : mouth
(C) fork : plate
(D) lace : boot
(E) curtain : window

14 ATLAS : MAPS ::
(A) manual : instructions
(B) directory : pages
(C) almanac : years
(D) dictionary : writers
(E) tome : books

15 DODO : BIRD ::
(A) horse : mule
(B) dinosaur : reptile
(C) venom : snake
(D) rooster : hen
(E) dog : puppy

16 PROCRASTINATE : ACTION ::
(A) reverse : direction
(B) postpone : event
(C) assign : choice
(D) endure : patience
(E) embezzle : fraud

17 LUMMOX : CLUMSY ::
(A) boon : beneficial
(B) egotist : conceited
(C) rascal : predictable
(D) maxim : hackneyed
(E) toady : important

18 SIREN : WARNING ::
(A) shovel : dirt
(B) alarm : clock
(C) barrier : intrusion
(D) signal : reception
(E) light : illumination

19 PREAMBLE : STATUTE ::
(A) interlude : musical
(B) conclusion : argument
(C) foreword : novel
(D) epilogue : address
(E) premiere : performance

20 HEDONISTIC : PLEASURE ::
(A) promising : achievement
(B) vindictive : vengeance
(C) precocious : youth
(D) concerned : empathy
(E) cruel : mercy

21 TOPIC : DISCOURSE ::
(A) title : play
(B) subject : digression
(C) guideline : policy
(D) theme : essay
(E) footnote : text

22 CONTEMPORARIES : AGE ::
(A) housemates : residence
(B) faculty : scholarship
(C) idols : worship
(D) kin : reunion
(E) authors : anthology

23 QUERULOUS : COMPLAIN ::
(A) silent : talk
(B) humorous : laugh
(C) dangerous : risk
(D) deceitful : cheat
(E) gracious : accept

GO ON TO THE NEXT PAGE

The passage below is followed by questions based on its content. Answer the questions on the basis of what is stated or implied in the passage and in any introductory material that may be provided.

Questions 24-35 are based on the following passage.

The excerpt below is from the introduction to a catalog of a recent museum exhibit of fake artworks and other kinds of forgeries.

Why, if what we value from a work of art is the aesthetic pleasure to be gained from it, is a successfully deceptive fake inferior to the real thing? Conscious of this problem, some have attempted to deny the importance of authorship. The great collector and scholar Richard Payne Knight, after discovering that an antique cameo* of the Roman goddess Flora might be a modern forgery, told the dealer who had sold it to him that it did not matter whether it was old or new, since its beauty was unaffected by its age. Similarly, the purchasers of a supposedly Renaissance bust of Lucrezia Donati expressed their pleasure, on discovering that it was a fake, that an artist of such talent was still alive. Indeed, in 1869 the Victoria and Albert Museum acquired the bust as an example of a forgery of exceptional quality, and at a price comparable to that paid for genuine Renaissance pieces. But it would be unwise to expect museums, dealers, or private collectors to take that attitude today.

What most of us suspect—that aesthetic appreciation is not the only engine of the art market—becomes evident when a well-known work of art is revealed as a fake. The work may not change in appearance, but it loses its value as a relic. It no longer provides a direct link to an artist of genius; it ceases to promise either spiritual refreshment to its viewer or status to its owner. Even though the work in question remains physically unaltered, our response to it is profoundly changed. In 1937 the art historian Abraham Bredius wrote of a painting entitled *Christ at Emmaus*, which he believed to be the work of the great seventeenth-century Dutch artist Vermeer, but which was in fact a forgery by a Dutch painter named Hans van Meegeren:

> It is a wonderful moment in the life of a lover of art when he finds himself suddenly confronted with a hitherto unknown painting by a great master, . . . on the original canvas, and without any restoration, just as it left the painter's studio! And what a picture! . . . What we have here is a —I am inclined to say—*the* masterpiece of Jan Vermeer of Delft.

After the exposure of van Meegeren, however, it became surprisingly apparent that his forgeries were grotesquely ugly and unpleasant paintings, altogether dissimilar to Vermeer's.

Van Meegeren's success seemed incredible to the experts. As one reviewer noted, "[h]ad van Meegeren been a better artist . . . he might just have succeeded in producing 'Vermeers' which would have fooled more people longer than the ones he created." Yet van Meegeren was exposed not because he ceased to fool people, but because he was forced to prove himself a forger in order to clear himself of the more serious charge of having sold a national treasure illegally.

What is extraordinary about van Meegeren's success is that the pattern revealed by his case is commonplace. The reaction of Bredius and his numerous distinguished colleagues, far from being exceptionally foolish, was normal; fakes are often greeted with rapture by well-informed experts and by the general public alike. It is generally true that forgers are known to us only because they have revealed themselves, overcoming considerable public and scholarly skepticism to prove the works in question are theirs, only to find that what was so admired as the work of another is now seen as trite and even maladroit.

It is clear that both private and public collections must contain many works by fakers more talented and fortunate than van Meegeren. And they will continue to do so. Some will be exposed by advances in scientific techniques; but many objects cannot be scientifically dated, and even where analysis is appropriate, its conclusions must be based on a control group of "genuine" objects that may itself be contaminated.

This is the main complaint against fakes. It is not that they cheat their purchasers of money, reprehensible though that is, but that they loosen our hold on reality, deform and falsify our understanding of the past. What makes them dangerous, however, also makes them valuable. The feelings of anger and shame they arouse among those who have been deceived are understandable, but the consequent tendency to dispose of or destroy fakes, once identified, is misguided. Even if the errors of the past only provided lessons for the future, they would be worthy of retention and study. But forgeries do more than that. As keys to understanding the changing nature of our vision of the past, as motors for the development of scholarly and scientific techniques of analysis, as subverters of aesthetic certainties, they deserve our closer attention. And as the most entertaining of monuments to the wayward talents of generations of gifted rogues, they certainly claim our reluctant admiration.

*A small medallion with a profiled head carved in relief

GO ON TO THE NEXT PAGE

24 The example of the antique cameo (line 7) is used to demonstrate that

(A) some collectors like to purchase forged pieces
(B) some collectors pay exorbitant prices for beautiful pieces
(C) some collectors prize beauty even more than authenticity
(D) most collectors refuse to buy from unscrupulous dealers
(E) most collectors correctly recognize forgeries

25 The first paragraph of the passage discusses conflict between

(A) artists and forgers
(B) collectors and museums
(C) an art collector and an art dealer
(D) perceived value and authenticity in artworks
(E) sellers of forgeries and the dealers who buy them

26 In line 25, "relic" most nearly means

(A) ancient custom
(B) fragile carcass
(C) venerated object
(D) remnant after decay
(E) souvenir of a famous place

27 In lines 24-25, the reference to an exposed forgery's value ("The work . . . a relic") suggests that the forgery

(A) is a financial loss to an investor
(B) is no less esteemed by some collectors than a contemporary work
(C) ceases to be seen as a symbol of the past
(D) should be prized for its historical significance
(E) provides less pleasure when its monetary value decreases

28 The passage implies that a viewer of a work of art will receive "spiritual refreshment" (line 27) only if the

(A) appearance of the work is unchanged
(B) experts have praised the beauty of the piece
(C) viewer is familiar with the artist
(D) work has been seen by only a few collectors
(E) work is considered genuine

29 The author quotes Bredius' opinion (lines 36-43) in order to show that

(A) unknown paintings by many famous artists are waiting to be found
(B) an artwork's history affects how people judge it
(C) the totality of a work is what makes it valuable
(D) no one has found the actual *Christ at Emmaus*
(E) any artist's work can be easily forged

30 According to paragraph 4 (lines 58-70), some forgers reveal themselves in order to

(A) avoid prosecution for forgery
(B) confound the art critics
(C) prove that forgery is commonplace
(D) rectify the confusion they have caused
(E) take credit for certain highly regarded works

31 The author's reference to "private and public collections" (line 71) suggests that

(A) museums cannot prevent forgeries from entering their collections
(B) museums sometimes seek out forgeries for their collections
(C) museums that knowingly purchase forgeries are foolish
(D) many valuable paintings have yet to be found in museum storerooms
(E) many valuable paintings have been replaced with forgeries in major museums

GO ON TO THE NEXT PAGE

32 The purpose of the "control group" (line 78) is to

(A) select forgeries to be tested by experts
(B) manage increases in market prices
(C) maintain a collection of forgeries in one location
(D) provide examples of genuine artworks
(E) test whether forgeries can deceive experts

33 Which of the following best exemplifies the "main complaint" mentioned in line 80 ?

(A) A counterfeit $1,000 bill used to pay a debt
(B) A crafty disguise used in a crime
(C) A false-bottomed trunk used to hide secret documents
(D) A fabricated letter from a past President
(E) A pseudonym used by an author

34 The author gives all of the following as reasons for preserving forgeries EXCEPT their ability to

(A) amuse us with the forger's cleverness
(B) challenge our convictions
(C) temper the rising price of original art
(D) serve as comparisons to genuine artworks
(E) shed light on how we view history

35 According to the final paragraph, forgeries are "valuable" (line 85) because they are

(A) artistically daring
(B) increasingly attempted
(C) rarely available
(D) relatively popular
(E) unusually instructive

IF YOU FINISH BEFORE TIME IS CALLED, YOU MAY CHECK YOUR WORK ON THIS SECTION ONLY. DO NOT TURN TO ANY OTHER SECTION IN THE TEST.

Section 4 4 4 4 4

Time—30 Minutes
25 Questions

This section contains two types of questions. You have 30 minutes to complete both types. You may use any available space for scratchwork.

Notes:

1. The use of a calculator is permitted. All numbers used are real numbers.
2. Figures that accompany problems in this test are intended to provide information useful in solving the problems. They are drawn as accurately as possible EXCEPT when it is stated in a specific problem that the figure is not drawn to scale. All figures lie in a plane unless otherwise indicated.

Reference Information

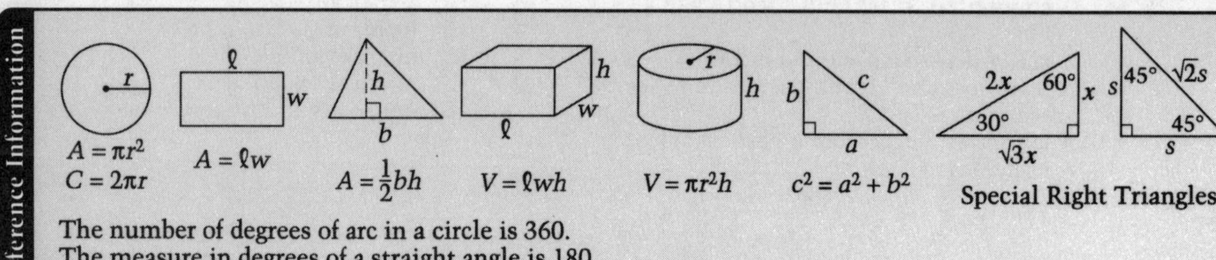

The number of degrees of arc in a circle is 360.
The measure in degrees of a straight angle is 180.
The sum of the measures in degrees of the angles of a triangle is 180.

Directions for Quantitative Comparison Questions

Questions 1-15 each consist of two quantities in boxes, one in Column A and one in Column B. You are to compare the two quantities and on the answer sheet fill in oval

A if the quantity in Column A is greater;
B if the quantity in Column B is greater;
C if the two quantities are equal;
D if the relationship cannot be determined from the information given.

AN E RESPONSE WILL NOT BE SCORED.

Notes:

1. In some questions, information is given about one or both of the quantities to be compared. In such cases, the given information is centered above the two columns and is not boxed.
2. In a given question, a symbol that appears in both columns represents the same thing in Column A as it does in Column B.
3. Letters such as x, n, and k stand for real numbers.

EXAMPLES

	Column A	Column B	Answers
E1	5^2	20	● Ⓑ Ⓒ Ⓓ Ⓔ
	150° x°		
E2	x	30	Ⓐ Ⓑ ● Ⓓ Ⓔ
	r and s are integers.		
E3	$r + 1$	$s - 1$	Ⓐ Ⓑ Ⓒ ● Ⓔ

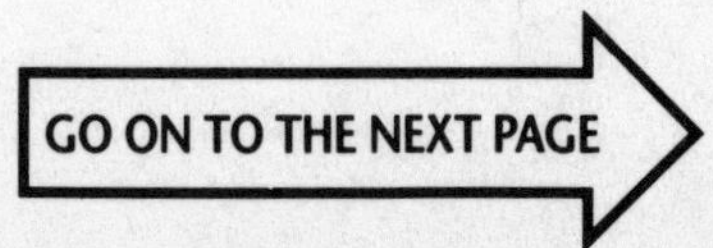

SUMMARY DIRECTIONS FOR COMPARISON QUESTIONS

Answer: A if the quantity in Column A is greater;
B if the quantity in Column B is greater;
C if the two quantities are equal;
D if the relationship cannot be determined from the information given.

	Column A	Column B
1	The value of x when $3x + 6 = 15$	The value of y when $3(y + 2) = 15$

One package of muffin mix makes 8 large muffins or 12 small muffins.

	Column A	Column B
2	The maximum number of small muffins that can be made with 3 packages of mix	The maximum number of large muffins that can be made with 4 packages of mix

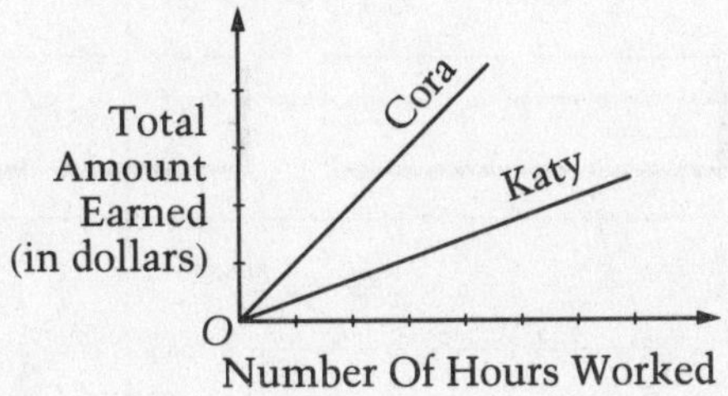

	Column A	Column B
3	The amount earned per hour by Cora	The amount earned per hour by Katy

$a + b = 0$

	Column A	Column B
4	$a \cdot a \cdot a$	$b \cdot b \cdot b$

	Column A	Column B
5	The length of a side of a square whose perimeter is 12	The length of one side of a rectangle whose perimeter is 12

$$\frac{42 \times k}{21} = 0$$

	Column A	Column B
6	$\frac{42 \times k}{7}$	6

Twice n equals 4 more than n.

	Column A	Column B
7	n	4

The 15th day of a certain 30-day month falls on a Wednesday.

	Column A	Column B
8	The number of Thursdays in that month before the 15th	The number of Thursdays in that month after the 15th

GO ON TO THE NEXT PAGE

SUMMARY DIRECTIONS FOR COMPARISON QUESTIONS

Answer: A if the quantity in Column A is greater;
B if the quantity in Column B is greater;
C if the two quantities are equal;
D if the relationship cannot be determined from the information given.

	Column A	Column B

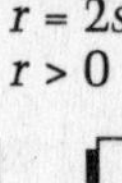

$r = 2s$
$r > 0$

	Column A	Column B
9	60% of r	30% of s
10	The total surface area of a box with dimensions 3 inches by 3 inches by 6 inches	The sum of the total surface areas of two cubes, each with dimensions 3 inches by 3 inches by 3 inches

$a > 0$

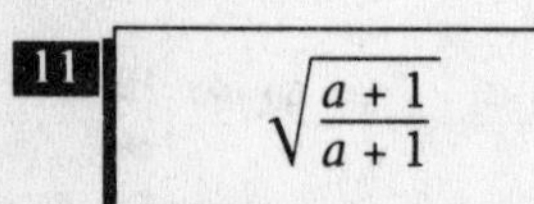

	Column A	Column B
11	$\sqrt{\frac{a+1}{a+1}}$	$\sqrt{\frac{a}{a}} + \sqrt{\frac{1}{1}}$

$S = \{-3, -2, 2, 3\}$

The members of a set T are the squares of numbers in set S.

	Column A	Column B
12	The number of members of S	The number of members of T

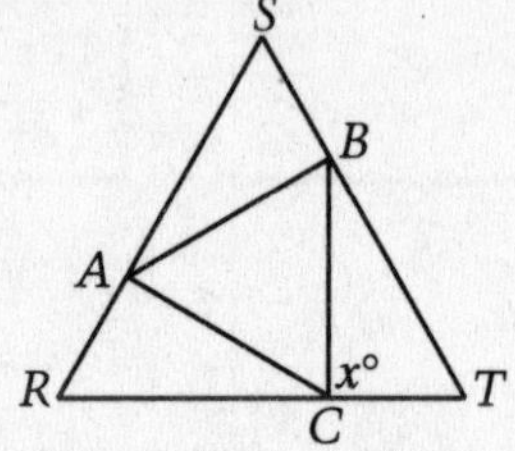

Note: Figure not drawn to scale.

Triangles ABC and RST are each equilateral.

	Column A	Column B
13	x	90

$n + p + v = 50$
$n + p - v = 20$

	Column A	Column B
14	v	15

In $\triangle ABC$, $AB = 3$, $BC = 4$, and $AC = 6$.

	Column A	Column B
15	The length of the altitude to base AB	The length of the altitude to base AC

GO ON TO THE NEXT PAGE

Directions for Student-Produced Response Questions

Each of the remaining 10 questions requires you to solve the problem and enter your answer by marking the ovals in the special grid, as shown in the examples below.

Answer: $\frac{7}{12}$ or 7/12

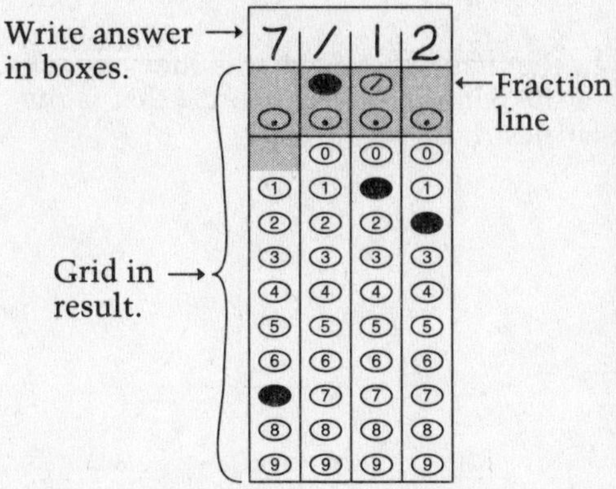

Answer: 2.5

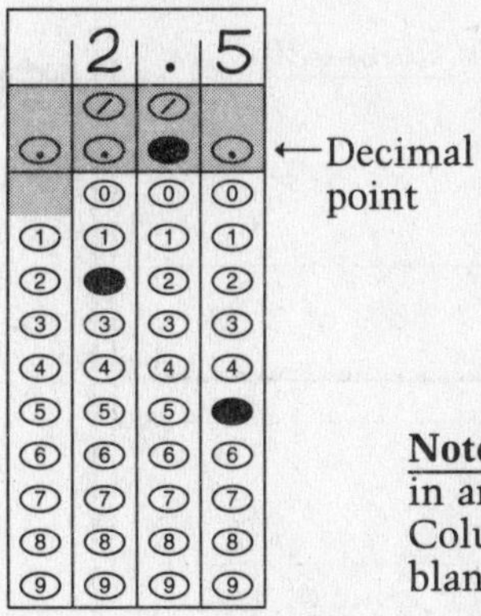

Answer: 201
Either position is correct.

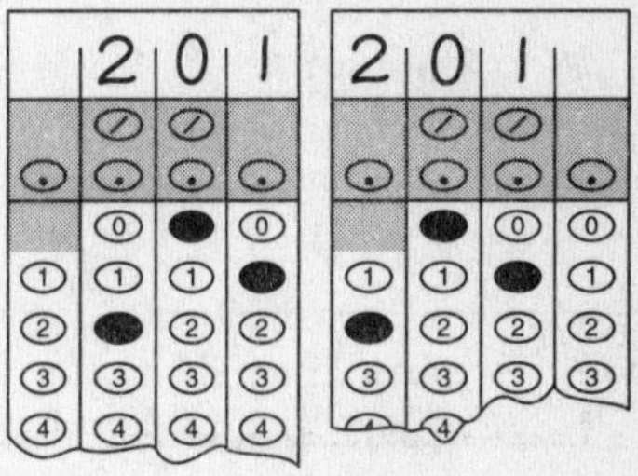

Write answer in boxes. → 7 / 1 2 ← Fraction line

Grid in result.

2 . 5 ← Decimal point

2 0 1 | 2 0 1

Note: You may start your answers in any column, space permitting. Columns not needed should be left blank.

- Mark no more than one oval in any column.
- Because the answer sheet will be machine-scored, **you will receive credit only if the ovals are filled in correctly.**
- Although not required, it is suggested that you write your answer in the boxes at the top of the columns to help you fill in the ovals accurately.
- Some problems may have more than one correct answer. In such cases, grid only one answer.
- No question has a negative answer.
- **Mixed numbers** such as $2\frac{1}{2}$ must be gridded as 2.5 or 5/2. (If 2 1 / 2 is gridded, it will be interpreted as $\frac{21}{2}$, not $2\frac{1}{2}$.)

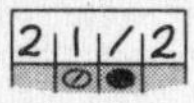

- **Decimal Accuracy:** If you obtain a decimal answer, **enter the most accurate value the grid will accommodate.** For example, if you obtain an answer such as 0.6666 . . . , you should record the result as .666 or .667. **Less accurate values such as .66 or .67 are not acceptable.**

Acceptable ways to grid $\frac{2}{3}$ = .6666 . . .

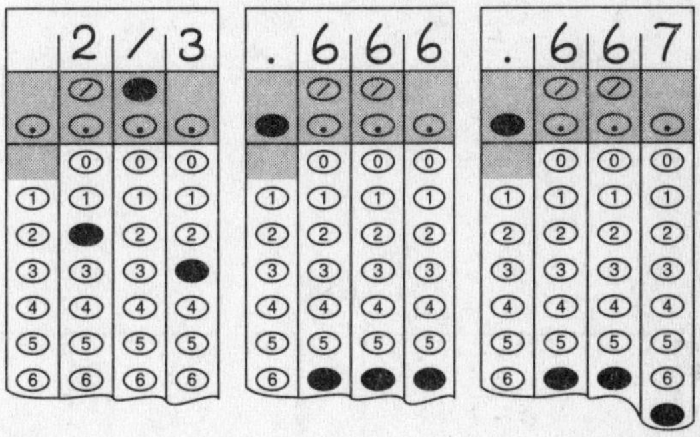

2 / 3 | . 6 6 6 | . 6 6 7

16 Four lines intersect in one point, forming 8 equal angles that are nonoverlapping. What is the measure, in degrees, of one of these angles?

17 The ratio of 1.5 to 32 is the same as the ratio of 0.15 to x. What is the value of x ?

GO ON TO THE NEXT PAGE

$$8 < x < 12$$
$$12 < y < 15$$

18 If x and y are <u>integers</u> that satisfy the conditions above, what is one possible value of xy ?

19 If $(3x^2 + 4x + 5)(3x + 6) = ax^3 + bx^2 + cx + d$ for all values of x, what is the value of c ?

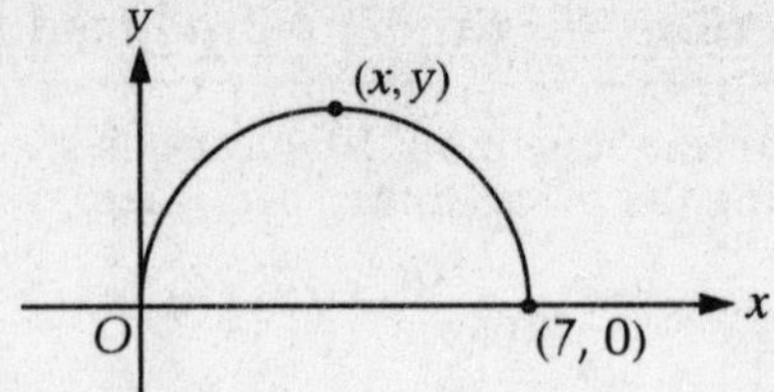

20 In the figure above, what is the y-coordinate of the point on the semicircle that is the farthest from the x-axis?

21 A plain white cube is marked with an "X" on exactly two adjacent faces as shown above. If the cube is tossed on a flat surface and the cube lands so that an "X" appears on the top face, what is the probability that the bottom face does not have an "X" on it?

GO ON TO THE NEXT PAGE

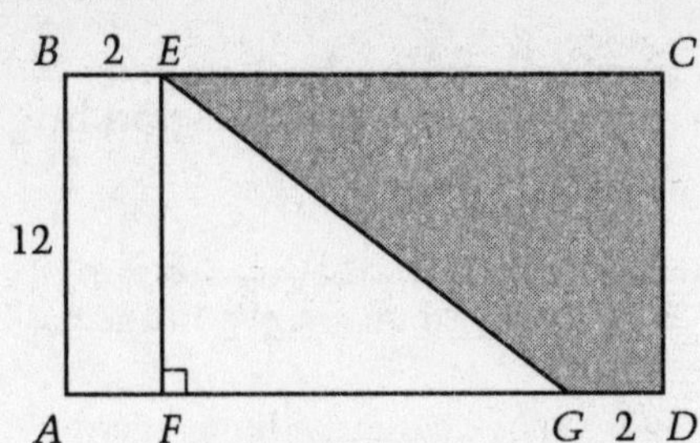

Note: Figure not drawn to scale.

22 If the area of the shaded region in rectangle $ABCD$ above is 90, what is the area of $\triangle EFG$?

$$(T \times 3^3) + (U \times 3^2) + (V \times 3) + W = 50$$

23 Each letter in the equation above represents a digit that is less than or equal to 2. What four-digit number does $TUVW$ represent?

24 A teacher is to be assigned to teach 5 different courses in 5 different class periods on Mondays. If exactly one course meets each period, how many different assignments of courses to these class periods are possible for Mondays?

25 If the average (arithmetic mean) of three different positive integers is 70, what is the greatest possible value of one of the integers?

IF YOU FINISH BEFORE TIME IS CALLED, YOU MAY CHECK YOUR WORK ON THIS SECTION ONLY. DO NOT TURN TO ANY OTHER SECTION IN THE TEST. **STOP**

Section 6 6 6 6

Time — 15 Minutes
12 Questions

For each question in this section, select the best answer from among the choices given and fill in the corresponding oval on the answer sheet.

The two passages below are followed by questions based on their content and on the relationship between the two passages. Answer the questions on the basis of what is stated or implied in the passages and in any introductory material that may be provided.

Questions 1-12 are based on the following passages.

The following adaptations from recent books discuss aspects of television news reportage. Both passages refer to English author George Orwell (1903-1950), whose 1949 novel entitled 1984 *warned against a totalitarian government that controlled all media and thus all "news" that was reported.*

Passage 1

Relaying information and images instantly, television newscasts have allowed viewers to form their own opinions about various political events and political leaders. In many instances, television newscasts have even fostered active dissent from established governmental policies. It is no coincidence that, in the 1960's, the civil rights movement took hold in the United States with the advent of television, which was able to convey both factual information and such visceral elements as outrage and determination. Only when all of America could see, on the nightly newscasts, the civil disobedience occurring in places like Selma and Montgomery did the issue of civil rights become a national concern rather than a series of isolated local events. By relaying reports from cities involved to an entire nation of watchers, television showed viewers the scope of the discontent and informed the disenfranchised that they were not alone.

The ability of television news to foster dissent has also been affected by increasingly widespread access to video cameras, so that the news presented on television now comes from the bottom up as well as from the top down. Across the world, dissidents have used video equipment to gather visual evidence of human rights abuses. Uncensored images and information have then been transmitted across otherwise closed borders by television newscasts.

One professor of popular culture, Jack Nachbar, views the personal video camera as a "truth-telling device that can cut through lies." That claim presumes, though, that the television viewer can believe what he or she sees. But the motivation of the photographer must always be taken into account, and the videotape that appears on television can, like still photography, be staged and even faked. When and if propagandists for some government utilize computer-generated effects, viewers will have more trouble believing what they see. However, even if seeing is not automatically believing, at least seeing is seeing — and in some repressive regimes, seeing is the fastest road to freedom.

"George Orwell was wrong," writes television newscaster Ted Koppel. Koppel's reasoning is persuasive: "The media, which Orwell predicted would become the instrument of totalitarian control, [have] become, instead, its nemesis."

Passage 2

"Now . . . this" is a phrase commonly used on television newscasts to indicate that what one has just heard or seen has no relevance to what one is about to hear or see, or possibly to anything one is ever likely to hear or see. The phrase acknowledges that the world as mapped by television news has no order or meaning and is not to be taken seriously. No earthquake is so devastating, no political blunder so costly, that it cannot be erased from our minds by a newscaster saying, "Now . . . this." Interrupted by commercials, presented by newscasters with celebrity status, and advertised like any other product, television newscasts transmit news without context, without consequences, without values, and therefore without essential seriousness; in short, news as pure entertainment. The resulting trivialization of information leaves television viewers well entertained, but not well informed or well prepared to respond to events.

The species of information created by television is, in fact, "disinformation." Disinformation does not mean false information, but misleading information — misplaced, irrelevant, fragmented, or superficial information — that creates the illusion of knowing something, but that actually leads one away from any true understanding. In the United States, television news does not deliberately aim to deprive viewers of a coherent understanding of their world. But when news is packaged as entertainment, no such understanding is possible. The problem is not that television viewers lack authentic information, but that they are losing their sense of what a complete body of information should include.

People are by now so thoroughly adjusted to the world of television news — a world of fragments,

GO ON TO THE NEXT PAGE

where events stand alone, stripped of any connection to the past, future, or other events—that all principles of coherence have vanished. And so has the notion of holding leaders accountable for contradictions in their policies. What possible interest could there be in comparing what the President says now and what the President said in the past? Such a comparison would merely rehash old news and could hardly be interesting or entertaining.

For all his perspicacity, George Orwell did not predict this situation; it is not "Orwellian." The government does not control the newscasts. Lies have not been defined as truth, nor truth as lies. All that has happened is that the public has adjusted to incoherence and has been entertained into indifference. The current situation fits the predictions of Aldous Huxley,* rather than those of Orwell: Huxley realized that the government need not conceal anything from a public that has become insensible to contradiction, that has lost any perspective from which to scrutinize government critically, and that has been rendered passive by technological diversions.

*English novelist and essayist (1894-1963)

1 Both passages are primarily concerned with ways in which

(A) television newscasts deliberately distort information
(B) television affects viewers by its presentation of news
(C) truth frustrates efforts by the media to constrain it
(D) viewers of television newscasts can sort out fact from fiction
(E) governments manage to control television newscasts

2 Which of the following, if true, would most clearly strengthen the assertion in Passage 1 about television and the civil rights movement (lines 11-15) ?

(A) Many filmed reports of civil disobedience were censored by television executives during the 1960's.
(B) Recent studies have questioned the objectivity with which television newscasts presented reports of civil disobedience during the 1960's.
(C) A biography of a major civil rights leader describes in detail the occasions on which the leader was featured in television newscasts of the 1960's.
(D) A 1960's poll shows that those Americans who considered civil rights a national priority had seen television newscasts of civil disobedience.
(E) Many of the reporting techniques used today originated in newscasts covering the 1960's civil rights movement.

3 In the context of lines 29-42, the reference to "still photography" (lines 35-36) serves to

(A) illustrate the accuracy with which current events can be documented
(B) develop a claim about the trustworthiness of television presentations
(C) demonstrate the progress that has been made in using computer-generated effects
(D) refute the argument that viewers are deceived by computer-generated effects
(E) emphasize that videotaped images have comparatively greater impact

4 The word "instrument" is used in line 46 to signify

(A) a gimmick
(B) an agent
(C) a navigational aid
(D) a musical device
(E) a legal document

GO ON TO THE NEXT PAGE

5 The use of the quotation in lines 43-47 can be considered a weakness of the argument in Passage 1 because

(A) an irrelevant reason is cited as evidence that television news is beneficial
(B) an attribute of the media that is labeled as beneficial is in fact destructive
(C) a work of fiction is cited as though it were scientific research
(D) a negative assessment of television news is left unchallenged
(E) a defense of television news is presented by a television newscaster

6 According to Passage 2, television news is presented in a manner that serves to

(A) hold leaders accountable for their policies
(B) entertain viewers
(C) define lies as truth
(D) make complex issues accessible
(E) exaggerate minor political blunders

7 The word "mapped" in line 53 most nearly means

(A) plotted on a chart (B) planned in detail (C) measured (D) defined (E) verified

8 According to Passage 2, the "disinformation" mentioned in line 68 affects television viewers by

(A) leading them to act on false information
(B) causing them to become skeptical about television news
(C) giving them the mistaken impression that they are knowledgeable
(D) making them susceptible to the commercials that accompany the news
(E) turning them against certain political leaders

9 Which of the following most accurately describes the organization of the last paragraph of Passage 2 ?

(A) One view of a situation is refuted and an alternative view is substituted.
(B) An assertion is made and is supported by means of historical evidence.
(C) Two authors with contrasting views are introduced and their views are reconciled.
(D) An argument in favor of one interpretation is set forth and an opposing interpretation is explained.
(E) A situation is described and a prediction about related future events is offered.

10 In each passage, the author assumes that viewers of television news tend to

(A) read about news events as well as watch them
(B) watch television programs other than newscasts
(C) lack a coherent understanding of their world
(D) follow only important events
(E) accept most of what they see as factual

11 The passages differ in their evaluations of television newscasts in that Passage 1 claims that

(A) newscasts seek mainly to criticize established governments, whereas Passage 2 warns that newscasts usually strengthen established governments
(B) television news inflames viewers' emotions, whereas Passage 2 warns that television news provides false information
(C) propagandists could falsify the news, whereas Passage 2 warns that television trivializes the news
(D) television news causes viewers to form hasty opinions, whereas Passage 2 warns that newscasts cause viewers to understand issues simplistically
(E) repressive governments are using television news as a means of control, whereas Passage 2 warns that commercial sponsorship biases the newscasts

12 Both passages refer to George Orwell's predictions in order to

(A) emphasize that the presentation of news has changed since Orwell's time
(B) show how aspects of Orwell's conception of the future have become reality
(C) point out that the government does not control television news
(D) warn against the control of news media exercised by governments worldwide
(E) illustrate public concerns that television newscasters themselves have begun to address

IF YOU FINISH BEFORE TIME IS CALLED, YOU MAY CHECK YOUR WORK ON THIS SECTION ONLY. DO NOT TURN TO ANY OTHER SECTION IN THE TEST. **STOP**

Section 7

Time—15 Minutes 10 Questions	**In this section solve each problem, using any available space on the page for scratchwork. Then decide which is the best of the choices given and fill in the corresponding oval on the answer sheet.**

Notes:

1. The use of a calculator is permitted. All numbers used are real numbers.

2. Figures that accompany problems in this test are intended to provide information useful in solving the problems. They are drawn as accurately as possible EXCEPT when it is stated in a specific problem that the figure is not drawn to scale. All figures lie in a plane unless otherwise indicated.

Reference Information

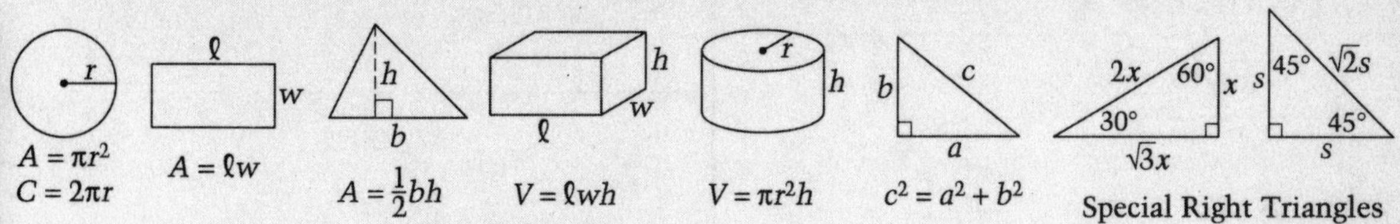

$A = \pi r^2$
$C = 2\pi r$

$A = \ell w$

$A = \frac{1}{2}bh$

$V = \ell wh$

$V = \pi r^2 h$

$c^2 = a^2 + b^2$

Special Right Triangles

The number of degrees of arc in a circle is 360.
The measure in degrees of a straight angle is 180.
The sum of the measures in degrees of the angles of a triangle is 180.

1 In Italy, when one dollar was approximately equal to 1,900 lire, a certain pair of shoes cost 60,000 lire. Of the following, which is the best approximation of the cost of these shoes, in dollars?

(A) \$20
(B) \$30
(C) \$60
(D) \$120
(E) \$300

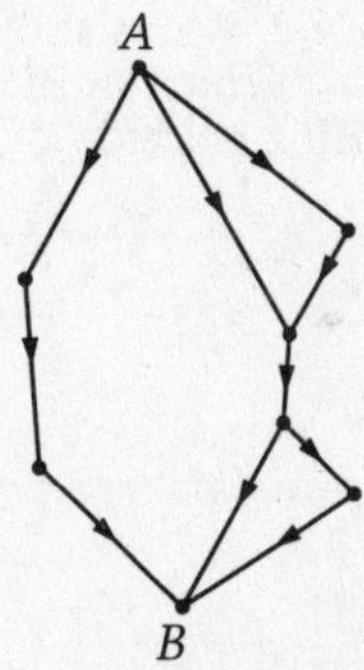

2 In the figure above, any path from A to B must follow the connected line segments in the direction shown by the arrows. How many different paths are there from A to B ?

(A) Five
(B) Six
(C) Seven
(D) Eight
(E) Nine

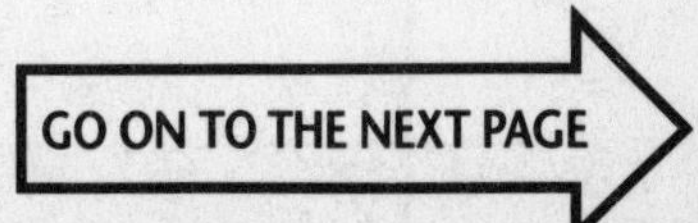

3 What is the least number of 2's that can be multiplied together to yield a number greater than 50 ?

(A) 4
(B) 5
(C) 6
(D) 7
(E) 10

4 The triangle in the figure above is to be reflected across the x-axis and then reflected across the y-axis. Which of the following shows the resulting position of the triangle?

(A)
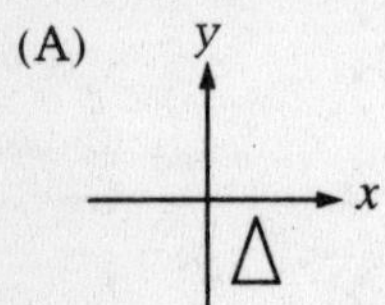

(B)
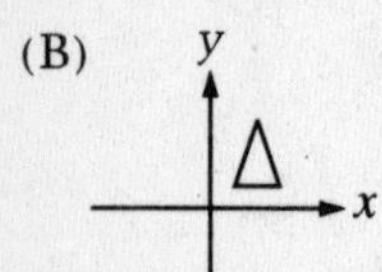

(C)
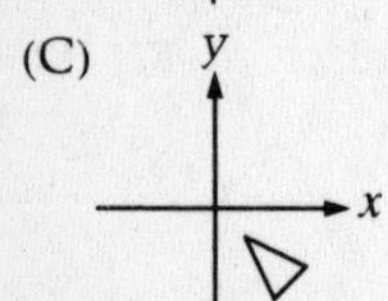

(D)
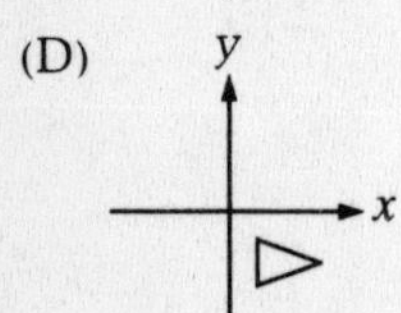

(E)
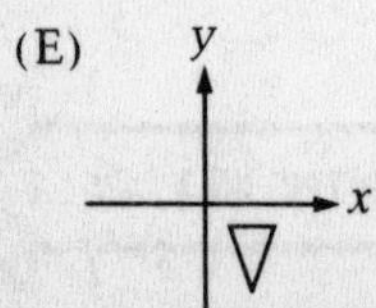

5 If e, f, g, and h are consecutive odd integers and $e < f < g < h$, then $g + h$ is how much greater than $e + f$?

(A) 2
(B) 3
(C) 4
(D) 5
(E) 8

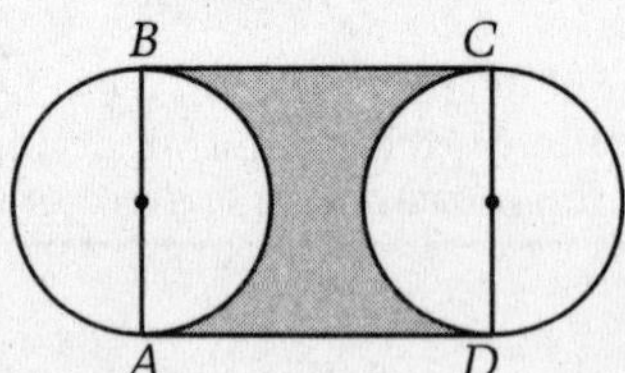

6 In rectangle $ABCD$ shown above, sides AB and CD pass through the centers of the two circles. If $AB = 12$ and $AD = 16$, what is the area of the shaded region?

(A) 120
(B) 156
(C) 192
(D) $192 - 36\pi$
(E) $192 - 72\pi$

GO ON TO THE NEXT PAGE

	Column 1	Column 2	Total
Row 1			53
Row 2			26
Row 3			21
Total	36	64	100

7 In the table above, each of the six empty boxes should contain a number entry so that the column and row totals are as given. Juan wants to complete the table. What is the least number of entries that he must ask for in order to complete the table?

(A) One
(B) Two
(C) Three
(D) Four
(E) Six

8 Ms. Clark drove from her home to the museum at an average speed of 40 miles per hour and returned home along the same route at an average speed of 35 miles per hour. If her total driving time for the trip was 2 hours, how many <u>minutes</u> did it take Ms. Clark to drive from <u>her home</u> to the museum?

(A) 70
(B) 60
(C) 56
(D) 45
(E) 40

GO ON TO THE NEXT PAGE

9 Two cities n miles apart are located s inches apart on a certain map that is drawn to scale. What is the distance, in inches, on the map between two cities that are $n + 1$ miles apart?

(A) $\frac{n}{s}$

(B) $\frac{(n + 1)}{s}$

(C) $\frac{s}{(n + 1)}$

(D) $\frac{s(n + 1)}{n}$

(E) $\frac{n}{s(n + 1)}$

10 If $3^x = y$, which of the following equals $9y$ in terms of x ?

(A) $3^{\frac{x}{2}}$

(B) 3^{2x}

(C) 3^{2+x}

(D) 3^{x^2}

(E) 27^x

IF YOU FINISH BEFORE TIME IS CALLED, YOU MAY CHECK YOUR WORK ON THIS SECTION ONLY. DO NOT TURN TO ANY OTHER SECTION IN THE TEST. **STOP**

SAT 1: Reasoning Test Answer Key
Saturday, November 1996

VERBAL

Section 1 — Five-choice Questions

	COR. ANS.	DIFF. LEV.
1.	D	1
2.	B	3
3.	C	2
4.	A	3
5.	C	4
6.	E	4
7.	A	3
8.	C	4
9.	A	5
10.	E	1
11.	D	2
12.	E	2
13.	A	5
14.	D	5
15.	E	5
16.	D	2
17.	B	1
18.	D	1
19.	E	3
20.	B	2
21.	E	3
22.	D	2
23.	D	5
24.	B	4
25.	D	3
26.	E	3
27.	C	3
28.	B	2
29.	A	3
30.	D	3
31.	A	3

______ no. correct

______ no. incorrect

Section 3 — Five-choice Questions

	COR. ANS.	DIFF. LEV.
1.	B	1
2.	E	1
3.	B	3
4.	C	2
5.	A	2
6.	B	3
7.	B	3
8.	D	5
9.	C	4
10.	A	5
11.	D	1
12.	D	1
13.	B	2
14.	A	2
15.	B	2
16.	B	3
17.	B	3
18.	E	3
19.	C	3
20.	B	5
21.	D	4
22.	A	4
23.	D	5
24.	C	1
25.	D	3
26.	C	3
27.	C	3
28.	E	2
29.	B	4
30.	E	3
31.	A	3
32.	D	3
33.	D	3
34.	C	4
35.	E	5

______ no. correct

______ no. incorrect

Section 6 — Five-choice Questions

	COR. ANS.	DIFF. LEV.
1.	B	3
2.	D	3
3.	B	3
4.	B	3
5.	E	4
6.	B	3
7.	D	3
8.	C	3
9.	A	4
10.	E	3
11.	C	5
12.	C	4

______ no. correct

______ no. incorrect

MATHEMATICAL

Section 2 — Five-choice Questions

	COR. ANS.	DIFF. LEV.
1.	C	1
2.	B	1
3.	E	1
4.	E	1
5.	C	1
6.	C	2
7.	A	2
8.	D	1
9.	A	2
10.	E	3
11.	A	3
12.	E	2
13.	C	3
14.	B	3
15.	E	3
16.	E	3
17.	D	3
18.	C	3
19.	B	3
20.	B	4
21.	A	4
22.	D	4
23.	A	4
24.	B	5
25.	E	5

______ no. correct

______ no. incorrect

Section 4 — Four-choice Questions

	COR. ANS.	DIFF. LEV.
1.	C	1
2.	A	1
3.	A	1
4.	D	2
5.	D	3
6.	B	2
7.	C	3
8.	B	3
9.	A	3
10.	B	4
11.	B	3
12.	A	5
13.	D	5
14.	C	4
15.	A	4

______ no. correct

______ no. incorrect

Section 7 — Five-choice Questions

	COR. ANS.	DIFF. LEV.
1.	B	1
2.	A	1
3.	C	2
4.	E	2
5.	E	3
6.	D	3
7.	B	3
8.	C	4
9.	D	5
10.	C	5

______ no. correct

______ no. incorrect

Section 4 — Student-Produced Response Questions

	COR. ANS.	DIFF. LEV.
16.	45	2
17.	3.2 or 16/5	2
18.	117, 126, 130, 140, 143 or 154	2
19.	39	3
20.	3.5 or 7/2	3
21.	1	4
22.	66	3
23.	1212	3
24.	120	4
25.	207	4

______ no. correct (16-25)

NOTE: Difficulty levels are estimates of question difficulty for a recent group of college-bound seniors. Difficulty levels range from 1 (easiest) to 5 (hardest).

The Scoring Process

Machine-scoring is done in three steps:

- *Scanning.* Your answer sheet is "read" by a scanning machine and the oval you filled in for each question is recorded on a computer tape.
- *Scoring.* The computer compares the oval filled in for each question with the correct response. Each correct answer receives one point; omitted questions do not count toward your score. For each wrong answer to the multiple-choice questions, a fraction of a point is subtracted to correct for random guessing. For questions with five answer choices, one-fourth of a point is subtracted for each wrong response; for questions with four answer choices, one-third of a point is subtracted for each wrong response. The SAT I verbal test has 78 questions with five answer choices each. If, for example, a student has 44 right, 32 wrong, and 2 omitted, the resulting raw score is determined as follows:

$$44 \text{ right} - \frac{32 \text{ wrong}}{4} = 44 - 8 = 36 \text{ raw score points}$$

Obtaining raw scores frequently involves the rounding of fractional numbers to the nearest whole number. For example, a raw score of 36.25 is rounded to 36, the nearest whole number. A raw score of 36.50 is rounded upward to 37.

- *Converting to reported scaled score.* Raw test scores are then placed on the College Board scale of 200 to 800 through a process that adjusts scores to account for minor differences in difficulty among different editions of the test. This process, known as equating, is performed so that a student's reported score is not affected by the edition of the test taken or by the abilities of the group with whom the student takes the test. As a result of placing SAT I scores on the College Board scale, scores earned by students at different times can be compared. For example, an SAT I verbal score of 400 on a test taken at one administration indicates the same level of developed verbal ability as a 400 score obtained on a different edition of the test taken at another time.

How to Score the Test

SAT I Verbal Sections 1, 3, and 6

Step A: Count the number of correct answers for *Section 1* and record the number in the space provided on the worksheet on the next page. Then do the same for the incorrect answers. (Do not count omitted answers.) To determine subtotal A, use the formula:

$$\text{number correct} - \frac{\text{number incorrect}}{4} = \text{subtotal A}$$

Step B: Count the number of correct answers and the number of incorrect answers for *Section 3* and record the number in the space provided on the worksheet. To determine subtotal B, use the formula:

$$\text{number correct} - \frac{\text{number incorrect}}{4} = \text{subtotal B}$$

Step C: Count the number of correct answers and the number of incorrect answers for *Section 6* and record the number in the space provided on the worksheet. To determine subtotal C, use the formula:

$$\text{number correct} - \frac{\text{number incorrect}}{4} = \text{subtotal C}$$

Step D: To obtain D, add subtotal A, subtotal B, and subtotal C, keeping any decimals. Enter the resulting figure on the worksheet.

Step E: To obtain E, your raw verbal score, round D to the nearest whole number. (For example, any number from 44.50 to 45.49 rounds to 45.) Enter the resulting figure on the worksheet.

Step F: To find your SAT 1 verbal score, look up the total raw verbal score you obtained in step E in the conversion table. Enter this figure on the worksheet.

SAT I Mathematical Sections 2, 4, and 7

Step A: Count the number of correct answers and the number of incorrect answers for *Section 2* and record the numbers in the spaces provided on the worksheet. To determine subtotal A, use the formula:

$$\text{number correct} - \frac{\text{number incorrect}}{4} = \text{subtotal A}$$

Step B: Count the number of correct answers and the number of incorrect answers for the *four-choice quantitative comparison questions (questions 1 through 15) in Section 4* and record the number in the space provided on the worksheet. Note: Do not count any E responses to questions 1 through 15 as correct or incorrect. Because these four-choice questions have no E answer choices, E responses to these questions are treated as omits. To determine subtotal B, use the formula:

$$\text{number correct} - \frac{\text{number incorrect}}{3} = \text{subtotal B}$$

Step C: Count the number of correct answers for the student-produced response questions *(questions 16 through 25)* in *Section 4* and record the number in the space provided on the worksheet. This is subtotal C.

Step D: Count the number of correct answers and the number of incorrect answers for *Section 7* and record the number in the space provided on the worksheet. To determine subtotal D, use the formula:

$$\text{number correct} - \frac{\text{number incorrect}}{4} = \text{subtotal D}$$

Step E: To obtain E, add subtotal A, subtotal B, subtotal C, and subtotal D, keeping any decimals. Enter the resulting figure on the worksheet.

Step F: To obtain F, your raw mathematical score, round E to the nearest whole number. (For example, any number from 44.50 to 45.49 rounds to 45.) Enter the resulting figure on the worksheet.

Step G: To find your SAT 1 mathematical score, look up the total raw mathematical score you obtained in step F in the conversion table. Enter this figure on the worksheet.

SAT I Scoring Worksheet

SAT I Verbal Sections

A. Section 1:	________ no. correct	–	(________ no. incorrect	÷ 4)	=	________ subtotal A
B. Section 3:	________ no. correct	–	(________ no. incorrect	÷ 4)	=	________ subtotal B
C. Section 6:	________ no. correct	–	(________ no. incorrect	÷ 4)	=	________ subtotal C
D. Total unrounded raw score (Total A + B + C)						________ D
E. Total rounded raw score (rounded to nearest whole number)						________ E
F. **SAT 1 verbal reported scaled score (See the conversion table)**						[ ] SAT I verbal score

SAT I Mathematical Sections

A. Section 2:	________ no. correct	–	(________ no. incorrect	÷ 4)	=	________ subtotal A
B. Section 4: Questions 1-15 (quantitative comparison)	________ no. correct	–	(________ no. incorrect	÷ 3)	=	________ subtotal B
C. Section 4: Questions 16-25 (student-produced response)	________ no. correct				=	________ subtotal C
D. Section 7:	________ no. correct	–	(________ no. incorrect	÷ 4)	=	________ subtotal D
E. Total unrounded raw score (Total A + B + C+ D)						________ E
F. Total rounded raw score (rounded to nearest whole number)						________ F
G. **SAT 1 mathematical reported scaled score (See the conversion table)**						[ ] SAT I mathematical score

Score Conversion Table
SAT 1: Reasoning Test
Saturday, November 1996
Recentered Scale

Raw Score	Verbal Scaled Score	Math Scaled Score	Raw Score	Verbal Scaled Score	Math Scaled Score
78	800		37	510	570
77	800		36	510	560
76	800		35	500	550
75	800		34	500	540
74	800		33	490	540
73	800		32	480	530
72	790		31	480	520
71	770		30	470	510
70	760		29	470	510
69	740		28	460	500
68	730		27	450	490
67	720		26	450	490
66	710		25	440	480
65	700		24	440	470
64	690		23	430	470
63	680		22	420	460
62	670		21	420	450
61	670		20	410	450
60	660	800	19	410	440
59	650	800	18	400	430
58	640	790	17	390	430
57	640	770	16	390	420
56	630	750	15	380	410
55	620	740	14	370	410
54	620	720	13	370	400
53	610	710	12	360	390
52	600	700	11	350	380
51	600	690	10	340	380
50	590	680	9	330	370
49	580	670	8	330	360
48	580	660	7	320	350
47	570	650	6	310	340
46	570	640	5	300	330
45	560	630	4	280	320
44	550	620	3	270	310
43	550	620	2	260	290
42	540	610	1	240	280
41	540	600	0	230	260
40	530	590	-1	210	250
39	520	580	-2	200	230
38	520	570	-3 and below	200	200

This table is for use only with this test.

SAT I: Reasoning Test

Saturday, January 1997

YOUR NAME (PRINT) ________________________________
LAST FIRST MI

TEST CENTER ________________________________
NUMBER NAME OF TEST CENTER ROOM NUMBER

SAT® I: Reasoning Test — General Directions

Timing

- You will have three hours to work on this test.
- There are five 30-minute sections and two 15-minute sections.
- You may work on only one section at a time.
- The supervisor will tell you when to begin and end each section.
- If you finish a section before time is called, check your work on that section. You may NOT turn to any other section.
- Work as rapidly as you can without losing accuracy. Don't waste time on questions that seem too difficult for you.

Marking Answers

- Carefully mark only one answer for each question.
- Make sure each mark is dark and completely fills the oval.
- Do not make any stray marks on your answer sheet.
- If you erase, do so completely. Incomplete erasures may be scored as intended answers.
- Use only the answer spaces that correspond to the question numbers.
- For questions with only four answer choices, an answer marked in oval E will not be scored.
- Use the test book for scratchwork, but you will not receive credit for anything written there.
- You may not transfer answers to your answer sheet or fill in ovals after time has been called.
- You may not fold or remove pages or portions of a page from this book, or take the book or answer sheet from the testing room.

Scoring

- For each correct answer, you receive one point.
- For questions you omit, you receive no points.
- For a wrong answer to a multiple-choice question, you lose a fraction of a point.
  - ► If you can eliminate one or more of the answer choices as wrong, however, you increase your chances of choosing the correct answer and earning one point.
  - ► If you can't eliminate any choice, move on. You can return to the question later if there is time.
- For a wrong answer to a math question that is not multiple-choice, you don't lose any points.

The passages for this test have been adapted from published material. The ideas contained in them do not necessarily represent the opinions of the College Board or Educational Testing Service.

IMPORTANT: The codes below are unique to your test book. Copy them on your answer sheet in boxes 8 and 9 and fill in the corresponding ovals exactly as shown.

8. Form Code

A	A	0	0	0
B	B	1	1	1
C	C	2	2	2
D	D	3	3	3
E	E	4	4	4
F	F	5	5	5
G	G	6	6	6
H	H	7	7	7
I	I	8	8	8
J	J	9	9	9
K	K			
L	L			
M	M			
N	N			
O	O			
P	P			
Q	Q			
R	R			
S	S			
T	T			
U	U			
V	V			
W	W			
X	X			
Y	Y			
Z	Z			

9. Test Form

DO NOT OPEN THIS BOOK UNTIL THE SUPERVISOR TELLS YOU TO DO SO.

THE COLLEGE BOARD — SAT I **Page 1**

Use a No. 2 pencil only. Be sure each mark is dark and completely fills the intended oval. Completely erase any errors or stray marks.

1. Your Name

First 4 letters of Last Name	First init.	Mid. init.
A–Z	A–Z	A–Z

2.
Your Name: ____________________ (Print) Last / First / M.I.

I agree to the conditions on the back of the SAT I test book.

Signature: ____________________ Date: ___/___/___

Home Address: ____________________ (Print) Number and Street

____________________ City / State / Zip Code

Center: ____________________ (Print) City / State / Center Number

IMPORTANT: Fill in items 8 and 9 exactly as shown on the back of test book.

3. Date of Birth

Month	Day	Year
Jan.	0–3	0–8
Feb.	0–9	0–9
Mar.		
Apr.		
May		
June		
July		
Aug.		
Sept.		
Oct.		
Nov.		
Dec.		

4. Social Security Number

(9 columns, 0–9)

5. Sex

Female ◯ Male ◯

6. Registration Number

(Copy from Admission Ticket.)

(7 columns, 0–9)

7. Test Book Serial Number

(Copy from front of test book.)

(6 columns, 0–9)

8. Form Code

(Copy and grid as on back of test book.)

(2 columns A–Z; 3 columns 0–9)

FOR ETS USE ONLY

9. Test Form

(Copy from back of test book.)

Start with number 1 for each new section. If a section has fewer questions than answer spaces, leave the extra answer spaces blank.

SECTION 1

1–40 Ⓐ Ⓑ Ⓒ Ⓓ Ⓔ

SECTION 2

1–40 Ⓐ Ⓑ Ⓒ Ⓓ Ⓔ

Q2778-06/2 CHW98324 11027 • 09132 • TF129M17.5eX I.N. 207158
1 2 3 4

Use a No. 2 pencil only. Be sure each mark is dark and completely fills the intended oval. Completely erase any errors or stray marks.

Start with number 1 for each new section. If a section has fewer questions than answer spaces, leave the extra answer spaces blank.

SECTION 3

1 Ⓐ Ⓑ Ⓒ Ⓓ Ⓔ through 40 Ⓐ Ⓑ Ⓒ Ⓓ Ⓔ

If section 3 of your test book contains math questions that are not multiple-choice, continue to item 16 below. Otherwise, continue to item 16 above.

ONLY ANSWERS ENTERED IN THE OVALS IN EACH GRID AREA WILL BE SCORED.
YOU WILL NOT RECEIVE CREDIT FOR ANYTHING WRITTEN IN THE BOXES ABOVE THE OVALS.

16 17 18 19 20

21 22 23 24 25

BE SURE TO ERASE ANY ERRORS OR STRAY MARKS COMPLETELY.

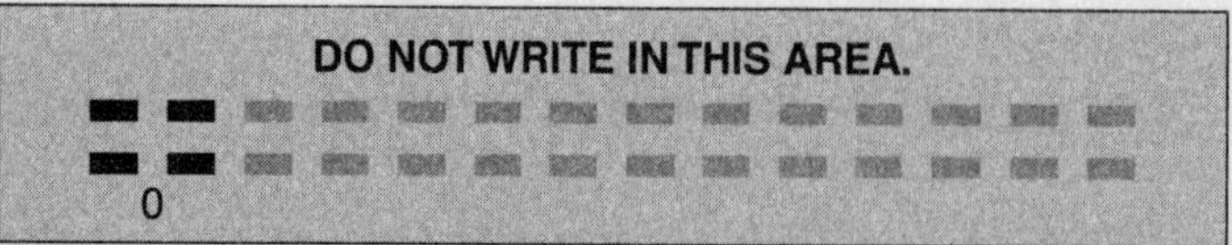

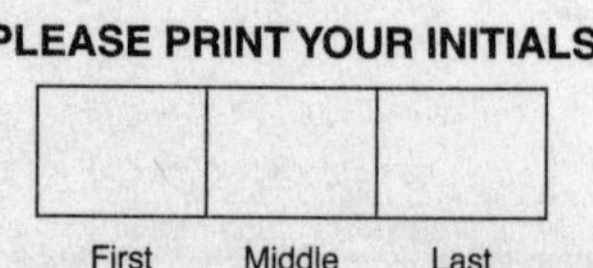

Use a No. 2 pencil only. Be sure each mark is dark and completely fills the intended oval. Completely erase any errors or stray marks.

Start with number 1 for each new section. If a section has fewer questions than answer spaces, leave the extra answer spaces blank.

SECTION 4

1 Ⓐ Ⓑ Ⓒ Ⓓ Ⓔ
2 Ⓐ Ⓑ Ⓒ Ⓓ Ⓔ
3 Ⓐ Ⓑ Ⓒ Ⓓ Ⓔ
4 Ⓐ Ⓑ Ⓒ Ⓓ Ⓔ
5 Ⓐ Ⓑ Ⓒ Ⓓ Ⓔ
6 Ⓐ Ⓑ Ⓒ Ⓓ Ⓔ
7 Ⓐ Ⓑ Ⓒ Ⓓ Ⓔ
8 Ⓐ Ⓑ Ⓒ Ⓓ Ⓔ
9 Ⓐ Ⓑ Ⓒ Ⓓ Ⓔ
10 Ⓐ Ⓑ Ⓒ Ⓓ Ⓔ
11 Ⓐ Ⓑ Ⓒ Ⓓ Ⓔ
12 Ⓐ Ⓑ Ⓒ Ⓓ Ⓔ
13 Ⓐ Ⓑ Ⓒ Ⓓ Ⓔ
14 Ⓐ Ⓑ Ⓒ Ⓓ Ⓔ
15 Ⓐ Ⓑ Ⓒ Ⓓ Ⓔ
16 Ⓐ Ⓑ Ⓒ Ⓓ Ⓔ
17 Ⓐ Ⓑ Ⓒ Ⓓ Ⓔ
18 Ⓐ Ⓑ Ⓒ Ⓓ Ⓔ
19 Ⓐ Ⓑ Ⓒ Ⓓ Ⓔ
20 Ⓐ Ⓑ Ⓒ Ⓓ Ⓔ
21 Ⓐ Ⓑ Ⓒ Ⓓ Ⓔ
22 Ⓐ Ⓑ Ⓒ Ⓓ Ⓔ
23 Ⓐ Ⓑ Ⓒ Ⓓ Ⓔ
24 Ⓐ Ⓑ Ⓒ Ⓓ Ⓔ
25 Ⓐ Ⓑ Ⓒ Ⓓ Ⓔ
26 Ⓐ Ⓑ Ⓒ Ⓓ Ⓔ
27 Ⓐ Ⓑ Ⓒ Ⓓ Ⓔ
28 Ⓐ Ⓑ Ⓒ Ⓓ Ⓔ
29 Ⓐ Ⓑ Ⓒ Ⓓ Ⓔ
30 Ⓐ Ⓑ Ⓒ Ⓓ Ⓔ
31 Ⓐ Ⓑ Ⓒ Ⓓ Ⓔ
32 Ⓐ Ⓑ Ⓒ Ⓓ Ⓔ
33 Ⓐ Ⓑ Ⓒ Ⓓ Ⓔ
34 Ⓐ Ⓑ Ⓒ Ⓓ Ⓔ
35 Ⓐ Ⓑ Ⓒ Ⓓ Ⓔ
36 Ⓐ Ⓑ Ⓒ Ⓓ Ⓔ
37 Ⓐ Ⓑ Ⓒ Ⓓ Ⓔ
38 Ⓐ Ⓑ Ⓒ Ⓓ Ⓔ
39 Ⓐ Ⓑ Ⓒ Ⓓ Ⓔ
40 Ⓐ Ⓑ Ⓒ Ⓓ Ⓔ

If section 4 of your test book contains math questions that are not multiple-choice, continue to item 16 below. Otherwise, continue to item 16 above.

ONLY ANSWERS ENTERED IN THE OVALS IN EACH GRID AREA WILL BE SCORED.
YOU WILL NOT RECEIVE CREDIT FOR ANYTHING WRITTEN IN THE BOXES ABOVE THE OVALS.

Grid-in items 16, 17, 18, 19, 20, 21, 22, 23, 24, 25 — each grid has four columns with ovals: / / (middle two columns); . . . . ; 0 0 0 (columns 2–4); 1–9 in all four columns.

BE SURE TO ERASE ANY ERRORS OR STRAY MARKS COMPLETELY.

DO NOT WRITE IN THIS AREA.

0

PLEASE PRINT YOUR INITIALS

First	Middle	Last

Use a No. 2 pencil only. Be sure each mark is dark and completely fills the intended oval. Completely erase any errors or stray marks.

Start with number 1 for each new section. If a section has fewer questions than answer spaces, leave the extra answer spaces blank.

SECTION 5

1 Ⓐ Ⓑ Ⓒ Ⓓ Ⓔ	11 Ⓐ Ⓑ Ⓒ Ⓓ Ⓔ	21 Ⓐ Ⓑ Ⓒ Ⓓ Ⓔ	31 Ⓐ Ⓑ Ⓒ Ⓓ Ⓔ
2 Ⓐ Ⓑ Ⓒ Ⓓ Ⓔ	12 Ⓐ Ⓑ Ⓒ Ⓓ Ⓔ	22 Ⓐ Ⓑ Ⓒ Ⓓ Ⓔ	32 Ⓐ Ⓑ Ⓒ Ⓓ Ⓔ
3 Ⓐ Ⓑ Ⓒ Ⓓ Ⓔ	13 Ⓐ Ⓑ Ⓒ Ⓓ Ⓔ	23 Ⓐ Ⓑ Ⓒ Ⓓ Ⓔ	33 Ⓐ Ⓑ Ⓒ Ⓓ Ⓔ
4 Ⓐ Ⓑ Ⓒ Ⓓ Ⓔ	14 Ⓐ Ⓑ Ⓒ Ⓓ Ⓔ	24 Ⓐ Ⓑ Ⓒ Ⓓ Ⓔ	34 Ⓐ Ⓑ Ⓒ Ⓓ Ⓔ
5 Ⓐ Ⓑ Ⓒ Ⓓ Ⓔ	15 Ⓐ Ⓑ Ⓒ Ⓓ Ⓔ	25 Ⓐ Ⓑ Ⓒ Ⓓ Ⓔ	35 Ⓐ Ⓑ Ⓒ Ⓓ Ⓔ
6 Ⓐ Ⓑ Ⓒ Ⓓ Ⓔ	16 Ⓐ Ⓑ Ⓒ Ⓓ Ⓔ	26 Ⓐ Ⓑ Ⓒ Ⓓ Ⓔ	36 Ⓐ Ⓑ Ⓒ Ⓓ Ⓔ
7 Ⓐ Ⓑ Ⓒ Ⓓ Ⓔ	17 Ⓐ Ⓑ Ⓒ Ⓓ Ⓔ	27 Ⓐ Ⓑ Ⓒ Ⓓ Ⓔ	37 Ⓐ Ⓑ Ⓒ Ⓓ Ⓔ
8 Ⓐ Ⓑ Ⓒ Ⓓ Ⓔ	18 Ⓐ Ⓑ Ⓒ Ⓓ Ⓔ	28 Ⓐ Ⓑ Ⓒ Ⓓ Ⓔ	38 Ⓐ Ⓑ Ⓒ Ⓓ Ⓔ
9 Ⓐ Ⓑ Ⓒ Ⓓ Ⓔ	19 Ⓐ Ⓑ Ⓒ Ⓓ Ⓔ	29 Ⓐ Ⓑ Ⓒ Ⓓ Ⓔ	39 Ⓐ Ⓑ Ⓒ Ⓓ Ⓔ
10 Ⓐ Ⓑ Ⓒ Ⓓ Ⓔ	20 Ⓐ Ⓑ Ⓒ Ⓓ Ⓔ	30 Ⓐ Ⓑ Ⓒ Ⓓ Ⓔ	40 Ⓐ Ⓑ Ⓒ Ⓓ Ⓔ

SECTION 6

1 Ⓐ Ⓑ Ⓒ Ⓓ Ⓔ	6 Ⓐ Ⓑ Ⓒ Ⓓ Ⓔ	11 Ⓐ Ⓑ Ⓒ Ⓓ Ⓔ	16 Ⓐ Ⓑ Ⓒ Ⓓ Ⓔ
2 Ⓐ Ⓑ Ⓒ Ⓓ Ⓔ	7 Ⓐ Ⓑ Ⓒ Ⓓ Ⓔ	12 Ⓐ Ⓑ Ⓒ Ⓓ Ⓔ	17 Ⓐ Ⓑ Ⓒ Ⓓ Ⓔ
3 Ⓐ Ⓑ Ⓒ Ⓓ Ⓔ	8 Ⓐ Ⓑ Ⓒ Ⓓ Ⓔ	13 Ⓐ Ⓑ Ⓒ Ⓓ Ⓔ	18 Ⓐ Ⓑ Ⓒ Ⓓ Ⓔ
4 Ⓐ Ⓑ Ⓒ Ⓓ Ⓔ	9 Ⓐ Ⓑ Ⓒ Ⓓ Ⓔ	14 Ⓐ Ⓑ Ⓒ Ⓓ Ⓔ	19 Ⓐ Ⓑ Ⓒ Ⓓ Ⓔ
5 Ⓐ Ⓑ Ⓒ Ⓓ Ⓔ	10 Ⓐ Ⓑ Ⓒ Ⓓ Ⓔ	15 Ⓐ Ⓑ Ⓒ Ⓓ Ⓔ	20 Ⓐ Ⓑ Ⓒ Ⓓ Ⓔ

SECTION 7

1 Ⓐ Ⓑ Ⓒ Ⓓ Ⓔ	6 Ⓐ Ⓑ Ⓒ Ⓓ Ⓔ	11 Ⓐ Ⓑ Ⓒ Ⓓ Ⓔ	16 Ⓐ Ⓑ Ⓒ Ⓓ Ⓔ
2 Ⓐ Ⓑ Ⓒ Ⓓ Ⓔ	7 Ⓐ Ⓑ Ⓒ Ⓓ Ⓔ	12 Ⓐ Ⓑ Ⓒ Ⓓ Ⓔ	17 Ⓐ Ⓑ Ⓒ Ⓓ Ⓔ
3 Ⓐ Ⓑ Ⓒ Ⓓ Ⓔ	8 Ⓐ Ⓑ Ⓒ Ⓓ Ⓔ	13 Ⓐ Ⓑ Ⓒ Ⓓ Ⓔ	18 Ⓐ Ⓑ Ⓒ Ⓓ Ⓔ
4 Ⓐ Ⓑ Ⓒ Ⓓ Ⓔ	9 Ⓐ Ⓑ Ⓒ Ⓓ Ⓔ	14 Ⓐ Ⓑ Ⓒ Ⓓ Ⓔ	19 Ⓐ Ⓑ Ⓒ Ⓓ Ⓔ
5 Ⓐ Ⓑ Ⓒ Ⓓ Ⓔ	10 Ⓐ Ⓑ Ⓒ Ⓓ Ⓔ	15 Ⓐ Ⓑ Ⓒ Ⓓ Ⓔ	20 Ⓐ Ⓑ Ⓒ Ⓓ Ⓔ

CERTIFICATION STATEMENT

Copy the statement below (do not print) and sign your name as you would an official document.

I hereby agree to the conditions set forth in the Registration Bulletin and certify that I am the person whose name and address appear on this answer sheet.

Signature: ______________________________ Date: ______________

Section 1 1 1 1 1 1 1

Time—30 Minutes
25 Questions

In this section solve each problem, using any available space on the page for scratchwork. Then decide which is the best of the choices given and fill in the corresponding oval on the answer sheet.

Notes:

1. The use of a calculator is permitted. All numbers used are real numbers.
2. Figures that accompany problems in this test are intended to provide information useful in solving the problems. They are drawn as accurately as possible EXCEPT when it is stated in a specific problem that the figure is not drawn to scale. All figures lie in a plane unless otherwise indicated.

Reference Information

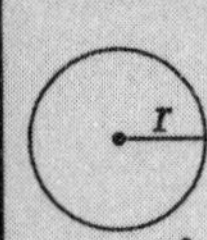

$A = \pi r^2$
$C = 2\pi r$

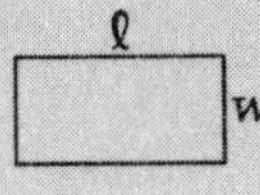

$A = \ell w$

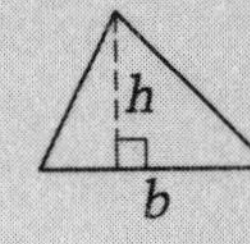

$A = \frac{1}{2}bh$

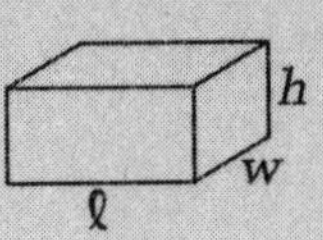

$V = \ell wh$

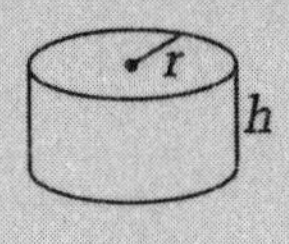

$V = \pi r^2 h$

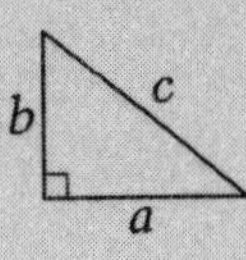

$c^2 = a^2 + b^2$

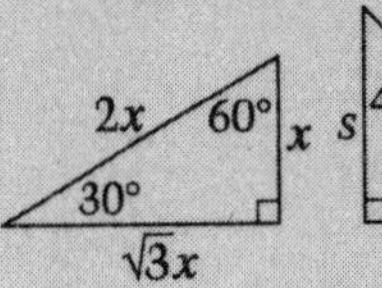

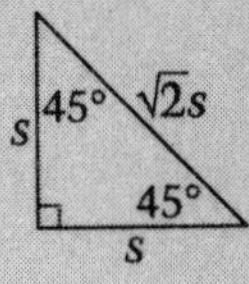

Special Right Triangles

The number of degrees of arc in a circle is 360.
The measure in degrees of a straight angle is 180.
The sum of the measures in degrees of the angles of a triangle is 180.

1 If $x + y = 5$ and $x = 3$, then $3y =$

(A) 6
(B) 9
(C) 12
(D) 15
(E) 18

2 If every digit of a whole number is either a 3 or a 5, the number must be

(A) prime
(B) odd
(C) even
(D) divisible by 3
(E) divisible by 5

3 If $2a - 6 = 10$, then $20 - 2a =$

(A) −16
(B) −12
(C) 4
(D) 14
(E) 16

GO ON TO THE NEXT PAGE

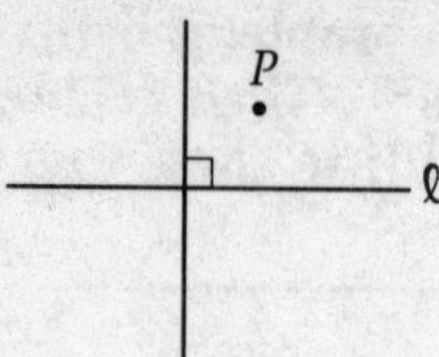

4 In the figure above, a line segment is to be drawn from point P perpendicular to line ℓ. Which of the following could be the resulting figure?

(A)

(B)

(C)

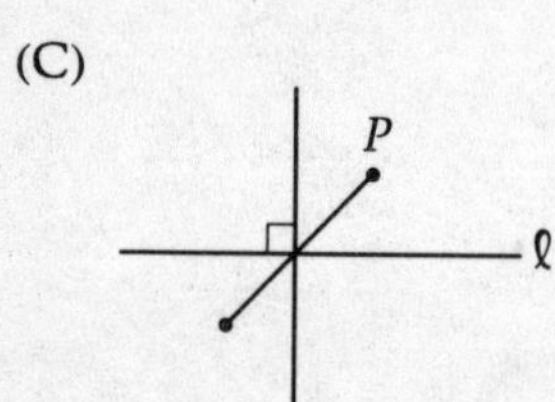

(D)

(E)

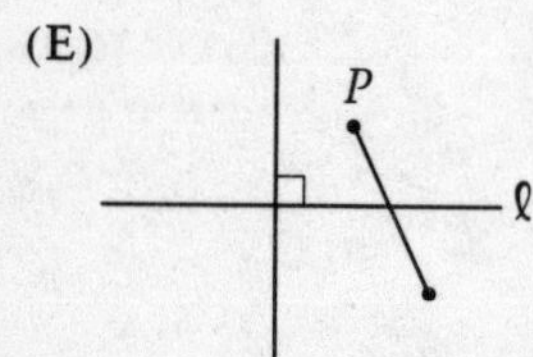

5 Which of the following groups contains three fractions that are equal?

(A) $\frac{1}{2}, \frac{1}{4}, \frac{1}{8}$

(B) $\frac{1}{2}, \frac{2}{4}, \frac{5}{8}$

(C) $\frac{2}{3}, \frac{4}{9}, \frac{8}{27}$

(D) $\frac{2}{3}, \frac{6}{9}, \frac{12}{18}$

(E) $\frac{4}{5}, \frac{7}{10}, \frac{16}{20}$

6 Sally buys a pen and a pencil for \$1.45. If the pen costs \$0.25 more than the pencil, how much does the pencil cost?

(A) \$0.25
(B) \$0.45
(C) \$0.60
(D) \$0.85
(E) \$1.20

If x and y are integers and $y \neq 0$, then $\frac{x}{y}$ is an integer.

7 Which of the following values of x and y proves that the statement above is not true?

(A) $x = 9, y = 3$

(B) $x = 10, y = 4$

(C) $x = 6, y = 3$

(D) $x = 5, y = 5$

(E) $x = 7, y = 1$

GO ON TO THE NEXT PAGE

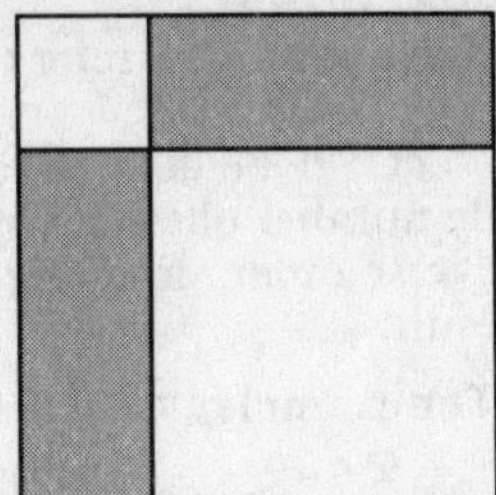

8 In the figure above, the large square is divided into two smaller squares and two shaded rectangles. If the perimeters of the two smaller squares are 8 and 20, what is the sum of the perimeters of the two shaded rectangles?

(A) 14
(B) 18
(C) 20
(D) 24
(E) 28

9 For which of the following sets of numbers is the average (arithmetic mean) greater than the median?

(A) {1, 2, 3, 4, 5}
(B) {1, 2, 3, 4, 6}
(C) {1, 3, 3, 3, 5}
(D) {−1, 2, 3, 4, 5}
(E) {−1, 2, 3, 4, 6}

10 Maple syrup leaks out of a container at the rate of ℓ liters in h hours. If the maple syrup costs 8 dollars per liter, how many dollars' worth will be lost in x hours?

(A) $\frac{8\ell x}{h}$
(B) $\frac{\ell x}{8h}$
(C) $\frac{8h}{\ell x}$
(D) $\frac{\ell h}{8x}$
(E) $\frac{hx}{\ell}$

11 75 percent of 88 is the same as 60 percent of what number?

(A) 100
(B) 103
(C) 105
(D) 108
(E) 110

GO ON TO THE NEXT PAGE

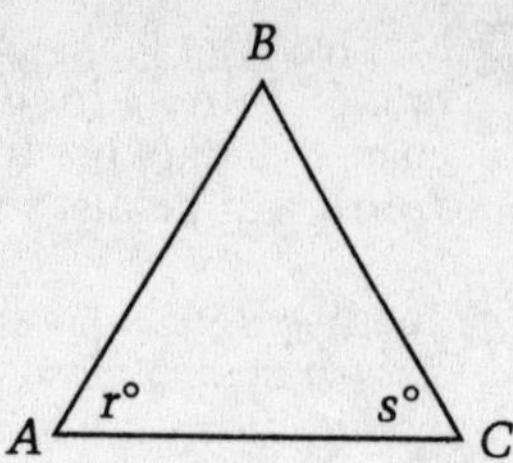

Note: Figure not drawn to scale.

12 In $\triangle ABC$ above, if $r > s$, which of the following must be true?

(A) $AB < BC$
(B) $AB < AC$
(C) $AB = BC$
(D) $AB > BC$
(E) $AB > AC$

Questions 13-15 refer to the following definition.

Let $^{\triangle}n$ be defined for any positive integer n as the number obtained by writing the digits of n in reverse order, dropping any leading zeros that result.

For example, $^{\triangle}5 = 5$, $^{\triangle}30 = 3$, and $^{\triangle}123 = 321$.

13 $^{\triangle}45{,}000 - {}^{\triangle}43{,}000 =$

(A) 2
(B) 20
(C) 200
(D) 2,000
(E) 20,000

14 Which of the following is equal to $^{\triangle}601 + {}^{\triangle}73$?

(A) $^{\triangle}53$
(B) $^{\triangle}134$
(C) $^{\triangle}143$
(D) $^{\triangle}341$
(E) $^{\triangle}638$

15 Which of the following must be true for all positive integers n ?

I. $^{\triangle}(^{\triangle}n) = n$
II. $^{\triangle}(10 \cdot n) < 10 \cdot n$
III. $^{\triangle}(1 + n) = 1 + {}^{\triangle}n$

(A) None
(B) I only
(C) II only
(D) I and II only
(E) I, II, and III

GO ON TO THE NEXT PAGE

16 If $x = 2y$, $y = 4z$, $2z = w$, and $w \neq 0$, then $\frac{x}{w} =$

(A) $\frac{1}{4}$

(B) $\frac{1}{2}$

(C) 1

(D) 2

(E) 4

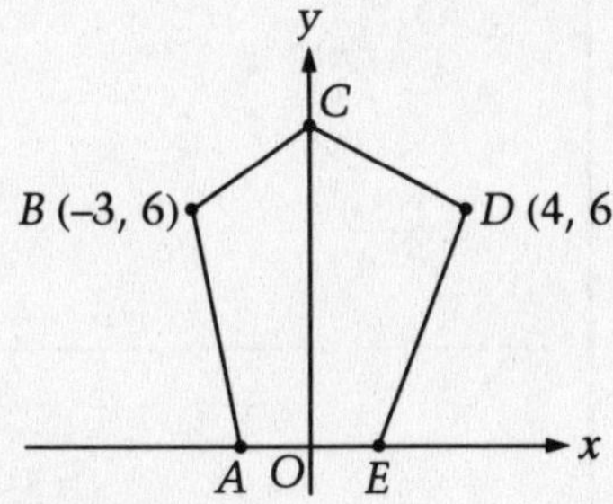

17 In pentagon $ABCDE$ above, how many diagonals with positive slope can be drawn?

(A) None
(B) One
(C) Two
(D) Three
(E) Four

18 Which of the following is equal to the sum of two consecutive even integers?

(A) 144
(B) 146
(C) 147
(D) 148
(E) 149

$0 \quad \frac{1}{3} \quad \frac{2}{3} \quad 1 \quad 1\frac{1}{3}$

19 Marks are equally spaced on a number line as shown above. How many marks would there be on this number line <u>between</u> the marks at 13 and 16 ?

(A) 3
(B) 6
(C) 7
(D) 8
(E) 9

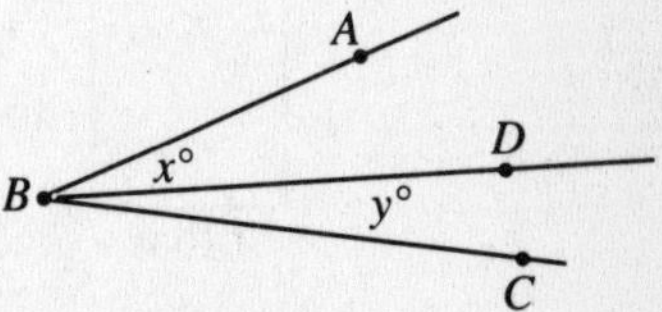

<u>Note:</u> Figure not drawn to scale.

20 In the figure above, point D is in the interior of $\angle ABC$ and the measure of $\angle ABD$ is $\frac{3}{5}$ the measure of $\angle ABC$. If $y = 24$, then $x =$

(A) 72
(B) 60
(C) 48
(D) 40
(E) 36

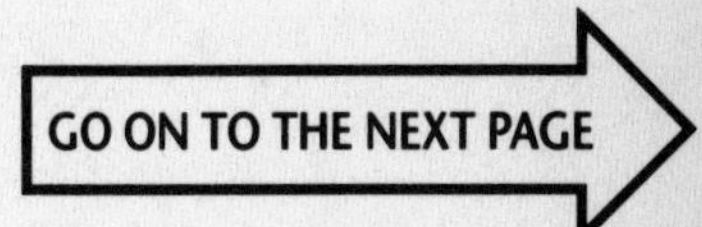

21 It takes Mia 5 hours, reading at a constant rate, to read a certain book containing 200 pages of reading material. If Samantha reads at twice this rate, how many minutes would it take her to read a book containing 100 pages of reading material?

(A) 75
(B) 85
(C) 90
(D) 120
(E) 150

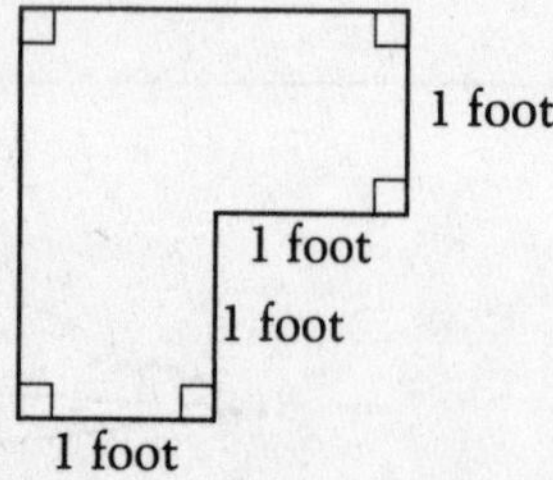

22 How many tiles of the size and shape shown above are needed to completely cover a rectangular floor measuring 30 feet by 20 feet?

(A) 120
(B) 150
(C) 200
(D) 250
(E) 300

23 If $x^2 + y^2 = 2xy$, then x must equal

(A) -1
(B) 0
(C) 1
(D) $-y$
(E) y

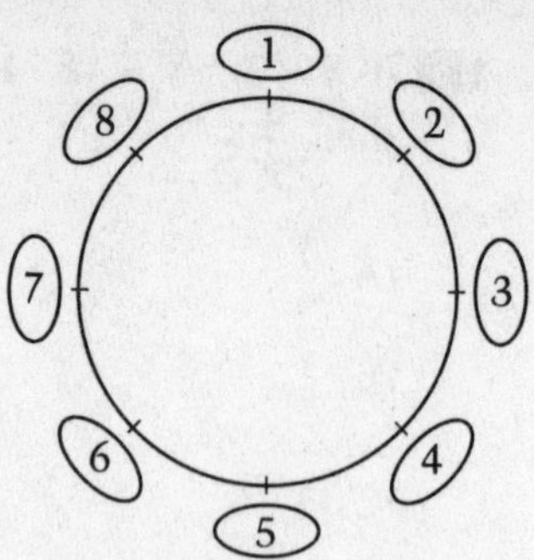

24 The figure above represents a circular table with 8 equally spaced chairs labeled 1 through 8. If two students are to sit directly opposite each other, leaving the other chairs empty, how many such arrangements of the two students are possible?

(A) 4
(B) 8
(C) 16
(D) 28
(E) 56

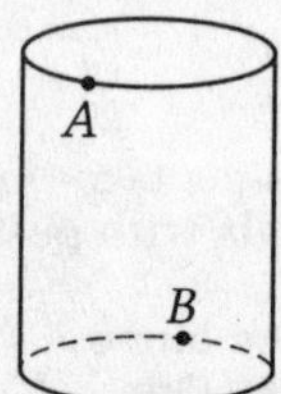

25 The figure above shows a cylinder with radius 2 and height 5. If points A and B lie on the circumference of the top and bottom of the cylinder, respectively, what is the greatest possible straight-line distance between A and B?

(A) 3

(B) 5

(C) 7

(D) $\sqrt{29}$

(E) $\sqrt{41}$

IF YOU FINISH BEFORE TIME IS CALLED, YOU MAY CHECK YOUR WORK ON THIS SECTION ONLY. DO NOT TURN TO ANY OTHER SECTION IN THE TEST. **STOP**

Section 2 2 2 2 2 2

Time — 30 Minutes
30 Questions

For each question in this section, select the best answer from among the choices given and fill in the corresponding oval on the answer sheet.

Each sentence below has one or two blanks, each blank indicating that something has been omitted. Beneath the sentence are five words or sets of words labeled A through E. Choose the word or set of words that, when inserted in the sentence, best fits the meaning of the sentence as a whole.

Example:

Medieval kingdoms did not become constitutional republics overnight; on the contrary, the change was ----.

(A) unpopular
(B) unexpected
(C) advantageous
(D) sufficient
(E) gradual 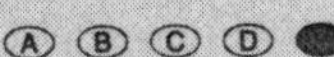

1 Hoping to ---- the dispute, negotiators proposed a compromise that they felt would be ---- to both labor and management.

(A) enforce. .useful
(B) end. .divisive
(C) overcome. .unattractive
(D) extend. .satisfactory
(E) resolve. .acceptable

2 Geneticist Olivia M. Pereira-Smith has published her findings on "immortal" cells, that is, cells that reproduce by dividing ----.

(A) indefinitely (B) occasionally (C) conclusively (D) periodically (E) precisely

3 The unusually large herb *Gunnera* is difficult to study because it is found only in ---- areas.

(A) fertile (B) hospitable (C) inaccessible (D) mundane (E) extensive

4 To ---- about craft clubs is not only ---- but foolish, for the focus of the clubs varies greatly from one town to another.

(A) brag. .necessary
(B) generalize. .difficult
(C) complain. .important
(D) rhapsodize. .fair
(E) learn. .unproductive

5 The female subject of this painting by Henri Matisse seems ----, as if Matisse sought to portray an unconquerable female spirit.

(A) ephemeral (B) indomitable (C) opulent (D) lithe (E) morose

6 Ironically, the same executives who brought bankruptcy to the coal fields were ---- by their contemporaries, who ---- the notion that these people were industrial heroes.

(A) celebrated. .cherished
(B) respected. .doubted
(C) ignored. .belied
(D) condemned. .rejected
(E) antagonized. .enjoyed

7 Even though some people feel historians have an exclusive right to act as the interpreters of bygone eras, most historians insist their profession has no ---- interpreting the past.

(A) interest in (B) responsibility in (C) consensus for (D) monopoly on (E) misgivings about

8 It is difficult to tell whether the attention new rock bands are receiving from audiences is that associated with ---- or that which indicates a durable ----.

(A) novelty. .popularity
(B) originality. .understanding
(C) success. .sensation
(D) longevity. .image
(E) creativity. .production

9 Fenster schemed and plotted for weeks and these ---- were rewarded when Griswold was fired and Fenster was promoted.

(A) circumlocutions (B) affiliations (C) gibberings (D) machinations (E) renunciations

GO ON TO THE NEXT PAGE

Each question below consists of a related pair of words or phrases, followed by five pairs of words or phrases labeled A through E. Select the pair that best expresses a relationship similar to that expressed in the original pair.

Example:

CRUMB : BREAD ::
(A) ounce : unit
(B) splinter : wood
(C) water : bucket
(D) twine : rope
(E) cream : butter

10 SEED : PLANT ::
(A) pouch : kangaroo
(B) root : soil
(C) drop : water
(D) bark : tree
(E) egg : bird

11 SANDAL : FOOTWEAR ::
(A) monarch : castle
(B) child : parent
(C) volume : bookcase
(D) watch : timepiece
(E) wax : candle

12 RENT : PROPERTY ::
(A) sue : lawyer
(B) hire : employee
(C) pose : painter
(D) pay : debtor
(E) purchase : buyer

13 VIRTUOSO : MUSIC ::
(A) bard : poetry
(B) crescendo : scale
(C) lyricist : melody
(D) portrait : photography
(E) critic : performance

14 AUDACIOUS : BOLDNESS ::
(A) anonymous : identity
(B) remorseful : misdeed
(C) deleterious : result
(D) impressionable : temptation
(E) sanctimonious : hypocrisy

15 LULL : TRUST ::
(A) balk : fortitude
(B) betray : loyalty
(C) cajole : compliance
(D) hinder : destination
(E) soothe : passion

GO ON TO THE NEXT PAGE

Each passage below is followed by questions based on its content. Answer the questions on the basis of what is stated or implied in each passage and in any introductory material that may be provided.

Questions 16-20 are based on the following passage.

In the following, a linguist reflects on changes in English language usage.

Linguistic manners are like any others. People have always found it worthwhile to reflect on how best to behave, for the sake of individual enlightenment and improvement. Since the eighteenth century, most of our great moralists have at one time or another turned their attention to the language, reflecting the conviction that the mastery of polite prose is a moral accomplishment to which we will be moved by appeals to our highest instincts.

The "improprieties" of traditional grammar are the usages that arise out of the natural drift of the meanings of words in the standard vocabulary. Obviously, we are not bound to use the language just as it was used a hundred years ago, but neither is it in our interest to change the language willy-nilly. Faced with a particular change, we need to ask if it involves real loss and if there is anything we can do to stop it.

The progressive loss of the distinction between the words *disinterested* (unbiased) and *uninterested* (apathetic) is regrettable; however, we might admit that the fight on behalf of the distinction is a lost cause. Nevertheless, I would not want to claim that there are no improprieties worth bothering about. Take the often-remarked use of *literally* to mean *figuratively*, as in, "We are literally drowning in red tape." If *literally* were going to shift its meaning away from *actually*, then it would have done so long ago; its stability is an indication that we are willing to reconsider our usage when the rationale is explained to us. Once the connection of *literal* with *letter* is made, the correct usage makes perfect sense. The distinction in this case is worth making.

Beyond the revision of traditional categories, new social conditions call for attention to aspects of language to which early grammarians were indifferent. Take the spoken language. Recent critics have been sensitive, with good reason, to the misuse of the phrases we use to orient the flow of talk, phrases like *I mean* and *you know*. In ordinary private conversation, the background of information we have in common is usually rich enough to enable us to fill in what is intended; and here we rarely notice whether *you know* is being used appropriately or not. I am struck by the misuse of such expressions only when I am listening to public discourse: television interviews, for example. What is otherwise a natural appeal to a shared background is distressing because we do not know who the speakers are, as we do in face-to-face conversation, and we cannot ask them for clarification. Just as attention to rules of written usage helps us to read intelligently, so an awareness of the abuse of *you know* in public forums makes us better listeners.

16 As used in line 20, "progressive" most nearly means

(A) improving
(B) reformist
(C) continuing
(D) freethinking
(E) futuristic

17 The author's attitude toward the loss of the distinction referred to in lines 20-22 is best described as

(A) indifference
(B) resignation
(C) resentment
(D) defiance
(E) puzzlement

18 It can be inferred from the passage that the author approves most of modern users of language who

(A) believe that meanings of words are purely arbitrary
(B) treat public conversation as if it were private
(C) recognize the reasons for particular usages
(D) consider "the natural drift" of language to be inescapable
(E) relax the rules of written usage

GO ON TO THE NEXT PAGE

19 It can be inferred that "early grammarians" (line 38) had little reason to concern themselves with

(A) the abuse of spoken language in public discourse
(B) declining moral values
(C) new and fascinating word meanings
(D) conflicting rules of usage
(E) the origins of linguistic rules

20 With which of the following statements relating to language usage today would the author be most likely to agree?

(A) Rules of grammar define usage.
(B) Television has little influence on language change.
(C) Opinions of traditionalists should be largely discounted.
(D) The study of polite prose is a moral accomplishment.
(E) Changes in the language ought to be questioned.

GO ON TO THE NEXT PAGE

Questions 21-30 are based on the following passage.

In this passage a painter and sculptor from the United States recounts her first visit to Paris, made when she was in her sixties.

January 19: I fly on the night of January 23rd. I know that as my foot crosses the threshold of the airplane, my spirit will lift. In my guidebook I have scouted out the topography of Paris so that when I arrive I can align myself north, south, east, west. And I continue to review my French.

French money is engraved with the portraits of artists: Delacroix, de La Tour, Montesquieu, Debussy; I am astounded, and catch a distant trumpet of an entirely new point of view. I wonder if, by way of similar extraordinary facts that I cannot predict, I may feel more at home in Europe than on my deeply loved stretches of land in the United States. Something stubborn in me hopes not, and in recognizing that part of me I suddenly know why I never sought out Europe when, for years of my life, I had ample opportunity: I am afraid of its wisdoms, leery of challenge to the little developments of my own that I have struggled for and the independence of which I cherish, perhaps inordinately.

I am slightly chagrined—but also delighted—that an astute English artist has already observed in me limitations I only today perceived for myself. She writes: "I hope you are looking forward to Paris. I am sure you will find it a revelation to be in Europe—you will recognize so many sources of your thinking."

January 24: Arrived at the airport in Paris at eight in the morning. Directed by three volubly helpful French people, I found a taxi which bore me to my daughter's hotel by way of the Place de la Concorde, the Tuileries Gardens, and the Louvre*: a space conceived on the level of a grand linear dream underwritten by power into reality. An American voice in me remarked coolly, even as I marveled, "Now I understand the French Revolution; it's *wrong* for any human being to have had this much power." But all that is really none of my business now. The architectural space of Paris is an astonishment to me because its scale so accurately attunes inhabited earth to sky that I can actually walk in a work of art. I feel in some subtle way eased. I find myself in a world ordered by people of like mind to my own, in a companionship rendered visible. As if for the first time in my life I could be content to be human without having to forego, because of that limitation, my intuition of divine order.

January 26: My daughter and I made our way, maps clutched in our hands, back to the Louvre.

The Louvre rolled up a lifetime's study of art into a pellet and spat it out in my ignorant face. Corridors dimensionless as those in nightmares were lined with art of such authority that I stood as much aghast as dazzled.

Whenever I have seen art in its land of origin, I have been struck by its reliance on place. In America, Japanese art looks withdrawn into itself, as if stiffened in self-defense; Australian Aboriginal art, unutterably powerful in Australia, loses meaning, can even look merely decorative, when carted off that continent, losing force as visibly as a rainbow trout fades when cast onto the bank of a river. The European art I have seen in America seems anemic in comparison to what I am seeing here. By the same token, I sometimes wish that photography were solely the domain of artists who photograph rather than a tool so commonly used for the reproduction of artworks. Reproduction fatally weakens the force of art, reducing its presence to mere information and thus rendering it accessible in a way that makes it easy to miss the point of it.

*Formerly a royal palace, the Louvre was turned into a public art museum after the French Revolution.

21 The passage creates an impression of the author as a person who is

(A) timid and indecisive
(B) bitter and full of regrets
(C) thoughtful and introspective
(D) headstrong and impetuous
(E) jovial and gregarious

22 In lines 7-10, the author discusses French money in order to make which point?

(A) Artists are held in esteem in French culture.
(B) People value art primarily as an investment.
(C) The author did not know what to expect in a foreign country.
(D) People in France are not as materialistically oriented as are people in the United States.
(E) The author's finances influenced her feelings about her trip.

GO ON TO THE NEXT PAGE

23 The concern expressed by the author in the second and third paragraphs (lines 7-28) centers on

(A) what she will discover about herself
(B) the uncertainty of the future
(C) the reception that her artworks will receive
(D) whether she should emigrate to Europe
(E) her relationships with other artists

24 "Something stubborn in me" (line 14) is used by the author as a reflection of her

(A) dislike of European styles of painting
(B) determination not to be identified as a foreigner
(C) desire to travel independently in a foreign city
(D) compulsion to master a new language and culture
(E) pride in her own accomplishments

25 The English artist's message (lines 25-28) indicates that artist's opinion that

(A) the author has been unaware of the extent to which European art has influenced her work
(B) the author's visit to Paris will radically alter the nature of her future work
(C) the author's previous work has been unduly dependent on European styles
(D) European artists have much to learn from the author
(E) all artists need to leave their own countries in order to gain perspective

26 The "American voice" described in lines 35-39 represents an attitude of

(A) awe aroused by the beauty of the Louvre
(B) eagerness to be enriched by new ideas about art
(C) painful insignificance when standing next to such a grand building
(D) critical evaluation of the Louvre in terms of its historical context
(E) surprise because American art seems decadent compared to European art

27 In line 62, the phrase "carted off" suggests a process of transporting objects that is

(A) inefficient and antiquated
(B) accomplished only with great effort
(C) slow and ponderous
(D) performed in a rough and thoughtless manner
(E) stealthy and possibly illegal

28 The author likens art to a "rainbow trout" (lines 63-64) in order to

(A) stress the importance of color in art
(B) suggest art's dependence on its environment
(C) mock those who prefer abstract painting
(D) argue that art must be grounded in a reverence for nature
(E) compare the activity of painting to mundane pursuits

29 The discussion of photography (lines 66-73) reveals the author's assumption that

(A) painting is superior to photography as an art form
(B) some viewers cannot distinguish a reproduction from an original
(C) the essence of an artwork cannot be conveyed through reproductions
(D) reproductions of famous paintings enable everyone to view them with insight
(E) works of art often are inexpertly reproduced

30 The author would be most likely to endorse an art education program that stressed

(A) the study of artworks in the context of their place of origin
(B) a thorough grounding in the artworks made in one's own region
(C) the use of reproductions of famous artworks
(D) creating original paintings rather than studying those of others
(E) analyzing a culture's history before studying its artistic tradition

IF YOU FINISH BEFORE TIME IS CALLED, YOU MAY CHECK YOUR WORK ON THIS SECTION ONLY. DO NOT TURN TO ANY OTHER SECTION IN THE TEST. **STOP**

Section 4 4 4 4 4

Time—30 Minutes
25 Questions

This section contains two types of questions. You have 30 minutes to complete both types. You may use any available space for scratchwork.

Notes:

1. The use of a calculator is permitted. All numbers used are real numbers.
2. Figures that accompany problems in this test are intended to provide information useful in solving the problems. They are drawn as accurately as possible EXCEPT when it is stated in a specific problem that the figure is not drawn to scale. All figures lie in a plane unless otherwise indicated.

Reference Information

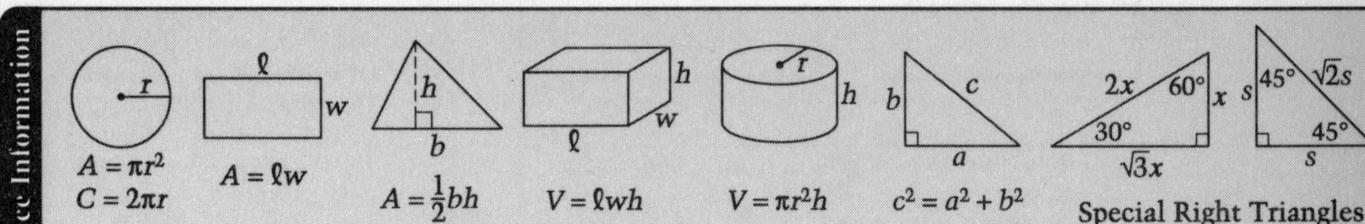

The number of degrees of arc in a circle is 360.
The measure in degrees of a straight angle is 180.
The sum of the measures in degrees of the angles of a triangle is 180.

Directions for Quantitative Comparison Questions

Questions 1-15 each consist of two quantities in boxes, one in Column A and one in Column B. You are to compare the two quantities and on the answer sheet fill in oval

A if the quantity in Column A is greater;
B if the quantity in Column B is greater;
C if the two quantities are equal;
D if the relationship cannot be determined from the information given.

AN E RESPONSE WILL NOT BE SCORED.

Notes:

1. In some questions, information is given about one or both of the quantities to be compared. In such cases, the given information is centered above the two columns and is not boxed.
2. In a given question, a symbol that appears in both columns represents the same thing in Column A as it does in Column B.
3. Letters such as x, n, and k stand for real numbers.

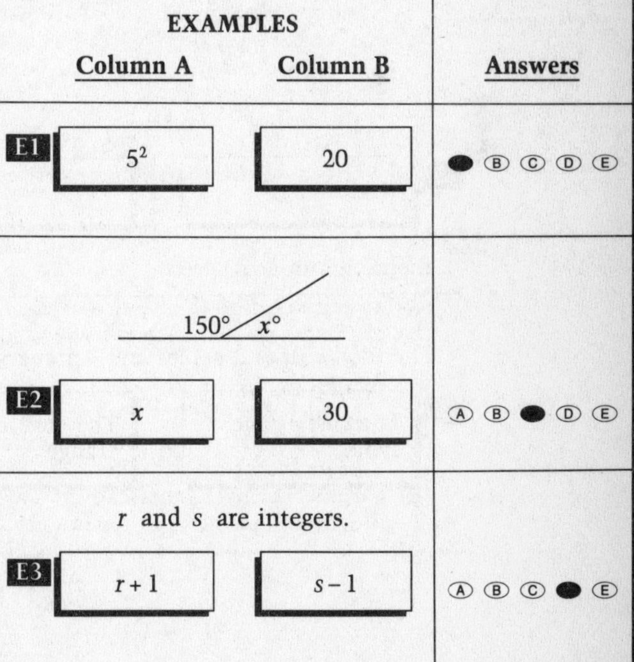

EXAMPLES
Column A
Column B
Answers
E1
5^2
20
E2
150°
$x°$
x
30
r and s are integers.
E3
$r + 1$
$s - 1$

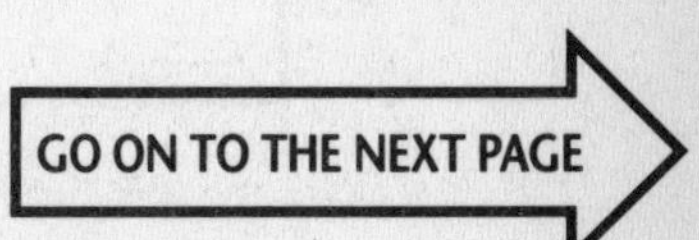

SUMMARY DIRECTIONS FOR COMPARISON QUESTIONS

Answer: A if the quantity in Column A is greater;
B if the quantity in Column B is greater;
C if the two quantities are equal;
D if the relationship cannot be determined from the information given.

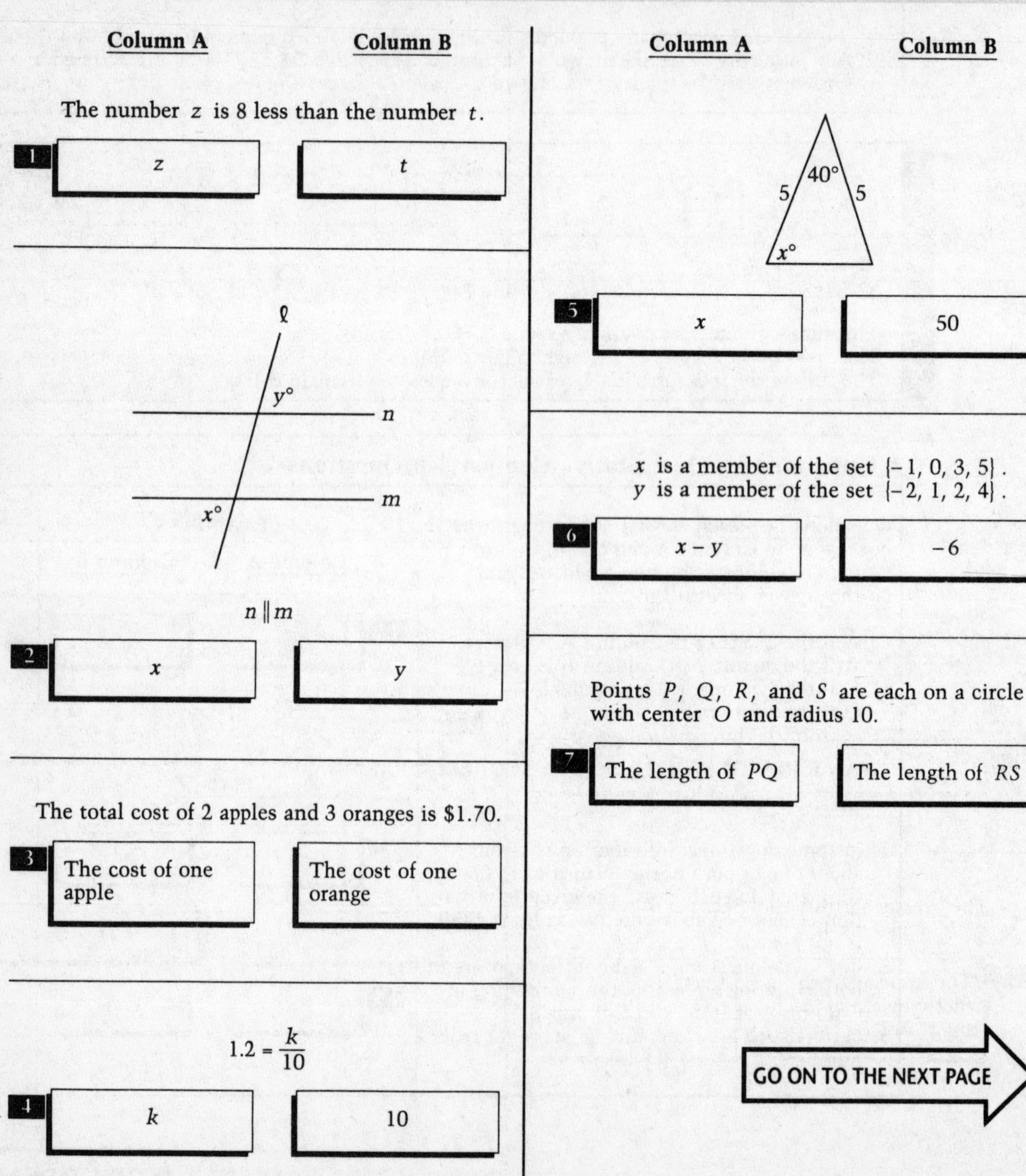

	Column A	Column B

The number z is 8 less than the number t.

	Column A	Column B
1	z	t

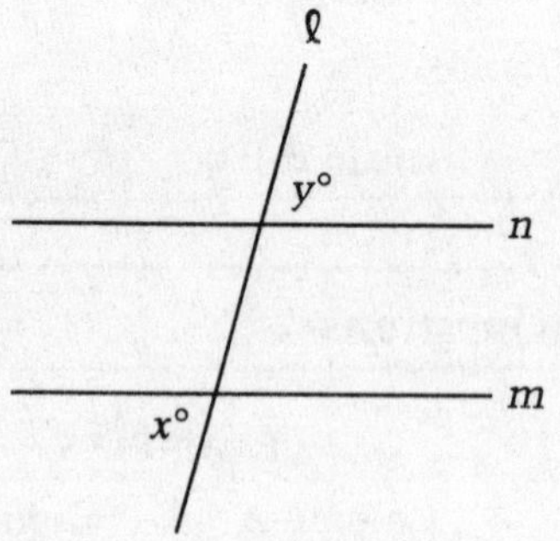

$n \parallel m$

	Column A	Column B
2	x	y

The total cost of 2 apples and 3 oranges is \$1.70.

	Column A	Column B
3	The cost of one apple	The cost of one orange

$1.2 = \frac{k}{10}$

	Column A	Column B
4	k	10

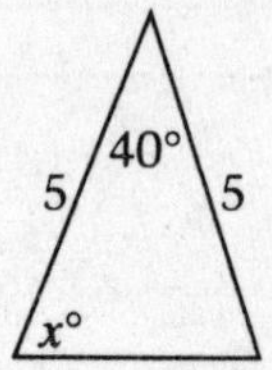

	Column A	Column B
5	x	50

x is a member of the set $\{-1, 0, 3, 5\}$.
y is a member of the set $\{-2, 1, 2, 4\}$.

	Column A	Column B
6	$x - y$	-6

Points P, Q, R, and S are each on a circle with center O and radius 10.

	Column A	Column B
7	The length of PQ	The length of RS

GO ON TO THE NEXT PAGE

SUMMARY DIRECTIONS FOR COMPARISON QUESTIONS

Answer: A if the quantity in Column A is greater;
B if the quantity in Column B is greater;
C if the two quantities are equal;
D if the relationship cannot be determined from the information given.

	Column A	Column B
	$\frac{s}{t} = \frac{2}{3}$	
8	$9s^2$	$4t^2$

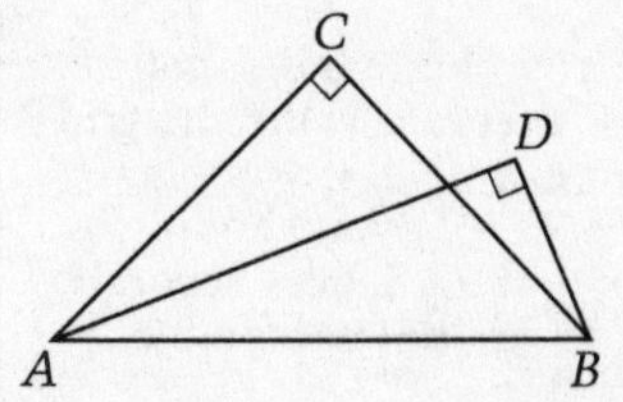

	Column A	Column B
9	$(AC)^2 + (BC)^2$	$(AD)^2 + (BD)^2$

$a = 3b$
$b > 0$

	Column A	Column B
10	$a + b$	$a \times b$

The average (arithmetic mean) of 3 integers a, b, and c is 40.

	Column A	Column B
11	The average (arithmetic mean) of a, b, c, and 39	40

$5 < 2x - 1 < 9$

	Column A	Column B
12	x	$\frac{9}{2}$

Twenty-seven white cubes of the same size are put together to form a larger cube. The larger cube is painted blue.

	Column A	Column B
13	The number of the smaller cubes that have exactly three blue faces	9

$w + x + y + z = 0$
$w \cdot x \cdot y \cdot z \neq 0$

	Column A	Column B
14	$w^2 + x^2 + y^2 + z^2$	$(w + x + y + z)^2$

$s - r = t - s = m - t = v - m = w - v$

	Column A	Column B
15	$t - r$	$(w - v) + (t - s)$

GO ON TO THE NEXT PAGE

Directions for Student-Produced Response Questions

Each of the remaining 10 questions requires you to solve the problem and enter your answer by marking the ovals in the special grid, as shown in the examples below.

Answer: $\frac{7}{12}$ or 7/12

Write answer in boxes. → 7/12 ← Fraction line

Grid in result.

Answer: 2.5

2.5 ← Decimal point

Answer: 201
Either position is correct.

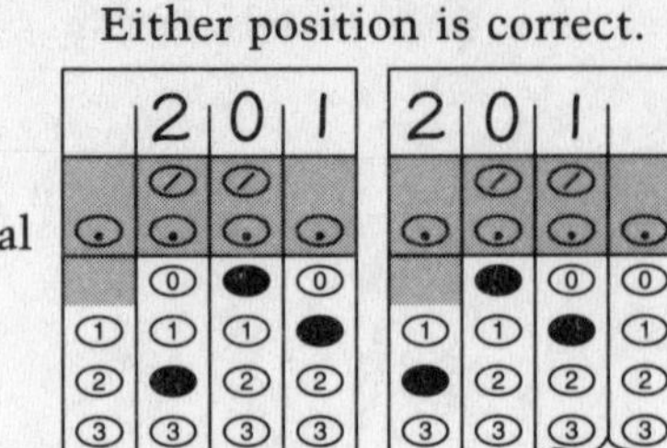

Note: You may start your answers in any column, space permitting. Columns not needed should be left blank.

- Mark no more than one oval in any column.
- Because the answer sheet will be machine-scored, **you will receive credit only if the ovals are filled in correctly.**
- Although not required, it is suggested that you write your answer in the boxes at the top of the columns to help you fill in the ovals accurately.
- Some problems may have more than one correct answer. In such cases, grid only one answer.
- No question has a negative answer.
- **Mixed numbers** such as $2\frac{1}{2}$ must be gridded as 2.5 or 5/2. (If 21/2 is gridded, it will be interpreted as $\frac{21}{2}$, not $2\frac{1}{2}$.)

- **Decimal Accuracy**: If you obtain a decimal answer, **enter the most accurate value the grid will accommodate.** For example, if you obtain an answer such as 0.6666 . . . , you should record the result as .666 or .667. **Less accurate values such as .66 or .67 are not acceptable.**

Acceptable ways to grid $\frac{2}{3} = .6666\ldots$

2/3 .666 .667

16 If $5ab + 1 = 1$, what is the value of ab ?

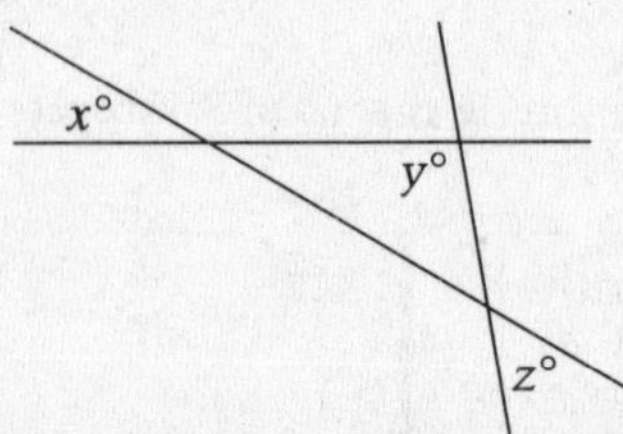

Note: Figure not drawn to scale.

17 In the figure above, if $x = 25$ and $z = 30$, what is the value of y ?

GO ON TO THE NEXT PAGE

18 The integer m is between 40 and 100. When m is divided by 3, the remainder is 2. When m is divided by 7, the remainder is 1. What is one possible value of m ?

19 In a group study on nutrition, the average daily intake of calories per person was 8 percent higher in April than it was in March. If this average was 3,200 calories in March, what was the average daily intake of calories per person in April?

20 Ten consecutive integers are arranged in order from least to greatest. If the sum of the first five integers is 200, what is the sum of the last five integers?

21 If the points $P(-2, 6)$, $Q(-2, 1)$, and $R(2, 1)$ are vertices of a triangle, what is the area of the triangle?

GO ON TO THE NEXT PAGE

22 If a pound of grass seed covers an area of 500 square feet and costs \$3.25, what is the cost, in dollars, of the seed needed to cover a level rectangular area that measures 200 feet by 300 feet? (Disregard \$ sign when gridding your answer.)

23 The expression $\frac{3x-1}{4} + \frac{x+6}{4}$ is how much more than x?

24 What is the least positive integer n for which $12n$ is the cube of an integer?

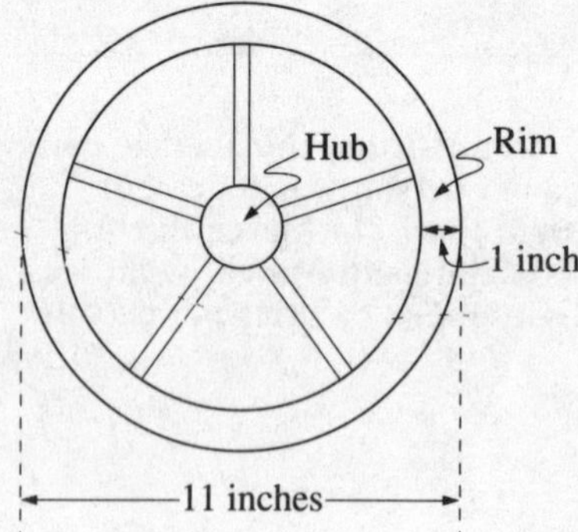

25 A wheel has an outer diameter of 11 inches, as shown above. The rim is 1 inch wide and the diameter of the hub is 2 inches. If each spoke extends $\frac{1}{2}$ inch into the hub and $\frac{1}{2}$ inch into the rim, what is the sum of the lengths of the five spokes, in inches?

IF YOU FINISH BEFORE TIME IS CALLED, YOU MAY CHECK YOUR WORK ON THIS SECTION ONLY. DO NOT TURN TO ANY OTHER SECTION IN THE TEST. **STOP**

Section 5 5

Time — 30 Minutes
35 Questions

For each question in this section, select the best answer from among the choices given and fill in the corresponding oval on the answer sheet.

Each sentence below has one or two blanks, each blank indicating that something has been omitted. Beneath the sentence are five words or sets of words labeled A through E. Choose the word or set of words that, when inserted in the sentence, best fits the meaning of the sentence as a whole.

Example:

Medieval kingdoms did not become constitutional republics overnight; on the contrary, the change was ----.

(A) unpopular
(B) unexpected
(C) advantageous
(D) sufficient
(E) gradual

Ⓐ Ⓑ Ⓒ Ⓓ ●

1 Whether Mitsuko Uchida is performing music or merely discussing it, the pianist's animated demeanor ---- her passion for her vocation.

(A) misrepresents (B) exaggerates (C) satisfies (D) reflects (E) disguises

2 One of the factors that ---- the understanding of the nature of cells was the limited resolution of early microscopes.

(A) aided (B) discredited (C) increased (D) contradicted (E) restricted

3 The congresswoman is very powerful: she has more ---- than any other member of the committee.

(A) integrity (B) influence (C) restraint (D) discrimination (E) pretense

4 Anyone who possesses perceptiveness, insight, and unflagging vitality has invaluable ----, but the rare individual who also possesses the ability to ---- these qualities through art has genius.

(A) prospects. .delegate
(B) gifts. .express
(C) traits. .forbid
(D) flaws. .impute
(E) visions. .bequeath

5 Each male mockingbird views his territory as ----; no other male of the same species is tolerated within its boundaries.

(A) circuitous (B) inviolable (C) dissipated (D) unparalleled (E) mandated

6 To summarize an article is to separate that which is ---- from the ---- material that surrounds it.

(A) notable. .primary
(B) undesirable. .encompassing
(C) fundamental. .vital
(D) essential. .supporting
(E) explanatory. .characteristic

7 Sometimes fiction is marred by departures from the main narrative, but Toni Morrison's *The Bluest Eye* is instead ---- by its ----, which add levels of meaning to the principal story.

(A) enhanced. .digressions
(B) harmed. .excursions
(C) adorned. .melodramas
(D) strengthened. .criticisms
(E) unaffected. .swervings

8 According to the report, the investment firm had ---- several customers, swindling them out of thousands of dollars.

(A) harassed (B) sullied (C) bilked (D) investigated (E) incriminated

9 Because this novel is not so narrowly concerned with ---- political issues, it seems as ---- today as it did two hundred years ago.

(A) momentary. .derivative
(B) evanescent. .nostalgic
(C) transient. .fresh
(D) sagacious. .wise
(E) dated. .quaint

10 Contemptuous of official myths about great men and women that had been taught to them in school, many postwar writers, with the skepticism expected of ----, advanced the idea that there was no such thing as greatness.

(A) idealists (B) well-wishers (C) dissemblers (D) nitpickers (E) debunkers

GO ON TO THE NEXT PAGE

Each question below consists of a related pair of words or phrases, followed by five pairs of words or phrases labeled A through E. Select the pair that best expresses a relationship similar to that expressed in the original pair.

Example:

CRUMB : BREAD ::
(A) ounce : unit
(B) splinter : wood
(C) water : bucket
(D) twine : rope
(E) cream : butter

Ⓐ ● Ⓒ Ⓓ Ⓔ

11 OSTRICH : BIRD ::
(A) lion : cat
(B) goose : flock
(C) ewe : sheep
(D) cub : bear
(E) primate : monkey

12 WORD : LANGUAGE ::
(A) paint : portrait
(B) poetry : rhythm
(C) note : music
(D) tale : story
(E) week : year

13 COOP : POULTRY ::
(A) aquarium : fish
(B) forest : wildlife
(C) crib : nursery
(D) fence : yard
(E) barn : tool

14 LEGEND : MAP ::
(A) subtitle : translation
(B) bar : graph
(C) figure : blueprint
(D) key : chart
(E) footnote : information

15 BILLBOARD : ADVERTISEMENT ::
(A) sculpture : museum
(B) store : window
(C) library : book
(D) canvas : painting
(E) theater : intermission

16 CUSTOM : SOCIETY ::
(A) hypothesis : evidence
(B) testimony : trial
(C) ballot : election
(D) rule : game
(E) contest : debate

17 TUNNEL : MINE ::
(A) conduit : fluid
(B) corner : intersection
(C) sign : detour
(D) aisle : seat
(E) corridor : building

18 DIVERSION : BOREDOM ::
(A) assurance : uncertainty
(B) enmity : hatred
(C) secrecy : curiosity
(D) reward : deed
(E) sluggishness : fatigue

19 THICKET : SHRUBS ::
(A) grove : trees
(B) orchard : apples
(C) pasture : cows
(D) reef : waves
(E) crop : plants

20 CONDESCENDING : RESPECT ::
(A) bashful : attention
(B) obliging : thanks
(C) insecure : doubt
(D) merciless : compassion
(E) pathetic : pity

21 LIVID : ANGER ::
(A) querulous : reconciliation
(B) forlorn : hope
(C) radiant : happiness
(D) graceful : posture
(E) marvelous : wonder

22 FATHOM : DEPTH ::
(A) amplify : volume
(B) overflow : capacity
(C) appraise : value
(D) stump : answer
(E) weigh : scale

23 REMUNERATION : LABOR ::
(A) gratuity : bonus
(B) apology : regret
(C) pledge : donation
(D) trophy : victory
(E) debt : loan

GO ON TO THE NEXT PAGE

The passage below is followed by questions based on its content. Answer the questions on the basis of what is stated or implied in the passage and in any introductory material that may be provided.

Questions 24-35 are based on the following passage.

The following excerpt by an anthropologist represents one point of view in the ongoing debate about cultural influences in the United States.

On a hot Friday afternoon in the last week of August, cars, pickup trucks, campers, and school buses slowly pull into a park on the edge of Fargo, North Dakota. Families carve out small pieces of territory around their vehicles, making the park into a series of encampments. As they have done for generations, American Indians of the Great Plains gather once again for an annual powwow. Donning their traditional clothing, Ojibwa, Lakota, and Dakota people assemble for several days of celebration and ceremony.

To an outside observer attending for the first time, this year's powwow may appear chaotic. Even though posted signs promise that dances will begin at four o'clock, there is still no dancing at five-thirty, and the scheduled drummers never arrive. No one is in charge; the announcer acts as a facilitator of ceremonies, but no chief rises to demand anything of anyone. Everyone shows great respect for the elders and for the dancers, who are repeatedly singled out for recognition, but at the same time children receive attention for dancing, as does the audience for watching. Eventually the program grows in an organic fashion as dancers slowly become activated by drums and singing. Each participant responds to the mood of the whole group but not to a single, directing voice, and the event flows in an orderly fashion like hundreds of powwows before it.

This apparent penchant for respectful individualism and equality within an American Indian group seems as strong today to a non-Indian observer in Fargo as it did five centuries ago to early European explorers. Much to the shock of the first European observers and to the dismay of bureaucratic individuals, American Indian societies have traditionally operated without strong positions of leadership or coercive political institutions.

Adventure novels and Hollywood films set in the past often portray strong chiefs commanding their tribes. More often, however, as in the case of the Iroquois people, a council of sachems, or legislators, ruled, and any person called the "head" of the tribe usually occupied a largely honorary position of respect rather than power. Chiefs mostly played ceremonial and religious roles rather than political or economic ones. Unlike the familiar words "caucus" and "powwow," which are Indian-derived and indicative of American Indian political traditions, the word "chief" is an English word of French origin that British officials tried to force onto American Indian tribes in order that they might have someone with whom to trade and sign treaties.

In seventeenth-century Massachusetts the British tried to make one leader, Metacom of the Wampanoag people, into King Philip, thereby imputing monarchy to the American Indian system when no such institution existed. Thus while certain English settlers learned from groups like the Iroquois people how to speak and act in group councils, others simultaneously tried to push American Indians toward a monarchical and therefore less democratic system.

By the late 1600's the Huron people of Canada had already interacted for decades with European explorers and traders and were thus able to compare their own way of life with that of the Europeans. The Hurons particularly decried the European obsession with money. By contrast, the Hurons lived a life of liberty and equality and believed that the Europeans lost their freedom in their incessant use of "thine" and "mine." One Huron explained to the French adventurer and writer Baron de La Hontan, who lived among the Hurons for eleven years, that his people were born free and united, each as great as the other, while Europeans were all the slaves of one sole person. "I am the master of my body," he said, ". . .I am the first and the last of my Nation . . . subject only to the great Spirit." These words recorded by La Hontan may have reflected the Frenchman's own philosophical bias, but his book rested on a solid factual base: the Huron people lived without social classes, without a government separate from their kinship system, and without private property. To describe this situation, La Hontan revived the Greek-derived word "anarchy," using it in the literal sense to mean "no ruler." La Hontan found

GO ON TO THE NEXT PAGE

an orderly society, but one lacking a formal government that compelled such order.

The descriptions by La Hontan and other European travelers of the so-called anarchy among the American Indians contributed to several different brands of anarchistic theory in the nineteenth century. Today, anarchism is often equated with terrorism and nihilism (denial of values), but early anarchism lacked those characteristics. Pierre Joseph Proudhon (1809-1865), the author of modern anarchistic theory, stressed the notion of "mutualism" in a society based on cooperation without the use of coercion from any quarter.

Like certain American plants that were introduced throughout the world and that found new surroundings in which to flourish, the examples of liberty and individuality in American Indian societies spread and survived in other surroundings. Today, in the ordered anarchy of a powwow in North Dakota, these same values are articulated more eloquently than in the writings of most political theorists.

24 The first two paragraphs (lines 1-29) serve all of the following purposes EXCEPT to

(A) provide a narrative account to serve as an introduction
(B) contrast American Indian social events with individual performances
(C) create a sense of the permanence of some American Indian customs
(D) inform the reader about the nature of a powwow
(E) lead to a discussion of an important political concept

25 In line 14, the author uses the word "promise" to reflect the

(A) outsider's misunderstanding of linguistic variations
(B) outsider's inability to be punctual
(C) outsider's inappropriate expectations
(D) announcer's frustration at the unexpected delay
(E) drummers' commitment to training a new generation in their art

26 Paragraph four (lines 40-55) suggests which of the following concerning Iroquois tribal "heads" of three hundred years ago?

(A) They were appointed by the European settlers.
(B) They were rarely present at ceremonial gatherings.
(C) Their people expected them to negotiate on their behalf.
(D) They did not wield as much power as the tribal councils did.
(E) They adjudicated conflicts within their own tribes.

27 Which conclusion concerning the term "caucus" (line 49) is most directly supported by the passage?

(A) Its use today reflects the influence of American Indian traditions.
(B) It is a word derived from French and transplanted to frontier America.
(C) It is a term synonymous with a European-style monarchy.
(D) It represents a misinterpretation of the idea of political anarchy.
(E) It refers to a convening of British officials and American Indian leaders.

28 The passage implies that the image of the monarchical American Indian leader originated in

(A) the writings of French political theorists
(B) the personal narratives of early American Indian leaders
(C) representative legends from diverse North American tribes
(D) European assumptions about social structure
(E) medieval European myths about undiscovered western lands

GO ON TO THE NEXT PAGE

29 In line 74, "thine" and "mine" are used to illustrate

(A) the mutual respect that Hurons felt for each other
(B) the verbal expression of liberating ideas
(C) a notion that La Hontan encouraged the Hurons to accept
(D) the importance of property in European society
(E) terms of address between French explorers and American Indians

30 In the context of the passage, the statement "I am the master . . . Spirit" (lines 80-82) implies that the person being quoted

(A) accepted political rebellion only as a measure of last resort
(B) thought of himself as the leader of his people
(C) had been designated to participate in the founding of a new nation
(D) believed that a class structure undermined individual freedom
(E) felt the weight of spiritual responsibility for humankind

31 If La Hontan's writing did, in fact, reflect his "philosophical bias" (line 84), it can be inferred that as a philosopher he was most likely motivated by a desire to

(A) misrepresent the Hurons' views about European society
(B) reform French society in order to gain more authority
(C) become a mentor to the Huron society
(D) describe an aspect of his many adventures
(E) encourage greater democracy in French society

32 Which statement best describes the relationship between Proudhon's theory and seventeenth century Huron practices discussed in lines 93-103?

(A) An influential idea was publicized by those who had helped formulate it.
(B) An intellectual argument was based on Proudhon's own experiences.
(C) Practical suggestions by nonspecialists were incorporated into a system of thought.
(D) A scholar's perceptions were modified only after comparison with a historical example.
(E) The development of an abstract concept was influenced by an observed phenomenon.

33 In line 96, "brands" most nearly means

(A) marks
(B) manufactures
(C) varieties
(D) logos
(E) identifications

34 In line 103, "quarter" is best understood as meaning

(A) fourth part
(B) monetary unit
(C) person or group
(D) dwelling place
(E) indefinite point or place

35 In the sentence beginning "Like certain . . ." (lines 104-108), the author's approach shifts from

(A) manipulating highly charged rhetoric to introducing a counterappeal
(B) supplying selected historical references to using figurative language
(C) analyzing a process unemotionally to suggesting mild disapproval
(D) expressing skepticism to invoking cautious praise
(E) employing veiled blame to summarizing concepts optimistically

IF YOU FINISH BEFORE TIME IS CALLED, YOU MAY CHECK YOUR WORK ON THIS SECTION ONLY. DO NOT TURN TO ANY OTHER SECTION IN THE TEST. **STOP**

Section 6 6 6 6

Time—15 Minutes
13 Questions

For each question in this section, select the best answer from among the choices given and fill in the corresponding oval on the answer sheet.

The two passages below are followed by questions based on their content and on the relationship between the two passages. Answer the questions on the basis of what is stated or implied in the passages and in any introductory material that may be provided.

Questions 1-13 are based on the following passages.

Radio astronomy, the science dealing with radio waves originating beyond the Earth's atmosphere, began with an accidental discovery made by Karl Jansky, an engineer at Bell Telephone Laboratories in New Jersey. Jansky was studying the sources of atmospheric radio static as part of an effort to improve overseas telephone transmission when, while scanning the sky with a shortwave antenna, he picked up a new kind of static. Passage 1 is from an article describing Jansky's work; Passage 2 is from a speech given in the early 1980's by Grote Reber, another pioneering radio astronomer.

Passage 1

In August 1931 Jansky first recognized a new, weak component of static, faintly audible with headphones. Like static at other frequencies, it was strongest around the time of electrical storms, but the source of this static moved across the southern sky in a regular east-to-west pattern. Jansky wrote in his work report: "The reason for this phenomenon is not yet known, but it is believed that a study of the known thunderstorm areas of the world will reveal the cause."

In August the static was a nighttime phenomenon, but when it persisted through the autumn and began to shift to different times of day, Jansky became intrigued. Early on, he called it "Sun static," for the direction of arrival seemed to coincide quite closely with the Sun's position. But by February its daily peak was preceding the Sun by as much as an hour.

In December 1932 Jansky reviewed his entire year's data and noticed the precision in the shift of the overall pattern. After one year the pattern had slipped exactly one day—the peak signal was now in the south at the same time of day as it had been the previous December. To an astronomer this kind of shift is a fact of life—a star or other source fixed in celestial coordinates rises four minutes earlier each day (with respect to the Sun) as a result of the Earth orbiting the Sun; after a year, this slippage amounts to one day. But to a communications engineer, the connection is not at all obvious. It may have been Jansky's friend Melvin Skellett who provided the key suggestion. Skellett was leading a highly unusual life, simultaneously working as a radio engineer for Bell Labs and pursuing graduate studies in astronomy. By late December, Jansky had consulted Skellett and had learned a good bit about astronomical coordinates. Jansky wrote in a letter: "I have taken more data which indicate definitely that the stuff, whatever it is, comes from something not only extraterrestrial, but from outside the Solar System."

Meanwhile, he began writing a paper about his findings, although apparently without much support from Harald Friis, his supervisor. In another letter Jansky wrote: "My records show that this static comes from a direction fixed in space. The evidence I have is conclusive and, I think, very startling. When I first suggested the idea of publishing something about it to Friis, he was somewhat skeptical and wanted more data. Frankly, I think he was scared."

Thus it is that Jansky's 1933 paper, one of the most important in the astronomy of this century, has the relatively cautious title "Electrical Disturbances Apparently of Extraterrestrial Origin."

In the paper Jansky proposed the center of the Milky Way galaxy as one possible origin of the static. Further study, however, proved confusing, for the daily time of arrival was not behaving as regularly (based on the assumption of a single source) as it should have. Soon Jansky realized that the static was coming not from the galactic center but from the entire galaxy.

GO ON TO THE NEXT PAGE

Passage 2

I have been asked about the early lack of interest in radio astronomy by the astronomical community. In retrospect, there appear to have been two difficulties. First, the astronomers had a nearly complete lack of knowledge of electronic apparatus, viewing it as magical and sinister. Second, and more important, the astrophysicists could not dream up any rational way by which the radio waves could be generated, and since they didn't know of such a process, the whole affair was at best a mistake and at worst a hoax. I've encountered this attitude at other times and places. If the why and how are not known, observations are discounted by the intelligentsia. By contrast, the engineering fraternity had a clear understanding of the electronic equipment. More important, they were not inhibited by mental hang-ups about the origin of the radio waves. On that subject, their attitude was—who cares?

The pundits of Marconi's* day said his ideas about wireless radio would not work because radio waves were similar to light and would not bend around the curvature of the Earth. Even after Marconi's successful transatlantic radio transmission in 1901, many doubted his results because there was no known way radio waves would perform as he reported. However, the telegraphic cable company believed him. They served him with a writ to cease and desist because they had an exclusive monopoly on transatlantic communication. As usual the intelligentsia fell flat on its face.

*Guglielmo Marconi (1874-1937), Nobel Prize-winning physicist and inventor of wireless radio

1 As described in the first paragraph of Passage 1 (lines 1-10), Jansky first became curious about the new static because

(A) its cause did not seem to be electrical
(B) its source moved in a distinctive pattern
(C) it was stronger than other static
(D) it occurred at all frequencies
(E) it was rarely observed during thunderstorms

2 The author of Passage 1 uses the phrase "a fact of life" (line 25) to indicate

(A) a challenge that every person must eventually confront
(B) an obstacle that astronomers must overcome
(C) part of an astronomer's body of basic knowledge
(D) something that is evident even to a child
(E) something that Jansky was afraid to face

3 Passage 1 suggests that Skellett played what role in Jansky's research?

(A) He spotted a flaw in Jansky's method of gathering data.
(B) He suggested a crucial improvement to Jansky's antenna.
(C) He corrected an error in Jansky's mathematical calculations.
(D) He helped Jansky to interpret the pattern of his data.
(E) He informed Jansky about new developments in theoretical physics.

4 What does Passage 1 suggest about the title of Jansky's 1933 paper (lines 52-55) ?

(A) It was entirely misleading.
(B) It did not convey the discovery's importance.
(C) It was unacceptable to Friis.
(D) It would have been comprehensible only to engineers.
(E) It made light of an important problem emerging in science.

5 In line 58, "proved" most nearly means

(A) turned out
(B) made clear
(C) tested
(D) verified
(E) refined

GO ON TO THE NEXT PAGE

6 In Passage 2, Reber suggests that the astronomers had which attitude toward electronic equipment (lines 67-69) ?

(A) They were impatient with its limitations.
(B) They took it for granted.
(C) They relied too heavily on it.
(D) They had an unreasonable aversion to it.
(E) They believed it would revolutionize their field.

7 In Passage 2, "the whole affair was at best a mistake" (lines 73-74) is presented as the opinion of

(A) Reber
(B) Jansky
(C) Marconi
(D) the engineers
(E) the astrophysicists

8 In Passage 2, Reber most likely believes that when attempting to interpret puzzling data one should

(A) reject the reports of previous observers
(B) derive new theoretical principles
(C) keep an open mind
(D) be especially on guard against a hoax
(E) assume that the most outlandish explanation is probably the most correct

9 In Passage 2, Reber describes Marconi's work chiefly in order to

(A) disparage the narrow-mindedness of some of the scientific community
(B) illustrate the dangers of commercial control over science
(C) suggest why Jansky's discovery was greater than Marconi's
(D) show that theoretical science is superior to applied science
(E) criticize the attitude of the industrialists of Marconi's day

10 The two passages approach radio astronomy differently in that Passage 1

(A) points out Jansky's originality while Passage 2 stresses his debt to his colleagues
(B) criticizes Friis while Passage 2 defends his reasoning
(C) emphasizes its inception while Passage 2 describes the early response to it
(D) is based on an assumption that Passage 2 reveals to be erroneous
(E) explores the theoretical aspect of science while Passage 2 stresses its danger to society

11 The passages differ in tone in that Passage 1 is

(A) enthusiastic while Passage 2 is cautious
(B) indignant while Passage 2 is nostalgic
(C) matter-of-fact while Passage 2 is sarcastic
(D) sensationalistic while Passage 2 is understated
(E) scornful while Passage 2 is uncritically admiring

12 Friis's attitude as presented in Passage 1 (lines 48-51) is most similar to whose attitude in Passage 2 ?

(A) Marconi's
(B) The cable company's
(C) The engineering fraternity's
(D) Reber's
(E) The intelligentsia's

13 Both passages illustrate the idea that scientists should

(A) resist the power of preconceived notions
(B) keep scrupulously accurate records
(C) make sure that their electronic equipment is up-to-date
(D) compare experimental results with those of other researchers
(E) achieve a solid grounding in theoretical principles

IF YOU FINISH BEFORE TIME IS CALLED, YOU MAY CHECK YOUR WORK ON THIS SECTION ONLY. DO NOT TURN TO ANY OTHER SECTION IN THE TEST. **STOP**

Section 7 7

Time—15 Minutes
10 Questions

In this section solve each problem, using any available space on the page for scratchwork. Then decide which is the best of the choices given and fill in the corresponding oval on the answer sheet.

Notes:

1. The use of a calculator is permitted. All numbers used are real numbers.
2. Figures that accompany problems in this test are intended to provide information useful in solving the problems. They are drawn as accurately as possible EXCEPT when it is stated in a specific problem that the figure is not drawn to scale. All figures lie in a plane unless otherwise indicated.

Reference Information

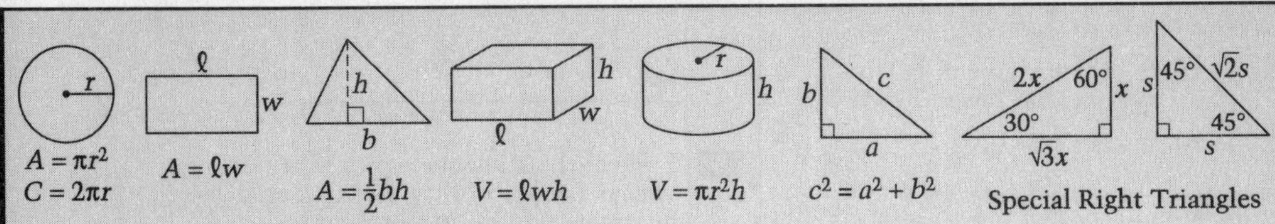

The number of degrees of arc in a circle is 360.
The measure in degrees of a straight angle is 180.
The sum of the measures in degrees of the angles of a triangle is 180.

1 If $a + 2 = 7$, then $(a + 3)^2 =$

(A) 25
(B) 36
(C) 49
(D) 64
(E) 81

$$\begin{array}{r} 13R \\ +\ R2 \\ \hline 19T \end{array}$$

2 R and T represent digits in the correctly worked addition problem above. What digit does T represent?

(A) 4
(B) 5
(C) 6
(D) 7
(E) 8

3 If $2^4 = 4^x$, then $x =$

(A) 1
(B) 2
(C) 4
(D) 5
(E) 8

GO ON TO THE NEXT PAGE

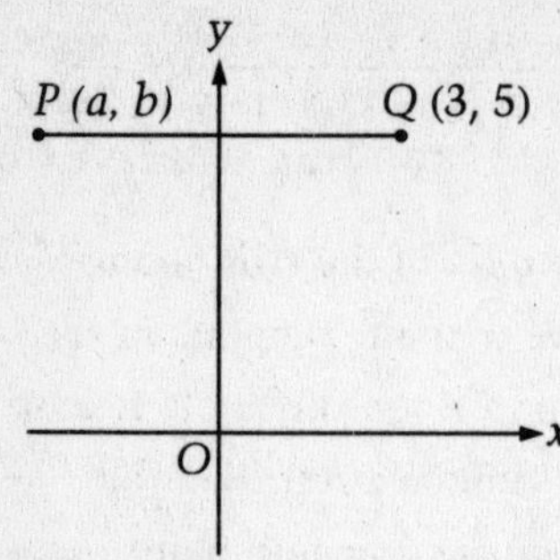

Note: Figure not drawn to scale.

4 In the figure above, if line segment PQ is parallel to the x-axis and has length 7, what is the value of a ?

(A) -4
(B) -3
(C) -2
(D) 3
(E) 5

Questions 5-6 refer to the following table.

Quiz Score	Number of Students Who Received That Score
0	3
1	6
2	7
3	4

A class of 20 students took a 3-question quiz. The table shows the possible scores on this quiz and the number of students who received each of these scores.

5 If one of the students is picked at random, what is the probability that that student's quiz score will be greater than 1 ?

(A) $\frac{1}{11}$

(B) $\frac{1}{2}$

(C) $\frac{11}{20}$

(D) $\frac{2}{3}$

(E) $\frac{7}{10}$

6 What is the average (arithmetic mean) of the scores for this class?

(A) 1.0
(B) 1.5
(C) 1.6
(D) 1.9
(E) 2.0

GO ON TO THE NEXT PAGE

1,234, . . . 1,920,21. . . ,484,950

7 The integer above is formed by writing the integers from 1 to 50, in order, next to each other. If the integer is read from left to right, what is the 50th digit from the left?

(A) 0
(B) 1
(C) 2
(D) 3
(E) 9

8 After Jean gave $10 to Irene and Irene gave $6 to Todd, Jean had $10 more than Irene and $20 more than Todd. Originally, how much more did Jean have than Irene and Todd?

(A) $14 more than Irene and $16 more than Todd
(B) $18 more than Irene and $24 more than Todd
(C) $18 more than Irene and $26 more than Todd
(D) $24 more than Irene and $26 more than Todd
(E) $24 more than Irene and $36 more than Todd

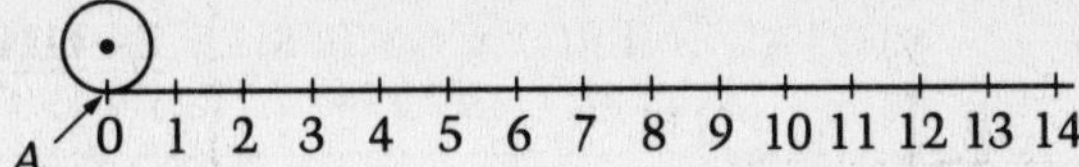

9 A circle of radius $\frac{2}{\pi}$ rolls to the right along the line shown above without slipping. In the starting position, point A on the circle touches the line for the first time at point 0 on the line. At what point on the line will point A touch the line for the fourth time?

(A) 12
(B) 10
(C) 8
(D) 6
(E) 4

GO ON TO THE NEXT PAGE

TOTAL ENERGY CONSUMED IN THE UNITED STATES
IN 1945 AND IN 1985

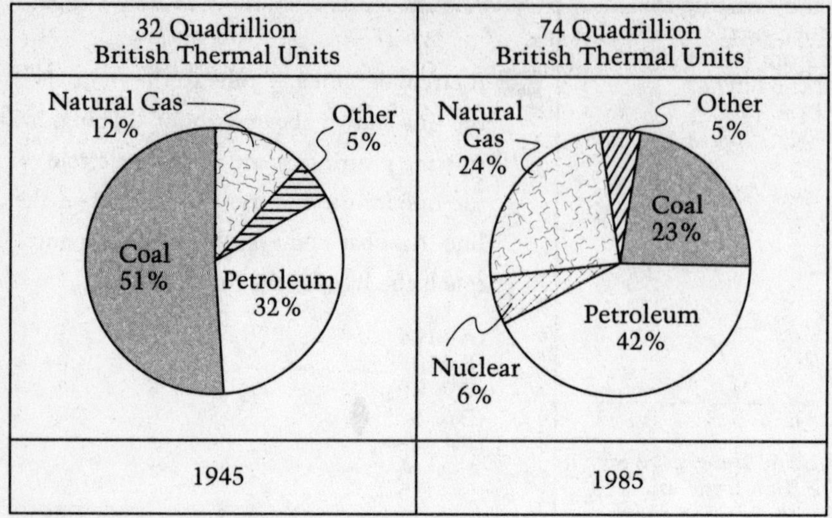

10 According to the graphs above, for which energy source was the actual amount of energy consumed, in British thermal units, nearly the same in 1985 as in 1945 ?

(A) Coal
(B) Natural gas
(C) Petroleum
(D) Nuclear
(E) Other

IF YOU FINISH BEFORE TIME IS CALLED, YOU MAY CHECK YOUR WORK ON THIS SECTION ONLY. DO NOT TURN TO ANY OTHER SECTION IN THE TEST. STOP

SAT 1: Reasoning Test Answer Key
Saturday, January 1997

VERBAL

Section 2

Five-choice Questions

	COR. ANS.	DIFF. LEV.
1.	E	1
2.	A	3
3.	C	2
4.	B	2
5.	B	3
6.	A	4
7.	D	5
8.	A	4
9.	D	5
10.	E	1
11.	D	1
12.	B	3
13.	A	4
14.	E	5
15.	C	5
16.	C	1
17.	B	5
18.	C	3
19.	A	4
20.	E	3
21.	C	3
22.	A	2
23.	A	3
24.	E	3
25.	A	3
26.	D	3
27.	D	3
28.	B	3
29.	C	3
30.	A	3

_____ no. correct

_____ no. incorrect

Section 5

Five-choice Questions

	COR. ANS.	DIFF. LEV.
1.	D	1
2.	E	2
3.	B	2
4.	B	1
5.	B	3
6.	D	2
7.	A	3
8.	C	4
9.	C	4
10.	E	5
11.	A	1
12.	C	1
13.	A	2
14.	D	2
15.	D	2
16.	D	3
17.	E	3
18.	A	3
19.	A	3
20.	D	3
21.	C	3
22.	C	4
23.	D	5
24.	B	4
25.	C	3
26.	D	3
27.	A	3
28.	D	3
29.	D	3
30.	D	3
31.	E	4
32.	E	5
33.	C	2
34.	C	3
35.	B	4

_____ no. correct

_____ no. incorrect

Section 6

Five-choice Questions

	COR. ANS.	DIFF. LEV.
1.	B	2
2.	C	2
3.	D	2
4.	B	4
5.	A	2
6.	D	3
7.	E	4
8.	C	3
9.	A	3
10.	C	4
11.	C	4
12.	E	4
13.	A	4

_____ no. correct

_____ no. incorrect

MATHEMATICAL

Section 1

Five-choice Questions

	COR. ANS.	DIFF. LEV.
1.	A	1
2.	B	1
3.	C	1
4.	B	1
5.	D	1
6.	C	2
7.	B	2
8.	E	3
9.	B	2
10.	A	3
11.	E	2
12.	A	3
13.	B	3
14.	D	3
15.	C	5
16.	E	3
17.	C	3
18.	B	3
19.	D	3
20.	E	4
21.	A	3
22.	C	3
23.	E	4
24.	B	4
25.	E	5

_____ no. correct

_____ no. incorrect

Section 4

Four-choice Questions

	COR. ANS.	DIFF. LEV.
1.	B	1
2.	C	1
3.	D	2
4.	A	2
5.	A	2
6.	A	2
7.	D	2
8.	C	3
9.	C	4
10.	D	4
11.	B	3
12.	D	4
13.	B	3
14.	A	4
15.	C	5

_____ no. correct

_____ no. incorrect

Section 7

Five-choice Questions

	COR. ANS.	DIFF. LEV.
1.	D	1
2.	E	2
3.	B	1
4.	A	3
5.	C	2
6.	C	3
7.	D	4
8.	E	5
9.	A	4
10.	A	5

_____ no. correct

_____ no. incorrect

Section 4

Student-Produced Response Questions

	COR. ANS.	DIFF. LEV.
16.	0	1
17.	125	2
18.	50, 71 or 92	3
19.	3456	2
20.	225	3
21.	10	3
22.	390	3
23.	1.25 or 5/4	4
24.	18	4
25.	22.5 or 45/2	4

_____ no. correct (16-25)

NOTE: Difficulty levels are estimates of question difficulty for a recent group of college-bound seniors. Difficulty levels range from 1 (easiest) to 5 (hardest).

The Scoring Process

Machine-scoring is done in three steps:

- *Scanning.* Your answer sheet is "read" by a scanning machine and the oval you filled in for each question is recorded on a computer tape.
- *Scoring.* The computer compares the oval filled in for each question with the correct response. Each correct answer receives one point; omitted questions do not count toward your score. For each wrong answer to the multiple-choice questions, a fraction of a point is subtracted to correct for random guessing. For questions with five answer choices, one-fourth of a point is subtracted for each wrong response; for questions with four answer choices, one-third of a point is subtracted for each wrong response. The SAT I verbal test has 78 questions with five answer choices each. If, for example, a student has 44 right, 32 wrong, and 2 omitted, the resulting raw score is determined as follows:

$$44 \text{ right} - \frac{32 \text{ wrong}}{4} = 44 - 8 = 36 \text{ raw score points}$$

Obtaining raw scores frequently involves the rounding of fractional numbers to the nearest whole number. For example, a raw score of 36.25 is rounded to 36, the nearest whole number. A raw score of 36.50 is rounded upward to 37.

- *Converting to reported scaled score.* Raw test scores are then placed on the College Board scale of 200 to 800 through a process that adjusts scores to account for minor differences in difficulty among different editions of the test. This process, known as equating, is performed so that a student's reported score is not affected by the edition of the test taken or by the abilities of the group with whom the student takes the test. As a result of placing SAT I scores on the College Board scale, scores earned by students at different times can be compared. For example, an SAT I verbal score of 400 on a test taken at one administration indicates the same level of developed verbal ability as a 400 score obtained on a different edition of the test taken at another time.

How to Score the Test

SAT I Verbal Sections 2, 5, and 6

Step A: Count the number of correct answers for *Section 2* and record the number in the space provided on the worksheet on the next page. Then do the same for the incorrect answers. (Do not count omitted answers.) To determine subtotal A, use the formula:

$$\text{number correct} - \frac{\text{number incorrect}}{4} = \text{subtotal A}$$

Step B: Count the number of correct answers and the number of incorrect answers for *Section 5* and record the number in the space provided on the worksheet. To determine subtotal B, use the formula:

$$\text{number correct} - \frac{\text{number incorrect}}{4} = \text{subtotal B}$$

Step C: Count the number of correct answers and the number of incorrect answers for *Section 6* and record the number in the space provided on the worksheet. To determine subtotal C, use the formula:

$$\text{number correct} - \frac{\text{number incorrect}}{4} = \text{subtotal C}$$

Step D: To obtain D, add subtotal A, subtotal B, and subtotal C, keeping any decimals. Enter the resulting figure on the worksheet.

Step E: To obtain E, your raw verbal score, round D to the nearest whole number. (For example, any number from 44.50 to 45.49 rounds to 45.) Enter the resulting figure on the worksheet.

Step F: To find your SAT 1 verbal score, look up the total raw verbal score you obtained in step E in the conversion table. Enter this figure on the worksheet.

SAT I Mathematical Sections 1, 4, and 7

Step A: Count the number of correct answers and the number of incorrect answers for *Section 1* and record the numbers in the spaces provided on the worksheet. To determine subtotal A, use the formula:

$$\text{number correct} - \frac{\text{number incorrect}}{4} = \text{subtotal A}$$

Step B: Count the number of correct answers and the number of incorrect answers for the *four-choice quantitative comparison questions (questions 1 through 15) in Section 4* and record the number in the space provided on the worksheet. Note: Do not count any E responses to questions 1 through 15 as correct or incorrect. Because these four-choice questions have no E answer choices, E responses to these questions are treated as omits. To determine subtotal B, use the formula:

$$\text{number correct} - \frac{\text{number incorrect}}{3} = \text{subtotal B}$$

Step C: Count the number of correct answers for the student-produced response questions *(questions 16 through 25)* in *Section 4* and record the number in the space provided on the worksheet. This is subtotal C.

Step D: Count the number of correct answers and the number of incorrect answers for *Section 7* and record the number in the space provided on the worksheet. To determine subtotal D, use the formula:

$$\text{number correct} - \frac{\text{number incorrect}}{4} = \text{subtotal D}$$

Step E: To obtain E, add subtotal A, subtotal B, subtotal C, and subtotal D, keeping any decimals. Enter the resulting figure on the worksheet.

Step F: To obtain F, your raw mathematical score, round E to the nearest whole number. (For example, any number from 44.50 to 45.49 rounds to 45.) Enter the resulting figure on the worksheet.

Step G: To find your SAT 1 mathematical score, look up the total raw mathemataical score you obtained in step F in the conversion table. Enter this figure on the worksheet.

SAT I Scoring Worksheet

SAT I Verbal Sections

A. Section 2:	________ no. correct	–	(________ no. incorrect ÷ 4)	=	________ subtotal A
B. Section 5:	________ no. correct	–	(________ no. incorrect ÷ 4)	=	________ subtotal B
C. Section 6:	________ no. correct	–	(________ no. incorrect ÷ 4)	=	________ subtotal C
D. Total unrounded raw score (Total A + B + C)					________ D
E. Total rounded raw score (rounded to nearest whole number)					________ E
F. SAT 1 verbal reported scaled score (See the conversion table)					[ ] SAT I verbal score

SAT I Mathematical Sections

A. Section 1:	________ no. correct	–	(________ no. incorrect ÷ 4)	=	________ subtotal A
B. Section 4: Questions 1-15 (quantitative comparison)	________ no. correct	–	(________ no. incorrect ÷ 3)	=	________ subtotal B
C. Section 4: Questions 16-25 (student-produced response)	________ no. correct			=	________ subtotal C
D. Section 7:	________ no. correct	–	(________ no. incorrect ÷ 4)	=	________ subtotal D
E. Total unrounded raw score (Total A + B + C+ D)					________ E
F. Total rounded raw score (rounded to nearest whole number)					________ F
G. SAT 1 mathematical reported scaled score (See the conversion table)					[ ] SAT I mathematical score

Score Conversion Table
SAT 1: Reasoning Test
Saturday, January 1997
Recentered Scale

Raw Score	Verbal Scaled Score	Math Scaled Score	Raw Score	Verbal Scaled Score	Math Scaled Score
78	800		37	520	570
77	800		36	510	560
76	800		35	510	550
75	800		34	500	540
74	780		33	500	540
73	760		32	490	530
72	750		31	490	520
71	730		30	480	520
70	720		29	470	510
69	710		28	470	500
68	700		27	460	500
67	690		26	460	490
66	680		25	450	480
65	670		24	450	480
64	670		23	440	470
63	660		22	430	460
62	650		21	430	460
61	640		20	420	450
60	640	800	19	420	440
59	630	800	18	410	440
58	630	770	17	400	430
57	620	750	16	390	420
56	610	740	15	390	410
55	610	720	14	380	410
54	600	710	13	370	400
53	600	700	12	360	390
52	590	690	11	360	380
51	590	680	10	350	370
50	580	670	9	340	370
49	580	660	8	330	360
48	570	650	7	320	350
47	570	640	6	310	340
46	560	630	5	290	320
45	560	630	4	280	310
44	550	620	3	260	300
43	550	610	2	250	280
42	540	600	1	220	270
41	540	600	0	200	250
40	530	590	-1	200	230
39	530	580	-2	200	210
38	520	570	-3 and below	200	200

This table is for use only with this test.

SAT I: Reasoning Test

Saturday, May 1997

YOUR NAME (PRINT) ______________________________
LAST FIRST MI

TEST CENTER ______________________________
NUMBER NAME OF TEST CENTER ROOM NUMBER

SAT® I: Reasoning Test — General Directions

Timing

- You will have three hours to work on this test.
- There are five 30-minute sections and two 15-minute sections.
- You may work on only one section at a time.
- The supervisor will tell you when to begin and end each section.
- If you finish a section before time is called, check your work on that section. You may NOT turn to any other section.
- Work as rapidly as you can without losing accuracy. Don't waste time on questions that seem too difficult for you.

Marking Answers

- Carefully mark only one answer for each question.
- Make sure each mark is dark and completely fills the oval.
- Do not make any stray marks on your answer sheet.
- If you erase, do so completely. Incomplete erasures may be scored as intended answers.
- Use only the answer spaces that correspond to the question numbers.
- For questions with only four answer choices, an answer marked in oval E will not be scored.
- Use the test book for scratchwork, but you will not receive credit for anything written there.
- You may not transfer answers to your answer sheet or fill in ovals after time has been called.
- You may not fold or remove pages or portions of a page from this book, or take the book or answer sheet from the testing room.

Scoring

- For each correct answer, you receive one point.
- For questions you omit, you receive no points.
- For a wrong answer to a multiple-choice question, you lose a fraction of a point.
  - ▶ If you can eliminate one or more of the answer choices as wrong, however, you increase your chances of choosing the correct answer and earning one point.
  - ▶ If you can't eliminate any choice, move on. You can return to the question later if there is time.
- For a wrong answer to a math question that is not multiple-choice, you don't lose any points.

IMPORTANT: The codes below are unique to your test book. Copy them on your answer sheet in boxes 8 and 9 and fill in the corresponding ovals exactly as shown.

8. Form Code

Ⓐ	Ⓐ	⓪	⓪	⓪
Ⓑ	Ⓑ	①	①	①
Ⓒ	Ⓒ	②	②	②
Ⓓ	Ⓓ	③	③	③
Ⓔ	Ⓔ	④	④	④
Ⓕ	Ⓕ	⑤	⑤	⑤
Ⓖ	Ⓖ	⑥	⑥	⑥
Ⓗ	Ⓗ	⑦	⑦	⑦
Ⓘ	Ⓘ	⑧	⑧	⑧
Ⓙ	Ⓙ	⑨	⑨	⑨
Ⓚ	Ⓚ			
Ⓛ	Ⓛ			
Ⓜ	Ⓜ			
Ⓝ	Ⓝ			
Ⓞ	Ⓞ			
Ⓟ	Ⓟ			
Ⓠ	Ⓠ			
Ⓡ	Ⓡ			
Ⓢ	Ⓢ			
Ⓣ	Ⓣ			
Ⓤ	Ⓤ			
Ⓥ	Ⓥ			
Ⓦ	Ⓦ			
Ⓧ	Ⓧ			
Ⓨ	Ⓨ			
Ⓩ	Ⓩ			

9. Test Form

The passages for this test have been adapted from published material. The ideas contained in them do not necessarily represent the opinions of the College Board or Educational Testing Service.

DO NOT OPEN THIS BOOK UNTIL THE SUPERVISOR TELLS YOU TO DO SO.

THE COLLEGE BOARD — SAT I Page 1

Use a No. 2 pencil only. Be sure each mark is dark and completely fills the intended oval. Completely erase any errors or stray marks.

1. Your Name

First 4 letters of Last Name | First init. | Mid. init.

2.

Your Name: (Print) Last First M.I.

I agree to the conditions on the back of the SAT I test book.

Signature: Date: / /

Home Address: (Print) Number and Street

City State Zip Code

Center: (Print) City State Center Number

IMPORTANT: Fill in items 8 and 9 exactly as shown on the back of test book.

8. Form Code

(Copy and grid as on back of test book.)

3. Date of Birth

Month | Day | Year

Jan. Feb. Mar. Apr. May June July Aug. Sept. Oct. Nov. Dec.

4. Social Security Number

5. Sex

Female Male

6. Registration Number

(Copy from Admission Ticket.)

7. Test Book Serial Number

(Copy from front of test book.)

FOR ETS USE ONLY

9. Test Form

(Copy from back of test book.)

Start with number 1 for each new section. If a section has fewer questions than answer spaces, leave the extra answer spaces blank.

SECTION 1

1–40 (A) (B) (C) (D) (E)

SECTION 2

1–40 (A) (B) (C) (D) (E)

Q2778-06/2 CHW98324 11027 • 09132 • TF129M17.5eX I.N. 207158

Use a No. 2 pencil only. Be sure each mark is dark and completely fills the intended oval. Completely erase any errors or stray marks.

Start with number 1 for each new section. If a section has fewer questions than answer spaces, leave the extra answer spaces blank.

SECTION 3

1 Ⓐ Ⓑ Ⓒ Ⓓ Ⓔ through 40 Ⓐ Ⓑ Ⓒ Ⓓ Ⓔ

If section 3 of your test book contains math questions that are not multiple-choice, continue to item 16 below. Otherwise, continue to item 16 above.

ONLY ANSWERS ENTERED IN THE OVALS IN EACH GRID AREA WILL BE SCORED.
YOU WILL NOT RECEIVE CREDIT FOR ANYTHING WRITTEN IN THE BOXES ABOVE THE OVALS.

16 17 18 19 20

21 22 23 24 25

BE SURE TO ERASE ANY ERRORS OR STRAY MARKS COMPLETELY.

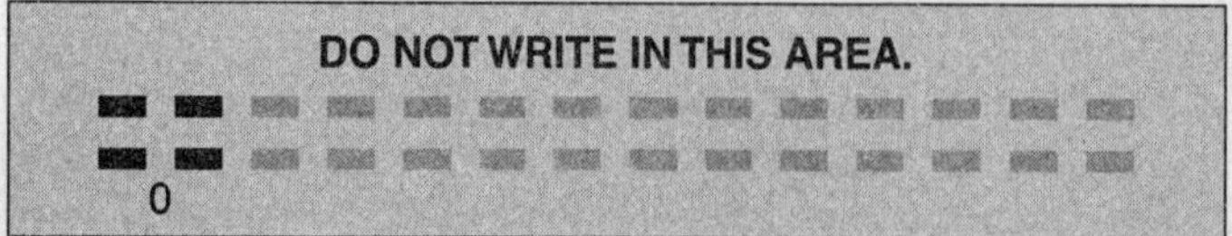

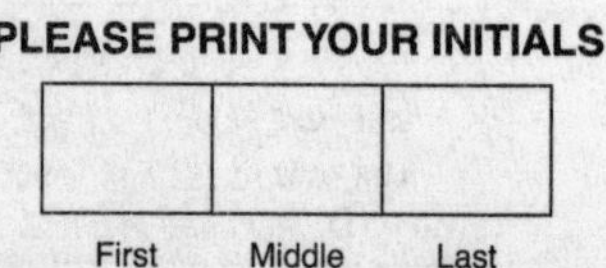

Use a No. 2 pencil only. Be sure each mark is dark and completely fills the intended oval. Completely erase any errors or stray marks.

Start with number 1 for each new section. If a section has fewer questions than answer spaces, leave the extra answer spaces blank.

SECTION 4

1 Ⓐ Ⓑ Ⓒ Ⓓ Ⓔ
2 Ⓐ Ⓑ Ⓒ Ⓓ Ⓔ
3 Ⓐ Ⓑ Ⓒ Ⓓ Ⓔ
4 Ⓐ Ⓑ Ⓒ Ⓓ Ⓔ
5 Ⓐ Ⓑ Ⓒ Ⓓ Ⓔ
6 Ⓐ Ⓑ Ⓒ Ⓓ Ⓔ
7 Ⓐ Ⓑ Ⓒ Ⓓ Ⓔ
8 Ⓐ Ⓑ Ⓒ Ⓓ Ⓔ
9 Ⓐ Ⓑ Ⓒ Ⓓ Ⓔ
10 Ⓐ Ⓑ Ⓒ Ⓓ Ⓔ
11 Ⓐ Ⓑ Ⓒ Ⓓ Ⓔ
12 Ⓐ Ⓑ Ⓒ Ⓓ Ⓔ
13 Ⓐ Ⓑ Ⓒ Ⓓ Ⓔ
14 Ⓐ Ⓑ Ⓒ Ⓓ Ⓔ
15 Ⓐ Ⓑ Ⓒ Ⓓ Ⓔ

16 Ⓐ Ⓑ Ⓒ Ⓓ Ⓔ
17 Ⓐ Ⓑ Ⓒ Ⓓ Ⓔ
18 Ⓐ Ⓑ Ⓒ Ⓓ Ⓔ
19 Ⓐ Ⓑ Ⓒ Ⓓ Ⓔ
20 Ⓐ Ⓑ Ⓒ Ⓓ Ⓔ
21 Ⓐ Ⓑ Ⓒ Ⓓ Ⓔ
22 Ⓐ Ⓑ Ⓒ Ⓓ Ⓔ
23 Ⓐ Ⓑ Ⓒ Ⓓ Ⓔ
24 Ⓐ Ⓑ Ⓒ Ⓓ Ⓔ
25 Ⓐ Ⓑ Ⓒ Ⓓ Ⓔ
26 Ⓐ Ⓑ Ⓒ Ⓓ Ⓔ
27 Ⓐ Ⓑ Ⓒ Ⓓ Ⓔ
28 Ⓐ Ⓑ Ⓒ Ⓓ Ⓔ
29 Ⓐ Ⓑ Ⓒ Ⓓ Ⓔ
30 Ⓐ Ⓑ Ⓒ Ⓓ Ⓔ

31 Ⓐ Ⓑ Ⓒ Ⓓ Ⓔ
32 Ⓐ Ⓑ Ⓒ Ⓓ Ⓔ
33 Ⓐ Ⓑ Ⓒ Ⓓ Ⓔ
34 Ⓐ Ⓑ Ⓒ Ⓓ Ⓔ
35 Ⓐ Ⓑ Ⓒ Ⓓ Ⓔ
36 Ⓐ Ⓑ Ⓒ Ⓓ Ⓔ
37 Ⓐ Ⓑ Ⓒ Ⓓ Ⓔ
38 Ⓐ Ⓑ Ⓒ Ⓓ Ⓔ
39 Ⓐ Ⓑ Ⓒ Ⓓ Ⓔ
40 Ⓐ Ⓑ Ⓒ Ⓓ Ⓔ

If section 4 of your test book contains math questions that are not multiple-choice, continue to item 16 below. Otherwise, continue to item 16 above.

ONLY ANSWERS ENTERED IN THE OVALS IN EACH GRID AREA WILL BE SCORED. YOU WILL NOT RECEIVE CREDIT FOR ANYTHING WRITTEN IN THE BOXES ABOVE THE OVALS.

16 17 18 19 20 21 22 23 24 25

(Each grid: / / ; . . . . ; 0 0 0 ; 1–9 in each of four columns)

BE SURE TO ERASE ANY ERRORS OR STRAY MARKS COMPLETELY.

DO NOT WRITE IN THIS AREA.

0

PLEASE PRINT YOUR INITIALS

First Middle Last

Use a No. 2 pencil only. Be sure each mark is dark and completely fills the intended oval. Completely erase any errors or stray marks.

Start with number 1 for each new section. If a section has fewer questions than answer spaces, leave the extra answer spaces blank.

SECTION 5

1 (A) (B) (C) (D) (E)	11 (A) (B) (C) (D) (E)	21 (A) (B) (C) (D) (E)	31 (A) (B) (C) (D) (E)
2 (A) (B) (C) (D) (E)	12 (A) (B) (C) (D) (E)	22 (A) (B) (C) (D) (E)	32 (A) (B) (C) (D) (E)
3 (A) (B) (C) (D) (E)	13 (A) (B) (C) (D) (E)	23 (A) (B) (C) (D) (E)	33 (A) (B) (C) (D) (E)
4 (A) (B) (C) (D) (E)	14 (A) (B) (C) (D) (E)	24 (A) (B) (C) (D) (E)	34 (A) (B) (C) (D) (E)
5 (A) (B) (C) (D) (E)	15 (A) (B) (C) (D) (E)	25 (A) (B) (C) (D) (E)	35 (A) (B) (C) (D) (E)
6 (A) (B) (C) (D) (E)	16 (A) (B) (C) (D) (E)	26 (A) (B) (C) (D) (E)	36 (A) (B) (C) (D) (E)
7 (A) (B) (C) (D) (E)	17 (A) (B) (C) (D) (E)	27 (A) (B) (C) (D) (E)	37 (A) (B) (C) (D) (E)
8 (A) (B) (C) (D) (E)	18 (A) (B) (C) (D) (E)	28 (A) (B) (C) (D) (E)	38 (A) (B) (C) (D) (E)
9 (A) (B) (C) (D) (E)	19 (A) (B) (C) (D) (E)	29 (A) (B) (C) (D) (E)	39 (A) (B) (C) (D) (E)
10 (A) (B) (C) (D) (E)	20 (A) (B) (C) (D) (E)	30 (A) (B) (C) (D) (E)	40 (A) (B) (C) (D) (E)

SECTION 6

1 (A) (B) (C) (D) (E)	6 (A) (B) (C) (D) (E)	11 (A) (B) (C) (D) (E)	16 (A) (B) (C) (D) (E)
2 (A) (B) (C) (D) (E)	7 (A) (B) (C) (D) (E)	12 (A) (B) (C) (D) (E)	17 (A) (B) (C) (D) (E)
3 (A) (B) (C) (D) (E)	8 (A) (B) (C) (D) (E)	13 (A) (B) (C) (D) (E)	18 (A) (B) (C) (D) (E)
4 (A) (B) (C) (D) (E)	9 (A) (B) (C) (D) (E)	14 (A) (B) (C) (D) (E)	19 (A) (B) (C) (D) (E)
5 (A) (B) (C) (D) (E)	10 (A) (B) (C) (D) (E)	15 (A) (B) (C) (D) (E)	20 (A) (B) (C) (D) (E)

SECTION 7

1 (A) (B) (C) (D) (E)	6 (A) (B) (C) (D) (E)	11 (A) (B) (C) (D) (E)	16 (A) (B) (C) (D) (E)
2 (A) (B) (C) (D) (E)	7 (A) (B) (C) (D) (E)	12 (A) (B) (C) (D) (E)	17 (A) (B) (C) (D) (E)
3 (A) (B) (C) (D) (E)	8 (A) (B) (C) (D) (E)	13 (A) (B) (C) (D) (E)	18 (A) (B) (C) (D) (E)
4 (A) (B) (C) (D) (E)	9 (A) (B) (C) (D) (E)	14 (A) (B) (C) (D) (E)	19 (A) (B) (C) (D) (E)
5 (A) (B) (C) (D) (E)	10 (A) (B) (C) (D) (E)	15 (A) (B) (C) (D) (E)	20 (A) (B) (C) (D) (E)

CERTIFICATION STATEMENT

Copy the statement below (do not print) and sign your name as you would an official document.

I hereby agree to the conditions set forth in the Registration Bulletin and certify that I am the person whose name and address appear on this answer sheet.

____

____

____

Signature: ____________________ Date: __________

Section 1 1 1 1 1 1 1

Time—30 Minutes
30 Questions

For each question in this section, select the best answer from among the choices given and fill in the corresponding oval on the answer sheet.

Each sentence below has one or two blanks, each blank indicating that something has been omitted. Beneath the sentence are five words or sets of words labeled A through E. Choose the word or set of words that, when inserted in the sentence, best fits the meaning of the sentence as a whole.

Example:

Medieval kingdoms did not become constitutional republics overnight; on the contrary, the change was ----.

(A) unpopular
(B) unexpected
(C) advantageous
(D) sufficient
(E) gradual

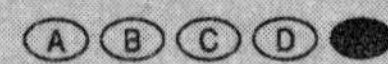

1. Residents of the secluded island fear that ---- commercial development will ---- their quiet way of life.

(A) widespread . . reinforce
(B) waning . . harm
(C) diminishing . . reform
(D) encroaching . . disturb
(E) further . . aid

2. Nicknamed the "contact lens," the device installed on the Hubble telescope successfully ---- its flawed vision, the result of a faulty mirror.

(A) corrected (B) displayed (C) generated (D) scrutinized (E) accentuated

3. Though it is often exclusively ---- Brazil, the Amazon jungle actually ---- parts of eight other South American countries.

(A) protected by . . threatens
(B) located in . . bypasses
(C) limited to . . touches
(D) surrounded by . . borders
(E) associated with . . covers

4. As an architect who rehabilitates older buildings, Roberta Washington objected to a city policy that resulted in the mass ---- of clearly ---- structures.

(A) demolition . . inconsequential
(B) renovation . . derelict
(C) razing . . salvageable
(D) protection . . venerable
(E) scouring . . grimy

5. Sandra Gilbert and Susan Gubar's recent book presents a ---- of detail, providing far more information than one can easily digest.

(A) modicum (B) discrepancy (C) surfeit (D) deficit (E) juxtaposition

6. On the verge of financial collapse, the museum was granted a ----, receiving a much-needed ---- of cash in the form of a government loan.

(A) reprieve . . infusion
(B) deferment . . inducement
(C) rebate . . advance
(D) hearing . . security
(E) procurement . . account

7. More ---- than her predecessor, Superintendent Reynolds would, many predicted, have a far less ---- term of office.

(A) phlegmatic . . apathetic
(B) conciliatory . . confrontational
(C) empathetic . . compassionate
(D) vigilant . . reputable
(E) penurious . . frugal

8. Rodolfo Gonzales was once described as ---- in body and mind because of the flexibility and grace apparent in both his boxing and his writing of poetry and plays.

(A) unyielding (B) tremulous (C) emphatic (D) lithe (E) fickle

9. Galloping technological progress has made consumers ----: advances undreamed of a generation ago are so common that they seem humdrum.

(A) flabbergasted (B) miffed (C) jaded (D) wary (E) embittered

GO ON TO THE NEXT PAGE

Each question below consists of a related pair of words or phrases, followed by five pairs of words or phrases labeled A through E. Select the pair that best expresses a relationship similar to that expressed in the original pair.

Example:

CRUMB : BREAD ::
(A) ounce : unit
(B) splinter : wood
(C) water : bucket
(D) twine : rope
(E) cream : butter

10 TUTOR : PUPIL ::
(A) patron : client
(B) coach : athlete
(C) waiter : diner
(D) driver : passenger
(E) novelist : writer

11 DECORATE : PLAIN ::
(A) create : talented
(B) mend : repaired
(C) cook : raw
(D) sing : vocal
(E) narrate : fictitious

12 PALLID : COLOR ::
(A) vital : energy
(B) parched : moisture
(C) restrained : limit
(D) measured : quantity
(E) deliberate : intention

13 DRIFT : MOVE ::
(A) sprint : run
(B) boil : heat
(C) ramble : walk
(D) evade : elude
(E) crawl : creep

14 CRASS : REFINEMENT ::
(A) inefficient : time
(B) prudent : discretion
(C) clairvoyant : perception
(D) inept : mistake
(E) pretentious : modesty

15 PARIAH : OSTRACISM ::
(A) idol : adulation
(B) gourmand : food
(C) scapegoat : symbol
(D) collector : ownership
(E) protagonist : narrative

GO ON TO THE NEXT PAGE

Each passage below is followed by questions based on its content. Answer the questions on the basis of what is stated or implied in each passage and in any introductory material that may be provided.

Questions 16-20 are based on the following passage.

This passage, about animal perception, was adapted from an essay by a writer who trains animals.

Anyone who trains animals recognizes that human and animal perceptual capacities are different. For most humans, seeing is believing, although we do occasionally brood about whether we can believe our eyes. The other senses are largely ancillary; most of us do not know how we might go about either doubting or believing our noses. But for dogs, scenting is believing. A dog's nose is to ours as the wrinkled surface of our complex brain is to the surface of an egg. A dog who did comparative psychology might easily worry about our consciousness or lack thereof, just as we worry about the consciousness of a squid.

We who take sight for granted can draw pictures of scent, but we have no language for doing it the other way about, no way to represent something visually familiar by means of actual scent. Most humans cannot know, with their limited noses, what they can imagine about being deaf, blind, mute, or paralyzed. The sighted can, for example, speak of a blind person as "in the darkness," but there is no corollary expression for what it is that we are in relationship to scent. If we tried to coin words, we might come up with something like "scent-blind." But what would it mean? It couldn't have the sort of meaning that "color-blind" and "tone-deaf" do, because most of us have experienced what "tone" and "color" mean in those expressions, but we don't know what "scent" means in the expression "scent-blind." Scent for many of us can be only a theoretical, technical expression that we use because our grammar requires that we have a noun to go in the sentences we are prompted to utter about animals' tracking. We don't have a sense of scent. What we do have is a sense of smell—for Thanksgiving dinner and skunks and a number of things we call chemicals.

So if Fido and I are sitting on the terrace, admiring the view, we inhabit worlds with radically different principles of phenomenology. Say that the wind is to our backs. Our world lies all before us, within a 180 degree angle. The dog's—well, we don't know, do we?

He sees roughly the same things that I see but he *believes* the scents of the garden behind us. He marks the path of the black-and-white cat as she moves among the roses in search of the bits of chicken sandwich I let fall as I walked from the house to our picnic spot. I can show *that* Fido is alert to the kitty, but not *how*, for my picture-making modes of thought too easily supply falsifyingly literal representations of the cat and the garden and their modes of being hidden from or revealed to me.

16 The phrase "other senses are largely ancillary" (lines 5-6) is used by the author to suggest that

(A) only those events experienced directly can be appreciated by the senses
(B) for many human beings the sense of sight is the primary means of knowing about the world
(C) smell is in many respects a more powerful sense than sight
(D) people rely on at least one of their other senses in order to confirm what they see
(E) the perceptual capacity of an animal is a function of its ability to integrate all of its senses

17 The example in the last paragraph suggests that "principles of phenomenology" mentioned in line 40 can best be defined as

(A) memorable things that happen
(B) behaviors caused by certain kinds of perception
(C) ways and means of knowing about something
(D) rules one uses to determine the philosophical truth about a certain thing
(E) effect of a single individual's perception on what others believe

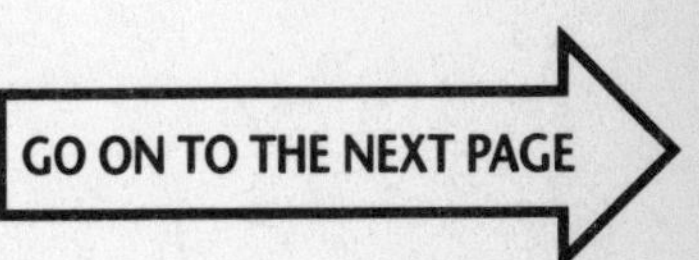

18 The missing phrase in the incomplete sentence "The dog's—well, we don't know, do we?" (lines 42-43) refers to

(A) color blindness
(B) depth perception
(C) perception of the world
(D) concern for our perceptions
(E) motivation for action

19 The author uses the distinction between *"that"* (line 49) and *"how"* (line 50) in order to suggest the difference between

(A) seeing and believing
(B) a cat's way and a dog's way of perceiving
(C) verifiable hypotheses and whimsical speculation
(D) awareness of presence and the nature of that awareness
(E) false representations and accurate representations

20 The example in the last paragraph is used to illustrate how

(A) a dog's perception differs from a human's
(B) human beings are not psychologically rooted in the natural world
(C) people fear nature but animals are part of it
(D) a dog's ways of seeing are superior to a cat's
(E) phenomenology is universal and constant

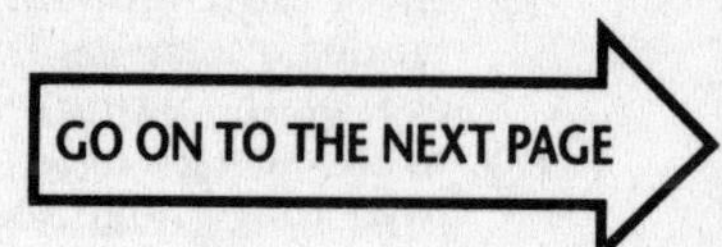

Questions 21-30 are based on the following passage.

First published in 1976, this passage discusses W. E. B. Du Bois and Marcus Garvey, two leaders of the Black American community in the 1910's and 1920's.

The concept of two warring souls within the body of the Black American was as meaningful for Du Bois at the end of his years as editor of *Crisis*, the official journal of the National Association for the Advancement of Colored People (NAACP), as when he had first used the image at the start of the century. The tension between race pride and identification with the nation as a whole was nowhere more dramatic than in the most controversial editorial ever printed in *Crisis*, "Close Ranks," which in July 1918 called on Black Americans to "forget our special grievances and close our ranks" with the White people "fighting for democracy" during the First World War. Bitterly criticized by Black people, Du Bois barely modified his statement when, two months later, he set the priorities for his readers: "first your Country, then your Rights!" Perhaps the editor had written more than he intended in using the word "forget," for *Crisis* before and after the editorial showed no diminution in its criticism of racism. But he distinguished between Allied and German ambitions, and declared that defeat of the former would be disastrous for that "United States of the World" to which he was most loyal.

Du Bois nevertheless saw danger in the negation of race pride, by those who did not recognize their own beauty as Black people, for example. The responsibility of *Crisis* was to arbitrate between those who advocated race pride and those who denied any differences between the races. The focal point of the magazine's efforts in this respect came with the rise of Marcus Garvey, the gifted Jamaican leader whose "back-to-Africa" movement, as it was popularly called, was founded on the premise, according to Du Bois, that "a black skin was in itself a sort of patent to nobility."

Garveyism, which flourished during the height of *Crisis'* influence and success, brought a formidable challenge to Du Bois. Garvey and his Universal Negro Improvement Association (UNIA), with its hostility to the interracial ideal and its scheme to have Black Americans emigrate to Africa, threw *Crisis* and the NAACP on the defensive by invoking the specter of self-doubt as characteristic of its Black members. Du Bois had first met Garvey on a visit to Jamaica in 1915, and *Crisis* announced Garvey's arrival in the United States the following year. Almost totally unknown in his new country, Garvey invited Du Bois to preside over his first public lecture; then in 1920 he asked permission to submit Du Bois's name as a candidate in the election of a "leader" of Black America at an international convention organized by the UNIA. Du Bois politely declined the former; "under no circumstances" would he allow the latter. Du Bois saw with amazement Garvey's success in persuading thousands of Black Americans of the legitimacy of his back-to-Africa movement and in collecting funds for the purchase of ships for his Black Star Line to transport people to Africa.

There were superficial similarities between Garvey's and Du Bois's commitment to race consciousness and economic empowerment; both men saw the world as comprising separate cultures, each reflecting a distinct heritage and demanding freedom of expression. But Garvey's fixed belief in the idea of Black racial purity, his obsession with Africa as the solution to the problems of its scattered peoples, and his refusal to allow any liberal idea to deflect his purpose differed greatly from Du Bois's ideals. Du Bois fantasized about Africa in at least one poem and wrote about the continent elsewhere, but he cultivated a scholar's knowledge of the land. He made the first of several visits there in 1923 and lived in Africa for the last two years of his life (1961-1963). In a cryptic piece in *Crisis* in 1922, Du Bois was surely referring to Garvey when he ominously predicted the rise of a demagogue who would "come to lead, inflame, lie, and steal" and when he commented that such a person would "gather large followings and then burst and disappear."

21 The primary purpose of the passage is to

(A) account for the rise of Black nationalism in the United States
(B) explain the charismatic appeal of two Black American leaders
(C) explain why Garvey refused to support Du Bois as a leader of Black America
(D) describe differences between the philosophies of Du Bois and Garvey
(E) describe Du Bois's quarrel and eventual reconciliation with Garvey

22 The image of "two warring souls" (line 1) refers to the struggle between

(A) democracy and dictatorship
(B) Du Bois's ideals and practical demands
(C) racial and national allegiances
(D) Du Bois's literary and political ambitions
(E) Allied and German goals

GO ON TO THE NEXT PAGE

23 It can be inferred that Du Bois's July 1918 editorial in *Crisis* was "Bitterly criticized" (line 14) because it seemed to

(A) devalue the specific concerns of Black Americans
(B) advocate military service for Black Americans
(C) support Garvey's back-to-Africa movement
(D) insist on racial rather than national priorities
(E) attack the official stance of the NAACP on race pride

24 As indicated in lines 17-24 ("Perhaps . . . loyal"), Du Bois advised Black Americans that

(A) they would be treated more equally in wartime than in peace
(B) racial harmony in the United States would improve after the war
(C) despite German military superiority, the Allies would win the war
(D) wartime provided economic opportunities for both Black and White Americans
(E) despite American racism, the effects of an Allied defeat would be even worse

25 That to which Du Bois was "most loyal" (line 24) is best described as

(A) the UNIA
(B) the NAACP
(C) *Crisis*
(D) global democracy
(E) a new African nation founded by Black Americans

26 According to Du Bois, "the premise" (line 34) underlying Garvey's movement was that

(A) racial issues are more significant than economic issues in the United States
(B) an entire group of people is inherently dignified and worthy
(C) many Black Americans are descended from African royalty
(D) education is more important than ethnicity in shaping a person's character
(E) loyalty to one's country takes precedence over all other matters in times of crisis

27 In line 36, "patent to" most nearly means

(A) copyright of
(B) safeguard of
(C) guarantee of
(D) hope for
(E) permission for

28 As described in lines 48-53, Garvey's actions suggest that he initially

(A) scorned Du Bois's advice
(B) doubted Du Bois's commitment
(C) envied Du Bois's fame
(D) admired Du Bois's writings
(E) appreciated Du Bois's influence

29 The information in lines 71-76 indicates that Du Bois

(A) valued Africa, but in a very different way than Garvey did
(B) lived in Africa, but finally returned to the United States to help Black Americans
(C) read about Africa, but benefited little from his visits there
(D) fantasized about escaping overseas from demagogues like Garvey
(E) supported radical solutions to racial problems in the United States

30 The passage implies that over time the relationship between Garvey and Du Bois changed from

(A) courteous to antagonistic
(B) professional to personal
(C) remote to close
(D) distrustful to ambivalent
(E) competitive to cooperative

IF YOU FINISH BEFORE TIME IS CALLED, YOU MAY CHECK YOUR WORK ON THIS SECTION ONLY. DO NOT TURN TO ANY OTHER SECTION IN THE TEST. **STOP**

Section 2

Time—30 Minutes
25 Questions

In this section solve each problem, using any available space on the page for scratchwork. Then decide which is the best of the choices given and fill in the corresponding oval on the answer sheet.

Notes:

1. The use of a calculator is permitted. All numbers used are real numbers.
2. Figures that accompany problems in this test are intended to provide information useful in solving the problems. They are drawn as accurately as possible EXCEPT when it is stated in a specific problem that the figure is not drawn to scale. All figures lie in a plane unless otherwise indicated.

Reference Information

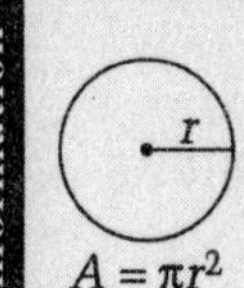

$A = \pi r^2$
$C = 2\pi r$

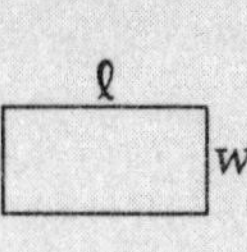

$A = \ell w$

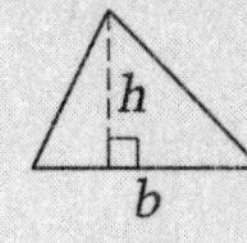

$A = \frac{1}{2}bh$

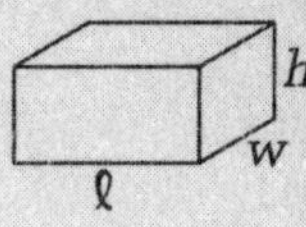

$V = \ell wh$

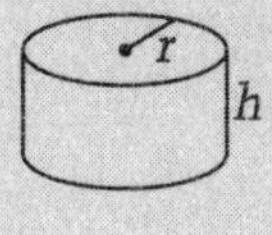

$V = \pi r^2 h$

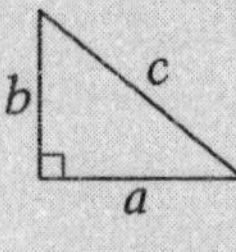

$c^2 = a^2 + b^2$

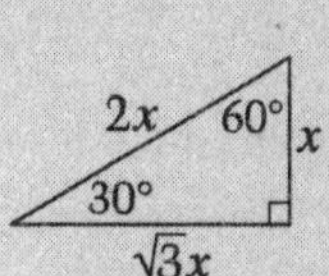

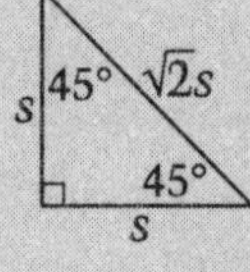

Special Right Triangles

The number of degrees of arc in a circle is 360.
The measure in degrees of a straight angle is 180.
The sum of the measures in degrees of the angles of a triangle is 180.

1 For which of the following values of k will the value of $3k - 1$ be greater than 10 ?

(A) 4
(B) 3
(C) 2
(D) 1
(E) 0

2 Which of the following numbers is between $\frac{1}{5}$ and $\frac{1}{4}$?

(A) 0.14
(B) 0.15
(C) 0.19
(D) 0.21
(E) 0.26

3 If $a \times k = a$ for all values of a, what is the value of k ?

(A) $-a$
(B) -1
(C) 0
(D) 1
(E) a

4 If $2x - 10 = 20$, then $x - 5 =$

(A) 5
(B) 10
(C) 15
(D) 20
(E) 30

GO ON TO THE NEXT PAGE

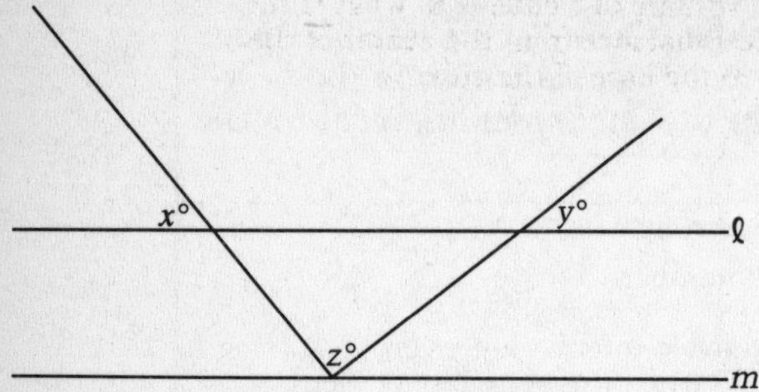

Note: Figure not drawn to scale.

5 In the figure above, $\ell \parallel m$. If $x = 80$ and $y = 70$, what is the value of z ?

(A) 30
(B) 60
(C) 75
(D) 90
(E) 150

6 If t represents an odd integer, which of the following expressions represents an even integer?

(A) $t + 2$
(B) $2t - 1$
(C) $3t - 2$
(D) $3t + 2$
(E) $5t + 1$

7 If there is no waste, how many square yards of carpeting is needed to cover a rectangular floor that is 12 feet by 18 feet? (1 yard = 3 feet)

(A) 8
(B) 16
(C) 24
(D) 30
(E) 216

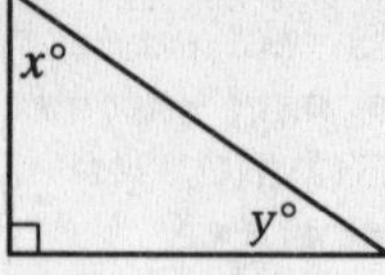

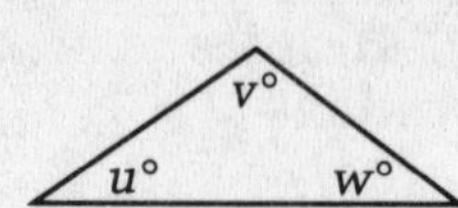

8 In the triangles above, what is the average (arithmetic mean) of u, v, w, x, and y ?

(A) 21
(B) 45
(C) 50
(D) 52
(E) 54

9 On a map, $\frac{1}{4}$ inch represents 16 feet. If a driveway is 40 feet long, what is its length, in inches, on the map?

(A) $\frac{3}{8}$
(B) $\frac{5}{8}$
(C) $\frac{3}{4}$
(D) $2\frac{1}{2}$
(E) 10

GO ON TO THE NEXT PAGE

10 If $m^x \cdot m^7 = m^{28}$ and $(m^5)^y = m^{15}$, what is the value of $x + y$?

(A) 7
(B) 12
(C) 14
(D) 24
(E) 31

11 A complete cycle of a traffic light takes 80 seconds. During each cycle, the light is green for 40 seconds, amber for 10 seconds, and red for 30 seconds. When a randomly chosen car arrives at the traffic light, what is the probability that the light will <u>not</u> be red?

(A) $\frac{7}{8}$

(B) $\frac{5}{8}$

(C) $\frac{4}{8}$

(D) $\frac{3}{8}$

(E) $\frac{1}{8}$

12 If n is a positive number, which of the following is equal to $8n$?

(A) $\sqrt{64n}$

(B) $\sqrt{8n^2}$

(C) $\sqrt{16n^2}$

(D) $2\sqrt{4n}$

(E) $4\sqrt{4n^2}$

13 If the volume of a cube is 8, what is the shortest distance from the center of the cube to the base of the cube?

(A) 1

(B) 2

(C) 4

(D) $\sqrt{2}$

(E) $2\sqrt{2}$

14 When a positive integer n is divided by 5, the remainder is 4. Which of the following expressions will yield a remainder of 2 when it is divided by 5?

(A) $n + 1$
(B) $n + 2$
(C) $n + 3$
(D) $n + 4$
(E) $n + 5$

GO ON TO THE NEXT PAGE

15 How many three-digit numbers have the hundreds digit equal to 3 and the units digit equal to 4 ?

(A) 10
(B) 19
(C) 20
(D) 190
(E) 200

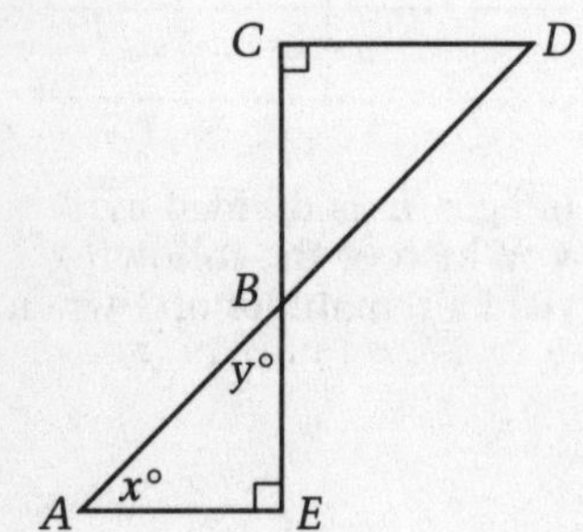

Note: Figure not drawn to scale.

16 In the figure above, AE and CD are each perpendicular to CE. If $x = y$, the length of AB is 4, and the length of BD is 8, what is the length of CE ?

(A) $3\sqrt{2}$ (approximately 4.24)

(B) $6\sqrt{2}$ (approximately 8.49)

(C) $8\sqrt{2}$ (approximately 11.31)

(D) $10\sqrt{2}$ (approximately 14.14)

(E) $12\sqrt{2}$ (approximately 16.97)

RATINGS OF CAR ENGINE OIL

Rating	Relative Speed of Flow
10W	Half as fast as 5W oil
15W	Half as fast as 10W oil
20W	Half as fast as 15W oil

17 According to the table above, car engine oil with a rating of 5W flows how many times as fast as car engine oil with a rating of 20W?

(A) 2
(B) 4
(C) 8
(D) 16
(E) 32

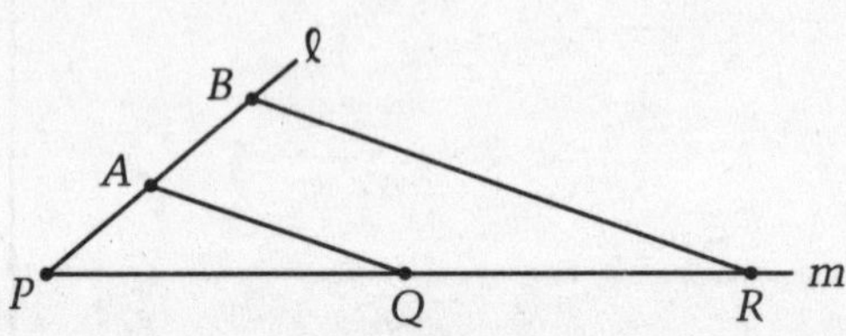

Note: Figure not drawn to scale.

18 In the figure above, points P, A, and B are equally spaced on line ℓ and points P, Q, and R are equally spaced on line m. If $PB = 4$, $PR = 6$, and $AQ = 4$, what is the perimeter of quadrilateral $QABR$?

(A) 13
(B) 14
(C) 15
(D) 16
(E) 17

GO ON TO THE NEXT PAGE

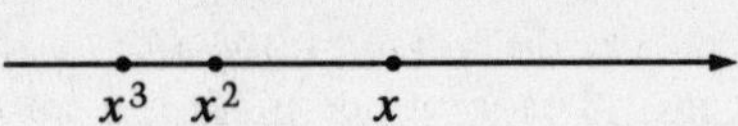

19 If x, x^2, and x^3 lie on a number line in the order shown above, which of the following could be the value of x ?

(A) -2

(B) $-\frac{1}{2}$

(C) $\frac{3}{4}$

(D) 1

(E) $\frac{3}{2}$

Questions 20-21 refer to the following definitions for integers n greater than 1.

$$\triangle\!\!\!\!\!\;n = n^2 + n$$

$$\boxed{n} = n^2 - n$$

20 $\triangle\!\!\!\!\!\;5 - \boxed{4} =$

(A) 0
(B) 8
(C) 10
(D) 18
(E) 32

---

21 If m is an integer greater than 1, then $\boxed{m+1} =$

(A) $\triangle\!\!\!\!\!\;m$

(B) $\triangle\!\!\!\!\!\;m + 1$

(C) $\triangle\!\!\!\!\!\;m - 1$

(D) $\boxed{m} + 1$

(E) $\boxed{m} - 1$

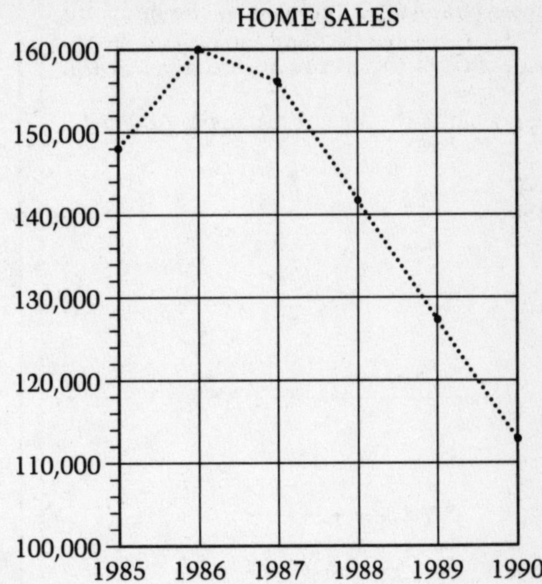

22 According to the graph above, which of the following is the closest approximation to the decrease per year in the number of homes sold between 1987 and 1990 ?

(A) 7,000
(B) 11,500
(C) 14,000
(D) 17,500
(E) 42,000

GO ON TO THE NEXT PAGE

23 In rectangle $ABCD$, point E is the midpoint of side BC. If the area of quadrilateral $ABED$ is $\frac{2}{3}$, what is the area of rectangle $ABCD$?

(A) $\frac{1}{2}$

(B) $\frac{3}{4}$

(C) $\frac{8}{9}$

(D) 1

(E) $\frac{8}{3}$

24 In a set of eleven different numbers, which of the following CANNOT affect the value of the median?

(A) Doubling each number
(B) Increasing each number by 10
(C) Increasing the smallest number only
(D) Decreasing the largest number only
(E) Increasing the largest number only

25 The price of ground coffee beans is d dollars for 8 ounces and each ounce makes c cups of brewed coffee. In terms of c and d, what is the dollar cost of the ground coffee beans required to make 1 cup of brewed coffee?

(A) $\frac{d}{8c}$

(B) $\frac{cd}{8}$

(C) $\frac{8c}{d}$

(D) $\frac{8d}{c}$

(E) $8cd$

IF YOU FINISH BEFORE TIME IS CALLED, YOU MAY CHECK YOUR WORK ON THIS SECTION ONLY. DO NOT TURN TO ANY OTHER SECTION IN THE TEST. **STOP**

Section 3 3 3 3 3 3 3

Time—30 Minutes
35 Questions

For each question in this section, select the best answer from among the choices given and fill in the corresponding oval on the answer sheet.

Each sentence below has one or two blanks, each blank indicating that something has been omitted. Beneath the sentence are five words or sets of words labeled A through E. Choose the word or set of words that, when inserted in the sentence, best fits the meaning of the sentence as a whole.

Example:

Medieval kingdoms did not become constitutional republics overnight; on the contrary, the change was ----.

(A) unpopular
(B) unexpected
(C) advantageous
(D) sufficient
(E) gradual

1 They use language not to explain but to ----; each statement is like a reflection in a warped mirror.

(A) preserve (B) distort (C) enlighten (D) negate (E) destroy

2 Many writers associated with the Harlem Renaissance were not originally from Harlem; drawn by the artistic community it provided, they ---- the place as home.

(A) neglected (B) adopted (C) avoided (D) criticized (E) encountered

3 Francis learned that by ---- his anger and resentment, and so avoiding ----, he could overcome opponents more successfully than could those who openly defied their adversaries.

(A) expressing . . hostility
(B) suppressing . . conflict
(C) stifling . . temperance
(D) disguising . . deceit
(E) rousing . . wrath

4 Colonial South Carolina was characterized by cultural ----: Europeans, Africans, and Native Americans each absorbed some customs of the other groups.

(A) tension (B) conservatism (C) integrity (D) convergence (E) eradication

5 Ellen Swallow Richards, a ---- environmental preservation in the United States, campaigned during the nineteenth century to ---- responsible practices in the discipline that has come to be known as ecology.

(A) foil for . . expose
(B) pioneer of . . implement
(C) resource on . . squelch
(D) mitigator of . . promote
(E) critic of . . exploit

6 Sleep actually occurs ----, though one may receive clues signaling its ---- for several minutes before one falls asleep.

(A) gradually . . abruptness
(B) erratically . . solace
(C) temporarily . . length
(D) inevitably . . approach
(E) instantaneously . . onset

7 Laila performed her tasks at the office with ----, completing all her projects in record time.

(A) alacrity (B) conformity (C) deliberation (D) recrimination (E) exasperation

8 Anna Freud's impact on psychoanalysis was ----, coming not from one brilliant discovery but from a lifetime of first-rate work.

(A) tangential (B) premature (C) exorbitant (D) indiscernible (E) cumulative

9 The treasurer was intimidated by the ---- demeanor of the auditors who neither spoke nor smiled when they arrived.

(A) amiable (B) ethical (C) glacial (D) taunting (E) nondescript

10 Critics say that the autobiographical work *Brothers and Keepers* by John Edgar Wideman is surprising in that it celebrates and yet ---- his own role in the life of his brother.

(A) censures (B) exacerbates (C) explores (D) duplicates (E) delineates

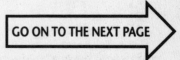

GO ON TO THE NEXT PAGE

Each question below consists of a related pair of words or phrases, followed by five pairs of words or phrases labeled A through E. Select the pair that best expresses a relationship similar to that expressed in the original pair.

Example:

CRUMB : BREAD ::
(A) ounce : unit
(B) splinter : wood
(C) water : bucket
(D) twine : rope
(E) cream : butter 

11 AUDIENCE : THEATER ::
(A) crew : ship
(B) scholars : library
(C) group : society
(D) spectators : arena
(E) actors : stage

12 QUART : VOLUME ::
(A) day : night
(B) mile : distance
(C) decade : century
(D) friction : heat
(E) part : whole

13 CARTOGRAPHER : MAPS ::
(A) architect : blueprints
(B) bibliographer : books
(C) curator : artworks
(D) traveler : countries
(E) surveyor : instruments

14 ABRASIVE : SKIN ::
(A) flammable : fire
(B) resilient : shock
(C) soluble : water
(D) corrosive : iron
(E) responsive : stimulus

15 CANAL : WATERWAY ::
(A) skyline : city
(B) bank : stream
(C) hub : wheel
(D) dam : river
(E) reservoir : lake

16 THRONG : PEOPLE ::
(A) game : players
(B) picnic : woods
(C) swarm : insects
(D) cat : kittens
(E) vase : flowers

17 FOOLHARDY : RECKLESSNESS ::
(A) defiant : complacency
(B) serene : tranquillity
(C) precious : worthlessness
(D) sociable : antagonism
(E) lucky : persistence

18 EMEND : FAULTY ::
(A) recruit : competent
(B) fracture : separable
(C) renovate : habitable
(D) purify : contaminated
(E) reproduce : copied

19 NEIGHBOR : PROXIMITY ::
(A) supervisor : obedience
(B) comrade : victory
(C) adversary : opposition
(D) traitor : loyalty
(E) teammate : competitiveness

20 HECKLER : DISCONCERT ::
(A) outcast : exclude
(B) firebrand : soothe
(C) performer : applaud
(D) monarch : depose
(E) lobbyist : persuade

21 VEER : COURSE ::
(A) swerve : obstacle
(B) blaze : paint
(C) bar : door
(D) emigrate : travel
(E) digress : subject

22 REVELER : MERRYMAKING ::
(A) hedonist : restraint
(B) demagogue : emotion
(C) anarchist : authority
(D) disputant : argument
(E) litigant : settlement

23 MALINGER : WORK ::
(A) escape : flight
(B) accuse : crime
(C) hide : discovery
(D) shun : ridicule
(E) guess : answer

GO ON TO THE NEXT PAGE

The two passages below are followed by questions based on their content and on the relationship between the two passages. Answer the questions on the basis of what is stated or implied in the passages and in any introductory material that may be provided.

Questions 24-35 are based on the following passages.

The California museum built by oil billionaire J. Paul Getty (1892-1976) to house his world-class art collection opened in 1974. Passage 1 describes some early reactions to the Getty Museum. Passage 2 is excerpted from Getty's autobiography.

Passage 1

It sits atop a wooded hillside overlooking the Pacific in Malibu, California. Critics have contemptuously compared it to Disneyland. "A plastic paradise in kitsch city," grumped one. "It outstrips any existing monument to expensive, aggressive bad taste, cultural pretension, and self-aggrandizement."

The building that houses the controversial new J. Paul Getty Museum is a re-creation of the Villa dei Papyri in Herculaneum, near Pompeii, which was destroyed by the eruption of Vesuvius in A.D. 79. Visitors and critics alike usually wind up being favorably impressed by the Getty collection, which specializes in classical antiquities. But it is the design of the building rather than the art itself that has ignited the most heated art controversy of the 1970's.

Criticism of the museum design is of two types. One school of thought holds that the museum building itself is not sufficiently neutral, that a museum ought not to be, of itself, a work of art, competing with the collection displayed therein. The other school of thought holds that while it is permissible for a museum to be a work of art, the Getty building fails miserably as art because it is neither tastefully conceived nor accurately reproduced. "It is a faithful replica of nothing that ever existed," wrote architecture critic John Pastier, "re-created by inappropriate technologies and frequently lacking in basic architectural design judgment. The details are all based on known Roman examples from various places, but they have been combined and executed in a manner that often negates their nature and purpose or creates an incongruous appearance."

Among the specific criticisms offered by Pastier and others dissatisfied with the museum-as-replica is that many interior walls and whole parts of the floor plan of the original villa have been shifted, and an entire wing of the original villa has been omitted. Perhaps the most devastating single criticism of the authenticity of the museum design has been that excavation of the original villa site has been so incomplete that there is insufficient knowledge available even to attempt a legitimate re-creation. "No one knows about its precise style and details, how many floors it had, or exactly how tall it was," wrote Pastier. The Getty Museum, he seemed to imply, is merely an exercise in guesswork.

Passage 2

Since I personally would be footing the bills for the new museum, the final question was put to me: Expand the existing facilities or construct an entirely new building? I listened to all the pros and cons. "Draw up plans for an entirely new building," I told the trustees. I made one reservation. "I refuse to pay for one of those concrete-bunker-type structures that are the fad among museum architects—nor for some tinted-glass-and-stainless-steel monstrosity." To my delight, the trustees beamed. They, too, wanted the museum building itself to be unique and a work of art.

The flouting of conventional wisdom and refusal to conform carry with them many risks. This is nowhere more true than in the Art World, certain quarters of which tend to be very much doctrinaire and elitist. However, I had calculated the risks—and, I say this with an admitted degree of arrogance, I disregarded them. Thus, I was neither shaken nor surprised when some of the early returns showed that certain critics sniffed at the new museum. The building did not follow the arbitrary criteria for "museum construction." There were those who thought it should have been more conventional—that is, I suppose, that it should have been built to look like some of the museum structures whose architecture can be best described as "Penitentiary Modern." In any event, for the first two months or so, the J. Paul Getty Museum building was called "controversial" in many Art World (or should I say Artsy-Craftsy?) quarters.

I have a fortunate capacity to remain unruffled. I also have had more than sufficient experience in many areas of life to know that the shrillest critics are not necessarily the most authoritative (and seldom the most objective). Beyond this, the very shrillness of their cries and howls very quickly exhausts their wind.

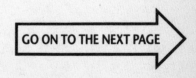

GO ON TO THE NEXT PAGE

24 In line 3, "plastic" most nearly means

(A) pliable
(B) artificial
(C) impermanent
(D) innovative
(E) inexpensive

25 The critics mentioned in the first paragraph of Passage 1 most probably consider the comparison of the museum to Disneyland appropriate because they believe that both places

(A) have aroused controversy in the press
(B) were built in picturesque areas
(C) celebrate imagination and innovation
(D) are garish and inauthentic in design
(E) were very expensive to maintain

26 In lines 26-34, Pastier's basic objection to the museum's design is that

(A) its separate parts do not create a coherent whole
(B) it is modeled on a building not worthy of imitation
(C) it does not sufficiently accommodate the needs of modern museum patrons
(D) its architectural style clashes with the styles of the artworks it houses
(E) it is not harmoniously integrated into the landscape that surrounds it

27 Lines 35-48 suggest that the excavation at the site of the Villa dei Papyri had revealed the original structure's

(A) domestic fixtures
(B) architectural embellishments
(C) shell, but not the location of its interior walls
(D) age, but neither its layout nor its purpose
(E) floor plan, but neither its height nor its details

28 Passage 1 indicates that Pastier and like-minded critics have arrived at some of their objections to the Getty Museum by

(A) evaluating the artworks it houses
(B) comparing it to other museums that house antiquities
(C) considering the Roman building on which it is modeled
(D) investigating the sources of Getty's personal fortune
(E) analyzing the character of J. Paul Getty

29 Getty indicates that the trustees "beamed" (line 58) because they were

(A) amused by Getty's cantankerousness
(B) accustomed to Getty's impulsiveness
(C) in accord with Getty's preferences
(D) pleased by Getty's unexpectedly generous donation
(E) impressed with Getty's financial acumen

30 When Getty mentions the "flouting of conventional wisdom" (line 61), he is referring to his opinions about the

(A) design of the museum building
(B) location of the museum
(C) museum's arrangement of displays
(D) financing of the museum
(E) floor plan of the museum building

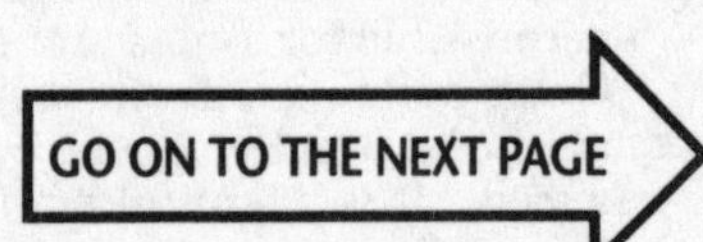

31 As indicated in Passage 2, Getty considered his choice of museum design an act of

(A) courageous defiance
(B) pointed satire
(C) spiteful mischief
(D) reluctant compromise
(E) justified indignation

32 On the basis of the information in Passage 2, which statement most accurately describes Getty's reaction to the art controversy mentioned in lines 13-16 ?

(A) He tabled plans to expand the museum's facilities.
(B) He felt that his intentions had been misunderstood by critics.
(C) He took the complaints seriously enough to consider redesigning the museum.
(D) He had anticipated the response and decided to ignore it.
(E) He engaged the most vehement of the critics in public debate.

33 Which aspect of the Getty Museum building seems to matter a great deal in Passage 1, but not in Passage 2 ?

(A) Its potential for future expansion
(B) Its convenience for visitors
(C) Its questionable authenticity
(D) Its unusual appearance
(E) Its practicality

34 Which statement best expresses an idea shared by one group of critics in Passage 1 and the trustees in Passage 2 ?

(A) A museum ought to concentrate on collecting artworks from only one historical period.
(B) Museums can be considered successful only if they attract a large enough segment of the population.
(C) The design of a building in which works of art are shown should resemble the style of those artworks.
(D) It is appropriate for a museum building to be a work of art in its own right.
(E) Museums that collect contemporary art experience fewer difficulties than those that collect classical art.

35 The final paragraph of Passage 2 suggests that Getty would predict which of the following about the critics referred to in Passage 1 ?

(A) Unless they offer more constructive advice, they will lose the chance to contribute.
(B) Unless they start to conform more closely to public opinion, they will lose their audience.
(C) Since they are widely read, they will continue to have an impact on museum attendance.
(D) Since they are taken seriously by the art world, they will continue to influence museum design.
(E) Although they are very loud, their influence will be short-lived.

IF YOU FINISH BEFORE TIME IS CALLED, YOU MAY CHECK YOUR WORK ON THIS SECTION ONLY. DO NOT TURN TO ANY OTHER SECTION IN THE TEST. STOP

Section 4 4 4 4 4

Time—30 Minutes
25 Questions

This section contains two types of questions. You have 30 minutes to complete both types. You may use any available space for scratchwork.

Notes:

1. The use of a calculator is permitted. All numbers used are real numbers.
2. Figures that accompany problems in this test are intended to provide information useful in solving the problems. They are drawn as accurately as possible EXCEPT when it is stated in a specific problem that the figure is not drawn to scale. All figures lie in a plane unless otherwise indicated.

Reference Information

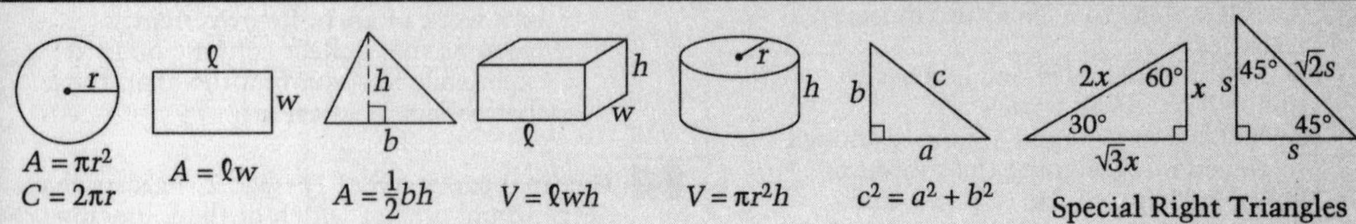

The number of degrees of arc in a circle is 360.
The measure in degrees of a straight angle is 180.
The sum of the measures in degrees of the angles of a triangle is 180.

Directions for Quantitative Comparison Questions

Questions 1-15 each consist of two quantities in boxes, one in Column A and one in Column B. You are to compare the two quantities and on the answer sheet fill in oval

A if the quantity in Column A is greater;
B if the quantity in Column B is greater;
C if the two quantities are equal;
D if the relationship cannot be determined from the information given.

AN E RESPONSE WILL NOT BE SCORED.

Notes:

1. In some questions, information is given about one or both of the quantities to be compared. In such cases, the given information is centered above the two columns and is not boxed.
2. In a given question, a symbol that appears in both columns represents the same thing in Column A as it does in Column B.
3. Letters such as x, n, and k stand for real numbers.

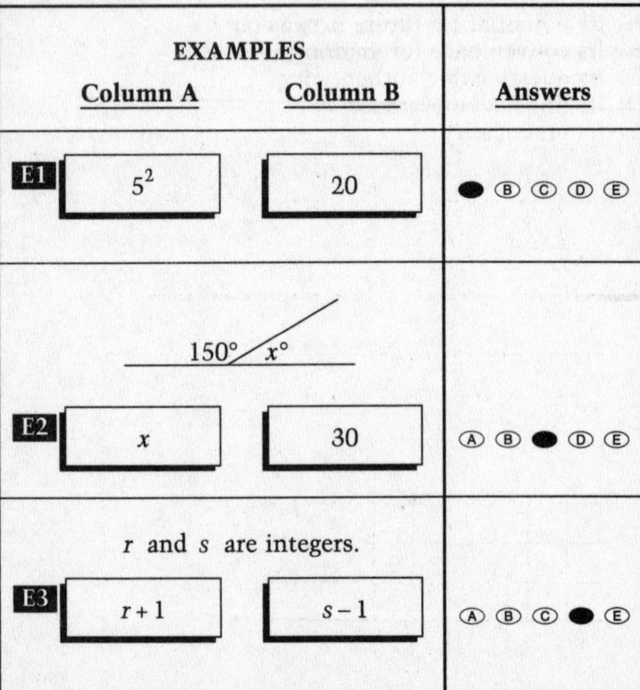

EXAMPLES
Column A
Column B
Answers
E1
5^2
20
150°
$x°$
E2
x
30
r and s are integers.
E3
$r + 1$
$s - 1$

GO ON TO THE NEXT PAGE

SUMMARY DIRECTIONS FOR COMPARISON QUESTIONS

Answer: A if the quantity in Column A is greater;
B if the quantity in Column B is greater;
C if the two quantities are equal;
D if the relationship cannot be determined from the information given.

	Column A	Column B

An entire 5-pound bag of sugar is to be divided equally among 3 students in a home economics class.

	Column A	Column B
1	The number of pounds of sugar each of these students will receive	$1\frac{1}{2}$

$x > 0$

	Column A	Column B
2	$\left(\sqrt{x}\right)^2$	$\sqrt{x^2}$

n is an integer greater than 1.

	Column A	Column B
3	$\frac{1}{n} - \frac{1}{2}$	$\frac{1}{2}$

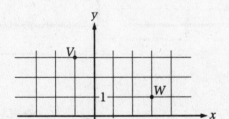

	Column A	Column B
4	The y-coordinate of point V	The x-coordinate of point W

	Column A	Column B
5	The increase in the area of circle A when its radius is increased by 1 inch	The increase in the area of circle B when its radius is increased by 1 inch

$2x + 15 = 4x - 1$

	Column A	Column B
6	$2x$	14

Tina and Jules both collect stamps. The number of stamps in Tina's collection is 3 less than 5 times the number in Jules's collection.

	Column A	Column B
7	The number of stamps in Tina's collection	The number of stamps in Jules's collection

t is 2 times r.

r is $\frac{1}{2}$ of p.

	Column A	Column B
8	t	p

GO ON TO THE NEXT PAGE

SUMMARY DIRECTIONS FOR COMPARISON QUESTIONS

Answer: A if the quantity in Column A is greater;
B if the quantity in Column B is greater;
C if the two quantities are equal;
D if the relationship cannot be determined from the information given.

	Column A	Column B
	$0.6 < x < 1.0$ $-0.6 < y < 1.0$	
9	x	y
	A bucket presently contains 20 liters of water and is $\frac{1}{4}$ full.	
10	The number of additional liters of water necessary to fill the bucket to capacity	60
11	The sum of the lengths of the dotted line segments	Half the perimeter of rectangle $ABCD$
	$4 < x < y < 5$	
12	25% of x	20% of y
	$m > 0$	
13	$\frac{m + m}{m}$	m
14	The sum of three different prime numbers if each number is less than 10	The sum of three different positive even integers if each integer is less than 10
	$AC > AB$	
15	BD	CE

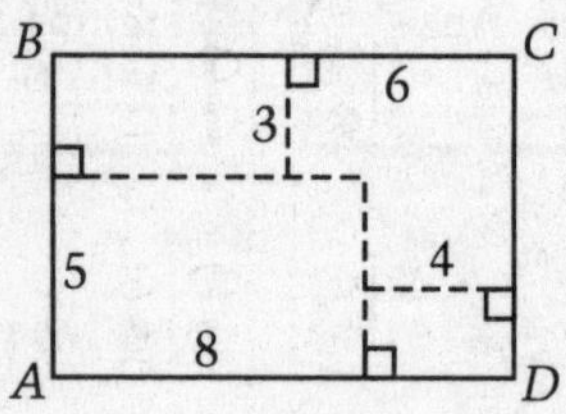

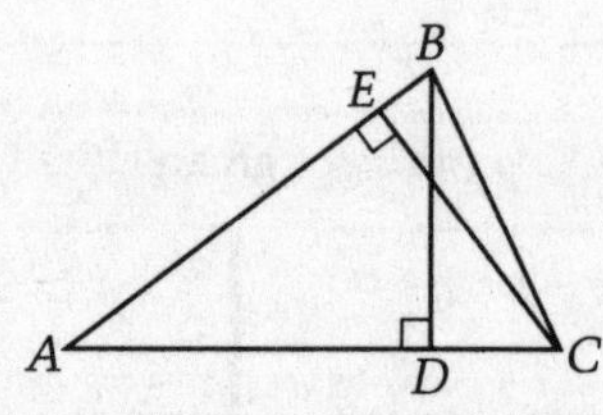

GO ON TO THE NEXT PAGE

Directions for Student-Produced Response Questions

Each of the remaining 10 questions requires you to solve the problem and enter your answer by marking the ovals in the special grid, as shown in the examples below.

Answer: $\frac{7}{12}$ or 7/12

Write answer → in boxes.

7/12

← Fraction line

Grid in → result.

Answer: 2.5

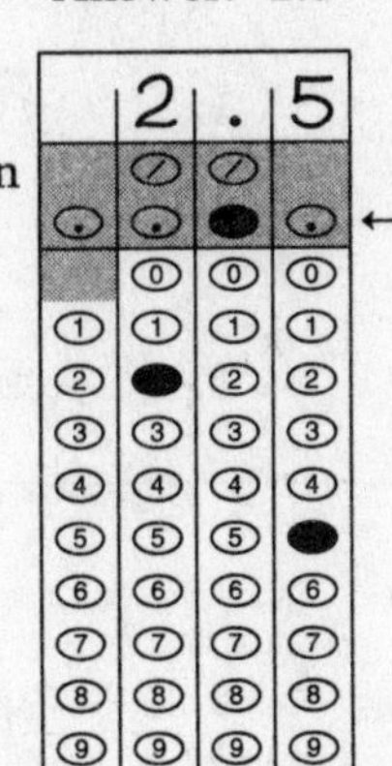

← Decimal point

Answer: 201
Either position is correct.

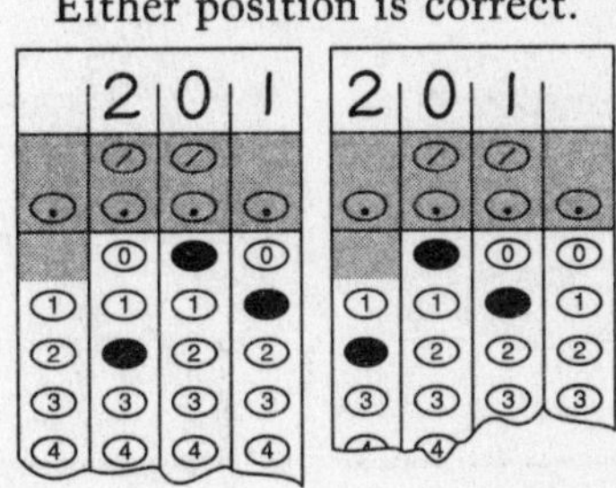

Note: You may start your answers in any column, space permitting. Columns not needed should be left blank.

- Mark no more than one oval in any column.
- Because the answer sheet will be machine-scored, **you will receive credit only if the ovals are filled in correctly.**
- Although not required, it is suggested that you write your answer in the boxes at the top of the columns to help you fill in the ovals accurately.
- Some problems may have more than one correct answer. In such cases, grid only one answer.
- No question has a negative answer.
- **Mixed numbers** such as $2\frac{1}{2}$ must be gridded as 2.5 or 5/2. (If 2 1 / 2 is gridded, it will be interpreted as $\frac{21}{2}$, not $2\frac{1}{2}$.)

- **Decimal Accuracy:** If you obtain a decimal answer, **enter the most accurate value the grid will accommodate.** For example, if you obtain an answer such as 0.6666 . . . , you should record the result as .666 or .667. **Less accurate values such as .66 or .67 are not acceptable.**

Acceptable ways to grid $\frac{2}{3}$ = .6666 . . .

2/3   .666   .667

16 If $\frac{10}{a} = \frac{b}{12}$, what is the value of ab ?

150, 30, 6, . . .

17 In the sequence above, each term after the 1st term is $\frac{1}{5}$ of the term preceding it. What is the 5th term of this sequence?

GO ON TO THE NEXT PAGE

18 Five points, A, B, C, D, and E, lie on a line, not necessarily in that order. Segment AB has a length of 24. Point C is the midpoint of AB, and point D is the midpoint of segment AC. If the distance between D and E is 5, what is one possible distance between A and E ?

19 What is the greatest of 5 consecutive integers if the sum of these integers equals 185 ?

20 A salesman's monthly gross pay consists of \$1,200 plus 20 percent of the dollar amount of his sales. If his gross pay for one month was \$2,500, what was the dollar amount of his sales for that month? (Disregard the \$ sign when gridding your answer.)

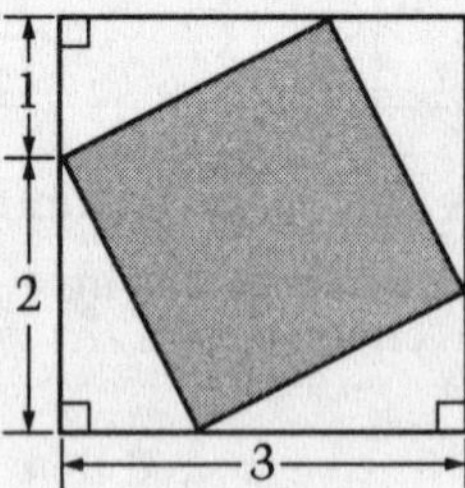

21 In the figure above, what is the area of the shaded square?

GO ON TO THE NEXT PAGE

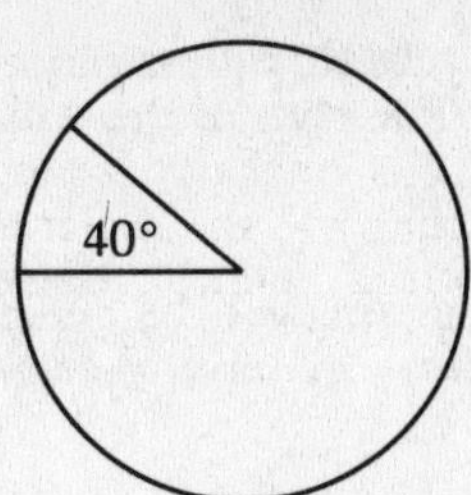

22 Naomi makes silver jewelry. For one style of earrings, she cuts wedges from a silver disk, as shown in the figure above. Each wedge makes a 40° angle at the center of the disk. If the weight of each uncut disk is a uniformly distributed 2.5 grams, how many grams does each wedge weigh?

23 If $x^2 - y^2 = 10$ and $x + y = 5$, what is the value of $x - y$?

24 For all positive integers j and k, let $j \boxed{R} k$ be defined as the whole number remainder when j is divided by k. If $13 \boxed{R} k = 2$, what is the value of k?

25 The average (arithmetic mean) of the test scores of a class of p students is 70, and the average of the test scores of a class of n students is 92. When the scores of both classes are combined, the average score is 86. What is the value of $\frac{p}{n}$?

IF YOU FINISH BEFORE TIME IS CALLED, YOU MAY CHECK YOUR WORK ON THIS SECTION ONLY. DO NOT TURN TO ANY OTHER SECTION IN THE TEST. **STOP**

Section 6 6 6 6

Time—15 Minutes
13 Questions

For each question in this section, select the best answer from among the choices given and fill in the corresponding oval on the answer sheet.

The passage below is followed by questions based on its content. Answer the questions on the basis of what is stated or implied in the passage and in any introductory material that may be provided.

Questions 1-13 are based on the following passage.

In this passage from a novel, the narrator has been reading letters of his grandmother, Susan Ward, and is reflecting on the meaning of certain events in her life. In about 1880, Susan Ward was a young woman—a writer and a mother—whose husband Oliver was working as a mining engineer in Leadville, in the West. Here, the narrator imagines Susan Ward as she spends the winter with her family in Milton, New York, before rejoining her husband in the spring.

From the parental burrow, Leadville seemed so far away it was only half real. Unwrapping her apple-cheeked son after a sleigh ride down the lane, she had difficulty in believing that she had ever lived anywhere but here in Milton.

She felt how the placid industry of her days matched the placid industry of all the days that had passed over that farm through six generations. Present and past were less continuous than synonymous. She did not have to come at her grandparents through a time machine. Her own life and that of the grandfather she was writing about showed her similar figures in an identical landscape. At the milldam where she had learned to skate she pulled her little boy on his sled, and they watched a weasel snow-white for winter flirt his black-tipped tail in and out of the mill's timbers. She might have been watching with her grandfather's eyes.

Watching a wintry sky die out beyond black elms, she could not make her mind restore the sight of the western mountains at sunset from her cabin door, or the cabin itself, or Oliver, or their friends. Who were those glittering people intent on raiding the continent for money or for scientific knowledge? What illusion was it that she bridged between this world and that? She paused sometimes, cleaning the room she had always called Grandma's Room, and thought with astonishment of the memory of Oliver's great revolver lying on the dresser when he, already a thoroughgoing Westerner, had come to the house to court her.

The town of Milton was dim and gentle, molded by gentle lives, the current of change as slow through it as the seep of water through a bog. More than once she thought how wrong those women in San Francisco had been, convinced that their old homes did not welcome them on their return. Last year when Oliver's professional future was uncertain, she would have agreed. Now, with the future assured in the form of Oliver's appointment as manager of the Adelaide mine in Leadville, the comfortable past asserted itself unchanged. Need for her husband, like worry over him, was tuned low. Absorbed in her child and in the writing of her book, she was sunk in her affection for home. Even the signs of mutability that sometimes jolted her—the whiteness of her mother's hair, the worn patience of her sister's face, the morose silences of her brother-in-law, now so long and black that the women worried about him in low voices—could not more than briefly interrupt the deep security and peace.

I wonder if ever again Americans can have that experience of returning to a home place so intimately known, profoundly felt, deeply loved, and absolutely submitted to? It is not quite true that you can't go home again. But it gets less likely. We have had too many divorces, we have consumed too much transportation, we have lived too shallowly in too many places. I doubt that anyone of my son's generation could comprehend the home feelings of someone like Susan Ward. Despite her unwillingness to live separately from her husband, she could probably have stayed on indefinitely in Milton, visited only occasionally by an asteroid husband. Or she would have picked up the old home and remade it in a new place. What she resisted was being a woman with no real home.

When frontier historians theorize about the uprooted, the lawless, the purseless, and the socially cut-off who emigrated to the West, they are not talking about people like my grandmother. So much that was cherished and loved, women like her had to give up; and the more they gave it up, the more they carried it helplessly with them. It was a process like ionization: what was subtracted from one pole was added to the other. For that sort of pioneer, the West was not a new country being created, but an old one being reproduced; in that sense our pioneer women were always more realistic than our pioneer men. The moderns, carrying little baggage of the cultural kind, not even living in traditional air, but breathing into their space helmets a scientific mixture of synthetic gases (and polluted at that) are the true pioneers. Their circuitry seems to include

GO ON TO THE NEXT PAGE

no domestic sentiment, they have had their empathy removed, their computers hum no ghostly feedback of Home, Sweet Home. How marvelously free they are! How unutterably deprived!

1 In line 1, the phrase "parental burrow" suggests

(A) a lack of luxurious accommodations
(B) an atmosphere of peaceful security
(C) the work required to sustain a home
(D) a lack of interest and stimulation
(E) the loss of privacy

2 It can be inferred that Ward "did not have to come at her grandparents through a time machine" (lines 10-11) because

(A) her parents had frequently told her stories of them
(B) she was deeply immersed in the history and literature of the period of their lives
(C) her life in Milton closely resembled theirs
(D) as a writer she could intuitively sense their lives
(E) she possessed written accounts of their lives

3 The reference to the grandfather's eyes in line 18 indicates that Ward

(A) longed to see nature as her ancestors did
(B) was unable to come to terms with her own life
(C) felt that her grandfather would approve of her life choices
(D) was seeing something her grandfather himself might well have seen
(E) longed to let her grandfather know what she was experiencing

4 The reference to a bog in line 34 serves to convey a sense of the

(A) natural setting of the town of Milton
(B) way in which Milton's residents earned their livelihoods
(C) deliberate pace of life in Milton
(D) confinement that Ward first felt in Milton
(E) vague foreboding that permeated Milton

5 Ward came to feel differently from "those women in San Francisco" (lines 35-36) because

(A) the rigors of life in the West made life in the East seem more pleasant
(B) the problems in her sister's life made her more content with the situation in her own life
(C) she had more free time as her son began to grow out of infancy
(D) her own career as a writer had become more important to her
(E) she was free to enjoy her surroundings now that she was confident about her husband's professional future

6 The word "sunk" in line 45 conveys the degree to which Ward

(A) is depressed about being separated from her husband
(B) is concerned about her son's social development
(C) feels powerless to help her sister's troubled marriage
(D) allows herself to be filled with a particular emotion
(E) lets down her defenses to free her creativity

7 The "feelings" referred to in line 61 might best be defined as

(A) an unwillingness to travel far
(B) the importance of property to self-esteem
(C) the emotional presence of one's ancestors
(D) deep knowledge and love of a place
(E) a yearning to recapture childhood

8 The narrator refers to "frontier historians" (line 69) primarily in order to

(A) add the weight of their authority to his assertion
(B) show his respect for their research
(C) suggest that instinct must be supplemented by formal training
(D) introduce a viewpoint he contradicts
(E) illustrate the nature of his own education

GO ON TO THE NEXT PAGE

9 The narrator characterizes the migration by people like his grandmother as chiefly a process of

(A) recreating a domestic haven
(B) developing new skills for physical survival
(C) shedding now-irrelevant concerns over status
(D) instilling a love of place in the young
(E) preserving the beauty of unspoiled nature

10 The reference to "little baggage" in line 81 serves to suggest which of the following about the narrator's view of modern people?

(A) They are not burdened by physical possessions.
(B) They are not affected by the values of the past.
(C) They are not interested in artistic tradition.
(D) They are not bearing their portion of responsibility.
(E) They are not respectful of the opinions of others.

11 In lines 85-89, the narrator describes members of the modern generation as the "true pioneers" because they

(A) have worthier motivations for breaking new ground
(B) build on the achievements of earlier generations
(C) have superior technology and training
(D) live in a violent and uncertain world
(E) regard life as no previous generation has done

12 The narrator apparently believes which of the following about the idea of home held by the new pioneers?

(A) They long to achieve their own sense of place.
(B) They scoff at the earlier generation's sense of place.
(C) They are free from hypocritical rhetoric about home.
(D) They are unable to experience the earlier generation's attachment to home.
(E) They are as deeply attuned to home as the earlier generation but in a distinctly different way.

13 What parallel between the narrator and Susan Ward does the passage reveal?

(A) Both openly resent the signs of change around them.
(B) Both have lived in many parts of the country.
(C) Both are writing about the life of a grandparent.
(D) Both feel alienated from their spouses.
(E) Both prefer solitude to company.

IF YOU FINISH BEFORE TIME IS CALLED, YOU MAY CHECK YOUR WORK ON THIS SECTION ONLY. DO NOT TURN TO ANY OTHER SECTION IN THE TEST. **STOP**

Section 7   7

Time—15 Minutes
10 Questions

In this section solve each problem, using any available space on the page for scratchwork. Then decide which is the best of the choices given and fill in the corresponding oval on the answer sheet.

Notes:

1. The use of a calculator is permitted. All numbers used are real numbers.
2. Figures that accompany problems in this test are intended to provide information useful in solving the problems. They are drawn as accurately as possible EXCEPT when it is stated in a specific problem that the figure is not drawn to scale. All figures lie in a plane unless otherwise indicated.

Reference Information

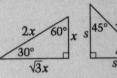

$A = \pi r^2$, $C = 2\pi r$; $A = \ell w$; $A = \frac{1}{2}bh$; $V = \ell wh$; $V = \pi r^2 h$; $c^2 = a^2 + b^2$; Special Right Triangles ($30°$–$60°$: x, $\sqrt{3}x$, $2x$; $45°$–$45°$: s, s, $\sqrt{2}s$)

The number of degrees of arc in a circle is 360.
The measure in degrees of a straight angle is 180.
The sum of the measures in degrees of the angles of a triangle is 180.

1 In a certain game, points are assigned to every word. Each q, x, and z in a word is worth 5 points, and all other letters are worth 1 point each. What is the sum of the points assigned to the word "exquisite"?

(A) 21
(B) 17
(C) 16
(D) 13
(E) 9

2 If $\frac{p}{r} = \frac{5}{2}$ and $\frac{r}{s} = \frac{2}{3}$, then $\frac{p}{s} =$

(A) $\frac{4}{15}$
(B) $\frac{2}{5}$
(C) $\frac{3}{5}$
(D) $\frac{5}{3}$
(E) $\frac{15}{4}$

A, B; $y°$; $x°$, $x°$, $x°$, $x°$, $x°$, $x°$, $x°$

3 In the figure above, if AB is a line, what is the value of y?

(A) 108
(B) 114
(C) 117
(D) 120
(E) 135

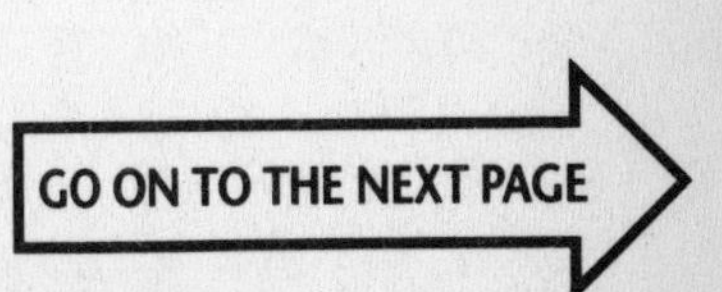

4 The scenic route to Mia's office is 5 kilometers longer than the direct route. When she goes by the scenic route and returns by the direct route, the round trip is 35 kilometers. How many kilometers is the direct route?

(A) 5

(B) $12\frac{1}{2}$

(C) 15

(D) 20

(E) $22\frac{1}{2}$

5 A certain scale for weighing food registers only weights above 6 pounds. A person who wanted to know the weight of 1 package each of chicken, beef, and turkey weighed every possible pair of these packages and got the following results.

The chicken and the beef weighed 7 pounds.
The chicken and the turkey weighed 8 pounds.
The beef and the turkey weighed 9 pounds.

What is the weight of the package of turkey?

(A) 2 pounds
(B) 3 pounds
(C) 4 pounds
(D) 5 pounds
(E) 6 pounds

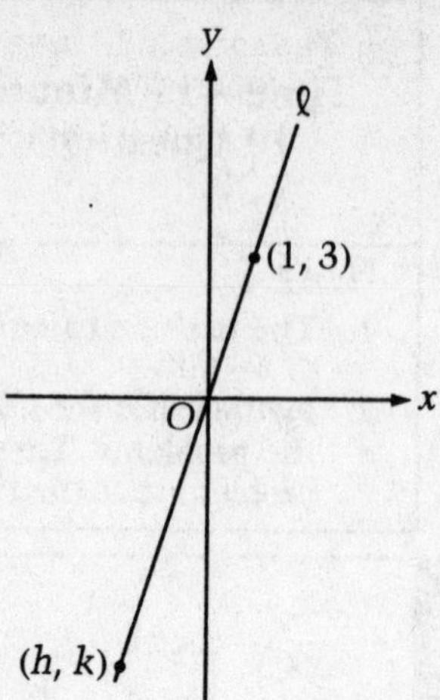

6 In the figure above, line ℓ passes through the origin. What is the value of $\frac{k}{h}$?

(A) 3

(B) 2

(C) $\frac{3}{2}$

(D) $-\frac{3}{2}$

(E) -3

GO ON TO THE NEXT PAGE

7 The integer 33 is to be expressed as a sum of n consecutive positive integers. The value of n could be which of the following?

I. 2
II. 3
III. 6

(A) I only
(B) II only
(C) I and II only
(D) I and III only
(E) I, II, and III

8 Points P, Q, R, S, T, and U are all different points lying in the same plane. Points P, Q, and U lie on the same line. The line through points P and Q is perpendicular to the line through points R and S. The line through points R and S is perpendicular to the line through points T and U. Which of the following sets contains points that must lie on the same line?

(A) $\{P, Q, R\}$
(B) $\{Q, R, S\}$
(C) $\{Q, R, T\}$
(D) $\{Q, T, U\}$
(E) $\{R, T, U\}$

GO ON TO THE NEXT PAGE

9 If $y = \frac{5x^3}{z}$, what happens to the value of y when both x and z are doubled?

(A) y is not changed.
(B) y is halved.
(C) y is doubled.
(D) y is tripled.
(E) y is multiplied by 4.

10 A store charges $28 for a certain type of sweater. This price is 40 percent more than the amount it costs the store to buy one of these sweaters. At an end-of-season sale, store employees can purchase any remaining sweaters at 30 percent off the store's cost. How much would it cost an employee to purchase a sweater of this type at this sale?

(A) $8.40
(B) $14.00
(C) $19.60
(D) $20.00
(E) $25.20

IF YOU FINISH BEFORE TIME IS CALLED, YOU MAY CHECK YOUR WORK ON THIS SECTION ONLY. DO NOT TURN TO ANY OTHER SECTION IN THE TEST. **STOP**

SAT 1: Reasoning Test Answer Key
Saturday, May 1997

VERBAL

Section 1

Five-choice Questions

	COR. ANS.	DIFF. LEV.
1.	D	1
2.	A	1
3.	E	3
4.	C	3
5.	C	3
6.	A	5
7.	B	5
8.	D	5
9.	C	5
10.	B	1
11.	C	1
12.	B	3
13.	C	5
14.	E	4
15.	A	4
16.	B	3
17.	C	3
18.	C	1
19.	D	3
20.	A	3
21.	D	3
22.	C	2
23.	A	3
24.	E	3
25.	D	3
26.	B	4
27.	C	3
28.	E	3
29.	A	3
30.	A	3

______ no. correct

______ no. incorrect

Section 3

Five-choice Questions

	COR. ANS.	DIFF. LEV.
1.	B	3
2.	B	1
3.	B	2
4.	D	2
5.	B	3
6.	E	3
7.	A	3
8.	E	2
9.	C	5
10.	A	5
11.	D	1
12.	B	2
13.	A	1
14.	D	3
15.	E	3
16.	C	3
17.	B	3
18.	D	3
19.	C	3
20.	E	4
21.	E	4
22.	D	4
23.	C	5
24.	B	1
25.	D	3
26.	A	3
27.	E	3
28.	C	3
29.	C	2
30.	A	2
31.	A	3
32.	D	3
33.	C	3
34.	D	3
35.	E	3

______ no. correct

______ no. incorrect

Section 6

Five-choice Questions

	COR. ANS.	DIFF. LEV.
1.	B	3
2.	C	3
3.	D	2
4.	C	3
5.	E	3
6.	D	3
7.	D	2
8.	D	3
9.	A	4
10.	B	3
11.	E	4
12.	D	3
13.	C	5

______ no. correct

______ no. incorrect

MATHEMATICAL

Section 2

Five-choice Questions

	COR. ANS.	DIFF. LEV.
1.	A	1
2.	D	1
3.	D	1
4.	B	1
5.	A	1
6.	E	2
7.	C	2
8.	E	3
9.	B	3
10.	D	3
11.	B	2
12.	E	3
13.	A	4
14.	C	3
15.	A	3
16.	B	4
17.	C	4
18.	E	4
19.	C	3
20.	D	3
21.	A	5
22.	C	3
23.	C	5
24.	E	5
25.	A	5

______ no. correct

______ no. incorrect

Section 4

Four-choice Questions

	COR. ANS.	DIFF. LEV.
1.	A	2
2.	C	2
3.	B	2
4.	C	2
5.	D	2
6.	A	3
7.	A	3
8.	C	3
9.	D	3
10.	C	3
11.	C	3
12.	A	4
13.	D	4
14.	D	4
15.	B	5

______ no. correct

______ no. incorrect

Section 7

Five-choice Questions

	COR. ANS.	DIFF. LEV.
1.	B	1
2.	D	1
3.	A	2
4.	C	2
5.	D	3
6.	A	3
7.	E	4
8.	D	4
9.	E	4
10.	B	5

______ no. correct

______ no. incorrect

Section 4

Student-Produced Response Questions

	COR. ANS.	DIFF. LEV.
16.	120	1
17.	6/25 or .24	2
18.	1 or 11	2
19.	39	2
20.	6500	3
21.	5	3
22.	5/18, .277 or .278	3
23.	2	4
24.	11	4
25.	3/8 or .375	5

______ no. correct (16-25)

NOTE: Difficulty levels are estimates of question difficulty for a recent group of college-bound seniors. Difficulty levels range from 1 (easiest) to 5 (hardest).

The Scoring Process

Machine-scoring is done in three steps:

- *Scanning.* Your answer sheet is "read" by a scanning machine and the oval you filled in for each question is recorded on a computer tape.
- *Scoring.* The computer compares the oval filled in for each question with the correct response. Each correct answer receives one point; omitted questions do not count toward your score. For each wrong answer to the multiple-choice questions, a fraction of a point is subtracted to correct for random guessing. For questions with five answer choices, one-fourth of a point is subtracted for each wrong response; for questions with four answer choices, one-third of a point is subtracted for each wrong response. The SAT I verbal test has 78 questions with five answer choices each. If, for example, a student has 44 right, 32 wrong, and 2 omitted, the resulting raw score is determined as follows:

$$44 \text{ right} - \frac{32 \text{ wrong}}{4} = 44 - 8 = 36 \text{ raw score points}$$

Obtaining raw scores frequently involves the rounding of fractional numbers to the nearest whole number. For example, a raw score of 36.25 is rounded to 36, the nearest whole number. A raw score of 36.50 is rounded upward to 37.

- *Converting to reported scaled score.* Raw test scores are then placed on the College Board scale of 200 to 800 through a process that adjusts scores to account for minor differences in difficulty among different editions of the test. This process, known as equating, is performed so that a student's reported score is not affected by the edition of the test taken or by the abilities of the group with whom the student takes the test. As a result of placing SAT I scores on the College Board scale, scores earned by students at different times can be compared. For example, an SAT I verbal score of 400 on a test taken at one administration indicates the same level of developed verbal ability as a 400 score obtained on a different edition of the test taken at another time.

How to Score the Test

SAT I Verbal Sections 1, 3, and 6

Step A: Count the number of correct answers for *Section 1* and record the number in the space provided on the worksheet on the next page. Then do the same for the incorrect answers. (Do not count omitted answers.) To determine subtotal A, use the formula:

$$\text{number correct} - \frac{\text{number incorrect}}{4} = \text{subtotal A}$$

Step B: Count the number of correct answers and the number of incorrect answers for *Section 3* and record the number in the space provided on the worksheet. To determine subtotal B, use the formula.

$$\text{number correct} - \frac{\text{number incorrect}}{4} = \text{subtotal B}$$

Step C: Count the number of correct answers and the number of incorrect answers for *Section 6* and record the number in the space provided on the worksheet. To determine subtotal C, use the formula:

$$\text{number correct} - \frac{\text{number incorrect}}{4} = \text{subtotal C}$$

Step D: To obtain D, add subtotal A, subtotal B, and subtotal C, keeping any decimals. Enter the resulting figure on the worksheet.

Step E: To obtain E, your raw verbal score, round D to the nearest whole number. (For example, any number from 44.50 to 45.49 rounds to 45.) Enter the resulting figure on the worksheet.

Step F: To find your SAT 1 verbal score, use the conversion table to look up the total raw verbal score you obtained in step E. Enter this figure on the worksheet.

SAT I Mathematical Sections 2, 4, and 7

Step A: Count the number of correct answers and the number of incorrect answers for *Section 2* and record the numbers in the spaces provided on the worksheet. To determine subtotal A, use the formula:

$$\text{number correct} - \frac{\text{number incorrect}}{4} = \text{subtotal A}$$

Step B: Count the number of correct answers and the number of incorrect answers for the *four-choice quantitative comparison questions (questions 1 through 15) in Section 4* and record the number in the space provided on the worksheet. Note: Do not count any E responses to questions 1 through 15 as correct or incorrect. Because these four-choice questions have no E answer choices, E responses to these questions are treated as omits. To determine subtotal B, use the formula:

$$\text{number correct} - \frac{\text{number incorrect}}{3} = \text{subtotal B}$$

Step C: Count the number of correct answers for the student-produced response questions *(questions 16 through 25)* in *Section 4* and record the number in the space provided on the worksheet. This is subtotal C.

Step D: Count the number of correct answers and the number of incorrect answers for *Section 7* and record the number in the space provided on the worksheet. To determine subtotal D, use the formula:

$$\text{number correct} - \frac{\text{number incorrect}}{4} = \text{subtotal D}$$

Step E: To obtain E, add subtotal A, subtotal B, subtotal C, and subtotal D, keeping any decimals. Enter the resulting figure on the worksheet.

Step F: To obtain F, your raw mathematical score, round E to the nearest whole number. (For example, any number from 44.50 to 45.49 rounds to 45.) Enter the resulting figure on the worksheet.

Step G. To find your SAT 1 mathematical score, use the conversion table to look up the total raw mathematical score you obtained in step F. Enter this figure on the worksheet.

SAT I Scoring Worksheet

SAT I Verbal Sections

A. Section 1:	______ no. correct	– (______ no. incorrect	÷ 4) =	______ subtotal A
B. Section 3:	______ no. correct	– (______ no. incorrect	÷ 4) =	______ subtotal B
C. Section 6:	______ no. correct	– (______ no. incorrect	÷ 4) =	______ subtotal C
D. Total unrounded raw score (Total A + B + C)				______ D
E. Total rounded raw score (Rounded to nearest whole number)				______ E
F. SAT 1 verbal reported scaled score (See the conversion table)				SAT I verbal score

SAT I Mathematical Sections

A. Section 2:	______ no. correct	– (______ no. incorrect	÷ 4) =	______ subtotal A
B. Section 4: Questions 1-15 (quantitative comparison)	______ no. correct	– (______ no. incorrect	÷ 3) =	______ subtotal B
C. Section 4: Questions 16-25 (student-produced response)	______ no. correct		=	______ subtotal C
D. Section 7:	______ no. correct	– (______ no. incorrect	÷ 4) =	______ subtotal D
E. Total unrounded raw score (Total A + B + C + D)				______ E
F. Total rounded raw score (Rounded to nearest whole number)				______ F
G. SAT 1 mathematical reported scaled score (See the conversion table)				SAT I mathematical score

Score Conversion Table
SAT 1: Reasoning Test
Saturday, May 1997
Recentered Scale

Raw Score	Verbal Scaled Score	Math Scaled Score	Raw Score	Verbal Scaled Score	Math Scaled Score
78	800		36	500	570
77	800		35	500	560
76	800		34	490	550
75	780		33	490	540
74	770		32	480	540
73	750		31	480	530
72	740		30	470	520
71	730		29	470	520
70	720		28	460	510
69	710		27	450	500
68	700		26	450	500
67	690		25	440	490
66	680		24	440	490
65	670		23	430	480
64	660		22	430	470
63	660		21	420	470
62	650		20	410	460
61	640		19	410	450
60	630	800	18	400	450
59	630	800	17	390	440
58	620	780	16	390	440
57	610	760	15	380	430
56	610	740	14	370	420
55	600	730	13	360	420
54	600	720	12	360	410
53	590	710	11	350	400
52	580	690	10	340	390
51	580	690	9	330	390
50	570	680	8	320	380
49	570	670	7	310	370
48	560	660	6	300	360
47	560	650	5	290	350
46	550	640	4	270	340
45	550	630	3	260	330
44	540	630	2	250	310
43	540	620	1	230	300
42	530	610	0	220	280
41	530	600	-1	200	260
40	520	590	-2	200	240
39	520	590	-3	200	210
38	510	580	-4	200	200
37	510	570	and below		

This table is for use only with this test.

SAT I: Reasoning Test

Sunday, May 1997

YOUR NAME (PRINT) ____
LAST FIRST MI

TEST CENTER ____
NUMBER NAME OF TEST CENTER ROOM NUMBER

SAT® I: Reasoning Test — General Directions

Timing

- You will have three hours to work on this test.
- There are five 30-minute sections and two 15-minute sections.
- You may work on only one section at a time.
- The supervisor will tell you when to begin and end each section.
- If you finish a section before time is called, check your work on that section. You may NOT turn to any other section.
- Work as rapidly as you can without losing accuracy. Don't waste time on questions that seem too difficult for you.

Marking Answers

- Carefully mark only one answer for each question.
- Make sure each mark is dark and completely fills the oval.
- Do not make any stray marks on your answer sheet.
- If you erase, do so completely. Incomplete erasures may be scored as intended answers.
- Use only the answer spaces that correspond to the question numbers.
- For questions with only four answer choices, an answer marked in oval E will not be scored.
- Use the test book for scratchwork, but you will not receive credit for anything written there.
- You may not transfer answers to your answer sheet or fill in ovals after time has been called.
- You may not fold or remove pages or portions of a page from this book, or take the book or answer sheet from the testing room.

Scoring

- For each correct answer, you receive one point.
- For questions you omit, you receive no points.
- For a wrong answer to a multiple-choice question, you lose a fraction of a point.
  - ► If you can eliminate one or more of the answer choices as wrong, however, you increase your chances of choosing the correct answer and earning one point.
  - ► If you can't eliminate any choice, move on. You can return to the question later if there is time.
- For a wrong answer to a math question that is not multiple-choice, you don't lose any points.

The passages for this test have been adapted from published material. The ideas contained in them do not necessarily represent the opinions of the College Board or Educational Testing Service.

IMPORTANT: The codes below are unique to your test book. Copy them on your answer sheet in boxes 8 and 9 and <u>fill in the corresponding ovals exactly as shown.</u>

8. Form Code

Ⓐ	Ⓐ	⓪	⓪	⓪
Ⓑ	Ⓑ	①	①	①
Ⓒ	Ⓒ	②	②	②
Ⓓ	Ⓓ	③	③	③
Ⓔ	Ⓔ	④	④	④
Ⓕ	Ⓕ	⑤	⑤	⑤
Ⓖ	Ⓖ	⑥	⑥	⑥
Ⓗ	Ⓗ	⑦	⑦	⑦
Ⓘ	Ⓘ	⑧	⑧	⑧
Ⓙ	Ⓙ	⑨	⑨	⑨
Ⓚ	Ⓚ			
Ⓛ	Ⓛ			
Ⓜ	Ⓜ			
Ⓝ	Ⓝ			
Ⓞ	Ⓞ			
Ⓟ	Ⓟ			
Ⓠ	Ⓠ			
Ⓡ	Ⓡ			
Ⓢ	Ⓢ			
Ⓣ	Ⓣ			
Ⓤ	Ⓤ			
Ⓥ	Ⓥ			
Ⓦ	Ⓦ			
Ⓧ	Ⓧ			
Ⓨ	Ⓨ			
Ⓩ	Ⓩ			

9. Test Form

DO NOT OPEN THIS BOOK UNTIL THE SUPERVISOR TELLS YOU TO DO SO.

THE COLLEGE BOARD — SAT I Page 1

Use a No. 2 pencil only. Be sure each mark is dark and completely fills the intended oval. Completely erase any errors or stray marks.

1. Your Name

First 4 letters of Last Name | First init. | Mid. init.

2.

Your Name: (Print) Last First M.I.

I agree to the conditions on the back of the SAT I test book.

Signature: Date: / /

Home Address: (Print) Number and Street

City State Zip Code

Center: (Print) City State Center Number

IMPORTANT: Fill in items 8 and 9 exactly as shown on the back of test book.

3. Date of Birth

Month | Day | Year

Jan. Feb. Mar. Apr. May June July Aug. Sept. Oct. Nov. Dec.

4. Social Security Number

5. Sex

Female Male

6. Registration Number

(Copy from Admission Ticket.)

7. Test Book Serial Number

(Copy from front of test book.)

8. Form Code

(Copy and grid as on back of test book.)

FOR ETS USE ONLY

9. Test Form

(Copy from back of test book.)

Start with number 1 for each new section. If a section has fewer questions than answer spaces, leave the extra answer spaces blank.

SECTION 1

1–40 (A) (B) (C) (D) (E)

SECTION 2

1–40 (A) (B) (C) (D) (E)

Q2778-06/2 CHW98324 11027 • 09132 • TF129M17.5eX I.N. 207158

Use a No. 2 pencil only. Be sure each mark is dark and completely fills the intended oval. Completely erase any errors or stray marks.

Start with number 1 for each new section. If a section has fewer questions than answer spaces, leave the extra answer spaces blank.

SECTION 3

1 (A) (B) (C) (D) (E)
2 (A) (B) (C) (D) (E)
3 (A) (B) (C) (D) (E)
4 (A) (B) (C) (D) (E)
5 (A) (B) (C) (D) (E)
6 (A) (B) (C) (D) (E)
7 (A) (B) (C) (D) (E)
8 (A) (B) (C) (D) (E)
9 (A) (B) (C) (D) (E)
10 (A) (B) (C) (D) (E)
11 (A) (B) (C) (D) (E)
12 (A) (B) (C) (D) (E)
13 (A) (B) (C) (D) (E)
14 (A) (B) (C) (D) (E)
15 (A) (B) (C) (D) (E)

16 (A) (B) (C) (D) (E)
17 (A) (B) (C) (D) (E)
18 (A) (B) (C) (D) (E)
19 (A) (B) (C) (D) (E)
20 (A) (B) (C) (D) (E)
21 (A) (B) (C) (D) (E)
22 (A) (B) (C) (D) (E)
23 (A) (B) (C) (D) (E)
24 (A) (B) (C) (D) (E)
25 (A) (B) (C) (D) (E)
26 (A) (B) (C) (D) (E)
27 (A) (B) (C) (D) (E)
28 (A) (B) (C) (D) (E)
29 (A) (B) (C) (D) (E)
30 (A) (B) (C) (D) (E)

31 (A) (B) (C) (D) (E)
32 (A) (B) (C) (D) (E)
33 (A) (B) (C) (D) (E)
34 (A) (B) (C) (D) (E)
35 (A) (B) (C) (D) (E)
36 (A) (B) (C) (D) (E)
37 (A) (B) (C) (D) (E)
38 (A) (B) (C) (D) (E)
39 (A) (B) (C) (D) (E)
40 (A) (B) (C) (D) (E)

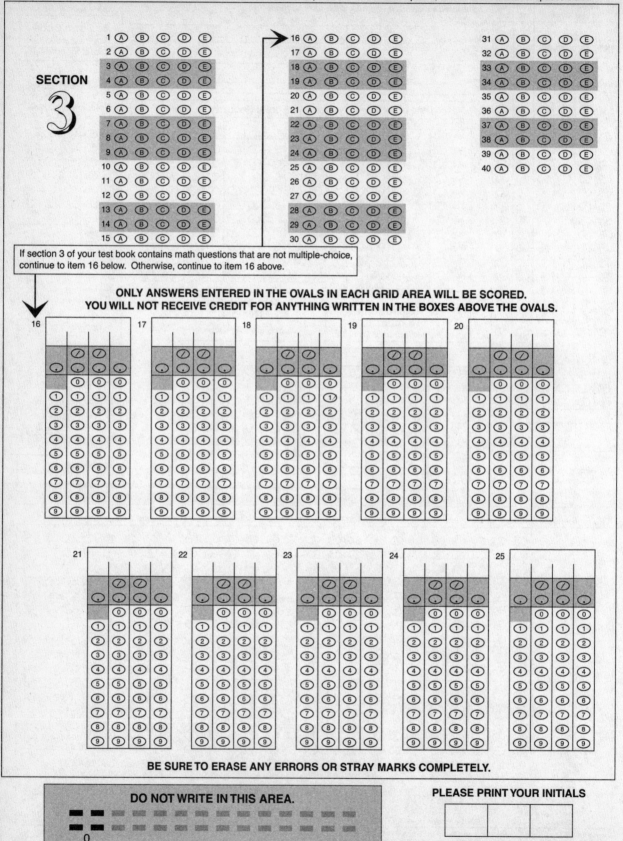

If section 3 of your test book contains math questions that are not multiple-choice, continue to item 16 below. Otherwise, continue to item 16 above.

ONLY ANSWERS ENTERED IN THE OVALS IN EACH GRID AREA WILL BE SCORED.
YOU WILL NOT RECEIVE CREDIT FOR ANYTHING WRITTEN IN THE BOXES ABOVE THE OVALS.

16 17 18 19 20

21 22 23 24 25

(Each grid: / / ; . . . . ; 0 0 0 ; 1 1 1 1 ; 2 2 2 2 ; 3 3 3 3 ; 4 4 4 4 ; 5 5 5 5 ; 6 6 6 6 ; 7 7 7 7 ; 8 8 8 8 ; 9 9 9 9)

BE SURE TO ERASE ANY ERRORS OR STRAY MARKS COMPLETELY.

DO NOT WRITE IN THIS AREA.

0

PLEASE PRINT YOUR INITIALS

First	Middle	Last

Use a No. 2 pencil only. Be sure each mark is dark and completely fills the intended oval. Completely erase any errors or stray marks.

Start with number 1 for each new section. If a section has fewer questions than answer spaces, leave the extra answer spaces blank.

SECTION 4

1 Ⓐ Ⓑ Ⓒ Ⓓ Ⓔ
2 Ⓐ Ⓑ Ⓒ Ⓓ Ⓔ
3 Ⓐ Ⓑ Ⓒ Ⓓ Ⓔ
4 Ⓐ Ⓑ Ⓒ Ⓓ Ⓔ
5 Ⓐ Ⓑ Ⓒ Ⓓ Ⓔ
6 Ⓐ Ⓑ Ⓒ Ⓓ Ⓔ
7 Ⓐ Ⓑ Ⓒ Ⓓ Ⓔ
8 Ⓐ Ⓑ Ⓒ Ⓓ Ⓔ
9 Ⓐ Ⓑ Ⓒ Ⓓ Ⓔ
10 Ⓐ Ⓑ Ⓒ Ⓓ Ⓔ
11 Ⓐ Ⓑ Ⓒ Ⓓ Ⓔ
12 Ⓐ Ⓑ Ⓒ Ⓓ Ⓔ
13 Ⓐ Ⓑ Ⓒ Ⓓ Ⓔ
14 Ⓐ Ⓑ Ⓒ Ⓓ Ⓔ
15 Ⓐ Ⓑ Ⓒ Ⓓ Ⓔ

16 Ⓐ Ⓑ Ⓒ Ⓓ Ⓔ
17 Ⓐ Ⓑ Ⓒ Ⓓ Ⓔ
18 Ⓐ Ⓑ Ⓒ Ⓓ Ⓔ
19 Ⓐ Ⓑ Ⓒ Ⓓ Ⓔ
20 Ⓐ Ⓑ Ⓒ Ⓓ Ⓔ
21 Ⓐ Ⓑ Ⓒ Ⓓ Ⓔ
22 Ⓐ Ⓑ Ⓒ Ⓓ Ⓔ
23 Ⓐ Ⓑ Ⓒ Ⓓ Ⓔ
24 Ⓐ Ⓑ Ⓒ Ⓓ Ⓔ
25 Ⓐ Ⓑ Ⓒ Ⓓ Ⓔ
26 Ⓐ Ⓑ Ⓒ Ⓓ Ⓔ
27 Ⓐ Ⓑ Ⓒ Ⓓ Ⓔ
28 Ⓐ Ⓑ Ⓒ Ⓓ Ⓔ
29 Ⓐ Ⓑ Ⓒ Ⓓ Ⓔ
30 Ⓐ Ⓑ Ⓒ Ⓓ Ⓔ

31 Ⓐ Ⓑ Ⓒ Ⓓ Ⓔ
32 Ⓐ Ⓑ Ⓒ Ⓓ Ⓔ
33 Ⓐ Ⓑ Ⓒ Ⓓ Ⓔ
34 Ⓐ Ⓑ Ⓒ Ⓓ Ⓔ
35 Ⓐ Ⓑ Ⓒ Ⓓ Ⓔ
36 Ⓐ Ⓑ Ⓒ Ⓓ Ⓔ
37 Ⓐ Ⓑ Ⓒ Ⓓ Ⓔ
38 Ⓐ Ⓑ Ⓒ Ⓓ Ⓔ
39 Ⓐ Ⓑ Ⓒ Ⓓ Ⓔ
40 Ⓐ Ⓑ Ⓒ Ⓓ Ⓔ

If section 4 of your test book contains math questions that are not multiple-choice, continue to item 16 below. Otherwise, continue to item 16 above.

ONLY ANSWERS ENTERED IN THE OVALS IN EACH GRID AREA WILL BE SCORED.
YOU WILL NOT RECEIVE CREDIT FOR ANYTHING WRITTEN IN THE BOXES ABOVE THE OVALS.

Grids 16, 17, 18, 19, 20, 21, 22, 23, 24, 25 (each with four columns):

/		⊘	⊘	
.	⊙	⊙	⊙	⊙
0		⓪	⓪	⓪
1	①	①	①	①
2	②	②	②	②
3	③	③	③	③
4	④	④	④	④
5	⑤	⑤	⑤	⑤
6	⑥	⑥	⑥	⑥
7	⑦	⑦	⑦	⑦
8	⑧	⑧	⑧	⑧
9	⑨	⑨	⑨	⑨

BE SURE TO ERASE ANY ERRORS OR STRAY MARKS COMPLETELY.

DO NOT WRITE IN THIS AREA.

0

PLEASE PRINT YOUR INITIALS

First	Middle	Last

Use a No. 2 pencil only. Be sure each mark is dark and completely fills the intended oval. Completely erase any errors or stray marks.

Start with number 1 for each new section. If a section has fewer questions than answer spaces, leave the extra answer spaces blank.

SECTION 5

1 (A) (B) (C) (D) (E)	11 (A) (B) (C) (D) (E)	21 (A) (B) (C) (D) (E)	31 (A) (B) (C) (D) (E)
2 (A) (B) (C) (D) (E)	12 (A) (B) (C) (D) (E)	22 (A) (B) (C) (D) (E)	32 (A) (B) (C) (D) (E)
3 (A) (B) (C) (D) (E)	13 (A) (B) (C) (D) (E)	23 (A) (B) (C) (D) (E)	33 (A) (B) (C) (D) (E)
4 (A) (B) (C) (D) (E)	14 (A) (B) (C) (D) (E)	24 (A) (B) (C) (D) (E)	34 (A) (B) (C) (D) (E)
5 (A) (B) (C) (D) (E)	15 (A) (B) (C) (D) (E)	25 (A) (B) (C) (D) (E)	35 (A) (B) (C) (D) (E)
6 (A) (B) (C) (D) (E)	16 (A) (B) (C) (D) (E)	26 (A) (B) (C) (D) (E)	36 (A) (B) (C) (D) (E)
7 (A) (B) (C) (D) (E)	17 (A) (B) (C) (D) (E)	27 (A) (B) (C) (D) (E)	37 (A) (B) (C) (D) (E)
8 (A) (B) (C) (D) (E)	18 (A) (B) (C) (D) (E)	28 (A) (B) (C) (D) (E)	38 (A) (B) (C) (D) (E)
9 (A) (B) (C) (D) (E)	19 (A) (B) (C) (D) (E)	29 (A) (B) (C) (D) (E)	39 (A) (B) (C) (D) (E)
10 (A) (B) (C) (D) (E)	20 (A) (B) (C) (D) (E)	30 (A) (B) (C) (D) (E)	40 (A) (B) (C) (D) (E)

SECTION 6

1 (A) (B) (C) (D) (E)	6 (A) (B) (C) (D) (E)	11 (A) (B) (C) (D) (E)	16 (A) (B) (C) (D) (E)
2 (A) (B) (C) (D) (E)	7 (A) (B) (C) (D) (E)	12 (A) (B) (C) (D) (E)	17 (A) (B) (C) (D) (E)
3 (A) (B) (C) (D) (E)	8 (A) (B) (C) (D) (E)	13 (A) (B) (C) (D) (E)	18 (A) (B) (C) (D) (E)
4 (A) (B) (C) (D) (E)	9 (A) (B) (C) (D) (E)	14 (A) (B) (C) (D) (E)	19 (A) (B) (C) (D) (E)
5 (A) (B) (C) (D) (E)	10 (A) (B) (C) (D) (E)	15 (A) (B) (C) (D) (E)	20 (A) (B) (C) (D) (E)

SECTION 7

1 (A) (B) (C) (D) (E)	6 (A) (B) (C) (D) (E)	11 (A) (B) (C) (D) (E)	16 (A) (B) (C) (D) (E)
2 (A) (B) (C) (D) (E)	7 (A) (B) (C) (D) (E)	12 (A) (B) (C) (D) (E)	17 (A) (B) (C) (D) (E)
3 (A) (B) (C) (D) (E)	8 (A) (B) (C) (D) (E)	13 (A) (B) (C) (D) (E)	18 (A) (B) (C) (D) (E)
4 (A) (B) (C) (D) (E)	9 (A) (B) (C) (D) (E)	14 (A) (B) (C) (D) (E)	19 (A) (B) (C) (D) (E)
5 (A) (B) (C) (D) (E)	10 (A) (B) (C) (D) (E)	15 (A) (B) (C) (D) (E)	20 (A) (B) (C) (D) (E)

CERTIFICATION STATEMENT

Copy the statement below (do not print) and sign your name as you would an official document.

I hereby agree to the conditions set forth in the Registration Bulletin and certify that I am the person whose name and address appear on this answer sheet.

____

____

____

Signature: ____________________ Date: __________

Section 1 1 1 1 1 1 1

Time—30 Minutes 25 Questions	**In this section solve each problem, using any available space on the page for scratchwork. Then decide which is the best of the choices given and fill in the corresponding oval on the answer sheet.**

Notes:

1. The use of a calculator is permitted. All numbers used are real numbers.
2. Figures that accompany problems in this test are intended to provide information useful in solving the problems. They are drawn as accurately as possible EXCEPT when it is stated in a specific problem that the figure is not drawn to scale. All figures lie in a plane unless otherwise indicated.

Reference Information

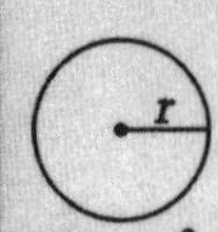

$A = \pi r^2$
$C = 2\pi r$

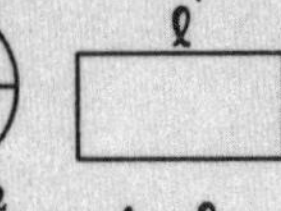
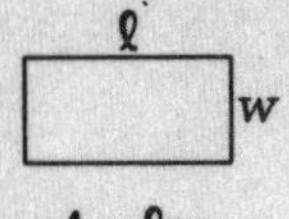

$A = \ell w$

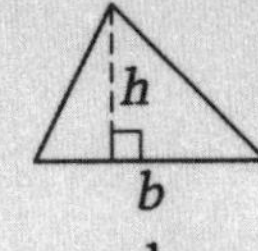

$A = \frac{1}{2}bh$

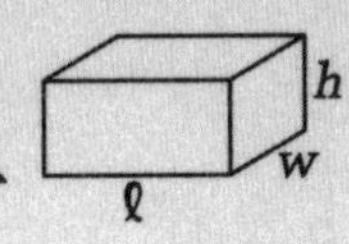

$V = \ell wh$

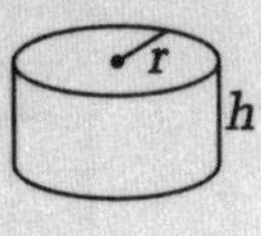

$V = \pi r^2 h$

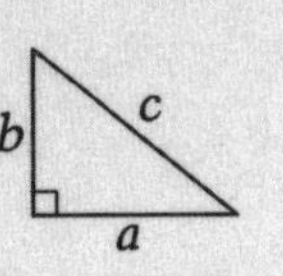

$c^2 = a^2 + b^2$

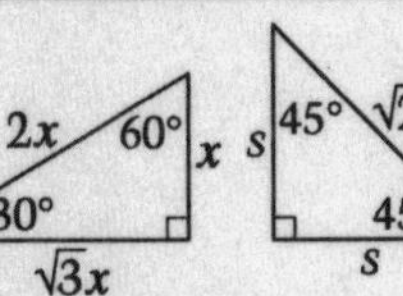

Special Right Triangles

The number of degrees of arc in a circle is 360.
The measure in degrees of a straight angle is 180.
The sum of the measures in degrees of the angles of a triangle is 180.

1 $(3 + 4)^2 =$

(A) $(2 \times 3) + (2 \times 4)$
(B) $3^2 + 4^2$
(C) 5^2
(D) 7^2
(E) $3^2 \times 4^2$

2 The average (arithmetic mean) of 3 numbers is 60. If two of the numbers are 50 and 60, what is the third number?

(A) 50
(B) 55
(C) 60
(D) 65
(E) 70

3 If $2x - 3y = 8$, what is the value of $4(2x - 3y)$?

(A) 32
(B) 16
(C) 12
(D) 4
(E) 2

4 On planet Urano, if each year has 8 months and each month has 16 days, how many full Urano years will have passed after 600 days?

(A) One
(B) Three
(C) Four
(D) Six
(E) Eight

GO ON TO THE NEXT PAGE

5 If $0 < x < 1$ and $0 < y < 1$, which of the following must be true?

(A) $xy > 0$
(B) $xy < 0$
(C) $\frac{x}{y} < 0$
(D) $x - y > 0$
(E) $x - y < 0$

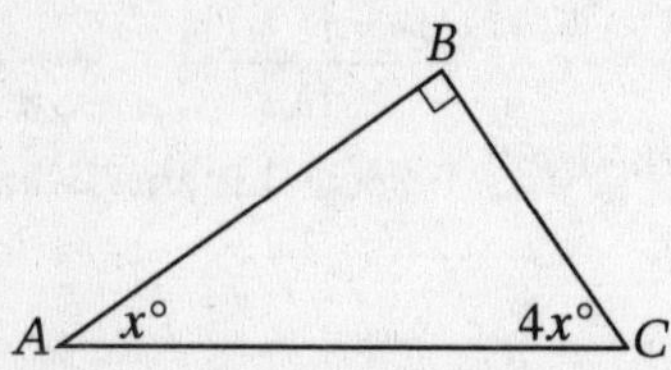

Note: Figure not drawn to scale.

6 In the right triangle above, what is the value of x ?

(A) 18
(B) $22\frac{1}{2}$
(C) 30
(D) 36
(E) 72

7 The cost of 3 sweatshirts is d dollars. At this rate, what is the cost, in dollars, of 30 sweatshirts?

(A) $\frac{10d}{3}$
(B) $\frac{d}{30}$
(C) $\frac{30}{d}$
(D) $10d$
(E) $30d$

8 If $\frac{3}{x} + \frac{5}{4} = 1$, what is the value of x ?

(A) −20
(B) −12
(C) −8
(D) 4
(E) 8

9 What percent of 50 is 6 ?

(A) 3%
(B) $8\frac{1}{3}$%
(C) 12%
(D) 30%
(E) $83\frac{1}{3}$%

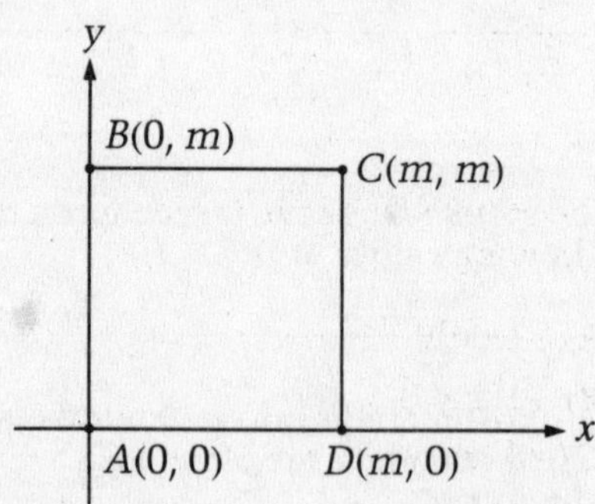

10 In the figure above, what is the area of square $ABCD$?

(A) m
(B) $2m$
(C) $4m$
(D) $\frac{1}{2}m^2$
(E) m^2

GO ON TO THE NEXT PAGE

11 The tens digit of a two-digit number is 3 and the units digit is H. If the two-digit number is divisible by H, which of the following CANNOT be the value of H ?

(A) 2
(B) 3
(C) 4
(D) 5
(E) 6

12 In a game, all tokens of the same color are worth the same number of points. If one player won 2 red tokens and 4 blue tokens for a total score of 24 points, and another player won 3 red tokens and 2 blue tokens for a total score of 16 points, how many points is a blue token worth?

(A) 2
(B) 4
(C) 5
(D) 6
(E) 8

$$(x + 3)^2 = (x - 1)^2$$

13 The statement above is true for which of the following values of x ?

(A) −1 only
(B) −1 and 3
(C) −3 and 1
(D) −3 and 3
(E) $-2\sqrt{2}$ and $2\sqrt{2}$ (approximately −2.83 and 2.83)

14 If $y = 5x$ and the value of x is increased by 4, then the value of y will increase by how much?

(A) 1
(B) 4
(C) 5
(D) 9
(E) 20

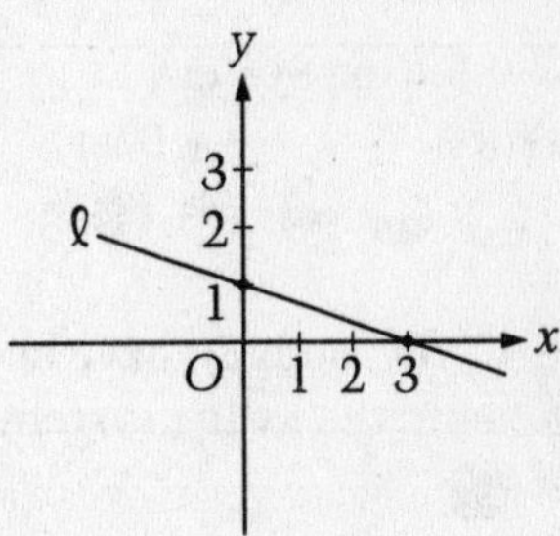

15 What is the slope of line ℓ shown in the figure above?

(A) −3
(B) $-\frac{1}{3}$
(C) 0
(D) $\frac{1}{3}$
(E) 3

GO ON TO THE NEXT PAGE

Questions 16-17 refer to the graph below.

CRASH PROTECTION RATINGS

Car	Driver Protection	Passenger Protection
A	○	⊖
B	⊖	⊖
C	◒	◓
D	⊖	○
E	●	◒

Rating System

Worst ⟷ Best

○ ◒ ⊖ ◓ ●

Five cars, *A*, *B*, *C*, *D*, and *E*, have been rated on crash protection using the rating system coded from worst ○ to best ●.

16 Which of the cars was rated worst in driver protection?

(A) *A*
(B) *B*
(C) *C*
(D) *D*
(E) *E*

17 If the rating system shown is used, how many different combinations of driver and passenger protection ratings is it possible for a car to receive?

(A) 5
(B) 10
(C) 15
(D) 20
(E) 25

18 The sum of ten positive odd integers is 22. Some of these integers are equal to each other. What is the greatest possible value of one of these integers?

(A) 21
(B) 13
(C) 11
(D) 9
(E) 7

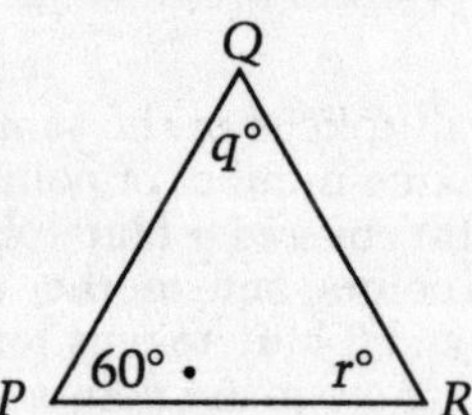

Note: Figure not drawn to scale.

19 In $\triangle PQR$ above, $PQ > QR$. Which of the following must be true?

(A) $PR = PQ$
(B) $PR < QR$
(C) $q = r$
(D) $q = 50$
(E) $q > 60$

GO ON TO THE NEXT PAGE

20 Let # be defined by $z \# w = z^w$. If $x = 5 \# a$, $y = 5 \# b$, and $a + b = 3$, what is the value of xy ?

(A) 15
(B) 30
(C) 75
(D) 125
(E) 243

−3, −2, −1, 0, 1, 2, 3

21 How many distinct sums can be obtained by adding any two different numbers shown above?

(A) 7
(B) 11
(C) 13
(D) 15
(E) 21

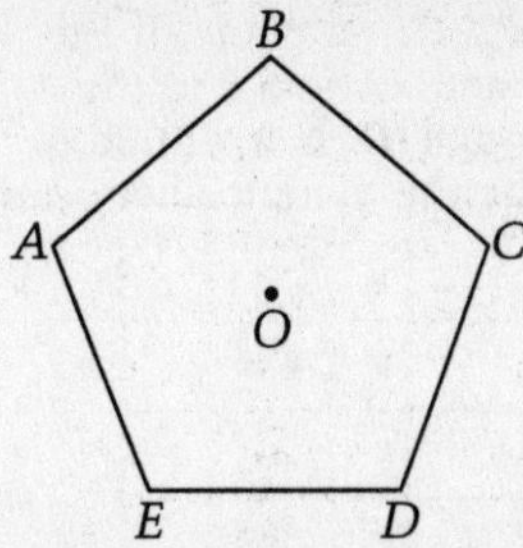

22 Pentagon $ABCDE$, shown above, has equal sides and equal angles. If O is the center of the pentagon, what is the degree measure of $\angle EOD$ (not drawn)?

(A) 60°
(B) 68°
(C) 70°
(D) 72°
(E) 75°

23 For every 1,000 cubic meters of air that comes through a filtering system, 0.05 gram of dust is removed. How many grams of dust are removed when 10^7 cubic meters of air have been filtered?

(A) 5
(B) 50
(C) 500
(D) 5,000
(E) 50,000

GO ON TO THE NEXT PAGE

24 Points P, Q, and R lie in a plane. If the distance between P and Q is 5 and the distance between Q and R is 2, which of the following could be the distance between P and R?

I. 3
II. 5
III. 7

(A) I only
(B) II only
(C) III only
(D) I and III only
(E) I, II, and III

25 The tip of a blade of an electric fan is 1.5 feet from the axis of rotation. If the fan spins at a full rate of 1,760 revolutions per minute, how many miles will a point at the tip of a blade travel in one hour? (1 mile = 5,280 feet)

(A) 30π
(B) 40π
(C) 45π
(D) 48π
(E) 60π

IF YOU FINISH BEFORE TIME IS CALLED, YOU MAY CHECK YOUR WORK ON THIS SECTION ONLY. DO NOT TURN TO ANY OTHER SECTION IN THE TEST. **STOP**

Section 2 2 2 2 2 2

**Time—30 Minutes
31 Questions**

For each question in this section, select the best answer from among the choices given and fill in the corresponding oval on the answer sheet.

Each sentence below has one or two blanks, each blank indicating that something has been omitted. Beneath the sentence are five words or sets of words labeled A through E. Choose the word or set of words that, when inserted in the sentence, best fits the meaning of the sentence as a whole.

Example:

Medieval kingdoms did not become constitutional republics overnight; on the contrary, the change was ----.

**(A) unpopular
(B) unexpected
(C) advantageous
(D) sufficient
(E) gradual**

1. She thought her ---- were amusing, but the others thought such tricks were irritating.

(A) anecdotes (B) researches (C) demands (D) pranks (E) debts

2. Though its wings look extremely ----, the butterfly is ---- enough to fly as high as 7,000 feet.

(A) vivid. .powerful
(B) iridescent. .skillful
(C) slender. .thick
(D) beautiful. .heavy
(E) fragile. .sturdy

3. Several medieval manuscripts that were improperly ----, and thus lost within the library itself since their acquisition, have been located and are finally ---- patrons.

(A) praised. .scrutinized by
(B) displayed. .comprehensible to
(C) labeled. .accessible to
(D) administered. .overlooked by
(E) cataloged. .unobtainable by

4. Using gestures and facial expressions rather than words, the performers eloquently communicated through the art of the ----.

(A) mediator (B) ensemble (C) elocutionist (D) pantomime (E) troubadour

5. The ability to treat stress-related illness is limited because many conditions can ---- stress, but none of them has been singled out as the ---- cause of stress.

(A) alleviate. .original
(B) relieve. .sole
(C) induce. .predominant
(D) inhibit. .actual
(E) produce. .partial

6. Company President Carmen Sanchez intends the ---- with which she works to be an example to her employees; as a result, they find that they are expected to apply themselves to their jobs most ----.

(A) sagacity. .unscrupulously
(B) leniency. .decorously
(C) nonchalance. .tenaciously
(D) acrimony. .cheerfully
(E) ardor. .assiduously

7. George was so eager to ---- his preconceptions that he grasped at any fact that seemed to ---- the undeniable gaps in his theory.

(A) reinforce. .strengthen (B) preserve. .bridge (C) convey. .widen (D) overcome. .plug (E) disregard. .destroy

8. That Virginia Woolf's criticism of prose is more astute than her criticism of poetry is most likely due to her ability, as a novelist and essayist, to approach prose as one of its ----.

(A) novices (B) neighbors (C) interpreters (D) practitioners (E) detractors

9. Since the opposing factions could reach no ---- the budget proposal, they decided to ---- it and to debate the hazardous waste bill instead.

(A) consensus on. .table
(B) opinion about. .enact
(C) decision about. .berate
(D) agreement on. .proclaim
(E) compromise on. .endorse

GO ON TO THE NEXT PAGE

Each question below consists of a related pair of words or phrases, followed by five pairs of words or phrases labeled A through E. Select the pair that best expresses a relationship similar to that expressed in the original pair.

Example:

CRUMB : BREAD ::
(A) ounce : unit
(B) splinter : wood
(C) water : bucket
(D) twine : rope
(E) cream : butter

Ⓐ ● Ⓒ Ⓓ Ⓔ

10 SHOVE : NUDGE ::
(A) vex : mutter
(B) calm : quell
(C) teach : lecture
(D) push : fight
(E) stare : glance

11 BARLEY : GRAIN ::
(A) yeast : bread
(B) pine : tree
(C) vine : fruit
(D) knot : rope
(E) twig : nest

12 LOCOMOTIVE : TRAIN ::
(A) horse : saddle
(B) tractor : plow
(C) rudder : rowboat
(D) camel : desert
(E) gasoline : automobile

13 ABRIDGE : NOVEL ::
(A) interrupt : conversation
(B) rehearse : play
(C) terminate : ending
(D) punctuate : sentence
(E) abbreviate : word

14 CHIEF : HIERARCHY ::
(A) office : rank
(B) platoon : army
(C) president : term
(D) lawyer : court
(E) summit : mountain

15 UNFETTER : PINIONED ::
(A) recite : practiced
(B) sully : impure
(C) enlighten : ignorant
(D) revere : unrecognized
(E) adore : cordial

GO ON TO THE NEXT PAGE

Each passage below is followed by questions based on its content. Answer the questions on the basis of what is stated or implied in each passage and in any introductory material that may be provided.

Questions 16-25 are based on the following passage.

The passage below discusses "evidence" in scientific research.

A woman from New Orleans who read the article on ravens that I wrote when I had just started to investigate whether and how ravens share, wrote me: "I did not have so much trouble as you did in showing that ravens share. I see them at my feeder—they even feed one another." There are no ravens in New Orleans, nor anywhere else in Louisiana. Perhaps what she actually saw were several large dark birds (crows? grackles?), one of which fed another one or two (probably their grown offspring traveling along with them).

People commonly confuse personal interpretations with factual observations. This tendency is a special bane in getting reliable observations on ravens because so much ingrained folklore about them exists that it is difficult to look at them objectively. I once read an article about a trapper/writer in Alaska. Knowing he would be familiar with ravens in the north, I wrote to ask him if he had seen ravens feeding in crowds. He had a lot of raven stories to tell. First, he said "everyone" he knew, knew that ravens share their food. He was surprised at the ignorance of us armchair scientists so far away, who would even question it. Ravens were "clever enough" to raid the fish he kept on racks for his dogs. They proved their cleverness by posting a "twenty-four-hour guard" at his cabin. (How did he distinguish this, I wondered, from birds waiting for an opportunity to feed?) As soon as he left the cabin, a raven was there to "spread the word." (Read: Flew away, and/or called.) He claimed that one raven "followed" him all day. (Read: He occasionally saw a raven.) It then "reported back" to the others so that they could all leave just before he got back from his day on the trapline. (Read: He saw several leave together, and there were none when he got back to the cabin door.) Many of the birds "raided" (fed from?) his fish rack, and his idea of their "getting out the word" to ravens for miles around is that the one who discovers the food calls, and thereby summons all the birds in neighboring territories, who then also call, in an ever-enlarging ring of information sharing. (An interesting *thought*.) It was no mystery to him why the birds would do this: they are "gossiping." "It seems obvious," he said, "that the birds get excited, and they simply cannot hold in their excitement—that lets others know." And why should they evolve such transparent excitement? That, too, was "obvious": "Because it is best for the species." This stock answer explains nothing.

It was disturbing to me to see anyone so facilely blur the distinction between observations and interpretations and then even go so far as to make numerous deductions without the slightest shred of evidence. When I was very young and did not "see" what seemed obvious to adults, I often thought I was stupid and unsuited for science. Now I sometimes wonder if that is why I make progress. I see the ability to *invent* interconnections as no advantage whatsoever where the discovery of truth is the objective.

There are those who believe that science consists entirely of disproving alternative hypotheses, as if when you eliminate the alternative views, the one you have left is right. The problem is that there is no way to think of all the possible hypotheses that nature can devise. More than that, you have to prove which is the *most* reasonable. But any one hypothesis can, with a limited data set, be reasonable. There is at least a touch of truth in the idea that any variable affects another. If you look long and determinedly enough you will find that almost any variable element you choose to examine apparently affects the behavior you are studying. You have to be able to skim over what is not important or relevant to your problem, and to concentrate long enough on the prime movers to unearth sufficient facts that, presuming they are recognized, add up to something.

16 The author's primary purpose in the passage is to

(A) assert the superiority of one approach to evaluating evidence
(B) consider sympathetically both sides of an argument
(C) convey an impression of a memorable experience
(D) explain a complex hypothesis
(E) propose a new solution to an old problem

NOTE: The reading passages in this test are brief excerpts or adaptations of excerpts from published material. The ideas contained in them do not necessarily represent the opinions of the College Board or Educational Testing Service. To make the text suitable for testing purposes, we may in some cases have altered the style, contents, or point of view of the original.

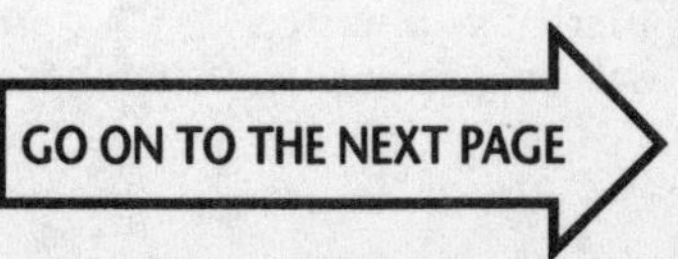

17 The author's parenthetical comments in lines 31-38 serve primarily to

(A) distinguish interpretation from observation
(B) translate a hypothesis into less technical terms
(C) provide facts that support generalizations
(D) emphasize the role of speculation in scientific observation
(E) supply information confirming the trapper's conclusions

18 In lines 49-50, "transparent" most nearly means

(A) invisible
(B) innocent
(C) extreme
(D) undisguised
(E) colorless

19 The author rejects as evidence the trapper's descriptions of ravens' behavior primarily because the trapper

(A) perpetuated common misconceptions about ravens
(B) did not compare his impressions with those of other trappers
(C) made subjective judgments from isolated incidents
(D) allowed his negative feelings about ravens to influence his observations
(E) was familiar with only a single community of ravens

20 The author suggests that the "adults" referred to in lines 57-59 made the mistake of

(A) failing to take a child's explanations seriously
(B) refusing to see obvious connections between facts
(C) giving a child unduly complex answers to straightforward questions
(D) making connections between events that may not have been related
(E) overemphasizing the importance of logic

21 In line 61, "progress" refers to the author's

(A) enhanced ability to see from an adult point of view
(B) adeptness at inventing interconnections between sets of data
(C) increasing acceptance by nonscientific observers
(D) popularity as a writer
(E) growth as a scientific researcher

22 Which of the following statements, if true, would contradict most directly the author's claim about "the ability to *invent* interconnections" (lines 61-62)?

(A) The ability to invent interconnections can be developed through training.
(B) Researchers who invent interconnections create lengthier investigations.
(C) The invention of interconnections is a comparatively recent phenomenon in scientific research.
(D) Interconnections can be discovered as well as invented.
(E) Inventing interconnections is an essential part of generating a valid hypothesis.

23 The author assumes that accurate knowledge of ravens' behavior is acquired through

(A) study of all research done on birds by behavioral specialists
(B) correlation of observed actions with notions of human motivation
(C) comparison of one's personal impressions with those of other researchers
(D) lifelong familiarity with ravens while living in the wilderness
(E) systematic observation combined with testing hypotheses

24 Which of the following statements best expresses the misconception criticized by the author in lines 64-67 ("There . . . right")?

(A) Illogical hypotheses are immediately rejected.
(B) Theoretical models are based solely on observations.
(C) Scientific truth is arrived at by default.
(D) Several hypotheses can be created to explain the same data.
(E) Scientific progress is based on the corroboration of previous research.

25 The author would consider which of the following statements to be an interpretation?

(A) Young ravens did not feed until the adults had finished feeding.
(B) The group of 25 ravens waited 40 minutes before trying the food left by the researchers.
(C) The group of ravens resented the intrusion of predators in their territory.
(D) No more than 20 ravens flew together as they approached the feeding site.
(E) Young ravens travel without their parents after the age of 18 months.

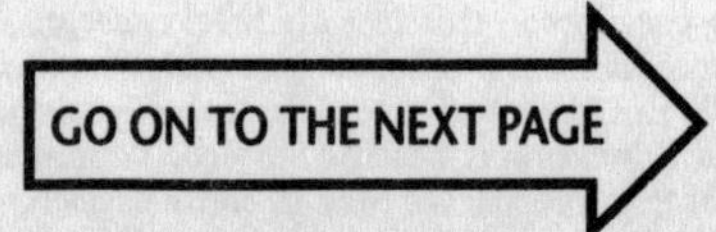

Questions 26-31 are based on the following passage.

The following passage, taken from an English novel published in 1910, describes events occurring after the announcement of the engagement of Margaret Schlegel, a financially independent young woman, to Henry Wilcox, a widower and successful businessman.

Margaret greeted Henry with peculiar tenderness. Mature as he was, she might yet be able to help him to the building of the rainbow bridge that should connect the prose in us with the passion. Without it we are meaningless fragments, half monks, half beasts, unconnected arches that are never joined into an individual. With it love is born, and alights on the highest curve, glowing against the fire. Happy are they who see from either aspect the glory of these outspread wings. The roads of their souls lie clear, and they and their friends shall find easy going.

It was hard going in the roads of Mr. Wilcox's soul. From boyhood he had neglected them. "I am not a fellow who bothers about my own inside." Outwardly he was cheerful, reliable, and brave; but within, all had reverted to chaos, ruled, so far as it was ruled at all, by an incomplete asceticism. Whether as boy, husband, or widower, he had always the sneaking belief that bodily passion is bad, a belief that is desirable only when held passionately. Religion had confirmed him. The words that were read aloud on Sunday to him and to other respectable persons were the words that had once kindled the souls of medieval mystics into a white-hot hatred of the carnal. He could not be as the saints and love the Infinite with a seraphic ardor, but he could be a little ashamed of loving a wife. *Amabat, amare timebat*.* And it was here that Margaret hoped to help him.

It did not seem so difficult. She would only point out the salvation that was latent in his own soul, and in the souls of every person. Only connect! That was the whole of her sermon. Only connect the prose and the passion, and both will be exalted, and human love will be seen at its height. Live in fragments no longer. Only connect, and the beast and the monk, robbed of the isolation that is life to either, will die.

Nor was the message difficult to give. It need not take the form of a good "talking." By quiet indications the bridge would be built and span their lives with beauty.

But at first she failed. For there was one quality in Henry for which she was never prepared, however much she reminded herself of it: his obtuseness. He simply did not notice things. He never noticed that her sister was hostile, or that her brother was not interested in currant plantations; he never noticed the lights and shades that exist in the greyest conversation, the milestones, the collisions, the illimitable views. Once she scolded him about it. Puzzled, he replied laughingly: "My motto is Concentrate. I've no intention of frittering away my strength on that sort of thing." "It isn't frittering away the strength," she protested. "It's enlarging the space in which you may be strong." He answered: "You're a clever little woman, but my motto's Concentrate."

Latin expression meaning "He loved, and he was afraid to love."

26 The "rainbow bridge" mentioned in line 3 should connect

(A) fear and bravery
(B) sanity and madness
(C) logic and emotion
(D) man and woman
(E) chaos and order

27 The author uses the terms "monks" and "beasts" in line 6 in order to

(A) distinguish between those who do and those who do not connect
(B) represent two extreme responses to desire
(C) suggest the impossibility of reconciling opposites
(D) remind the reader of the difference between animals and humans
(E) indicate the emotional phases through which an individual passes

28 The characteristic of Henry that Margaret has to struggle with most is his

(A) general lack of perceptiveness
(B) blindness to her love for him
(C) intense preoccupation with religion
(D) overemphasis on his career
(E) susceptibility to outside influences

GO ON TO THE NEXT PAGE

29 In context, the term "latent" (line 32) most nearly means

(A) emergent
(B) vanquished
(C) inherent
(D) struggling
(E) unshaped

30 The author's statement that Henry never noticed "lights and shades" (line 50) serves to

(A) demonstrate the manner in which Henry relates to others
(B) repudiate Margaret's theory that Henry was a good listener
(C) illustrate one of Henry's social strengths
(D) emphasize Henry's lack of fear in any situation
(E) contrast with Henry's final judgment of Margaret

31 Henry's comment to Margaret in lines 58-59 emphasizes his

(A) condescending refusal to take Margaret's comments seriously
(B) overt hostility toward Margaret and her views
(C) appreciation of Margaret's efforts to change him
(D) belief that Margaret agrees with him
(E) decision to treat Margaret as a full partner

IF YOU FINISH BEFORE TIME IS CALLED, YOU MAY CHECK YOUR WORK ON THIS SECTION ONLY. DO NOT TURN TO ANY OTHER SECTION IN THE TEST. **STOP**

Section 3 3 3 3 3 3 3

Time—30 Minutes
25 Questions

This section contains two types of questions. You have 30 minutes to complete both types. You may use any available space for scratchwork.

Notes:

1. The use of a calculator is permitted. All numbers used are real numbers.
2. Figures that accompany problems in this test are intended to provide information useful in solving the problems. They are drawn as accurately as possible EXCEPT when it is stated in a specific problem that the figure is not drawn to scale. All figures lie in a plane unless otherwise indicated.

Reference Information

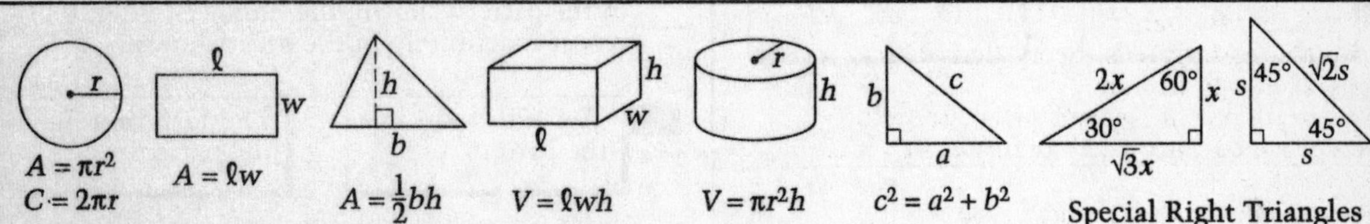

The number of degrees of arc in a circle is 360.
The measure in degrees of a straight angle is 180.
The sum of the measures in degrees of the angles of a triangle is 180.

Directions for Quantitative Comparison Questions

Questions 1-15 each consist of two quantities in boxes, one in Column A and one in Column B. You are to compare the two quantities and on the answer sheet fill in oval

A if the quantity in Column A is greater;
B if the quantity in Column B is greater;
C if the two quantities are equal;
D if the relationship cannot be determined from the information given.

AN E RESPONSE WILL NOT BE SCORED.

Notes:

1. In some questions, information is given about one or both of the quantities to be compared. In such cases, the given information is centered above the two columns and is not boxed.
2. In a given question, a symbol that appears in both columns represents the same thing in Column A as it does in Column B.
3. Letters such as x, n, and k stand for real numbers.

EXAMPLES

	Column A	Column B	Answers
E1	5^2	20	● Ⓑ Ⓒ Ⓓ Ⓔ
	150° x°		
E2	x	30	Ⓐ Ⓑ ● Ⓓ Ⓔ
	r and s are integers.		
E3	$r + 1$	$s - 1$	Ⓐ Ⓑ Ⓒ ● Ⓔ

GO ON TO THE NEXT PAGE

SUMMARY DIRECTIONS FOR COMPARISON QUESTIONS

Answer: A if the quantity in Column A is greater;
B if the quantity in Column B is greater;
C if the two quantities are equal;
D if the relationship cannot be determined from the information given.

	Column A	Column B
	A number n increased by 8 is equal to 35.	
1	n	43
	$k > 0$	
2	$\frac{2+k}{3}$	$\frac{2-k}{3}$
	$x > 0$ $y > 0$	
3	20% of x	20% of y

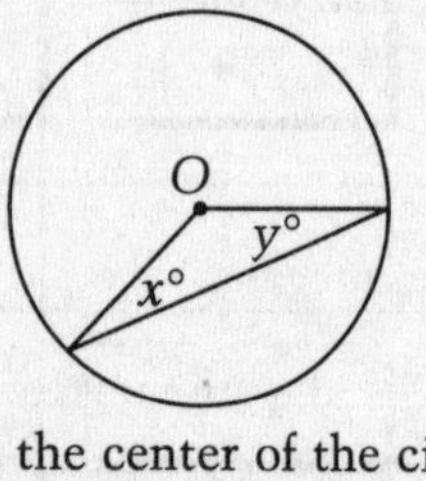

O is the center of the circle.

	Column A	Column B
4	x	y

$-1, 1, 0, -1, 1, 0, \ldots$

In the pattern shown, the numbers $-1, 1, 0$ repeat indefinitely in the order shown.

	Column A	Column B
5	The 19th term in the pattern	The 17th term in the pattern

$$(x+1)^2 = 16$$
$$y^2 = 9$$

	Column A	Column B
6	x	y

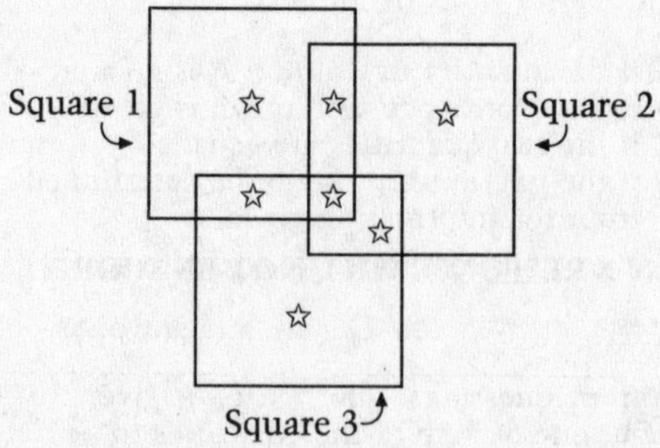

	Column A	Column B
7	The number of stars that are in Square 1	The number of stars that are in Square 2 or Square 3 but are not in Square 1

GO ON TO THE NEXT PAGE

SUMMARY DIRECTIONS FOR COMPARISON QUESTIONS

Answer: A if the quantity in Column A is greater;
B if the quantity in Column B is greater;
C if the two quantities are equal;
D if the relationship cannot be determined from the information given.

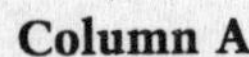

Column A	Column B

The square has side of length 1 and diagonal of length d.

8	d^2	3

9	$(a^5)^6(a^6)^6$	$(a^{11})^6$

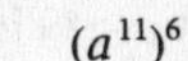

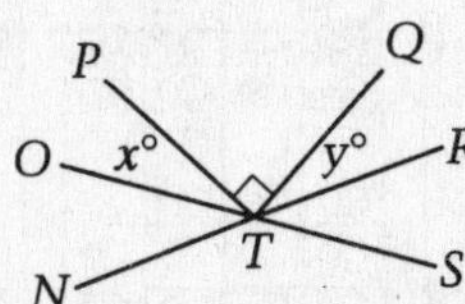

Note: Figure not drawn to scale.

NR and OS are straight lines.

10	x	y

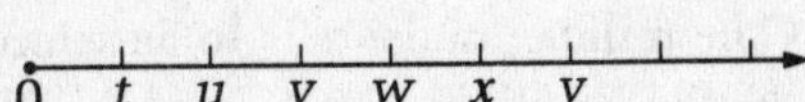

Integers t, u, v, w, x, and y are equally spaced on the number line.

$$y - t = 30$$

11	$v - u$	6

	Column A	Column B
12	The number of ways that 0 can be expressed as a product of two different one-digit integers	The number of ways that 12 can be expressed as a product of two different one-digit integers

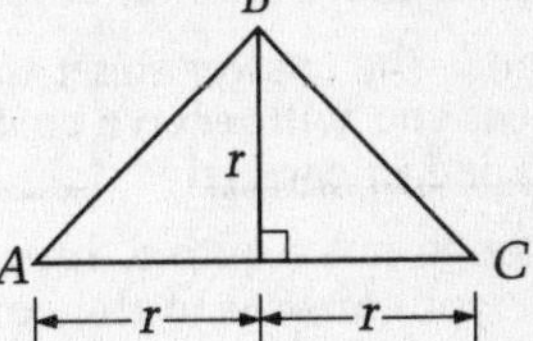

13	Twice the area of $\triangle ABC$	The area of a circle with radius r

The average (arithmetic mean) of 5 positive integers is 70.

14	The median of the 5 integers	70

x and y are positive and $x \neq y$.

15	$(x - y)^2$	$-2xy$

GO ON TO THE NEXT PAGE

Directions for Student-Produced Response Questions

Each of the remaining 10 questions requires you to solve the problem and enter your answer by marking the ovals in the special grid, as shown in the examples below.

Answer: $\frac{7}{12}$ or 7/12 — Answer: 2.5 — Answer: 201 Either position is correct.

Write answer in boxes. → 7/12 — Fraction line — Grid in result.

2.5 — Decimal point

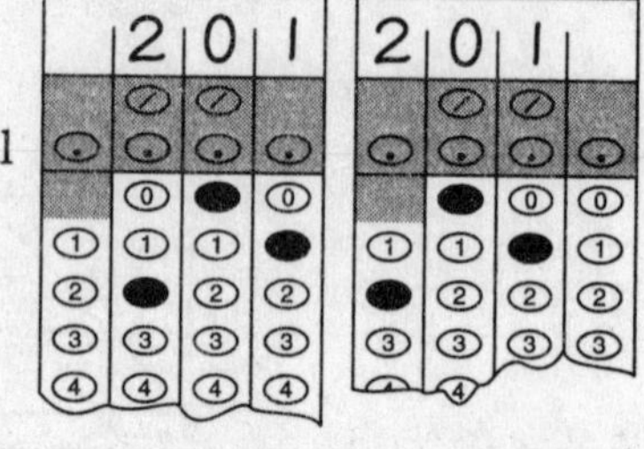

Note: You may start your answers in any column, space permitting. Columns not needed should be left blank.

- Mark no more than one oval in any column.
- Because the answer sheet will be machine-scored, **you will receive credit only if the ovals are filled in correctly.**
- Although not required, it is suggested that you write your answer in the boxes at the top of the columns to help you fill in the ovals accurately.
- Some problems may have more than one correct answer. In such cases, grid only one answer.
- No question has a negative answer.
- **Mixed numbers** such as $2\frac{1}{2}$ must be gridded as 2.5 or 5/2. (If 2 1/2 is gridded, it will be interpreted as $\frac{21}{2}$, not $2\frac{1}{2}$.)

- **Decimal Accuracy:** If you obtain a decimal answer, **enter the most accurate value the grid will accommodate.** For example, if you obtain an answer such as 0.6666 . . . , you should record the result as .666 or .667. **Less accurate values such as .66 or .67 are not acceptable.**

Acceptable ways to grid $\frac{2}{3} = .6666\ldots$

2/3 — .666 — .667

16 If $4x = 10 - x$, what is the value of x?

17 There are 360 students in a certain high school. One of these students is to be selected at random to be a student representative. If the probability that a senior will be selected is $\frac{3}{8}$, how many seniors are in the school?

GO ON TO THE NEXT PAGE

18 If x and y are each different positive integers and $x + y = 5$, what is one possible value of $4x + 9y$?

19 Five of the 12 members of a club are girls and the rest are boys. What is the ratio of boys to girls in the club? (Grid your ratio as a fraction.)

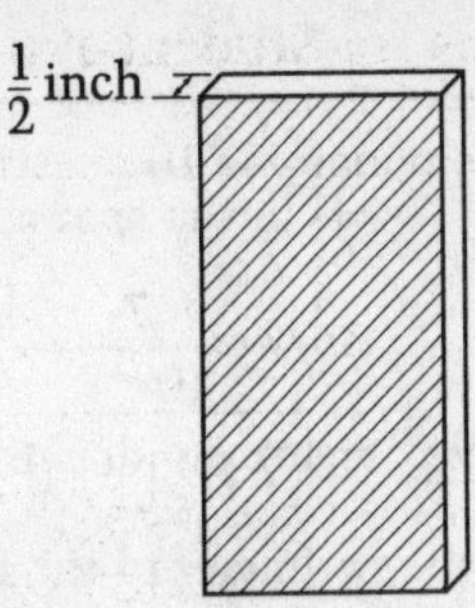

20 If the volume of the rectangular solid shown above is 64 cubic inches and its depth is $\frac{1}{2}$ inch, what is the area, in square inches, of the shaded face?

21 Luis can select one or more of the following 3 toppings for his ice cream: nuts, whipped cream, cherries. If he selects one or more, how many different combinations of toppings are possible? (Assume that the order of the toppings does not matter.)

GO ON TO THE NEXT PAGE

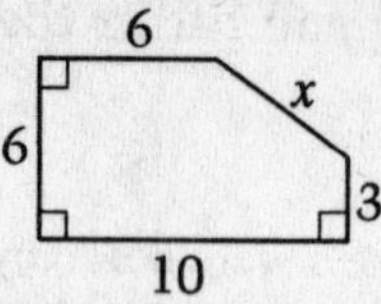

Note: Figure not drawn to scale.

22 What is the perimeter of the figure shown above?

23 For all positive integers n, let $\boxed{n}$ equal the greatest prime number that is a divisor of n. What does $\frac{\boxed{10}}{\boxed{12}}$ equal?

MAPLE AVENUE TREES	
Number of Trees	Trimming Time per Tree
7	20 minutes
8	40 minutes
10	80 minutes
15	100 minutes

24 How many hours will it take to trim all 40 trees listed in the table above?

25 Points A, B, C, and D lie on a line in that order. If $\frac{AD}{AC} = \frac{2}{1}$ and $\frac{AD}{AB} = \frac{3}{1}$, what is the value of $\frac{AC}{BD}$?

IF YOU FINISH BEFORE TIME IS CALLED, YOU MAY CHECK YOUR WORK ON THIS SECTION ONLY. DO NOT TURN TO ANY OTHER SECTION IN THE TEST.

Section 5 5

Time—30 Minutes
35 Questions

For each question in this section, select the best answer from among the choices given and fill in the corresponding oval on the answer sheet.

Each sentence below has one or two blanks, each blank indicating that something has been omitted. Beneath the sentence are five words or sets of words labeled A through E. Choose the word or set of words that, when inserted in the sentence, best fits the meaning of the sentence as a whole.

Example:

Medieval kingdoms did not become constitutional republics overnight; on the contrary, the change was ----.

(A) unpopular
(B) unexpected
(C) advantageous
(D) sufficient
(E) gradual

1. Pat made the descent with unusual caution, placing each foot first ----, then firmly.

(A) heavily (B) clumsily (C) tentatively (D) confidently (E) languidly

2. Because the geometry course ---- the principles governing solid structures, it was especially popular with students specializing in ----.

(A) emphasized. .architecture
(B) deleted. .geology
(C) reversed. .literature
(D) revealed. .history
(E) attacked. .economics

3. As their enemy grew weaker, the confidence of the allies increased and the ---- predictions they had made at the beginning of the war began to seem justified.

(A) imperceptive (B) belated (C) everlasting (D) optimistic (E) useless

4. Typically, an environmental problem worsens little by little until finally its effects can no longer be ----; organizations then emerge to raise public consciousness and to press vociferously for ---- action.

(A) preserved. .immediate
(B) disregarded. .gradual
(C) ignored. .remedial
(D) observed. .governmental
(E) distorted. .scientific

5. The workers were bored by the mindless routine of their jobs; their performance, therefore, was mechanical, no more than ----.

(A) querulous (B) perfunctory (C) diffuse (D) irresolute (E) transient

6. In the style of some ancient Chinese poets, Asian American poet Li-Young Lee speaks ---- but ----: he meditates on abstract issues while using everyday language in his writing.

(A) clearly. .simply
(B) pompously. .nonchalantly
(C) philosophically. .colloquially
(D) diffidently. .cunningly
(E) sternly. .profoundly

7. They were not ---- misfortune, having endured more than their share of ----.

(A) cognizant of. .calamity
(B) superstitious about. .prosperity
(C) jealous of. .success
(D) oblivious to. .happiness
(E) unacquainted with. .adversity

8. It is perilously easy to decry so ---- a historical figure without trying to understand the motives for his reprehensible actions.

(A) exemplary (B) astute (C) efficacious (D) prosaic (E) villainous

9. Because that testimony had been the ---- the prosecutor's case, when it was ruled inadmissible the case collapsed.

(A) scapegoat for (B) linchpin of (C) bane of (D) conundrum of (E) buffer against

10. Samantha's distinguishing trait is her ----: she gives liberally to those less fortunate than herself.

(A) amicability (B) inexorableness (C) frivolity (D) munificence (E) venerability

GO ON TO THE NEXT PAGE

Each question below consists of a related pair of words or phrases, followed by five pairs of words or phrases labeled A through E. Select the pair that best expresses a relationship similar to that expressed in the original pair.

Example:

CRUMB : BREAD ::
(A) ounce : unit
(B) splinter : wood
(C) water : bucket
(D) twine : rope
(E) cream : butter (A) ● (C) (D) (E)

11 WING : AIR ::
(A) arm : hand
(B) lung : breath
(C) flipper : water
(D) cloud : sky
(E) engine : jet

12 CONDENSE : SHORT ::
(A) shrink : wet
(B) measure : equal
(C) magnify : invisible
(D) deflate : flat
(E) increase : boundless

13 ORATOR : SPEECH ::
(A) protagonist : story
(B) chronicler : events
(C) playwright : stage
(D) comedian : jokes
(E) vocalist : voice

14 JUBILATION : JOY ::
(A) exaggeration : truth
(B) compassion : sympathy
(C) security : instability
(D) fortitude : danger
(E) emotion : anger

15 DINGY : BUILDING ::
(A) shabby : clothes
(B) discolored : bruise
(C) devastated : city
(D) vacant : apartment
(E) chapped : lips

16 RANGERS : FOREST ::
(A) panel : contest
(B) corps : army
(C) members : board
(D) police : precinct
(E) climbers : mountain

17 STIMULANT : ACTIVITY ::
(A) symptom : disease
(B) food : hunger
(C) fertilizer : growth
(D) diagnosis : treatment
(E) gravity : force

18 PARAMOUNT : IMPORTANCE ::
(A) debatable : quality
(B) inaccurate : correction
(C) modulated : pitch
(D) unheralded : publicity
(E) precious : value

19 RAUCOUS : SOUND ::
(A) dim : light
(B) noisy : uproar
(C) tanned : leather
(D) rough : texture
(E) hard : granite

20 TOURNIQUET : BLEEDING ::
(A) relapse : condition
(B) lotion : skin
(C) hoist : elevating
(D) splint : movement
(E) inflation : expanding

21 CLOYING : SWEETNESS ::
(A) shiny : polish
(B) pale : hue
(C) raspy : softness
(D) enchanting : desire
(E) garish : brightness

22 PERFIDIOUS : TREACHERY ::
(A) philanthropic : destitution
(B) servile : submissiveness
(C) truculent : temperament
(D) bereft : consolation
(E) resplendent : drabness

23 CORROBORATE : CLAIM ::
(A) document : assertion
(B) disprove : evidence
(C) sentence : punishment
(D) promise : advancement
(E) disseminate : information

GO ON TO THE NEXT PAGE

The passage below is followed by questions based on its content. Answer the questions on the basis of what is stated or implied in the passage and in any introductory material that may be provided.

Questions 24-35 are based on the following passage.

In the following excerpt from an article, the author considers the new possibilities for changing the human body that modern technology and medicine have made available, along with the accompanying conviction that one can—and should—have the sort of body one wants.

In a culture in which organ transplants, life-extension machinery, microsurgery, and artificial organs have entered everyday medicine, we seem to be on the verge of realization of the seventeenth-century European view of the body as a machine. But if we seem to have realized that conception, it can also be argued that we have in a sense turned it inside out. In the seventeenth century, machine imagery reinforced the notion of the human body as a totally determined mechanism whose basic functionings the human being is helpless to alter. The then-dominant metaphors for this body — clocks, watches, collections of springs—imagined a system that is set, wound up, whether by nature or God the watchmaker, ticking away in a predictable, orderly manner, regulated by laws over which the human being has no control. Understanding the system, we can help it perform efficiently and intervene when it malfunctions, but we cannot radically alter the configuration of things.

Western science and technology have now arrived, paradoxically but predictably (for it was a submerged, illicit element in the mechanistic conception all along), at a new, postmodern conception of human freedom from bodily determination. Gradually and surely, a technology that was first aimed at the replacement of malfunctioning parts has generated an industry and a value system fueled by fantasies of rearranging, transforming, and correcting, an ideology of limitless improvement and change, defying the historicity, the mortality, and indeed the very materiality of the body. In place of that materiality, we now have what I call "cultural plastic." In place of God the watchmaker, we now have ourselves, the master sculptors of that plastic.

"Create a masterpiece; sculpt your body into a work of art," urges *Fit* magazine. "You visualize what you want to look like, and then you create that form." The precision technology of body sculpting, once the secret of the Arnold Schwarzeneggers and Rachel McLishes of the professional bodybuilding world, has now become available to anyone who can afford the price of membership in a health club. On the medical front, plastic surgery, whose repeated and purely cosmetic employment has been legitimated by popular music and film personalities, has become a fabulously expanding industry, extending its domain from nose jobs, face lifts, and tummy tucks to collagen-plumped lips and liposuction-shaped ankles and calves. In 1989, 681,000 procedures were done, up by 80 percent since 1981; over half of these were performed on patients between the ages of 18 and 35. The trendy *Details* magazine described such procedures as just "another fabulous [fashion] accessory" and used to invite readers to share their cosmetic surgery experiences in the monthly column "Knifestyles of the Rich and Famous."

Popular culture does not apply any brakes to these fantasies of rearrangement and transformation. "The proper diet, the right amount of exercise, and you can have, pretty much, any body you desire," claims an ad for a bottled mineral water. Of course, the rhetoric of choice and self-determination and the breezy analogies comparing cosmetic surgery to fashion accessorizing are deeply misleading. They efface not only the inequalities of privilege, money, and time that prohibit most people from indulging in these practices, but also the desperation that characterizes the lives of those who do. "I will do anything, *anything*, to make myself look and feel better," says a contributor to the "Knifestyles" column. Medical science has now designated a new category of "polysurgical addicts" (or, as more casually referred to, "scalpel slaves") who return for operation after operation, in perpetual quest of that elusive yet ruthlessly normalizing goal, the "perfect" body. The dark underside of the practices of body transformation and rearrangement reveals botched and sometimes fatal operations, exercise addictions, and eating disorders.

We are surrounded by homogenizing and normalizing images whose content is far from arbitrary but is instead suffused with dominant gender, class, racial, and other cultural archetypes. The very advertisements whose copy speaks of choice and self-determination visually legislate the effacement of individual and cultural differences and thereby circumscribe our choices. Despite the claims of the mineral water ad, one cannot have *any* body that one wants—for not every body will *do*. Yet most contemporary understandings of the

GO ON TO THE NEXT PAGE

behaviors I have been describing do not recognize that cultural imagery functions in this way, and seek to preempt precisely such a critique as my own. Moreover, they represent, on the level of discourse and interpretation, the same principles that body sculptors act on: a construction of life as plastic possibility and weightless choice, undetermined by history, social location, or even individual biography.

24 The author's analysis of cosmetic surgery supports the proposition that

(A) only the rich should undergo such procedures
(B) doctors should worry about medicine, not ethics
(C) advertising should accurately reflect popular culture
(D) such surgery should never be covered by health insurance
(E) nature should not be tampered with unnecessarily

25 In line 10, "determined" most nearly means

(A) identified
(B) judged
(C) measured
(D) programmed
(E) understood

26 The last sentence of the first paragraph (lines 17-21) is intended to express the

(A) current consensus regarding human physiology
(B) author's formulation of the proper way to think about the body
(C) belief that humanity's fate depends directly on divine will
(D) conception of the body held in the seventeenth century
(E) view of the body that might achieve dominance in the future

27 Which best expresses the change since the seventeenth century in the perception people have of their relationship to their bodies?

(A) From beneficiary to benefactor
(B) From preserver to despoiler
(C) From observer to investigator
(D) From caretaker to creator
(E) From admirer to detractor

28 The ad for mineral water (lines 64-66) is cited as an example of the way popular culture

(A) promotes symbols of status
(B) excludes those unwilling to consume
(C) fosters unrealistic expectations
(D) co-opts the role of nutritionists
(E) discourages political dissent

29 According to the passage, one reason why the rhetoric of choice and self-determination is "misleading" (line 70) is that it does not acknowledge that

(A) free will has been shown to be an illusory concept
(B) many people lack the money needed to pursue bodily perfection
(C) profit is the main motive behind the self-improvement industry
(D) most people resist having to conform to an ideal
(E) those who popularize it are themselves less than perfect

30 The author implies that those who indulge in "these practices" (lines 72-73) should be seen as

(A) individuals who are to be pitied
(B) examples of extreme self-control
(C) artists who creatively transform themselves
(D) people of unprecedented daring
(E) thrill seekers who crave novelty

GO ON TO THE NEXT PAGE

31 The remark by the "Knifestyles" contributor (lines 74-76) is used to illustrate the

(A) obsessiveness displayed by certain cosmetic surgery patients
(B) disparity between those who can afford cosmetic surgery and those who cannot
(C) cynical greed of the cosmetic surgeons who accommodate habitual patients
(D) role played by magazine editors who promote particular surgeons
(E) growth of the cosmetic surgery business in the last decade

32 The author implies that the "normalizing images" (line 87) we are surrounded with have the effect of

(A) ensuring that antisocial impulses flourish in secret
(B) encouraging mediocrity instead of excellence
(C) enabling individuals to free themselves from anxiety
(D) promoting solidarity among disparate social groups
(E) bolstering the supremacy of a narrow range of values

33 It can be inferred from the passage that in place of the clock as the dominant metaphor for the body, contemporary culture has substituted

(A) advanced technology
(B) the universe
(C) impressionable clay
(D) the surgeon's scalpel
(E) modern manufacturing

34 The author's attitude toward the belief that the human body can be redesigned at will is one of

(A) aesthetic revulsion
(B) strong opposition
(C) passive detachment
(D) cautious optimism
(E) awestruck appreciation

35 The author's analysis of the impulse toward bodily transformation is most weakened by a failure to explore the

(A) psychological benefits of an improved appearance
(B) point of view of psychologists who treat "scalpel slaves"
(C) difference between competent and incompetent plastic surgeons
(D) dangers of injury stemming from misuse of bodybuilding equipment
(E) relative effects on the viewer of print and television advertising

IF YOU FINISH BEFORE TIME IS CALLED, YOU MAY CHECK YOUR WORK ON THIS SECTION ONLY. DO NOT TURN TO ANY OTHER SECTION IN THE TEST. **STOP**

Section 6 6 6 6

Time—15 Minutes
10 Questions

In this section solve each problem, using any available space on the page for scratchwork. Then decide which is the best of the choices given and fill in the corresponding oval on the answer sheet.

Notes:

1. The use of a calculator is permitted. All numbers used are real numbers.
2. Figures that accompany problems in this test are intended to provide information useful in solving the problems. They are drawn as accurately as possible EXCEPT when it is stated in a specific problem that the figure is not drawn to scale. All figures lie in a plane unless otherwise indicated.

Reference Information

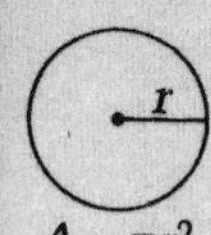

$A = \pi r^2$
$C = 2\pi r$

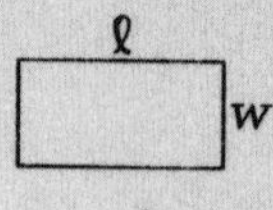

$A = \ell w$

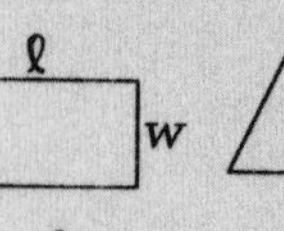

$A = \frac{1}{2}bh$

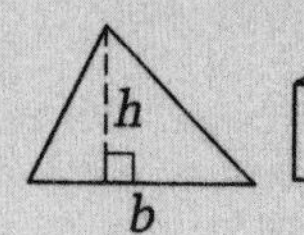

$V = \ell wh$

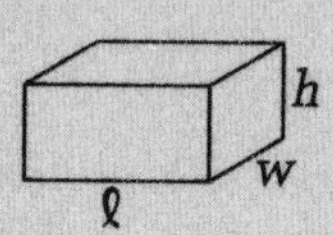

$V = \pi r^2 h$

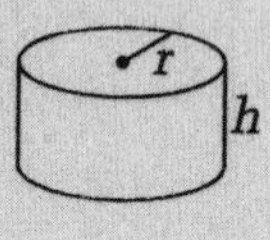

$c^2 = a^2 + b^2$

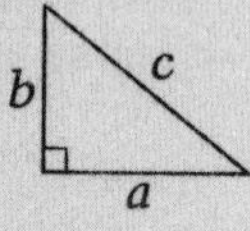

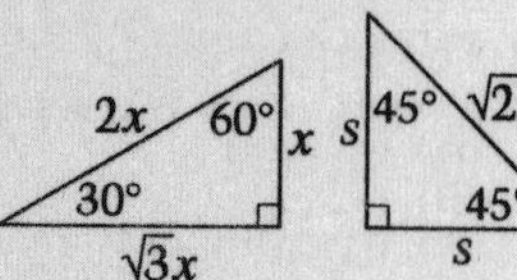

Special Right Triangles

The number of degrees of arc in a circle is 360.
The measure in degrees of a straight angle is 180.
The sum of the measures in degrees of the angles of a triangle is 180.

1 If $3(x - 30) = 2(x - 30)$, what is the value of x ?

(A) 1
(B) 2
(C) 10
(D) 15
(E) 30

2 Which of the following numbers disproves the statement "A number that is divisible by 3 and by 6 is also divisible by 9" ?

(A) 18
(B) 30
(C) 36
(D) 54
(E) 90

GO ON TO THE NEXT PAGE

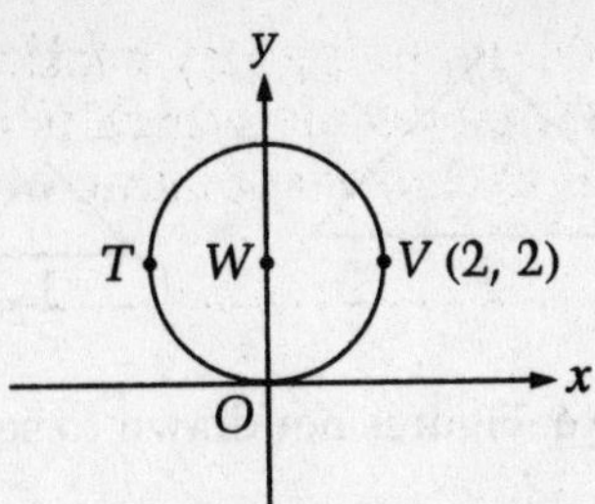

3 In the circle with center W shown above, T and V are endpoints of a diameter that is parallel to the x-axis. What are the coordinates of point T?

(A) (−2, −2)
(B) (−2, 2)
(C) (0, 2)
(D) (2, −2)
(E) (2, 2)

2		
	5	3
	x	8

4 In the figure above, one of the nine integers from 1 to 9 is to be placed in each of the nine small squares so that the sums of the three integers in all rows, columns, and diagonals are equal. What is the value of x?

(A) 1
(B) 4
(C) 6
(D) 7
(E) 9

5 Airplane P and airplane Q fly along parallel paths each 3,000 miles long. If they start at the same time and if P flies at a constant speed of 600 miles per hour and Q flies at a constant speed of 580 miles per hour, how many miles will Q have left to fly after P completes its flight?

(A) 20
(B) 60
(C) 100
(D) 120
(E) 150

GO ON TO THE NEXT PAGE

6 If m and n are both negative numbers, m is less than -1, and n is greater than -1, which of the following gives all possible values of the product mn ?

(A) All negative numbers
(B) All negative numbers less than -1
(C) All negative numbers greater than -1
(D) All positive numbers
(E) All positive numbers less than 1

7 Pat has s grams of strawberries and uses 40 percent of the strawberries to make pies, each of which requires p grams. The rest of the strawberries are used to make pints of jam, each of which requires j grams. Which of the following gives the number of pints of jam Pat can make?

(A) $\frac{2s}{5p}$

(B) $\frac{2s}{5j}$

(C) $\frac{3s}{5j}$

(D) $\frac{3p}{5s}$

(E) $\frac{3sj}{5}$

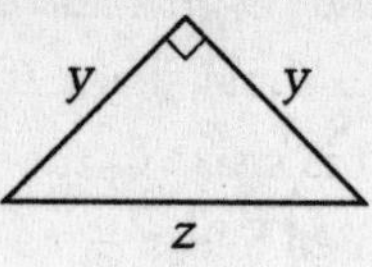

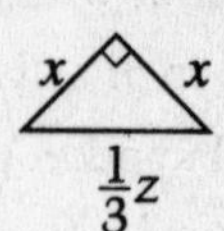

Note: Figures not drawn to scale.

8 In the figures above, what is the value of y in terms of x ?

(A) $\sqrt{2}x$ (approximately $1.41x$)
(B) $2x$
(C) $2\sqrt{2}x$ (approximately $2.83x$)
(D) $3x$
(E) $3\sqrt{2}x$ (approximately $4.24x$)

GO ON TO THE NEXT PAGE

9 A business is owned by 3 men and 1 woman, each of whom has an equal share. If one of the men sells $\frac{1}{2}$ of his share to the woman, and another of the men keeps $\frac{2}{3}$ of his share and sells the rest to the woman, what fraction of the business will the woman own?

(A) $\frac{5}{24}$

(B) $\frac{11}{24}$

(C) $\frac{1}{2}$

(D) $\frac{13}{24}$

(E) $\frac{11}{6}$

10 How many solid wood cubes, each with a total surface area of 96 square centimeters, can be cut from a solid wood cube with a total surface area of 2,400 square centimeters if no wood is lost in the cutting?

(A) 5
(B) 25
(C) 30
(D) 80
(E) 125

IF YOU FINISH BEFORE TIME IS CALLED, YOU MAY CHECK YOUR WORK ON THIS SECTION ONLY. DO NOT TURN TO ANY OTHER SECTION IN THE TEST. **STOP**

Section 7 7

Time—15 Minutes
12 Questions

For each question in this section, select the best answer from among the choices given and fill in the corresponding oval on the answer sheet.

The two passages below are followed by questions based on their content and on the relationship between the two passages. Answer the questions on the basis of what is stated or implied in the passages and in any introductory material that may be provided.

Questions 1-12 are based on the following passages.

Below are two excerpts that consider the relationship between works of literature and social conditions. The first is from a book published in 1974 and written by a Black male scholar about Black American literature. The second is from a book published in 1979 and written by two White female scholars about literature written by women in the nineteenth century.

Passage 1

One of the most notable aspects of the Black narrative tradition is that at the beginning of the narrative the main character is usually in a state of bondage or imprisonment, either physical or mental or both. The main action of the narrative involves the character's attempt to break out of this narrow arena. By the end of the narrative, however, the character has seldom achieved a state of ideal freedom; often it is a mixture of hope and despair, madness and sanity, repleteness and longing. *The Narrative of the Life of Frederick Douglass, An American Slave, Written by Himself* (1845) offers a case in point.

In his autobiography Douglass describes his journey from "the prison house of slavery" to the North and the abolitionist movement. As a slave he was in a condition of bondage, deprivation, and injustice. The young Douglass does not know his father, sees his mother only two or three times before she dies, and is confronted early and often by the nakedness of the power wielded by White people.

A climactic point in the *Narrative* occurs when Douglass complains to his White master about the brutal treatment he has received at the hands of another White man to whom he has been consigned. He asks for just treatment, but is informed that he must go back to the other man "come what might" and that he will be punished severely if he ever complains again. This encounter, in which the only tribunal before which a slave can demand justice consists of a slaveholder, who acts as both judge and jury, is representative of the patterns of justice that the book describes.

It is Douglass' expanding awareness of the exclusiveness of White justice that leads to subtle rebellion, physical revolt, and finally an escape from slavery. When he first arrives in New York, Douglass is still unsure of himself and fearful of the omnipresent threat of capture. He changes his name in order to avoid the thoroughgoing "justice" of the White world. He moves to Massachusetts before he feels somewhat secure. Douglass comes to feel, however, that the security offered by Massachusetts is not enough. He must join the abolitionist movement to find sanctuary: the entire system must change before he can be free.

The final positions of Frederick Douglass and the protagonists of other Black narratives carry us toward a more elevated conception of the human condition. We have not only the insights and the liberating strategies that illuminate the course of the narration but also the honest complexity of endings that indicate no solution is final until the basis of the White court's power has been destroyed. The Black narrative does not offer a comfortable majority report. It speaks of the enduring struggle of those who have been unjustly judged and restricted and yet have sought to evolve humane standards of existence. There is suffering involved, but ultimately the process augurs well for some essential human dignity.

Passage 2

Dramatizations of imprisonment and escape are so all-pervasive in nineteenth-century literature by women that we believe they represent a uniquely female tradition in this period. Interestingly, though works in this tradition generally begin by using houses as primary symbols of female imprisonment, they also use much of the other paraphernalia of "woman's place" to enact their central symbolic drama of enclosure and escape. Ladylike veils and costumes, mirrors, paintings, statues, locked cabinets, drawers, trunks, strongboxes, and other domestic furnishings appear and reappear in women's novels and poems. They signify the woman writer's sense that, as Emily Dickinson put it, her "life" has been "shaven and fitted to a frame," a confinement she can tolerate only by believing that "the soul has moments of escape / When bursting all the doors / She dances like a bomb abroad." Significantly, too, the explosive

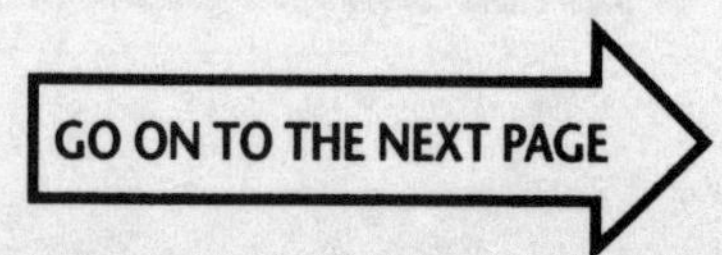

violence of these "moments of escape" that women writers continually imagine for themselves reminds us of the phenomenon of the mad double* that so many of these women have projected into their works. For it is, after all, through the violence of the double that the female author enacts her own raging desire to escape male houses and male constructs, while at the same time it is through the double's violence that the author articulates for herself the costly destructiveness of anger repressed until it can no longer be contained.

*mad double: a literary device in which a seemingly insane character represents certain aspects of a conventional character's personality

1 Both passages are primarily concerned with the themes of

(A) madness and sanity
(B) rescue and deliverance
(C) weakness and strength
(D) captivity and escape
(E) memory and forgetfulness

2 Passage 1 is developed primarily through

(A) quotations from specific texts
(B) references to the truths expressed by myths
(C) the interpretation of symbols
(D) extended treatment of a specific example
(E) the presentation of abstract principles

3 How do the pairs of nouns in lines 9-11 of Passage 1 ("hope and . . . longing") support the author's generalization about the endings of Black narratives?

(A) They convey the complex, unresolved nature of the endings.
(B) They illustrate the contradictions that are explained in the endings.
(C) They evoke the heightened sense of power expressed by the author.
(D) They describe the extremes of emotions that the endings avoid.
(E) They suggest that readers will find the endings climactic.

4 When he first arrived in New York, Frederick Douglass behaved most like someone who

(A) acts more confident about his accomplishments than the facts warrant
(B) is aware of the tenuous nature of his freedom
(C) objects to being praised publicly, even though such praise is justified
(D) is constantly afraid of things that offer no real threat
(E) takes risks when the occasion seems to justify them

5 The word "thoroughgoing" (line 41) emphasizes Douglass' perception that the justice system is

(A) an efficient mechanism for protecting human rights
(B) a pervasive system of oppression
(C) a local, rather than a federal, system
(D) a comprehensive set of abstract beliefs
(E) an inescapable pretext for violence

6 The statement in lines 56-57 ("The Black . . . report") suggests that the Black narrative

(A) offers a subjective, and therefore unrevealing, view of social reality
(B) delivers in a new way truths that are obvious to the unbiased
(C) reveals unpleasant truths that many would prefer not to face
(D) has important things to say, even though it is not read widely enough
(E) confirms discouraging facts already familiar to most readers

7 In Passage 2, the list of objects in lines 71-74 serves to suggest

(A) the lavishness of domestic furnishings
(B) the precarious economic position of women
(C) society's concern with surface rather than underlying truth
(D) the limitations placed on women
(E) the threat of violence in the home sometimes faced by women

GO ON TO THE NEXT PAGE

8 In Passage 2, Dickinson's perception (lines 77-81) is similar to views expressed by other women writers of her era in that it

(A) hints at the intensity of the urge to be free
(B) asserts that only those who have experienced freedom directly can appreciate it
(C) conveys the impression of belonging to a larger whole
(D) affirms that there is but one correct way to behave
(E) suggests that only those who work well with others will be able to achieve freedom

9 In Passage 2, the inclusion of Dickinson's description of the soul (lines 79-81) reinforces the suggestion that women's desire for escape is

(A) a potentially violent longing
(B) suppressed during childhood
(C) not a common wish
(D) worth risking danger to achieve
(E) hardly ever realized

10 In Passage 2, the word "constructs" (line 89) refers to

(A) literature written by men
(B) definitions of masculinity
(C) physical objects men have created
(D) rules for building and architecture men admire
(E) sets of ideas established by men

11 The central focus of the two passages suggests that Frederick Douglass and the women writers most significantly share a

(A) heightened awareness of the past
(B) feeling of optimism
(C) belief in the power of literature
(D) desire for freedom and power
(E) determination to improve their economic circumstances

12 Which statement most accurately describes a difference between the two passages?

(A) Passage 1 deals more with general cases than does Passage 2.
(B) Passage 1 is more concerned with the role of language in combating oppression than is Passage 2.
(C) Passage 1 ends with an expression of optimism and Passage 2 does not.
(D) Passage 1 deals less directly with political and legal considerations than does Passage 2.
(E) Passage 1 mentions specifically the category of people who are the oppressors, and Passage 2 does not.

IF YOU FINISH BEFORE TIME IS CALLED, YOU MAY CHECK YOUR WORK ON THIS SECTION ONLY. DO NOT TURN TO ANY OTHER SECTION IN THE TEST.

SAT 1: Reasoning Test Answer Key
Sunday, May 1997

VERBAL

Section 2

Five-choice Questions

	COR. ANS.	DIFF. LEV.
1.	D	1
2.	E	1
3.	C	1
4.	D	1
5.	C	3
6.	E	3
7.	B	4
8.	D	4
9.	A	4
10.	E	1
11.	B	3
12.	B	3
13.	E	3
14.	E	4
15.	C	5
16.	A	3
17.	A	3
18.	D	3
19.	C	3
20.	D	4
21.	E	3
22.	E	3
23.	E	3
24.	C	4
25.	C	3
26.	C	3
27.	B	4
28.	A	3
29.	C	4
30.	A	3
31.	A	4

______ no. correct

______ no. incorrect

Section 5

Five-choice Questions

	COR. ANS.	DIFF. LEV.
1.	C	2
2.	A	1
3.	D	1
4.	C	3
5.	B	3
6.	C	3
7.	E	3
8.	E	3
9.	B	4
10.	D	5
11.	C	1
12.	D	1
13.	D	2
14.	B	2
15.	A	3
16.	D	3
17.	C	3
18.	E	3
19.	D	3
20.	D	3
21.	E	5
22.	B	5
23.	A	5
24.	E	2
25.	D	2
26.	D	5
27.	D	2
28.	C	3
29.	B	3
30.	A	3
31.	A	2
32.	E	4
33.	C	5
34.	B	3
35.	A	3

______ no. correct

______ no. incorrect

Section 7

Five-choice Questions

	COR. ANS.	DIFF. LEV.
1.	D	1
2.	D	3
3.	A	3
4.	B	3
5.	B	3
6.	C	3
7.	D	3
8.	A	2
9.	A	3
10.	E	2
11.	D	2
12.	C	3

______ no. correct

______ no. incorrect

MATHEMATICAL

Section 1

Five-choice Questions

	COR. ANS.	DIFF. LEV.
1.	D	1
2.	E	1
3.	A	2
4.	C	1
5.	A	2
6.	A	2
7.	D	3
8.	B	3
9.	C	3
10.	E	3
11.	C	3
12.	C	3
13.	A	3
14.	E	3
15.	B	3
16.	A	1
17.	E	3
18.	B	4
19.	B	4
20.	D	4
21.	B	5
22.	D	4
23.	C	3
24.	E	5
25.	E	5

______ no. correct

______ no. incorrect

Section 3

Four-choice Questions

	COR. ANS.	DIFF. LEV.
1.	B	1
2.	A	1
3.	D	2
4.	C	2
5.	B	2
6.	D	5
7.	A	1
8.	B	3
9.	C	3
10.	D	4
11.	C	3
12.	A	3
13.	B	3
14.	D	5
15.	A	3

______ no. correct

______ no. incorrect

Section 6

Five-choice Questions

	COR. ANS.	DIFF. LEV.
1.	E	1
2.	B	1
3.	B	2
4.	A	2
5.	C	3
6.	D	3
7.	C	4
8.	D	3
9.	B	5
10.	E	5

______ no. correct

______ no. incorrect

Section 3

Student-Produced Response Questions

	COR. ANS.	DIFF. LEV.
16.	2	1
17.	135	2
18.	25, 30, 35 or 40	2
19.	7/5 or 1.4	2
20.	128	3
21.	7	3
22.	30	3
23.	5/3, 1.66 or 1.67	4
24.	46	3
25.	3/4 or .75	4

______ no. correct (16-25)

NOTE: Difficulty levels are estimates of question difficulty for a recent group of college-bound seniors. Difficulty levels range from 1 (easiest) to 5 (hardest).

The Scoring Process

Machine-scoring is done in three steps:

- *Scanning*. Your answer sheet is "read" by a scanning machine and the oval you filled in for each question is recorded on a computer tape.
- *Scoring*. The computer compares the oval filled in for each question with the correct response. Each correct answer receives one point; omitted questions do not count toward your score. For each wrong answer to the multiple-choice questions, a fraction of a point is subtracted to correct for random guessing. For questions with five answer choices, one-fourth of a point is subtracted for each wrong response; for questions with four answer choices, one-third of a point is subtracted for each wrong response. The SAT I verbal test has 78 questions with five answer choices each. If, for example, a student has 44 right, 32 wrong, and 2 omitted, the resulting raw score is determined as follows:

$$44 \text{ right} - \frac{32 \text{ wrong}}{4} = 44 - 8 = 36 \text{ raw score points}$$

Obtaining raw scores frequently involves the rounding of fractional numbers to the nearest whole number. For example, a raw score of 36.25 is rounded to 36, the nearest whole number. A raw score of 36.50 is rounded upward to 37.

- *Converting to reported scaled score.* Raw test scores are then placed on the College Board scale of 200 to 800 through a process that adjusts scores to account for minor differences in difficulty among different editions of the test. This process, known as equating, is performed so that a student's reported score is not affected by the edition of the test taken or by the abilities of the group with whom the student takes the test. As a result of placing SAT I scores on the College Board scale, scores earned by students at different times can be compared. For example, an SAT I verbal score of 400 on a test taken at one administration indicates the same level of developed verbal ability as a 400 score obtained on a different edition of the test taken at another time.

How to Score the Test

SAT I Verbal Sections 2, 5, and 7

Step A: Count the number of correct answers for *Section 2* and record the number in the space provided on the worksheet on the next page. Then do the same for the incorrect answers. (Do not count omitted answers.) To determine subtotal A, use the formula:

$$\text{number correct} - \frac{\text{number incorrect}}{4} = \text{subtotal A}$$

Step B: Count the number of correct answers and the number of incorrect answers for *Section 5* and record the number in the space provided on the worksheet. To determine subtotal B, use the formula:

$$\text{number correct} - \frac{\text{number incorrect}}{4} = \text{subtotal B}$$

Step C: Count the number of correct answers and the number of incorrect answers for *Section 7* and record the number in the space provided on the worksheet. To determine subtotal C, use the formula:

$$\text{number correct} - \frac{\text{number incorrect}}{4} = \text{subtotal C}$$

Step D: To obtain D, add subtotal A, subtotal B, and subtotal C, keeping any decimals. Enter the resulting figure on the worksheet.

Step E: To obtain E, your raw verbal score, round D to the nearest whole number. (For example, any number from 44.50 to 45.49 rounds to 45.) Enter the resulting figure on the worksheet.

Step F: To find your SAT 1 verbal score, use the conversion table to look up the total raw verbal score you obtained in step E. Enter this figure on the worksheet.

SAT I Mathematical Sections 1, 3, and 6

Step A: Count the number of correct answers and the number of incorrect answers for *Section 1* and record the numbers in the spaces provided on the worksheet. To determine subtotal A, use the formula:

$$\text{number correct} - \frac{\text{number incorrect}}{4} = \text{subtotal A}$$

Step B: Count the number of correct answers and the number of incorrect answers for the *four-choice quantitative comparison questions (questions 1 through 15) in Section 3* and record the number in the space provided on the worksheet. Note: Do not count any E responses to questions 1 through 15 as correct or incorrect. Because these four-choice questions have no E answer choices, E responses to these questions are treated as omits. To determine subtotal B, use the formula:

$$\text{number correct} - \frac{\text{number incorrect}}{3} = \text{subtotal B}$$

Step C: Count the number of correct answers for the student-produced response questions *(questions 16 through 25)* in *Section 3* and record the number in the space provided on the worksheet. This is subtotal C.

Step D: Count the number of correct answers and the number of incorrect answers for *Section 6* and record the number in the space provided on the worksheet. To determine subtotal D, use the formula:

$$\text{number correct} - \frac{\text{number incorrect}}{4} = \text{subtotal D}$$

Step E: To obtain E, add subtotal A, subtotal B, subtotal C, and subtotal D, keeping any decimals. Enter the resulting figure on the worksheet.

Step F: To obtain F, your raw mathematical score, round E to the nearest whole number. (For example, any number from 44.50 to 45.49 rounds to 45.) Enter the resulting figure on the worksheet.

Step G. To find your SAT 1 mathematical score, use the conversion table to look up the total raw mathematical score you obtained in step F. Enter this figure on the worksheet.

SAT I Scoring Worksheet

SAT I Verbal Sections

A. Section 2: ______ – (______ ÷ 4) = ______
no. correct — no. incorrect — subtotal A

B. Section 5: ______ – (______ ÷ 4) = ______
no. correct — no. incorrect — subtotal B

C. Section 7: ______ – (______ ÷ 4) = ______
no. correct — no. incorrect — subtotal C

D. Total unrounded raw score
(Total A + B + C) ______ D

E. Total rounded raw score
(Rounded to nearest whole number) ______ E

F. **SAT 1 verbal reported scaled score**
(See the conversion table)

[ ] SAT I verbal score

SAT I Mathematical Sections

A. Section 1: ______ – (______ ÷ 4) = ______
no. correct — no. incorrect — subtotal A

B. Section 3:
Questions 1-15 (quantitative comparison) ______ – (______ ÷ 3) = ______
no. correct — no. incorrect — subtotal B

C. Section 3:
Questions 16-25 (student-produced response) ______ = ______
no. correct — subtotal C

D. Section 6: ______ – (______ ÷ 4) = ______
no. correct — no. incorrect — subtotal D

E. Total unrounded raw score
(Total A + B + C + D) ______ E

F. Total rounded raw score
(Rounded to nearest whole number) ______ F

G. **SAT 1 mathematical reported scaled score**
(See the conversion table)

[ ] SAT I mathematical score

Score Conversion Table
SAT 1: Reasoning Test
Sunday, May 1997
Recentered Scale

Raw Score	Verbal Scaled Score	Math Scaled Score	Raw Score	Verbal Scaled Score	Math Scaled Score
78	800		37	510	560
77	800		36	510	560
76	800		35	500	550
75	800		34	500	540
74	790		33	490	540
73	770		32	480	530
72	760		31	480	520
71	750		30	470	510
70	730		29	470	510
69	720		28	460	500
68	710		27	460	490
67	700		26	450	490
66	690		25	440	480
65	690		24	440	470
64	680		23	430	470
63	670		22	430	460
62	660		21	420	450
61	650		20	410	450
60	650	800	19	410	440
59	640	790	18	400	430
58	630	770	17	390	430
57	630	750	16	390	420
56	620	730	15	380	410
55	610	720	14	370	400
54	610	710	13	360	400
53	600	690	12	360	390
52	590	680	11	350	380
51	590	670	10	340	370
50	580	670	9	330	360
49	580	660	8	320	350
48	570	650	7	310	340
47	570	640	6	300	330
46	560	630	5	290	320
45	560	620	4	280	310
44	550	620	3	270	300
43	540	610	2	260	290
42	540	600	1	250	270
41	530	590	0	230	250
40	530	590	-1	210	240
39	520	580	-2	200	220
38	520	570	-3 and below	200	200

This table is for use only with this test.

SAT I: Reasoning Test

Saturday, January 2000

YOUR NAME (PRINT) ____
LAST FIRST MI

TEST CENTER ____
NUMBER NAME OF TEST CENTER ROOM NUMBER

SAT® I: Reasoning Test — General Directions

Timing

- You will have three hours to work on this test.
- There are five 30-minute sections and two 15-minute sections.
- You may work on only one section at a time.
- The supervisor will tell you when to begin and end each section.
- If you finish a section before time is called, check your work on that section. You may NOT turn to any other section.
- Work as rapidly as you can without losing accuracy. Don't waste time on questions that seem too difficult for you.

Marking Answers

- Carefully mark only one answer for each question.
- Make sure each mark is dark and completely fills the oval.
- Do not make any stray marks on your answer sheet.
- If you erase, do so completely. Incomplete erasures may be scored as intended answers.
- Use only the answer spaces that correspond to the question numbers.
- For questions with only four answer choices, an answer marked in oval E will not be scored.
- Use the test book for scratchwork, but you will not receive credit for anything written there.
- You may not transfer answers to your answer sheet or fill in ovals after time has been called.
- You may not fold or remove pages or portions of a page from this book, or take the book or answer sheet from the testing room.

Scoring

- For each correct answer, you receive one point.
- For questions you omit, you receive no points.
- For a wrong answer to a multiple-choice question, you lose a fraction of a point.
  - ► If you can eliminate one or more of the answer choices as wrong, however, you increase your chances of choosing the correct answer and earning one point.
  - ► If you can't eliminate any choice, move on. You can return to the question later if there is time.
- For a wrong answer to a math question that is not multiple-choice, you don't lose any points.

The passages for this test have been adapted from published material. The ideas contained in them do not necessarily represent the opinions of the College Board or Educational Testing Service.

IMPORTANT: The codes below are unique to your test book. Copy them on your answer sheet in boxes 8 and 9 and <u>fill in the corresponding ovals exactly as shown.</u>

8. Form Code

A	A	0	0	0
B	B	1	1	1
C	C	2	2	2
D	D	3	3	3
E	E	4	4	4
F	F	5	5	5
G	G	6	6	6
H	H	7	7	7
I	I	8	8	8
J	J	9	9	9
K	K			
L	L			
M	M			
N	N			
O	O			
P	P			
Q	Q			
R	R			
S	S			
T	T			
U	U			
V	V			
W	W			
X	X			
Y	Y			
Z	Z			

9. Test Form

DO NOT OPEN THIS BOOK UNTIL THE SUPERVISOR TELLS YOU TO DO SO.

THE COLLEGE BOARD — SAT I **Page 1**

Use a No. 2 pencil only. Be sure each mark is dark and completely fills the intended oval. Completely erase any errors or stray marks.

1. Your Name

First 4 letters of Last Name				First init.	Mid. init.
A–Z	A–Z	A–Z	A–Z	A–Z	A–Z

2.

Your Name: (Print) _____ Last _____ First _____ M.I.

I agree to the conditions on the back of the SAT I test book.

Signature: _____ Date: ___ / ___ / ___

Home Address: (Print) _____ Number and Street

_____ City _____ State _____ Zip Code

Center: (Print) _____ City _____ State _____ Center Number

IMPORTANT: Fill in items 8 and 9 exactly as shown on the back of test book.

3. Date of Birth

Month	Day		Year	
Jan.				
Feb.				
Mar.	0	0	0	0
Apr.	1	1	1	1
May	2	2	2	2
June	3	3	3	3
July		4	4	4
Aug.		5	5	5
Sept.		6	6	6
Oct.		7	7	7
Nov.		8	8	8
Dec.		9	9	9

4. Social Security Number

(9 columns, each 0–9)

5. Sex

Female Male

6. Registration Number

(Copy from Admission Ticket.)

(7 columns, each 0–9)

7. Test Book Serial Number

(Copy from front of test book.)

(6 columns, each 0–9)

8. Form Code

(Copy and grid as on back of test book.)

(2 columns A–Z; 3 columns 0–9)

FOR ETS USE ONLY

9. Test Form

(Copy from back of test book.)

Start with number 1 for each new section. If a section has fewer questions than answer spaces, leave the extra answer spaces blank.

SECTION 1

1 Ⓐ Ⓑ Ⓒ Ⓓ Ⓔ	11 Ⓐ Ⓑ Ⓒ Ⓓ Ⓔ	21 Ⓐ Ⓑ Ⓒ Ⓓ Ⓔ	31 Ⓐ Ⓑ Ⓒ Ⓓ Ⓔ
2 Ⓐ Ⓑ Ⓒ Ⓓ Ⓔ	12 Ⓐ Ⓑ Ⓒ Ⓓ Ⓔ	22 Ⓐ Ⓑ Ⓒ Ⓓ Ⓔ	32 Ⓐ Ⓑ Ⓒ Ⓓ Ⓔ
3 Ⓐ Ⓑ Ⓒ Ⓓ Ⓔ	13 Ⓐ Ⓑ Ⓒ Ⓓ Ⓔ	23 Ⓐ Ⓑ Ⓒ Ⓓ Ⓔ	33 Ⓐ Ⓑ Ⓒ Ⓓ Ⓔ
4 Ⓐ Ⓑ Ⓒ Ⓓ Ⓔ	14 Ⓐ Ⓑ Ⓒ Ⓓ Ⓔ	24 Ⓐ Ⓑ Ⓒ Ⓓ Ⓔ	34 Ⓐ Ⓑ Ⓒ Ⓓ Ⓔ
5 Ⓐ Ⓑ Ⓒ Ⓓ Ⓔ	15 Ⓐ Ⓑ Ⓒ Ⓓ Ⓔ	25 Ⓐ Ⓑ Ⓒ Ⓓ Ⓔ	35 Ⓐ Ⓑ Ⓒ Ⓓ Ⓔ
6 Ⓐ Ⓑ Ⓒ Ⓓ Ⓔ	16 Ⓐ Ⓑ Ⓒ Ⓓ Ⓔ	26 Ⓐ Ⓑ Ⓒ Ⓓ Ⓔ	36 Ⓐ Ⓑ Ⓒ Ⓓ Ⓔ
7 Ⓐ Ⓑ Ⓒ Ⓓ Ⓔ	17 Ⓐ Ⓑ Ⓒ Ⓓ Ⓔ	27 Ⓐ Ⓑ Ⓒ Ⓓ Ⓔ	37 Ⓐ Ⓑ Ⓒ Ⓓ Ⓔ
8 Ⓐ Ⓑ Ⓒ Ⓓ Ⓔ	18 Ⓐ Ⓑ Ⓒ Ⓓ Ⓔ	28 Ⓐ Ⓑ Ⓒ Ⓓ Ⓔ	38 Ⓐ Ⓑ Ⓒ Ⓓ Ⓔ
9 Ⓐ Ⓑ Ⓒ Ⓓ Ⓔ	19 Ⓐ Ⓑ Ⓒ Ⓓ Ⓔ	29 Ⓐ Ⓑ Ⓒ Ⓓ Ⓔ	39 Ⓐ Ⓑ Ⓒ Ⓓ Ⓔ
10 Ⓐ Ⓑ Ⓒ Ⓓ Ⓔ	20 Ⓐ Ⓑ Ⓒ Ⓓ Ⓔ	30 Ⓐ Ⓑ Ⓒ Ⓓ Ⓔ	40 Ⓐ Ⓑ Ⓒ Ⓓ Ⓔ

SECTION 2

1 Ⓐ Ⓑ Ⓒ Ⓓ Ⓔ	11 Ⓐ Ⓑ Ⓒ Ⓓ Ⓔ	21 Ⓐ Ⓑ Ⓒ Ⓓ Ⓔ	31 Ⓐ Ⓑ Ⓒ Ⓓ Ⓔ
2 Ⓐ Ⓑ Ⓒ Ⓓ Ⓔ	12 Ⓐ Ⓑ Ⓒ Ⓓ Ⓔ	22 Ⓐ Ⓑ Ⓒ Ⓓ Ⓔ	32 Ⓐ Ⓑ Ⓒ Ⓓ Ⓔ
3 Ⓐ Ⓑ Ⓒ Ⓓ Ⓔ	13 Ⓐ Ⓑ Ⓒ Ⓓ Ⓔ	23 Ⓐ Ⓑ Ⓒ Ⓓ Ⓔ	33 Ⓐ Ⓑ Ⓒ Ⓓ Ⓔ
4 Ⓐ Ⓑ Ⓒ Ⓓ Ⓔ	14 Ⓐ Ⓑ Ⓒ Ⓓ Ⓔ	24 Ⓐ Ⓑ Ⓒ Ⓓ Ⓔ	34 Ⓐ Ⓑ Ⓒ Ⓓ Ⓔ
5 Ⓐ Ⓑ Ⓒ Ⓓ Ⓔ	15 Ⓐ Ⓑ Ⓒ Ⓓ Ⓔ	25 Ⓐ Ⓑ Ⓒ Ⓓ Ⓔ	35 Ⓐ Ⓑ Ⓒ Ⓓ Ⓔ
6 Ⓐ Ⓑ Ⓒ Ⓓ Ⓔ	16 Ⓐ Ⓑ Ⓒ Ⓓ Ⓔ	26 Ⓐ Ⓑ Ⓒ Ⓓ Ⓔ	36 Ⓐ Ⓑ Ⓒ Ⓓ Ⓔ
7 Ⓐ Ⓑ Ⓒ Ⓓ Ⓔ	17 Ⓐ Ⓑ Ⓒ Ⓓ Ⓔ	27 Ⓐ Ⓑ Ⓒ Ⓓ Ⓔ	37 Ⓐ Ⓑ Ⓒ Ⓓ Ⓔ
8 Ⓐ Ⓑ Ⓒ Ⓓ Ⓔ	18 Ⓐ Ⓑ Ⓒ Ⓓ Ⓔ	28 Ⓐ Ⓑ Ⓒ Ⓓ Ⓔ	38 Ⓐ Ⓑ Ⓒ Ⓓ Ⓔ
9 Ⓐ Ⓑ Ⓒ Ⓓ Ⓔ	19 Ⓐ Ⓑ Ⓒ Ⓓ Ⓔ	29 Ⓐ Ⓑ Ⓒ Ⓓ Ⓔ	39 Ⓐ Ⓑ Ⓒ Ⓓ Ⓔ
10 Ⓐ Ⓑ Ⓒ Ⓓ Ⓔ	20 Ⓐ Ⓑ Ⓒ Ⓓ Ⓔ	30 Ⓐ Ⓑ Ⓒ Ⓓ Ⓔ	40 Ⓐ Ⓑ Ⓒ Ⓓ Ⓔ

Q2778-06/2 CHW98324 11027 • 09132 • TF129M17.5eX I.N. 207158
1 2 3 4

Use a No. 2 pencil only. Be sure each mark is dark and completely fills the intended oval. Completely erase any errors or stray marks.

Start with number 1 for each new section. If a section has fewer questions than answer spaces, leave the extra answer spaces blank.

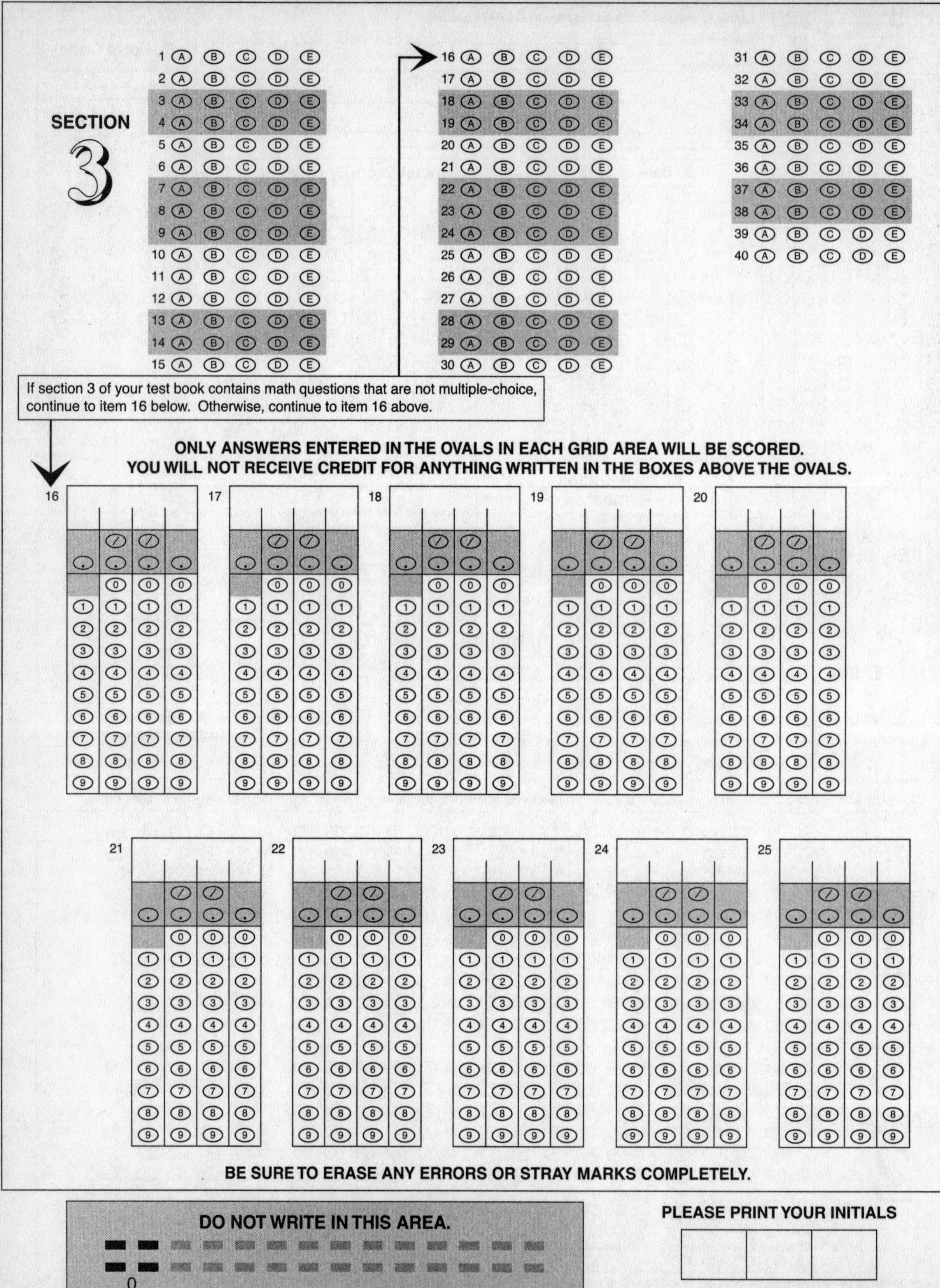

SECTION 3
If section 3 of your test book contains math questions that are not multiple-choice, continue to item 16 below. Otherwise, continue to item 16 above.
ONLY ANSWERS ENTERED IN THE OVALS IN EACH GRID AREA WILL BE SCORED.
YOU WILL NOT RECEIVE CREDIT FOR ANYTHING WRITTEN IN THE BOXES ABOVE THE OVALS.
BE SURE TO ERASE ANY ERRORS OR STRAY MARKS COMPLETELY.

DO NOT WRITE IN THIS AREA.

0

PLEASE PRINT YOUR INITIALS

First Middle Last

Use a No. 2 pencil only. Be sure each mark is dark and completely fills the intended oval. Completely erase any errors or stray marks.

Start with number 1 for each new section. If a section has fewer questions than answer spaces, leave the extra answer spaces blank.

SECTION 4

1–40: Ⓐ Ⓑ Ⓒ Ⓓ Ⓔ

If section 4 of your test book contains math questions that are not multiple-choice, continue to item 16 below. Otherwise, continue to item 16 above.

ONLY ANSWERS ENTERED IN THE OVALS IN EACH GRID AREA WILL BE SCORED.
YOU WILL NOT RECEIVE CREDIT FOR ANYTHING WRITTEN IN THE BOXES ABOVE THE OVALS.

16 17 18 19 20

21 22 23 24 25

BE SURE TO ERASE ANY ERRORS OR STRAY MARKS COMPLETELY.

DO NOT WRITE IN THIS AREA.

0

PLEASE PRINT YOUR INITIALS

First Middle Last

THE COLLEGE BOARD – SAT I   Page 4

Use a No. 2 pencil only. Be sure each mark is dark and completely fills the intended oval. Completely erase any errors or stray marks.

Start with number 1 for each new section. If a section has fewer questions than answer spaces, leave the extra answer spaces blank.

SECTION 5

1 Ⓐ Ⓑ Ⓒ Ⓓ Ⓔ	11 Ⓐ Ⓑ Ⓒ Ⓓ Ⓔ	21 Ⓐ Ⓑ Ⓒ Ⓓ Ⓔ	31 Ⓐ Ⓑ Ⓒ Ⓓ Ⓔ
2 Ⓐ Ⓑ Ⓒ Ⓓ Ⓔ	12 Ⓐ Ⓑ Ⓒ Ⓓ Ⓔ	22 Ⓐ Ⓑ Ⓒ Ⓓ Ⓔ	32 Ⓐ Ⓑ Ⓒ Ⓓ Ⓔ
3 Ⓐ Ⓑ Ⓒ Ⓓ Ⓔ	13 Ⓐ Ⓑ Ⓒ Ⓓ Ⓔ	23 Ⓐ Ⓑ Ⓒ Ⓓ Ⓔ	33 Ⓐ Ⓑ Ⓒ Ⓓ Ⓔ
4 Ⓐ Ⓑ Ⓒ Ⓓ Ⓔ	14 Ⓐ Ⓑ Ⓒ Ⓓ Ⓔ	24 Ⓐ Ⓑ Ⓒ Ⓓ Ⓔ	34 Ⓐ Ⓑ Ⓒ Ⓓ Ⓔ
5 Ⓐ Ⓑ Ⓒ Ⓓ Ⓔ	15 Ⓐ Ⓑ Ⓒ Ⓓ Ⓔ	25 Ⓐ Ⓑ Ⓒ Ⓓ Ⓔ	35 Ⓐ Ⓑ Ⓒ Ⓓ Ⓔ
6 Ⓐ Ⓑ Ⓒ Ⓓ Ⓔ	16 Ⓐ Ⓑ Ⓒ Ⓓ Ⓔ	26 Ⓐ Ⓑ Ⓒ Ⓓ Ⓔ	36 Ⓐ Ⓑ Ⓒ Ⓓ Ⓔ
7 Ⓐ Ⓑ Ⓒ Ⓓ Ⓔ	17 Ⓐ Ⓑ Ⓒ Ⓓ Ⓔ	27 Ⓐ Ⓑ Ⓒ Ⓓ Ⓔ	37 Ⓐ Ⓑ Ⓒ Ⓓ Ⓔ
8 Ⓐ Ⓑ Ⓒ Ⓓ Ⓔ	18 Ⓐ Ⓑ Ⓒ Ⓓ Ⓔ	28 Ⓐ Ⓑ Ⓒ Ⓓ Ⓔ	38 Ⓐ Ⓑ Ⓒ Ⓓ Ⓔ
9 Ⓐ Ⓑ Ⓒ Ⓓ Ⓔ	19 Ⓐ Ⓑ Ⓒ Ⓓ Ⓔ	29 Ⓐ Ⓑ Ⓒ Ⓓ Ⓔ	39 Ⓐ Ⓑ Ⓒ Ⓓ Ⓔ
10 Ⓐ Ⓑ Ⓒ Ⓓ Ⓔ	20 Ⓐ Ⓑ Ⓒ Ⓓ Ⓔ	30 Ⓐ Ⓑ Ⓒ Ⓓ Ⓔ	40 Ⓐ Ⓑ Ⓒ Ⓓ Ⓔ

SECTION 6

1 Ⓐ Ⓑ Ⓒ Ⓓ Ⓔ	6 Ⓐ Ⓑ Ⓒ Ⓓ Ⓔ	11 Ⓐ Ⓑ Ⓒ Ⓓ Ⓔ	16 Ⓐ Ⓑ Ⓒ Ⓓ Ⓔ
2 Ⓐ Ⓑ Ⓒ Ⓓ Ⓔ	7 Ⓐ Ⓑ Ⓒ Ⓓ Ⓔ	12 Ⓐ Ⓑ Ⓒ Ⓓ Ⓔ	17 Ⓐ Ⓑ Ⓒ Ⓓ Ⓔ
3 Ⓐ Ⓑ Ⓒ Ⓓ Ⓔ	8 Ⓐ Ⓑ Ⓒ Ⓓ Ⓔ	13 Ⓐ Ⓑ Ⓒ Ⓓ Ⓔ	18 Ⓐ Ⓑ Ⓒ Ⓓ Ⓔ
4 Ⓐ Ⓑ Ⓒ Ⓓ Ⓔ	9 Ⓐ Ⓑ Ⓒ Ⓓ Ⓔ	14 Ⓐ Ⓑ Ⓒ Ⓓ Ⓔ	19 Ⓐ Ⓑ Ⓒ Ⓓ Ⓔ
5 Ⓐ Ⓑ Ⓒ Ⓓ Ⓔ	10 Ⓐ Ⓑ Ⓒ Ⓓ Ⓔ	15 Ⓐ Ⓑ Ⓒ Ⓓ Ⓔ	20 Ⓐ Ⓑ Ⓒ Ⓓ Ⓔ

SECTION 7

1 Ⓐ Ⓑ Ⓒ Ⓓ Ⓔ	6 Ⓐ Ⓑ Ⓒ Ⓓ Ⓔ	11 Ⓐ Ⓑ Ⓒ Ⓓ Ⓔ	16 Ⓐ Ⓑ Ⓒ Ⓓ Ⓔ
2 Ⓐ Ⓑ Ⓒ Ⓓ Ⓔ	7 Ⓐ Ⓑ Ⓒ Ⓓ Ⓔ	12 Ⓐ Ⓑ Ⓒ Ⓓ Ⓔ	17 Ⓐ Ⓑ Ⓒ Ⓓ Ⓔ
3 Ⓐ Ⓑ Ⓒ Ⓓ Ⓔ	8 Ⓐ Ⓑ Ⓒ Ⓓ Ⓔ	13 Ⓐ Ⓑ Ⓒ Ⓓ Ⓔ	18 Ⓐ Ⓑ Ⓒ Ⓓ Ⓔ
4 Ⓐ Ⓑ Ⓒ Ⓓ Ⓔ	9 Ⓐ Ⓑ Ⓒ Ⓓ Ⓔ	14 Ⓐ Ⓑ Ⓒ Ⓓ Ⓔ	19 Ⓐ Ⓑ Ⓒ Ⓓ Ⓔ
5 Ⓐ Ⓑ Ⓒ Ⓓ Ⓔ	10 Ⓐ Ⓑ Ⓒ Ⓓ Ⓔ	15 Ⓐ Ⓑ Ⓒ Ⓓ Ⓔ	20 Ⓐ Ⓑ Ⓒ Ⓓ Ⓔ

CERTIFICATION STATEMENT

Copy the statement below (do not print) and sign your name as you would an official document.

I hereby agree to the conditions set forth in the Registration Bulletin and certify that I am the person whose name and address appear on this answer sheet.

____

____

____

Signature: ________________________ Date: ____________

Section 1 1 1 1 1 1 1

Time—30 Minutes 25 Questions	**In this section solve each problem, using any available space on the page for scratchwork. Then decide which is the best of the choices given and fill in the corresponding oval on the answer sheet.**

Notes:

1. The use of a calculator is permitted. All numbers used are real numbers.

2. Figures that accompany problems in this test are intended to provide information useful in solving the problems. They are drawn as accurately as possible EXCEPT when it is stated in a specific problem that the figure is not drawn to scale. All figures lie in a plane unless otherwise indicated.

Reference Information

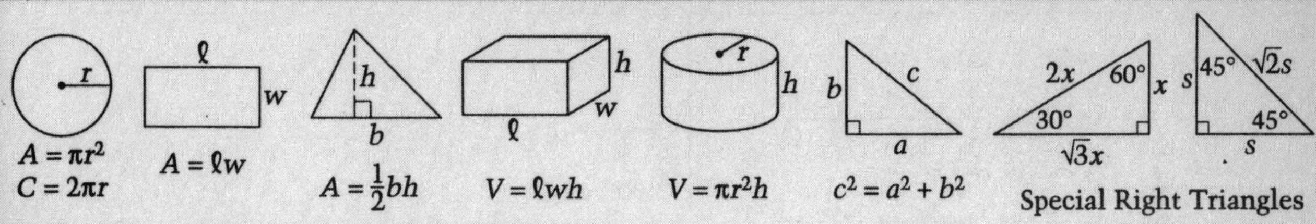

$A = \pi r^2$
$C = 2\pi r$ $A = \ell w$ $A = \frac{1}{2}bh$ $V = \ell wh$ $V = \pi r^2 h$ $c^2 = a^2 + b^2$ Special Right Triangles

The number of degrees of arc in a circle is 360.
The measure in degrees of a straight angle is 180.
The sum of the measures in degrees of the angles of a triangle is 180.

1 If $4 + y = 7$, what is the value of $4 \times y$?

(A) 3
(B) 12
(C) 28
(D) 44
(E) 49

WORKDAY ABSENCES AT EMPIRE PROCESSING PLANT

Month	1994	1995
January	18	12
February	22	16
March	19	16
April	20	12
May	21	14

2 According to the table above, what was the total decrease from 1994 to 1995 in workday absences for the months shown?

(A) 31
(B) 30
(C) 29
(D) 28
(E) 26

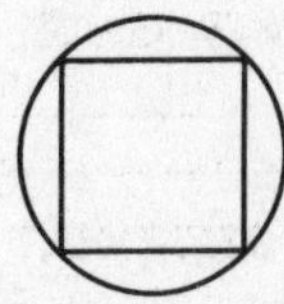

3 A square is inscribed in a circle as shown in the figure above. What is the least number of lines that must be added to the figure so that the resulting figure consists of two right triangles inscribed in the circle?

(A) One
(B) Two
(C) Three
(D) Four
(E) Five

4 A printing press produces 4,200 posters per hour. At this rate, in how many minutes can the printing press produce 840 posters?

(A) 0.2
(B) 1.5
(C) 5
(D) 12
(E) 70

GO ON TO THE NEXT PAGE

5 If $p = 3$, what is $4r(3 - 2p)$ in terms of r?

(A) $-12r$
(B) $-8r$
(C) $-7r$
(D) $12r - 6$
(E) $12r$

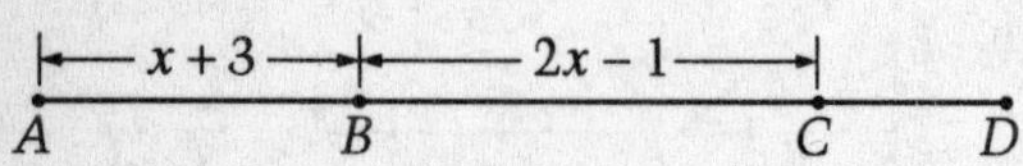

6 In the figure above, if the length of AD is $3x + 7$, what is the length of CD?

(A) $x + 2$
(B) $x + 5$
(C) 2
(D) 4
(E) 5

7 If r is 35 percent of p and s is 45 percent of p, what is $r + s$ in terms of p?

(A) $0.4p$
(B) $0.5p$
(C) $0.6p$
(D) $0.7p$
(E) $0.8p$

8 A bucket holds 4 quarts of popcorn. If $\frac{1}{3}$ cup of corn kernels makes 2 quarts of popcorn, how many buckets can be filled with the popcorn made from 4 cups of kernels?

(A) 96
(B) 24
(C) 6
(D) 3
(E) $1\frac{1}{2}$

9 On a number line, if point P has coordinate -2 and point Q has coordinate 10, what is the coordinate of the point that is located $\frac{1}{4}$ of the way from P to Q?

(A) $-1\frac{1}{2}$
(B) -1
(C) $-\frac{1}{2}$
(D) 1
(E) $2\frac{1}{2}$

GO ON TO THE NEXT PAGE

10 A group of s children has collected 650 bottle caps. If each child collects w more bottle caps per day for the next d days, which of the following represents the number of bottle caps that will be in the group's collection?

(A) $650sw$

(B) $650 + \frac{dw}{s}$

(C) $650 + \frac{ds}{w}$

(D) $650 + sw + d$

(E) $650 + dsw$

11 Set T contains only the integers 1 through 50. If a number is selected at random from T, what is the probability that the number selected will be greater than 30 ?

(A) $\frac{1}{4}$

(B) $\frac{1}{3}$

(C) $\frac{2}{5}$

(D) $\frac{3}{5}$

(E) $\frac{2}{3}$

12 If an integer k is divisible by 2, 3, 6, and 9, what is the next larger integer divisible by these numbers?

(A) $k + 6$
(B) $k + 12$
(C) $k + 18$
(D) $k + 30$
(E) $k + 36$

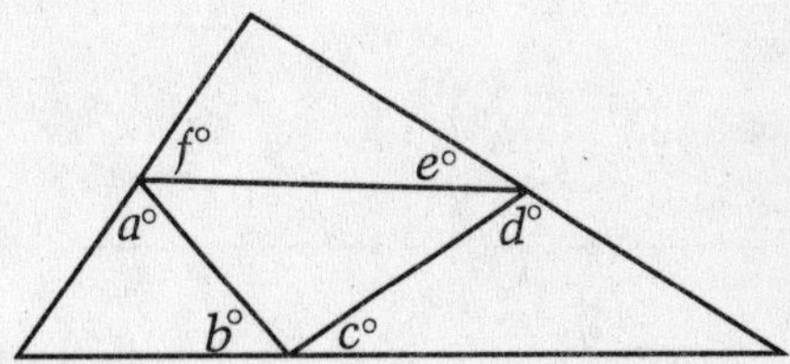

13 In the figure above, what is the value of $a + b + c + d + e + f$?

(A) 180
(B) 270
(C) 360
(D) 450
(E) 540

GO ON TO THE NEXT PAGE

14 If x is $\frac{2}{3}$ of y and y is $\frac{3}{5}$ of z, what is the value of $\frac{x}{z}$?

(A) $\frac{2}{5}$
(B) $\frac{5}{8}$
(C) $\frac{9}{10}$
(D) $\frac{10}{9}$
(E) $\frac{5}{2}$

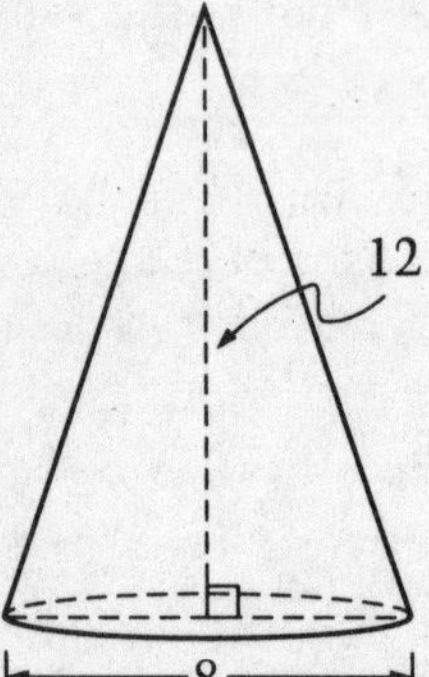

15 The right circular cone shown above is to be cut by a plane parallel to the base to form a new, smaller cone. If the diameter of the base of the smaller cone is 3, what is its height?

(A) 4
(B) 4.5
(C) 5
(D) 5.5
(E) 6

16 In how many different ways can 5 people arrange themselves in the 5 seats of a car for a trip if only 2 of the people can drive?

(A) 12
(B) 15
(C) 26
(D) 48
(E) 120

17 If $2^x = 7$, then $2^{2x} =$

(A) 3.5
(B) 7
(C) 14
(D) 28
(E) 49

GO ON TO THE NEXT PAGE

<u>Questions 18-20</u> refer to the following definition.

A positive integer is called a palindrome if it reads the same forward as it does backward. For example, 959 and 8228 are palindromes, whereas 1332 is not. Neither the first nor the last digit of a palindrome can be 0.

18 Which of the following integers is a palindrome?

(A) 550
(B) 2255
(C) 2525
(D) 2552
(E) 5002

---

19 How many three-digit palindromes are there?

(A) 19
(B) 20
(C) 90
(D) 100
(E) 810

---

20 The next two palindromes greater than 50805 are m and p, where $m < p$. What is the value of $p - m$?

(A) 10
(B) 90
(C) 100
(D) 110
(E) 210

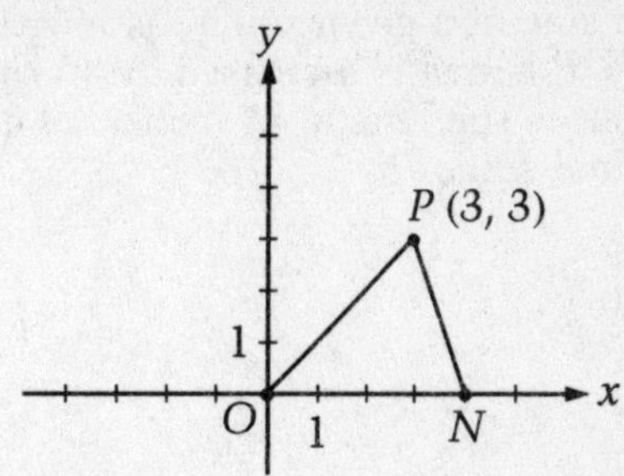

21 In the figure above, for which of the following coordinates of a point T (not shown) will $\triangle OTN$ have the same perimeter as $\triangle OPN$?

(A) (0, 3)
(B) (1, 3)
(C) (2, 3)
(D) (4, 3)
(E) (5, 3)

---

22 A person slices a pie into k equal pieces and eats one piece. In terms of k, what percent of the pie is left?

(A) $100(k - 1)\ \%$

(B) $\dfrac{100(k-1)}{k}\ \%$

(C) $\dfrac{100k}{k-1}\ \%$

(D) $\dfrac{k-1}{100}\ \%$

(E) $\dfrac{k-1}{100k}\ \%$

GO ON TO THE NEXT PAGE

23 When each side of a given square is lengthened by 2 inches, the area is increased by 40 square inches. What is the length, in inches, of a side of the original square?

(A) 4
(B) 6
(C) 8
(D) 9
(E) 10

24 If a and b are positive, then the solution to the equation $\frac{bx}{a-x} = 1$ is $x =$

(A) $\frac{a}{b+1}$

(B) $\frac{a+1}{b+1}$

(C) $\frac{b-1}{a}$

(D) $\frac{b}{a+1}$

(E) $\frac{b+1}{a}$

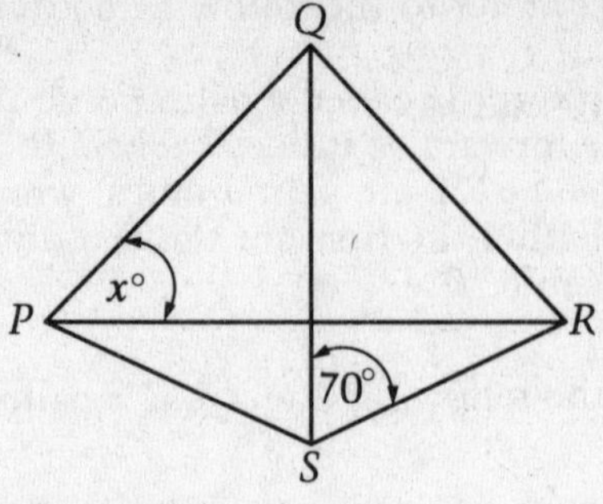

Note: Figure not drawn to scale.

25 In the quadrilateral above, if $PQ = SQ = RQ$ and $PS = SR$, then $x =$

(A) 30
(B) 40
(C) 50
(D) 60
(E) 70

IF YOU FINISH BEFORE TIME IS CALLED, YOU MAY CHECK YOUR WORK ON THIS SECTION ONLY. DO NOT TURN TO ANY OTHER SECTION IN THE TEST. STOP

Section 2 2 2 2 2 2

Time—30 Minutes
31 Questions

For each question in this section, select the best answer from among the choices given and fill in the corresponding oval on the answer sheet.

Each sentence below has one or two blanks, each blank indicating that something has been omitted. Beneath the sentence are five words or sets of words labeled A through E. Choose the word or set of words that, when inserted in the sentence, best fits the meaning of the sentence as a whole.

Example:

Medieval kingdoms did not become constitutional republics overnight; on the contrary, the change was ----.

(A) unpopular
(B) unexpected
(C) advantageous
(D) sufficient
(E) gradual

1 Although he can ---- isolated facts, he is no scholar: he is able to ---- information but cannot make sense of it.

(A) regurgitate . . synthesize
(B) memorize . . recite
(C) falsify . . denounce
(D) misinterpret . . acquire
(E) recall . . disregard

2 The use of tools among chimpanzees is learned behavior: young chimpanzees become ---- by ---- others.

(A) socialized . . overcoming
(B) dominant . . obeying
(C) vocal . . mimicking
(D) adept . . imitating
(E) agile . . following

3 The speech was a ---- of random and contradictory information that could not be integrated into ----, consistent whole.

(A) collage . . a rambling
(B) development . . an ambiguous
(C) hodgepodge . . a coherent
(D) morass . . an amorphous
(E) harangue . . an unintelligible

4 The prosecutor termed the defendants' actions ---- because there was no justification for their intentional disregard for the law.

(A) indefensible (B) surreptitious (C) indefatigable (D) comprehensive (E) corrective

5 Acid rain is damaging lakes in ---- way, causing the virtually unnoticed ---- of these aquatic ecosystems.

(A) a manifest . . eradication
(B) a nefarious . . polarization
(C) an insidious . . destruction
(D) a methodical . . amalgamation
(E) an obvious . . stagnation

6 The new concert hall proved to be a ----: it was costly, acoustically unsatisfactory, and far too small.

(A) colossus (B) milestone (C) debacle (D) consecration (E) fabrication

7 A hypocrite may ---- reprehensible acts but escape discovery by affecting ----.

(A) abhor . . profundity
(B) condone . . enthusiasm
(C) commit . . innocence
(D) perform . . immorality
(E) condemn . . repentance

8 The review was ----, recounting the play's felicities and its flaws without unduly emphasizing one or the other.

(A) equitable (B) immoderate (C) cumulative (D) unproductive (E) adulatory

9 Rosita Perú, who rose to become the highest-ranking female in the television industry, was ---- recruited: Spanish language program-producers courted her persistently.

(A) indiscriminately (B) enigmatically (C) vicariously (D) rancorously (E) assiduously

GO ON TO THE NEXT PAGE

Each question below consists of a related pair of words or phrases, followed by five pairs of words or phrases labeled A through E. Select the pair that best expresses a relationship similar to that expressed in the original pair.

Example:

CRUMB : BREAD ::
(A) ounce : unit
(B) splinter : wood
(C) water : bucket
(D) twine : rope
(E) cream : butter

10 LUBRICANT : SLIDE ::
(A) battery : discharge
(B) glue : adhere
(C) stain : cleanse
(D) poison : ingest
(E) water : drink

11 STOMP : WALK ::
(A) devour : starve
(B) shout : speak
(C) run : scamper
(D) prepare : finish
(E) deliberate : conclude

12 INDEX : TOPICS ::
(A) agenda : meeting
(B) diary : secrets
(C) roster : names
(D) manual : equipment
(E) ledger : numbers

13 MENDICANT : BEG ::
(A) sycophant : demean
(B) braggart : boast
(C) parasite : contribute
(D) hero : worship
(E) dissembler : believe

14 PRUDENT : INDISCRETION ::
(A) frugal : wastefulness
(B) proud : accomplishment
(C) generous : wealth
(D) disqualified : competition
(E) disgruntled : cynicism

15 VISCOUS : FLOW ::
(A) transparent : see
(B) stationary : stop
(C) arid : rain
(D) stiff : bend
(E) damp : soak

GO ON TO THE NEXT PAGE

Each passage below is followed by questions based on its content. Answer the questions on the basis of what is <u>stated</u> or <u>implied</u> in each passage and in any introductory material that may be provided.

Questions 16-24 are based on the following passage.

This passage on Navajo sandpainting was published in 1989 by a scholar of Navajo traditions who was trying to interpret them for non-Navajo readers. Sandpaintings are made by trickling fine, multi-colored sands onto a base of neutral-colored sand.

We cannot fully appreciate some Native American objects we consider art without also appreciating the contexts in which they are produced. When our understanding of art is heavily focused on objects, we tend to look in the wrong place for art. We find only the leavings or by-products of a creative process.

The concerns I have are deepened as I begin to compare how we, as outsiders, view sandpaintings with how the Navajo view them, even just from a physical perspective. Let me list several points of comparison. We have only representations of sandpaintings drawn or painted on paper or canvas, which we enjoy as objects of art. The Navajo strictly forbid making representations of sandpaintings, and they are never kept as aesthetic objects. Even the use of figures from sandpaintings in the sand-glue craft has not met with the approval of most Navajo traditionalists. Sandpaintings must be destroyed by sundown on the day they are made. They are not aesthetic objects; they are instruments of a ritual process. The sandpainting rite is a rite of re-creation in which a person in need of healing is symbolically remade in a way corresponding to his or her ailment. This person sits at the center of the very large painting and identifies with the images depicted, experiencing the complexity and the diversity, the dynamics and the tension, represented in the surrounding painting. The illness is overcome when the person realizes that these tensions and oppositions can be balanced in a unity that signifies good health and beauty.

In terms of visual perspective, we traditionally view sandpainting from a position as if we were directly above and at such a distance that the whole painting is immediately graspable, with each side equidistant from our eyes. This view is completely impossible for the Navajo. I got a laugh when I asked some Navajo if anyone ever climbed on the roof of a hogan* to look at a sandpainting through the smoke hole. When a painting 6 feet in diameter, or even larger, is constructed on the floor of a hogan only 20 feet in diameter, the perspective from the periphery is always at an acute angle to the surface. A sandpainting cannot be easily seen as a whole. The most important point of view is that of the person for whom the painting is made, and this person sees the painting from the inside out because he or she sits in the middle of it. These differences are basic and cannot be dismissed. The traditional Navajo view is inseparable from the significance that sandpainting has for the Navajo.

I think we can say that for the Navajo the sandpainting is not the intended product of the creative process in which it is constructed. The product is a healthy human being or the re-creation of a well-ordered world. The sandpainting is but an instrument for the creative act, and perhaps it is the wisdom of the Navajo that it be destroyed in its use so that the obvious aesthetic value of the instrument does not supplant the human and cosmic concern. The confinement of our attention to the reproduction of sandpaintings is somewhat analogous to hanging paint-covered artists' palettes on the wall to admire, not acknowledging that these pigment-covered boards are not paintings but the means to create them. There is a certain aesthetic value in artists' palettes, I suppose, but surely most would think of this action as foolishly missing the point.

* A traditional Navajo dwelling

16 According to Navajo tradition, the most significant perspective on a sandpainting is that of the

(A) group that requests the sandpainting's creation
(B) persons represented by the sandpainting figures
(C) Navajo leader conducting the sandpainting rite
(D) artists who conceive and design the sandpainting
(E) person for whom the sandpainting is made

17 As used in line 8, "deepened" most nearly means

(A) darkened
(B) heightened
(C) immersed
(D) made distant
(E) made obscure

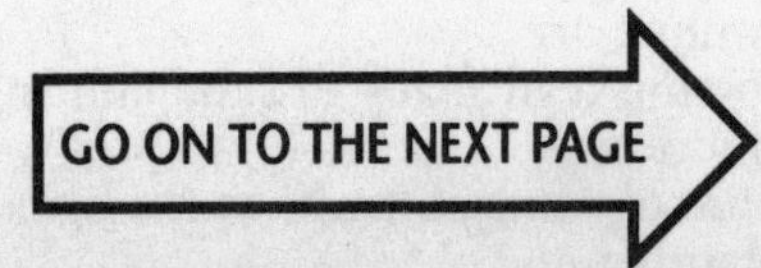

18 What would happen if Navajo practices regarding sandpaintings (lines 14-20) were strictly observed?

(A) Only the Navajo would be permitted to exhibit sandpaintings as works of art.
(B) All sandpaintings would be destroyed before the rite of re-creation.
(C) The sandpaintings could be viewed only during the sandpainting rite.
(D) The sand-glue craft would be the only art form in which figures from sandpaintings could appear.
(E) The Navajo would be able to focus exclusively on the sandpaintings' images of unity.

19 Why did the Navajo listeners mentioned in line 39 laugh?

(A) It would be dangerous for a person to climb onto the roof of a hogan.
(B) The view from the periphery is more amusing than the view from the center of the paintings.
(C) Only the person in need of healing should act in the way suggested by the author.
(D) Critical details in the sandpaintings would be imperceptible from such a distance.
(E) A bird's-eye perspective is irrelevant to the intended function of the paintings.

20 The phrase "obvious aesthetic value" (line 60) suggests that

(A) despite an attempt to separate sandpaintings from the realm of art, the author recognizes their artistic qualities
(B) imposing artistic rules on sandpaintings diminishes their symbolic value
(C) the Navajo believe the sandpaintings' artistic qualities to be as important as their function
(D) the author discourages artistic elitism, yet acknowledges the esteemed reputation that sandpainters enjoy within the Navajo community
(E) aesthetic value should be associated with objects of natural beauty as well as with things created by humans

21 The author's discussion of artists' palettes (lines 62-69) emphasizes the

(A) array of colors in the creation of sandpaintings
(B) insight required to appreciate technically unique art
(C) growing legitimacy of sandpainting reproductions
(D) value of sandpaintings as a means rather than an end
(E) benefit of combining several components to produce a single painting

22 The information in the passage suggests that a museum's exhibition of reproduced Navajo sandpaintings would

(A) undermine the effectiveness of sandpaintings in the healing process
(B) help to safeguard the traditions and treasures of Navajo civilization
(C) devalue the representations of sandpainting figures in the sand-glue craft
(D) discourage non-Navajo people from preserving actual sandpaintings
(E) perpetuate the importance of a painting's form rather than its function

23 Which of the following would the author consider to be most similar to a non-Navajo person's appreciation of sandpainting, as it is discussed in the passage?

(A) Savoring the taste of a cake that someone else has baked
(B) Enjoying a book written by an anonymous author
(C) Admiring an ancient structure without comprehending its historical context
(D) Praising a concert performance without knowing how to play a musical instrument
(E) Appreciating a building without having contributed to its construction

24 Which statement best summarizes the author's perspective on the appreciation of sandpainting?

(A) We should not revere ceremonial art objects because such reverence is a kind of tyranny that stifles the full expression of ideas.
(B) We must understand that the materials of the object and the design it takes are at the core of its meaning.
(C) We cannot fully understand sandpaintings until we witness their healing powers.
(D) We must understand the process by which an object was created and the purpose it serves in order to grasp its significance.
(E) Our usual way of looking at art objects should be augmented by knowledge of the artists' personal history.

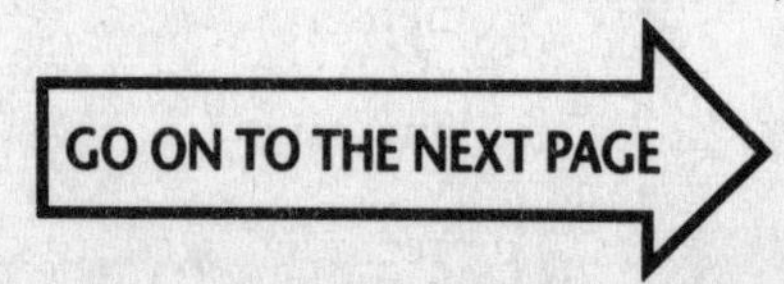

Questions 25-31 are based on the following passage.

During the nineteenth century privileged travelers from England and the United States often published accounts of their journeys to foreign lands. Some of these travelers were women who wrote travel books.

For most women of the leisure class, immobilized as they were by the iron hoops of convention, the term "abroad" had a dreamlike, talismanic quality. It conjured up a vision composed of a whole cluster of myths, half-myths, and truths—of sunlight, liberty, the fantastic and the healing, the unknown and the mysterious—all those concepts that stood in direct contrast to domesticity. When women who had the time and means traveled to India, China, or Africa, their real destination, more often than not, was a restorative idea rather than a place on the map.

Though this restorative idea sometimes led them to endure long, uncomfortable journeys to remote places where few of their compatriots had penetrated before them, there was little intent to imitate the male fashion for exploration, which was such a feature of the time. It is apparent that discovery was not the aim of most women travelers, nor did their wanderings inspire other expeditions of greater size or ambition.

What, *specifically*, were these women seeking "abroad"? From their diaries, letters, and published accounts, travel seems to have been the individual gesture of the previously housebound, male-dominated, wealthy lady. Desperate for an emotional outlet, she often found it through travel. Aboard a boat, perched atop a camel or an elephant, paddling an outrigger, away for months on end, she could enjoy a sense of control and a freedom of action and thought unthinkable at home. Travel offered the kind of adventure imaginable to her heretofore only in the Gothic or romantic novels of the day—encounters with the exotic, the exciting, the self-fulfilling. The challenges and new experiences increased confidence and allowed the woman within to emerge, at least temporarily.

But the motive for going abroad was more than a quest for the extraordinary. Travel satisfied that established Victorian passion for improvement—of oneself and of others. This passion, once regarded as the property of men only, was shared by these "new" women. Touring or residing in foreign lands, they learned history, geography, languages, and politics. Many vivid images were imprinted upon the memory that would have been poorer without them. The recorded accounts of their adventures—mountain climbing in Japan, outdoor bathing in Finland, monkey watching in India, canoeing along the Nile—helped to educate British and American readers. Simply said, the women travelers brought back a powerful commodity—knowledge.

History put these women travelers in a unique position, and they responded in a unique way: they created a small but impressive library of first-person narratives that combined genuine learning with the spirit of individualism. The succeeding generations of women travelers—the daughters and granddaughters of these pioneers—were impelled by essentially the same impetus, the desire for independence and enlightenment. These were the twin forces that crystallized in the ongoing movement for equal rights. Thus, the once-lowly travel book rather unexpectedly became an important instrument for the emancipation of women.

25 The primary purpose of the passage is to

(A) evaluate women's travel books and journals from a literary perspective
(B) contrast nineteenth-century women travelers with male explorers of the same period
(C) describe changes in travel opportunities for wealthy women in the nineteenth century
(D) examine the motives that some nineteenth-century women had for traveling
(E) analyze the historical significance of women travelers' books and journals

26 In line 2, "iron hoops" primarily signify the

(A) strict codes governing the social behavior of women
(B) unbecoming styles of Victorian fashion
(C) lack of mobility within society
(D) household implements disdained by Victorian women
(E) barriers to a woman's right to travel alone

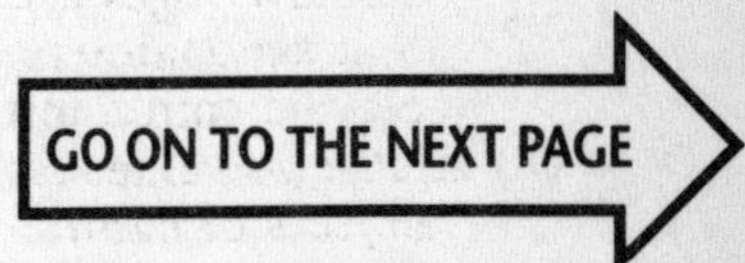

27 The main reason certain women traveled abroad during the nineteenth century was to

(A) seek the companionship of like-minded women
(B) satisfy a desire for freedom and adventure
(C) explore remote and uncharted places
(D) research and publish travel guides
(E) visit countries about which they had only read

28 In line 62, "crystallized" most nearly means

(A) refracted
(B) metamorphosed
(C) glittered
(D) sharpened
(E) solidified

29 In what way was a certain type of travel book an "instrument" (lines 64-65) ?

(A) It conveyed an impression of beauty.
(B) It revealed what would otherwise have been hidden.
(C) It was an agent that helped bring about a change.
(D) It registered a cataclysmic change in society.
(E) It was an implement wielded by an expert.

30 The author's conclusion would be most directly supported by additional information that

(A) described the details of particular journeys of women travelers
(B) revealed the number and titles of travel journals published by women
(C) indicated how nineteenth-century travel writers influenced the future status of women
(D) discussed the accuracy of the travel information included in women's journals and books
(E) discussed the effect of nineteenth-century travel writers on modern women writers

31 The author suggests that the travel books written by nineteenth-century women are significant primarily because they

(A) reflect the expanding role women were soon to assume in Britain and America
(B) were "once-lowly" and are now prized by book collectors
(C) helped women to achieve economic independence
(D) were richly illustrated and helped to educate people about life abroad
(E) are valuable historical sources that describe nineteenth-century travel

IF YOU FINISH BEFORE TIME IS CALLED, YOU MAY CHECK YOUR WORK ON THIS SECTION ONLY. DO NOT TURN TO ANY OTHER SECTION IN THE TEST.

Section 4 4 4 4 4

Time—30 Minutes
25 Questions

This section contains two types of questions. You have 30 minutes to complete both types. You may use any available space for scratchwork.

Notes:

1. The use of a calculator is permitted. All numbers used are real numbers.
2. Figures that accompany problems in this test are intended to provide information useful in solving the problems. They are drawn as accurately as possible EXCEPT when it is stated in a specific problem that the figure is not drawn to scale. All figures lie in a plane unless otherwise indicated.

Reference Information

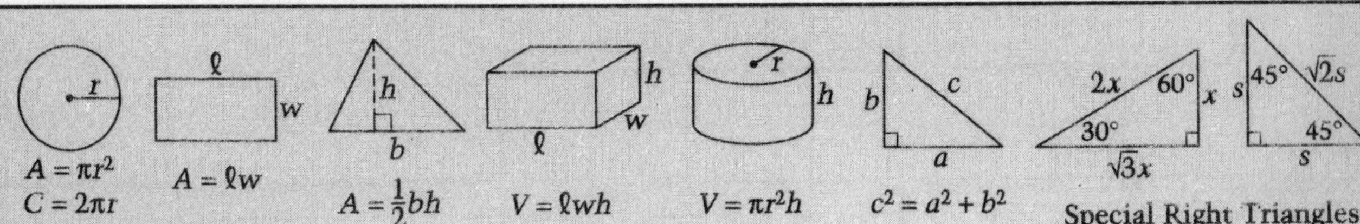

The number of degrees of arc in a circle is 360.
The measure in degrees of a straight angle is 180.
The sum of the measures in degrees of the angles of a triangle is 180.

Directions for Quantitative Comparison Questions

Questions 1-15 each consist of two quantities in boxes, one in Column A and one in Column B. You are to compare the two quantities and on the answer sheet fill in oval

A if the quantity in Column A is greater;
B if the quantity in Column B is greater;
C if the two quantities are equal;
D if the relationship cannot be determined from the information given.

AN E RESPONSE WILL NOT BE SCORED.

Notes:

1. In some questions, information is given about one or both of the quantities to be compared. In such cases, the given information is centered above the two columns and is not boxed.
2. In a given question, a symbol that appears in both columns represents the same thing in Column A as it does in Column B.
3. Letters such as x, n, and k stand for real numbers.

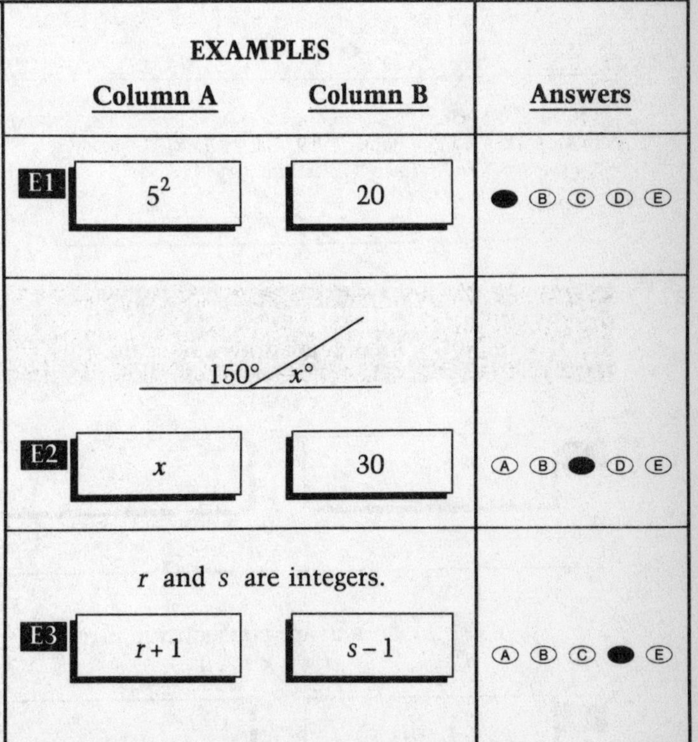

GO ON TO THE NEXT PAGE

SUMMARY DIRECTIONS FOR COMPARISON QUESTIONS

Answer: A if the quantity in Column A is greater;
B if the quantity in Column B is greater;
C if the two quantities are equal;
D if the relationship cannot be determined from the information given.

	Column A	Column B

$3n - 6 = 21$

1	n	5

2	The average (arithmetic mean) of 3, 4, and 5	The average (arithmetic mean) of 2, 3, 7, and 8

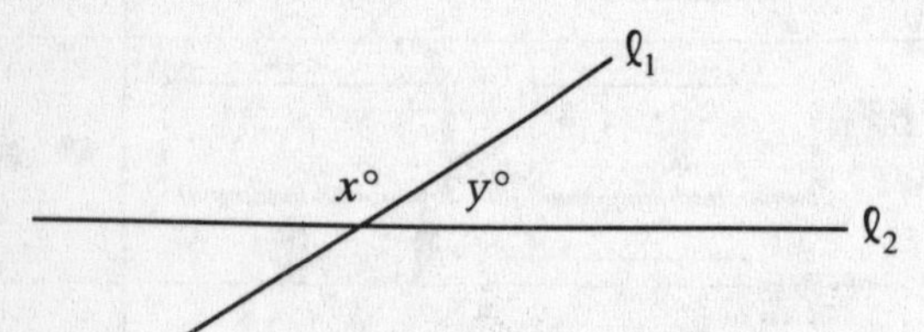

Note: Figure not drawn to scale.

$x > 90$

3	y	30

r, s, t, and u are consecutive integers.
$r < s < t < u$

4	$r + u$	$s + t$

	Column A	Column B

Ian has x dollars in a savings account.
$x > 0$

5	Twice the number of dollars that Ian has in the account	$200x$

$y = ax^2 + bx$
$x = 1$
$y = 3$

6	b	1

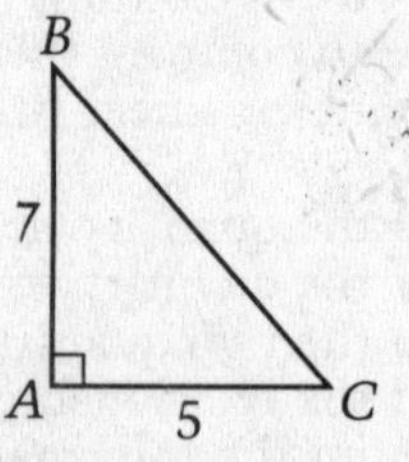

7	The length of BC	9

$(x - 3)(x + 2) < 0$

8	x	3

GO ON TO THE NEXT PAGE

SUMMARY DIRECTIONS FOR COMPARISON QUESTIONS

Answer: A if the quantity in Column A is greater;
B if the quantity in Column B is greater;
C if the two quantities are equal;
D if the relationship cannot be determined from the information given.

	Column A	Column B

$$\begin{array}{r} PW \\ -\,WP \\ \hline 72 \end{array}$$

P and W represent different nonzero digits in the correctly solved subtraction problem.

	Column A	Column B
9	P	W

u, v, and w are positive numbers.

	Column A	Column B
10	$u + v + w$	uvw

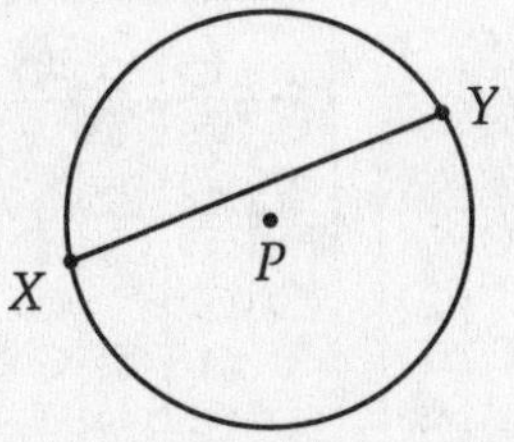

The circle has center P and area 5π.

	Column A	Column B
11	The length of XY	5

$x = y + 1$
x is a positive odd integer.

	Column A	Column B
12	$2x$	$3y - 1$

	Column A	Column B

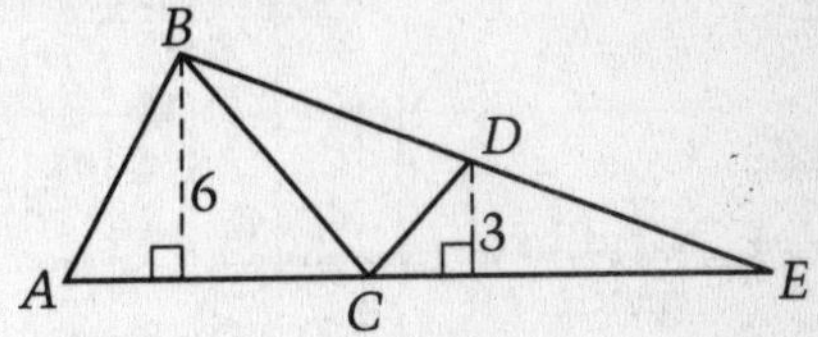

Note: Figure not drawn to scale.

$AE = 27$
$AC = 9$

	Column A	Column B
13	The area of $\triangle ABC$	The area of $\triangle CDE$

When the square of $2m$ is multiplied by 2, the result is g.

$m > 0$

	Column A	Column B
14	$\frac{g}{4m}$	m

p and r are different prime numbers.

	Column A	Column B
15	The number of positive integer divisors of p^3	The number of positive integer divisors of pr

GO ON TO THE NEXT PAGE

Directions for Student-Produced Response Questions

Each of the remaining 10 questions requires you to solve the problem and enter your answer by marking the ovals in the special grid, as shown in the examples below.

Answer: $\frac{7}{12}$ or 7/12

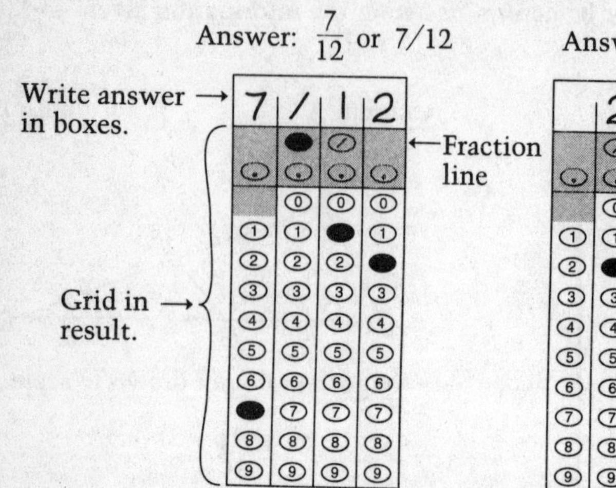

Answer: 2.5

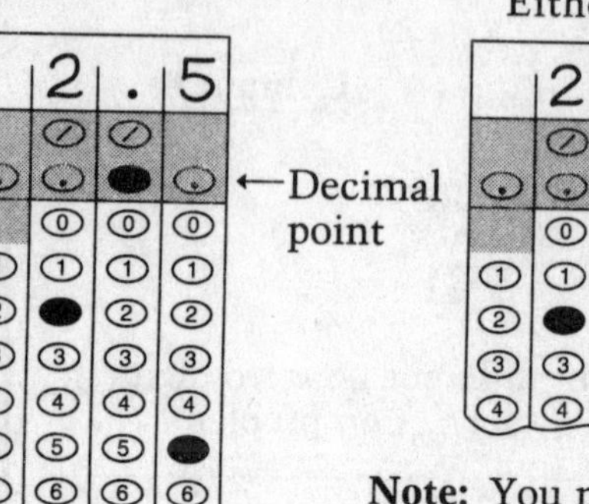

Answer: 201
Either position is correct.

Note: You may start your answers in any column, space permitting. Columns not needed should be left blank.

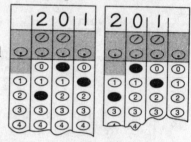

- Mark no more than one oval in any column.
- Because the answer sheet will be machine-scored, **you will receive credit only if the ovals are filled in correctly.**
- Although not required, it is suggested that you write your answer in the boxes at the top of the columns to help you fill in the ovals accurately.
- Some problems may have more than one correct answer. In such cases, grid only one answer.
- No question has a negative answer.
- **Mixed numbers** such as $2\frac{1}{2}$ must be gridded as 2.5 or 5/2. (If 21/2 is gridded, it will be interpreted as $\frac{21}{2}$, not $2\frac{1}{2}$.)
- **Decimal Accuracy**: If you obtain a decimal answer, **enter the most accurate value the grid will accommodate.** For example, if you obtain an answer such as 0.6666 . . . , you should record the result as .666 or .667. **Less accurate values such as .66 or .67 are not acceptable.**

Acceptable ways to grid $\frac{2}{3}$ = .6666 . . .

2/3   .666   .667

16 A certain car's gasoline tank holds 20 gallons when full. The tank is $\frac{3}{4}$ full. At \$1.20 a gallon, how many dollars worth of gasoline must be purchased to fill the remainder of the tank? (Disregard the \$ sign when gridding your answer.)

17 If $(3 \times 10^3) + (2 \times 10^2) = a \times 10^3$, what is the value of a?

GO ON TO THE NEXT PAGE

18 If $2x + y = 14$ and $4x + y = 20$, what is the value of $3x + y$?

19 What is the number that satisfies the following three conditions?

- It is an integer greater than 999 and less than 1,234.
- The sum of its digits is 14.
- Its tens and units digits are the same.

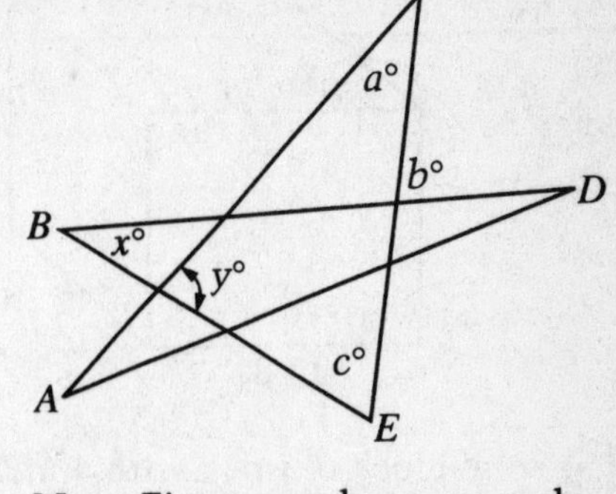

Note: Figure not drawn to scale.

20 In the figure above, AC, CE, EB, BD, and DA are line segments. If $a = 40$, $b = 70$, and $c = 50$, what is the value of $x + y$?

21 For all integers x, let $\boxed{x}$ be defined as follows:

$$\boxed{x} = \frac{x}{2} \text{ if } x \text{ is even.}$$

$$\boxed{x} = x^2 \text{ if } x \text{ is odd.}$$

If $\boxed{2} + \boxed{3} = y$, what is the value of y^3 ?

GO ON TO THE NEXT PAGE

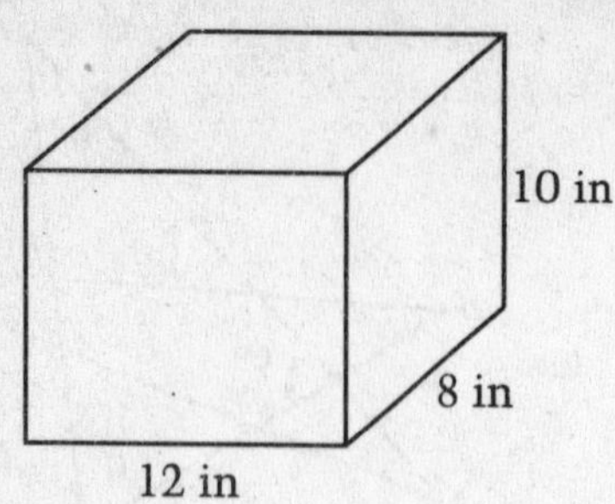

22 A solid block of wood with dimensions as shown in the figure above is to be painted on all of its faces. What is the total area (in square inches) to be painted?

23 Hakim and Chris began running a 50-yard race at the same time. When Hakim finished the race, Chris was 4 yards behind him. If Hakim ran the race in 7 seconds, what was the difference in their rates in yards per second for those 7 seconds?

24 What is one possible value for the slope of a line passing through point $(-1, 1)$ and passing <u>between</u> points $(1, 3)$ and $(2, 3)$ but not containing either of them?

25 If the average (arithmetic mean) of x, $2x - 8$, $2x + 2$, $3x - 1$, and $4x + 1$ is 6, what is the value of the mode of these numbers?

IF YOU FINISH BEFORE TIME IS CALLED, YOU MAY CHECK YOUR WORK ON THIS SECTION ONLY. DO NOT TURN TO ANY OTHER SECTION IN THE TEST. **STOP**

Section 5 5

Time—30 Minutes
35 Questions

For each question in this section, select the best answer from among the choices given and fill in the corresponding oval on the answer sheet.

Each sentence below has one or two blanks, each blank indicating that something has been omitted. Beneath the sentence are five words or sets of words labeled A through E. Choose the word or set of words that, when inserted in the sentence, best fits the meaning of the sentence as a whole.

Example:

Medieval kingdoms did not become constitutional republics overnight; on the contrary, the change was ----.

(A) unpopular
(B) unexpected
(C) advantageous
(D) sufficient
(E) gradual

1 Mammals of temperate zones often give birth in the spring, thereby ---- their offspring to ---- the season's abundant food.

(A) subjecting . . subsist on
(B) encouraging . . compete for
(C) tempting . . abstain from
(D) forcing . . forage for
(E) enabling . . benefit from

2 While the dome of the nineteenth-century city hall once ---- the city's skyline, a much taller new office building now ---- the old landmark.

(A) overshadowed . . enhances
(B) dominated . . dwarfs
(C) punctuated . . resembles
(D) cluttered . . destroys
(E) beautified . . uplifts

3 Ancient cloth makers probably could not twist flax fibers until they had dipped the fibers into water to make them ----.

(A) solvent (B) supple (C) nonporous (D) immutable (E) invisible

4 In an effort to ---- people's physical discomforts, modern medicine sometimes wrongly treats the body's defense mechanisms as ---- and in need of corrective intervention.

(A) cure . . complex
(B) prescribe . . symptomatic
(C) diagnose . . suppressive
(D) relieve . . defective
(E) analyze . . medicinal

5 *Crazy Love*, by Elías Miguel Muñoz, is an ---- novel: it takes the form of a series of letters.

(A) archetypal (B) epistolary (C) inauspicious (D) inconspicuous (E) illusory

6 The meal had ---- effect on the famished travelers: their energy was restored almost instantly.

(A) a tonic
(B) a cloying
(C) an indefinite
(D) a debilitating
(E) an intemperate

7 While cynics may ---- the goal of international disarmament as utopian, others believe that laughing contemptuously at idealism leads nowhere.

(A) exalt (B) confirm (C) renew (D) deride (E) defend

8 Although his memoirs contained scathing criticisms of his opponents, the politician ---- vindictiveness as his motive.

(A) disavowed
(B) claimed
(C) disparaged
(D) substantiated
(E) evaluated

9 Even in her most casual conversation, one detects the impulse to ----, to impart knowledge systematically to her listener.

(A) mystify (B) instruct (C) insinuate (D) embellish (E) meditate

10 Ms. Turner was an ---- opponent, one who never swerved from her purpose and would never compromise or yield.

(A) inexorable
(B) ambivalent
(C) eloquent
(D) impassive
(E) obstreperous

GO ON TO THE NEXT PAGE

Each question below consists of a related pair of words or phrases, followed by five pairs of words or phrases labeled A through E. Select the pair that best expresses a relationship similar to that expressed in the original pair.

Example:

CRUMB : BREAD ::
(A) ounce : unit
(B) splinter : wood
(C) water : bucket
(D) twine : rope
(E) cream : butter

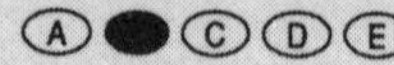

11 MAP : NAVIGATE ::
(A) manuscript : submit
(B) license : revoke
(C) writing : erase
(D) blueprint : build
(E) receipt : pay

12 SKULL : HEAD ::
(A) heart : organ
(B) finger : hand
(C) skeleton : body
(D) elbow : joint
(E) scalp : hair

13 ACCOMPLICE : CRIME ::
(A) inmate : prison
(B) detective : clue
(C) employer : work
(D) salesperson : store
(E) partner : business

14 BARRICADE : ACCESS ::
(A) heal : illness
(B) demand : due
(C) bind : movement
(D) complete : task
(E) chat : conversation

15 ENSEMBLE : DANCER ::
(A) clique : outsider
(B) band : musician
(C) gymnasium : athlete
(D) museum : curator
(E) audience : performer

16 CONSIDER : CONTEMPLATE ::
(A) smile : greet
(B) write : compose
(C) complain : bicker
(D) examine : scrutinize
(E) ignore : notice

17 CONGEAL : SOLID ::
(A) heat : fire
(B) breathe : air
(C) immunize : disease
(D) melt : liquid
(E) push : resistance

18 SHEAR : WOOL ::
(A) reap : wheat
(B) whittle : wood
(C) sweep : broom
(D) prune : tree
(E) rake : leaves

19 EPILOGUE : BOOK ::
(A) sequel : movie
(B) conclusion : title
(C) tiff : quarrel
(D) intermission : play
(E) finale : symphony

20 GLUTTON : MODERATION ::
(A) thief : larceny
(B) peer : nobility
(C) scoundrel : virtue
(D) gambler : luck
(E) benefactor : gift

21 AFFECTATION : BEHAVIOR ::
(A) speech : topic
(B) tension : violence
(C) façade : appearance
(D) buffoonery : action
(E) pretense : honesty

22 EXHORTATION : URGE ::
(A) division : unite
(B) agreement : dissent
(C) eulogy : praise
(D) travesty : reproduce
(E) charity : donate

23 COOPERATION : COLLUSION ::
(A) evidence : proof
(B) achievement : reward
(C) damage : compensation
(D) imitation : forgery
(E) emotion : ecstasy

GO ON TO THE NEXT PAGE

The passage below is followed by questions based on its content. Answer the questions on the basis of what is stated or implied in the passage and in any introductory material that may be provided.

Questions 24-35 are based on the following passage.

The following passage, first published in 1960, is adapted from an essay in which the author, an anthropologist, discusses his recent visit to a lake.

Not long ago I visited a New England lake that has been preempted and civilized by human beings. All day long in the vacation season high-speed motorboats, driven with the reckless abandon common to the young of our society, speed back and forth. The shores echo to the roar of powerful motors and the delighted screams of young people with uncounted horsepower surging under their hands. If I had had some desire to swim or to canoe in the older ways of the great forest that once lay about this region, either notion would have been folly. I would have been gaily chopped to ribbons by young people whose eyes were always immutably fixed on the far horizons of space, or on the dials which indicated the speed of their passing. There was another world, I was to discover, along the lake shallows and under the boat dock, where the motors could not come.

As I sat there one sunny morning when the water was peculiarly translucent, I saw a dark shape moving swiftly over the bottom. It was the first sign of life I had seen in this lake, whose shores seemed to yield little but washed-in beer cans. By and by the gliding shadow ceased to scurry from stone to stone over the bottom. Unexpectedly, it headed almost directly for me. A furry nose with gray whiskers broke the surface. Below the whiskers, green water foliage trailed out in an inverted V as long as his body. A muskrat still lived in the lake. He was bringing in his breakfast. I sat very still in the strips of sunlight under the pier. To my surprise, the muskrat came almost to my feet with his little breakfast of greens. He was young, and it rapidly became obvious to me that he was laboring under an illusion of his own, that he thought animals and people were still living in the Garden of Eden. He gave me a friendly glance from time to time as he nibbled his greens. Once, even, he went out into the lake again and returned to my feet with more greens. He had not, it seemed, heard very much about people. I shuddered. Only the evening before I had heard my neighbor describe with triumphant enthusiasm how he had killed a muskrat in the garden because the creature had dared to nibble his petunias.

On this pleasant shore a war existed and would go on until nothing remained but human beings. Yet this creature with the gray, appealing face wanted very little: a strip of shore to coast up and down, sunlight and moonlight, some weeds from the deep water. He was an edge-of-the-world dweller, caught between a vanishing forest and a deep lake preempted by unpredictable machines full of chopping blades. He eyed me nearsightedly, a green leaf poised in his mouth. Plainly he had come with some poorly instructed memory about the lion and the lamb.*

"You had better run away now," I said softly, making no movement in the shafts of light. "You are in the wrong universe and must not make this mistake again. I am really a very terrible and cunning beast. I can throw stones." With this I dropped a little pebble at his feet.

He looked at me half blindly, with eyes much better adjusted to the wavering shadows of his lake bottom than to sight in the open air. He made almost as if to take the pebble up into his forepaws. Then a thought seemed to cross his mind: perhaps after all this was not Eden. His nose twitched carefully; he edged toward the water.

As he vanished in an oncoming wave, there went with him a natural world, distinct from the world of young people and motorboats. . . . It was a world of sunlight he had taken down into the water weeds. It hovered there, waiting for my disappearance.

* The lion lying down with the lamb is a Biblical image of ideal peace.

24 The passage as a whole can best be described as an expression of

(A) amusement at the behavior of muskrats
(B) regret at the impact of humans on the lake
(C) scorn for the people who use the lake
(D) optimism about the future of the lake
(E) irritation at the modern obsession with speed

25 Lines 3-9 indicate that the word "civilized" (line 2) is being used

(A) cautiously
(B) sarcastically
(C) humorously
(D) hopefully
(E) wistfully

GO ON TO THE NEXT PAGE

26 The underlying sentiment in the sentence beginning "If I had" (lines 9-12) is the author's

(A) nostalgia for experiences that are no longer possible
(B) grudging admiration for young people
(C) regret for something he had failed to do
(D) amusement at his own foolishness
(E) feeling of moral paralysis

27 In lines 12-15, the author suggests that the young people are

(A) competitive
(B) violent
(C) self-absorbed
(D) rebellious
(E) uninformed

28 In line 27, "broke" most nearly means

(A) destroyed
(B) surpassed
(C) weakened
(D) pierced
(E) tamed

29 In the sentence beginning in line 33 ("He was young . . . Garden of Eden"), the author suggests that

(A) in this lake, few muskrats have the chance to reach maturity
(B) an older, wiser muskrat would have learned to fear people
(C) the muskrat was only one of several types of animals living in the lake
(D) at one time the lake had been home to a variety of animals
(E) some parts of the lake had remained unchanged for centuries

30 In line 35, "laboring under" most nearly means

(A) moving with great effort
(B) being exploited by
(C) striving to achieve
(D) working for
(E) suffering from

31 The author probably "shuddered" (line 41) because

(A) he was afraid of the muskrat
(B) he envisioned what could happen to the muskrat
(C) he was sitting in shade under the boat dock
(D) the behavior of the young people in the motorboats frightened him
(E) he wondered what else could happen to undermine the ecology of the lake

32 The phrase "dared to" in line 45 emphasizes the author's belief that

(A) the muskrat was dangerous
(B) the muskrat was insolent
(C) humans will eventually destroy all life in the lake
(D) the neighbor's behavior was uncalled for
(E) the author felt intimidated by his neighbor

33 The quotation in lines 58-62 primarily serves as a warning about the

(A) threat from the author
(B) behavior of humans in general
(C) predatory nature of many wild animals
(D) inevitable destruction of the natural world
(E) callousness of the young people in the motorboats

GO ON TO THE NEXT PAGE

34 Which of the following best describes the author's action in lines 62-63 ("With this . . . at his feet") as compared to his words in lines 58-62 ?

(A) His action exaggerates his words.
(B) His action is more admirable than his words.
(C) His action reveals a hidden dimension to his words.
(D) His action parallels the severity of his words.
(E) His action is much less emphatic than his words.

35 In the last sentence (lines 75-76), the author implies that

(A) he himself does not belong to the natural world
(B) his fears have been unfounded
(C) his behavior has been unacceptable
(D) humans will eventually learn to behave responsibly toward nature
(E) there is no future for the young muskrat

IF YOU FINISH BEFORE TIME IS CALLED, YOU MAY CHECK YOUR WORK ON THIS SECTION ONLY. DO NOT TURN TO ANY OTHER SECTION IN THE TEST.

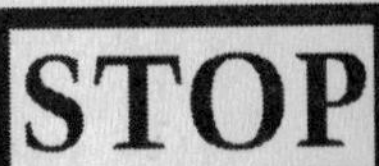

Section 6 6 6 6

Time—15 Minutes
10 Questions

In this section solve each problem, using any available space on the page for scratchwork. Then decide which is the best of the choices given and fill in the corresponding oval on the answer sheet.

Notes:

1. The use of a calculator is permitted. All numbers used are real numbers.

2. Figures that accompany problems in this test are intended to provide information useful in solving the problems. They are drawn as accurately as possible EXCEPT when it is stated in a specific problem that the figure is not drawn to scale. All figures lie in a plane unless otherwise indicated.

Reference Information

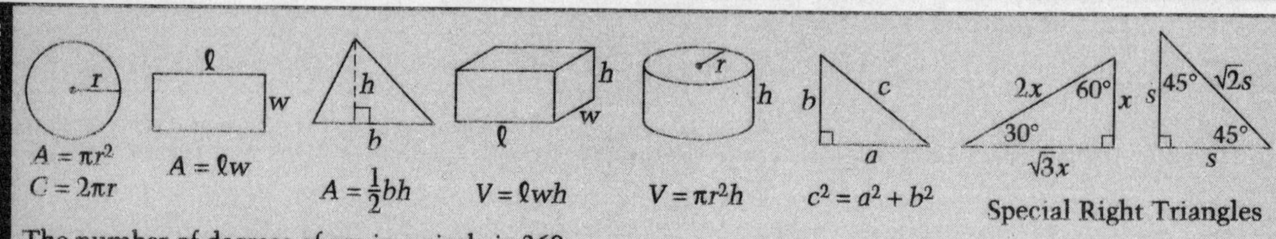

The number of degrees of arc in a circle is 360.
The measure in degrees of a straight angle is 180.
The sum of the measures in degrees of the angles of a triangle is 180.

1 If $x = 2y$ and $y = \frac{10}{z}$, what is the value of x when $z = 4$?

(A) 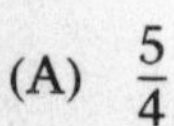 $\frac{5}{4}$

(B) $\frac{5}{2}$

(C) 5

(D) 8

(E) 20

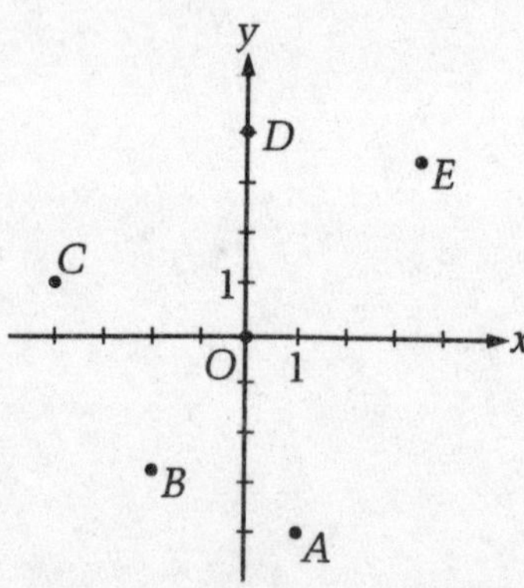

2 In the figure above, which lettered point, other than point O, lies in the interior of a circle with center O and radius 4 ?

(A) A
(B) B
(C) C
(D) D
(E) E

GO ON TO THE NEXT PAGE

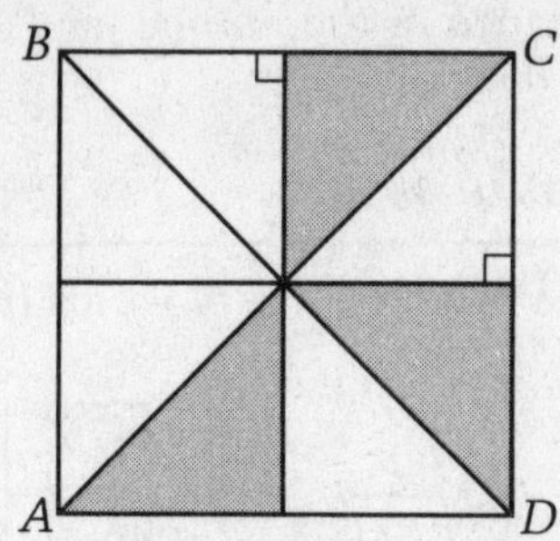

3 In the figure above, $ABCD$ is a square. What percent of the square is shaded?

(A) 25%

(B) $33\frac{1}{3}\%$

(C) $37\frac{1}{2}\%$

(D) 40%

(E) 50%

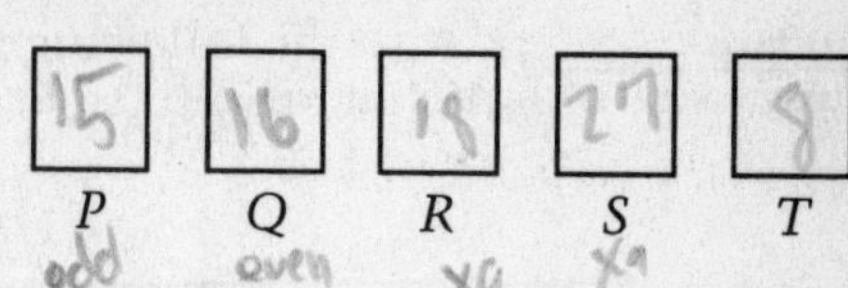

4 Each of the boxes above must contain one number from the set {8, 15, 16, 18, 27}. A different number is to be placed in each box so that the following conditions are met.

(1) Box P contains an odd number.
(2) Box Q contains an even number.
(3) Boxes R and S each contain a number that is a multiple of 9.
(4) The number in box P is less than the number in box Q.

What number must be in box T?

(A) 8
(B) 15
(C) 16
(D) 18
(E) 27

Questions 5-6 refer to the following graphs, which show the change in the number and average (arithmetic mean) size of farms in the United States during the years 1940-1990.

UNITED STATES FARMS, 1940–1990

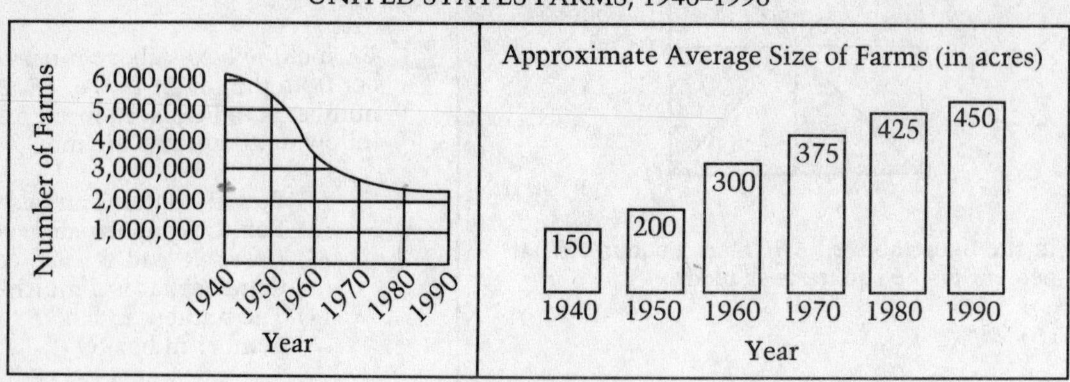

5 Which of the following is NOT a valid conclusion from the information shown in the graphs?

(A) From 1950 to 1960, the number of farms decreased by approximately 2,000,000.
(B) From 1940 to 1990, the number of farms decreased.
(C) From 1940 to 1990, the average size of farms increased each decade.
(D) In 1980, there were about 2,500,000 farms.
(E) From 1950 to 1960, the average size of farms increased by approximately 100%.

6 According to the graphs, which of the following is the best estimate of the total acreage of farms in 1950 ?

(A) 200,000
(B) 1,100,000
(C) 5,500,000
(D) 1,100,000,000
(E) 11,000,000,000

GO ON TO THE NEXT PAGE

7 In the exact middle of a certain book, when the page numbers on the facing pages, x and $x + 1$, are multiplied together, the product is 210. If all of the pages are numbered in order, how many numbered pages are in the book?

(A) 24
(B) 26
(C) 28
(D) 32
(E) 34

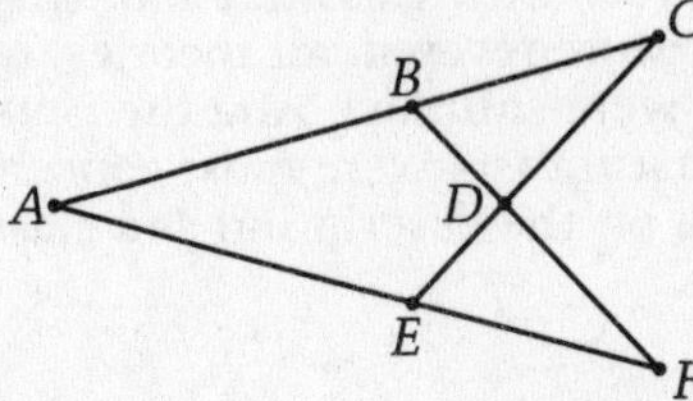

8 Segments AC, AF, BF, and EC intersect at the labeled points as shown in the figure above. Define two points as "independent" if they do not lie on the same segment in the figure. Of the labeled points in the figure, how many pairs of independent points are there?

(A) None
(B) One
(C) Two
(D) Three
(E) Four

9 If a and b are positive integers, which of the following expressions is equivalent to $\frac{(3^a)^b}{3^a}$?

(A) 1^b
(B) 3^b
(C) 3^{ab-1}
(D) $3^{ab} - 3^a$
(E) $(3^a)^{b-1}$

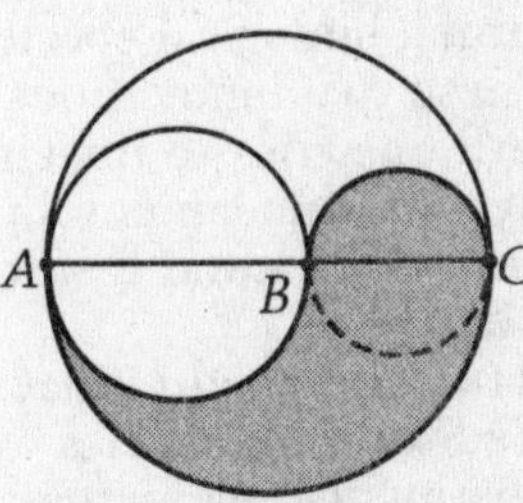

Note: Figure not drawn to scale.

10 AB, BC, and AC are diameters of the three circles shown above. If $BC = 2$ and $AB = 2BC$, what is the area of the shaded region?

(A) 12π

(B) 6π

(C) $\frac{9}{2}\pi$

(D) 3π

(E) 2π

IF YOU FINISH BEFORE TIME IS CALLED, YOU MAY CHECK YOUR WORK ON THIS SECTION ONLY. DO NOT TURN TO ANY OTHER SECTION IN THE TEST. **STOP**

Section 7 7

Time—15 Minutes
12 Questions

For each question in this section, select the best answer from among the choices given and fill in the corresponding oval on the answer sheet.

The two passages below are followed by questions based on their content and on the relationship between the two passages. Answer the questions on the basis of what is stated or implied in the passages and in any introductory material that may be provided.

Questions 1-12 are based on the following passages.

The following adaptations from late-twentieth-century works offer perspectives on the work of botanist Carolus Linnaeus (1707-1778), who taught at the University of Uppsala, Sweden.

Passage 1

Linnaeus' enormous and essential contribution to natural history was to devise a system of classification whereby any plant or animal could be identified and slotted into an overall plan. In creating this system, Linnaeus also introduced a method of naming biological species that is still used today. These two innovations may sound unexciting until one tries to imagine a scientific world without these fundamental tools—as was indeed the case with natural history before the Linnaean system.

Previous naturalists (and Linnaeus himself in his youth) had tried to name species by enumerating all of a species' distinguishing features. Often these multiword names had to be expanded when similar related species were discovered, and the names differed from author to author and language to language. Naturalists therefore had difficulty understanding and building on one another's work. It became crucial that every species have the same name in all languages. In using Latin for naming species, Linnaeus followed the custom of his time, but in reducing the name of each species to two words—the genus, common to every species within the genus, and the species name itself—he made an invaluable break with the past. For instance, a shell with earlier names such as "Marbled Jamaica Murex with Knotty Twirls (Petiver)" became simply *Strombus gigas* L. ("L" for Linnaeus).

Yet the invention of a system of nomenclature, vital as it has come to seem, was trivial by comparison with Linnaeus' main achievement: devising a classification system for all organisms, so that scientists no longer had to list every species individually. Linnaeus' universally understood classification of species also enabled scientists to retrieve information, make predictions, and understand traits by association. Linnaeus divided each kingdom (animal, vegetable, and mineral) into hierarchies that are still, with some additions, followed today. His classifications reflect an eighteenth-century concept of nature in which all organisms, graded from lower to higher, formed a ladder or "great chain of being," with the human species at the summit.

Linnaeus himself would probably have been the first to admit that classification is only a tool, and not the ultimate purpose, of biological inquiry. Unfortunately, this truth was not apparent to his immediate successors, and for the next hundred years biologists were to concern themselves almost exclusively with classification. All facts, however trivial, were revered; all theories, however stimulating, were shunned. And the facts with which these naturalists were most concerned were those bearing on the description and classification of species.

Passage 2

A few years ago I stood in a historic place—a neat little eighteenth-century garden, formally divided by gravel walks, with a small wooden house in one corner where the garden's owner had once lived. This garden, which lies in the old Swedish university town of Uppsala, was owned by the warehouse clerk and great indexer of nature, Linnaeus, who between 1730 and 1760 docketed, or attempted to docket, most of the biological world. Perhaps nothing is more moving at Uppsala than the actual smallness and ordered simplicity of that garden, as compared to the immense consequences that sprang from it in terms of the way humans see and think about the external world. For all its air of gentle peace, this garden is closer to an explosion whose reverberations continue to resonate inside the human brain; it is the place where an intellectual seed landed and has now grown to a tree that shadows the entire globe.

GO ON TO THE NEXT PAGE

I am a heretic about Linnaeus. I do not dispute the value of the tool he gave natural science, but am wary about the change it has effected in humans' relationship to the world. From Linnaeus on, much of science has been devoted to providing specific labels, to explaining specific mechanisms — to sorting masses into individual entities and arranging the entities neatly. The cost of having so successfully itemized and pigeonholed nature, of being able to name names and explain behaviors, is to limit certain possibilities of seeing and apprehending. For example, the modern human thinks that he or she can best understand a tree (or a species of tree) by examining a single tree. But trees are not intended to grow in isolation. They are social creatures, and their society in turn creates or supports other societies of plants, insects, birds, mammals, and microorganisms, all of which make up the whole experience of the woods. The true woods is the sum of all its phenomena.

Modern humans have come to adopt the scientific view of the external world as a way of understanding their everyday experience in it. Yet that experience is better understood as a synthesis, a complex interweaving of strands, past memories and present perceptions, times and places, private and public history, that is hopelessly beyond science's powers to analyze. It is quintessentially "wild": irrational, uncontrollable, incalculable. Despite modern humans' Linnaeus-like attempts to "garden" everyday experience, to invent disciplining social and intellectual systems for it, in truth it resembles wild nature, the green chaos of the woods.

1 In the first paragraph of Passage 1, the attitude of the author toward Linnaeus' legacy is one of

(A) nostalgia
(B) appreciation
(C) delight
(D) bafflement
(E) resentment

2 The word "case" as it is used in line 10 most nearly means

(A) example
(B) lawsuit
(C) convincing argument
(D) set of circumstances
(E) situation under investigation

3 The discussion of "a shell" in lines 26-29 serves primarily to illustrate

(A) what types of Latin names were commonly used for biological species in Linnaeus' day
(B) why the Linnaean system of naming was trivial in comparison to another innovation
(C) why other naturalists initially opposed the Linnaean system of naming
(D) how the Linnaean system helped naturalists identify previously unknown species
(E) how the Linnaean system simplified the names of biological species

4 As used in line 31, "vital" most nearly means

(A) animated
(B) invigorating
(C) essential
(D) necessary to maintaining life
(E) characteristic of living beings

5 Passage 1 indicates that Linnaeus' classification of the natural kingdom was based on

(A) the conclusions of previous naturalists
(B) a conception of nature's order
(C) the idea that classifying forms the basis of biological inquiry
(D) close observation of nature's patterns
(E) a theory about how biological species developed over time

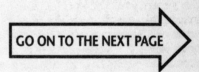

GO ON TO THE NEXT PAGE

6 In Passage 2, the author mentions that the garden "is closer to an explosion" (line 72) in order to

(A) illustrate the impact that Linnaeus' fame had on the town of Uppsala
(B) emphasize the influence that Linnaeus has had on human thought
(C) call attention to the profusion of growth in the small garden
(D) note that the seeds that Linnaeus planted in the garden have grown into large trees
(E) express concern about the destructive potential of scientific advancement

7 The author of Passage 2 characterizes "much of science" (line 81) as

(A) reductive
(B) innovative
(C) controversial
(D) idealistic
(E) obscure

8 As used in lines 87-88, "apprehending" most nearly means

(A) seizing
(B) anticipating
(C) fearing
(D) understanding
(E) doubting

9 The author of Passage 2 suggests that the "scientific view of the external world" (lines 97-98) involves

(A) perceiving the actual chaos of nature
(B) recognizing that plants and animals are social creatures
(C) limiting one's understanding of the world
(D) appreciating nature only for its usefulness to humans
(E) performing experiments with potentially destructive results

10 Which of the following techniques is used in each of the last two sentences of Passage 2 (lines 104-109) ?

(A) Comparison and contrast
(B) Personal anecdote
(C) Elaboration of terms
(D) Summary of opposing arguments
(E) Illustration by example

11 The approaches of the two passages to the topic of Linnaeus differ in that only Passage 2 uses

(A) second-person address to the reader
(B) several specific examples of Linnaean nomenclature
(C) an anecdote from the author's personal experience
(D) references to other authors who have written about Linnaeus
(E) a comparison between Linnaeus' system and other types of scientific innovations

12 Both passages emphasize which of the following aspects of Linnaeus' work?

(A) The extent to which it represented a change from the past
(B) The way in which it limits present-day science
(C) The degree to which it has affected humans' reverence toward nature
(D) The decisiveness with which it settled scientific disputes
(E) The kinds of scientific discoveries on which it built

IF YOU FINISH BEFORE TIME IS CALLED, YOU MAY CHECK YOUR WORK ON THIS SECTION ONLY. DO NOT TURN TO ANY OTHER SECTION IN THE TEST. **STOP**

Correct Answers and Difficulty Levels

VERBAL

Section 2

Five-choice Questions

	COR. ANS.	DIFF. LEV.
1.	B	1
2.	D	2
3.	C	3
4.	A	2
5.	C	2
6.	C	3
7.	C	3
8.	A	4
9.	E	5
10.	B	1
11.	B	1
12.	C	2
13.	B	3
14.	A	4
15.	D	5
16.	E	3
17.	B	3
18.	C	4
19.	E	3
20.	A	5
21.	D	4
22.	E	4
23.	C	3
24.	D	2
25.	D	3
26.	A	3
27.	B	2
28.	E	3
29.	C	3
30.	C	3
31.	A	4

______ no. correct

______ no. incorrect

Section 5

Five-choice Questions

	COR. ANS.	DIFF. LEV.
1.	E	1
2.	B	3
3.	B	3
4.	D	2
5.	B	3
6.	A	4
7.	D	4
8.	A	4
9.	B	4
10.	A	5
11.	D	1
12.	C	2
13.	E	3
14.	C	2
15.	B	3
16.	D	3
17.	D	3
18.	A	3
19.	E	3
20.	C	3
21.	C	4
22.	C	4
23.	D	5
24.	B	2
25.	B	3
26.	A	2
27.	C	3
28.	D	3
29.	B	3
30.	E	4
31.	B	1
32.	D	3
33.	B	2
34.	E	4
35.	A	3

______ no. correct

______ no. incorrect

Section 7

Five-choice Questions

	COR. ANS.	DIFF. LEV.
1.	B	1
2.	D	3
3.	E	2
4.	C	1
5.	B	4
6.	B	3
7.	A	5
8.	D	1
9.	C	4
10.	C	4
11.	C	3
12.	A	5

______ no. correct

______ no. incorrect

MATHEMATICAL

Section 1

Five-choice Questions

	COR. ANS.	DIFF. LEV.
1.	B	1
2.	B	1
3.	A	1
4.	D	2
5.	A	1
6.	E	2
7.	E	2
8.	C	3
9.	D	3
10.	E	3
11.	C	3
12.	C	3
13.	C	3
14.	A	3
15.	B	3
16.	D	5
17.	E	3
18.	D	1
19.	C	4
20.	D	4
21.	B	4
22.	B	4
23.	D	4
24.	A	5
25.	C	5

12 no. correct

13 no. incorrect

Section 4

Four-choice Questions

	COR. ANS.	DIFF. LEV.
1.	A	1
2.	B	1
3.	D	3
4.	C	2
5.	B	3
6.	D	3
7.	B	3
8.	B	3
9.	A	3
10.	D	4
11.	B	4
12.	D	4
13.	C	3
14.	A	4
15.	C	5

9 no. correct

6 no. incorrect

Section 6

Five-choice Questions

	COR. ANS.	DIFF. LEV.
1.	C	1
2.	B	2
3.	C	2
4.	A	1
5.	E	3
6.	D	3
7.	C	3
8.	D	4
9.	E	5
10.	D	5

5 no. correct

5 no. incorrect

Section 4

Student-Produced Response Questions

	COR. ANS.	DIFF. LEV.
16.	6	1
17.	3.2 or 16/5	2
18.	17	2
19.	1166	3
20.	150	4
21.	1000	3
22.	592	3
23.	4/7 or .571	4
24.	2/3<x<1 or .666<x<1	4
25.	8	5

4 no. correct (16-25)

NOTE: Difficulty levels are estimates of question difficulty for a recent group of college-bound seniors. Difficulty levels range from 1 (easiest) to 5 (hardest).

The Scoring Process

Machine-scoring is done in three steps:

- *Scanning.* Your answer sheet is "read" by a scanning machine and the oval you filled in for each question is recorded on a computer tape.
- *Scoring.* The computer compares the oval filled in for each question with the correct response. Each correct answer receives one point; omitted questions do not count toward your score. For each wrong answer to the multiple-choice questions, a fraction of a point is subtracted to correct for random guessing. For questions with five answer choices, one-fourth of a point is subtracted for each wrong response; for questions with four answer choices, one-third of a point is subtracted for each wrong response. The SAT I verbal test has 78 questions with five answer choices each. If, for example, a student has 44 right, 32 wrong, and 2 omitted, the resulting raw score is determined as follows:

$$44 \text{ right} - \frac{32 \text{ wrong}}{4} = 44 - 8 = 36 \text{ raw score points}$$

Obtaining raw scores frequently involves the rounding of fractional numbers to the nearest whole number. For example, a raw score of 36.25 is rounded to 36, the nearest whole number. A raw score of 36.50 is rounded upward to 37.

- *Converting to reported scaled score.* Raw test scores are then placed on the College Board scale of 200 to 800 through a process that adjusts scores to account for minor differences in difficulty among different editions of the test. This process, known as equating, is performed so that a student's reported score is not affected by the edition of the test taken or by the abilities of the group with whom the student takes the test. As a result of placing SAT I scores on the College Board scale, scores earned by students at different times can be compared. For example, an SAT I verbal score of 400 on a test taken at one administration indicates the same level of developed verbal ability as a 400 score obtained on a different edition of the test taken at another time.

How to Score the Test

SAT I Verbal Sections 2, 5, and 7

Step A: Count the number of correct answers for *Section 2* and record the number in the space provided on the worksheet on the next page. Then do the same for the incorrect answers. (Do not count omitted answers.) To determine subtotal A, use the formula:

$$\text{number correct} - \frac{\text{number incorrect}}{4} = \text{subtotal A}$$

Step B: Count the number of correct answers and the number of incorrect answers for *Section 5* and record the numbers in the spaces provided on the worksheet. To determine subtotal B, use the formula:

$$\text{number correct} - \frac{\text{number incorrect}}{4} = \text{subtotal B}$$

Step C: Count the number of correct answers and the number of incorrect answers for *Section 7* and record the numbers in the spaces provided on the worksheet. To determine subtotal C, use the formula:

$$\text{number correct} - \frac{\text{number incorrect}}{4} = \text{subtotal C}$$

Step D: To obtain D, add subtotal A, subtotal B, and subtotal C, keeping any decimals. Enter the resulting figure on the worksheet.

Step E: To obtain E, your raw verbal score, round D to the nearest whole number. (For example, any number from 44.50 to 45.49 rounds to 45.) Enter the resulting figure on the worksheet.

Step F: To find your SAT I verbal score, use the conversion table on page 39 to look up the total raw verbal score you obtained in step E. Enter this figure on the worksheet.

SAT I Mathematical Sections 1, 4, and 6

Step A: Count the number of correct answers and the number of incorrect answers for *Section 1* and record the numbers in the spaces provided on the worksheet. To determine subtotal A, use the formula:

$$\text{number correct} - \frac{\text{number incorrect}}{4} = \text{subtotal A}$$

Step B: Count the number of correct answers and the number of incorrect answers for the *four-choice quantitative comparison questions (questions 1 through 15) in Section 4* and record the numbers in the spaces provided on the worksheet. Note: Do not count any E responses to questions 1 through 15 as correct or incorrect. Because these four-choice questions have no E answer choices, E responses to these questions are treated as omits. To determine subtotal B, use the formula:

$$\text{number correct} - \frac{\text{number incorrect}}{3} = \text{subtotal B}$$

Step C: Count the number of correct answers for the student-produced response questions *(questions 16 through 25)* in *Section 4* and record the number in the space provided on the worksheet. This is subtotal C.

Step D: Count the number of correct answers and the number of incorrect answers for *Section 6* and record the numbers in the spaces provided on the worksheet. To determine subtotal D, use the formula:

$$\text{number correct} - \frac{\text{number incorrect}}{4} = \text{subtotal D}$$

Step E: To obtain E, add subtotal A, subtotal B, subtotal C, and subtotal D, keeping any decimals. Enter the resulting figure on the worksheet.

Step F: To obtain F, your raw mathematical score, round E to the nearest whole number. (For example, any number from 44.50 to 45.49 rounds to 45.) Enter the resulting figure on the worksheet.

Step G: To find your SAT I mathematical score, use the conversion table on page 39 to look up the total raw mathematical score you obtained in step F. Enter this figure on the worksheet.

SAT I Scoring Worksheet

SAT I Verbal Sections

A. Section 2:	____ no. correct	–	(____ no. incorrect ÷ 4)	=	____ subtotal A
B. Section 5:	____ no. correct	–	(____ no. incorrect ÷ 4)	=	____ subtotal B
C. Section 7:	____ no. correct	–	(____ no. incorrect ÷ 4)	=	____ subtotal C
D. Total unrounded raw score (Total A + B + C)					____ D
E. Total rounded raw score (Rounded to nearest whole number)					____ E
F. SAT I verbal reported scaled score (See the conversion table.)					☐ SAT I verbal score

SAT I Mathematical Sections

A. Section 1:	12 no. correct	–	(13 no. incorrect ÷ 4)	=	8.75 subtotal A
B. Section 4: Questions 1-15 (quantitative comparison)	9 no. correct	–	(6 no. incorrect ÷ 3)	=	7 subtotal B
C. Section 4: Questions 16-25 (student-produced response)	4 no. correct			=	4 subtotal C
D. Section 6:	6 no. correct	–	(5 no. incorrect ÷ 4)	=	3.75 subtotal D
E. Total unrounded raw score (Total A + B + C + D)					23.5 E
F. Total rounded raw score (Rounded to nearest whole number)					24 F
G. SAT I mathematical reported scaled score (See the conversion table.)					490 SAT I mathematical score

Should you have any questions on these scoring instructions, you may call the phone number below. If, after following the above scoring directions and checking your work at least twice, your results disagree with the SAT I verbal or SAT I mathematical score reported on your score report, you may request rescoring of your answer sheet. If rescoring confirms that an error had been made (resulting in either higher or lower scores than those originally reported), corrected reports will be sent to all recipients of your original scores. Please indicate whether it is your SAT I verbal or SAT I mathematical answers, or both, that you want to have rescored. When you write, please include a copy of this scoring worksheet that shows your calculations. Please send your request to:

College Board SAT Program
Attention: Rescore Request
P.O. Box 6200
Princeton, NJ 08541-6200

Telephone: 609-771-7600

SAT I Score Conversion Table

Raw Score	Verbal Scaled Score	Math Scaled Score	Raw Score	Verbal Scaled Score	Math Scaled Score
78	800		36	500	570
77	800		35	490	560
76	800		34	490	560
75	800		33	480	550
74	800		32	480	540
73	790		31	470	540
72	780		30	460	530
71	760		29	460	520
70	750		28	450	510
69	740		27	450	510
68	730		26	440	500
67	710		25	440	490
66	700		24	430	490
65	700		23	420	480
64	690		22	420	470
63	680		21	410	470
62	670		20	410	460
61	660		19	400	450
60	650	800	18	390	440
59	640	800	17	390	440
58	640	790	16	380	430
57	630	770	15	370	420
56	620	760	14	370	420
55	620	740	13	360	410
54	610	730	12	350	400
53	600	720	11	340	390
52	600	710	10	340	380
51	590	700	9	330	370
50	580	690	8	320	360
49	580	680	7	310	350
48	570	670	6	300	340
47	560	660	5	280	330
46	560	650	4	270	320
45	550	640	3	260	310
44	540	640	2	240	290
43	540	630	1	220	280
42	530	620	0	200	260
41	530	610	-1	200	240
40	520	600	-2	200	220
39	520	600	-3	200	200
38	510	590	and		
37	500	580	below		

This table is for use only with the test in this booklet.

SAT I: Reasoning Test

Sunday, May 2000

YOUR NAME (PRINT) ______________________ LAST FIRST MI

TEST CENTER ______________________ NUMBER NAME OF TEST CENTER ROOM NUMBER

SAT® I: Reasoning Test — General Directions

Timing

- You will have three hours to work on this test.
- There are five 30-minute sections and two 15-minute sections.
- You may work on only one section at a time.
- The supervisor will tell you when to begin and end each section.
- If you finish a section before time is called, check your work on that section. You may NOT turn to any other section.
- Work as rapidly as you can without losing accuracy. Don't waste time on questions that seem too difficult for you.

Marking Answers

- Carefully mark only one answer for each question.
- Make sure each mark is dark and completely fills the oval.
- Do not make any stray marks on your answer sheet.
- If you erase, do so completely. Incomplete erasures may be scored as intended answers.
- Use only the answer spaces that correspond to the question numbers.
- For questions with only four answer choices, an answer marked in oval E will not be scored.
- Use the test book for scratchwork, but you will not receive credit for anything written there.
- You may not transfer answers to your answer sheet or fill in ovals after time has been called.
- You may not fold or remove pages or portions of a page from this book, or take the book or answer sheet from the testing room.

Scoring

- For each correct answer, you receive one point.
- For questions you omit, you receive no points.
- For a wrong answer to a multiple-choice question, you lose a fraction of a point.
  - ► If you can eliminate one or more of the answer choices as wrong, however, you increase your chances of choosing the correct answer and earning one point.
  - ► If you can't eliminate any choice, move on. You can return to the question later if there is time.
- For a wrong answer to a math question that is not multiple-choice, you don't lose any points.

IMPORTANT: The codes below are unique to your test book. Copy them on your answer sheet in boxes 8 and 9 and fill in the corresponding ovals exactly as shown.

8. Form Code

A	A	0	0	0
B	B	1	1	1
C	C	2	2	2
D	D	3	3	3
E	E	4	4	4
F	F	5	5	5
G	G	6	6	6
H	H	7	7	7
I	I	8	8	8
J	J	9	9	9
K	K			
L	L			
M	M			
N	N			
O	O			
P	P			
Q	Q			
R	R			
S	S			
T	T			
U	U			
V	V			
W	W			
X	X			
Y	Y			
Z	Z			

9. Test Form

The passages for this test have been adapted from published material. The ideas contained in them do not necessarily represent the opinions of the College Board or Educational Testing Service.

DO NOT OPEN THIS BOOK UNTIL THE SUPERVISOR TELLS YOU TO DO SO.

THE COLLEGE BOARD — SAT I Page 1

Use a No. 2 pencil only. Be sure each mark is dark and completely fills the intended oval. Completely erase any errors or stray marks.

1. Your Name

First 4 letters of Last Name				First init.	Mid. init.
A–Z	A–Z	A–Z	A–Z	A–Z	A–Z

2.
Your Name: ____________________ (Print) Last First M.I.

I agree to the conditions on the back of the SAT I test book.

Signature: ____________________ Date: ___ / ___ / ___

Home Address: ____________________ (Print) Number and Street

____________________ City State Zip Code

Center: ____________________ (Print) City State Center Number

IMPORTANT: Fill in items 8 and 9 exactly as shown on the back of test book.

3. Date of Birth

Month	Day		Year	
Jan.				
Feb.				
Mar.	0	0	0	0
Apr.	1	1	1	1
May	2	2	2	2
June	3	3	3	3
July		4	4	4
Aug.		5	5	5
Sept.		6	6	6
Oct.		7	7	7
Nov.		8	8	8
Dec.		9		9

4. Social Security Number

(9 columns, each 0–9)

5. Sex

Female ◯ Male ◯

6. Registration Number

(Copy from Admission Ticket.)

(7 columns, each 0–9)

7. Test Book Serial Number

(Copy from front of test book.)

(6 columns, each 0–9)

8. Form Code

(Copy and grid as on back of test book.)

(2 columns A–Z, 3 columns 0–9)

FOR ETS USE ONLY

9. Test Form

(Copy from back of test book.)

Start with number 1 for each new section. If a section has fewer questions than answer spaces, leave the extra answer spaces blank.

SECTION 1

1–40: Ⓐ Ⓑ Ⓒ Ⓓ Ⓔ

SECTION 2

1–40: Ⓐ Ⓑ Ⓒ Ⓓ Ⓔ

Q2778-06/2 CHW98324 11027 • 09132 • TF129M17.5eX I.N. 207158
1 2 3 4

Use a No. 2 pencil only. Be sure each mark is dark and completely fills the intended oval. Completely erase any errors or stray marks.

Start with number 1 for each new section. If a section has fewer questions than answer spaces, leave the extra answer spaces blank.

SECTION 3

1 Ⓐ Ⓑ Ⓒ Ⓓ Ⓔ	16 Ⓐ Ⓑ Ⓒ Ⓓ Ⓔ	31 Ⓐ Ⓑ Ⓒ Ⓓ Ⓔ
2 Ⓐ Ⓑ Ⓒ Ⓓ Ⓔ	17 Ⓐ Ⓑ Ⓒ Ⓓ Ⓔ	32 Ⓐ Ⓑ Ⓒ Ⓓ Ⓔ
3 Ⓐ Ⓑ Ⓒ Ⓓ Ⓔ	18 Ⓐ Ⓑ Ⓒ Ⓓ Ⓔ	33 Ⓐ Ⓑ Ⓒ Ⓓ Ⓔ
4 Ⓐ Ⓑ Ⓒ Ⓓ Ⓔ	19 Ⓐ Ⓑ Ⓒ Ⓓ Ⓔ	34 Ⓐ Ⓑ Ⓒ Ⓓ Ⓔ
5 Ⓐ Ⓑ Ⓒ Ⓓ Ⓔ	20 Ⓐ Ⓑ Ⓒ Ⓓ Ⓔ	35 Ⓐ Ⓑ Ⓒ Ⓓ Ⓔ
6 Ⓐ Ⓑ Ⓒ Ⓓ Ⓔ	21 Ⓐ Ⓑ Ⓒ Ⓓ Ⓔ	36 Ⓐ Ⓑ Ⓒ Ⓓ Ⓔ
7 Ⓐ Ⓑ Ⓒ Ⓓ Ⓔ	22 Ⓐ Ⓑ Ⓒ Ⓓ Ⓔ	37 Ⓐ Ⓑ Ⓒ Ⓓ Ⓔ
8 Ⓐ Ⓑ Ⓒ Ⓓ Ⓔ	23 Ⓐ Ⓑ Ⓒ Ⓓ Ⓔ	38 Ⓐ Ⓑ Ⓒ Ⓓ Ⓔ
9 Ⓐ Ⓑ Ⓒ Ⓓ Ⓔ	24 Ⓐ Ⓑ Ⓒ Ⓓ Ⓔ	39 Ⓐ Ⓑ Ⓒ Ⓓ Ⓔ
10 Ⓐ Ⓑ Ⓒ Ⓓ Ⓔ	25 Ⓐ Ⓑ Ⓒ Ⓓ Ⓔ	40 Ⓐ Ⓑ Ⓒ Ⓓ Ⓔ
11 Ⓐ Ⓑ Ⓒ Ⓓ Ⓔ	26 Ⓐ Ⓑ Ⓒ Ⓓ Ⓔ	
12 Ⓐ Ⓑ Ⓒ Ⓓ Ⓔ	27 Ⓐ Ⓑ Ⓒ Ⓓ Ⓔ	
13 Ⓐ Ⓑ Ⓒ Ⓓ Ⓔ	28 Ⓐ Ⓑ Ⓒ Ⓓ Ⓔ	
14 Ⓐ Ⓑ Ⓒ Ⓓ Ⓔ	29 Ⓐ Ⓑ Ⓒ Ⓓ Ⓔ	
15 Ⓐ Ⓑ Ⓒ Ⓓ Ⓔ	30 Ⓐ Ⓑ Ⓒ Ⓓ Ⓔ	

If section 3 of your test book contains math questions that are not multiple-choice, continue to item 16 below. Otherwise, continue to item 16 above.

ONLY ANSWERS ENTERED IN THE OVALS IN EACH GRID AREA WILL BE SCORED.
YOU WILL NOT RECEIVE CREDIT FOR ANYTHING WRITTEN IN THE BOXES ABOVE THE OVALS.

Grid-in items 16, 17, 18, 19, 20, 21, 22, 23, 24, 25 (each grid: / / ; . . . . ; 0 0 0 ; 1–9 in each of four columns)

BE SURE TO ERASE ANY ERRORS OR STRAY MARKS COMPLETELY.

DO NOT WRITE IN THIS AREA.

0

PLEASE PRINT YOUR INITIALS

First	Middle	Last

Use a No. 2 pencil only. Be sure each mark is dark and completely fills the intended oval. Completely erase any errors or stray marks.

Start with number 1 for each new section. If a section has fewer questions than answer spaces, leave the extra answer spaces blank.

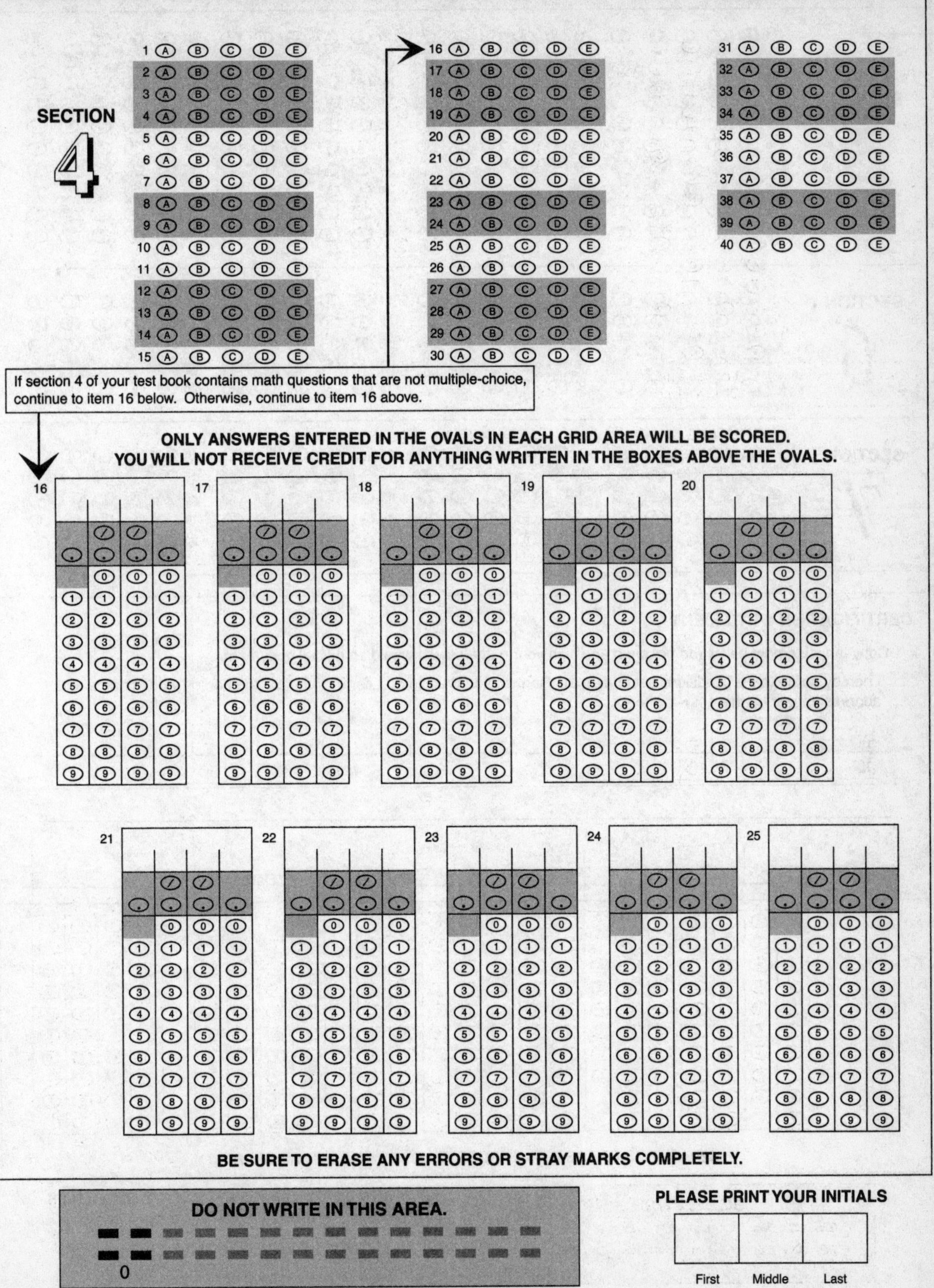

SECTION 4
If section 4 of your test book contains math questions that are not multiple-choice, continue to item 16 below. Otherwise, continue to item 16 above.
ONLY ANSWERS ENTERED IN THE OVALS IN EACH GRID AREA WILL BE SCORED.
YOU WILL NOT RECEIVE CREDIT FOR ANYTHING WRITTEN IN THE BOXES ABOVE THE OVALS.
BE SURE TO ERASE ANY ERRORS OR STRAY MARKS COMPLETELY.

DO NOT WRITE IN THIS AREA.

PLEASE PRINT YOUR INITIALS

First Middle Last

Use a No. 2 pencil only. Be sure each mark is dark and completely fills the intended oval. Completely erase any errors or stray marks.

Start with number 1 for each new section. If a section has fewer questions than answer spaces, leave the extra answer spaces blank.

SECTION 5

1 Ⓐ Ⓑ Ⓒ Ⓓ Ⓔ	11 Ⓐ Ⓑ Ⓒ Ⓓ Ⓔ	21 Ⓐ Ⓑ Ⓒ Ⓓ Ⓔ	31 Ⓐ Ⓑ Ⓒ Ⓓ Ⓔ
2 Ⓐ Ⓑ Ⓒ Ⓓ Ⓔ	12 Ⓐ Ⓑ Ⓒ Ⓓ Ⓔ	22 Ⓐ Ⓑ Ⓒ Ⓓ Ⓔ	32 Ⓐ Ⓑ Ⓒ Ⓓ Ⓔ
3 Ⓐ Ⓑ Ⓒ Ⓓ Ⓔ	13 Ⓐ Ⓑ Ⓒ Ⓓ Ⓔ	23 Ⓐ Ⓑ Ⓒ Ⓓ Ⓔ	33 Ⓐ Ⓑ Ⓒ Ⓓ Ⓔ
4 Ⓐ Ⓑ Ⓒ Ⓓ Ⓔ	14 Ⓐ Ⓑ Ⓒ Ⓓ Ⓔ	24 Ⓐ Ⓑ Ⓒ Ⓓ Ⓔ	34 Ⓐ Ⓑ Ⓒ Ⓓ Ⓔ
5 Ⓐ Ⓑ Ⓒ Ⓓ Ⓔ	15 Ⓐ Ⓑ Ⓒ Ⓓ Ⓔ	25 Ⓐ Ⓑ Ⓒ Ⓓ Ⓔ	35 Ⓐ Ⓑ Ⓒ Ⓓ Ⓔ
6 Ⓐ Ⓑ Ⓒ Ⓓ Ⓔ	16 Ⓐ Ⓑ Ⓒ Ⓓ Ⓔ	26 Ⓐ Ⓑ Ⓒ Ⓓ Ⓔ	36 Ⓐ Ⓑ Ⓒ Ⓓ Ⓔ
7 Ⓐ Ⓑ Ⓒ Ⓓ Ⓔ	17 Ⓐ Ⓑ Ⓒ Ⓓ Ⓔ	27 Ⓐ Ⓑ Ⓒ Ⓓ Ⓔ	37 Ⓐ Ⓑ Ⓒ Ⓓ Ⓔ
8 Ⓐ Ⓑ Ⓒ Ⓓ Ⓔ	18 Ⓐ Ⓑ Ⓒ Ⓓ Ⓔ	28 Ⓐ Ⓑ Ⓒ Ⓓ Ⓔ	38 Ⓐ Ⓑ Ⓒ Ⓓ Ⓔ
9 Ⓐ Ⓑ Ⓒ Ⓓ Ⓔ	19 Ⓐ Ⓑ Ⓒ Ⓓ Ⓔ	29 Ⓐ Ⓑ Ⓒ Ⓓ Ⓔ	39 Ⓐ Ⓑ Ⓒ Ⓓ Ⓔ
10 Ⓐ Ⓑ Ⓒ Ⓓ Ⓔ	20 Ⓐ Ⓑ Ⓒ Ⓓ Ⓔ	30 Ⓐ Ⓑ Ⓒ Ⓓ Ⓔ	40 Ⓐ Ⓑ Ⓒ Ⓓ Ⓔ

SECTION 6

1 Ⓐ Ⓑ Ⓒ Ⓓ Ⓔ	6 Ⓐ Ⓑ Ⓒ Ⓓ Ⓔ	11 Ⓐ Ⓑ Ⓒ Ⓓ Ⓔ	16 Ⓐ Ⓑ Ⓒ Ⓓ Ⓔ
2 Ⓐ Ⓑ Ⓒ Ⓓ Ⓔ	7 Ⓐ Ⓑ Ⓒ Ⓓ Ⓔ	12 Ⓐ Ⓑ Ⓒ Ⓓ Ⓔ	17 Ⓐ Ⓑ Ⓒ Ⓓ Ⓔ
3 Ⓐ Ⓑ Ⓒ Ⓓ Ⓔ	8 Ⓐ Ⓑ Ⓒ Ⓓ Ⓔ	13 Ⓐ Ⓑ Ⓒ Ⓓ Ⓔ	18 Ⓐ Ⓑ Ⓒ Ⓓ Ⓔ
4 Ⓐ Ⓑ Ⓒ Ⓓ Ⓔ	9 Ⓐ Ⓑ Ⓒ Ⓓ Ⓔ	14 Ⓐ Ⓑ Ⓒ Ⓓ Ⓔ	19 Ⓐ Ⓑ Ⓒ Ⓓ Ⓔ
5 Ⓐ Ⓑ Ⓒ Ⓓ Ⓔ	10 Ⓐ Ⓑ Ⓒ Ⓓ Ⓔ	15 Ⓐ Ⓑ Ⓒ Ⓓ Ⓔ	20 Ⓐ Ⓑ Ⓒ Ⓓ Ⓔ

SECTION 7

1 Ⓐ Ⓑ Ⓒ Ⓓ Ⓔ	6 Ⓐ Ⓑ Ⓒ Ⓓ Ⓔ	11 Ⓐ Ⓑ Ⓒ Ⓓ Ⓔ	16 Ⓐ Ⓑ Ⓒ Ⓓ Ⓔ
2 Ⓐ Ⓑ Ⓒ Ⓓ Ⓔ	7 Ⓐ Ⓑ Ⓒ Ⓓ Ⓔ	12 Ⓐ Ⓑ Ⓒ Ⓓ Ⓔ	17 Ⓐ Ⓑ Ⓒ Ⓓ Ⓔ
3 Ⓐ Ⓑ Ⓒ Ⓓ Ⓔ	8 Ⓐ Ⓑ Ⓒ Ⓓ Ⓔ	13 Ⓐ Ⓑ Ⓒ Ⓓ Ⓔ	18 Ⓐ Ⓑ Ⓒ Ⓓ Ⓔ
4 Ⓐ Ⓑ Ⓒ Ⓓ Ⓔ	9 Ⓐ Ⓑ Ⓒ Ⓓ Ⓔ	14 Ⓐ Ⓑ Ⓒ Ⓓ Ⓔ	19 Ⓐ Ⓑ Ⓒ Ⓓ Ⓔ
5 Ⓐ Ⓑ Ⓒ Ⓓ Ⓔ	10 Ⓐ Ⓑ Ⓒ Ⓓ Ⓔ	15 Ⓐ Ⓑ Ⓒ Ⓓ Ⓔ	20 Ⓐ Ⓑ Ⓒ Ⓓ Ⓔ

CERTIFICATION STATEMENT

Copy the statement below (do not print) and sign your name as you would an official document.

I hereby agree to the conditions set forth in the Registration Bulletin and certify that I am the person whose name and address appear on this answer sheet.

____

____

____

Signature: ______________________________ Date: ________________

Time—30 Minutes
30 Questions

For each question in this section, select the best answer from among the choices given and fill in the corresponding oval on the answer sheet.

Each sentence below has one or two blanks, each blank indicating that something has been omitted. Beneath the sentence are five words or sets of words labeled A through E. Choose the word or set of words that, when inserted in the sentence, best fits the meaning of the sentence as a whole.

Example:

Medieval kingdoms did not become constitutional republics overnight; on the contrary, the change was ----.

(A) unpopular
(B) unexpected
(C) advantageous
(D) sufficient
(E) gradual

1 Lacking self-assurance, he was too ---- to ---- controversial topics with people he did not know well.

(A) impassioned . . analyze
(B) timid . . discuss
(C) cautious . . suppress
(D) knowledgeable . . disregard
(E) perceptive . . defend

2 After winning the lottery, John bought sports cars, built a mansion, and wore designer suits, but, by thus ---- his ----, he alienated his friends.

(A) enduring . . hardship
(B) flaunting . . prosperity
(C) undermining . . image
(D) calculating . . successes
(E) moderating . . consumption

3 Ballads often praise popular figures who have performed feats that many perceive as ----, such as defending the poor or resisting ---- authority.

(A) modest . . acceptable
(B) inescapable . . legitimate
(C) insufficient . . overpowering
(D) admirable . . unjust
(E) unbelievable . . tolerable

4 As ---- as the disintegration of the Roman Empire must have seemed, that disaster nevertheless presented some ---- aspects.

(A) momentous . . formidable
(B) decisive . . unavoidable
(C) unexpected . . ambiguous
(D) advantageous . . beneficial
(E) catastrophic . . constructive

5 Predictably, detail-oriented workers are ---- keeping track of the myriad particulars of a situation.

(A) remiss in (B) adept at
(C) humorous about (D) hesitant about
(E) contemptuous of

6 The beauty of Mount McKinley is usually cloaked: clouds ---- the summit nine days out of ten.

(A) release (B) elevate (C) entangle
(D) shroud (E) attain

7 In the opening scene, the playwright creates such a strong impression of the ---- of the main characters that none of their subsequent, apparently honorable actions can ---- these characters in the eyes of the audience.

(A) integrity . . discredit
(B) conviction . . justify
(C) corruption . . redeem
(D) dignity . . excuse
(E) degradation . . convict

8 By allowing one printer to be used by several computers, this device ---- the need for many separate printers.

(A) accelerates (B) predetermines
(C) substantiates (D) precludes
(E) anticipates

9 In an attempt to malign and misrepresent their opponents, some candidates resort to ----.

(A) arbitration (B) narcissism
(C) calumny (D) tenacity
(E) solicitude

GO ON TO THE NEXT PAGE

Each question below consists of a related pair of words or phrases, followed by five pairs of words or phrases labeled A through E. Select the pair that best expresses a relationship similar to that expressed in the original pair.

Example:

CRUMB : BREAD ::
(A) ounce : unit
(B) splinter : wood
(C) water : bucket
(D) twine : rope
(E) cream : butter

10 GAZE : OBSERVER ::
(A) hear : listener
(B) banish : exile
(C) separate : joint
(D) operate : doctor
(E) sprain : ankle

11 ODOMETER : DISTANCE ::
(A) microscope : size
(B) decibel : loudness
(C) orchestra : instrument
(D) computer : data
(E) scale : weight

12 COPYRIGHT : BOOK ::
(A) franchise : license
(B) lease : owner
(C) patent : design
(D) trademark : registration
(E) brand : manufacturer

13 FEIGN : DECEIVE ::
(A) flee : elude
(B) dangle : drop
(C) send : receive
(D) contract : lengthen
(E) publish : write

14 ETHOS : VALUES ::
(A) accord : nations
(B) code : principles
(C) policy : officials
(D) debate : opinions
(E) offense : criminals

15 TORPID : SLUGGISH ::
(A) wrong : apologetic
(B) refracted : direct
(C) comic : funny
(D) sad : empathetic
(E) merry : morose

GO ON TO THE NEXT PAGE

Each passage below is followed by questions based on its content. Answer the questions on the basis of what is <u>stated</u> or <u>implied</u> in each passage and in any introductory material that may be provided.

Questions 16-20 are based on the following passage.

This excerpt from a novel by a Chinese American author is about a Chinese American woman named June. During a family dinner party attended by some of June's Chinese American friends, Waverly, a tax attorney, discusses an advertisement that June wrote for her.

Waverly laughed in a lighthearted way. "I mean, really, June." And then she started in a deep television-announcer voice: "*Three* benefits, *three* needs, *three* reasons to buy . . . . Satisfaction *guaranteed* . . . ."

She said this in such a funny way that everybody thought it was a good joke and laughed. And then, to make matters worse, I heard my mother saying to Waverly: "True, one can't teach style. June is not sophisticated like you. She must have been born this way."

I was surprised at myself, how humiliated I felt. I had been outsmarted by Waverly once again, and now betrayed by my own mother.

. . . .

Five months ago, some time after the dinner, my mother gave me my "life's importance," a jade pendant on a gold chain. The pendant was not a piece of jewelry I would have chosen for myself. It was almost the size of my little finger, a mottled green and white color, intricately carved. To me, the whole effect looked wrong: too large, too green, too garishly ornate. I stuffed the necklace in my lacquer box and forgot about it.

But these days, I think about my life's importance. I wonder what it means, because my mother died three months ago, six days before my thirty-sixth birthday. And she's the only person I could have asked to tell me about life's importance, to help me understand my grief.

I now wear that pendant every day. I think the carvings mean something, because shapes and details, which I never seem to notice until after they're pointed out to me, always mean something to Chinese people. I know I could ask Auntie Lindo, Auntie An-mei, or other Chinese friends, but I also know they would tell me a meaning that is different from what my mother intended. What if they tell me this curving line branching into three oval shapes is a pomegranate and that my mother was wishing me fertility and posterity? What if my mother really meant the carvings were a branch of pears to give me purity and honesty?

And because I think about this all the time, I always notice other people wearing these same jade pendants—not the flat rectangular medallions or the round white ones with holes in the middle but ones like mine, a two-inch oblong of bright apple green. It's as though we were all sworn to the same secret covenant, so secret we don't even know what we belong to. Last weekend, for example, I saw a bartender wearing one. As I fingered mine, I asked him, "Where'd you get yours?"

"My mother gave it to me," he said.

I asked him why, which is a nosy question that only one Chinese person can ask another; in a crowd of Caucasians, two Chinese people are already like family.

"She gave it to me after I got divorced. I guess my mother's telling me I'm still worth something."

And I knew by the wonder in his voice that he had no idea what the pendant really meant.

16 In lines 1-5, Waverly characterizes June's advertisement as being

(A) unsophisticated and heavy-handed
(B) somber and convoluted
(C) clear and concise
(D) humorous and effective
(E) clever and lively

GO ON TO THE NEXT PAGE

17 In the context of the passage, the statement "I was surprised at myself" (line 12) suggests that June

(A) had been unaware of the extent of her emotional vulnerability
(B) was exasperated that she allowed Waverly to embarrass her in public
(C) was amazed that she could dislike anyone so much
(D) had not realized that her mother admired her friend Waverly
(E) felt guilty about how much she resented her own mother

18 For June, a significant aspect of what happened at the dinner party is that

(A) her mother had taken great pains to make Waverly feel welcome
(B) her mother had criticized her for arguing with Waverly
(C) her mother had sided against her in front of family and friends
(D) Waverly had angered June's mother
(E) Waverly had lied to June's mother

19 The description of June's encounter with the bartender primarily serves to suggest that

(A) the relationship of mother and son is different from that of mother and daughter
(B) June is not the only one who ponders the meaning of a jade pendant
(C) a jade pendant symbolizes the mystery of life and death
(D) June finally understands the true meaning of her jade pendant
(E) strangers are easier to talk to than family members and friends

20 The passage indicates that the act of giving a jade pendant can best be described as

(A) a widely observed tradition
(B) a mother's plea for forgiveness
(C) an example of a mother's extravagance
(D) an unprecedented act of generosity
(E) an unremarkable event in June's life

GO ON TO THE NEXT PAGE

Questions 21-30 are based on the following passage.

The author of this excerpt discusses the relationship of art to history and politics, particularly during the period of political violence, persecution, and upheaval immediately preceding the Second World War.

In his famous poem on the death of the Irish poet and visionary W. B. Yeats, the English poet W. H. Auden wrote, "Ireland has her madness and her weather still / For poetry makes nothing happen." Elsewhere, Auden, with his characteristic and endearing honesty, commented that all the verse he wrote, all the political views that he expressed in the 1930's did not save a single Jewish person from Nazi persecution. "Those attitudes," he wrote, "only help oneself":

> Artists and politicians would get along better at a time of crisis like the present, if the latter would only realize that the political history of the world would have been the same if not a poem had been written, nor a picture painted, nor a bar of music composed.

This of course is an empirical claim, and it is difficult to know how true it is because it is difficult to explain in historical terms. In any case, as we know, even works intended to prick our consciousness to political concern have tended to provoke at best an admiration for the works themselves and a moral self-admiration on the part of those who admired them. During the Spanish Civil War (1936-1939), the cynical bombing of the Spanish town of Guernica by Nazi warplanes made the painting *Guernica*, which expressed the horror of the event, happen. Therefore, it was not merely wit when *Guernica's* painter, Pablo Picasso, answered a Nazi officer who showed him a postcard of the painting and asked, "Did you do that?" with "No, you did." Everyone knew who did what and why: the bombing was an atrocity meant by its perpetrators to be perceived as an atrocity committed by ruthless fighters. The painting was used as a fund-raiser for the victims of the war in Spain, but those who paid money for the privilege of filing past it only used it as a mirror to reflect attitudes *already* in place, and in later years it required art-historical knowledge to know what was going on: it hung in the Museum of Modern Art as a handsome backdrop, and it was sufficiently attractive in its gray and black harmonies that an article on interior decoration described how a copy of the painting ornamented a sophisticated modern kitchen where fancy meals were concocted for bright and brittle guests. So in the end it did about as much for the devastated townspeople as Auden's verses did for the people and causes he wrote about, making nothing relevant happen, simply memorializing, enshrining, spiritualizing, about at the same level as a solemn ritual whose function is to confess the extreme limitation of our powers to make anything happen.

Fine, some would say. But if the sole political role of poetry is this deflected, consolatory, ceremonial—not to say reliquary—office, why is the political attitude that *art is dangerous* so pervasive in our society? The history of art is the history of the suppression of art. This suppression is itself a kind of futility if the art that one seeks to cast in chains has no effectiveness whatsoever, and one confers upon the art the illusion of competency by treating as dangerous what would make nothing happen if it were allowed to be free. Where, if Auden is right, does the belief in the dangerousness of art come from? Indeed, construing art, as Auden does, as a causally or politically neutered activity is itself an act of neutralization. Representing art as something that in its nature can make nothing happen is not so much a view opposed to the view that art is dangerous as it is a way of responding to the sensed danger of art by treating art as though it were nothing to be afraid of.

21 The author's main point about the relationship between art and politics is that

(A) Auden's view of the role of art is more widely accepted than the view that art is dangerous
(B) Auden's denial of the political impact of art is somewhat misleading
(C) artists such as Auden and Yeats incorporate political concerns in their art
(D) artists and the people who admire their creations have different ideas about the political role of art
(E) politicians suppress art that has the potential to cause undesirable political changes

22 Auden believed that artists and politicians would "get along better at a time of crisis" (lines 11-12) if politicians would

(A) heed the messages that artists convey through art
(B) remember the contributions that artists have made to culture through the ages
(C) admit that art speaks in a language that is incomprehensible to politicians
(D) recognize that art does not affect the course of history
(E) acknowledge the role of artists in shaping the consciousness of a nation

GO ON TO THE NEXT PAGE

23 The author emphasizes the word "already" (line 38) in order to stress the point that

(A) Picasso's painting was perceived as just another artist's depiction of war
(B) Picasso's political attitudes were widely known
(C) Picasso's painting did not cause a change in political attitudes
(D) Picasso did not expect his painting to be so controversial
(E) Picasso had not thought his painting would be so quickly acclaimed

24 The author refers to "art-historical knowledge" (lines 39-40) in order to emphasize which point about Picasso's *Guernica* ?

(A) Most art historians share Auden's view of art.
(B) The original purpose of the painting gradually became obscure.
(C) The painting continues to memorialize those who were killed in the bombing of Guernica.
(D) Art historians continue to discuss the artistic merits of the painting.
(E) The Museum of Modern Art is an appropriate setting for the painting.

25 The tone of the description in lines 42-46 ("and it was . . . guests") is one of

(A) sorrow
(B) admiration
(C) indifference
(D) sympathy
(E) sarcasm

26 In discussing Picasso's *Guernica*, the author indicates that the painting's ultimate accomplishment was

(A) providing a politically effective condemnation of an atrocity
(B) heightening political consciousness among its viewers
(C) commemorating a terrible event
(D) gaining Picasso recognition as a political activist
(E) revealing the versatility of Picasso's artistic talent

27 The author would probably characterize "some" (line 54) as being

(A) understandably content to follow a practical course of action
(B) relieved that a difficult decision has been made
(C) agreeable to a compromise that would weaken the author's argument
(D) reluctant to compare the concerns of artists with those of politicians
(E) convinced that art has a limited political role

28 In line 68, the word "neutralization" refers to an act of

(A) making objective
(B) blending with something that counteracts
(C) bringing to destruction
(D) rendering ineffective
(E) prohibiting conflict

29 The author concludes that "Representing art as something that in its nature can make nothing happen" (lines 68-70) is actually

(A) proof that art is subversive
(B) an activity that in itself is inconsequential
(C) the only valid response to art
(D) a reaction to perceptions about art's power
(E) an act of defiance in response to political pressures

30 The author's strategy in the passage is best described as

(A) relating an incident and then explaining its significance
(B) refuting an argument and then examining a counterargument
(C) presenting a position and then criticizing it
(D) summarizing an achievement and then analyzing it
(E) describing several examples and then explaining how they differ from one another

NOTE: The reading passages in this test are brief excerpts or adaptations of excerpts from published material. The ideas contained in them do not necessarily represent the opinions of the College Board or Educational Testing Service. To make the text suitable for testing purposes, we may in some cases have altered the style, contents, or point of view of the original.

IF YOU FINISH BEFORE TIME IS CALLED, YOU MAY CHECK YOUR WORK ON THIS SECTION ONLY. DO NOT TURN TO ANY OTHER SECTION IN THE TEST. **STOP**

Section 2

2 2 2 2 2

Time—30 Minutes
25 Questions

In this section solve each problem, using any available space on the page for scratchwork. Then decide which is the best of the choices given and fill in the corresponding oval on the answer sheet.

Notes:

1. The use of a calculator is permitted. All numbers used are real numbers.

2. Figures that accompany problems in this test are intended to provide information useful in solving the problems. They are drawn as accurately as possible EXCEPT when it is stated in a specific problem that the figure is not drawn to scale. All figures lie in a plane unless otherwise indicated.

Reference Information

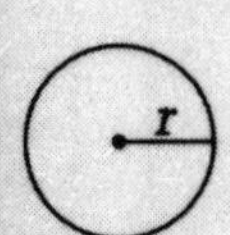
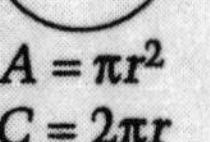

$A = \pi r^2$
$C = 2\pi r$

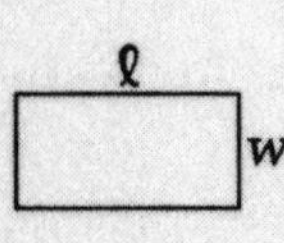

$A = \ell w$

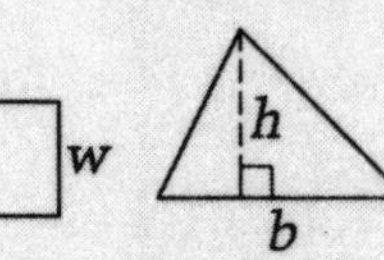

$A = \frac{1}{2}bh$

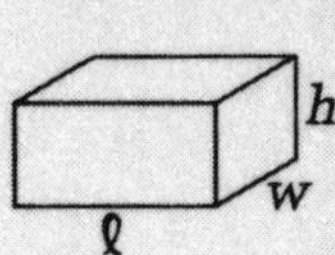

$V = \ell wh$

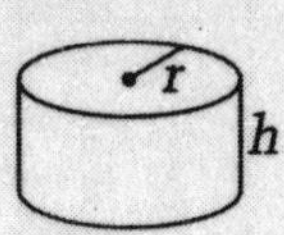

$V = \pi r^2 h$

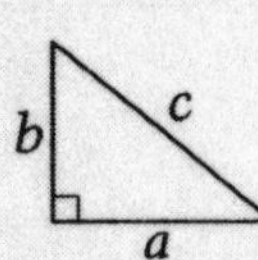

$c^2 = a^2 + b^2$

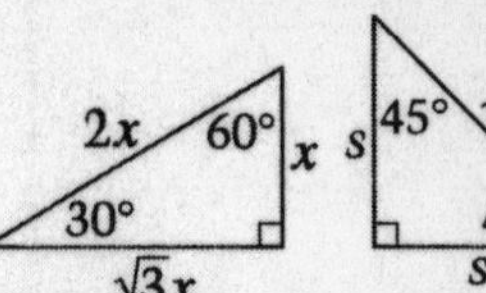

Special Right Triangles

The number of degrees of arc in a circle is 360.
The measure in degrees of a straight angle is 180.
The sum of the measures in degrees of the angles of a triangle is 180.

1 If $n + n + n + n + 1 = 2 + n + n + n$, what is the value of n?

(A) 1
(B) 2
(C) 3
(D) 4
(E) 7

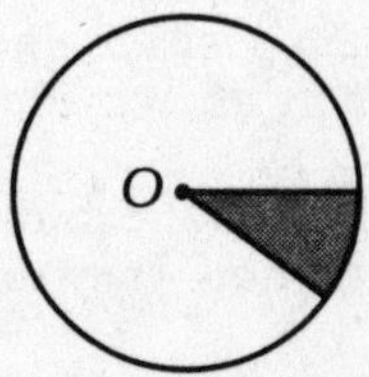

2 O is the center of the circle above. Approximately what percent of the circle is shaded?

(A) 1%
(B) 10%
(C) 25%
(D) 50%
(E) 75%

3 Which of the following numbers is greater than 0.428 ?

(A) 0.053
(B) 0.42
(C) 0.43
(D) 0.419
(E) 0.4228

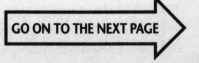

GO ON TO THE NEXT PAGE

4 Karen's salary is greater than Margot's but less than Henrietta's. If k, m, and h represent each of their salaries, respectively, which of the following is true?

(A) $h < k < m$
(B) $k < h < m$
(C) $k < m < h$
(D) $m < h < k$
(E) $m < k < h$

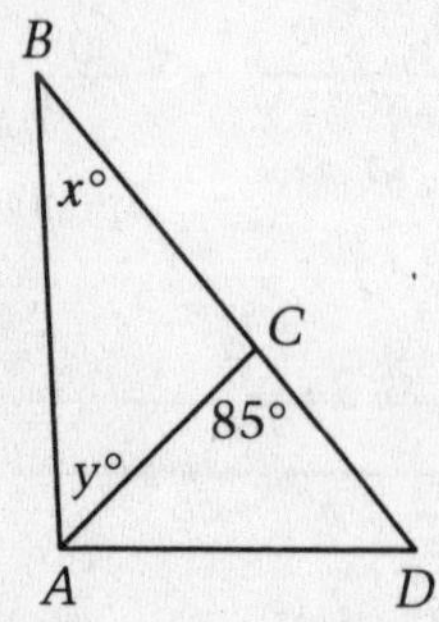

Note: Figure not drawn to scale.

5 In $\triangle ABD$ above, if $y = 40$, what is the value of x?

(A) 25
(B) 30
(C) 35
(D) 40
(E) 45

6 Chuck is writing the page number on the bottom of each page of a 25-page book report, starting with 1. How many digits will he have written after he has written the number 25?

(A) 35
(B) 40
(C) 41
(D) 49
(E) 50

7 Tim had $2b$ books for sale at a price of k dollars each. If y is the number of books he did not sell, which of the following represents the total dollar amount he received in sales from the books?

(A) $k(2b - y)$
(B) $k(y - 2b)$
(C) $ky - 2b$
(D) $2b - ky$
(E) $2bk - y$

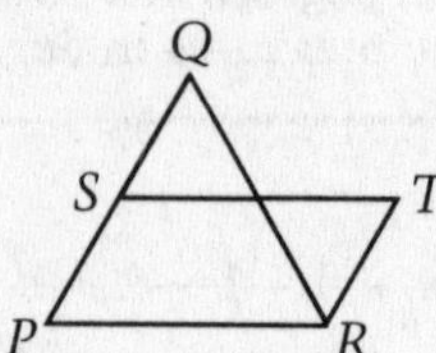

8 In the figure above, $\triangle PQR$ is equilateral and $PSTR$ is a parallelogram. If S is the midpoint of PQ and the perimeter of $\triangle PQR$ is 6, what is the perimeter of $PSTR$?

(A) 9
(B) 8
(C) 6
(D) 4
(E) 3

GO ON TO THE NEXT PAGE

9 Five balls, each of radius $2\frac{1}{2}$ inches, are placed side by side in a straight row with adjacent balls touching. What is the distance, in inches, between the center of the first ball and the center of the last ball?

(A) 15

(B) $17\frac{1}{2}$

(C) 20

(D) $22\frac{1}{2}$

(E) 25

10 The average (arithmetic mean) of nine numbers is 9. When a tenth number is added, the average of the ten numbers is also 9. What is the tenth number?

(A) 0

(B) $\frac{9}{10}$

(C) $\frac{10}{9}$

(D) 9

(E) 10

$$\begin{array}{r} 1A \\ +\ \ A \\ \hline 2B \end{array}$$

11 In the correctly solved addition problem above, A and B represent digits. If A is not equal to B, how many different digits from 0 through 9 could A represent?

(A) Two
(B) Three
(C) Five
(D) Seven
(E) Nine

12 When 247 is divided by 6, the remainder is r, and when 247 is divided by 12, the remainder is s. What is the value of $r - s$?

(A) -6
(B) -1
(C) 0
(D) 1
(E) 6

GO ON TO THE NEXT PAGE

<u>Questions 13-14</u> refer to the following coordinate system.

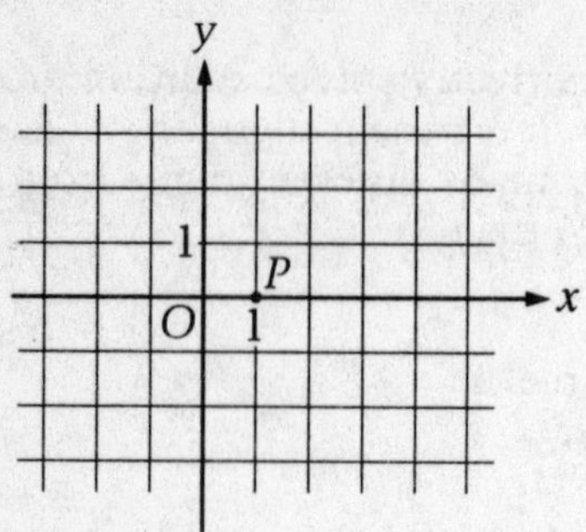

13 Point T (not shown) is located by beginning at P, moving 1 unit up and then moving 2 units to the right. What is the slope of line PT ?

(A) $\frac{1}{3}$

(B) $\frac{1}{2}$

(C) 1

(D) 2

(E) 3

---

14 Line ℓ (not shown) contains point P and has slope 5. Which of the following points is on line ℓ ?

(A) (0, 5)
(B) (1, 5)
(C) (2, 5)
(D) (5, 1)
(E) (5, 5)

15 The quantity (3×8^{12}) is how many times the quantity (3×8^{5}) ?

(A) 7
(B) 8
(C) 21
(D) 8^7
(E) 3×8^7

---

16 The dogs in a certain kennel are fed Brand A and Brand B dog food only. Of these dogs, 6 dogs eat Brand A and 15 dogs eat Brand B. If 4 of the dogs that eat Brand B also eat Brand A, how many dogs are in the kennel?

(A) 17
(B) 19
(C) 21
(D) 25
(E) 29

---

17 On a number line, point A has coordinate -3 and point B has coordinate 12. Point P is $\frac{2}{3}$ of the way from A to B. What is the coordinate of point P ?

(A) -1
(B) 2
(C) 6
(D) 7
(E) 10

GO ON TO THE NEXT PAGE

18 If the ratio of two positive integers is 3 to 2, which of the following statements about these integers CANNOT be true?

(A) Their sum is an odd integer.
(B) Their sum is an even integer.
(C) Their product is divisible by 6.
(D) Their product is an even integer.
(E) Their product is an odd integer.

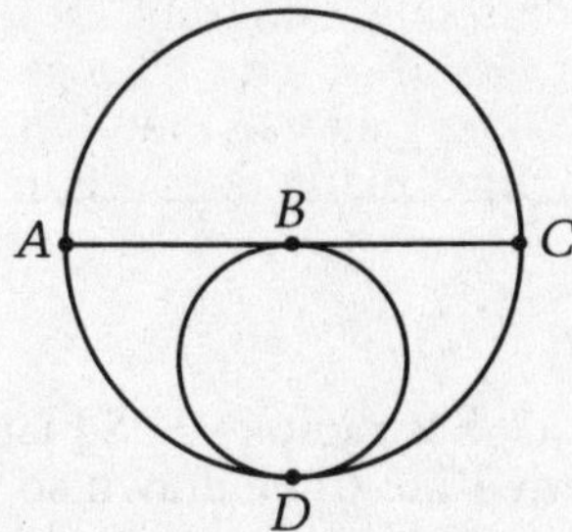

19 In the figure above, B is the center of the larger circle. The smaller circle is tangent to the larger circle at D and contains point B. If the length of diameter AC is 12, what is the area of the smaller circle?

(A) 6π
(B) 9π
(C) 12π
(D) 16π
(E) 36π

x	1	2	3	4
y	$\frac{(0)(2)}{3}$	$\frac{(1)(3)}{5}$	$\frac{(2)(4)}{7}$	$\frac{(3)(5)}{9}$

20 Of the following equations, which describes the relationship between x and y in the table above?

(A) $y = \dfrac{2x - 2}{x + 2}$

(B) $y = \dfrac{2x - 1}{x + 3}$

(C) $y = \dfrac{(x - 1)(x + 1)}{2x + 1}$

(D) $y = \dfrac{(x - 1)(2x - 2)}{2x + 1}$

(E) $y = \dfrac{2^x}{2x + 1}$

21 S is the sum of the first 100 consecutive positive even integers, and T is the sum of the first 100 consecutive positive integers. S is what percent greater than T?

(A) 100%
(B) 50%
(C) 10%
(D) 2%
(E) 1%

GO ON TO THE NEXT PAGE

Product	Number of People Choosing Product
W	37
X	51
Y	m
Z	n

22 The table above shows the results of a survey of 200 people in which each person chose exactly 1 of 4 products. If m and n are positive integers, what is the greatest possible value of n ?

(A) 12
(B) 56
(C) 111
(D) 112
(E) 200

23 If $kn \neq k$ and $n = \frac{1}{k}$, which of the following expressions is equivalent to $\frac{1-k}{1-n}$?

(A) $-n$
(B) $-k$
(C) 1
(D) k
(E) n

24 The first two numbers of a sequence are 1 and 3, respectively. The third number is 4, and, in general, every number after the second is the sum of the two numbers immediately preceding it. How many of the first 1,000 numbers in this sequence are odd?

(A) 333
(B) 500
(C) 665
(D) 666
(E) 667

25 Circle C has radius $\sqrt{2}$. Squares with sides of length 1 are to be drawn so that, for each square, one vertex is on circle C and the rest of the square is inside circle C. What is the greatest number of such squares that can be drawn if the squares do not have overlapping areas?

(A) None
(B) One
(C) Two
(D) Three
(E) Four

IF YOU FINISH BEFORE TIME IS CALLED, YOU MAY CHECK YOUR WORK ON THIS SECTION ONLY. DO NOT TURN TO ANY OTHER SECTION IN THE TEST. **STOP**

Section 3 3 3 3 3 3 3

Time—30 Minutes
36 Questions

For each question in this section, select the best answer from among the choices given and fill in the corresponding oval on the answer sheet.

Each sentence below has one or two blanks, each blank indicating that something has been omitted. Beneath the sentence are five words or sets of words labeled A through E. Choose the word or set of words that, when inserted in the sentence, best fits the meaning of the sentence as a whole.

Example:

Medieval kingdoms did not become constitutional republics overnight; on the contrary, the change was ----.

(A) unpopular
(B) unexpected
(C) advantageous
(D) sufficient
(E) gradual

1 The stage director insisted that before the next performance the set be ---- to eliminate its dinginess.

(A) requisitioned (B) enlarged (C) refurbished (D) demolished (E) relocated

2 Most pioneers ---- this valley on their journey to the West because its rugged terrain and frequent landslides made it a ---- place for travelers.

(A) flanked . . fascinating
(B) avoided . . necessary
(C) encompassed . . curious
(D) enjoyed . . troublesome
(E) skirted . . hazardous

3 Most people would be amazed to discover how ---- their recollections are, even those memories of which they are most ----.

(A) unpleasant . . frightened
(B) repressed . . unaware
(C) inaccurate . . certain
(D) amorphous . . unsure
(E) trustworthy . . confident

4 Perhaps the most visible sign of the ---- nature of the Cherokee nation was the fact that the women who led each clan picked the chief.

(A) stoic (B) matriarchal (C) defensive (D) caustic (E) didactic

5 Castillo's poetry has generated only enthusiastic response: praise from the general public and ---- from the major critics.

(A) condemnation (B) sarcasm (C) plaudits (D) irony (E) pathos

6 Many scientists have such specialized expertise that they look only at ---- aspects of nature, but ecologists are concerned with the ---- of the natural environment.

(A) complex . . purity
(B) detailed . . paradox
(C) isolated . . totality
(D) universal . . balance
(E) distant . . erosion

7 Notoriously ---- regarding issues of national security, the Prime Minister dumbfounded her opponents when she ---- a defense appropriations bill they had expected her to contest.

(A) evenhanded . . muddled
(B) compliant . . conceded on
(C) pacific . . opposed
(D) intransigent . . compromised on
(E) rancorous . . railed against

8 Leslie thoroughly ---- the text to avoid any lawsuits that might arise because of the new obscenity law.

(A) condensed (B) delineated (C) exterminated (D) expurgated (E) transcribed

9 The skepticism of some ancient philosophers ---- and helps to elucidate varieties of nihilism that appeared in the early nineteenth century.

(A) suppresses (B) disseminates (C) undermines (D) confounds (E) foreshadows

10 The doctor ---- so frequently on disease-prevention techniques that her colleagues accused her of ----.

(A) vacillated . . inconsistency
(B) sermonized . . fidelity
(C) wavered . . steadfastness
(D) experimented . . inflexibility
(E) relied . . negligence

GO ON TO THE NEXT PAGE

Each question below consists of a related pair of words or phrases, followed by five pairs of words or phrases labeled A through E. Select the pair that best expresses a relationship similar to that expressed in the original pair.

Example:

CRUMB : BREAD ::
(A) ounce : unit
(B) splinter : wood
(C) water : bucket
(D) twine : rope
(E) cream : butter

Ⓐ ● Ⓒ Ⓓ Ⓔ

11 RULER : LINE ::
(A) stamp : letter
(B) period : dot
(C) key : door
(D) compass : circle
(E) thermometer : degree

12 CATNAP : SLEEP ::
(A) exhaustion : slumber
(B) blink : eye
(C) snack : meal
(D) swallow : bite
(E) feast : banquet

13 MANAGER : STORE ::
(A) technician : laboratory
(B) student : school
(C) administrator : hospital
(D) spectator : arena
(E) president : electorate

14 WALLET : MONEY ::
(A) safe : lock
(B) suitcase : clothing
(C) camera : film
(D) setting : jewel
(E) car : engine

15 LUBRICATE : SMOOTHLY ::
(A) weigh : heavily
(B) assist : grudgingly
(C) speak : softly
(D) muffle : quietly
(E) absorb : quickly

16 BIRD : AVIAN ::
(A) plant : tropical
(B) meat : carnivorous
(C) snake : slippery
(D) dog : canine
(E) lung : amphibian

17 IRRATIONAL : LOGIC ::
(A) unrealistic : understanding
(B) unethical : morality
(C) illegible : erasure
(D) infinite : expansion
(E) factual : verification

18 CONSTELLATION : STARS ::
(A) construction : houses
(B) honey : bees
(C) map : boundaries
(D) train : passengers
(E) range : mountains

19 CALCULATOR : COMPUTE ::
(A) plug : insert
(B) clamp : grip
(C) saddle : straddle
(D) bridge : suspend
(E) incinerator : warm

20 EXTRAVAGANT : SPEND ::
(A) belligerent : fight
(B) remarkable : surprise
(C) charitable : receive
(D) antagonistic : agree
(E) persuasive : believe

21 ARCHITECT : BLUEPRINT ::
(A) instructor : blackboard
(B) graduate : diploma
(C) musician : note
(D) painter : brush
(E) composer : score

22 WEAVE : FABRIC ::
(A) illustrate : manual
(B) hang : picture
(C) sew : thread
(D) bake : oven
(E) write : text

23 TESTIMONY : WITNESS ::
(A) leadership : follower
(B) proof : theorist
(C) expertise : authority
(D) contradiction : investigator
(E) confiscation : official

GO ON TO THE NEXT PAGE

The two passages below are followed by questions based on their content and on the relationship between the two passages. Answer the questions on the basis of what is stated or implied in the passages and in any introductory material that may be provided.

Questions 24-36 are based on the following passages.

The New England town meeting, discussed in these passages, is an institution of local government that had its origins in the 1600's.

Passage 1

In their remoteness from the seat of government in London, colonial New Englanders necessarily created simple new forms of self-government. The New England town meetings had an uncertain precedent in the vestry meetings of parishes in rural England, but New World circumstances gave town meetings comprehensive powers and a new vitality.

The New England town meetings, which met first weekly, then monthly, came to include all the men who had settled the town. At first, the meetings seem to have been confined to men labeled "freemen," those who satisfied the legal requirements for voting in the colony. Soon the towns developed their own sort of "freemen"—a group larger than those whom the General Court of the colony recognized as those granted rights to land. While the town meetings proved to be lively and sometimes acrimonious debating societies, they were more than that. They distributed town lands used by individuals on a rotating basis, they levied local taxes, they made crucial decisions about schools, roads, and bridges, and they elected the selectmen, constables, and others to conduct town affairs between meetings.

The laws of one colony, the Massachusetts Bay colony, gradually gave form to the town meetings. A law of 1692 required that meetings be held annually in March and enumerated the officers to be elected. A law of 1715 required the selection of moderators, gave them the power to impose fines on those who spoke without permission during meetings, and authorized any ten or more property owners to put items on the agenda. But as the movement for independence gathered momentum, a British Parliamentary Act of 1774 decreed that no town meeting should be held to discuss affairs of government without written permission from the royal governor.

Passage 2

Nationalistic pride in the myth of the venerable New England town meeting is entirely understandable. Nothing else so embodies the democratic ideal in the United States. Who can resist the thought that life would be better if we the people could just run our own affairs the way they used to in the old-fashioned New England town meetings?

A mainstay of the New England mythology is the presumption that at town meetings everybody was allowed to vote. But the impression that the town meetings of old were free, democratic, and civilized is far too simplistic. For one thing, the "everybody" who could vote did not include women, Black people, American Indians, and White men who did not own property. In the seventeenth century it was not "the people" who ran the town meetings; it was the town selectmen. It was they who levied the taxes, passed the laws, punished the disorderly, and settled disputes between neighbors.

However, in early colonial Dedham, Massachusetts, there was a time when the townsfolk themselves actually made all the big decisions at town meetings. Here was the direct, participatory democracy in which Americans take such pride. A great and noble experiment, it lasted all of three years and was abandoned by 1639, soon after the town was established.

Historians who study the operation of the town meetings have revealed that the people in the colonial era exercised little control at all over their own affairs. For one thing, meetings were held so infrequently that townsfolk had little opportunity even to monitor their elected representatives. On average, two meetings were held a year. When meetings were called, it was the selectmen who set the agenda and they who controlled the discussion. Only rarely did townsfolk challenge the decisions the selectmen made.

Ultimately the power did rest with the townsfolk if they wanted it. But frequently, they did not. The people were too busy plowing their fields and clearing the forests to bother with government. More importantly, many did not think they were equipped for governing. In Dedham, people willingly left governing up to those who were well-off, old, and devout. Once elected, selectmen tended to be elected over and over again, remaining in office for decades.

GO ON TO THE NEXT PAGE

It can be argued that because the selectmen were elected by the townspeople, the process was indirectly democratic. It was. The statistics show, for example, that in the 1640's up to 90 percent of the adult males could vote in Dedham in town elections. Some historians go so far as to say that anybody could vote. All one had to do, they say, was show up, even if one could not meet the legal property qualifications.

Perhaps, but the suffrage laws must have meant something, and through the seventeenth century, the suffrage was increasingly restricted. While upward of 90 percent of adult White males could vote in Massachusetts in the 1630's, by the 1680's, says colonial historian Kenneth Lockridge, "a majority of men held no suffrage whatsoever."

24 Passage 1 is best described as a

(A) tactful response to a controversial question
(B) personal assessment of a confusing situation
(C) scathing condemnation of an outdated concept
(D) general overview of a political institution
(E) theoretical statement about the value of self-government

25 Passage 1 suggests that the most significant innovation of the town meeting was the

(A) rejection of the parish as being equivalent to the town
(B) collective decision-making by ordinary citizens
(C) creation of a local arena for discussion of issues of national interest
(D) community approval of taxes and expenditures
(E) definition of "freemen" as a new group in rural society

26 In passage 1, the author's attitude toward the participants in town meetings is best described as

(A) admiration of their loyalty to a political ideal
(B) respect for their active involvement in local government
(C) sympathy with their frustration with meeting at infrequent intervals
(D) affection for their naïve trust in purely democratic institutions
(E) amusement at their willingness to carry petty arguments to local officials

27 The author of Passage 1 refers to the Parliamentary Act of 1774 to make the point that town meetings

(A) were perceived as fostering political self-determination
(B) were regarded as forums for class conflict
(C) enjoyed prestige only in New England
(D) had no counterparts in local English government
(E) represented a long tradition of local self-rule

28 In Passage 2, the author attempts to

(A) compare two erroneous views
(B) perpetuate old-fashioned historical beliefs
(C) explain reasons underlying a poor decision
(D) correct a misconception
(E) argue for changing a deplorable situation

29 In lines 39-45, the author of Passage 2 expresses which of the following for supporters of the myth?

(A) Scorn
(B) Impatience
(C) Dismay
(D) Admiration
(E) Sympathy

30 In lines 53-55, ("In . . . selectmen"), the author of Passage 2 distinguishes between the

(A) general population and a small group
(B) earliest colonizers and the earliest inhabitants
(C) rural population and the population of towns
(D) agricultural labor force and an aristocratic class
(E) highly educated elite and an illiterate minority

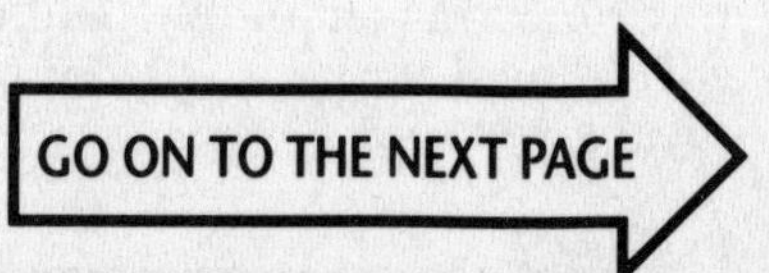

31 In Passage 2, the author describes the "experiment" (line 63) in a tone that

(A) objectively summarizes crucial events in a typical town
(B) enthusiastically reveals a startling discovery
(C) mildly scolds historians who support inaccurate interpretations
(D) gently mocks false notions about town meetings
(E) sharply criticizes the disastrous errors of the first settlers

32 The discussion of Dedham (lines 58-65) serves what function in the development of the argument in Passage 2 ?

(A) It provides a detailed examination of a case that illustrates an overall pattern.
(B) It refers to an expert to confirm the author's viewpoint.
(C) It gives an example of a fact uncovered only recently by historians.
(D) It compares an atypical, verified example with an inaccurate generalization.
(E) It contrasts a historical incident with a legendary event.

33 Passage 2 suggests that the statement in lines 8-10 ("The New England . . . . town") should be qualified by which additional information?

(A) The group was based on a definition set by rural English parishes.
(B) The classification was significantly altered by the British legislation of 1774.
(C) The tradition rejected the claims of female residents of Dedham to full voting rights.
(D) The standard did not recognize property owners as substantial contributors of tax revenues.
(E) The category did not include numerous adults of the community.

34 Which detail discussed in Passage 1 is most consistent with the generalization in lines 72-76 ("When . . . made")?

(A) The existence of vestry meetings in English parishes
(B) The amenities on which tax revenues were spent
(C) The limit on attendance at town meetings to those designated as freemen
(D) The Massachusetts Bay colony law of 1715
(E) The Parliamentary Act of 1774

35 Both passages support which generalization about the seventeenth-century town meeting?

(A) Voters were well informed about political issues.
(B) Participants had to have certain qualifications.
(C) Town leaders were frequently replaced after an election.
(D) Meetings discussed matters of national interest.
(E) The most heated debates were about taxes.

36 Which statement best describes a significant difference between the two interpretations of how local taxes were set and collected?

(A) Passage 1 discusses the burden on taxpayers; Passage 2, the expenses to be met.
(B) Passage 1 emphasizes details of the process; Passage 2, the results of the process.
(C) Passage 1 analyzes seventeenth-century patterns; Passage 2, eighteenth-century patterns.
(D) Each passage presents a different justification for local taxes.
(E) Each passage identifies a different part of the community as having authority over taxes.

IF YOU FINISH BEFORE TIME IS CALLED, YOU MAY CHECK YOUR WORK ON THIS SECTION ONLY. DO NOT TURN TO ANY OTHER SECTION IN THE TEST. **STOP**

Section 4 4 4 4 4

Time—30 Minutes
25 Questions

This section contains two types of questions. You have 30 minutes to complete both types. You may use any available space for scratchwork.

Notes:

1. The use of a calculator is permitted. All numbers used are real numbers.
2. Figures that accompany problems in this test are intended to provide information useful in solving the problems. They are drawn as accurately as possible EXCEPT when it is stated in a specific problem that the figure is not drawn to scale. All figures lie in a plane unless otherwise indicated.

Reference Information

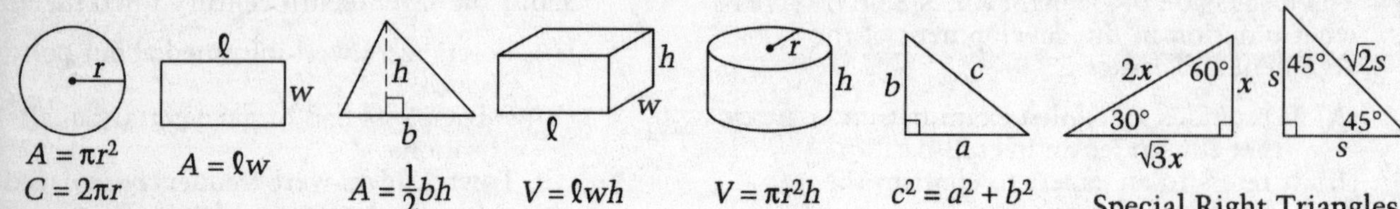

The number of degrees of arc in a circle is 360.
The measure in degrees of a straight angle is 180.
The sum of the measures in degrees of the angles of a triangle is 180.

Directions for Quantitative Comparison Questions

Questions 1-15 each consist of two quantities in boxes, one in Column A and one in Column B. You are to compare the two quantities and on the answer sheet fill in oval

A if the quantity in Column A is greater;
B if the quantity in Column B is greater;
C if the two quantities are equal;
D if the relationship cannot be determined from the information given.

AN E RESPONSE WILL NOT BE SCORED.

Notes:

1. In some questions, information is given about one or both of the quantities to be compared. In such cases, the given information is centered above the two columns and is not boxed.
2. In a given question, a symbol that appears in both columns represents the same thing in Column A as it does in Column B.
3. Letters such as x, n, and k stand for real numbers.

EXAMPLES

	Column A	Column B	Answers
E1	5^2	20	● Ⓑ Ⓒ Ⓓ Ⓔ
	150° x°		
E2	x	30	Ⓐ Ⓑ ● Ⓓ Ⓔ
	r and s are integers.		
E3	$r + 1$	$s - 1$	Ⓐ Ⓑ Ⓒ ● Ⓔ

GO ON TO THE NEXT PAGE

SUMMARY DIRECTIONS FOR COMPARISON QUESTIONS

Answer: A if the quantity in Column A is greater;
B if the quantity in Column B is greater;
C if the two quantities are equal;
D if the relationship cannot be determined from the information given.

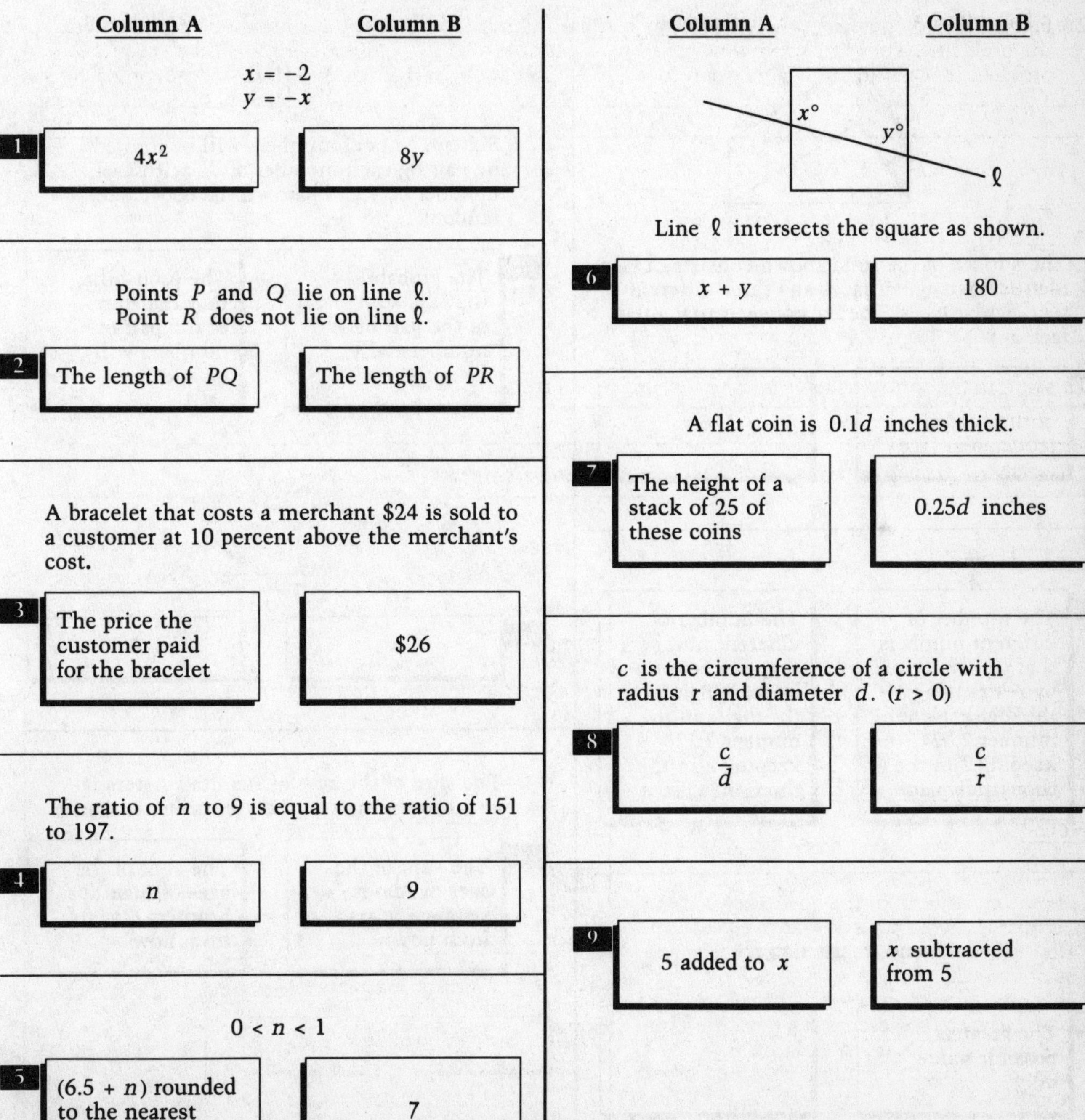

	Column A	Column B
	$x = -2$, $y = -x$	
1	$4x^2$	$8y$
	Points P and Q lie on line ℓ. Point R does not lie on line ℓ.	
2	The length of PQ	The length of PR
	A bracelet that costs a merchant \$24 is sold to a customer at 10 percent above the merchant's cost.	
3	The price the customer paid for the bracelet	\$26
	The ratio of n to 9 is equal to the ratio of 151 to 197.	
4	n	9
	$0 < n < 1$	
5	$(6.5 + n)$ rounded to the nearest whole number	7

Line ℓ intersects the square as shown.

	Column A	Column B
6	$x + y$	180
	A flat coin is $0.1d$ inches thick.	
7	The height of a stack of 25 of these coins	$0.25d$ inches
	c is the circumference of a circle with radius r and diameter d. $(r > 0)$	
8	$\frac{c}{d}$	$\frac{c}{r}$
9	5 added to x	x subtracted from 5

GO ON TO THE NEXT PAGE

SUMMARY DIRECTIONS FOR COMPARISON QUESTIONS

Answer: A if the quantity in Column A is greater;
B if the quantity in Column B is greater;
C if the two quantities are equal;
D if the relationship cannot be determined from the information given.

Column A	Column B

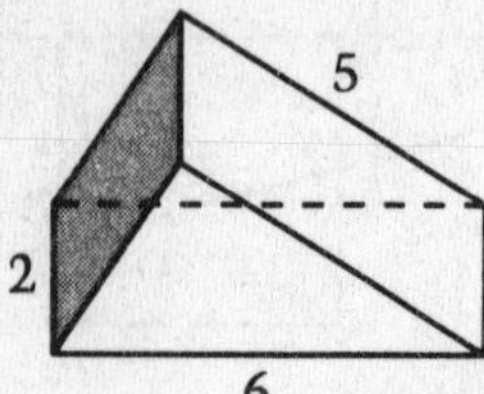

The surface of the solid shown consists of two identical triangular faces and three different rectangular faces. The area of each triangular face is 9.

	Column A	Column B
10	The perimeter of the shaded rectangular face	6

$2x + y = 26$
x and y are integers.
$y < 0$

	Column A	Column B
11	The number of different numbers that can be formed by rearranging the digits in the number 2,024, keeping 2 in the thousands place	The number of different numbers that can be formed by rearranging the digits in the number 2,224, keeping 2 in the thousands place
12	The greatest possible value of y	−1

Column A	Column B

$X = \{1, 3, 5, 7\}$
$Y = \{2, 4, 6, 8\}$

Sixteen pairs of numbers will be formed by pairing each member of X with each member of Y. A pair will be chosen at random.

	Column A	Column B
13	The probability that the sum of the pair of numbers will be even	The probability that the sum of the pair of numbers will be odd

$a > 1$

$\frac{a^{16}}{a^x} = \frac{a^x}{a^4}$

	Column A	Column B
14	x	8

The sum of the ages of Juanita's sisters is equal to the sum of the ages of her brothers.

	Column A	Column B
15	The sum of the ages of Juanita's sisters 5 years from now	The sum of the ages of Juanita's brothers 6 years from now

GO ON TO THE NEXT PAGE

Directions for Student-Produced Response Questions

Each of the remaining 10 questions requires you to solve the problem and enter your answer by marking the ovals in the special grid, as shown in the examples below.

Answer: $\frac{7}{12}$ or 7/12

Write answer → in boxes.

7 / 1 2

←Fraction line

Grid in → result.

Answer: 2.5

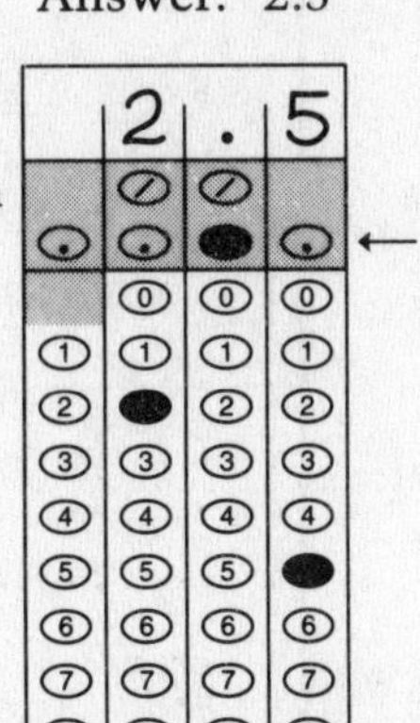

←Decimal point

Answer: 201
Either position is correct.

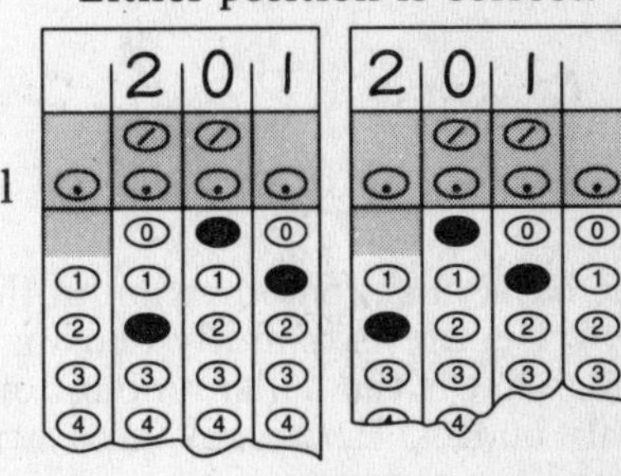

Note: You may start your answers in any column, space permitting. Columns not needed should be left blank.

- Mark no more than one oval in any column.
- Because the answer sheet will be machine-scored, **you will receive credit only if the ovals are filled in correctly.**
- Although not required, it is suggested that you write your answer in the boxes at the top of the columns to help you fill in the ovals accurately.
- Some problems may have more than one correct answer. In such cases, grid only one answer.
- No question has a negative answer.
- **Mixed numbers** such as $2\frac{1}{2}$ must be gridded as 2.5 or 5/2. (If 2 1 / 2 is gridded, it will be interpreted as $\frac{21}{2}$, not $2\frac{1}{2}$.)

- **Decimal Accuracy**: If you obtain a decimal answer, **enter the most accurate value the grid will accommodate.** For example, if you obtain an answer such as 0.6666 . . . , you should record the result as .666 or .667. **Less accurate values such as .66 or .67 are not acceptable.**

Acceptable ways to grid $\frac{2}{3}$ = .6666 . . .

2 / 3   . 6 6 6   . 6 6 7

16 If $x = 16$ is a solution to the equation $9x - k = 130$, where k is a constant, what is the value of k ?

17 If $xy = 10$, $yz = 30$, and $y^2 = \frac{1}{9}$, what is the value of xz ?

GO ON TO THE NEXT PAGE

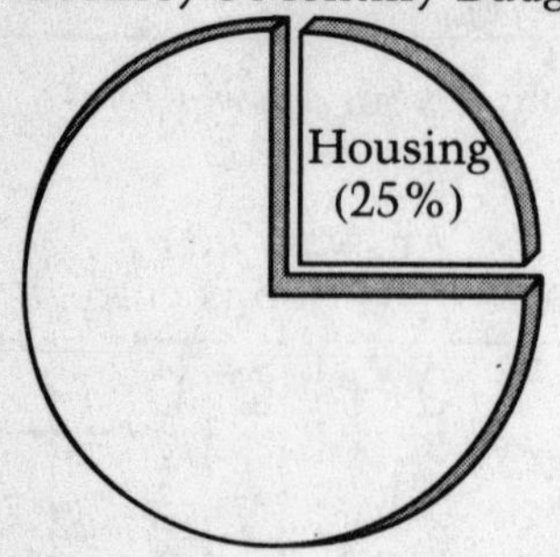

18 On the basis of the information in the graph above, if Geoffrey's monthly housing budget is $650, what is the dollar amount of his total monthly budget? (Disregard the $ sign when gridding your answer.)

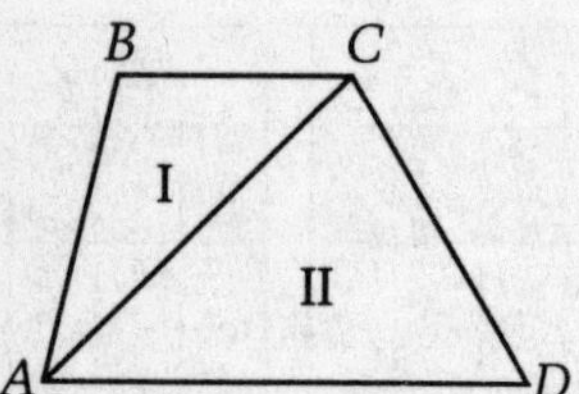

19 In the figure above, the area of triangle I is $\frac{1}{2}$ the area of triangle II. If $BC \parallel AD$ and the sum of the lengths of BC and AD is 18, what is the length of AD?

20 What is one possible value of x for which $x < 2 < \frac{1}{x}$?

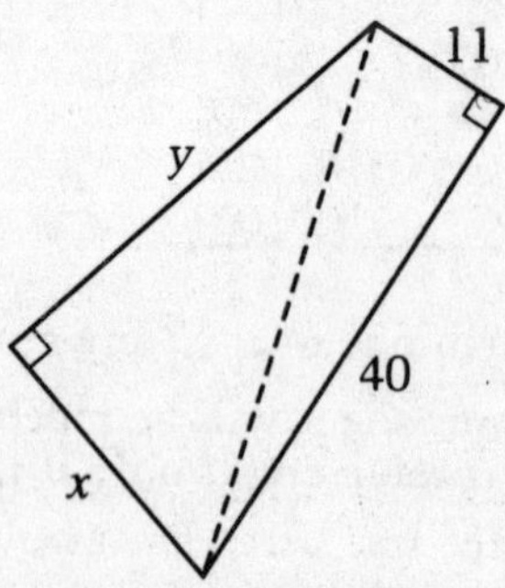

21 In the figure above, what is the value of $x^2 + y^2$?

GO ON TO THE NEXT PAGE

22 For all numbers x and y, where $x \neq y$, let $x \blacktriangle y$ be defined as $\frac{x + y}{x - y}$. If $8 \blacktriangle w = \frac{4}{3}$, what is the value of w?

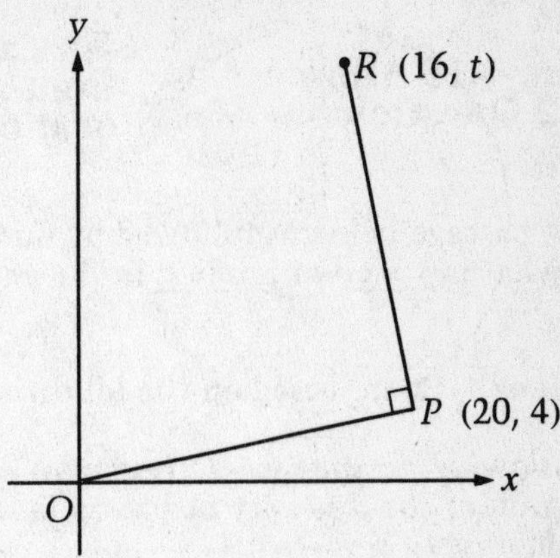

24 In the xy-plane above, $OP = PR$. What is the value of t?

23 Roberta rode her bicycle a total of 169 miles in 13 days. Each day after the first day she rode 1 mile farther than the day before. What was the difference between the average (arithmetic mean) number of miles she rode per day and the median number of miles she rode during the 13 days?

25 A flock of geese on a pond were being observed continuously. At 1:00 P.M., $\frac{1}{5}$ of the geese flew away. At 2:00 P.M., $\frac{1}{8}$ of the geese that remained flew away. At 3:00 P.M., 3 times as many geese as had flown away at 1:00 P.M. flew away, leaving 28 geese on the pond. At no other times did any geese arrive or fly away. How many geese were in the original flock?

IF YOU FINISH BEFORE TIME IS CALLED, YOU MAY CHECK YOUR WORK ON THIS SECTION ONLY. DO NOT TURN TO ANY OTHER SECTION IN THE TEST. **STOP**

Time—15 Minutes
12 Questions

For each question in this section, select the best answer from among the choices given and fill in the corresponding oval on the answer sheet.

The passage below is followed by questions based on its content. Answer the questions on the basis of what is stated or implied in the passage and in any introductory material that may be provided.

Questions 1-12 are based on the following passage.

The following passage is adapted from a biologist's discussion of the diversity of life on Earth (first published in 1992).

The most wonderful mystery of life may well be the means by which it created so much diversity from so little physical matter. The biosphere, all organisms combined, makes up only about one part in ten billion of Earth's mass. It is sparsely distributed through a kilometer-thick layer of soil, water, and air stretched over a half billion square kilometers of surface. If the world were the size of an ordinary desktop globe and its surface were viewed edgewise an arm's length away, no trace of the biosphere could be seen with the naked eye. Yet life has divided into millions of species, the fundamental units, each playing a unique role in relation to the whole.

For another way to visualize the tenuousness of life, imagine yourself on a journey upward from the center of Earth, taken at the pace of a leisurely walk. For the first twelve weeks you travel through furnace-hot rock and magma devoid of life. Three minutes to the surface, five hundred meters to go, you encounter the first organisms, bacteria feeding on nutrients that have filtered into the deep water-bearing strata of the rock. You breach the surface and for ten seconds glimpse a dazzling burst of life, tens of thousands of species of microorganisms, plants, and animals within horizontal line of sight. Half a minute later almost all are gone. Two hours later only the faintest traces remain, consisting largely of people in airliners who are filled in turn with bacteria.

The hallmark of life is this: a struggle among an immense variety of organisms weighing next to nothing for a vanishingly small amount of energy. Life operates on less than 10 percent of the Sun's energy reaching Earth's surface, that portion fixed by the photosynthesis* of green plants. That energy is then sharply discounted as it passes through the food webs from one organism to the next: very roughly 10 percent passes to the caterpillars and other herbivores that eat the plants and bacteria, 10 percent of that to the spiders and other low-level carnivores that eat the herbivores, 10 percent of the residue to the warblers and other middle-level carnivores that eat the low-level carnivores, and so on upward to the top carnivores, which are consumed by no one except parasites and scavengers. Top carnivores, including eagles, tigers, and sharks, are predestined by their perch at the apex of the food web to be big in size and sparse in number. They live on such a small portion of life's available energy as always to skirt the edge of extinction, and they are the first to suffer when the ecosystem around them starts to erode.

A great deal can be learned about biological diversity by noticing that species in the food web are arranged in two hierarchies. The first hierarchy is the energy pyramid, a straightforward consequence of the law of diminishing energy flow as noted—a relatively large amount of the Sun's energy that strikes Earth goes into the plants at the bottom. This energy then tapers to a minute quantity for the big carnivores at the top level.

The second hierarchy is a pyramid composed of biomass, the weight of organisms. By far the largest part of the physical bulk of the living world is contained in plants. The second largest amount belongs to the scavengers and other decomposers, from bacteria to fungi and termites, which together extract the last bit of fixed energy from dead tissue and waste at every level in the food web. These scavengers and decomposers then return degraded nutrient chemicals to the plants. Each level above the plants diminishes thereafter in biomass until you come to the top carnivores, which are so scarce that the very sight of one in the wild is memorable. No one looks twice at a sparrow or a squirrel, or even once at a dandelion, but glimpsing a peregrine falcon or a mountain lion is a lifetime experience. And not just because of their size (think of a cow) or ferocity (think of a house cat).

*photosynthesis: a chemical process by which green plants turn the energy in sunlight into food

GO ON TO THE NEXT PAGE

1 The exercise involving the desktop globe (lines 8-11) is meant to

(A) suggest that a determined student can master the complexities of ecology
(B) compare the diversity of life on different continents
(C) reiterate the comparatively small size of Earth
(D) emphasize that most of life on Earth is invisible to the naked eye
(E) illustrate the extent of the biosphere relative to the size of Earth

2 The reference to "ten seconds" in line 24 primarily serves to

(A) show the consequences of a single action
(B) suggest the brief life spans of many species
(C) illustrate the space occupied by most life
(D) demonstrate the invulnerability of life on Earth
(E) indicate the frustration of snatching brief insights

3 In line 29, the author mentions "airliners" to illustrate that

(A) natural biorhythms are routinely disrupted
(B) life on Earth is mostly limited to the surface
(C) humans are the most mobile species
(D) intelligence affects the survival of a species
(E) life-forms just above the surface of Earth are diverse

4 The author argues that the central aspect of the "hallmark of life" (line 31) is essentially

(A) competition for energy
(B) competition for sunlight
(C) competition for space
(D) efficient use of energy
(E) an incessant flow of energy

5 In line 37, "discounted" most nearly means

(A) devalued
(B) disregarded
(C) discredited
(D) reduced
(E) underestimated

6 In line 48, the author uses "predestined" to convey the

(A) unavoidable influence of change in the natural world
(B) intensity of the instincts of carnivores
(C) inevitability of the size and number of certain organisms
(D) outcome of predictable conflicts between animals of different sizes
(E) consistency of behavior across species

GO ON TO THE NEXT PAGE

7 The passage indicates that which group receives the smallest amount of energy?

(A) Green plants
(B) Herbivores
(C) Low- and middle-level carnivores
(D) Top-level carnivores
(E) Bacteria

8 The two pyramids described in the passage are similar in which of the following ways?

I. Green plants are at the bottom.
II. Decomposers are at the second level.
III. Large carnivores are at the top.

(A) I only
(B) III only
(C) I and II only
(D) I and III only
(E) I, II, and III

9 In lines 75-76, "No one looks twice" emphasizes that certain animal species are

(A) unappealing
(B) short-lived
(C) timid
(D) small
(E) plentiful

10 Which animal would be the most appropriate example to add to the two special animals mentioned in lines 77-78 ?

(A) Racehorse
(B) Grizzly bear
(C) Garden snake
(D) Pigeon
(E) Rat

11 The author assumes that a house cat (line 80) is

(A) aggressive
(B) pampered
(C) playful
(D) interesting
(E) endangered

12 The tone of the passage is primarily one of

(A) detached inquiry
(B) playful skepticism
(C) mild defensiveness
(D) informed appreciation
(E) urgent entreaty

IF YOU FINISH BEFORE TIME IS CALLED, YOU MAY CHECK YOUR WORK ON THIS SECTION ONLY. DO NOT TURN TO ANY OTHER SECTION IN THE TEST.

Section 7

7

Time—15 Minutes 10 Questions	**In this section solve each problem, using any available space on the page for scratchwork. Then decide which is the best of the choices given and fill in the corresponding oval on the answer sheet.**

Notes:

1. The use of a calculator is permitted. All numbers used are real numbers.
2. Figures that accompany problems in this test are intended to provide information useful in solving the problems. They are drawn as accurately as possible EXCEPT when it is stated in a specific problem that the figure is not drawn to scale. All figures lie in a plane unless otherwise indicated.

Reference Information

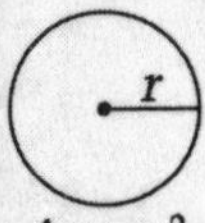
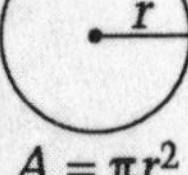
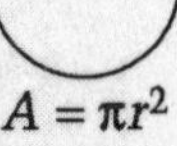
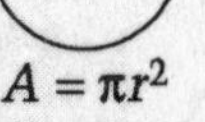

$A = \pi r^2$
$C = 2\pi r$

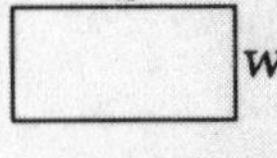
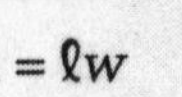

$A = \ell w$

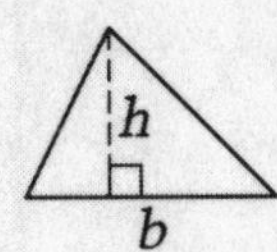
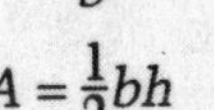

$A = \frac{1}{2}bh$

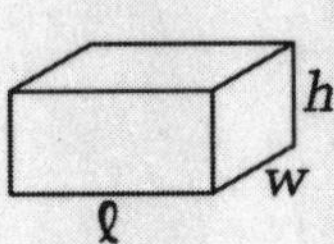

$V = \ell wh$

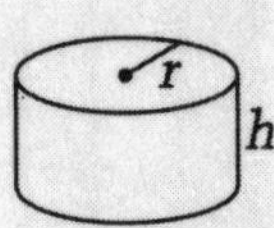

$V = \pi r^2 h$

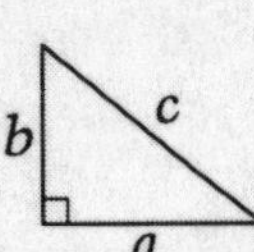

$c^2 = a^2 + b^2$

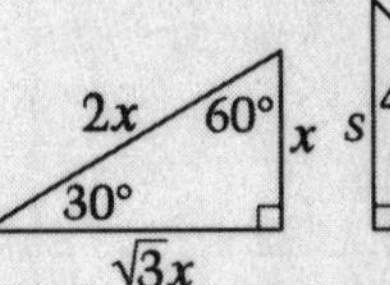

Special Right Triangles

The number of degrees of arc in a circle is 360.
The measure in degrees of a straight angle is 180.
The sum of the measures in degrees of the angles of a triangle is 180.

1 If $x + 2y = 8$ and $4y = 4$, what is the value of x ?

(A) 0
(B) 2
(C) 4
(D) 6
(E) 7

2 What is the least positive integer that is a multiple of 4, 15, and 18 ?

(A) 30
(B) 60
(C) 180
(D) 360
(E) 1,080

GO ON TO THE NEXT PAGE

3 Which of the following is an expression for 10 less than the product of x and 2 ?

(A) $x^2 - 10$
(B) $2(x - 10)$
(C) $(x + 2) - 10$
(D) $10 - 2x$
(E) $2x - 10$

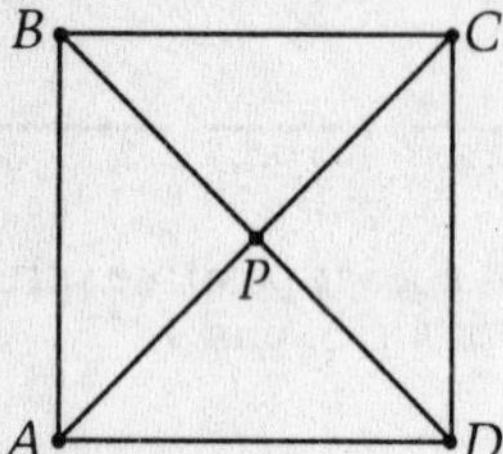

4 The figure above shows a square and five labeled points. What is the least number of these five points that need to be moved so that all five points lie on the same circle?

(A) One
(B) Two
(C) Three
(D) Four
(E) Five

5 How many minutes are required for a car to go 10 miles at a constant speed of 60 miles per hour?

(A) 600
(B) 100
(C) 60
(D) 10
(E) 6

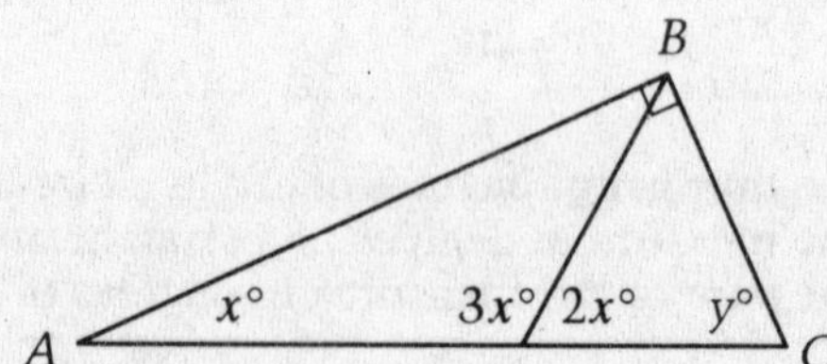

Note: Figure not drawn to scale.

6 In right triangle ABC above, what is the value of y ?

(A) 45
(B) 48
(C) 54
(D) 60
(E) 72

GO ON TO THE NEXT PAGE

Questions 7-8 refer to the following information.

1	2	3
4	5	6

The diagram above represents six building lots along a street. There are no other residential sites in the area. Five families—*v*, *w*, *x*, *y*, and *z*—are each interested in purchasing a lot, with the following restrictions.

v will occupy lot 6.

y and *z* will live on different sides of the street.

w and *x* will live on the same side of the street, and *x* will be the only next-door neighbor that *w* has.

One lot will remain unsold.

7 If all five families purchased lots and fulfilled all the restrictions, which of the following pairs of lots could be the ones purchased by *y* and *z* ?

(A) 1 and 2
(B) 1 and 3
(C) 2 and 3
(D) 3 and 5
(E) 3 and 6

8 If all five families purchased lots and fulfilled all the restrictions and if *y* purchased lot 3, which of the following must be true?

I. *w* purchased lot 1.
II. *x* purchased lot 4.
III. *z* purchased lot 5.

(A) I only
(B) II only
(C) III only
(D) I and III
(E) II and III

GO ON TO THE NEXT PAGE

7

9 In a plane, lines are drawn through a given point O so that the measure of each non-overlapping angle formed about point O is 60°. How many different lines are there?

(A) Two
(B) Three
(C) Four
(D) Five
(E) Six

10 For how many different positive integer values of k does $(kx - 6)^2 = 0$ have integer solutions?

(A) None
(B) One
(C) Two
(D) Four
(E) Six

IF YOU FINISH BEFORE TIME IS CALLED, YOU MAY CHECK YOUR WORK ON THIS SECTION ONLY. DO NOT TURN TO ANY OTHER SECTION IN THE TEST. **STOP**

SAT I: Reasoning Test Answer Key
Sunday, May 2000

VERBAL

Section 1

Five-choice Questions

	COR. ANS.	DIFF. LEV.
1.	B	1
2.	B	1
3.	D	1
4.	E	3
5.	B	3
6.	D	3
7.	C	3
8.	D	4
9.	C	5
10.	A	1
11.	E	2
12.	C	2
13.	A	3
14.	B	3
15.	C	5
16.	A	3
17.	A	3
18.	C	1
19.	B	2
20.	A	3
21.	B	5
22.	D	3
23.	C	3
24.	B	3
25.	E	3
26.	C	3
27.	E	5
28.	D	4
29.	D	4
30.	C	5

_____ no. correct

_____ no. incorrect

Section 3

Five-choice Questions

	COR. ANS.	DIFF. LEV.
1.	C	2
2.	E	1
3.	C	2
4.	B	2
5.	C	3
6.	C	3
7.	D	3
8.	D	4
9.	E	4
10.	A	5
11.	D	1
12.	C	1
13.	C	3
14.	B	2
15.	D	2
16.	D	2
17.	B	3
18.	E	2
19.	B	3
20.	A	3
21.	E	3
22.	E	4
23.	C	5
24.	D	3
25.	B	3
26.	B	3
27.	A	3
28.	D	3
29.	E	5
30.	A	3
31.	D	4
32.	D	4
33.	E	3
34.	D	5
35.	B	3
36.	E	4

_____ no. correct

_____ no. incorrect

Section 6

Five-choice Questions

	COR. ANS.	DIFF. LEV.
1.	E	3
2.	C	3
3.	B	4
4.	A	2
5.	D	3
6.	C	3
7.	D	3
8.	D	4
9.	E	3
10.	B	2
11.	A	3
12.	D	3

_____ no. correct

_____ no. incorrect

MATHEMATICAL

Section 2

Five-choice Questions

	COR. ANS.	DIFF. LEV.
1.	A	1
2.	B	1
3.	C	1
4.	E	1
5.	E	2
6.	C	2
7.	A	2
8.	C	2
9.	C	3
10.	D	3
11.	C	3
12.	A	3
13.	B	2
14.	C	4
15.	D	3
16.	A	3
17.	D	4
18.	E	4
19.	B	3
20.	C	3
21.	A	5
22.	C	4
23.	B	5
24.	E	5
25.	E	4

_____ no. correct

_____ no. incorrect

Section 4

Four-choice Questions

	COR. ANS.	DIFF. LEV.
1.	C	3
2.	D	1
3.	A	1
4.	B	2
5.	C	3
6.	C	3
7.	A	3
8.	B	3
9.	D	3
10.	A	3
11.	A	3
12.	B	5
13.	B	3
14.	A	5
15.	D	5

_____ no. correct

_____ no. incorrect

Section 7

Five-choice Questions

	COR. ANS.	DIFF. LEV.
1.	D	1
2.	C	1
3.	E	2
4.	A	3
5.	D	3
6.	C	3
7.	D	1
8.	A	4
9.	B	4
10.	D	5

_____ no. correct

_____ no. incorrect

Section 4

Student-Produced Response Questions

	COR. ANS.	DIFF. LEV.
16.	14	1
17.	2700	3
18.	2600	1
19.	12	3
20.	0<x<1/2 or 0<x<.5	3
21.	1721	3
22.	8/7 or 1.14	4
23.	0	4
24.	24	4
25.	280	5

_____ no. correct (16-25)

NOTE: Difficulty levels are estimates of question difficulty for a recent group of college-bound seniors. Difficulty levels range from 1 (easiest) to 5 (hardest).

The Scoring Process

Machine-scoring is done in three steps:

- *Scanning.* Your answer sheet is "read" by a scanning machine and the oval you filled in for each question is recorded on a computer tape.
- *Scoring.* The computer compares the oval filled in for each question with the correct response. Each correct answer receives one point; omitted questions do not count toward your score. For each wrong answer to the multiple-choice questions, a fraction of a point is subtracted to correct for random guessing. For questions with five answer choices, one-fourth of a point is subtracted for each wrong response; for questions with four answer choices, one-third of a point is subtracted for each wrong response. The SAT I verbal test has 78 questions with five answer choices each. If, for example, a student has 44 right, 32 wrong, and 2 omitted, the resulting raw score is determined as follows:

$$44 \text{ right} - \frac{32 \text{ wrong}}{4} = 44 - 8 = 36 \text{ raw score points}$$

Obtaining raw scores frequently involves the rounding of fractional numbers to the nearest whole number. For example, a raw score of 36.25 is rounded to 36, the nearest whole number. A raw score of 36.50 is rounded upward to 37.

- *Converting to reported scaled score.* Raw test scores are then placed on the College Board scale of 200 to 800 through a process that adjusts scores to account for minor differences in difficulty among different editions of the test. This process, known as equating, is performed so that a student's reported score is not affected by the edition of the test taken or by the abilities of the group with whom the student takes the test. As a result of placing SAT I scores on the College Board scale, scores earned by students at different times can be compared. For example, an SAT I verbal score of 400 on a test taken at one administration indicates the same level of developed verbal ability as a 400 score obtained on a different edition of the test taken at another time.

How to Score the Test

SAT I Verbal Sections 1, 3, and 6

Step A: Count the number of correct answers for *Section 1* and record the number in the space provided on the worksheet on the next page. Then do the same for the incorrect answers. (Do not count omitted answers.) To determine subtotal A, use the formula:

$$\text{number correct} - \frac{\text{number incorrect}}{4} = \text{subtotal A}$$

Step B: Count the number of correct answers and the number of incorrect answers for *Section 3* and record the numbers in the spaces provided on the worksheet. To determine subtotal B, use the formula:

$$\text{number correct} - \frac{\text{number incorrect}}{4} = \text{subtotal B}$$

Step C: Count the number of correct answers and the number of incorrect answers for *Section 6* and record the numbers in the spaces provided on the worksheet. To determine subtotal C, use the formula:

$$\text{number correct} - \frac{\text{number incorrect}}{4} = \text{subtotal C}$$

Step D: To obtain D, add subtotal A, subtotal B, and subtotal C, keeping any decimals. Enter the resulting figure on the worksheet.

Step E: To obtain E, your raw verbal score, round D to the nearest whole number. (For example, any number from 44.50 to 45.49 rounds to 45.) Enter the resulting figure on the worksheet.

Step F: To find your SAT I verbal score, use the conversion table on page 39 to look up the total raw verbal score you obtained in step E. Enter this figure on the worksheet.

SAT I Mathematical Sections 2, 4, and 7

Step A: Count the number of correct answers and the number of incorrect answers for *Section 2* and record the numbers in the spaces provided on the worksheet. To determine subtotal A, use the formula:

$$\text{number correct} - \frac{\text{number incorrect}}{4} = \text{subtotal A}$$

Step B: Count the number of correct answers and the number of incorrect answers for the *four-choice quantitative comparison questions (questions 1 through 15) in Section 4* and record the numbers in the spaces provided on the worksheet. Note: Do not count any E responses to questions 1 through 15 as correct or incorrect. Because these four-choice questions have no E answer choices, E responses to these questions are treated as omits. To determine subtotal B, use the formula:

$$\text{number correct} - \frac{\text{number incorrect}}{3} = \text{subtotal B}$$

Step C: Count the number of correct answers for the student-produced response questions *(questions 16 through 25)* in *Section 4* and record the number in the space provided on the worksheet. This is subtotal C.

Step D: Count the number of correct answers and the number of incorrect answers for *Section 7* and record the numbers in the spaces provided on the worksheet. To determine subtotal D, use the formula:

$$\text{number correct} - \frac{\text{number incorrect}}{4} = \text{subtotal D}$$

Step E: To obtain E, add subtotal A, subtotal B, subtotal C, and subtotal D, keeping any decimals. Enter the resulting figure on the worksheet.

Step F: To obtain F, your raw mathematical score, round E to the nearest whole number. (For example, any number from 44.50 to 45.49 rounds to 45.) Enter the resulting figure on the worksheet.

Step G: To find your SAT I mathematical score, use the conversion table on page 39 to look up the total raw mathematical score you obtained in step F. Enter this figure on the worksheet.

SAT I Scoring Worksheet

SAT I Verbal Sections

A. Section 1:	________ no. correct	–	(________ no. incorrect	÷ 4) =	________ subtotal A
B. Section 3:	________ no. correct	–	(________ no. incorrect	÷ 4) =	________ subtotal B
C. Section 6:	________ no. correct	–	(________ no. incorrect	÷ 4) =	________ subtotal C
D. Total unrounded raw score (Total A + B + C)					________ D
E. Total rounded raw score (Rounded to nearest whole number)					________ E
F. SAT I verbal reported scaled score (See the conversion table.)					[ ] SAT I verbal score

SAT I Mathematical Sections

A. Section 2:	________ no. correct	–	(________ no. incorrect	÷ 4) =	________ subtotal A
B. Section 4: Questions 1-15 (quantitative comparison)	________ no. correct	–	(________ no. incorrect	÷ 3) =	________ subtotal B
C. Section 4: Questions 16-25 (student-produced response)	________ no. correct			=	________ subtotal C
D. Section 7:	________ no. correct	–	(________ no. incorrect	÷ 4) =	________ subtotal D
E. Total unrounded raw score (Total A + B + C + D)					________ E
F. Total rounded raw score (Rounded to nearest whole number)					________ F
G. SAT I mathematical reported scaled score (See the conversion table.)					[ ] SAT I mathematical score

Score Conversion Table
SAT I: Reasoning Test
Sunday, May 2000
Recentered Scale

Raw Score	Verbal Scaled Score	Math Scaled Score	Raw Score	Verbal Scaled Score	Math Scaled Score
78	800		37	510	580
77	800		36	510	570
76	800		35	500	560
75	800		34	500	550
74	800		33	490	550
73	780		32	480	540
72	760		31	480	530
71	750		30	470	520
70	740		29	470	520
69	720		28	460	510
68	710		27	460	500
67	700		26	450	490
66	690		25	450	490
65	680		24	440	480
64	680		23	430	470
63	670		22	430	470
62	660		21	420	460
61	650		20	410	450
60	640	800	19	410	440
59	640	800	18	400	440
58	630	800	17	390	430
57	620	780	16	390	420
56	620	760	15	380	410
55	610	740	14	370	400
54	610	730	13	360	390
53	600	720	12	360	390
52	590	710	11	350	380
51	590	700	10	340	370
50	580	690	9	330	360
49	580	680	8	320	350
48	570	670	7	310	340
47	570	660	6	300	320
46	560	650	5	290	310
45	550	640	4	280	300
44	550	630	3	270	290
43	540	630	2	250	270
42	540	620	1	240	260
41	530	610	0	220	240
40	530	600	-1	210	220
39	520	590	-2 and below	200	200
38	520	590			

This table is for use only with this test.

Notes

Notes

Notes

Notes

Notes

Notes

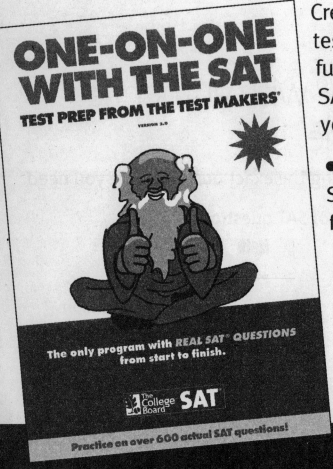

Get a 20% discount!

Pay only $15 for *Real SAT® II: Subject Tests,* $23.95 for *One-on-One with the SAT®*.

After you try the mini-SAT on the CD-ROM enclosed, try the complete software! Order *One-on-One with the SAT®* (item #006747), and get over 600 practice questions, plus a full-length posttest to see how you've improved. Only $23.95 with this coupon (regularly $29.95).

Planning to take the SAT II? Order *Real SAT® II: Subject Tests* (item #006771), with practice tests in each subject. Only $15 with this coupon (regularly $18.95).

For ordering information, call 800 323-7155 and mention operator code SAP2202A to get the discount.

Offer valid until December 31, 2002.
No other discounts apply.
One coupon per customer. Only one of each product may be ordered at the discounted price.

We'd love to get your feedback! Please take a moment to fill out this survey and drop the card in the mail. (No postage necessary.)

1. How did you learn about *10 Real SAT®s*?

❑ Bookstore ❑ Online
❑ SAT prep course ❑ Friend/Family Member
❑ Teacher/Counselor ❑ College Board Web site
❑ Other Web site (please specify)

____

2. Who purchased *10 Real SAT®s*?

❑ You ❑ Parent/Guardian
❑ School ❑ SAT prep course

3. Would you recommend (or have you recommended) this book to other students who are preparing for the SAT?

❑ yes ❑ no

If yes, why ________________________

If no, why ________________________

4. Did you use the CD in the back of this book?

❑ yes ❑ no

5. Do you plan to purchase *One-on-One with the SAT®*?

❑ yes ❑ no

6. Would you purchase an online SAT prep service by the College Board?

❑ yes ❑ no

7. If you are a student, what grade are you in?

❑ 9th ❑ 10th ❑ 11th
❑ 12th ❑ other

If you're not a student, what is your occupation?

____

8. What is your household income?

❑ $25,000 or below ❑ $25,001–$50,000
❑ $50,001–$75,000 ❑ $75,001–$100,000
❑ Above $100,001

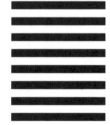

BUSINESS REPLY MAIL

FIRST-CLASS MAIL PERMIT NO. 9151 NEW YORK, NY

POSTAGE WILL BE PAID BY ADDRESSEE

Dept. SATAA
The College Board
45 Columbus Avenue
New York, NY 10133-0035